D0761248

RACE AND REUNION: The Civil War in American Memory
By David W. Blight
Publication Date: February 2001
Price: $29.95
ISBN: 0-674-00332-2
576 pages, 32 halftones
Harvard University Press/Belknap

For more information, please contact:
Mary Kate Maco
Publicity Director
Phone 617.495.4713
Fax 617.496.2550

Visit our Web site
www.hup.harvard.edu

RACE AND REUNION

RACE
AND
REUNION

THE CIVIL WAR IN
AMERICAN MEMORY

DAVID W. BLIGHT

The BELKNAP PRESS of
HARVARD UNIVERSITY PRESS
Cambridge, Massachusetts and London, England 2001

Library of Congress Cataloging-in-Publication Data
Blight, David W.
Race and reunion: the Civil War in American memory / David W. Blight.
p. cm.
Includes bibliographical references (p.) and index.
ISBN 0-674-00332-2 (alk. paper)
1. United States—History—Civil War, 1861–1865—Influence. 2. United
States—History—Civil War, 1861–1865—Social aspects. 3. United States—History—Civil
War, 1861–1865—Afro-Americans. 4. Reconstruction—Social aspects. 5. War and
society—United States—History. 6. Memory—Social aspects—United States—History. 7.
Reconciliation—Social aspects—United States—History. 8. United States—Race relations.
I. Title.

E468.9 .B58 2001

973.7—dc21   00-042918

"The People made their recollection fit in with their sufferings."
—THUCYDIDES, History of the Peloponnesian War

CONTENTS

RACE AND REUNION

Prologue

History . . . does not refer merely to the past . . .
history is literally *present* in all that we do.

—JAMES BALDWIN, "Unnameable Objects, Unspeakable Crimes," 1965

"THE CIVIL WAR is our *felt* history—history lived in the national imagination," wrote Robert Penn Warren in his *Legacy of the Civil War* (1961). "Somewhere in their bones," he declared, most Americans have a storehouse of "lessons" drawn from the Civil War. Exactly what those lessons should be, and who should determine them, has been the most contested question in American historical memory since 1863, when Robert E. Lee retreated back into Virginia, Abraham Lincoln went to Gettysburg to explain the meaning of the war, and Frederick Douglass announced "national regeneration" as the "sacred significance" of the war. Among those lessons, wrote Warren, is the realization that "slavery looms up mountainously" in the story, "and cannot be talked away." But Warren acknowledged another lesson of equal importance for Americans of all persuasions: "When one is happy in forgetfulness, facts get forgotten." Or as William Dean Howells once put it: "What the American public always wants is a tragedy with a happy ending."[1]

This book is a history of how Americans remembered their most divisive and tragic experience during the fifty-year period after the Civil War. It probes the interrelationship between the two broad themes of race and reunion in American culture and society from the turning point in the war (1863) to the culmination of its semicentennial in 1915. This is necessarily, therefore, a synthetic and selective work on a vast topic. I am primarily concerned with the ways that contending memories clashed or intermingled in public memory, and not in a developing professional historiography of the

Civil War. All historians make research decisions and impose categories on the infinity of evidence and on the enormous variety of human stories embedded in their subjects. This book is no exception: Reconstruction politics, reunion literature, soldiers' memory, the reminiscence industry, African American memory, the origins and uses of Memorial Day, and the Southern Lost Cause receive considerable attention in this work, while other important forms and voices of memory do not, such as monument-building, late-nineteenth-century presidential politics, business enterprise, or the gendered character of America's romance with reunion. I have ignored none of these themes, but in every chapter have kept my eye on race as the central problem in how Americans made choices to remember and forget their Civil War. Throughout, I tell the stories of Civil War memory with the divergent voices of North and South, black and white, joined in the same narrative. And in every chapter I have tried to tell stories by using the power and variety of American voices: presidents and generals, men and women, former foot soldiers and ex-slaves, master novelists and essayists as well as the thousands who crafted ordinary reminiscences, romantics and realists, the victors and the vanquished.

Three overall visions of Civil War memory collided and combined over time: one, the reconciliationist vision, which took root in the process of dealing with the dead from so many battlefields, prisons, and hospitals and developed in many ways earlier than the history of Reconstruction has allowed us to believe; two, the white supremacist vision, which took many forms early, including terror and violence, locked arms with reconciliationists of many kinds, and by the turn of the century delivered the country a segregated memory of its Civil War on Southern terms; and three, the emancipationist vision, embodied in African Americans' complex remembrance of their own freedom, in the politics of radical Reconstuction, and in conceptions of the war as the reinvention of the republic and the liberation of blacks to citizenship and Constitutional equality. In the end this is a story of how the forces of reconciliation overwhelmed the emancipationist vision in the national culture, how the inexorable drive for reunion both used and trumped race. But the story does not merely dead-end in the bleakness of the age of segregation; so much of the emancipationist vision persisted in American culture during the early twentieth century, upheld by blacks and a fledgling neo-abolitionist tradition, that it never died a permanent death on the landscape of Civil War memory. That persistence made the revival of the emancipationist memory of the war and the transformation of American society possible in the last third of the twentieth century.

Americans faced an overwhelming task after the Civil War and emancipation: how to understand the tangled relationship between two profound ideas—*healing* and *justice*. On some level, both had to occur; but given the potency of racial assumptions and power in nineteenth-century America, these two aims never developed in historical balance. One might conclude that this imbalance between outcomes of sectional healing and racial justice was simply America's inevitable historical condition, and celebrate the remarkable swiftness of the reunion, as Paul Buck did in his influential book, *The Road to Reunion* (1937).[2] But theories of inevitability—of irrepressible conflicts or irrepressible reconciliations—are rarely satisfying. Human reconciliations—when tragically divided people unify again around aspirations, ideas, and the postive bonds of nationalism—are to be cherished. But sometimes reconciliations have terrible costs, both intentional and unseen. The sectional reunion after so horrible a civil war was a political triumph by the late nineteenth century, but it could not have been achieved without the resubjugation of many of those people whom the war had freed from centuries of bondage. This is the tragedy lingering on the margins and infesting the heart of American history from Appomattox to World War I.

For many whites, especially veterans and their family members, healing from the war was simply not the same proposition as doing justice to the four million emancipated slaves and their descendants. On the other hand, a simple justice, a fair chance to exercise their basic rights, and secure access to land and livelihood were all most blacks ever demanded of Reconstruction and beyond. They sought no official apologies for slavery, only protection, education, human recognition, a helping hand. The rub, of course, was that there were many warring definitions of healing in the South and the nation's collective memory had never been so shattered. In the wake of the Civil War, there were no "Truth and Reconciliation" commissions through which to process memories of either slavery or the experience of total war. Defeated white Southerners and black former slaves faced each other on the ground, seeing and knowing the awful chasm between their experiences, unaware that any path would lead to *their* reconciliation. Yankee and Confederate soldiers, however, would eventually find a smoother path to bonds of fraternalism and mutual glory. As is always the case in any society trying to master the most conflicted elements of its past, healing and justice had to happen *in history*

— 3 —

and *through politics.* Reinhold Niebuhr wrote with insight about this historical dilemma that has so plagued modern nations. "The processes of historical justice," said Niebuhr, "are . . . not exact enough to warrent the simple confidence in the moral character of history . . . Moral judgments are executed in history, but never with precision . . . every execution of moral judgments in history is inexact because of its necessary relation to the morally irrelevant fact of power."[3] Americans have had to work through the meaning of their Civil War in its rightful place—in the politics of memory. And as long as we have a politics of race in America, we will have a politics of Civil War memory.

In many ways, this is a story of how in American culture romance triumphed over reality, sentimental remembrance won over ideological memory. For Americans broadly, the Civil War has been a defining event upon which we have often imposed unity and continuity; as a culture, we have often preferred its music and pathos to its enduring challenges, the theme of reconcilied conflict to resurgent, unresolved legacies. The greatest enthusiasts for Civil War history and memory often displace complicated consequences by endlessly focusing on the contest itself. We sometimes lift ourselves out of historical time, above the details, and render the war safe in a kind of national Passover offering as we view a photograph of the Blue and Gray veterans shaking hands across the stone walls at Gettysburg. Deeply embedded in an American mythology of mission, and serving as a mother lode of nostalgia for antimodernists and military history buffs, the Civil War remains very difficult to shuck from its shell of sentimentalism. Over time, Americans have needed deflections from the deeper meanings of the Civil War. It haunts us still; we feel it, to borrow from Warren, but often do not face it.

In the half century after the war, as the sections reconciled, by and large, the races divided. The intersectional wedding that became such a staple of mainstream popular culture, especially in the plantation school of literature, had no interracial counterpart in the popular imagination. Quite the opposite: Race was so deeply at the root of the war's causes and consequences, and so powerful a source of division in American social psychology, that it served as the antithesis of a culture of reconciliation. The memory of slavery, emancipation, and the Fourteenth and Fifteenth Amendments never fit well into a developing narrative in which the Old and New South were romanticized and welcomed back to a new nationalism, and in which devotion alone made everyone right, and no one truly wrong, in the remembered Civil War. Persistent discussion of the "race problem" across the political and ideological spectrum throughout the late nineteenth century meant that American society could not easily remember its "Civil War problem" or a "Blue-Gray problem."

In a popular novel, *Cease Firing* (1912), Southern writer Mary Johnston, a Virginian imbued with Lost Cause tradition and a determination to represent its complexity (as well as a progressive woman and a suffragist), imagined a telling dialogue that may have captured the memory that most Americans, then and even now, want to embrace about the Civil War. On the last page of the book, Robert E. Lee's Army of Northern Virginia is retreating west toward its final collapse and surrender at Appomattox in the last week of the war. The April breezes are not yet warm, and the rivers to be forded still run cold. One Confederate soldier asks another what he thinks it all means. "I think that we were both right and both wrong," says the veteran of many battles, "and that, in the beginning, each side might have been more patient and much wiser. Life and history, and right and wrong and minds of men look out of more windows than we used to think! Did you never hear of the shield that had two sides and both were precious metal?" There was, of course, no lack of honor on either side in that fateful and compassionate surrender at Appomattox in 1865. And Johnston captured an honest soldiers' sentiment that had reverberated through veterans' memory for decades. But outside of this pathos and the endearing mutuality of sacrifice among soldiers that came to dominate national memory, another process was at work—the denigration of black dignity and the attempted erasure of emancipation from the national narrative of what the war had been about. That other process led black scholar and editor W. E. B. Du Bois to conclude in the same year as Johnston's novel that "this country has had its appetite for facts on the Negro problem spoiled by sweets."[4] Deflections and evasions, careful remembering and necessary forgetting, and embittered and irreconcilable versions of experience are all the stuff of historical memory.

If Du Bois was at all correct in his famous 1903 assertion that "the problem of the twentieth century is the problem of the color line," then we can begin to see how the problems of "race" and "reunion" were trapped in a tragic, mutual dependence.[5] This book is the story of that dependence, and its consequences, in America's collective memory.

ONE

The Dead and the Living

> And so good-bye to the war. I know not how it may
> have been, or may be, to others—to me the main in-
> terest I found, (and still, on recollection, find) in the
> rank and file of the armies, both sides, and in those
> specimens amid the hospitals, and even the dead on
> the field.
>
> —WALT WHITMAN, *Specimen Days,* 1882

THE LONG AND TROUBLED career of Civil War memory began well before the conflict ended. It took root in the dead and the living. The living
were compelled to find meaning in the dead and, as in most wars, the dead
would have a hold on the living. In his Gettysburg Address, Abraham Lincoln referred to the "brave men" who had "consecrated" the ground of that
battlefield above the "power" of his words to "add or detract."[1] Implied in the
rest of that speech was the notion that the difference between the living and
the dead was that the living were compelled to remember, and from the stuff
of memory, create a new nation from the wreckage of the old.

ON JULY 3, 1913, a day of withering heat in Washington, D.C., President
Woodrow Wilson took a cruise aboard the *Mayflower* down the Potomac
River toward Chesapeake Bay. A small party of aides and journalists accompanied a harassed President who was eager to be a historical tourist for a day
at the Yorktown Revolutionary War battlefield. The following day, July 4,

Wilson was to address an extraordinary gathering of Union and Confederate veterans at America's most famous battlefield—Gettysburg, Pennsylvania.

During his visit to the Yorktown sites, Wilson went almost entirely unrecognized by the variety of local people he encountered. Only a young white girl recognized the President as she offered to be his guide through the house that had served as Lord Cornwallis's headquarters. Neither the clerk at the court house, nor the local sheriff, who had a campaign photograph of Wilson on his own wall, recognized their famous visitor. Most poignantly, as Wilson entered and returned to the wharf he met several blacks who called him "Uncle" but did not recognize the President. According to press reports, a "group of old-fashioned darkies sitting around some equally old-fashioned scales" offered to weigh the tourists. After a jaunty exchange, Wilson consented and tipped the scales at 181 pounds. The next morning at Gettysburg Wilson would weigh in on another matter, speaking to the world about the meaning of the Civil War and of fifty years of the nation's remembering and forgetting. That he had gone virtually unrecognized on either side of the color line in a small corner of Virginia the day before may hardly have mattered much to the President. But perhaps the unnamed, and almost invisible, blacks hanging around a Potomac River wharf near a great historic site of Old Virginia (Wilson's home state) represent an appropriate backdrop for the resounding event that Wilson would visit within twenty-four hours. The ignorance of the clerk and sheriff is remarkable. But it is hardly surprising that rural black Virginians would not know Wilson; since 1904 none of them had been able to vote in the state without passing literacy tests, paying poll taxes, and meeting all but impossible property restrictions. They spent so much of their segregated lives being "disrecognized" by whites that recognizing a President might take special knowledge.[2]

President Wilson had initially declined to appear at the fiftieth-anniversary Blue-Gray reunion to be held in the Pennsylvania town July 1–4, preferring a vacation trip with his family in Cornish, New Hampshire. But circumstances, and the urgings of Congressman A. Mitchell Palmer, made him "constrained to consent to be present at the fiftieth anniversary of the Battle of Gettysburg," as he wrote to his wife, Ellen. Wilson realized that this reunion "was something we had to take very seriously indeed. It is no ordinary celebration." Wilson privately expressed his awareness of being the first Southerner elected President since the Civil War. "Both blue and gray are to be there," he observed. "It is to celebrate the end of all feeling as well as the end of all strife between the sections." Wilson was also acutely aware that he followed Abraham Lincoln's footsteps to Gettysburg. "Fifty years ago, almost, also on the fourth of July, Mr. Lincoln was there (in the midst of business of the most serious and pressing kind, and at great personal cost and sacrifice to himself). If the President should refuse to go this time . . . it would be hotly resented . . . it would be suggested that he is a Southerner and out of sympathy with the occasion."[3] Sometime between changing his plans on June 28, when he announced that he would attend the reunion, and July 4, Wilson wrote his own short, restrained Gettysburg address.

The 1913 reunion at Gettysburg was a ritual like none other that had occurred in America. It had been designed to be a festival of sectional reconciliation and patriotism. The states appropriated some $1,750,000 to pay the transportation of any Civil War veteran from any part of the country. The federal government, through Congress and the War Department, appropriated approximately $450,000 to build a "Great Camp" to house and feed the veterans. A total of 53,407 veterans attended the reunion, and as many spectators were estimated to have descended on the town of Gettysburg during the week of the event, all riding the special cars of some forty-seven railroad companies operating in or through Pennsylvania. As it stood in American culture in the early twentieth century, Civil War memory never saw a more fully orchestrated expression than at Gettysburg on the battle's semicentennial.[4]

Once the old men had arrived in their uniforms, decked out in ribbons and graced with silver beards, the tent city on the battlefield became one of the most extraordinary spectacles Americans had ever seen. For most observers, the veterans were men out of another time, icons that stimulated a sense of pride, history, and amusement all at once. They were an irresistible medium through which Americans could envision part of their inheritance and be deflected by it at the same time. They were at once the embodiment of Civil War nostalgia, symbols of a lost age of heroism, and the fulfillment of that most human of needs—civic and spiritual reconciliation.

As bands played, suffragettes lobbied the tented grounds, shouting "votes for women." The recently formed Boy Scouts of America served as aides to the old soldiers, and members of the regular U.S. Army guarded the proceedings. Newspapers gushed with amazement. "You may search the world's history in vain for such a spectacle," announced the *Columbus Citizen* (Ohio). The sense of completeness of the national reunion was especially prevalent in the newspapers. The *National Tribune* (an official organ of the Grand Army of the Republic, GAR) rejoiced over the "death of sectionalism" and the on-going "obliterating of Mason and Dixon's line." And the *Confederate Veteran* could declare with full confidence that "the day of differences and jealousies is past." The *London Times* of England marveled that, however pathetic their feebleness, the mingled veterans were "eradicating forever the scars of the civil war in a way that no amount of preaching or political maneuvering could have done." Glorious remembrance was all but overwhelmed by an even more glorious forgetting. "Thank God for Gettysburg, hosanna!" proclaimed the *Louisville Courier-Journal.* "God bless us everyone, alike the Blue and the Gray, the Gray and the Blue! The world ne'er witnessed such a sight as this. Beholding, can we say happy is the nation that hath no history?"[5]

On the third day of the reunion, July 3, the governors of the various states spoke in a giant tent constructed on the field where Pickett's Charge had occurred fifty years earlier. Governor William Hodges Mann of Virginia struck the most meaningful chord of memory: "We are not here to discuss the Genesis of the war, but men who have tried each other in the storm and smoke of battle are here to discuss this *great fight* . . . we came here, I say, *not to discuss what caused the war of 1861–65,* but to talk over the events of the battle here as man to man" (emphasis added).[6] Like the politics of reconciliation, which was several decades old by 1913, this reunion was about forging unifying myths and making remembering safe. Neither space nor time was allowed at Gettysburg for considering the causes, transformations, and results of the war; no place was reserved for the legacies of emancipation or the conflicted and unresolved history of Reconstruction. Because the planners had allowed no space for surviving black veterans, they had also left no space on the programs for a discussion of that second great outcome of the war—the failures of racial reconciliation.

Of course, nations rarely commemorate their disasters and tragedies, unless compelled by forces that will not let the politics of memory rest. One should not diminish the profoundly meaningful experiences of the veterans themselves at such a reunion; the nation, through the psyches of old soldiers, had achieved a great deal of healing. But the 1913 "Peace Jubilee," as the organizers called it, was a Jim Crow reunion, and white supremacy might be said to have been the silent, invisible master of ceremonies. At a time when lynching had developed into a social ritual of its own horrifying kind, and when the American apartheid had become fully entrenched, many black leaders and editors found the sectional love feast at Gettysburg more than they could bear. "A Reunion of whom?" asked the *Washington Bee.* Only those who "fought for the preservation of the Union and the extinction of human slavery," or also those who "fought to destroy the Union and perpetuate slavery, and who are now employing every artifice and argument known to deceit and sophistry to propagate a national sentiment in favor of their nefarious contention that emancipation, reconstruction and enfranchisement are a dismal failure?"[7] Black responses to such reunions as that at Gettysburg in 1913, and a host of similar events, demonstrated how fundamentally at odds black memories were with the national reunion. In that disconnection lay an American tragedy not yet fully told by 1913, and one utterly out of place at Blue-Gray reunions.

Woodrow Wilson did not likely think of this disconnection between black and white memories as he arrived at the Gettysburg train station on the morning of July 4. Wilson did not come to Gettysburg as a historian probing the past. Whisked in a car out to the battlefield where the great tent awaited with several thousand veterans crammed inside, Wilson, the Virginian-President, stood before the entrance, flanked by a Union veteran in long beard, holding a small U.S. flag, and a Confederate veteran in long mustache, holding a small Confederate flag. Behind him, Governors John K.

On July 4, 1913, Woodrow Wilson, the first Southerner elected President since the Civil War, spoke on the battlefield at Gettysburg during the fiftieth anniversary Blue-Gray reunion and declared the war America's "quarrel forgotten." (Record Group 25, Pennsylvania State Archives)

Tener (Pennsylvania) and William H. Mann (Virginia) followed him into the tent, as the President doffed his top hat. As the assembled throng of old veterans rose on the ground and in high-rise bleachers, Wilson strode to the stage. Wilson stood without a podium, the great beams of the tent arched behind him, the script in his left hand, and began to speak. He had not come to discuss the genesis or the results of the war. He declared it an "impertinence to discourse upon how the battle went, how it ended," or even "what it signified." Wilson's charge, he claimed, was to comprehend the central question: What had the fifty years since the battle meant? His answer struck the mystic chord of memory that most white Americans were prepared to hear:

> They have meant peace and union and vigor, and the maturity and might of a great nation. How wholesome and healing the peace has been! We have found one another again as brothers and comrades, in arms, enemies no longer, generous friends rather, our battles long past, the *quarrel forgotten*—except that we shall not forget the splendid valor, the manly devotion of the men then arrayed against one another, now grasping hands and smiling into each other's eyes. How complete the union has become and how dear to all of us, how unquestioned, how benign and majestic, as state after state has been added to this, our great family of free men! (emphasis added)[8]

Wilson strained to look ahead and not to the past, to call the younger generation to a moral equivalent of war, doing battle "not with armies but with principalities and powers and wickedness in high places." He appealed to a new "host" for a new age, not the "ghostly hosts who fought upon these battlefields long ago and are gone." That new host was the teeming masses of the Progressive era, "the great and the small without class or difference of kind or race or origin; and undivided in interest." Wilson's great gift for mixing idealism with ambiguity was in perfect form. After this sole mention of race, and probably without the slightest thought of Jim Crow's legal reign, Wilson proclaimed that "our constitutions are their [the people's] articles of enlistment. The orders of the day are the laws upon our statute books." After the obligatory endorsement of the valor of the past, Wilson devoted the majority of his fifteen-minute speech to the present and the future. "The day of our country's life has but broadened into morning," he concluded. "Do not put uniforms by. Put the harness of the present on."[9] These were telling words for the future war President who had studied the Civil War with keen interest.

After the playing of the "Star Spangled Banner," Governor Tener immediately escorted Wilson to his car and back to the train station. In all, Wilson had spent less than an hour in Gettysburg; before noon he was on his private car en route to New York City, and eventually on to a New Hampshire retreat with his family. Within fifteen minutes of the conclusion of Wilson's speech, the closing ceremony of the reunion took place. At high noon, all across the town and hillsides of Gettysburg, cooks and generals, Boy Scouts and veterans, journalists and tourists, Congressmen and latrine cleaners, all came to attention. The colors were lowered to half mast at all the regimental or unit headquarters throughout the tent city. A lone bugle played taps, and in the distance a battery of cannon fired intermittently. Then, for the next five minutes, the vast crowd stood in utter silence and paid the "Tribute to Our Honored Dead."[10] As Wilson's train sped away in retreat, and as the fifty thousand assembled veterans tried to look down through what the President had called "those fifty crowded years" to fathom the meaning of the war and its aftermath, the dead and the living, the memories and the sun-baked oblivion, who can know what stories played on their hearts? In collective silence what memories careened back and forth between gleaming monuments and flapping flags? How did the silence of the honored dead speak?

THE FIVE MINUTES of silence to honor the dead on July 4, 1913, was two minutes longer than Abraham Lincoln's famous speech on November 19, 1863, dedicating an unfinished cemetery for more than twelve thousand soldiers (many whose names were unknown) still in the process of being properly reburied. Since the battle nearly five months before, Gettysburg had been a community in shock and a macabre scene. Makeshift graves had been hastily dug all over the fields where men fell; others had been dug up by families looking for loved ones. Serious health hazards had threatened the local population, and hogs had fed on human body parts protruding from the ground. The horror that was the real battle of Gettysburg was to be transformed into something proper, solemn, perhaps even exalted by the carefully planned cemetery to be dedicated in November. The struggle to define the Civil War in America and determine its meaning did not begin at Gettysburg on that late autumn day, but it did receive an important ideological infusion.

Lincoln's brief speech followed the official address—a long funeral oration by one of the nation's premier orators, Edward Everett. Rich in detail about the battle and its participants, partisan and unflinching in its descriptions of the carnage, Everett's nearly two-hour effort held the audience of twenty thousand in his customary spell. Drawing inspiration from Pericles's funereal oration during the Peloponnesian War, Everett established America's ancient lineage of sacred bloodletting. He laid responsibility for the "crime of rebellion," and therefore, all the death, in the hands of Southern leaders. But no matter how long the war or the scale of death, Everett saw a future of "reconciliation," a revived spirit of Union forged in such apocalyptic and necessary sacrifice.[11]

As Lincoln assumed his function in the dedication (intended to be largely ceremonial), only about one-third of the Gettysburg dead had actually been buried in the new cemetery. Lincoln's address contained no local details of the battle or cemetery preparations. He never mentioned the town of Gettysburg, nor that year's other great document—the Emancipation Proclamation—which had changed the character of the war. Lincoln assumed the task of offering an assessment of the graves' deepest meanings. As President, he would try to explain the war to audiences far beyond Cemetery Hill. It is as if Lincoln, beleaguered by death on a scale he could no longer control, could only discuss *why* it had happened.

Although Lincoln's speech must have seemed abstract to many auditors, an ideological explanation of the Civil War flowed through the brief address. The United States was an idea, Lincoln argued, a republic fated to open its doors, however unwillingly, by one of its founding creeds, the "proposition that all men are created equal." History had caught up with the contradictions to that creed and all but killed the idea. Only in the killing, and yet more killing if necessary, would come the rebirth—a *new* birth—of the freedoms that a republic makes possible. Humankind will forever debate what kinds of ideas men should be asked to die for. But Lincoln did not lack clarity at Gettysburg. The sad-faced Lincoln looked beyond Appomattox to the "unfinished work" of the "living." When he said "the world . . . can never forget what they did here," he anticipated not an endless remembrance of soldiers' valor, not a bloodletting purified and ennobled by extraordinary courage and manly sacrifice alone.[12] He envisioned an ideological struggle over the meaning of the war, a society's tortured effort to know the real character of the tragedy festering in the cold and in the stench of all those bodies awaiting burial. Lincoln seemed to see fitfully that the rebirth would be rooted in the challenge of human *equality* in a nation, ready or not, governed somehow by and for *all* the people. This was an idea that might make most future orators at monuments, reunions, and memorial days flinch and seek refuge in the pleasing pathos of soldiers' mutual valor. This was an idea so startling that, as the years went by, the forces of reunion would be marshaled in its defiance.

If Garry Wills is at all correct in his exuberant praise of Lincoln's Gettysburg Address as a speech that "revolutionized the revolution" and offered the nation a "refounding" in the principle of equality, then Woodrow Wilson, on his day at Gettysburg fifty years later, provided a subtle and strikingly less revolutionary response. According to Wills, Lincoln had suggested a new constitution at Gettysburg, "giving people a new past to live with that would change their future indefinitely." So did Wilson in his very different context of 1913. But that new past at the semicentennial was one in which all sectional strife was gone, and in which racial strife was covered over in Wilson's pose as a Progressive reformer. His moral equivalent of war had nothing to do with the creed of racial equality. Lincoln's "rebirth of freedom" had become in fifty years Wilson's forward-looking "righteous peace." The potential embedded in the idea of the Second American Revolution had become the "quarrel forgotten" on the statute books of Jim Crow America.[13]

Wilson, of course, did not believe he was speaking for or about the ravages of segregation, or other aspects of racial division in America, on his day at Gettysburg. He was acutely aware of his Southernness and eager to leave the mysticism of the reunion to others' rhetoric. He was still negotiating the uneasy terrain of a minority President elected by only 42 percent of the popular vote in the turbulent four-way election of 1912. Educated by events, and compelled to explain the totalizing character of the war, Lincoln had soared above the "honored dead" in 1863 to try to imagine a new future in America. Wilson soared above the honored veterans and described a present and a future in 1913 in which white patriotism and nationalism flourished, in which society seemed threatened by disorder, and in which the principle of equality might be said, by neglect and action, to be living a social death. Wilson's ambiguity paled in the shadow of Lincoln's clarity. But as the *New York Times* reported, "it is a difficult and disconcerting task for any statesman these days to deliver an address on the battlefield at Gettysburg, especially for any President of the United States." The *Times* declared the speech "good," but a "trifle academic in its argument." Wilson was interrupted only twice by "perfunctory" applause. Some observers thought the speech "out of place" for the occasion.[14] Whether in 1863 or in 1913, Gettysburg haunted American memory, both as a reminder of the war's revolutionary meanings and as the locus of national reconciliation.

FROM WELL BEFORE Lincoln's Gettysburg Address, from the first attempts to recruit black soldiers, from the initial waves of "contraband" slaves who escaped to an increasingly less abstract "freedom" in 1861–62, and simply from an ever-lengthening war that tested the life of slavery as much as the life of the Union, Americans, North and South, white and black, would forever possess and deny an ideological memory of their Civil War. No contemporary Northerner contributed more to the war's ideological meaning and memory than Frederick Douglass. An abolitionist orator-editor with few equals, Douglass had, by 1863–64, waged an all-out propaganda campaign to help foment a holy war on the South and on slavery; he had given his own Gettysburg Address many times over during the war. If Lincoln "revolutionized the revolution" at Gettysburg, if his speech engineered a "correction of the spirit" that cleared the "infected air of American history itself," as Wills boldly asserts, then Frederick Douglass was his stalking horse and his minister of propaganda. On the level of ideology, Douglass was the President's unacknowledged and unpaid alter ego, the intellectual godfather of the Gettysburg Address.[15] The Northern postwar ideological memory of the conflict as a transformation in the history of freedom, as an American second founding, was born in the rhetoric of 1863 fashioned by Douglass, Lincoln, and others whose burden it was to explain how the war's first purpose (preservation of the Union) had transfigured into the second (emancipation of the slaves).

In a speech delivered in Philadelphia only two weeks after Lincoln had dedicated the cemetery at Gettysburg, Douglass made an aggressive appeal for what he repeatedly called an "Abolition War." During the first year and a half of the war, Douglass had been one of Lincoln's fiercest critics among abolitionists, scolding the President on many occasions for his resistance to a policy of emancipation. Much had changed with the Emancipation Proclamation and the recruiting of black troops in 1863. The all-out war on southern society and on slaveholders that Douglass had so vehemently advocated had come to fruition. The war could still be lost on the battlefield, at impending elections, or in political compromise. But Douglass felt confident that history itself had taken a mighty turn. He took the pressure off Lincoln.

"We are not to be saved by the captain," he declared, "but by the crew. We are not to be saved by Abraham Lincoln, but by the power behind the throne, greater than the throne itself." The supreme "testing" of that "government of the people" about which Lincoln had spoken so carefully at Gettysburg was precisely Douglass's subject as well. In language far more direct than Lincoln's, Douglass announced that the "abolition war" and "peace" he envisioned would never be "completed until the black men of the South, and the black men of the North, shall have been admitted, fully and completely, into the body politic of America."[16] Here, in late 1863, he demanded immediate suffrage for blacks. In such expressions of equality, Douglass, too, looked beyond Appomattox to the long struggle to preserve in reality and memory what the war could create.

Douglass's Philadelphia speech took place on the occasion of the thirtieth anniversary meeting of the American Antislavery Society, the organization in which his own career began. While reminiscing with his old colleagues, he did not miss an opportunity to invoke the symbol of Gettysburg and tell the story of his first meeting with Lincoln, which had occurred in August 1863. He remembered traveling twenty years earlier to a meeting of the same society "along the vales and hills of Gettysburg," when local antislavery friends warned him to travel only by night, lest he be kidnapped back into slavery across the Maryland border. This year, however, he had journeyed "down there" all the way to Washington, where "the President of the United States received a black man at the White House." Douglass spoke with enormous pride about how he "felt big there" after secretaries admitted him to Lincoln's office ahead of a long line of solicitors strewn through the hallway. The President received Douglass with "a kind cordiality and a respectful reserve." "Mr. Douglass, I know you, I have read about you," said the standing Lincoln. With Douglass at ease, Lincoln remarked that he had read one of the black man's speeches where he had complained about the "tardy, hesitating, vacillating policy of the President of the United States" (toward emancipation). According to Douglass, Lincoln responded with complete sincerity: "Mr. Douglass, I am charged with vacillating . . ., but I do not think that charge can be sustained; I think it cannot be shown that when I have once taken a position, I have ever retreated from it."[17]

The abolitionist had gone to Washington in August to confront Lincoln and Secretary of War Edwin M. Stanton about the unequal pay and other discriminations suffered by black soldiers. Lincoln engaged Douglass in a conversation about how the whole idea of blacks in uniform had needed much "preparatory work." The President unflinchingly told black America's leader that he had feared that "all the hatred which is poured on the head of the Negro race would be visited on his administration." Moreover, Lincoln looked Douglass in the eye and said, "remember this . . . remember that Milliken's Bend, Port Hudson and Fort Wagner are recent events; and that these were necessary to prepare the way for this very proclamation of mine."[18]

In this encounter, narrated to an audience in early December 1863, Douglass constructed his own proud mutuality with Lincoln. However falteringly, by whatever unjust means blacks had to die in uniform to be acknowledged as men, Douglass was determined to demonstrate that his own ideological war aims had now become Lincoln's as well. The "rebirth" they were imagining was one both clearly understood as a terrible ordeal, but one from which there was no turning back. Douglass came away from this extraordinary meeting with the conclusion that Lincoln's position was "reasonable," but more important, that he would go down in history as "Honest Abraham." By invoking the sacred ground of Gettysburg, the symbolic space of the White House, and recounting his direct conversation with Lincoln, Douglass was declaring his rightful place at the new founding. Near the end of his Philadelphia speech, he asserted that "the old Union, whose canonized bones we so quietly inurned under the shattered walls of Sumter, can never come to life again. It is dead and you cannot put life in it."[19] During those last weeks of that horrible year, Douglass and Lincoln seemed to be speaking with the same voice about what had been buried and what was being reborn. Douglass would outlive Lincoln by thirty years and carry the burden of preserving their mutual vision.

On December 8, 1863, only four days after Douglass spoke in Philadelphia, Lincoln delivered his Annual Message to Congress. Lincoln still labeled the war in limited terms, calling it an "inexcusable insurrection." But the last five pages of the document demonstrate his understanding of the revolutionary turn in the character of the war. Recounting the past year, "the policy of emancipation, and of employing black soldiers," he declared, "gave to the future a new aspect, about which hope, and fear, and doubt contended in uncertain conflict." Lincoln wrote admiringly of the one hundred thousand "slaves at the beginning of the rebellion . . . now in the United States military service." Emancipation, said the President, had turned the nation's "great trial" into its "new reckoning," and had made the cause of the Union and a "total revolution of labor throughout whole states" one and the same. In the last lines of Lincoln's message, he stressed the iron necessity of the "war power" and paid tribute to the soldiers to whom "the world must stand indebted for the home of freedom disenthralled, regenerated, enlarged, and perpetuated."[20]

Lincoln's language makes a striking comparison to a speech Douglass wrote sometime late that fall and delivered many times across the North throughout the winter and spring, 1863–64. In "The Mission of the War," Douglass summed up more than two years of his war propaganda, his sense of the Civil War as America's cleansing tragedy and bloody rebirth. However long the "shadow of death" cast over the land, however ugly the "weeds of mourning," said Douglass, Americans should not forget the moral "grandeur" of the war's mission. "What we now want is a country—a free country," said Douglass, "a country not saddened by the footprints of a single slave—and nowhere cursed by the presence of a slaveholder. We want a country which shall not brand the Declaration of Independence as a lie."[21]

The dreamer calling men to die for grand ideas drew upon one of the deepest strains of American mission. "It is the manifest destiny of this war," cried Douglass, "to unify and reorganize the institutions of the country" and thereby give the scale of death its "sacred significance." "The mission of this war," he concluded, "is National regeneration."[22] Douglass spoke as though he and Lincoln had practiced from the same script, albeit one of them with the restrained tones of official state papers and the other in the fiery tones of a prophet. One spoke almost always with an eye on the fickleness of public opinion, and the other as though he were the national evangelist carrying the "Battle Hymn of the Republic" to that public in literal terms. Between them, Lincoln and Douglass provided the passive and the declarative voices of the Second American Revolution at its inception. This revolutionary—*regenerative*—conception of the war launched black freedom and future equality on its marvelous, but always endangered, career in American history and memory. All future discussion of the meaning and memory of this fundamental turning point in American history had to either confront or deflect the words, the laws, and the social realities the war had wrought in 1863.

Words alone did not give the nation its potential rebirth. To borrow from the word-master supreme, Walt Whitman, perhaps the "dead, the dead, the dead, our dead—or South or North, ours all" remade America. So did thousands of surviving soldiers, liberated freedpeople enduring near starvation in contraband camps, and women on both homefronts who performed all manner of war work and tried to sustain farms, households, and the human spirit as their men were asked to die for ideas, self-defense, retribution, manly values, or some abstract notion of their community's future. In time, the war itself remade America. As Ralph Waldo Emerson put it in 1862, "the war is a new glass to see all our old things through," and "our sole and doleful instructor."[23]

There were millions of individual stories unfolding at the end of this transforming war that gave real-life meaning to all the metaphors of death and rebirth. In all the material and human wreckage, in shattered families and psyches, new life was to take form. Countless private memories began to collide, inexorably, with the politics of collective memory. Contrary to Whitman's famous prediction, the "real war" would eventually "get into the books" because historians and writers have learned so much in the twentieth century about unearthing and telling the stories of real people.[24] Americans on both sides had experienced an authentic tragedy of individual and collective proportions. How people of both sections and races would come to define and commemorate that tragedy, where they would find heroism and villainy, and how they would decide what was lost and what was won, would have a great deal to do with determining the character of the new society that they were to build.

The initial task was to find meaning in the war's grisly scale of death. Death was all around in 1865, and no one tried to comprehend its meaning more passionately than the poet from Brooklyn, who worked more than two years in soldiers' hospitals. By his own estimation, Walt Whitman, after moving to Washington, D.C., in 1862 to investigate the fate of his brother, George, made some six hundred visits to hospitals and attended to between eighty thousand and one hundred thousand sick and dying soldiers. What Whitman witnessed profoundly shaped and inspired him for the rest of his life. He saw, and one might say, intellectually and emotionally ingested, the horrible results of the "real war." When asked in old age if he ever went "back to those days," Whitman replied, "I have never left them. They are here now, while we are talking together—real, terrible, beautiful days." Whitman spoke the truth when he declared that "the war saved me: what I saw in the war set me up for all time—the days in those hospitals."[25]

In poetry, and especially in prose remembrance, Whitman left a literary testament to the war. In all the shattered limbs and lives, in all the youths he watched as they became voiceless, and then breathless, Whitman found authentic tragedy, as well as his own Homeric sense of self. "The war had much to give," he later wrote, and it served as the "very centre, circumference, umbilicus, of my whole career." He compared himself to Achilles in Homer's *Iliad* who, when warned not to "act unwisely," declares, "No, let what must, come; I must cut up my capers." As though representing the thousands of veterans who would tell their increasingly sanitized stories to each other, and anticipating the endless obsessions of Civil War buffs in later generations who long for some transplanted, heroic place in the nineteenth century, he concluded, "I would not for all the rest have missed those three or four years."[26] Whitman could mix reality with nostalgia like no other writer; in so doing, he built and illuminated the literary avenue to reunion.

In "A Backward Glance o'er Travelled Roads" (1888), Whitman remembered first reading the *Iliad* on a peninsula at "the northeast end of Long Island, in a sheltered hollow of rocks and sand, with the sea on each side." Nestled in the "full presence of Nature," the young romantic had read the ultimate war book. In old age, though, he quickly converted such a remembrance into a statement of how war became his own great subject. "Although I had made a start before," he wrote, "only from the occurrence of the Secession War, and what it showed me by flashes of lightning, with the emotional depths it sounded and arous'd (of course, I don't mean in my own heart only, I saw it just as plainly in others, in millions)—that only from the flare and provocation of that war's sights and scenes the final reasons-for-being of an autochthonic and passionate song definitely came forth." Believing he spoke for millions (and in some ways he probably did), Whitman understood the war as America's own tragic recreation, a whole people reborn as something new by tearing themselves inside out. Words alone did not remake America, but they were mighty weapons in the myth-making that the Civil War inevitably produced. Whitman's own favorite descriptive word for the Civil War's character, if not its meaning, was "*convulsiveness.*"[27] That "autochthonic . . . song," though, has had many discordant verses.

Whitman was certainly a Yankee partisan, but while he cheered the Union cause, the horror scenes he almost unrelievedly witnessed gave rise to his own spirit of reconciliation. Whitman hated the war's capacity to mangle the bodies of young men, but he made few distinctions between the combatants themselves, or between their leaders. "What an awful thing war is!" he wrote home in March 1864. "Mother, it seems not men but a lot of devils and butchers butchering each other." Whitman's letters to his mother about his hospital work are a remarkable example of the very kind of experience (for so many women nurses as well) that demanded resolution over time in Civil

War memory. Writing at the peak of Grant's campaign against Lee in Virginia in June 1864, Whitman described the waves of wounded flowing into Washington hospitals: "We receive them here with their wounds full of worms—some all swelled and inflamed. Many of the amputations have to be done over again." He gave his mother a full picture of the hideous refuse of modern war. "One new feature," he said, "is that many of the poor afflicted young men are crazy. Every ward has some in it that are wandering. They have suffered too much, and it is perhaps a privilege that they are out of their senses." When he came to write in retrospect in *Specimen Days,* Whitman did not sanitize the "hell-scenes." He seemed to relish the descriptions of his soldiers, who were "horribly mutilated . . . groaning and moaning." They could be multiplied, he argued, and lit "with every lurid passion, the wolf's, the lion's lapping thirst for blood—the passionate, boiling volcanoes of human revenge for comrades, brothers slain—with the light of burning farms, and heaps of smutting, smouldering black embers—and in the human heart everywhere black, worse embers—and you have an inkling of this war."[28] In such honest language, a mix of memory and his own raw documentation, Whitman did speak for millions. This was the recurring national nightmare lurking beneath the revolution of black freedom and the quest for reunion. And these were the memories the nation would have to work through in the years ahead.

Whitman's war was rooted in his own brand of mystical Unionism. He almost never called the conflict a "civil war"; it was to him forever the "Secession War."[29] He threw blame for the war's outbreak, which he welcomed, on all those who had ever threatened America's unified destiny. Whitman loathed Southern "fireaters" and Northern "abolitionists" with equal disdain. He nursed, wrote letters for, and admired black troops, but only within the narrowly racist confines of his views on black capacities, and as a peculiar poetic subject. Whitman's "real war" did not ultimately include the revolution in black freedom of 1863; his own myriad uses of rebirth metaphors did not encompass black equality. This poet of democracy, whose work can and has been used to advance an antiracist tradition, never truly faced the long-term implications of emancipation.

During the seven pivotal years after the war, Whitman worked as a clerk in the U.S. Attorney General's office in Washington, D.C. Part of his job was processing the pardons that President Andrew Johnson proffered to ex-Confederates. Politically, Whitman became a devotee of Johnson and his lenient, state-rights approach to Reconstruction policy.[30] Whitman did not believe blacks capable of exercising the suffrage, and he viewed radical Reconstruction policies with the same contempt he had felt for abolitionists. "The republicans have exploited the Negro too intensely," he wrote to his mother in 1868, "and there comes a reaction." By 1875, Whitman had described Reconstruction racial affairs in words that would become with time the staple mythology of white Southern, and much Northern, comprehension of the aftermath of emancipation. "The black domination," he wrote, "but little above the beasts—viewed as a temporary, deserv'd punishment for their [Southern whites'] Slavery and Secession sins, may perhaps be admissible; but as a permanency of course is not to be consider'd for a moment."[31] Here again, Whitman spoke for a growing consensus. The image of Reconstruction as black domination, radical ideology taken too far, would become one of the deepest strains of American historical consciousness in the next generation.

Walt Whitman's never-ending quest to comprehend the convulsiveness of the Civil War can serve as a mirror of the larger culture's tendencies toward a reconciliation that would postpone, or evade altogether, its racial reckoning. Whitman never absorbed the anti-Southern political feeling of the prewar decade. In 1860 he declared his love of the South's natural beauty and its contradictions:

> O magnet-South! O glistening perfumed South! my South!
> O quick mettle, rich blood, impulse and love! good and evil! O all dear
> to me!

In such prewar poems as "O Magnet-South," in his war fever poetry of 1861–62, and in his immediate postwar verse, Whitman wrote of a war that would purge and unify the whole nation. Southerners were never really enemies to Whitman; they were family members to be nursed to their necessary deaths or revived to health. His hospital sketches were thoroughly nonpartisan descriptions of a shared agony. "How impressive was the fact of their [soldiers'] likeness," Whitman recorded after the war, "their uniformity of essential nature—the same basic traits in them all—in the Northern man, in the Southern man, in the Western man—all of one instinct, one color, addicted to the same vices, ennobled by the same virtues." In these compelling pictures of common soldiers as the shattered victims of modern war, Whitman depoliticized such suffering. Much partisan hatred dissolved on those cots where lads from Mississippi and Ohio were consumed by the same pneumonia, gangrene, or mercury poisoning. If an American nation was to survive this *civil* war, and if all the rhetoric of "national regeneration" was ultimately to make sense beyond 1865, then America's own "cult of the fallen soldier" was destined in time to be the basis of a new civil religion, and therefore, of the reunion itself.[32]

One of Whitman's close friends, John Burroughs, described him after the war as "the lover, the healer, the reconciler . . . a great tender mother-man." This notion of the "reconciler," a role forged in the care of dying soldiers of both armies, as well as in the reversal of gender expectations implied in the label "mother-man," makes Whitman representative of the earliest root of sectional reconciliation—the mutuality of soldiers' death and the need to mourn, commemorate, and memorialize all of that death on both sides. In the 1866 poem "Reconciliation" Whitman captured the theme:

> Word over all, beautiful as the sky,
> Beautiful that war and all its deeds of carnage must in time be utterly
>   lost,
> That the hands of the sisters Death and Night incessantly softly wash
>   again, and ever again, this soil'd world;
> For my enemy is dead, a man divine as myself is dead,
> I look where he lies white-faced and still in the coffin—I draw near,
> Bend down and touch lightly with my lips the white face in the coffin.[33]

Whitman no doubt never intended one irony embedded in this poem: in the shared divinity—a virtual kinship—of all the "white-faced" dead brothers rested that "beautiful" idea of *reconciliation*, as well as the ultimate betrayal of the dark-faced folk whom the dead had shared in liberating. Whitman's poetry and prose contained an infinity of truths, including those they masked.

IN THE FINAL MONTHS of the Civil War, all participants knew they were living through transformations. This was especially true for blacks. Black soldiers at the front wrote of their palpable expectations of a new future. Full of bravado and Biblical justification, Thomas B. Wester wrote in December 1864 from a camp hear Bermuda Hundred, Virginia, that he and his comrades were overthrowing "Pharoah" as "in the days of old." Wester made clear why blacks were fighting. "We are fighting as hard to restore the Union as the white man is," he said. "Why then should we not have equal rights with a foreigner, who comes to this country to fight for the preservation of the Government?" Wester looked ahead and imagined a legacy he would embody: "If we live to have families, we can sit down by the side of our wives, with our children around us, and relate to them what we have endured and witnessed upon the battlefields, to help restore this now-broken Union. We can recount to them the privations and sufferings endured by both white and black soldiers in the rebellion." Another black soldier, Henry C. Hoyle, wrote from near Richmond, Virginia, on January 15, 1865, looking forward to the day when he and comrades could "surround our cheerful firesides, and relate to our wives and children, parents and friends, what we have witnessed during this struggle for freedom, liberty and equal rights." Black men too expected a soldier's due out of this war—safe firesides, public recognition, and a place in at least some form of reconciliation between blacks and whites. Indeed, both Wester and Hoyle, like the more famous Douglass before them, were convinced that in equal suffering, if not in natural law, the country might discover the roots of equal rights. In this sense, for black soldiers and their future families, *equality* was another word for reconciliation. These black soldiers had no trouble defining the meaning of freedom and the war; they were only beginning the long struggle to protect the memory of their story, one they already considered comparable to the older conquest of "Pharoah and his host."[34] They knew the older story well: Moses did not make it to the promised land, but many of his foot soldiers and his people did.

On the evening of January 12, 1865, in the headquarters of General William Tecumseh Sherman in Savannah, Georgia, an extraordinary meeting took place. All present seemed aware of how unusual and historic the occasion might prove to be. Sherman's famous March to the Sea—the conquest of the Georgia countryside and the destruction of its resources from Atlanta to Savannah—had ended just three weeks earlier with the Confederate evacuation of the coastal city. The march and its wave of property destruction had liberated and displaced thousands of ex-slaves. Sherman faced a tremendous dilemma: what to do with so many refugee freedpeople, and how to begin to define their status. He and Secretary of War Edwin Stanton decided to ask the opinions of the representative black leadership of Savannah and of the very Georgia counties through which Sherman's troops had wreaked devastation. Twenty black ministers, most of whom had been slaves at some time in their lives, and some of whom had achieved freedom only in the past month at the hands of the Union armies, sat in a room together, face to face with Sherman and Stanton. Twelve carefully worded questions were written out and read aloud to the ministers. The answers as well were "written down in . . . exact words" and "read over" by each participant so as to determine "concurrence or dissent."[35] These words, like the Gettysburg Address, might not remake America, but everyone present seemed to understand that their articulation was a part of that process.

Garrison Frazier, a sixty-seven-year-old Baptist minister, served as the blacks' spokesman. For $1,000 in gold and silver Frazier had bought his freedom and that of his wife in 1857. The interrogatories in this meeting form an enduring testament to the meaning of the revolution of 1863–65; the exchange laid down for all time what would be both cherished and denied in Civil War memory. When asked for his "understanding" of President Lincoln's Emancipation Proclamation, Frazier delivered a definition in historical context. It had been Lincoln's offer to the "Rebellious States . . . that if they would lay down their arms, and submit to the laws of the United States before the first of January, 1863, all should be well; but if they did not, then all the slaves in the Rebel States should be free henceforth and forever." Asked next for his definition of "slavery" and the "freedom" given by the Proclamation, Frazier spoke from the deep past and to the future: "Slavery is, receiving by irresistible power the work of another man, and not by his consent. The freedom . . . promised by the proclamation, is taking us from under the yoke of bondage, and placing us where we could reap the fruit of our own labor, take care of ourselves and assist the Government in maintaining our freedom." Asked how the freedpeople could best take care of themselves and assist the government, Frazier provided a motto for the early struggles of Reconstruction: "The way we can best take care of ourselves," said Frazier, "is to have land . . . we want to be placed on land until we are able to buy it and make it our own." To assist the government in executing this revolution, "the young men should enlist in the service . . . and serve in such manner as they may be wanted."[36]

Frazier's shortest answer came to the query whether there was "intelligence enough" among the ex-slaves to maintain themselves and live peacefully with their neighbors. "I think there is sufficient intelligence among us to do so," he said directly. Then Frazier was asked to examine the "causes and object" of the war itself, and he responded with a poignant history lecture:

> I understand, as to the war, that the South is the aggressor. President Lincoln was elected President by a majority of the United States, which guaranteed him the right of holding the office and exercising that right over the whole United States. The South,

without knowing what he would do, rebelled. . . . The object of the war was not at first to give the slaves their freedom, but the sole object of the war was at first to bring the rebellious states back into the Union and their loyalty to the laws of the United States. Afterward, knowing the value set on the slaves by the Rebels, the President thought that his Proclamation would stimulate them to lay down their arms, reduce them to obedience, and help to bring back the Rebel States; and their not doing so has now made the freedom of the slaves a part of the war. It is my opinion that there is not a man in this city that could be started to help the Rebels one inch, for that would be suicide.

After several exchanges about the character and degree of black enlistment in the Union armies, Sherman then left the room as Frazier was asked the group's opinion of the general. Frazier declared Sherman "a man in the Providence of God set apart to accomplish this work."[37]

This ceremonial and substantive exchange between the freedmen ministers and the military leadership of the United States was unprecedented. The interview had lasted three hours in all. According to James Lynch, a northern-born missionary and one of the youngest ministers, the colloquy was unforgettable. "We expressed our opinions freely," wrote Lynch, "and dwelt, with interest, upon every word that fell from the Secretary's lips." Lynch described Frazier's performance as "a splendid expression of Southern colored men's opinion of the war and its policy." The meeting had provided an unusual kind of council of war. It represented much of the interior meaning of Sherman's March to the Sea. Earlier in 1864, a report of the American Freedmen's Inquiry Commission had described the "state of . . . transformation" in some sections of the South that brought former masters and former slaves "face to face in the presence of the great revolution and of the trials to which it summons both." In Savannah, the conflict's greatest symbol of cruel war sat face to face with twenty "colored Georgians," as Lynch put it, hearing in many ways the same summons.[38] The career of Civil War memory over the next fifty years is, in part, the story of how these extraordinary face-to-face encounters gave way to a reunion in which General Sherman, and the soldiers he defeated, would be remembered for their noble fight, and how the Reverend Frazier, and his words, were forgotten. With time, face-to-face encounters between blacks and whites would rarely dwell upon those meanings discussed that night in Savannah.

There can be no mistake, though, that black Civil War memory, as well as national and sectional memories, took deep root in those final months of the war. Much of that memory took hold in the bitter experiences of soldiers bearing up to discriminations and unequal pay and of the hundreds of thousands of refugees who found their first homes in freedom in contraband camps all over the upper South and in regions occupied by Union forces. The hardships in those camps, the struggle to work and survive, to relocate family members, all were to become part of black remembrance. So too would memory rooted in the experience of military laborers building corduroy roads for Union forces in Georgia, or digging canals from the James River in Virginia.[39] Several thousand had labored in the camps and on the fortifications of both armies almost from the beginning of the war.

Other kinds of hardship would be remembered. The Louisiana freedwoman Emily Waters wrote to her husband (who was still in the army in the wake of the war's end) that the master of Roseland Plantation had come home from the Confederate army and threatened to turn the freedpeople on his land "out on the levee" if they did not pay eight dollars per month in "house rent." "I have no money of any account," Waters wrote, "and I want you to get a furlough as soon as you can and come home and find a place for us to live in." Waters was in dire straits: "My children are going to school, but I find it very hard to feed them all." Emily Waters's husband did get a furlough and returned to his home just in time to find a provost guard "at his house for the purpose of ousting his wife and children." "Persecution is the order of the day . . . against the colored race," complained Hugh P. Beach, an officer in Waters's company, to a Freedmen's Bureau agent. As Ezra Adams, an ex-slave in South Carolina, remembered some seventy years later, "dat somethin' called freedom" had to include what people could "eat, wear, and sleep in. Yes, sir, they soon found out dat freedom, ain't nothin', 'less you is got somethin' to live on and a place to call home." Moreover, a Virginia freedwoman, Catherine Massey, wrote to Secretary of War Stanton in July 1865, begging him to find and force her negligent husband to send her money. "I am his lawful wife and he has neglected to treat me as a husband should," wrote Massey. "I think it no more than right than that he should be made to do what he has never yet done and that is to help me support myself as I . . . naturally did support him before he came in the army."[40] For many freedpeople, emancipation meant the struggle to survive in the new, chaotic social order, and it provided few if any occasions for celebration in the short term.

But in other places, especially churches, and at less formal gatherings in contraband camps or at soldiers' campfires, celebration was in order. Northern black churches held official celebrations of the anniversary of the Emancipation Proclamation as early as January 1865. In New Haven, Connecticut, at the AME Bethel Church (African Methodist Episcopal), religious fervor and patriotism mixed as perhaps never before in that free black community's history. A choir sang the old hymn "Blow Ye the Trumpet Blow," and then after a prayer for the preservation of the Union, it sang several verses of "America." Reverend S. V. Berry made a speech in which he linked the Proclamation and the Declaration of Independence in the same unified history. "As our forefathers fought, bled, and conquered for the Declaration of Independence," declared Berry, "just so hard are we now fighting for the Emancipation Proclamation." To great applause, and just before the singing of "Oh! Be True to Our Flag," Berry concluded with the idea that all present could now entertain: "The time is fast approaching, when we as citizens of the United States, will be respected as such."[41]

On the same day out west, in Chester, Illinois, the AME Church was decorated as never before. "Wreaths and evergreens . . . and the stars and stripes hung from almost every part of the room." The Proclamation, "beautifully framed in gilt, and containing the likeness of President Lincoln," hung above the pulpit. In Chester, they too began by singing "Blow Ye the Trumpet Blow," followed by "My Country, 'Tis of Thee." The Proclamation was then read in full. Following the first oration of the day, the congregation sang the "Battle Cry of Freedom," according to the recorder, "with a will." Speech after speech followed, one of them entertaining the audience with rousing metaphors about the "beast of slavery" being ushered through its stages of death. Similar to New Haven, the Chester celebration ended with a resolution to carry on the war for the "principles" in the Proclamation and the Declaration, including a recitation of Thomas Jefferson's preamble.[42]

In these remarkable commemorations taking place before the war had even ceased, blacks were preparing the script and forging the arguments for a long struggle over the memory of the events they were living through. They could not know how difficult that struggle would be. But in their unblinking medley of Negro hymns and the war-inspired national hymns, in their folding of the Proclamation and the Declaration into one seamless story, they named their text. In their understanding, and here they surely spoke for the Garrison Fraziers and the Emily Waterses in the South, America's rebirth was one and the same with their own rebirth as "citizens." Words had become deeds, or so they had a right to believe.

FROM THE MOST mournful experience at the war's ending, Lincoln's assassination, Walt Whitman crafted unforgettable images of life and death on a mutual journey. In "When Lilacs Last in the Dooryard Bloomed," the poet gave to grief (his own and the nation's) a mood and a setting. The mood is a calming, depoliticized contemplation of the "fathomless . . . sure-enwinding arms of cool-enfolding death." Whitman imagines a warbling in a secluded swamp singing a solitary "song of the bleeding throat, / Death's outlet song of life, (for well dear brother I know, / If thou wast not granted to sing thou would'st surely die.)" The poet speaks for millions of Americans in 1865 who were wondering how to remember and forget: "How shall I warble myself for the dead one there I loved?" As an offering, Whitman picks a "sprig of lilac" and places Abraham Lincoln's funeral train in the setting of "ever-returning spring" across the vast landscape of America from the East to the prairie:

> Over the breast of spring, the land, amid cities,
> Amid lanes and through old woods, where lately the violets peep'd from the ground, spotting the gray debris,
> Amid the grass in the fields each side of the lanes, passing the endless grass,
> Passing the yellow-speared wheat, every grain from its shroud in the dark-brown fields uprisen,
> Passing the apple-tree blows of white and pink in the orchards,
> Carrying a corpse to where it shall rest in the grave,
> Night and day journeys a coffin.

As the bird sings its "carol of death," the poet tries to give words to the music. Yet one senses that even Whitman could not match the warbling's power to deliver "that powerful psalm in the night"—to capture the meaning of the death caused by the Civil War. He is left with visions of "battle corpses . . . debris of all the slain soldiers of the war." The funeral train passes by all the images the poet can muster and he is left to say: "The living remained and suffer'd."[43] Whitman leaves his sprig of lilac in the dooryard and takes hope from the fragrance of spring.

"Lilacs" is not a poem about victory through death. It is more of a contemplation, a psalm about Lincoln's death at the nation's new beginning. But the nation is the land, and redemption comes from nature, not so much from the people or their politics. Whitman wrote a victory/death poem of a sort in "O Captain, My Captain." But the mood and the setting of "Lilacs" may best represent the numbed horror that so many Americans (Northerners and blacks at least) felt at Lincoln's murder. This was profound mourning without politics; the warbling, the lilacs, and the fields of grass gave the best eulogies.[44]

That April, in Vicksburg, Mississippi, as in a thousand other places, a large crowd of ex-slaves, in silence and tears, gathered in front of a store window that contained a photograph of Lincoln. A black correspondent from Chicago tried to characterize the scene of Lincoln's funeral procession in that city. "The grandeur was beyond description," he remarked. "The colored citizens turned out in full force, and were well-received . . . We can only look on in breathless silence, and think of the great change." A month after the assassination, a black Union soldier, Corporal William Gibson of the Twenty-eighth U.S. Colored Troops, wrote from City Point, Virginia, worrying that his home state of Indiana might not remove its old "Black Laws" from its statute books. Gibson seemed flushed with hope and anxiety over the "rights" he believed his "old 28th" had earned. "We ask to be made equal before the law," said the veteran, "grant us this, and we ask no more. Let the friends of freedom canvass the country on this subject. Let the sound go into all the earth." The politics of rebirth mixed with all the mourning that could be felt, if not explained. With Whitman, the nation had "the knowledge of death as walking one side of me, / And the thought of death close-walking the other side of me, / And I in the middle . . . as holding the hands of companions."[45] But the new nation awaiting rebirth also had the thought of black equality on one side, the knowledge of sectional reunion on the other side, and no muse yet in the middle holding their hands.

TWO

Regeneration and Reconstruction

'Tis far the best that the rebels have been pounded
instead of negotiated into a peace. They must remember it . . . I fear that the high tragic historic justice which the nation . . . should execute, will be
softened and dissipated and toasted away at dinner
tables. But the problems that now remain to be
solved are very intricate and perplexing.

—RALPH WALDO EMERSON, *Journal*, April 1865

RECONSTRUCTION WAS one long referendum on the meaning and memory of the verdict at Appomattox. The great challenge of Reconstruction was to determine how a national blood feud could be reconciled at the same time a new nation emerged out of war and social revolution. The survivors on both sides, winners and losers in the fullest sense, would still inhabit the same land and eventually, the same government. The task was harrowing: how to make the logic of sectional reconciliation compatible with the logic of emancipation, how to square black freedom and the stirrings of racial equality with a cause (the South's) that had lost almost everything except its unbroken belief in white supremacy. Such an effort required both remembering and forgetting. During Reconstruction, many Americans increasingly realized that remembering the war, even the hatreds and deaths on a hundred battlefields—facing all those graves on Memorial Day—became, with time, easier than struggling over the enduring ideas for which those battles had been fought.

Writing in 1935, W. E. B. Du Bois argued that general understanding of the Reconstruction era in American historical memory was the product of a "field devastated by passion and belief." Like most other historians of his time, Du Bois wrote in a tradition that assumed nations were built on collective self-understandings. In America, he contended, the nation's central turning point had been misshapen by white supremacy and the necessity of a mythology of reunion. According to Du Bois, the war and Reconstruction had left too many "terrible wounds" unhealed; in school textbooks, popular culture, and scholarship, the nation suffered from a "searing of the memory" of that period.[1]

That searing of national memory had occurred over many decades. Reconstruction itself, 1865–77, was not only a time of political and constitutional strife, but also an era of unprecedented clashes between raw memories of war, extreme suffering, grand political ambitions, and revolutionary turns in race relations and human rights. The traumatic impact of the war bred a language of personal and national regeneration, and of malleable rebirth metaphors that served the ends of rapid reunion, lenient reconstruction, and resistance to revolutions in race relations. But it also bred a notion of regeneration in which the South was remade in the North's image and harshly punished, the freedpeople enfranchised as citizens, and the Constitution rewritten. Some thought regeneration might be rapid, done in a season, while others foresaw a long, perennial process of reforming the country's civic ideology and its political institutions. Moreover, the emotional and material lives of the defeated, as well as the victors, had to be regenerated. Along with mourning the dead, this contested definition of regeneration was one of the earliest challenges to Civil War memory. Virtually everyone confronted its meanings in one way or another, whether they were traveling journalists, famous writers, defeated Southern planters, freedpeople trying to adjust to new labor arrangements, soldiers commemorating their experiences, or politicians in Congress debating Reconstruction policy. The struggle ensued not only over whose understanding of the Civil War would determine the character of Reconstruction, but also over whose definition of regeneration would prevail in the emerging political culture of the postwar era.

IN 1865, DUE TO the devastation of the war, America was truly a land with ruins. America's natural landscapes, especially in the West, had inspired imagery of ruins. But to European sensibilities, however beautiful a natural landscape, it was "uninteresting compared to a historic landscape."[2] Unlike the haunting, destroyed abbeys of the English Civil War of the seventeenth century or Rome's ancient, majestic city of ruins, America's destruction was brand new, but instantaniously historic, and at many battlefields and burial grounds, sacred. America was still not old; its ruins were not those made hoary by years and beautified through decay. But it was a country that had torn itself asunder—physically, politically, and spiritually. Some of its cities lay in rubble, large stretches of the southern countryside were depopulated and defoliated, and thousands of people were refugees from any sense of home. Americans were now a people with so much tragic, bloody history that their modern society would forever be burdened by its historical memory. America's "historic landscapes" became more *interesting* because of the Civil War.

No one understood this more deeply than defeated white Southerners, but their ruins inspired different reactions depending upon time and perspective. In October 1865, just after his release from a five-month imprisonment in Boston, former Confederate vice-president Alexander H. Stephens rode a slow train southward. In northern Virginia, he found "the desolation of the country from Alexandria to near Charlottesville was horrible to behold." When Stephens reached northern Georgia, his native state, he was again shocked: "War has left a terrible impression on the whole country to Atlanta. The desolation is heart-sickening. Fences gone, fields all a-waste, houses burnt." Father Abram Ryan, known as the "Poet Priest of the Lost Cause," eventually found inspiration and a sense of spiritual renewal in the South's ruins. "A land without ruins is a land without memories," said the itinerant preacher at the end of Reconstruction, "a land without memories is a land without liberty. A land that wears a laurel crown may be fair to see; but twine a few sad cypress leaves around the brow of any land, and, be that land barren, beautiless, and bleak, it becomes lovely in its consecrated cornet of sorrow, and it wins the sympathy of the heart and of history." From such melancholia and desolation, Stephens's political career, like that of many ex-Confederates, would revive—in the U.S. Congress and in the governor's chair of Georgia. It would also provide a defeated South with an exotic and romantic niche in the American popular imagination.[3]

In the wake of the war, thousands of northern readers learned about the material and political condition of the defeated South, from the writings of northern travelers. In *The South: A Tour of Its Battlefields and Ruined Cities* (1866), the novelist and poet John T. Trowbridge wrote the longest and most lyrical of the many travel accounts published in the immediate postwar years. As one of the first battlefield tourists, Trowbridge began his journeys in late August 1865 in Pennsylvania. Trowbridge encountered many "lively reminiscences of those terrible times" in the countryside surrounding Gettysburg. Upon his arrival at a hotel in the town square of Gettysburg, he asked the route to the battleground of the "world famous fight." The hotel keeper informed him, "you are on it now," and directed him to a house nearby with a "Rebel shell embedded in the brick wall."[4] The pilgrimages of American Civil War enthusiasts, relic hunters, veterans, statesmen, and historians to the sacred ground of Gettysburg had begun.

Guided by a local civilian hero of the battle, John Burns, Trowbridge began his tour on Cemetery Hill. The supreme "stillness" of the summer day was broken only by the "perpetual click-click" sound of stonecutters preparing headstones in the soldiers' cemetery. The scene moved Trowbridge deeply; it was already "the time-hallowed place of the dead." He felt an "overpowering sense of the horror and wickedness of war" as he watched workmen still digging trenches and laying foundations for headstones. He watched a veritable production line producing stones lettered "Unknown," and wondered whether regeneration could ever happen:

> Grown accustomed to the waste of life through years of war, we learn to think too lightly of such sacrifices. "So many killed," —with that brief sentence we glide over the unimaginably fearful fact, and pass on to other details. We indulge in pious commonplaces,—"They have gone to a better world; they have their reward," and the like . . . But the future, with all our faith, is vague and uncertain. It lies before us like one of those unidentified heroes, hidden from sight, deep-buried, mysterious, its headstone lettered "Unknown."

The curiosity and partisanship with which Trowbridge's northern readers probably devoured his book (and he supplied plenty of Yankee contempt for Rebels and images of the exotic, destroyed South) may not have allowed for much reflection on the tragic dimension of the Gettysburg cemetery. But in that late summer, 1865, Trowbridge pondered warily the nation's rebirth. "Will it ever rise?" he asked. The "uncounted thousands" of dead soldiers, he wrote, had "confronted, for their country's sake, that awful uncertainty." Strolling among the cemetery workmen, Trowbridge "looked into one of the trenches . . . and saw the ends of the coffins protruding. It was silent and dark down there." It was as though the illusive meaning of the war was in that trench; the coffin captured the observer as no abstract monument ever could. "I chose out one coffin from among the rest," remembered Trowbridge, "and thought of him whose dust it contained,—your brother and mine, although we never knew him." The author tried to think of the man's childhood, his parents and siblings, "his home, his heart-life." But he could only conclude: "I could not know; in this world, none will ever know."[5] Trowbridge altered his gaze, resumed his tour, and moved on to "other details."

Trowbridge saw his first real ruins in Chambersburg, Pennsylvania, the town that had been burned in a Confederate raid in 1864. At first it appeared as a "doomed and desolated place." It seemed a town with only "skeletons of houses" where "sightless windows . . . stared at us with their empty eye-sockets, and yawned at us with their fanged and jagged jaws." But the traveler saw rebuilding beginning all around. "There is no loss without gain," Trowbridge concluded. "Chambersburg will in the end be greatly benefitted by

Main Street in Richmond, the Confederate capital, April 1865. (Cook Collection, Valentine Museum, Richmond, Virginia)

the fire . . . So let it be with our country; fearful as our loss has been, we shall build better anew."[6] Such was the assurance and the regeneration of the victors.

When Trowbridge reached Richmond by mid-September, he found himself surprised at the beauty of the city, "although she appeared to be mourning for her sins at the time in dust and ashes." Here Trowbridge encountered a vast "burnt district" left from the great fire of April 3, 1865. Among the "beds of cinders . . ., broken and blackened walls, impassable streets deluged with debris," Trowbridge found laborers, the majority of whom were black, beginning the work of rebuilding. In a morality tale about free and slave labor, rubble and reconstruction, Trowbridge described how black masons and carpenters, "sitting down amid the ruins, broke the mortar from the old bricks and put them up in neat piles ready for use." The author talked with one twenty-one-year-old laborer, married and the father of two children, making a dollar and a half per day. The young ex-slave described himself as a "heap better off" than under slavery, and he expected to get his "rights" soon. He was not certain of what those rights would be, but he thought "land" from his former master was in order. "I worked for him for twelve years," said the laborer, "and I think something is due me." Trowbridge fashioned many images of a regenerative Richmond: white Virginians, their faces "with a dazed look . . ., groping about, as if they had lost something, or were waiting for something"; and black Virginians amid ruins, hopeful and industrious, rebuilding the city. What the future held for such images remained to be seen.[7]

Another northern traveler, John R. Dennett, commissioned by the new magazine the *Nation,* arrived in Richmond even earlier than Trowbridge. Among Dennett's many conversations with Virginians was one long talk with an old planter, identified only as "Mr. K," who had owned 115 slaves prior to the war. Most of his "servants" had left him by the end of the war, and the planter now worked parts of his fifteen hundred acres in Amelia County with hired hands. "I suppose someone else has hired mine," complained Mr. K. The planter saw no future for blacks as free laborers. "The Negro," offered Mr. K, "is doomed to undergo extinction. Less than a hundred years of freedom will see the race practically exterminated." Dennett's talk with the old planter lasted through a long boat ride on the James River and encompassed many topics, especially the future of the freedmen. Their conversation became so "pleasant" that Dennett asked the planter if he did not expect all the antagonism of the war to quickly subside and the "old friendly feeling" to resume between the sections. He was surpised at the bitterness of Mr. K's answer: "No sir, never. The people of the South feel they have been . . . most tyranically oppressed by the North. All our rights have been trampled upon. We knew that we had a perfect right to go and leave you. We were only carrying out the principles of the Revolution."[8] Dennett's conversation with the planter exhibited both the flickerings of reunion as well as how much that reunion owed to white Southern desires to control the lives of Southern blacks.

In Richmond hotel parlors Dennett encountered a steady stream of white Southerners obsessed with the relationship of race to reunion. Virtually all acknowledged their "subjugation" by war, but warned the Yankee observer that they would never submit to "Negro suffrage" or "nigger regiments . . . put over them." Dennett also spoke with two local black leaders preparing for a state convention. Both were self-improvement advocates, although they were convinced that the new "relations between capital and labor could not safely be left to natural laws." "Legislation," the two black spokesmen told Dennett, "if not used in behalf of the colored laborer, would be used against him."[9] Driving every conversation Dennett had in the former Confederate capital was the awareness that a new social and political world had to rise out of the ashes of war. Raw memory pushed against the uncertain future, retribution collided with grudging admiration, vows to never forget and the sounds of rebuilding vied to be heard all at once. The forces of race and reunion were shaping one another even before Reconstruction policies were implemented.

On December 9, 1865, the *Richmond Dispatch* resumed publication, its facilities having been consumed in the fire during the fall of the city. In its opening editorial, "The Past and the Present," the paper announced itself "endowed with the Promethean fire." Reborn, it vowed to carry on its prewar mission of the "improvement" of Richmond and Virginia. As the foundation of its new life, the *Dispatch* declared an early, if moderate, version of Lost Cause ideology. The South had fought from a "sense of rights under the Constitution," maintained the editors, "and a conscientious conviction of the justice of their position." The founding fathers had bequeathed the inevitable war to the country because they had left as an unfinished question the proper relation of the states to the federal government. In effect, the South, the paper argued, had sacrificed itself in order for the country to find an answer. The South had fought with unparalleled "courage and constancy," and borrowing from Robert E. Lee's farewell to his troops (a cardinal tenet of Lost Cause faith), it had submitted to "the fates" only because its armies had been "overwhelmed by superior numbers and resources."[10] In the tone and substance of the *Dispatch's* Promethean rebirth, one finds virtually all the ingredients (except organizations and rituals) that would form the Lost Cause: a public memory, a cult of the fallen soldier, a righteous political cause defeated only by superior industrial might, a heritage community awaiting its exodus, and a people forming a collective identity as victims and survivors. Nowhere in the paper's reflection on the "Past and the Present" was there a single mention of slavery or black freedom. That evasion would be critical in Southern memory of the war.

In the North the language of rebirth intoned in many voices. The *Nation* celebrated the Fourth of July, 1865, aware that for so many families mourning their dead, "the brightest picture has its dark side." But with a victor's self-congratulation, the new magazine announced: "It is not simply the birth of the nation which we now commemorate, but its regeneration." "We see the dawn of a new era," wrote Ralph Waldo Emerson in his *Journal* in the summer of 1865, "worth to mankind all the treasure and all the lives it has cost, yes, worth to the world the lives of all this generation of American men, if they had been demanded." The war Emerson celebrated with such bravado was a thoroughly moral experience. The conflict had "*moralized* many of our regiments, and not only so, but *moralized* cities and states." By November 1865, as the political crises over Reconstruction began, Emerson waxed more pessimistic. "We hoped that in the peace, after such a war," he confided, "a great expansion would follow in the mind of the country: grand views in every direction—true freedom in politics, in religion, in social science, in thought. But the energy of the nation seems to have expended itself in the war."[11] As Reconstruction conflicts and economic revival and expansion began to dominate American consciousness, many commentators lamented a war-induced loss of moral bearings.

Harriet Beecher Stowe interpreted the last days of the war in confident, apocalyptic terms. Writing in 1865, and relying on a thoroughly Christian sense of history, Stowe portrayed the American nation as God's own afflicted family—sundered, but about to rise in new form:

> The prophetic visions of Nat Turner, who saw the leaves drop blood and the land darkened, have been fulfilled. The work of justice which he predicted is being executed to the uttermost. But when this strange work of judgment and justice is consummated, when our country, through a thousand battles and ten thousands

of precious deaths, shall have come forth from this long agony, redeemed and regenerated, then God himself shall return and dwell
with us, and the Lord God shall wipe away all tears from all faces,
and the rebuke of his people shall he utterly take away.

Perhaps the most extraordinary element of Stowe's confidence about regeneration was the easy way she imagined that, once all the tears were wiped away,
the "country" might even agree that Nat Turner had been one of its great
prophets. Abolitionists were to enjoy a few years in which they aspired to
shape the memory of the war.[12] But revolutionary violence has never found a
stable place in the mainstream of American memory.

In October 1866, at an early soldiers' reunion, a Vermont officer addressed
assembled veterans and families in the state legislative hall in Montpellier. In
a fiercely patriotic address, Colonel Wheelock G. Veazey signaled a thousand
such speeches to follow through the years. For the veterans the historical moment was a "post-revolutionary period," and the South's "treason" the revolutionary act. A majority had beaten a minority "at the ballot" and "with the
bayonet." Veazey's understanding of the war reflected the widespread Northern belief that the struggle had been prosecuted to the end to save the whole
society from dismemberment and disorder. "But out of this revolution grew a
reform," announced the Vermonter. "Instead of overturning the Republic, its
fires purified the nation. Instead of destroying free government, it resulted in
making the subjects of the government free. Instead of enslaving the free, it
freed the slave. This is the reformation, the national regeneration." Colonel
Veazey's certainties, not unlike Stowe's, included the destruction of slavery
and some notions of black equality. "The army has done the work of regeneration," said Veazey; "there remains to it to do the work of re-organization."
And such an effort would have to include the "full rights of freedom."[13]

In 1865–66, white Southerners faced utter defeat as perhaps no other
Americans ever have. Surviving soldiers and planter families held few certainties as their world dissolved. The metaphor of purifying "fires," so prevalent
in Northern rhetoric, was a real experience to Southern whites, many of
whom fled from their plantations and farms before the Union armies in
Georgia, the lower Mississippi River valley, or Virginia. White Southern
memory of the war was forever animated by this profound sense of loss in
1865. The conquered filled their letters and diaries with a combination of
defiance, despair, and fear.

In Tyler, Texas, on April 28, 1865, while living in exile from her Louisiana plantation home, Kate Stone wrote in her journal of General Robert E. Lee's rumored surrender. "All are fearfully depressed," she reported. "I cannot bear to hear them talk of defeat," Stone continued. "It seems a reproach to our gallant dead." With last-gasp bravado, she hoped that "the thousands of grass-grown mounds heaped on mountainside and in every valley of our country" would still rally the South "to be free or die." On May 15, Stone opened a journal entry with a definition of the South's immediate fate that no doubt spoke for many, especially women living in isolation and physical hardship. "*Conquered, Submission, Subjugation* are the words that burn into my heart, and yet I feel that we are doomed to know them in all their bitterness." She looked ahead and saw her class and her race as "slaves, yes slaves, of the Yankee Government." Stone's fears were quite specific as she described her people's "unendurable" fate: "Submission to the Union (how we hate the word!), Confiscation, and Negro equality—or a bloody unequal struggle to last we know not how long." While rocking a baby in July 1865, and singing all the songs she could remember, she found the "war songs sicken me; the sound is like touching a new wound. I cannot bear to think of it all—forget when I can."[14]

In Kate Stone's struggles to cope with the personal and collective elements of defeat, we can see the beginnings of white Southern Civil War memory. But we can also see how life, inevitably, revived. When Stone returned to the family plantation, Brokenburn, in late 1865, she was unable to reconcile herself to paying wages to black laborers. She later declared herself "deadly afraid" of the black soldiers who "strutted around in their uniforms" at Brokenburn in September 1867. But as old neighbors gathered to talk over their mutual trials, she found a new social life reborn. "I felt like I did not want to see anybody or ever dance again," confided Stone. But "after a good cry," she found that the "burden . . . slipped from my shoulders, and I was young again." Regeneration came in many forms. With extraordinary emotional resilience, Stone, who had lost two brothers in the war and watched a third (also a veteran) suffer in almost utter silence, survived. In 1869, she married Lieutenant Henry Holmes, with whom she bore four children. Kate Stone died in 1907, but not before revising her famous journal in 1900 and becoming a leader of the United Daughters of the Confederacy and the Confederate memorial movement in Tallulah, Louisiana.[15] She represented thousands of women and men among the conquered who converted their defeat into a triumphant remembrance.

In Georgia, the extended planter family of the Reverend Charles Colcock

Jones Sr. and Mary Jones provided another experience of white Southern defeat and early memory. Their plantation world in Liberty County, with hundreds of slaves, slowly began to dissolve during the war, and then was crushed in Sherman's march toward Savannah in early 1865. At war's end, with her husband dead, Mary Jones looked around her beloved plantation, Montevideo, and surveyed the destruction left by a Union cavalry raid. "Memory's buried stories lie all exhumed before my eye," she lamented. She found solace only in the great trees that remained. "These living memorials remain, but the hands that placed them there are moldering where no work nor device is found . . . The servants that used to faithfully . . . wait around us are (many of them) dead or scattered or sadly and willfully changed. All things are altered."[16]

Mrs. Jones's daughters-in-law confirmed such gloom. On April 30, 1865, Caroline S. Jones described her family as "almost paralyzed here [Augusta, Georgia] by the rapid succession of strange and melancholy incidents." Caroline took solace from the "righteous retribution upon Lincoln." "One sweet drop among so much that is painful," she said, "is that he at least cannot raise a howl of diabolical triumph over us." In shock that "slavery is entirely abolished," Eva B. Jones felt an "all enveloping sorrow." She coped, however, and "uninterruptedly sought forgetfulness" by reading, she claimed, in "fourteen volumes of history." Eva discovered, though, that "the study of human nature from the earliest epochs affords one little comfort." These were Confederate women undergoing the disaster and humiliation out of which much of white Southern Civil War memory was formed.[17]

In the wake of the war, Charles Jones Jr. and his mother struggled to hold on to their lands and their laborers. They had always considered themselves paternalistic slaveholders. But their feeble attempts to adjust to free labor were financially disastrous. Most of their freedpeople abandoned them. Charles moved to New York City at the end of 1865 to pursue a legal career. He maintained an absentee landlord's interest in the family's lands as they experienced annual failure. Charles and his mother complained incessantly about ungrateful ex-slaves who fled, put on airs, and refused to work in any of the old ways. The freedpeople were making their own decisions in late 1865, and according to Charles, "the women are the controlling spirits." Charles never believed in free black labor. He admitted that "we will have to recognize the fact at once that our former slaves have been set free . . . and that if they continue with us we must pay for their services rendered." Paying wages to blacks, though, was, to him, an "absolute experiment," one that white Southerners could only hope to "control . . . to at least a limited extent."[18] That distaste for wage labor, coupled with resistance to black political rights, eventually blunted the egalitarian aims of radical Reconstruction.

In 1877 Charles Jr. left a successful law practice in New York and returned to the politically "redeemed" Georgia. Life for this ex-Confederate family regenerated in a variety of ways. Jones and his family took up residence in an antebellum mansion near Augusta. He pursued a literary career and the law over the next decade. As a historian, Jones wrote several books on his native state, on the war, and about black folklore on the Georgia coast. In 1879, Jones founded the Confederate Survivors' Association of Augusta, served as the organization's only president until his death in 1893, and delivered at least a dozen annual Memorial Day addresses.[19]

Jones became an "ambivalent irreconciliable." He celebrated the Confederacy at every opportunity and wrote with deep nostalgia about the Old South. In 1870, on one of his annual visits back to Montevideo (the old plantation), Jones noted particularly "faithful" servants who had "done their best" to keep the place functioning. By 1882, the "old homestead" was "filled with memories pure and consecrated." Here were ruins of a civilization, not just of the destroyed sections of cities Northern travelers had seen. He feared that "inexorable decay" would turn into "something near akin to nothingness." His was an angry, if private, nostalgia. "Even the trees are growing old," lamented Jones. "The entire region is strangely changed. It is peopled only with the phantoms of things that were, and present images are a mockery of the blessed idols once here enshrined." In public, though, Jones mixed his unreconstructed zeal for Confederate memory with a pragmatic embrace of life as it was: his twelve years practicing law in New York, an honorary degree from the New York University Law School, and an application by his son for an appointment at West Point. What Jones rejected were the "commercial methods" used in the economic expansion of the New South. In 1887, in the Confederate cemetery in Augusta, Jones called for "a remembrance and an observance of the patriotism, the purity, of the manhood . . . of the days that are gone." The words he most detested, said Jones, were "*The New South* and *Boom*."[20] Jones's Confederate memory combined a new reconciliation with an old value system; he found his own terms on which to accept reunion. In the South, private nostalgia, public memory, and Reconstruction politics coalesced among whites to produce an increasingly lethal environment for the experiment in black equality forged out of the war.

Blacks experienced renewal through their newly earned rights, as well as in an extraordinary new attachment to the nation. Their expectations of citizenship allowed them to rejoice and complain. Private R. D. Hicks, a soldier in the Thirty-third U.S. Colored Troops, formerly the First South Carolina Volunteers, the first regiment composed exclusively of ex-slaves, wrote in August 1865 from a dusty road on a long march from Augusta, Georgia, to Anderson, South Carolina, that all they were doing was "luging they knapsacks from one side of the country to the other." Hicks insisted they deserved better because they were "noble hearted mans who have left theirs homes and familys come honorable and volunteer themsealvs in the United States service as Soldiers to fight for freedom." With clear-eyed reason, Hicks gave a black soldier's weary description of national regeneration: "this Regiment has been the cause of victory being restored to the United States." In February 1866, John T. Harper, a black veteran who had lost a leg in the war, wrote to Congressman and radical Republican leader Thaddeus Stevens, demanding that blacks be given officers' commissions in new regiments formed for Southern occupation duty. As Reconstruction plans were hotly debated, Harper wanted Stevens to know "how galling it was to me and to many of my comrades to be stopped from promotion . . . to the . . . rank of commissioned officer." In the new nation's army, he hoped, "competent colored men—may I say *gentlemen!*—shall be appointed as *captains* and *lieutenants*."[21]

To Frederick Douglass, renewal during Reconstruction required a full accounting for the past. To him, the new republic could not be reborn if blacks simply forgave and forgot. The political challenge of Reconstruction, Douglass maintained at the end of 1866, was "whether the tremendous war so heroically fought . . . shall pass into history a miserable failure," or whether the victors would gain the "rightful reward of victory over treason . . . a solid nation, entirely delivered from all contradictions . . . based upon loyalty, liberty, and equality." In grave but hopeful words, Douglass defined the problem of Reconstruction as the "great work of national regeneration and entire purification."[22]

In all of this language of regeneration, irreconcilable memories and expectations were still very much at war. The armies had virtually all disbanded, and the country was sick of war. Thus the conflicting conceptions of justice, victory, defeat, liberty, labor, and rights had to be worked through in the only arena available—politics. The outcome of the Second American Revolution would be, in part, a struggle for power between competing versions of what the war and emancipation had meant. In Ernest Renan's classic essay on nationalism, "What Is a Nation?" (1882) he aptly described a nation as "a large-scale solidarity . . . a daily plebiscite" constantly negotiated between "memories" and "present-day consent" and requiring a great deal of "forgetting."[23] Such was the situation and the fate of Reconstruction America.

THE CONFEDERACY WAS decisively defeated in the Civil War, and American slavery was unmistakably destroyed. But the great challenge of Reconstruction was to determine just how defeated the South really was, and to establish how free the emancipated slaves really were. During the struggle between President Andrew Johnson's lenient and the radical Republicans' harsh Reconstruction plans (1865–68), a crucial factor was just how pliant or defiant white Southerners chose to be. As the *Chicago Tribune* announced in April 1865, "the most important feature attending the regeneration of these States is the temper and disposition of the Southern people."[24]

In the immediate aftermath of the war, defeated and prostrate, it appeared to many that white Southerners would accept virtually any conditions or terms laid upon them. This was the initial conclusion of the northern journalist Whitelaw Reid, who believed that even black suffrage would be "promptly accepted"—that is, until he observed white Southern defiance revived by President Johnson's conciliatory Reconstruction measures. After his Southern tour, Reid left a mixed warning to policymakers about the disposition of white Southerners in 1866. "The simple truth is," Reid concluded, "they stand ready to claim everything, if permitted, and to accept anything, if required." Other Northern journalists observing the South reached similar conclusions. The initial war-bludgeoned compliance on the part of white Southerners gave way within a year to what Trowbridge called a "loyalty . . . of a negative sort: it is simply disloyalty subdued." A correspondent for the *New York Tribune* reported from Raleigh, North Carolina, that "the spirit of the Rebellion is not broken though its power is demolished." And a Northerner who had just returned from six months in South Carolina and Georgia informed Thaddeus Stevens in February 1866 that "the spirit which actuated the traitors . . . during the late rebellion is only subdued and *allows* itself to be *nourished* by *leniency.*"[25]

Against this backdrop, Andrew Johnson offered to the South his rapid Reconstruction policy. In late May 1865, Johnson announced his plan for the readmission of Southern states. It included a broad provision for amnesty and pardon for those participants in the rebellion who would take a loyalty oath to the Union. High-ranking ex-Confederate government officials were excluded from pardons for the time being, as were all Southerners who owned $20,000 or more worth of property. The latter group had to apply personally to the President for a pardon. Johnson's plan further required each former Confederate state to call a convention to revise its antebellum constitution, renounce secession, and accept the Thirteenth Amendment abolishing slavery; they would then be promptly restored to the Union.[26]

Johnson's plan put enormous authority back in the hands of white Southerners, but without any provisions for black civil or political rights. Indeed, Johnson himself was a thoroughgoing white supremacist and a doctrinaire state rightist. He openly encouraged the South to draft its notorious Black Codes, laws enacted across the South by the fall of 1865 that denied the freedmen political liberty and restricted their economic options and physical mobility. Designed as labor controls and a means for plantation discipline, such laws were part of the new constitutions produced by these "Johnson governments," and they expressed clearly white Southerners' refusal to face the deeper meanings of emancipation.[27] Presidential Reconstruction, as it evolved in 1865, allowed Southerners to recreate governments of and for white men. Moreover, Johnson was openly hostile to the Freedmen's Bureau, the agency created by Congress in the last months of the war to provide food, medical care, schools, and labor contract adjudication for the freedpeople. The President overruled military and Freedmen's Bureau efforts to redistribute some land from masters to ex-slaves. By the fall of 1865, pardoned ex-Confederates were reclaiming their lands, and with such presidential encouragement, reclaiming political power.

More than fifteen thousand Southerners submitted applications for individual pardons, with many applicants visiting the White House in person. By September 1865, pardons were being issued wholesale, occasionally hundreds in a single day. By 1866, seven thousand ex-Confederates excluded under the $20,000 provision had received pardons. The politics of forgetting seemed to be the order of the day. Many of the white Southerners who appeared to return to political power in their states were "Unionists" who had opposed secession in 1861 and still carried an allegiance to the old Whig Party in the South. Some of these Southern Unionists were bitterly anti-Confederate or anti-planter, but by and large, they did not support freedmen's rights, especially if the federal government allowed them [whites] a free hand in designing their political institutions. Indeed, every governor whom Johnson appointed to head the new state governments opposed black suffrage. Governor William Marvin of Florida told blacks in his state not to "delude themselves" into believing that emancipation would result in their political rights. He urged them to return to their plantations, work hard, and "call your old Master—'Master.'"[28]

Profoundly different memories and expectations collided in 1865–67, as presidential Reconstruction collapsed and the Republicans in Congress wrested control of the process away from Johnson. "These people [white Southerners] are not loyal; they are only conquered," wrote Union Brigadier General James S. Brisbin to Thaddeus Stevens in December 1865. "I tell you there is not as much loyalty in the South today as there was the day Lee surrendered to Grant. The moment they lost their cause in the field they set about to gain by politics what they had failed to obtain by force of arms." Brisbin thought the Black Codes would "reduce the blacks to a slavery worse than that from which they have just escaped."[29] Johnson's leniency seemed only to restore an old order and risk losing the very triumph that the Union forces had just won with so much sacrifice.

Thousands wondered, along with the *Nation,* whether Johnson's scheme was a "plan of reconstruction or reconciliation." Warning of ex-Confederate leaders who under the cover of presidential Reconstruction now urged their fellow Southerners to accept "restoration," the *Nation* designated "partisans of a restoration . . . the most extreme of extremists." Charles Sumner, the Republican leader in the U.S. Senate, developed his own harsher view of Reconstruction, writing, "Never was so great an opportunity lost as our President has flung away." Sumner's ire toward the South was never hidden. "The rebels must be broken in character as in battle," he wrote as early as May 1865. Much was at stake, and Sumner practiced in private what would soon be a public determination: "This republic cannot be lost. Therefore the policy of the President must fail." The tragedy of Reconstruction came not so much from the radical measures by which the South eventually was forced to reenter the Union, but from the irreconcilable character of the warring memories and motivations of the postwar years. "Perhaps a very low farce was thought necessary," Stevens wrote to Sumner early in the process, "amidst so many bloody tragedies."[30]

Johnson and the Republican leadership thus took divergent roads to Reconstruction. "Reconstruction is a very delicate question," Stevens wrote to President Johnson in 1865 with resounding understatement. "While I think we shall agree with you almost unanimously on the main objects you have in view I fear we may differ as to the manner of effecting them."[31] The conflict between Johnson and Congress from late 1865 to 1868 was an unprecedented

Constitutional struggle over the function of the federal government, the meaning of the war, the meaning of emancipation, and the character of Reconstruction policy. In December 1865, as Congress reconvened, Republicans seized authority and refused to seat the newly elected members from ex-Confederate states. They established the Joint Committee on Reconstruction, held extensive hearings in the first months of 1866, and began the redirection of Reconstruction policy that ultimately included black suffrage, a full declaration of citizenship for the freedmen, temporary disfranchisement for ex-Confederates, and a short-term military occupation of the South.

The radical Republicans had a genuine plan for Reconstruction. Their ideology was grounded in the notion of an activist federal government, a redefinition of American citizenship that guaranteed equal political rights for black men, and faith in free labor in a competitive capitalist system. The radicals greatly expanded federal authority, fixing their vision, as Sumner put it, on "the general principles" of "a national security and a national faith."[32] Their cardinal principle was *equality before the law*, which in 1866 they enshrined in the Fourteenth Amendment, expanding citizenship to all those born in the United States without regard to race. The same year Congress renewed the Freedmen's Bureau over Johnson's veto and passed the first civil rights act in American history.

Such legislation became reality because most Northerners were not ready to forget the results, and especially the sacrifices, of the war. The Southern states' rejection of the Fourteenth Amendment and Johnson's repeated vetoes of Reconstruction measures (as well as his repudiation at the polls in the Congressional elections of 1866) gave the radicals increased control over federal policy. In 1867 Congress divided the ex-Confederate states into five miitary districts and made black suffrage a condition of readmission to the Union. By 1870 all ex-Confederate states had rejoined the Union, and in most, the Republican Party—built as a coalition of "carpetbaggers" (Northerners who moved South), "scalawags" (native Southerners who gave allegiance to the new order), and thousands of black voters—held the reins of state government. Indeed black voters were the core constituency of Southern Republicanism and the means to power in 1867–68.

In monumental Congressional debates, in electoral politics, and in the daily lives of blacks and whites in the South, the heavy weight of the past did constant battle with the new day dawning during these pivotal Reconstruction years. In North Carolina, Thomas Settle Jr. demonstrated the diversity of white Southern outlook in the wake of the war. Settle had been a Democrat before the war and initially opposed secession. But as war came, he joined the Thirteenth North Carolina regiment. One year into the conflict he left the army, and for three bitter years, opposed the war and urged peace. By 1867, Settle had emerged as a prominent scalawag and helped create the Republican Party in his state. On opening night of the Republican convention in Raleigh in March 1867, Settle declared a position that would remain a tortured one in Southern memory for a long time. "The war," said the former slaveowner, "was commenced to perpetuate slavery. It went the other way, contrary to all the leaders of the rebellion. Therefore, slavery is forever dead . . . This has been the work of God, and I can say that it *is* for the best." The changes seemed breathtaking. "The old crust of ideas" rooted in slavery, he declared, had "broken up in a thousand fragments." Settle spoke for all sides in this transporting historical moment: "one month flings a greater flood of light upon the world than fifty years."[33]

Although Settle was not alone in his sentiments, the dominant white Southern attitude of the late 1860s is probably represented by some of those who wrote to their emerging arch-villian, Thaddeus Stevens. A sarcastic Virginian asked Stevens to send him some Congressional documents, including "your own *colored* speeches," since "you will not allow our so-called representative to get into your circus." Calling Stevens a "good *hater*," the correspondent asked the radical leader a direct question: "Which feeling is strongest and uppermost in your Abrahamic bosom,—*love* of the *negro,* or *hatred* of the *white man* of the south?" The Virginian concluded his insults by telling "dear Thad" to "let the Southern States alone for a little while, till they can catch their breath and go to work." Another Southerner wrote to Stevens thanking him for unifying the white South. "You have the thanks of every Southerner with whom I am acquainted," said A. Conroe, "for . . . your constant foulest abuse of this country." Conroe warned Stevens that the North had only "been able to *overwhelm not* conquer" the South. With prescience, he sent the radicals a challenge: "if any thing should unite such a people the language you use and the infamous measures proposed, are certain to do so."[34] No seeds of reconciliation took root in these exchanges.

Southern Unionists also wrote long letters to Republican Congressmen, often urging a radical approach to Reconstruction and pleading their personal cases of loyalty. Stevens must have been greatly encouraged by the white South Carolinian who suggested that the things to be forgotten in the South were the Johnson governments. Claiming he had been "*forced* into the ranks of the rebellion," Simon Corley wrote as if from the very text of radical

Reconstruction. "Give us then a Provisional government," he pleaded, "and 'let bygones be bygones' as far as the President's policy is concerned . . . organize a loyal state government of *republican form,* where all *loyal* men . . . shall have a voice *without reference to color or caste.*" Corley even offered to wait "twenty years for reinstatement to full citizenship" if Congress so deemed it necessary. A Virginian who had joined a Pennsylvania regiment in 1864 and had returned home to Madison County begged for federal protection of loyalists. "I do seek protection but find none," wrote Charles J. Smith. "Rebellion is as rife here now as it ever was . . . No loyal citizen is at all regarded. Since I came home I have been derided, avoided, and insulted." A Texan reported to Stevens that mob violence against Unionists had been rampant in his state. "Nearly every live oak on our premises stands a silent monument to mob-law," wrote A. J. Evans from Waco, "for at the foot of nearly every one is the uncoffined grave of some Union man." And from North Carolina, Stevens heard of the perils of political rule by ex-rebels. "The war is over," wrote Marion Roberts. "But we have no peace. The officers throughout the whole state organization . . . are filled almost entirely by original secessionists." In many places in the South, these local civil wars carried on for years.[35] From such local raw memories the national crisis over Reconstruction took its sustenance.

Political mobilization in Southern black communities was a stunning achievement in 1867–68. At the state and local levels black and white Republicans helped to establish public school systems, more equitable taxation, bargaining mechanisms between laborers and planters, and economic development. Union Leagues, originally founded as Northern patriotic clubs during the war, were the nexus of a remarkable political awakening. Racially integrated meetings, huge and small, occurred all over the South, especially in the spring of 1867. The freedpeople were self-consciously part of a new history. In the Houses Creek district of North Carolina, a racially mixed crowd gathered near a mill in "a beautiful grove" and amidst "loud and deafening cheers" held a flag-raising of the stars and stripes on a seventy-five-foot pole. In such a season of hope, blacks enjoyed a freedom of expression that they had only dreamed of, and claimed, as did an Alabama meeting, "exactly the same rights, privileges, and immunities as are enjoyed by white men—we ask nothing more . . . the law no longer knows white or black, but simply men." These Alabamians were fully aware of their adversaries, but such were their spectacular hopes that it seemed the past might be banished, that freedom might triumph over memory. They organized, acted, and dreamed. "The sad memories of the past will be forgotten," they concluded, "amid the joys of the present and the prospects of the future."[36] For most Southern blacks, remembrance and forgetting marched in step.

As Congress and the President tangled mercilessly for two years over how to reconstruct the Confederate states, Northerners of all backgrounds debated what it meant. A Vermonter wrote to Stevens in 1866, urging the radicals to "banish forever" the spirit of the Confederate South. A Union veteran from Missouri deeply resented the conciliation of the South and worried about the future public memory in America. "The attempts of the reactionary elements in this country to write history backwards," demanded Samuel Holmes, "must be stopped." In 1867, abolitionist Wendell Phillips urged his fellow reformers not to forsake the old cause. He counseled rejection of "all this milk and water conciliation, all this forgetting of the lessons of thirty years . . . and bring to the front again the frank speech . . . no matter what chips fly in our faces."[37]

But already in these early Reconstruction years, among a growing number of Northerners, sectional reconciliation was embedded in their very support of the Republican Reconstruction of the South. Calling Republicans to moderation in 1867, the *Buffalo Express* announced that "at some period in our history we must reach the point of forgiveness of the South, and when we dictate terms of restoration, and they accept them . . . that is the fitting time for the introduction of that virtue." Horace Greeley, reknowned editor of the *New York Tribune,* fashioned himself as a spokesman for the spirit of reunion. "There is a difference of opinion among Republicans as to Reconstruction," wrote Greeley in May 1867. He claimed all wanted "full justice to the Freedmen," but were "yet anxious for an early and general amnesty for Rebels and for the prompt restoration of the states."[38] The will to enforce Reconstruction and the desire for reconciliation with the South, especially in the interest of renewed commerce, gave many Northerners conflicting motivations. A genuine reunion was still premature.

On a long speaking tour of the South in 1867, Republican Senator Henry Wilson of Massachusetts tried desperately to combine the principles of radical Reconstruction (then ascendant) with a "spirit of kindness." "We of the North have won in the field, have won in the public councils," Wilson declared to an audience in New Bern, North Carolina. Northerners and Southerners had done their duty, "front to front, face to face" on many battlefields, Wilson remembered. But the long "conflict of ideas" was over. The time had arrived for "the passions, prejudices, and bitter memories engendered by the great struggle" to be "forgotten." Such forgetting in many circles certainly came with time, but not yet, especially regarding the "ideas" over which the war was fought. While the Reconstruction struggle ensued in Washington and across the South, Edward A. Pollard, wartime editor of the *Richmond Examiner,* wrote his long manifesto, *The Lost Cause,* published in 1867. Pollard issued a warning to all who would ever try to shape the memory of the Civil War, much less Reconstruction policy. "All that is left the South," wrote Pollard, "is the war of ideas." The war may have decided the "restoration of the union and the excision of slavery," declared Pollard, "but the war did not decide Negro equality."[39] Reconstruction was at once a struggle over ideas, interests, and memory.

As Congress engaged in the fateful debates over national policy in 1866–67, the floors of the House and Senate became arenas of warring memories. Many Republicans were clearly driven by a combination of retribution against the South, a desire to remake the Constitution based on black equality, and a quest for long-term political hegemony. Stevens left no doubt of his personal attitude toward ex-slaveholders and ex-Confederates. "The murderers must answer to the suffering race," he said on May 8, 1866. "A load of misery must sit heavily upon their souls." The public debate in Congress was often sanguinary; it challenged everyone's ability to convert primal memory into public policy. "I know that there is a morbid sensibility, sometimes called mercy," declared Stevens, "which affects a few of all classes, from the priest to the clown, which has more sympathy for the murderer on the gallows than for his victim." Yankee retribution never had a more vehement voice than Stevens, and no one ever waved the "bloody shirt" with greater zeal. "I am willing they shall come in when they are ready," Stevens pronounced. "Do not, I pray you, admit those who have slaughtered half a million of our countrymen until their clothes are dried, and until they are reclad. I do not wish to sit side by side with men whose garments smell of the blood of my kindred."[40]

"Bloody shirt" rhetoric lasted a long time in American politics; it was more than a slogan, and in these early years, it had many uses and diverse practitioners. As both raw personal memory and partisan raw material, the "bloody shirt" was a means to establish war guilt and a method through which to express war-induced hatreds. Whether the Southern states were to be reverted to conquered provinces and forced to languish while Congress reconceived their institutions, or whether a degree of forgiveness should lead to "immediate reunion" without Constitutional transformations as a Pennsylvania Democrat put it, depended in large measure on how politicians remembered or forgot the "blood" from the war. Congressman Charles E. Phelps, a Maryland Democrat, portrayed the South as "formerly possessed of the devil," but now as a defeated land, the "tormented and bleeding victim" had been exorcised of its evil core—"slavery." Phelps urged Republicans not to "manacle and cuff and curse the rescued, regenerated, and emancipated South." He imagined a new South, no longer "gnashing among the tombs" but already "sitting, clothed and in his right mind." Republican Ebon C. Ingersoll of Illinois, however, had no patience with such metaphors of devils coming to their senses, nor with leniency toward ex-Confederates. "The rebels were not made rebels in a day, and they cannot be made patriots in a day," demanded Ingersoll. "In my opinion, they must be born again. The only difference is this: during the war the rebel had a musket, now he has none. The difference is in the musket, not in the rebel."[41] Reconstruction was both a struggle among the living over the meaning of the dead and a fierce political fight to determine just what was alive or dead in the new order born from the war.

During Congressional debates over Reconstruction, members accused each other of favoring "revolutionary" measures. Two Ohioans, Democrat William E. Finck and Republican James A. Garfield, squared off in May 1866 over the enforcement measures in the Fourteenth Amendment. Finck accused the radicals of a "monstrous and revolutionary . . . scheme" designed to exclude the Southern states from the next several elections. Finck's favored image of the South was that of a humbled and acquiescent family member who had already "fully and completely yielded obedience to the Constitution." Like so many to follow him in the reunion politics of the rest of the nineteenth century, he folded the idea of evil Republican retribution into the litany of reasons for sectional reconciliation. "The time has come," declared Finck, "when the feelings of sectional hate and animosity should give way to the higher and nobler principles of magnanimity." Garfield countered by accusing his colleague of being a Copperhead, a Southern sympathizer whose wartime loyalties had followed him into Reconstruction. "It is not the first time that gentlemen on that side of the House," Garfield charged, "have asked the South to rally against the North." The war was not yet over between these two Ohioans.[42]

Democrats too displayed bloody shirts. Only rapid and "complete restoration," said Finck, could assuage the "oceans of blood and treasure" Americans had "poured out like water." He insisted, "The North and South are destined to live together as one people, in the same Union." And the way to rebuild that unity, in his view, was in the "noble example of our brave armies in the field, who, when the conflict had ended, no longer regarded the Southern people as enemies, but as friends." A reunion forged around the mutual valor and respect of soldiers did not lack advocates from as early as the surrender fields of Appomatox, and even earlier amidst the shared despair of hospital wards. Democrats who denounced radical Reconstruction and demanded immediate reunion without black rights and a rewritten Constitution were nevertheless insistent on their own place in the remembrance of wartime sacrifice. "No one party can rightfully boast of having saved the country," declared Benjamin Boyer of Pennsylvania in May 1866, "and those who are the most bloody-minded and proscriptive in the uses of victory, as a general rule, have shed the least blood in its achievement."[43] The long battle to define and own the legacies of the war had begun in full force.

In 1866–67, all sides in the epic Reconstruction debates seemed to hear and speak in the tones of a requiem. But this requiem was badly out of tune, its harmony discordant. Many earnestly sought healing and forgiveness as well as a speedy reunion. But the Republicans temporarily in control sought, from a variety of motives, a reimagined republic and a new South that could never again threaten the stability of the nation. Some Democrats, like Charles Eldridge of Wisconsin, argued that reconciliation was more a matter of the heart than of policy. "There is an agreement," Eldridge asserted, "that we will forgive them [Southerners], and if the fraternal union of our fathers is ever restored we must." Eldridge contended that the obligation to "forget and forgive" rested with Republicans, not Southerners. Eldridge's rhetoric was one of sections, of Yankees and Rebels, not one of ideas and issues.[44] Much more had to be reconciled than the blood and anguish of war. The blood had been shed over something fundamental. Reconstruction, therefore, was not about the timing and manner of forgiveness. Not yet, anyway. It was about the politics of retribution and the politics of rights, the profound questions involving race, before there could be a reunion.

Whenever Congressmen engaged the subject of race, they revealed the deepest source of their dilemma. In the *Nation*, E. L. Godkin had predicted this with remarkable insight. "The Negro's success in assuming a prominent position in the political arena," said the editor, "seems to be in the inverse ratio of the earnestness with which it is sought to suppress him and put him out of sight. Everybody is heartily tired of discussing his condition and his rights, and yet little else is talked about, and none talk about him so much as those who are most convinced of his insignificance." Such was the reality on the floor of both houses of Congress in 1866–68. In the final days of debate before the passage of the Fourteenth Amendment, Democrat Samuel J. Randall of Pennsylvania wished his colleagues could "leave the war-path, and return to the ways of friendship and peace." The Republicans' aim to establish "an equality in every respect between the two races" offended the Congressman's state rights faith, as well as his racial prejudices.[45] At stake in Reconstruction were fundamentally different conceptions of the war's results, and especially of the place of the freedmen in the new polity. Much hinged on this evolving core memory of the war. Randall and the radical Republicans had witnessed different wars.

During the two crucial years that the radicals held sway, they did seek to make the nation paramount over the states, and at least to root the idea of racial equality in the American imagination. Equality before the law is as profound and as threatening a principle as American politicians had faced since throwing off monarchy and inventing a republic. Without the Civil War and emancipation facing them as overwhelming realities, and the 4.5 million freedpeople confronting them as living challenges, the great Reconstruction measures (three Constitutional amendments and a variety of civil rights laws) would never have been passed in the 1860s and 1870s. But words alone could not remake America. "Something" made many of his colleagues "nervous," said Republican senator James W. Nye of Nevada. "There is some parting of old ties; there is something in the breeze that they snuff." That something was in the word "liberty," Nye suggested, especially as possessed by blacks. But to those who wished for peace and speedy reconciliation, Nye counseled that a country "turned upside down . . . upheaved in every part," could never be quieted and settled by the word."[46]

But words were potent weapons in these debates, and race was the anxious subject. Words became policy and action, and hence wrought the establishment of black suffrage, the expansion of citizenship, and the enactment of military rule over the ex-Confederate states as provided in the First Reconstruction Act of 1867. Republican Congressman Fernando Beaman of Michigan urged his colleagues in 1866 not to "forget justice, and remember only mercy." He hoped to "see the rights of the freedmen completely established." Democrat Andrew Rogers of New Jersey reacted with a stunning defense of the South's "revolution" that would fit comfortably into almost any Lost Cause rally two or three decades later. To Beaman's charge that Confederates had "murdered hundreds of thousands" of loyal Americans, Rogers countered: "they are not murderers, they are not thieves, they are not felons; they are simply political convicts before the altar of patriotism." He insisted that the American govenment "was made for white men and white women." Republican Reconstruction, in Rogers's view, could never overturn God's "edict" against a "social equality between the black race and the white race." Rogers struck to the heart of the matter in his resistance to the Fourteenth Amendment, a resistance that every ex-Confederate state imitated. "It is but the negro again," he said, "appearing in the background." Indeed, in backgrounds and foregrounds, the presence of free black folk was the preoccupation of early Civil War memory. By the end of 1866, Frederick Douglass had reached an exhilarating conclusion about the place of blacks in political affairs. "Men denounce the negro for his prominence," declared Douglass, "but it is no fault of his that in peace as in war, that in conquering Rebel armies as in reconstructing States, the right of the negro is the true solution of our national troubles."[47]

The freedpeople sought a justice adequate enough to procure personal dignity and economic independence. Many Americans, white and black, North and South, sought to heal the country and its people in body and soul. But there were many warring definitions of healing at play in the late 1860s. True collective healing required more of the country's shattered collective memory than it could bear. When the radicals sought to lay down permanent solutions to the war's results, they acted for a version of justice against formidable forces of reaction. To most Republicans, their vague sense of "justice" consisted of providing the ballot to the freedmen. Only suffrage, according to Senator William M. Stewart of Nevada, could surmount the two great obstacles to reunion—"hatred of rebels" and "hatred of the negro." The ballot would be the path to "justice," said Stewart, because blacks would then "have plenty of white friends, for the people of the United States love votes and office more than they hate negroes."[48] This thoroughgoing political liberalism, which saw all solutions as political and ignored economic reality, in time served both the aims of retribution and reconciliation; it claimed a grip at least on both justice and healing.

But in the minds of radical leaders healing could wait. As the House of Representatives was about to vote on the Fourteenth Amendment, Stevens declared: "in rebuilding, it is necessary to clear away the rotten and defective portions of the old foundations, and to sink deep and found the repaired edifice upon the firm foundation of eternal justice." Likewise, a year later, in fighting for passage of the First Reconstruction Act, James Garfield saw himself present at the new creation. "It is now our turn to act," he announced.

"They [Southerners] would not cooperate with us in rebuilding what they destroyed. We must remove the rubbish and rebuild from the bottom."[49] Republican Reconstruction was at least the attempt to build a new house—a reinvented republic. The citizens who lived in it would have to find ways to heal at the same time they learned to live in a more just world. The tragedy of Reconstruction is rooted in this American paradox: the imperative of healing and the imperative of justice could not, ultimately, cohabit the same house. The one was the prisoner of memory, the other a creature of law.

A RITUAL ILLUSTRATING the tormented relationship between healing and justice occurred in Richmond, Virginia, in May 1867. Former Confederate president Jefferson Davis was released from prison, remanded from civil to military authority, given bail, and freed. On May 11, an emaciated, gray-bearded, and feeble Davis road aboard the steamer *Sylvester* up the James River from the place of his two years' imprisonment, Fortress Monroe, to Richmond. Along the way, well-wishers cheered and wept, and some brought bouquets of flowers to the wharves. Davis's imprisonment had become an embarrassment to the federal government, and an increasingly bitter bone of political contention between President Johnson and the radical Republicans. The Reconstruction process was now firmly in Congress's hands with the passage of the First Reconstruction Act in March, and Johnson had more than once hinted that he would pardon Davis, the only remaining Confederate leader still in federal custody. Formerly charged and indicted for treason, he had not yet stood trial. Davis eagerly wanted a trial and refused all consideration of a pardon. By the spring of 1867, he was something of a pawn in Reconstruction politics, and more so, an idealized tragic hero who provided ex-Confederates a symbol of their suffering. As Reconstruction seemed ever harsher, Davis remained in his cell at Fortress Monroe, refusing to acknowledge that secession could ever be construed as treason and embodying continuing Confederate defiance.[50] But now distinguished Yankees paid his bail and Jeff Davis could be seen.

Fifty cavalry, a detachment of infantry, and untold numbers of police guarded the streets as Davis, his wife, Varina, and a small party rode from the Richmond wharf to the Spotswood Hotel. There the Davises occupied the

After his release from prison, Jefferson Davis was photographed in a Richmond studio on July 3, 1867. (Cook Collection, Valentine Museum, Richmond, Virginia)

same rooms as in the spring of 1861, when the Mississippian had come to Richmond to lead the Confederacy. Spectators were everywhere, including a large crowd of blacks. Rumors had abounded for days that Richmond blacks would "riot" in reaction to the release of Davis. On Sunday, May 12, as Davis received an endless train of well-wishers and flowers at his hotel, at least one disturbance did occur between blacks and Richmond police. Four policemen were allegedly beaten and eighteen rioters captured. Squads of police were placed at all the black churches that Sunday. At a meeting of blacks held the night before Davis's arrival (May 10), a visiting speaker from Massachusetts, Jedekiah K. Haywood, was arrested for his incendiary speech. He had allegedly advised Richmond blacks that, in the wake of Davis's release, they should "hold high carnival, or do what you please . . . for great bodies do as they have a mind to." Haywood's bail was placed at $3,000.[51] No riot ensued; the only carnival might be said to have occurred in the courtroom drama of Davis's bailing and release.

On May 13, before federal Judge John Underwood, Jefferson Davis entered a courtroom in the very building where he had often presided over the Confederate war effort. The men assembled to pass judgment on his freedom were surrounded by walls that only a little over two years earlier had held military campaign maps. An integrated crowd of between three hundred and four hundred swelled the chambers. A grand jury composed of blacks and whites sat to the right of the judge. Among the many ex-Confederates who came to lend moral support were former generals Fitzhugh Lee and John Imboden. Davis was dressed in a plain white and black plaid suit, wore green kid gloves, and walked with a cane. Judge Underwood quickly moved to the matter at hand. He declared Davis's case "bailable." Underwood tried to provide a tone of reconciliation, assuring the crowd "that we are about to enter on a peace more permanent than ever before."[52] In this atmosphere of anxiety and celebration, eighteen men stepped forward to post Davis's $100,000 bail. But Davis never did receive his coveted trial. As his release became official, supporters threw open the windows of the courthouse to the May afternoon and shouted the news to crowds in the street. As the former Confederate president, in all his frailty, slowly departed the building, a huge crowd cheered; many observed that it was the first time since the war that the "rebel yell" had been heard.

Among the men who made bail for Jefferson Davis were three wealthy and prominent Northerners: former radical abolitionist Gerrit Smith, entrepeneur and business tycoon Cornelius Vanderbilt (by proxy), and the indefatigable Horace Greeley. Smith had long exhibited a turbulent personality, but the spectacle of this former supporter of John Brown (who had been mentor and friend to so many black abolitionists) making bail for Davis was a strange sideshow in this early ritual of reunion. In August 1866, Smith had written to Andrew Johnson, declaring Davis's confinement "an insult to the South . . . and a no less deep dishonor to the Government." Two months before going to Richmond, Smith wrote to William Lloyd Garrison detailing his support of reconciliation on moral grounds. He longed for "a heart-union between the North and the South," said Smith. He opposed all harsh measures toward the conquered states. "Let our terms of Reconstruction be full of love and generosity as well as of justice, and we shall be able to pin the South to us." Smith did not grasp just how out of place such moral suasion was in Reconstruction politics. Later, in a retrospective attempt to explain his motives, Smith walked, at least rhetorically, right into the arms of unreconstructed Southerners. "A sufficient reason we should not punish the conquered South," he said, "is that the North was quite as responsible as the South for the chief cause of the war . . . the mercenary North coolly reckoned the political, commercial, and ecclesiastical profits of slavery."[53] The men who made bail for Davis had complicated motives for doing so. A sincere desire for reunion undoubtedly guided their action, but all knew, as well, that a renewal of commercial ties between North and South necessitated these emotional rituals of reunion.

Horace Greeley's presence in Richmond was the most important and controversial. At least as early as the fall of 1866 in the *New York Tribune*, Greeley had urged Northern sympathy toward Davis. Varina Davis had written emotional appeals to Greeley, seeking his influence with the federal government. "I have come to look upon you my dear sir," she wrote from Fortress Monroe in October 1866, "as one who would gladly lighten my burthen if it were in your power." Mrs. Davis described her husband's "deprivations" in some detail. According to his wife, Davis had been "chained, starved, kept awake systematically, almost blinded by light and tortured by the ingenuity of a cruel jailor." Although these accusations were only marginally true, Varina Davis did make a point that, no doubt, affected Greeley and others: in prolonged confinement, the prisoner had never "been tried."[54]

In 1866–67, Greeley began to build a political career around the grand aim of sectional reunion. He was still a Republican in his support of the Fourteenth Amendment and black suffrage, but he zealously pursued reconciliation. Greeley believed that rapid reunion was essentially a matter of political skill, management, and human will. "The truth is," he wrote in December 1866, "there is but one question of moment remaining to be settled; and that is manhood suffrage." Like so many other Americans, he saw the vote as the essence of liberty; order, commerce, and a new, mystic unity would somehow flow from the expansion of suffrage. "What is needed," said Greeley, "is that the matter shall be so fine-scented that we do not seem to force Negro Suffrage on the South at the point of the bayonet, but suffer her to unite with us in pacifying the country and fixing forever one uniform rule for suffrage throughout the Union." It was a matter of commitment. "We can get the Negro out of politics and into complete manhood *this winter,*" he concluded. Greeley broke with the radicals in his peculiar taste for moderation. As he set about to make Southern friends, his personal quest to convince the nation to "clasp hands across the bloody chasm" carried him all the way through a disastrous presidential run in 1872.[55]

During Davis's discharge in Richmond, in May 1867, Greeley walked to the front of the courtroom to sign the bond. There he and Davis met for the first time and exchanged warm conversation. The following evening, the Exchange Hotel gave a banquet for all the dignitaries, journalists, and lawyers who had participated in the release. The Richmond hosts offered an opening toast to "a reunited North and South," to which Greeley responded, as formal chairman: "to the brave men on both sides." Toasts followed to Confederate and Union generals as journalists from New York, Boston, London, and Richmond and other Southern cities raised their tumblers. The *Richmond Whig* celebrated the day's events, announcing that Northern "magnanimity" had in "one moment levelled barriers that might otherwise have remained for years."[56]

Most remarkable, however, was a meeting held at an African Methodist Episcopal Church in Richmond, to which Greeley was invited as the chief speaker. Blacks and whites attended in large numbers to hear Greeley's beguiling case for freedmen's rights and rapid reunion. The speech set a tone, and given its setting, provided a kind of founding text for sectional reconciliation; variations on its themes would echo for decades with profound political consequences. *"Shall the sword devour forever?"* asked Greeley, rising to the occasion. "So asked of old a Hebrew prophet, standing amid the ruins of his desolated country":

> So, I an American citizen, standing amid some of the ruins of our
> great civil war, encircled by a hundred thousand graves of men

who fell on this side and that, in obedience to what they thought the dictates of duty and of patriotism, shall speak in the spirit of that prophet, asking you whether the time has not fully come when all the differences, all the heart-burnings, all the feuds and the hatreds which necessarily grew up in our great struggle, should be abandoned forever?

Greeley denounced the Black Codes of 1865 and claimed that such "outrages" had been the chief impediment to an "early and genuine reconstruction of the Union." He received a rousing ovation from blacks when he pronounced that "no reconstruction would be real and enduring which did not include guaranties for the rights of the colored people of the South." He cleverly appealed to white Southerners to join in making "equal rights" for blacks the "cornerstone" of Reconstruction, not merely because it was right, but because of the "general deportment" of slaves—their alleged devotion to their masters and their eschewal of insurrection—during the war. Appealing to the hearts of his listeners, Greeley longed "to be done with the topic at once . . . to say that we have settled forever the question of black men's rights by imbedding them in the constitutions of the states and the nation."[57] In such sincere wish fulfillment lay the seeds of a real reunion.

The sword Greeley asked Americans to lay down was double-edged. As he neared the end of his Richmond speech, the voice of the *New York Tribune* asked his audience to engage in a purposeful forgetting. "Men of Virginia!" he shouted. "I entreat you to forget the years of slavery, and secession, and civil war now happily past . . . forget that some of you have been masters, others slaves,—some for disunion, others against it,—and remember only that you are Virginians, and all now and henceforth freemen." How dearly the Richmond blacks in that AME Church that night must have wanted to believe in Greeley's words. They heard his call to "Republicans and Conservatives, whites and blacks, to bury the dead past in mutual and hearty good-will . . . and exalt the glory of our . . . reunited, magnificent country."[58] If only Horace Greeley could have spoken a world into being!

Greeley's performance in Richmond garnered him condemnation from many corners of the North, among black and white Republicans and among veterans. The Union League Club of New York called a special meeting to consider sanctioning its famous member, an action they never took. The *New York Herald* feared that the Northern people would now have to conclude that "if there is no treason the war was all wrong, and the national debt is a national swindle." The *Nation* reacted to Greeley's conduct in Richmond with "repulsiveness" and accused him of "a love of notoriety." Greeley had too easily forgotten, said the *Nation,* that "the last six years' . . . struggle" had not been merely to "settle a political difference, but . . . between moral right and moral wrong." Greeley's premature reconciliation plans led the humorist Petroleum Nasby to recount in the *Toledo Blade* the scenes in Richmond with Confederates standing misty-eyed and cheering at every turn: "'Three cheers for Jeff'son Greely and Horris Davis—one and inseprable, now and forever!' shouted one enthusistic Confedrit." In New York, Post No. 8 of the Grand Army of the Republic (the principle Union veterans' organization) met on Bowery Street and condemned Greeley's role in the release of Davis, who, in their official response, they called "the fell Moloch of the Southern rebellion." And black Methodists across the country read of the "unspeakable disgust" of the *Christian Recorder.* "The nation ought to put a legal brand upon this representative of the so-called Confederacy," wrote its editor, Benjamin Tanner.[59] Coming as it did in the wake of passage of the First Reconstruction Act in March, during the intensification of the impeachment movement against Andrew Johnson, and as enormous optimism swept through black communities, the release of Jefferson Davis seemed, to many, an incongruent step in Reconstruction.

Almost as telling as the outrage were the expressions of support Greeley received from all corners of the country and beyond. "Blessed are the peace makers," B. F. White, a Louisianan and a Christian minister, wrote from Zurich, Switzerland, thanking Greeley for his "noble and philanthropic course." U.S. Supreme Court Justice Richard G. Parsons admired Greeley's Richmond speech in part because it provided a moderate path to reunion, one that would blunt radical designs of Southern land "confiscation." Parsons feared that genuine property confiscation would push "to madness the present unfortunate condition of the Southern mind." Greeley's case for Davis's amnesty, and for a collective reunion of the heart, seemed for many a way out of the confusions and challenges of Reconstruction. "If such frank, manly, noble utterances," said Parsons, "do not have a powerful tendency to heal the terrible wounds of this civil war and bring back reason and honest effort to the hearts of the broken people, nothing will."[60]

For many whites, the most affecting element in Greeley's widely reprinted speech was his bold assertion that slavery was something all sides could forget—if they only willed it so. Writing as the corresponding secretary of the Society of Loyal Sons of Maryland in New York City, J. E. Snodgrass gushed with admiration for Greeley's speech. He interpreted Greeley's "all-controlling idea as touching Slavery and its incidents . . . that both races involved in it were alike, though not to the same degree of wrong, *victims* of a false state of things." As time passed, no more effective way emerged for evading the meaning of the American Civil War than in this understanding of slavery and "its incidents." History carries no responsibilities when everyone can carry the mantle of a victim of false forces. "Now that the victimizer is dead," wrote Snodgrass, "there is nothing left to feel wrath about." All sides, black and white, North and South, could now share a "sense of their similar if not coequal misfortune in the past."[61] With time, and as part of the rise and fall of Reconstruction, such private expressions of how Americans could escape their past developed into public rituals.

On a national political scale, Greeley's brand of reconciliation—to secure black rights under law, give universal amnesty to Southerners, and then forget the past—was still too premature to form any consensus among a people only two years out of war. But the need for new economic expansion, an abiding racism, and a defiant South lay in the immediate future. Greeley's bold stroke for reconciliation demonstrated that in place as early as 1867 were the desire as well as the arguments necessary for Americans to find a collective road to reunion that might bypass the heart of the Civil War's meaning. Greeley saw himself as a healer; he and others thought that such healing could be achieved by jettisoning, or simply refashioning, the past. Not so, said an article from the *Toledo Blade,* reprinted in Greeley's own paper the week before the editor went to Richmond to help release Jefferson Davis. In a story concerning a white Virginia lawyer who, in an effort to win votes from blacks, appealed to former slaves with stories of how he had loved his black mammy, the paper concluded: "They are laying it on too thick. The backs of the audience addressed by the Richmond lawyer have not yet had time to heal; and every one of them has either been upon the auction-block or seen his relatives there."[62] Radical Reconstruction still had its days of triumph, and it would leave an indelible legacy of racial democracy. But the true healing of the nation's soul that so many wished for in the 1860s eluded America.

THREE

Decoration Days

> The procession went on, and stopped here and there
> at the little graveyards on the farms, leaving their
> bright flags to flutter through summer and winter
> rains and snows, and to bleach in the wind and sun-
> shine. . . They sent flags to all the distant graves, and
> proud were those households who claimed kinship
> with valor.
>
> —SARAH ORNE JEWETT, "Decoration Day," 1892

AT THE END OF the Civil War the American people faced an enormous challenge of memorialization. Their war of limited aims in 1861 had become an all-out struggle of conquest and survival between the largest armies the western hemisphere had ever seen. Approximately 620,000 soldiers died in the war, 60 percent on the Union side and 40 percent Confederate. American deaths in all other wars combined through the Korean conflict totaled 606,000. Death and mourning were everywhere in America in 1865; hardly a family had escaped its pall. In the North, 6 percent of white males aged 13–43 had died in the war; in the South, 18 percent were dead. Of the 180,000 African Americans who served in the Union army and navy, 20 percent perished. Diseases such as typhoid, dysentery, and pneumonia claimed more than twice as many soldiers as did battle. The most immediate legacy of the war was its slaughter and how to remember it.[1]

Death on such a scale demanded meaning. During the war, soldiers in countless remote arbors, or on awful battlefield landscapes, had gathered to mourn and bury their comrades, even while thousands remained unburied, their skeletons lying about on the killing fields of Virginia, Tennessee, or Georgia. Women had begun rituals of burial and remembrance in informal ways well before the war ended, both in towns on the homefront and sometimes at the battlefront. Americans carried flowers to graves or to makeshift monuments representing their dead, and so was born the ritual of "Decoration Day," known eventually also as Memorial Day.

In most places, the ritual was initially a spiritual practice. But very soon, remembering the dead and what they died for developed partisan fault lines. The evolution of Memorial Day during its first twenty years or so became a contest between three divergent, and sometimes overlapping, groups: blacks and their white former abolitionist allies, white Northerners, and white Southerners. With time, in the North, the war's two great results—black freedom and the preservation of the Union—were rarely accorded equal space. In the South, a uniquely Confederate version of the war's meaning, rooted in resistance to Reconstruction, coalesced around Memorial Day practice. Decoration Day, and the ways in which it was observed, shaped Civil War memory as much as any other cultural ritual. The story of the origins of this important American day of remembrance is central to understanding how the reconciliationist practices overtook the emancipationist legacies of the Civil War.

BLACK SOUTH CAROLINIANS and their white Northern abolitionist allies were primarily responsible for the founding of Decoration Day. In Charleston, South Carolina, where the war had begun, the first collective ceremony, involving a parade and the decoration of the graves of the dead with spring flowers, took place on May 1, 1865. The May Day event was the culmination of a series of extraordinary ceremonies in Charleston, where in the last months of the war the planters' world, with their jewel of a city, had been turned upside down. After a long seige, a prolonged and devastating bombardment, and numerous fires, the lower half of Charleston was in ruins by February 18, 1865, when it was finally evacuated. Ringing the harbor, Forts Sumter, Moultrie, and Ripley, as well as Castle Pinckney, had held out valiantly with small Confederate garrisons through more than a year and a half of seige and shelling.

From the battery at the harbor to Calhoun Street, Charleston had become the domain of mobs and anarchy. Above Calhoun Street, remnants of the city's white population (most had fled) tried to maintain a society through the long seige. By the end of 1864, wrote Mrs. St. Julien Ravenal, one of its chroniclers, the city had an "extraordinary appearance . . . it was awfully biblical! . . . to pass from this bustling, crowded scene to the lower part of the town was . . . like going from life to death." Another Charlestonian called the lower section "a city of the dead." As the city was abandoned, fires broke out everywhere, many of which were ignited in bales of cotton left in huge stockpiles in public squares, as if they were the funeral pyres of a dying civilization. Among the first Union troops to enter Charleston was the Twenty-first U.S. Colored regiment; their commander, Lieutenant Colonel A. G. Bennett, received the formal surrender of the city from its mayor, and the troops helped put out fires in those first days of occupation. As the black soldiers marched up Meeting Street singing liberation songs, they left indelible memories on all who saw them.[2]

For black Charlestonians this was a time of celebration and of ritual role reversals. On March 3, a large crowd of blacks gathered in Marion Square to watch as thirteen black women, elegantly dressed to represent the thirteen original states, presented the Union Commander, General Quincy A.

Charleston, South Carolina, in ruins, 1865. (Photo by George N. Barnard, Hallmark Photographic Collection, Hallmark Cards, Inc.)

Gillmore, with a flag, a bouquet of flowers, and a fan for Mrs. Lincoln. On March 29, approximately four thousand blacks marched in an unprecedented victory parade. Companies of soldiers were followed by tailors, coopers, butchers, sailors, and many other tradesmen. Eight companies of firemen marched, as did some eighteen hundred schoolchildren with their teachers, some of whom were from the Northern freedmen's aid societies that had been active on the Carolina coast for nearly two years. Then, dramatically, two carts rolled along in the procession, one carrying an auction block and an auctioneer selling two black women and their children. The second cart contained a coffin with a sign announcing the "death of slavery" and that "Sumter dug his grave on the 13th of April, 1861."[3]

In such collective public performances, blacks in Charleston proclaimed their freedom and converted destruction into new life. In richly symbolic parades and other ceremonies they announced their rebirth; whatever the new order would bring in their lives, they drew a line of demarcation between past and present. These were days of awe and wonderment, of sorrow and gaiety. The freedpeople of Charleston had converted Confederate ruin into their own festival of freedom. They provided the images and metaphors, even the objects and places with which to establish the earliest "theaters of memory" for the transition from slavery to freedom.[4]

On April 14, a celebration took place at the mouth of the harbor, in Fort Sumter itself. Four years to the day after the surrender of the fort, General Robert Anderson returned to Charleston with many Northern dignitaries to raise the flag he had lowered in 1861. Three thousand African Americans crammed on to the island fortress for the ceremony. In attendance were abolitionist William Lloyd Garrison and President Lincoln's secretary, John G. Nicolay. Also among the throng was Martin Delaney, an abolitionist and writer, and now a major in the Union army; the son of Denmark Vesey, the leader of a slave rebellion who was executed in Charleston in 1822, was there as well. The former slave and boat pilot Robert Smalls was near Fort Sumter aboard the *Planter* (which was filled with a contingent of freedpeople), the steamer he had commandeered and sailed out of Charleston to freedom during the war. The Reverend Henry Ward Beecher, orator of the day, condemned South Carolina's secessionists to eternal damnation: the South's "remorseless traitors" were held fully responsible for the war. Speaking to Southern leaders, Beecher promised vengeance, that they would be "whirled aloft and plunged downward forever and forever in endless retribution." To other white Southerners, Beecher promised forgiveness and fellowship. Many in that special audience hoped for guidance from Beecher about the confused and delicate questions of Reconstruction, but on that count they heard little in what unfolded as primarily a festival of victory, thanksgiving, and celebration. When hearing a regimental band play "John Brown's Body," Garrison, who two decades earlier had a price put on his life by the state of South Carolina, broke down and wept.[5]

Flowers were blooming everywhere amidst the ruins of Charleston; for so many, remembrance at this early date was but a fragrance full of warring emotions. As the flag reached its height on the staff in the fort, guns all around Charleston harbor opened up in a salute. The grand day ended that evening at a banquet in the city as Anderson, among others, offered many toasts, some of which were to President Lincoln, who was that very night assassinated in Ford's Theater in Washington.

During the next two weeks in Charleston, as elsewhere, mourning over Lincoln's death swept through the community of blacks and their Unionist and white abolitionist allies. Death required attention all over the land. A Union quartermaster general's report shortly after Appomattox noted that only about one-third of the Union dead in the war were interred in identifiable graves. The federal government instituted an elaborate program of locating and burying the Union dead all over the South in newly created national cemeteries, and by 1870, some 300,000 Northern soldiers had been reinterred in seventy-three national cemeteries, with 58 percent identified. Retrieval and recognition of the Confederate dead took much longer due to inadequate resources. Early Reconstruction policies had not extended the federal program of reinterrment to Confederates.[6] All of this death on the battlefield, as well as the deaths of thousands of soldiers in prisons and hundreds of nameless freedpeople in contraband camps, presented an overwhelming burden for memorialization.

Charleston had more than its share of this burden. During the final year of the war, the Confederate command in the city had converted the planters' Race Course (horse-racing track) into a prison. Union soldiers were kept in terrible conditions in the interior of the track, without tents or other coverings. At least 257 died from exposure and disease and were hastily buried without coffins in unmarked graves behind the former judge's stand. After the fall of the city, Charleston's blacks, many of whom had witnessed the suffering at the horse-track prison, insisted on a proper burial of the Union dead. The symbolic power of the planter aristocracy's Race Course (where they had displayed their wealth, leisure, and influence) was not lost on the freedpeople. In conjunction with James Redpath and the missionaries and teachers among three freedmen's relief associations at work in Charleston, blacks planned a May Day ceremony that a *New York Tribune* correspondent called "a procession of friends and mourners as South Carolina and the United States never saw before."[7]

The "First Decoration Day," as this event came to be recognized in some circles in the North, involved an estimated ten thousand people, most of them black former slaves. During April, twenty-eight black men from one of the local churches built a suitable enclosure for the burial ground at the Race Course. In some ten days, they constructed a fence ten feet high, enclosing the burial ground, and landscaped the graves into neat rows. The wooden fence was whitewashed and an archway was built over the gate to the enclosure. On the arch, painted in black letters, the workmen inscribed "Martyrs of the Race Course." At nine o'clock in the morning on May 1, the procession to this special cemetery began as three thousand black schoolchildren (newly enrolled in freedmen's schools) marched around the Race Course, each with an armload of roses and singing "John Brown's Body." The children were followed by three hundred black women representing the Patriotic

African Americans founded Decoration Day here, at the graveyard of 257 Union soldiers labeled "Martyrs of the Race Course," May 1, 1865, Charleston, South Carolina. (Sketch by A. R. Ward, *Harper's Weekly*, May 18, 1867)

Association, a group organized to distribute clothing and other goods among the freedpeople. The women carried baskets of flowers, wreaths, and crosses to the burial ground. The Mutual Aid Society, a benevolent association of black men, next marched in cadence around the track and into the cemetery, followed by large crowds of white and black citizens. All dropped their spring blossoms on the graves in a scene recorded by a newspaper correspondent: "when all had left, the holy mounds—the tops, the sides, and the spaces between them—were one mass of flowers, not a speck of earth could be seen; and as the breeze wafted the sweet perfumes from them, outside and beyond . . . there were few eyes among those who knew the meaning of the ceremony that were not dim with tears of joy." While the adults marched around the graves, the children were gathered in a nearby grove, where they sang "America," "We'll Rally around the Flag," and "The Star-Spangled Banner."[8]

The official dedication ceremony was conducted by the ministers of all the black churches in Charleston. With prayers, the reading of biblical passages, and the singing of spirituals, black Charlestonians gave birth to an American tradition. In so doing, they declared the meaning of the war in the most public way possible—by their labor, their words, their songs, and their solemn parade of roses, lilacs, and marching feet on the old planters' Race Course. One can only guess at which passages of scripture were read at the graveside on this first Memorial Day. But among the burial rites the spirit of Leviticus was surely there: "For it *is* the jubilee; it shall be holy unto you . . . in the year of this jubilee ye shall return every man unto his possession."[9]

After the dedication, the crowds gathered at the Race Course grandstand to hear some thirty speeches by Union officers, local black ministers, and abolitionist missionaries, all chaired by James Redpath, the director of freedmen's education in the coastal region. Picnics ensued around the grounds, and in the afternoon, a full brigade of Union infantry, including the Fifty-fourth Massachusetts and the Thirty-fifth and 104th U.S. Colored Troops, marched in double column around the martyrs' graves and held a drill on the infield of the Race Course.[10] The war was over, and Memorial Day had been founded by African Americans in a ritual of remembrance and consecration. But the struggle to own the meaning of Memorial Day in particular, and of Civil War memory in general, had only begun.

According to a reminiscence written long after the fact, "several slight disturbances" occurred during the ceremonies on this first Decoration Day, as well as "much harsh talk about the event locally afterward." But a measure of how white Charlestonians suppressed from memory this founding in favor of their own creation of the practice a year later came fifty-one years afterward, when the president of the Ladies Memorial Association of Charleston received an inquiry for information about the May 1, 1865, parade. A United Daughters of the Confederacy official wanted to know if it was true that blacks and their white abolitionist friends had engaged in such a burial rite. Mrs. S. C. Beckwith responded tersely: "I regret that I was unable to gather any official information in answer to this."[11] In Southern and national memory, the first Decoration Day was nearly lost in a grand evasion.

As a Northern ritual of commemoration, Memorial Day officially took hold in May 1868 and 1869, when General John A. Logan, commander-in-chief of the Grand Army of the Republic (GAR), called on all Union veterans to conduct ceremonies and decorate the graves of their dead comrades. In general orders issued each of the two springs, Logan called for a national commemoration unlike anything in American experience save possibly the Fourth of July. In "almost every city, village, and hamlet church-yard in the land," charged Logan's circular, those who died to "suppress the late rebellion" were to be honored annually "while a survivor of the war remains." On May 30, 1868, when flowers were plentiful, funereal ceremonies were attended by thousands of people in 183 cemeteries in twenty-seven states. The following year, some 336 cities and towns in thirty-one states (including the South) arranged Decoration Day parades and orations. The observance grew manifold with time. In 1873, the New York legislature designated May 30 a legal holiday, and by 1890 every other Northern state had followed its lead.[12]

By the early 1870s, and for at least two decades thereafter, as late spring arrived and flowers were in full supply, one could not live in or near an American city or village, North or South, and remain unaware of the ritual of decorating the graves of the Civil War dead. In most communities, women carried the primary responsibility of gathering flowers and mobilizing people, including huge turnouts of schoolchildren, for Decoration Day ceremonies. The Northern Women's Relief Corps (WRC), which evolved out of this memorial work in the 1860s and 1870s, claimed a membership of one hundred thousand by 1890, only seven years after its founding. The WRC's persistence kept Memorial Day focused on sorrow and loss in many communities into the late nineteenth century, when the holiday also became the occasion of amusement and sport. With time, the WRC attracted women of varying persuasions—suffragists, anti-suffragists, those who saw their roles as essentially moral and religious, and those who were political activists—but all, by and large, found unity in their duties as guardians of the memory of the Union dead.[13]

Due to Memorial Day, the ancient art of funereal orations and sermons gained a new life in America. The Decoration Day speech became an American genre that ministers, politicians, and countless former soldiers tried to master. In some communities, these orations remained for decades primarily an occasion of sacred bereavement. But early on, such speeches also assumed a political character; the dead and the lilacs were ever useful for the collective remembering and forgetting that Memorial Day helped to foster.

Many a widow or mother at Memorial Day observances must have strained for forbearance of endless expressions of joyous death on the altars of national survival. Northern speeches tended to be mournful, celebratory, and fiercely patriotic all at once. They mixed religion and nationalism in a victory cult that provided Northern Christians with a narrative through which to understand their sacrifice of kin and friends. Their soldiers had died necessary deaths; they had saved the republic, and their blood had given the nation new life. In the Christian cosmology and the apocalyptic sense of history through which many Americans, white and black, interpreted the scale of death in the war, Memorial Day provided a means to achieve both spiritual recovery and historical understanding. In the cult of the fallen soldier, a nineteenth-century manly ideal of heroism was redefined for coming generations. And in a thousand variations, the Union dead—and soon the Confederate dead with them—served as saviors and founders, the agents of the death of an old social order and birth of a new one. Memorial Day became a legitimizing ritual of the new American nationalism forged out of the war.

In Cincinnati in 1869, a crowd of thirty thousand gathered in a cemetery to observe the decoration of 745 graves of that community's war dead. Among the processions was a disciplined line of hundreds of women, all dressed in "purest white" and carrying baskets of flowers. At a signal, each woman stepped forward and cast her flowers on a grave. The scale of such an event would dwarf an All Saints Day procession in some European cities. Ohio Lieutenant Governor J. C. Lee was orator of the day. With words that modern anthropologists might endorse, Lee opened his speech: "Every act has its language, whether the act be of an individual, a society, a city, a state, or a nation, it has its language." Lee warned against the moral degeneration that the war's legacies might foster. Too many people understood the war, he maintained, as "nothing more than a material, visible matching of arms and physical force . . . that nothing is achieved beyond that involved in a prize-ring." He reaffirmed that the central meaning of the war was that an "evil"—slavery—had been overthrown. The dead represented "something higher, something more enduring."[14] One has to read carefully to find such explicitly moral expressions, but good and evil, as well as the emancipationist legacy, were very much a part of early Memorial Day rhetoric.

Many Memorial Day ceremonies tingled with local and state pride, and all were collective expressions of genuine mourning. Some reflected the spirit of pastoral outings: an observer at the Antietam battlefield in 1869 described small crowds "strolling" a landscape where "scarcely a scar made by the great conflict can be seen," yet where many knew those scars from published wartime photographs. The tradition of Memorial Day picnics began on these battlefields, not yet preserved as national parks, and in the ever-expanding rural cemeteries. To many orators, the dead were not gone at all—they survived in countless blood metaphors. "They are not dead," declared a speaker in Kenduskeag, Maine, in 1869; "the early manhood of this nation retains its majesty by their fall, and the black stain of slavery has been effaced from the bosom of this fair land by martyr blood." At many ceremonies a line of orphans commonly marched in the cemetery procession, as in Baltimore, where some fifty children from the Union Orphan Asylum, led by their matrons, dropped flowers on their fathers' graves.[15]

However numbing the rhetoric, many a speech flowed with reconciliation as it honored the dead. In Little Rock, Arkansas, the 1869 orator, one A. W. Bishop, pushed his audience to turn "from the past to the present" as quickly as they could. "The future is too full of opportunity," he said, "to be frittered away by a pointless antagonism." Reunion, especially its alleged permanence, was the theme of many Northern addresses in 1869 as well. At Matoon, Illinois, an orator honored soldiers' heroism in the customary manner by reflexively denouncing the rebellion but then rejoicing with certainty that the nation had "secured a lasting peace" and had cemented a "common ancestry, one destiny, one heart."[16] Memorial Day rituals did their part in helping many Northerners become early believers in reunion, at least its ultimate necessity, while majorities still voted for the "bloody shirt."

Americans now had their Homeric tales of great war to tell. Within five years of the conflict, speakers gave the Union veterans their place in a direct line from Thermopylae to Gettysburg, from the "storied Wallace" and the Scottish tribes to "Sheridan's ride" and "Sherman's march to the sea." Americans now had a defining past of mythic battles, as the 1869 orator in

Hornellsville, New York, put it, that would "stir the heart of the Irishman at home or abroad."[17] Such speeches undoubtedly inspired many of the veterans who first heard them. These were tales of glory, epics they had lived and created, their future claim on the hearts and budgets of the nation. Thousands of those veterans would, in time, try their own hands at telling the story. Their individual narratives, which had exploded as a reminiscence industry by the 1880s, were rooted in a decade and more of Memorial Day speechifying and monument dedications.

Many events and orators emphasized the *democratic* character of the war and its memorialization. To a minister in Ogdensburg, New York, in 1869, the Union dead had broken down class barriers by their sacrifice. They did not come "from any one class or station of life, but from all," said L. L. Wood. "They came from the homes of refinement, of piety, and influence, as well as ignorance, poverty, and distress. They are all our own." In Wilmington, Delaware, in 1869, Memorial Day included an extraordinary interracial, interethnic, and interfaith procession to Brandywine Cemetery. Methodists, Episcopalians, Baptists, Unitarians, and Catholics marched together, representing the various churches of the city. White GAR posts marched in the same parade with a black post, and the "Mount Vernon Cornet Band (colored)" kept step and time with the "Irish Nationalists with the harp and the sunburst flag of Erin." The Reverend Fielder Israel of the First Unitarian Church, keeping alive a sense of the enemy of this composite gathering, broke from the conciliatory oratorical norm. Following the choir's rendition of the "Battle Hymn of the Republic," Reverend Israel laid the war's guilt squarely at the feet of Southerners, "the murderers of those whose memories we were here to honor."[18]

In other ceremonies sectional partisanship dissolved into celebration of the ethnic diversity of the fallen. "Our adopted citizens from other lands have been more thoroughly Americanized . . . by the few years of war," said a speaker in Winona, Minnesota, "than they could have been by a long life-time of peace." Sacred battlefields and hillsides full of graves gave some Americans the experience through which to define the nation as multiethnic and multiracial as never before. Indeed, a definition of citizenship that was civic (enshrined in the Fourteenth Amendment), rather than ethnic/racial, emerged in some Memorial Day oratory. "The gallant German . . ., the brave and generous Irishman, the sturdy Scandinavian," said the Minnesota minister, "and the various other nationalities who have fought by the side of our white and our black Americans . . . are by this fact forever identified with its

destinies." This variation on the emancipationist legacy—the idea of a people's war for an expanding free labor society—was a real and abiding part of
Civil War commemoration. In this vision, the descendants of all the Union
dead were "no longer strangers and foreigners, but are, by this baptism of
blood . . ., consecrated citizens of America forever."[19] Decoration Day was,

Carl Hirschberg's *Decoration Day* (1885) portrays a common scene at Northern Memorial Day
celebrations, one that illustrates the marginal place of blacks in white Civil War memory. (Private collection)

indeed, America's first multiracial, multiethnic commemoration. Along with emancipation celebrations, Memorial Day (and its derivatives) emerged as the Independence Day of the Second American Republic.

On Memorial Day, 1870, at Jefferson Barracks in St. Louis, Missouri, General I. F. Shepard spoke as the representative Yankee soldier remembering how emancipation evolved as a central result of the war. Freedom to the slaves did not come by any simple playing out of destiny. Frail humanity had to be bludgeoned by divine power. Emancipation, said Shepard, "was heralded in the thunders of battlefields." It was a turning point in history "only second in sublimity to that upon Sinai's awful front, when the Decalogue was given in fire and smoke." Shepard then celebrated the war's transforming power as a victory over nativism. At length he identified the immigrant groups and declared the war unwinnable without the nation's "adopted sons." From the usual rhetoric about a new, single nationality now "bathed" in baptismal blood, Shepard then moved to blacks, whom he characterized as pure victims of slavery: crushed, but now the "ransomed menials" of the transforming war. Shepard's racist image of the freedpeople—a "differing species"—nevertheless portrayed them as beknighted heroes, due their rights of "coequal privilege."[20] In such visions of the war's democratic legacy, blacks had a place at Memorial Day processions, though the visions contained no plan yet for how an African American future would be secured.

At the dedication of a monument in the Soldiers' National Cemetery at Gettysburg, July 1, 1869, Reverend Henry Ward Beecher drew apocalyptic imagery, "heroic devotion," "mothers," and "orphans" into a single prayerful message to the next generation. "May the soldiers' children never prove unworthy of their fathers' name," said Beecher; "let them be willing to shed their blood, to lay down their lives, for the sake of their country." The transfer of a nationalistic legacy of heroism to the next generation took hold early. Veterans would struggle with this burden—as they laid it on their children—for decades. The orator at Gettysburg that day, though, Governor Oliver P. Morton of Indiana, left no doubts about the meaning of the sacrifice. Morton linked Thermopylae not only to the fields of Gettysburg, but also to emancipation and the Fifteenth Amendment (which had just passed Congress). A Yankee partisan who had helped invent "bloody shirt" rhetoric, Morton refused to pay equal honor to the "rebel dead" and the Union dead. Of course, Southerners had fought with "courage," and he would "drop a tear to their memory." But his subject was war guilt more than the romance of heroism. "The rebellion was madness," declared Morton. "It was the insanity of States, the delirium of millions, brought on by the pernicious influence of human slavery." In his long-windedness, Morton was more Edward Everett than Abraham Lincoln; but his subject was precisely that of the former President six years earlier. "From the tomb of the rebellion a nation had been born again," Morton maintained. He gave the emancipationist meaning of the war full definition: "The rebellion, the offspring of slavery, hath murdered its unnatural parent, and the perfect reign of liberty is at hand."[21]

FOR WHITE SOUTHERNERS, Memorial Day was born amidst the despair of defeat and the need for collective expressions of grief. By 1866, local memorial associations had formed in many Southern communities, organized largely by women. Some new cemeteries were founded near battlefields, while existing ones in towns and cities were expanded enormously to accommodate the dead. In both sections, but especially in the South, the first monuments erected tended to be placed in cemeteries—the obvious sites of bereavement. By the 1890s, hardly a city square, town green, or even some one-horse crossroads lacked a Civil War memorial of some kind. But through most of the Reconstruction years, the cemetery remained the public site of memorialization; obelisks and stone pyramids appeared as markers of the recent past that so haunted every community. Often directed by social elites who could fund monuments, the Southern "memorial movement . . . helped the South assimilate the fact of defeat," as Gaines Foster writes, without repudiating the defeated."[22] Memorialization functioned as a ritual, a way of coping with loss on a profound scale. Elite women did much of the daily work of organizing memorialization, ostensibly keeping it in the realm of sentiment.

During Reconstruction, federal troops did very little to inhibit this process of Southern memorialization. Confederate Memorial Day had several independent origins in 1866. Different dates were recognized in different parts of the South. The deep South tended to honor the dead on April 26, the day of Joseph E. Johnston's surrender to William Tecumseh Sherman, while communities in South and North Carolina adopted May 10, the anniversary of Stonewall Jackson's death. Virginia towns chose days ranging from May 10 to mid-June. The spectrum of dates caused some local ladies memorial associations to compete over which days were most proper. By 1916, ten Southern states officially observed Memorial Day on June 3, Jefferson Davis's birthday.

In both North and South, participants and orators often drew a comparison to the old Catholic European custom of All Saints Day, where whole villages and towns marched to churchyards to decorate the graves of generations of dead loved ones. Lizzie Rutherford, of Columbus, Georgia, recommended adopting All Saints Day as a model in 1866 after returning from decorating the graves of Confederate dead and reading a German novel that described the custom in detail. At the Winona, Minnesota, Memorial Day ceremony in 1869, Reverend William McKinley stood in the cemetery of the local Union dead and proclaimed: "This day may without impropriety be called our American All-Saints day."[23]

Memorialization could not forever be kept separate from civic life; it was itself part of the process of determining the meanings of the war and, therefore, inherently linked to the politics of memory. Some Southern orators tried hard to avoid "political utterances," but soon many began to connect the cause of Confederate independence with the struggle over Reconstruction. Southern vindicationists may not have dominated Memorial Day oratory in the early years, but they certainly had their say. "Here let us look away from the gloom of political bondage," declared the Georgian Henry D. Capers in 1869, "and fix our vision upon a coming day of triumph, when principles, born of truth and baptized in the blood of our brothers, shall out live the persecution of a merciless enemy and the treachery of unhallowed ambition."[24] The postbellum war of ideas crept into the mournful processions and the silent grief on Southern Memorial Days, and on many days between.

By the early 1870s, a group of ex-Confederate officers in Virginia had forged a coalition of memorial groups that quickly took over the creation of the Lost Cause tradition. They did so through print as much as through ritual commemorations. In 1866, former Confederate general Daniel H. Hill founded the magazine *The Land We Love,* a periodical devoted to demonstrating the skill and prowess of Confederate armies against all odds. By 1869, Hill's journal had become *Southern Magazine,* and most importantly, the Southern Historical Society (SHS) was founded as the vehicle for presenting the Confederate version of the war to the world. By 1876, the SHS began publishing its regular *Southern Historical Society Papers,* a series that ran for fourteen years under the editorship of a former Confederate chaplain, John William Jones. The driving ideological and emotional force behind the SHS was the former Confederate general Jubal Early. Early had fled to Mexico at the end of the war and vowed never to return to his native Virginia under the federal flag. Despite such bluster, and because of threatening poverty, Early returned to his hometown of Lynchburg in 1869. He made himself, as Gaines Foster observes, into the "prototypical unreconstructed Rebel."[25] His principle aim was not only to vindicate Southern secession and glorify the Confederate soldier, but also to launch a propaganda assault on popular history and memory.

With millennial zeal and a conspiratorial vision, Early warned that Northern apologists were riveting a Unionist-emancipationist narrative of the war deep into American memory, an interpretation that portrayed Southern Confederates as traitors. He and his minions would do their best to burn the Unionist and emancipationist narratives out of Southern and national memory. Early saw this Unionist-emancipationist version of the war as a journalistic and pedagogical threat to destroy Southern honor, and he launched a counteroffensive.[26] The spirit of the Southern people would be redeemed, in Early's view, through the story of the irrepressible and heroic Confederate soldier. Black people would eventually have a place in the Confederate narrative, but only as time-warped, loyal antebellum slaves. In the Confederate version of the story, blacks would have to stay in the past, frozen in time, so that ex-Confederates could take their sick souls to a safe place for rehabilitation.

In 1873, Early and others gained control of the SHS and brought its operations to Virginia. At an August 14, 1873, meeting of some fifty-four delegates from twelve states held in White Sulphur Springs, West Virginia, Early gave the keynote address. Attired in his uniform, with Confederate flag cufflinks, Early forged defeat and victimhood into a passionate, heroic history. He argued that Confederate soldiers never lost on the battlefield, and that secession had been right and honorable. At the "bar" of history, claimed Early, Southerners would "appear . . . as patriots demanding our rights and vindicating the true principles of the government founded by our fathers." The nobler side had lost the war, maintained Early, and its case had to be advanced boldly in the public memory. "The men who by their deeds caused so many battlefields of the South to blaze with a glory unsurpassed in the annals of the world," maintained Early, "cannot be so recreant to the principles for which they fought . . . as to abandon the tribunal to those before whose immense numbers and physical power alone they were finally compelled to yield from mere exhaustion." Early's targets included not only Northern historical writing and Memorial Day eulogies, but "their legislation and government policy."[27]

As ex-Confederates organized to vindicate their war experience and to forge the Lost Cause tradition, they sought a usable past in the battles over Reconstruction. Heroic victims of colossal Yankee machines and venal Republican tyranny now would have a well-rehearsed historical memory for the long struggle ahead. As the Southern Historical Society published its battle accounts and vindications of why the war happened, Southern terror succeeded in overthrowing Reconstruction on the ground, where myth-making held sway in the hearts and minds of citizens.

In the South, monument unveiling days took on a significance equal to, if not greater than, Memorial Day. In Richmond, Virginia, on October 26, 1875, Confederate veterans by the thousands staged their first major coming-out as a collective force. At the unveiling of the first significant monument to a Confederate hero, a standing statue of Stonewall Jackson sculpted by the British artist T. H. Foley, nearly fifty thousand people gathered for an unprecedented parade and a ceremony. As a public ritual and a mass statement of the meaning of Confederate defeat and Southern revival, the event had enormous political significance. A group of Englishmen had funded and launched the effort to create the monument in 1863, shortly after Jackson's death. The sculptor, Foley, was preoccupied with many commitments, and fortuitously for Virginia could not finish the work until the 1870s. It is hard to imagine such a ceremony in Richmond before 1874, when Republican Party rule was overthrown and ex-Confederate general James L. Kemper, who had been wounded in Pickett's Charge at Gettysburg, was elected the Democratic governor of the state.[28]

The day dawned as balmy Indian summer in Richmond. The city was decorated and festooned with flags, flowers, and streamers all along the parade route. Hundreds of doors and windows displayed portraits of Jackson. Everyday life and business were completely suspended; the stage was set for a public drama. Former Confederate general D. H. Hill described the scene as a "mournful but still a gala day." The crowds on the streets and on housetops watched the "imposing pageant," according to Hill, "with solemn faces and subdued feeling, as though looking at the funeral of the nation that died in 1865." Perhaps this was the celebratory funeral that the old Confederacy had been edging toward through nearly a decade of Memorial Days and resistance to Reconstruction. Despite the balmy skies, Hill found in the autumn leaves a "fading" and a "withering . . . a requiem to the Lost Cause." Hill saw painful contrasts of the old and new everywhere in the procession. Flags especially caught his symbolic eye. "The battle-torn banners in the procession were conquered banners," Hill wrote. "The new, bright flags . . . were the

flags of the conqueror. Those maimed and mutilated soldiers . . . were pa-
roled prisoners. Those in tasteful uniforms were subjects of the conqueror.
The flag that floats over the Capitol-grounds is the flag of the conqueror. The
conquered banner is wrapped around the dead hero's body in the dead hero's
grave." Deeply conscious of loss, General Hill seems to have discovered in
such a public display of remembrance a sense of what was truly gone. But in
his commentary, he also anticipates Robert Penn Warren's notion of how "in
the moment of its death the Confederacy entered upon its immortality."[29]

At major intersections on the parade route, veterans, ladies memorial associations, and "the indefatigable K.K.K." (Ku Klux Klan) had assembled arti-
sans to construct arches and towers with elaborate decorations honoring
Jackson. The largest arch, at Grace and Eighth Streets, included huge letters
that read: "Warrior, Christian, Patriot." Above the inscription was a painting
representing a stone wall, "upon which was resting a bare sabre, a Bible, and a
Confederate cap." On either side of this arch stood two towers. "The most
decided effect in any of the decorations," according to a journalist, "was produced by placing two Confederate soldiers, dressed in their genuine, old, tattered Confederate garments, upon two pedestals just in front of each tower.
They leaned upon reversed muskets, and were as immovable as statues; indeed, many people could not believe that they were living individuals."[30] Perhaps it was this sense of theater—living Confederate veterans in faded wool,
standing as ersatz statues—that prompted D. H. Hill to hear the dirges for a
dead nation.

One dispute among the planners of the Jackson statue unveiling nearly de-
railed the event. Governor Kemper was the grand marshal of the ceremonies
and had carefully planned the parade to the Capitol Square in Richmond.
Kemper was nervous that "nothing shall appear on the 26th to hurt the
party" (Democrats). He feared that the "least excess" in the Confederate celebration would give yet another "bloody shirt" to Northern Republicans, and
he asked the leaders of the Confederate veterans to restrain their displays of
battle flags. Only days before the big event, Jubal Early wrote to Kemper
complaining of rumors that black militia companies and civilians were to be
"allowed in the procession." "I am inexpressibly shocked at the idea," said
Early. He considered the involvement of blacks "an indignity to the memory
of Jackson and an insult to the Confederates." Black Richmonders, the total
of which Early judged to be between twenty thousand and thirty thousand,
would swarm into the square, he believed, and whites would be forced to
"struggle for place with buck negroes . . . anxious to show their conse-

This statue of Stonewall Jackson was unveiled in Richmond on Capitol Square, October 26, 1875, in the first large parade of Confederate veterans held after the war. (The Museum of the Confederacy, Richmond, Virginia)

quence." Believing that blacks would wave "pictures of Lincoln and Fifteenth Amendment banners," Early threatened not to attend, and to take other veterans with him, if Kemper executed the plan.[31]

In ferocious responses, Kemper told Early to mind his own business and begged him to "stay at home." Black militia officers and ministers in Richmond had petitioned Kemper to take part in the procession. For racial "peace" in the city, the governor accepted the petitioners' request. The small contingent of blacks were placed at the extreme rear of a parade several miles long, numbering many thousands of white marchers. By the time the crowd had assembled in the square for the unveiling speeches, Kemper felt certain that it would "have very far fewer negroes in it than would be there in case of no such formation." Since the blacks had promised to "humbly" honor Jackson, Kemper judged the situation as "calculated to vindicate our white people against Radical lies." To avoid any exhibition of racial mixing, Kemper even eliminated the Virginia General Assembly from the march, where a few black Republicans still served. Kemper kept the program as planned, and Early attended, though he washed his hands of any responsibility for its arrangements. The black militia companies, perhaps anticipating their humiliation, did not march in the event. The only blacks who participated formally were a contingent of former slave workers who had been in the Stonewall Brigade during the war.[32] In the racial ordering fiercely disputed behind the scenes by these two former Confederate generals, we can see much of what was at stake in Southern memorialization as it went public. The position of blacks in this bitter argument between the ultimate irreconcilable and a redeemer-reconciliationist governor remained utterly subordinate. One would eliminate them altogether from Confederate memory; the other would declare them loyal and dispatch them to the rear of parades. In the long history of Lost Cause tradition, both got their wish.

As the immense crowd assembled at the state capitol grounds where the Jackson monument was to be unveiled, Kemper welcomed them as the Democrat-redeemer governor of Virginia. He announced that Jackson was a national hero, not merely a Southern saint, whose memory was to be a "common heritage of glory" for both sections. The massive ceremony served as the South's reminder to the North of its insistence on "respect." The unveiling declared, in effect, that Reconstruction, as Northern Republicans had imagined it, was over. "It [the monument]," said Kemper, "stands forth a mute protest before the world against the rule of tyrants which, wanting faith in the instincts of honor, would distrust and degrade a brave and proud but unfortunate people, which would bid them repent, in order to be forgiven, of such deeds and achievements as heroes rejoice to perform." The whole event, declared Kemper, was the harbinger of "actual reconciliation" and the "equal honor and equal liberties of each section."[33] The war had been about sections, and the one conquered was back in the fold, with some of its old leadership at the helm.

As orator of the day, the Virginia legislature chose the Reverend Moses Drury Hoge, pastor of the Richmond Second Presbyterian Church. During the war, Hoge had given the daily prayer at the Confederate Congress and served as a blockade runner as well as chaplain at a Richmond training camp. Confederate defeat had apparently crushed Hoge psychologically in 1865. But ten years later, on that bright autumn day, he rose to the occasion and announced that Southerners were living in a "new era of our history." Preparing Lost Causers for the long haul, Hoge declared "defeat" the "discipline which trains the truly heroic soul." In his finale, Hoge reached his most important theme: the overthrow of Reconstruction and the demand for a political return to a *status quo antebellum.* "If it be objected that we have already entered upon one of those political revolutions that never go backward," Hoge proclaimed, "then I ask, who gave to anyone the authority to say so?" Hoge summoned the audience to return to the old ways, to the old nation. Their duty in the new era was to return to "a Union as our fathers framed . . . the Constitution in its old supremacy."[34] Amidst a massive performance of Confederate remembrance on this day, neither the Gettysburg Address nor the Thirteenth, Fourteenth, and Fifteenth Amendments existed. In short, the civic meaning of emancipation itself fell among the litter on the streets of Richmond. As Southerners mourned their dead hero and their dead Confederacy, they rejoiced in their emerging victory over the peace.

DURING THE 1870S, perhaps as a way of escaping the rancor of Reconstruction politics, Northerners and Southerners began to participate together in Memorial Day rituals. Strikingly early, in 1867, Frances Miles Finch published his widely popular poem, "The Blue and the Gray," in the *Atlantic Monthly,* which gave to the cause of reconciliation verses of sweetness, mutual sympathy, and the universality of death and mourning. How true his simple lines must have seemed to the thousands who would hear them recited down through the years at Decoration Days and Blue-Gray reunions:

Sadly, but not with upbraiding,
   The generous deed was done;
In the storm of the years that are fading,
   No braver battle was won;—
     Under the sod and the dew,
      Waiting the judgment day;—
     Under the blossoms, the Blue,
      Under the garlands, the Gray.[35]

But beyond the pain and pathos of individual mourners, the emerging reunionism served many social and political aims.

In the South, collective pride in the Confederate past returned in public outpourings on recurring Memorial Days. That pride was often local as well as Southern. In Guilford, North Carolina, on Confederate Memorial Day (May 10) in 1873, John A. Gilmer, urging "pride" in "our own Guilford dead," invoked the memory of local commanders, regiments, and battles that had special associations for his audience. But mostly, Gilmer celebrated the "rapidly returning sense of right in our own people." Southerners need no longer have any "hesitation" or "reluctance" about their Memorial Day, said Gilmer. The world had "*conceded* to Southern courage, Southern devotion, Southern skill, and Southern power, as displayed in that war."[36]

A year later, in Wilmington, North Carolina, on the federal Memorial Day, Albion Tourgée delivered a different, though conciliatory, address to a crowd of five thousand in the local national cemetery. A former Union soldier, carpetbagger, and federal district judge in Greensboro, Tourgée was deeply committed to Reconstruction and to the rights of the freedpeople. In 1874, he was still embroiled in North Carolina politics, struggling to survive the terror of the Ku Klux Klan and to hold a dying Republican Party together in that state. Tourgée would emerge later as one of the most eloquent proponents of the emancipationist legacy of the war. But his Memorial Day effort in Wilmington in 1874 was, for him, extraordinarily generous toward ex-Confederates. He welcomed the ex-Confederates who had come to the ceremony that day as "those . . . who sit no longer on the 'sounding shore' of memory, and nurse the madness of the past—but as those who bow to the issue of war, and honor the valor which prevailed." Tourgée confronted the reality that the war had been one "between kindred—between brothers speaking the same tongue, worshipping the same God." It is doubtful that many ex-Confederates were comfortable with Tourgée's terms of reconciliation. He lectured at some length on how slavery lay at the root of the war and argued that the "emancipation of the slave" had been a principle aim of the struggle and not, as had become "fashionable" to say, "forced upon the government." To the freedmen in his audience, Tourgée declared the day their own. "These . . . are your dead," he announced, "they are those who fell in the wilderness between the Egypt of your bondage and the Promised Land of your freedom!"[37] On the ground in the South, in a national cemetery at this interracial Memorial Day, the vexations and divisions of Civil War memory had become manifest.

In 1874–75, Union and Confederate veterans began to participate in Memorial Day exercises together in both North and South. In the wake of Memorial Day, 1875, in North Carolina, a black citizen in Raleigh, Osborne Hunter, anxiously observed in a letter to a newspaper "a noticeable spirit of reconciliation pervading the political atmosphere of both the Republican and Democratic parties of this state." In August 1874, the Democrats had regained power in North Carolina, and the highly racialized election had hinged, in part, on Southern resistance to federal enforcement of black civil rights. Until May 1875, blacks in Raleigh had always played a major role in Decoration Day ceremonies in that city. That year they were discouraged from participating, as the occasion was declared to be only a "soldier's turn-out." At the mark of a "decade in the history of freedom," concluded Hunter, Decoration Day seemed to be only an occasion for "ignoring the colored citizen and the colored voter."[38]

Up North, Memorial Day orators increasingly struck chords of reconciliation, especially around the theme of shared soldiers' valor. On Decoration Day in Boston in 1874, the Charles Russell Lowell Encampment of the Grand Army of the Republic (GAR) assembled for a sermon in West Church by the Reverend C. A. Bartol. In an effort entitled "The Soldier's Motive," Bartol honored the blind faith of warriors who forget themselves in devotion to a cause. Conviction, duty, and obedience with an "abandonment that neither reserves its resources nor counts the cost," said Bartol, "is the all-surpassing reason for our approval and love." This theme, what Oliver Wendell Holmes Jr., would later famously term the "Soldier's Faith," would become a standard feature of memorial and reunion rhetoric. The soldierly virtue of devotion, whatever the cause, was within a decade of the war already well-rehearsed as a means to sectional peace. Indeed, it became a rhetorical weapon of great potency in the retreat from and overthrow of Reconstruction.[39]

The disputed election of 1876 and the electoral crisis that culminated in the Compromise of 1877 brought the Republican Rutherford B. Hayes to the presidency, as well as the final three remaining Southern states not under Democratic control into that party's fold. Reconciliation seemed to sweep over the country's political spirit, as the Union survived another potential severing by sectional and partisan strife. Although it was hardly the first time that commentators in both sections had declared the final conclusion to the issues of the war, the political settlement of 1877 easily took its place as the traditional "end" of Reconstruction (a label it has carried ever since).

On Memorial Day, May 30, 1877, New York City experienced an array of parades and ceremonies unprecedented since the formal inception of the holiday nine years earlier. Virtually every orator and editorial writer declared the day one of forgetting, forgiveness, and equality of the Blue and the Gray veterans. The *New York Herald* set the tone for the occasion a day in advance by offering a vision of an American character free of the burdens of the past: "The man whose memory dates back over a month is voted a bore, and accused of being interested in ancient history." With an unabashed sense of finality, the *Herald* declared that "all the issues on which the war of the rebellion was fought seem dead, and the late effort to manufacture political sentiment out of them was a signal failure. American eyes have a characteristic tendency to look forward and let the past be with itself." In this atmosphere of national reunion, massive parades thronged New York's streets, and tens of thousands of citizens visited every cemetery in the region to lay flowers at the graves of the Union and Confederate dead.[40]

An "immense multitude" filled the streets of Manhattan to watch the Decoration Day parades. Detachments of city police, fire engine companies, the New York National Guard, the Association of Mexican War Veterans, and seventeen GAR posts assembled along Fourth Avenue between Sixteenth and Twentieth Streets. In each block several decorated floral wagons, a choir, a drum corps, and carriages for invited guests (some of whom were War of 1812 veterans) were positioned among the Civil War veterans. The parade was blessed with a late spring morning "so beautiful," reported the *Tribune*, "that it rested on the city like a benediction." Each detachment had a specific destination for the day's march—a cemetery or a monument in Brooklyn or lower Manhattan where they would conduct ceremonies and lay the traditional flowers on the graves of the dead.[41]

In Union Square and Madison Square, floral decorations adorned the statues of George Washington, Abraham Lincoln, Marquis de Lafayette, and

William H. Seward. The Lincoln statue drew the most attention and the most elaborate display of flowers. With a laurel wreath atop Lincoln's head, and amidst wisteria sprays, begonias, and greenery all around, white carnations were used to write the word "Emancipation" across a panel in the center of the monument. As the Abraham Lincoln Post No. 13 gathered, the black abolitionist and Presbyterian minister Henry Highland Garnet gave an opening prayer. A black militia group, the Skidmore Guards, occupied a prominent position in the ceremony, as did members of Garnet's congregation from Shiloh Church. The orator of the morning, General John Cochrane, veteran of many battles and vice-presidential running mate of John C. Fremont in the 1864 election bid to unseat Lincoln from within the Republican Party, celebrated the recent national compromise, no doubt without any sense of irony, as "the birth of constitutional liberty." The restoration of home rule in the South and the cessation of hostilities between the sections was to Cochrane "a purely American emancipation . . . a new nation burst into life, whose centennial glories embrace the liberalization of government." Cochrane spoke proudly of the fact that it was the Lincoln GAR post that had three years before, in a ceremony at this very statue, advocated that "the graves equally of the Union and Confederate dead be decorated by loyal hands." Cochrane said they should not lose their sense of which cause had been right and which wrong, but that as soldiers all Confederates, dead and alive, were their "brothers."[42] On this day, the only meanings of the war given public airing were those that emancipated former foes to mutual honor and liberated the nation from division to a sense of political peace.

In late morning, the New York parade headed south for twenty spectacular blocks on Fifth Avenue. One GAR post carried twelve stained and torn battle flags, and on the sides of one floral wagon, a veterans unit had displayed photographs of dead comrades. Following close behind all the hook and ladder companies of the fire department was a regiment of black troops, led by an all–African American marching band. After passing in front of a large grandstand on the west side of Madison Square, and marching a short distance on Broadway, the parade turned and went down to the ferry docks on the East River. The several divisions of the parade rode ferry boats across to the Brooklyn shore, where via the Long Island Railroad and other conveyances they were transported to the Cypress Hills, Calvary, and Greenwood cemeteries.[43]

A crowd estimated at nearly fifty thousand gathered along the roadways and near the gothic arches at the entrance to Greenwood, one of the first such "rural" cemeteries designed in the United States. The long procession encircled the Soldiers' Monument (a typical symbol now on the landscapes of many American cemeteries, and increasingly in town and city squares) erected in memory of the 148,000 New Yorkers who had served the Union cause. As a band played intermittently between various prayers and speeches, individuals and family members walked forward from the crowds and placed wreaths at the base of the monument. The chief orator, Colonel A. W. Baxter, closed with an appeal for unity, calling all to "over the grave of buried bygones rejoice that, now, as soldiers and citizens, we know no North, no South, no East, no West—only one country and one flag.[44] In the bucolic setting of Greenwood Cemetery, vast numbers of the mourners stayed until nearly sunset.

At Calvary Cemetery, also in Brooklyn, similar ceremonies occurred amidst huge crowds. The obliteration of any sectional identity or animosity was the theme of poems and speeches. To the press the most striking feature of the Calvary ceremonies was that the day before a palmetto tree had been planted at the grave of a South Carolinian, James G. Kelly, a Confederate soldier buried in New York. The tree had been sent by friends from South Carolina, and the gesture seemed to many to capture the meaning of the occasion.[45] On these landscapes of Civil War memory, devotion to the Lost Cause had already gained a special place in the American imagination—the alleged nobility of losers in a desperate struggle carried an enduring fascination in an age increasingly characterized by cynical politics, amoral machines, and the impersonal leviathan of industrialization. Political necessity combined with deep cultural need to produce an almost irresistible Decoration Day spirit of reunion.

Decoration Day, 1877 in New York culminated with a special indoor event at the Brooklyn Academy of Music. The planning committee, dominated by Democrats, had invited the prominent ex-Confederate general, lawyer, and then Brooklyn resident Roger A. Pryor to be orator of the evening. A committee member, Joseph Neilson, opened the proceedings with an explicit appeal for reconciliation. Neilson declared all the "causes" of the "late domestic contention" forgotten. As the voice of "healing," Pryor took the podium before an audience of nearly one thousand to deliver his extraordinary address, "The Soldier, the Friend of Peace and Union."[46]

Pryor, a Virginian, had been a fiery secessionist in 1861 and served in the Confederate Congress at the outset of the war. He enlisted in the Confederate army and rose to the rank of brigadier general. Due to casualties his brigade was dissolved in 1863, whereupon Pryor reenlisted as a private in Fitzhugh Lee's cavalry and was captured near Petersburg in November 1864. In September 1865, Pryor, who would refuse a pardon until 1880, moved to New York, where Democratic Party friends helped him establish a legal career. He published articles defending the South's cause in the *Daily News*, sometimes under a pseudonym because he feared arrest. Republican newspapers referred to him as "the Rebel Pryor" for his advocacy of the Lost Cause. By the 1870s, Pryor had achieved membership in the Manhattan Club, a prominent Democratic Party organization, and had begun a long political career that would land him a seat by 1890 on the New York Court of Common Pleas, and in 1896, an appointment to the state supreme court. The man asked to be the chief speaker on Decoration Day in Brooklyn was the most prominent among a growing and influential group of what many called the "Confederate carpetbaggers" of New York and other Northern cities.[47] Pryor, along with his wife, Sarah Rice Pryor, who eventually became a significant writer and memoirist, never retreated from the righteousness of the South's cause as they accepted some of the war's results.

As the embodiment of a sectional reunion forged out of business enterprise and a Reconstruction that sustained white supremacy, Pryor did not squander his opportunity in the spotlight. After thanking the organizers for their "overture of reconciliation," Pryor delivered an unreconstructed Southerner's demand for recognition of the equality and nobility of the Confederate soldier, as well as a ringing statement of the "needless war" doctrine that would become popular among some historians in the twentieth century. "The bloody work of secession," announced the former ardent secessionist, "was wholly the act of professed men of peace—the politicians." Soldiers were simply men of honor and duty, serving the dictates of history, and therefore the suffering victims of fate. The Confederate veteran especially deserved the sympathy of the American people. The orator touched a chord that would resonate for decades in Civil War memory. "From the reproach of conscious wrong the soldier of the South is free," declared Pryor.[48] The greatest heroes were those who fought for the cause lost; devotion alone merited a reunited nation's gratitude.

But Pryor did not restrict himself merely to the subject of the heroic soldier. Given such a forum, the Confederate partisan gave a full-throated condemnation of Reconstruction as "that dismal period—massacres of the helpless, violations of the ballot, usurpations of force on the popular will and the independence of the States." Pryor fashioned a beguiling version of the evil image of Reconstruction. The Reconstruction years were a time, he said, of "alien rule and federal domination by which sovereign states were reduced to the impotence of satrapies." The reunion now possible after the Compromise of 1877 was, therefore, a victory over Reconstruction, over racial equality, and over federal enforcement against the South. "Fallen it [Reconstruction] is at last," declared Pryor, "fallen like Lucifer never to hope again; fallen by the thunderbolt of the people's wrath."[49] Twelve years after Appomattox, a former Confederate general and voice of the Lost Cause explained to his Yankee audience, many of whom were Union veterans, that the South's vindication was the nation's triumph. Long live the new Union, Pryor in effect announced—a Union saved from the Devil of radical Republicanism and black suffrage by the Confederate veteran. Over the next four decades, this theme would continue to flourish in new literary and political forms.

Unlike many Memorial Day orators, Pryor did not hide the issue of race behind a rhetoric of reunion. The war had nothing directly to do with slavery, he proclaimed, in what became an article of faith to Southern vindicationists and their Northern allies. Southerners were comfortably reconciled to the destruction of slavery because it had only been the "occasion not the cause of secession." Slavery was an impersonal force in history, a natural phenomenon subject only to divine control and beyond all human responsibility. It was good while it lasted, good once it was gone; no Southerner fought in its defense, and no Northerner died to end it. It just went away, like a change in the weather. Pryor declared with audacious confidence that "impartial history will record that slavery fell not by any effort of man's will, but by the immediate intervention and act of the Almighty himself; and in the anthem of praise ascending to heaven for the emancipation of four million human beings, the voice of the Confederate soldier mingles its note of devout gratulation."[50] In such selective and politically charged uses of memory, the devout could claim anything. Everyone responsible for slavery—and the war—had already achieved absolution, even a resurrection.

To Pryor, Southerners were the best Unionists because they understood fully how radical Reconstruction had been a scheme "devised to balk the ambition of the white race." Southerners knew best how their own "shelter and support" lay within the Union because of the fear of "the havoc and carnage of a war aggravated by a conflict between races and issuing inevitably in the catastrophe of a remorseful subjugation." The reunion taking hold by 1877 was none other than a national victory over the potential of race war. As Pryor concluded his performance, he folded "Grant and Lee . . . Stonewall and Sherman" into the same mystic remembrance, and placed the future safety of the Union in the "blended memories" of the Confederate and Union veterans. At the end of his speech, according to the *Tribune*, Pryor bowed before the "prolonged applause" of his New York audience.[51]

Following Pryor, former Union general Isaac S. Catlin delivered the final address of the evening. In full sympathy with the former Confederate's speech, Catlin spoke of military pathos and glory, of the victimhood and heroism of all soldiers on both sides. "I love the memory of a soldier," said Catlin. "I love the very dust that covers his mouldering body." Catlin called on all to be "exultant" that slavery was dead. "Is this not enough?" he asked. "Is it not enough that we are all American citizens, that our country is saved, that our country is one?" In this doctrine of "enough," the emancipationist legacy of the war had become bad taste among gentlemen soldiers. The "divine doctrine of forgiveness and conciliation" was the order of the day.[52]

Dissent from this Blue-Gray reconciliationist version of the war's memory, while now on the margins, was by no means silenced in the larger culture or in New York. One year later, as though they had decided to invite a direct response to Pryor and his ilk, the integrated Abraham Lincoln Post of the GAR asked Frederick Douglass to address them in Madison Square on Decoration Day. As he did on so many occasions during the last quarter of his life, Douglass rose to the challenge with fire and indignation, offering an alternative, emancipationist memory of the war. "There was a right side and a wrong side in the late war," insisted Douglass, "that no sentiment ought to cause us to forget." As though he were answering Pryor in a debate, Douglass declared that "he [the Southerner] must not glory in his shame, and boast his non-repentance." In Douglass's view, the subject of Memorial Day should be the "moral character of the war." Sickened at the increasingly defensive posture of those Northerners who saw the war as a triumph for black freedom and the birth of a new republic, Douglass stood before Lincoln's statue and demanded that his audience "not be asked to be ashamed of our part in the war." The reconciliationists were using memory to send the nation down the wrong road to reunion, he believed. Douglass had no patience for endless tales of Southern woes. "The South has suffered to be sure," he said, "but she has been the author of her own suffering."[53]

Douglass called on his listeners not to cave in to pathos and sentiment, not to seek reunion in the mutuality of soldiers' sacrifice, hard as that might be in the climate of the late 1870s. In their processions to the graves, Douglass called white and black Union veterans to a different remembrance. The struggle had not been one of mere "sectional character," he asserted. "It was a war of ideas, a battle of principles . . . a war between the old and new, slavery and freedom, barbarism and civilization." The war was "not a fight," he concluded, "between rapacious birds and ferocious beasts, a mere display of brute courage and endurance, but it was a war between men of thought as well as of action, and in dead earnest for something beyond the battlefield."[54]

As the passions evident in the speeches of Pryor and Douglass revealed, the conflicted memory of the Civil War lived at the heart of American political culture. To mourn is to yearn for healing, but the extent of the healing often depends on the freedom and power of the mourners on the day after the grief ritual. By the late 1870s, many Northern orators and commentators, even the most famous, clearly felt themselves on the defensive in the struggle over the memory of the war. In an interview in 1878, Ulysses S. Grant complained about "historians" who kept rehearsing the argument that the Union forces had "overwhelmed the South" with numbers, especially foreign immigrants. Grant took umbrage at the claim that the Union had won with "hirelings and Hessians." "This is the way public opinion was made during the war," said Grant, "and this is the way history is made now. We never overwhelmed the South . . . What we won from the South we won by hard fighting." Grant turned the argument around on Southern apologists and vindicationists in an ironic way. He complained that the "4,000,000 of negroes" who "kept the farms, protected the families, supported the armies, and were really a reserve force" were "never counted in any summary of the forces of the South."[55]

Moreover, General William Tecumseh Sherman, who was orator for the evening ceremonies at the Booth Theater on Memorial Day in New York, 1878, responded to the incessant demand that all the loss in life and treasure from the war "should be forgotten." Southerners had "long since been forgiven," Sherman answered. They were "our equals" in the councils of government and in "all attributes of citizenship." Indeed, the South's welcome back into the "family group," the general wondered, might have "gone too far" and constituted "one of the great political questions now on trial." What Sherman, who was no friend of Reconstruction and black rights, would not yet extend to Southerners was an equal "measure of honor and glory" merely because their "motives were pure." He insisted that whatever else Southerners had achieved in the reunion, they had to live with being on the "wrong" side in the war. "Abstract right and abstract wrong" mattered as a question of history, he maintained. Sherman insisted that Northerners not "tear from the history of our country the pages which record the great events from 1860 to 1865" and that they "never apologize for the deeds done."[56]

The fervor with which Americans practiced the rituals of Memorial Day began to fade in the late 1870s and early 1880s. "Graceful popular ceremonies," declared the *New York Tribune* in May 1878, no longer fit in a society characterized by "the pioneers of the prairie and the speculators in railway stock." Bitterness had waned, and as "individual sorrow for the fallen fades away," said the *Tribune,* Decoration Day "gradually loses its best significance." By 1880, the same paper editorialized on how Decoration Day had "become coarser and more blurred" in its meaning, and how it had fallen into the "slough of politics." In the Gilded Age, the *Tribune* claimed that the truly "loyal" would continue to honor the Civil War dead, but also make every "effort to put out of sight the causes of the war, the hate and bitterness which we thought immortal." At stake now was the next generation and the social and moral order. Civil War memorialization should not be used for political purposes among the children born since the war, claimed the *Tribune,*

A group of black children on their way to school stop for *A Lesson in History-Decoration Day,* 1881. (*Harper's Weekly,* June 4, 1881, drawn by W. G. McCutcheon)

but the sacrifice of soldiers should very much be used as lessons in morality and patriotism. "The days they [postwar children] have been born in are not heroic," declared the *Tribune*, "they are full of fraud, corruption, bargain, and sale. Men are not pushing to the battlefield to die for an idea; they are pushing into place." As an antidote to America's "sordid expertness in money-getting," the editors spoke for a large cross-section of the culture that now looked to the Civil War dead, as well as to living veterans, as the alternative to their unheroic age, as sources of honest passion, higher morality, something "noble and true . . . kept for our children."[57]

By the 1880s, Americans needed a social and moral equivalent of war. They would achieve this, of a kind, in the realm of sentiment—in a resurgent cult of manliness and soldierly virtues recycled in thousands of veterans' papers, speeches, and reminiscences. But such a moral equivalent of war came increasingly to exalt the soldier and his sacrifice, disembodied from the causes and consequences of the war. Returning to his hometown of Lancaster, Massachusetts, to speak on Memorial Day in 1880, veteran John D. Washburn announced that he could not speak of "abstract themes." "Even questions of present duty and the rights of man are too harsh," he said. The day was now reserved, in his view, only for "grateful love and tender recollection" of his dead comrades.[58]

Although it became dominant, such a mode of commemoration continued to spawn its dissenters in a turbulent contest over the meaning of Decoration Days and monument building. In 1879, in Stillwater, Minnesota, a veteran, Colonel Thomas Barr, offered his "utter dissent "from what he considered the "false sentimentality" of reconciliation based on a "blue and gray . . . fraternity." Echoing many of Frederick Douglass's postwar speeches, Barr insisted, "Our tributes are not paid to courage . . . it was no gladiatorial contest in which we were engaged—a test of physical prowess of sections. It was a death grapple between right and wrong." Barr was one Union veteran who believed that too much forgiveness had been extended the South. Identifying the destruction of slavery in particular as a central result of the war, and the plight of the freedmen's rights an ugly legacy, Barr argued that "treason" should have been "so punished . . . that it might never come to be eulogized as true loyalty."[59] More than one Lost Cause contended for space on the landscape of Civil War memory as the conflict receded into the past, and into the realm of organized recollection mixed with imagination.

In the North of the 1880s, Oliver Wendell Holmes Jr. came to represent as forcefully as anyone the dominant, nonideological mode of Civil War memory. The spirit of reconciliation as a method of forgetting had no greater spokesman than the great jurist from Massachusetts. Wounded at Antietam, horrified by what he called "an infamous butchery" at the battle of Fredericksburg in 1862, and worried for his own sanity during his experiences of the Wilderness campaign in 1864, Holmes had resigned his commission before the war ended. Deeply troubled in the immediate aftermath of the war by his experiences of combat, Holmes's changing attitudes toward war mirrored the social climate. By 1884, Holmes was a regular orator at Memorial Days and veterans' reunions. At Keene, New Hampshire, in 1884, he opened a Decoration Day address with the statement that a young man had recently asked him why people still "kept up Memorial Day." His memorable and writerly answer was not overtly about reconciliation, nor was there a hint of the war's causes. The young needed to hear the veterans' stories, contended Holmes, because "the generation that carried on the war has been set apart by its experience." In what are now famous lines, Holmes spoke a kind of prose anthem of the American reunion:

> Through our great good fortune, in our youth our hearts were touched with fire. It was given to us to learn at the outset that life is a profound and passionate thing. While we are permitted to scorn nothing but indifference, and do not pretend to undervalue the worldly rewards of ambition, we have seen with our own eyes beyond and above the gold fields the snowy heights of honor, and it is for us to bear the report to those who come after us.

In Holmes's vision, Union and Confederate veterans were one in feeling and experience. "The soldiers of the war need no explanations," Holmes declared, "they can join in commemorating a soldier's death with feelings not different in kind, whether he fell toward them or by their side."[60] Whoever was honest in his devotion and courage was *right*. Such a mutual feeling among soldiers on opposite sides has emerged from every modern war. Holmes described many truths. But rarely from a civil war of such violence and scale has such a reconciliation forged in remembered valor taken hold so quickly, and with such political consequences.

The Holmesian mode of memory—passion and heroism immunized from motive—did not go unchallenged as Memorial Day reached its twentieth anniversary. No one criticized Memorial Days devoted to Blue-Gray reconciliation more than Albion Tourgée. In a series of articles that appeared in the *Chicago Inter-Ocean* during 1884–85 and were called "The Veteran and His

Pipe," Tourgée satirized a reunion based on soldierly honor alone. Writing as a lone Union veteran speaking to his pipe, "Blower," Tourgée dissented repeatedly from sectional reconciliation if it meant the obliteration of the emancipationist meaning of the war, or for that matter, any other sense of ideology or cause. In a column entitled "Memorial Day," Tourgée resented that the original name, "Decoration Day," had waned and that the "festival of flowers" had been ransomed for "a little cheap laudation, in silly deference to a sickly sentimentality." The holiday had become one only of calculated forgetting, the veteran moaned into his pipe. "To dwell upon the hero's sufferings and ignore the motive which inspired his acts," he wrote, "is to degrade him to the level of the mercenary. Fame dwells in purpose as well as in achievement. Fortitude is sanctified only by its aim."[61]

The story of Civil War memory and the ritual of Decoration Days continued well beyond 1885 with the emancipationist legacy fighting endless rearguard actions against a Blue-Gray reconciliation that was to sweep through American culture. Those who remembered the war as the rebirth of the republic in the name of racial equality would continue to do battle with the growing number who would remember it as the nation's test of manhood and the South's struggle to sustain white supremacy. Rituals such as Memorial Day parades, ceremonies, and speeches are the means by which real and ideal worlds meet in most cultures. As Clifford Geertz has written, "in a ritual, the world as lived and the world as imagined, fused under the agency of a single set of symbolic forms, turn out to be the same world."[62] Because the meaning of the Civil War remained so unsettled in American culture for so long, memorialization became just such a set of rituals whereby the dead continued to mingle among the living—in small stone monuments, symbolic bloody shirts, terrorists' white hoods, patriotic songs and speeches, veterans' fraternal bonds, women's Memorial Day committees, and, ultimately, in the tangible form of election ballots.

FOUR

Reconstruction and Reconciliation

If war among the whites brought peace and liberty to
blacks, what will peace among the whites bring?

—FREDERICK DOUGLASS, July 5, 1875

IN THE AMERICAN ELECTIONS from 1868 to 1876, the vast majority of
voters were participants, survivors, or freedmen whose adult lives and political sensibilities had been shaped by the war and the struggle over Reconstruction. Hence even as the reunion took root during the years surrounding these
elections, each campaign served as a referendum on both the sectional and
the racial meanings of the war. Bloody shirts still waved everywhere as politicians sought to permanently bury the issues of the war and simultaneously
used those very issues to fan the flames of political difference. The differences
were real, and the issues could not yet be buried, at least until the mid-1870s.
The nation was healing, but not yet healed.

Some historians have argued that postwar elections in America were
driven by a "partisan imperative"—the deep-seated political habits and loyalties (forged since the crises of the 1850s) vested in the Democratic and Republican parties. According to this argument, habitual party connections,
with their institutional and communal relationships, especially locally, were
more important than events or ideas in shaping voter behavior. Conservative
Republicans, disenchanted with their own party's radicalism by 1868, just
could not abide mingling with Democrats. More so, the party on the defensive, the Democrats, especially moderates seeking a new legitimacy, could not
abide even the antiradical elements of the party of Lincoln. With intense partisanship, both parties waged political warfare that replaced real warfare. But

if the aim of both parties "was to reinvigorate the memories of these party relations," perhaps it is worth examining what the *memories* were all about.[1]

On May 20, 1868, only a week after President Andrew Johnson had been acquitted in his impeachment trial in the U.S. Senate, the Republican Party gathered in Chicago to nominate Ulysses S. Grant for President. Although inexperienced in formal politics, Grant was the principal war hero of the Union cause. Republican managers put his name forward as the candidate of harmony in a season of bitter political discord. The week before the Republican convention, a soldiers and sailors gathering of Civil War veterans had met in Chicago, endorsing Grant and providing an exuberant welcome to delegates and politicos. Grant, who remained appropriately aloof from convention affairs, was in Washington, D.C., on May 29, when he received delegations informing him of the nomination. Reaching for unity, and trying to sidestep all controversy, especially the unpopular issue of black suffrage, Grant issued a statement: "I shall have no policy of my own to interfere against the will of the people." More enduring, if no more direct, was his concluding passage, which became the splendidly ambiguous slogan of his campaign: "Let us have Peace."[2]

Grant had committed himself to Congressional control of Reconstruction policy, and in vague terms at least, he supported black voting rights. But as Thaddeus Stevens lay dying that summer, the historical moment of the radical Republicans was passing just as it had triumphed. In 1868, the Republican Party retrenched onto a platform of order and stability; they would now be protectors of a status quo rather than innovators. Yet Republicans were pilloried with the charge of "radicalism" by Democrats, as well as by white Southerners generally, some of whom sat out this election willfully, and others because they were still disenfranchised. After the Democrats made startling gains in the off-year elections of 1867, the authors of the 1868 Republican platform struck conservative chords. Black suffrage was necessary in the South for the purposes "of public safety, of gratitude, and of justice." Black voting rights in the North were left to the whims of each state. Reconstruction would continue, and the Southern states would be restored to the Union. But with the general at its helm, the Republican Party had a new image. They were now the party of sound money, economic growth and prosperity, and eventual reunion.[3] It all depended on how "Let us have peace" was interpreted, and that slogan had very different meanings across the political landscape.

The Democrats held their convention in July, and instead of reaching for a new, moderate coalition that might accommodate some realities of Reconstruction, they nominated candidates Horatio Seymour and Frank Blair, who represented the opposite. Seymour, New York's former governor, had openly supported the draft rioters in New York City in 1863, whose actions led to the murder of many blacks; his record of opposition to the war gave the Republicans a perfect target. Blair, a Missourian and an avowed white supremacist, announced that a Democratic administration would declare the Reconstruction Acts "null and void" and turn the clock back to white Southern home rule. Although many Democrats professed their loyalty and sacrifice in the war, rhetoric from the top of the Democratic ticket seemed to threaten a second civil war. The Democrats opposed every element of Congressional Reconstruction and favored immediate reunion based on white Southern autonomy.[4]

In rhetoric and reality, the stakes of the election of 1868 were the essential results of the war. Republicans may have been hasty and "unwise," at times, concluded the *Nation*, "but we more firmly believe that if the positions of the Democratic party are adopted, the war for nationality will have been turned into a farce." Even more directly, blacks saw their freedom and their future at stake; their own partisan imperative required only short-term memory. Benjamin Tanner, editor of the *Christian Recorder*, called on black men as voters to exercise a stern partisanship. In an imaginary dialogue with Democrats, Tanner gave that charged term "Negro manhood" deep political meaning:

> Negro manhood says, "I am an American citizen." Modern Democracy says, "You are not." Negro manhood says, "I demand all my rights, civil and political." Modern Democracy says: "You have no rights except what I choose to give you." Negro manhood says, "I must build churches for myself, and school houses for my children." Modern Democracy says, "If you do I will burn them down." Negro manhood says, "I will exercise the rights vouchsafed." Modern Democracy says, "If you do I will mob and murder you."[5]

Blacks prepared to vote their hopes and interests as self-evident truths in spite of, and as part of, the rhetoric about "peace."

The memory-laden peace in 1868 was still the creation of the war. As some Democratic newspapers threatened repeal of the Thirteenth and Fourteenth Amendments and denounced the Reconstruction Acts, one among them, the

New York Herald, worried about its own party's extremism. At stake, the *Herald* made clear, "was what the war has written into the Constitution." But "what Constitution?" it asked in August. "The Constitution as it was or the Constitution as it is?" In the deep South, newspapers made clear the grounds on which whites would support the Democrats (and they had plenty of Northern allies on this question). "Let us have the Constitution as it was," proclaimed the Milledgeville, Georgia, *Federal Union*. "Let us stand square up to the old Constitution and we can conquer."[6] From this election forward, the enduring political character of Civil War memory thrived on this sort of contest over just who had won the war and what had been its verdict.

Many Northerners wondered about the level of forgiveness and forgetting they would be expected to extend to the South. One Republican paper bristled at the South's audacity to portray itself as "a wronged and outraged people." "It has forgotten all that has happened since 1860," declared the *New York Tribune*. Another paper captured the way ex-Confederates were already seeking control over the nation's memory. "There is something ineffably cool in the way the extremists of the Democracy have of saying they are willing to let by-gones be by-gone," complained the *Cincinnati Commercial*. "It is like one convicted of an 'unpleasantness' in business, asking to be placed in a situation of trust, and, when his past character is inquired into, drawing himself up with dignity and saying that he . . . will not insist upon a discussion of such old events."[7] As yet, the table for the banquet of sectional reconciliation could not be set.

White supremacy was the cornerstone of the Democrats' strategy in 1868, and with vice-presidential candidate Blair leading the offensive, they conducted one of the most explicitly racist presidential campaigns in American history. Republicans had oppressed the South, claimed Blair in one speech, by subjecting it to the rule of a "semi-barbarous race of blacks who are . . . poligamists" and destined to "subject the white women to their unbridled lust." The specter of black equality animated the Democratic press across the land. "Let white men rule America!" screamed an editorial in the Louisville *Daily Courier*, arguing that Republicans preferred "native negroes to native whites." In the minds of many Democratic editors, race theory and racial fear worked hand in hand with antiradical politics. Republican misrule, went the argument, had stolen the rights of whites and disrupted the natural place of blacks in society. Fear of the "amalgamation of the races," combined with the "monstrous . . . negro equality doctrine," as the Louisville editor put it, provided the Democrats a potent political ideology.[8] Whatever the result of this election and others to follow, the road to reunion would pass through endless miles in the dangerous wilderness of American racial thought.

Mingling honor, state rights, and racism, Southern Democrats initiated the arguments and tactics that eventually led to the "redemption" of their states in the 1870s. In July 1868 in Atlanta, a former Confederate senator from Georgia, Benjamin H. Hill, portrayed a South under tyrannical, oppressive rule by a "foreign power," driven by "hate" and determined to "dishonor an unarmed people." Amidst all the South had lost—property, cities, loved ones—Hill admonished his fellow Georgians never to surrender their "honor as a people." In language understood across white class lines, he declared that any Georgians who acquiesced in radical Reconstruction were rendered "slaves" to the Republican Congress, and among their fellow Southerners, they were simply "becoming a negro." The presidential election of 1868, Hill insisted, turned "upon the glorious ancestral doctrine that the States are equal and that white blood is superior."[9] Memories rooted in such creeds of blood, soil, state equality, and honor (products of both defeat in war and a developing sense of victory over Reconstruction) provided the political fuel for the white South's long struggle to win the peace.

White Southern editors used the election of 1868 to advance the image of the beknighted South—conquered, violated, but unbowed. "We had hoped," said the Athens, Georgia, *Southern Watchman,* "that after the surrender we would have peace." Southerners "quietly submitted to the harsh terms . . . although a violation of the plighted faith of the United States Government, and . . . humiliating to their pride and ruinous to their interests." The Southern bloody shirt was a populist weapon of white solidarity. *"Radicalism,"* announced another *Southern Watchman* editorial, "has murdered your sons, brothers, husbands and fathers" and "proposes to elevate the negro above the white race." According to some Southern editors, the coming election and Republican rule threatened race war, and such a prospect united former foes in racial solidarity. "When a war of races commences," declared the Savannah *Daily News and Herald,* "the 'rebels' who under Lee were victorious on many a hard-fought field and the soldiers under Grant who received their surrender at Appomattox . . . the veterans of Sherman and the heroes of Beauregard . . . will march shoulder to shoulder in battle array in defense of their race and kindred."[10] In this language, the bloody shirt became a white man's talisman, not merely a Yankee politician's appeal to stay in office.

But no one surpassed the bloody shirt rhetoric of Republican orators and editors in 1868. If war is politics by other means, then postwar American politics was still war by other means. At the beginning of the campaign, George William Curtis wrote a public letter in which he likened Grant's campaign to a Union army still in the field. "Grant will enter the White House next year as surely as he entered Richmond three years ago," announced Curtis, "and against the same opposition." Curtis asked voters to remember "the bloody years from Sumter to Appomattox, to reflect [on] who and what made those years," and then "bring the rebellion at the polls, as it had already brought it in the field, to 'unconditional surrender.'" Near the end of the campaign, the abolitionist Wendell Phillips gave a speech in Boston in which he demanded an ideological focus to the Republican cause. "We have just finished a war between two ideas," said Phillips. "We sent our armies to South Carolina to carry our ideas. If we had no right to carry our ideas we had no right to send our armies." Only Republican victory could hold together the revolution in ideas (racial equality, public schools) just begun in the South. "Seymour's election," declared Phillips, "is Lee's triumphing at Appomattox." The *New York Tribune* kept the theme of war memories on a personal level for Northern voters, declaring that across the North, "empty sleeves" blew in the wind "against broken ribs" and "about crippled bodies."[11]

Black spokesmen as well could wave the bloody shirt. Black voters should throw themselves into the canvass, argued the *Christian Recorder,* with their own memories of "their brothers' lifeless and mutilated bodies piled a hundred deep upon the body of their brave and noble leader before the walls of bloody Wagner." Black Republicans took special exception at ex-Confederate Democrats "stalking abroad throughout the country, before the widows of their murdered and starved victims have left off their habiliments of mourning." The black bloody shirt included "remembering the prayers of the poor slaves down in the cotton fields . . . in the canebrakes, and in the rebel trenches."[12] But at the heart of such rhetoric was the realization, on all sides, that at stake in these elections was just who and what had triumphed in the war.

The role of most ex-Confederates in the Democratic campaign, especially those who came North as speakers, was to build a line of defiance against radical Republicanism and to turn the country away from Reconstruction. But some Democrats tried to use the election of 1868 to forge reconciliation through the prestige of former generals from both sides. In August 1868, former Union general and Democrat William S. Rosecrans went to White Sulphur Springs, West Virginia, for an orchestrated meeting with Robert E. Lee and some thirty other ex-Confederates. Rosecrans came, he said, with his heart in his hand to forge a soldiers' peace. But his aims were thoroughly political. At stake in the struggle over Reconstruction, he claimed, was "credit and currency," the "vast business and commerce of the country." Control over race relations in the postwar South should be left to the former Confederate leaders, who "have the interest and the power to employ, protect, educate, and elevate the poor freedmen."[13] Rosecrans's gesture was an appeal for Lee's imprimatur in the new campaign against Grant, an argument for rapid reconciliation as good business, and an embrace of state rights and white supremacy.

Lee's public letter of response, signed by three dozen Southerners on holiday, including P. G. T. Beauregard and Alexander H. Stephens, was an expression of national peace and healing on Southern terms. Lee admitted that secession and "African slavery" were "questions . . . decided by the war." Were it not for certain radical policies, namely black suffrage and the "oppressive misrule" of Northern occupation during the previous three years, Lee contended, "this old irritation would have passed away, and the wounds inflicted by the war would have been in great measure healed." With a paternalistic grace that vast numbers of Americans found appealing, Lee described Southern blacks as "the important part of our laboring population." The "two races" were "necessary to each other," and "relations . . . would soon adjust themselves on a basis of mutual kindness and advantage."[14] The two generals seemed almost to be writing from the same script; they postured as though above politics, while participating in a strategy of intersectional cooperation to abruptly end Reconstruction.

Such a strategy did not win at the polls in 1868, but it was a harbinger of things to come. Many Southern newspapers were disappointed with the White Sulphur Springs meeting. The *Columbus Sun* (Georgia) declared it a "nine days wonder for newspaperdom." The *Sun's* editor was especially contemptuous of the "apostasy" of former Confederate general James Longstreet, who, though he attended the gathering, refused to sign Lee's letter. Instead, Longstreet embraced the "twaddle of radicalism" by going to New York to participate in a Republican meeting. He was lured, said the Georgia paper, by "a pimp of the *New York Tribune*." Republican newspapers ridiculed the Rosecrans-Lee exchange. Rosecrans wanted to achieve a "true and enduring peace," said the *New York Tribune*, "by disfranchising the Blacks and giving all power to the Rebels." The image of the South as victimized and blameless did not wash with Northern voters in 1868. Northerners who had sacrificed loved ones to the Union cause were not yet ready, declared the *Cincinnati*

Commercial, to allow any level of soldiers' mutual sentiment to "put the hands of the dial back a few years." Reconstruction as reconciliation, a process already latent in the postwar culture, was not yet politically acceptable. The Cincinnati editor captured the stakes of the 1868 election: "recognizing the citizenship of all the people of the United States . . . and lodging in the Constitution other results growing out of the conflict of arms."[15] Within a decade or so, however, soldiers' memories profoundly influenced political affairs and helped forge a level of popular forgetting that enabled the Rosecrans-Lee script for reconciliation to reach a new consensus.

Grant's election victory in 1868 gave Republicans an unwarranted sense of permanence and optimism. Especially with the passage in February 1869 of the Fifteenth Amendment (declaring the right to vote regardless of race, but not outlawing qualification tests), Northern Republicans seemed ready to declare Reconstruction over. In April 1869, Henry Adams wrote that Reconstruction, due to Southern acquiescence in the election results as well as to a growing prosperity, "has lost much of its old prominence in politics." In the aftermath of the election, Republicans felt released to engage in triumphal retrospection. According to Greeley in the *New York Tribune,* all the issues of the war—the permanence of the Union, black freedom, and equal civil and political rights—were "settled forever by the election of Grant." The *Christian Recorder* celebrated Grant's election as the "day of burial" not only for "slavery . . ., treason," and "the doctrine of State Rights," but "of that, which like a demon has vexed the nation more than all these, *the burial of the demon of American prejudice* against the negro."[16] Given the strong belief in America that the solutions to all problems are essentially political, such faith in the doctrine of guaranteed rights before law is understandable in 1868–69. Moreover, the sheer power of religious faith in black communities, bolstered now by experience, reinforced African American optimism. The sense of finality about Reconstruction by the end of the 1860s was a combination of wish fulfillment and a reasonable summing up of a decade of profound change. At the very least, many Republicans, black and white, seemed to breathe a sigh of relief; they took a victors' holiday of celebration and thanksgiving.

But voices of caution and alarm also joined the celebration, and soon their warnings assumed an angry tone. At a speech in Boston in December 1869, Wendell Phillips rejoiced in the creation of black citizenship but demanded federal enforcement of all Reconstruction measures in the South. Phillips called for "a squad of soldiers in every voting district in the thirty-eight States," regardless of the risks. "Better despotism than anarchy." Most of all,

Phillips warned against the new mood overtaking national memory. "We have got an idea that forgiveness of everybody," said Phillips, "is a virtue. We have got an idea that Christianity consists in putting our own eyes out, not knowing good from bad . . . just from unjust." Phillips's urgent demand of the new Congress was that they "fortify against the coming magnanimity."[17]

In 1870, as he began to edit the *New National Era* in Washington, D.C., Frederick Douglass tried to build an ideological fire wall against the new magnanimity. With the resurgence of the Democratic Party in the South, and the waning of radicalism in the Republican Party, Douglass described the American people as "destitute of political memory." If Republicans would stand as the party of memory, Douglass was happy to carry their banner. He comprehended Reconstruction as a political and moral challenge to save the emancipationist results of the war. Like so many others in the South and North, Douglass understood that, as time passed, those who controlled the political legacies of the war could shape America. On Memorial Day, 1871, Douglass delivered a speech in the newly created Arlington Cemetery, just across the Potomac River from Washington, D.C. Standing at the mass grave of the unknown Union dead, on the former property of Robert E. Lee, the old abolitionist raged against forgetfulness:

> We are sometimes asked in the name of patriotism to . . . remember with equal admiration those who struck at the nation's life, and those who struck to save it—those who fought for slavery and those who fought for liberty and justice. I am no minister of malice . . ., I would not repel the repentant, but . . . may my tongue cleave to the roof of my mouth if I forget the difference between the parties to that . . . bloody conflict . . . I may say if this war is to be forgotten, I ask in the name of all things sacred what shall men remember?[18]

By 1870, most white Southerners viewed Reconstruction as a hated, imposed regime. In an editorial taking stock of the decade of the 1860s, the *Louisville Courier-Journal* never mentioned the end of slavery. The Louisville editor glorified state rights, on the ruins of which "this thing called Reconstruction" had been built. The "peace" that reigned was "only that . . . which is a cessation of actual hostilities . . . the peace of the empire." The suffering South, he said, was ruled by bayonets and "obnoxious constitutional amendments." An exchange between the Louisville paper and the *Cleveland Herald* demonstrated the raw animosity out of which an unstable peace grew.

The Ohio paper rejoiced in the election of the African American Hiram Revels from Mississippi to the U.S. Senate. Revels's appearance in the Senate, said the *Herald,* provided the "exclamation point of the rebellion." Definitions of war guilt and causation were at stake. "The origin of our 'late unpleasantness'—way back in the past," declared the Cleveland paper, "was a determination on the part of the slaveowners to nationalize human bondage." But in the Louisville editor's understanding, "the war originated in nothing the slaveowners did . . . or desired to do." The war's cause was the "destruction . . . the moral gangrene which curses every community in which New England's influence is felt."[19] In such venomous differences over the causes of the war, one can see why the most vigorous advocates of reconciliation believed they had to banish slavery and race from the discussion. The bitter experiences of Reconstruction, and the impossibility of a postwar consensus on the war's causes, all but guaranteed the irresolution deep at the heart of Civil War memory.

As military Reconstruction neared its end, and as most ex-Confederate states were restored to the Union, many radicals acquiesced in the limited character of the Fifteenth Amendment (its lack of restrictions against voter qualification tests, and its avoidance of black suffrage rights in the North). With its ratification in spring 1870, the voting rights amendment absorbed a quick reputation as the final act of Reconstruction. Even Wendell Phillips rejoiced in April that blacks were now "panoplied in all the rights of citizenship." Republicans had provided blacks with an "ample shield" for their political security, even if more had to be done for their economic security. "Ploughing its laborious, but no longer doubtful, course through heavy seas," Phillips concluded, "the bark of that race nears a safe harbor."[20] Such optimism from radicals soon seemed strangely out of place as violence and fraud began to crush black political liberty in much of the South.

African American spokesmen uttered many warnings during these years of declining radicalism, the ascendant white counter-revolution in the South, and the need for black forbearance. In a public letter to the "National Convention of Colored Citizens of the United States," held in Washington, D.C., in 1869, AME bishop Daniel Alexander Payne called blacks to political vigilance and moral and material uplift all at once. "In no portion of the Southern States where the whites are in majority," wrote Payne, "is the life of a colored person safe, unless he or she exhibits both in word, and deed, the spirit of a slave . . . the heel of the oppressor is still upon the neck of the colored American." A few months earlier, Benjamin Tanner had answered his own headline question, "After Emancipation and Enfranchisement, What?" by reminding blacks of their "special . . . history," in which slavery had given them a different cultural and educational starting line than whites. Anticipating Phillips's "ship" metaphor, Tanner suggested that only the earliest chapters of black destiny in America had been written. "A ship beating about the shore," he wrote, "with bow and stern inverted, cannot be said to have begun her voyage."[21]

Yet black political optimism and self-assertion in these transforming years had to coexist with fear of white reaction. As blacks adjusted their collective and individual memories to the new age, they did what all peoples have done while undergoing revolutionary change—they marched ahead, seizing new hopes and skills as they could and worrying about the weight of their past. The new dawn of freedom was on one side of the scale of their destiny, and slavery's many legacies occupied the other side. As they looked backward and forward and imagined their "ship" of fate, most probably saw it in midcourse, neither floundering on its orginal shore nor anchored in a safe harbor. Theirs was an ongoing struggle for which they were newly equipped and uniquely burdened.

IN MANY AREAS of the South, part of the burden that blacks carried was living with violence, both real and threatened. Terror, organized and random, was a persistent part of politics in the postwar South. Black folklore, fiction, and reminiscence have reflected the legacy of violence that began during Reconstruction. Many ex-slaves remembered the Ku Klux Klan as part of a continuum from former slave patrols to lynchings to numerous forms of vigilante violence in the South well into the twentieth century. "They used to be the Ku Klux Klan organization," recollected Charles Anderson in the 1930s. "That was the pat-rollers, then they called them the Night Riders, and at one time the Regulators." South Carolinian Frances Andrews told of how "after the war, the 'bush-whackers,' called Ku Klux, rode there [Wallace plantation, Newberry, South Carolina]. Preacher Pitts' brother was one. They went to negro houses and killed the people. They wore caps over their head and eyes." Klan lawlessness and black vulnerability were so ubiquitous for periods in South Carolina that eighty-seven-year-old Anderson Bates answered an interviewer's query: "Does I 'member anything 'bout de Ku Kluxes? Jesus yes! My old marster, de doctor, in goin' 'round, say out loud to people dat Ku Kluxes was doin' some things they ought not do, by 'stortin money out of niggers just 'cause they could."[22] In that phrase, "just 'cause they could," Bates captured one of the meanings violence attained as an integral part of Reconstruction. Protection of freedmen's rights and safety was so lacking that attacks and intimidation became an all too regular element of Southern life.

Mob violence and eventually lynching were so deeply embedded in black folk memory that virtually every major African American writer since emancipation has made these subjects central to his or her work in poetry and prose. The sheer persistence of themes of ritualized violence in black writing indicates, as one critic has argued, that a form of "racial memory" took hold, that the black writer has served as a "kind of ritual priest in ever keeping before his black audience the essence of one of the forces that have shaped their lives." Such a literary tradition began at least as early as William Wells Brown's novel *Clotel* (1853), in which an "impudent" slave is ritually executed, indeed burned, before a crowd of four thousand slaves brought from nearby plantations to witness the spectacle. Such stories were repeated time and again in numerous novels such as Charles Chesnutt's *The Marrow of Tradition* (1901), which retells in fiction the story of the 1898 racial massacre in Wilmington, North Carolina, and Pauline Hopkins's *Contending Forces* (1900), which made central themes of mob violence, the rape of black women, and the intergenerational transmission of such a history. Walter White's *The Fire in the Flint* (1924) ends with a ritualized burning of a mutilated lynching victim in the public square of a Southern town, in front of the local Confederate monument.[23]

Most poignantly, James Weldon Johnson's *The Autobiography of an Ex-Colored Man* (1912) recounts the story of a young black intellectual passing for white and traveling through the South. The ex-colored man's journey ends shockingly as he witnesses a lynching in a Southern railroad yard. As though he spoke for the black post-Reconstruction generation's inescapable memory of such violence, both real and threatened, Johnson's protagonist describes the scene:

> A railroad tie was sunk into the ground, the rope was removed, and a chain brought and securely coiled round the victim and the stake. There he stood, a man only in form and stature . . . His eyes were full and vacant, indicating not a single ray of thought. Fuel was brought from everywhere, oil, the torch; the flames crouched for an instant as though to gather strength, then leaped up as high as their victim's head. He squirmed, he writhed, strained at his

chains, then gave out cries and groans that *I shall always hear . . .* his eyes, bulging from their sockets, rolled from side to side, appealing in vain for help . . . I was fixed to the spot where I stood, powerless to take my eyes from what *I did not want to see.*[24] (emphasis added)

In black folk memory over time, the violence of slavery, the mob terror of the Reconstruction years, and the long history of lynching that took on highly ritualized forms by the 1890s had to be remembered and exorcised all at once. As Johnson's character says, these were stories people did "not want to see" but could "always hear."

The bulk of white Southerners had experienced the psychological trauma of defeat; their world had been turned upside down, and they simply could not abide the presence of assertive blacks wearing uniforms and carrying guns, organizing Union Leagues, or voting and serving in the legislature and on the judicial bench. Most white Southerners found intolerable the collective and individual demonstrations by blacks of their public identities as *citizens* during the years of radical Reconstruction. White rage led quickly to individual and organized violence against the churches, schools, homes, farmsteads, and bodies of black citizens, as well as against their white Republican allies. As historian George Rable has written, altering Clausewitz's famous dictum, "for the South, peace became war carried on by other means."[25]

Violence left Reconstruction's most difficult and twisted legacy. Few white Southern intellectuals wrote as directly, if defensively, about the peculiar Southern proclivity to violence as Wilbur Cash. In *The Mind of the South* (1941), Cash maintained that the South of Reconstruction became the new "frontier the Yankee made." White Southerners, even the "better men," unleashed on emancipated blacks a fury born of lost battles, lost mastery, alleged political repression, and the necessity of finding the "scapegoat" through which to "strike at Yankeedom." Stranded in time and circumstances seemingly created by the conquerors, white Southerners, in Cash's terms, "let their own hate run." Evil almost always has a historical logic, and therefore an explanation. Historian Sheldon Hackney has suggested that the source of Southern violence rests in "a Southern world view that defines the social, political, and physical environment as hostile and casts the white Southerner in the role of passive victim of malevolent forces." To locate the significance of Reconstruction violence in American memory, we must seek it not only in the darkness of evil, but as Hackney says, in "the sense of grievance that is at the heart of the Southern identity," however mythical that grievance's origins or horrible its outcomes.[26]

In Southern lore, in formal history, and eventually in popular culture, the Klan, as the saviors of Southern society, racial order, and white womanhood, attained a heroic image in American memory, a place from which the organization could be dislodged only during the latter half of the twentieth century. As Primo Levi has written of the memory of genocidal violence, "the end point of the deformation of the memory of a committed fault is its complete suppression." Such suppressions of memory and responsibility can be the result of a "deliberate intent to lie, but in other cases we are faced with a fossilized lie, an ancient lie frozen into a formula." Nothing in the popular Southern and national image of Reconstruction by the turn of the century caused more spirited defense or aggressive evasion than the role of the Klan and violence in the white South's overthrow of Reconstruction.[27]

In two widely popular books, *The Leopard's Spots* (1902) and *The Clansman* (1905), Thomas Dixon Jr., a North Carolinian born during the war, provided the Klan and its violence with its most enduring romantic mythology. *The Clansman* became a popular success as a stage production as well as a novel, and provided the basis for D. W. Griffith's epic film *Birth of a Nation* (a collaboration with Dixon) in 1915. Dixon's vicious version of the idea that blacks had caused the Civil War by their very presence, and that Northern radicalism during Reconstruction failed to understand that freedom had ushered blacks as a race into barbarism, neatly framed the story of the rise of heroic vigilantism in the South. Reluctantly, Klansmen—white men—had to take the law into their own hands in order to save Southern white womanhood from the sexual brutality of black men. Dixon's vision captured the attitudes of thousands and forged in story form a collective memory of how the war may have been lost but Reconstruction was won—by the South and by a reconciled nation. Riding as masked cavalry, the Klan stopped corrupt government, prevented the anarchy of "Negro rule," and most of all, saved white supremacy.[28] They were the noble founders of a new, reunited nation, the white Lancelots of the American reunion. The Klan thus found a place as a frozen formula (Levi's "fossilized lie") in the mainstream of American historical consciousness.

With time Dixon's brand of radical racism became an embarrassment within the genteel South. But at the turn of the century, the theory of black retrogression and the sympathetic explanation of Southern violence during

Reconstruction were widely held assumptions about American history. *Dixie after the War* (1906), a popular history of the Reconstruction era by a Virginian, Myrta Lockett Avary, nurtured the popular legends of Reconstruction. "With freedom," she announced, "the negro, *en masse*, relapsed promptly into the voodooism of Africa. Emotional extravaganzas, which for the sake of his health and sanity, if for nothing else, had been held in check by his owners, were indulged without restraint." Avary derided the political activity of blacks in Union Leagues, claiming that these "secret" societies committed acts of oppression against white Southerners far worse than anything the Klan ever did. According to Avary, "the swing back to savagery the instant the master-hand was removed" provided the "inflammable material upon which political sharpers played without scruple" upon Southern blacks.[29]

Avary plied the Southern imagination about Reconstruction with an indiscriminate use of quotation marks from her personal sources and with a flood of alleged "facts" about black rapists and white female victims. According to Avary, Southern white women lived during the postwar years as "prisoners of fear." She detailed one story of an 1870 lynching where a heroic mob followed strict orders not to drink liquor and not to mutilate the body of the executed. Avary took pride in writing dialect. After the black man pleads for his life, saying "But fo' Gawd, gent'mun, ef a white man f'om de Norf hadn't put't in my hade dat a white 'oman warn' none too good fuh," Avary clinically describes how "word was given, and he dropped into eternity." She decried the pattern of lynching in more recent times when the "moderation" of the Reconstruction era had collapsed into "orgies of vengeance." But she felt assured of the legacy of the earlier era, and portrayed the original Klan as a necessary, if unfortunate, outcome of social chaos and an arm of community justice. In the spirit of reconciliation, Avary placed the racial violence of Reconstruction in the comfort zone of national progress. "Informed Northerners," she opined, "will concede that the evils of the day justified or excused the Klan's existence. For my part, I believe that this country owes a heavy debt to its noiseless white horsemen, shades of a troubled past."[30]

Troubled indeed. The vision of Dixon, Avary, and other Klan apologists deformed the reality of the white counterrevolution during Reconstruction. The Ku Klux Klan was founded as a social club composed of young Confederate veterans looking for amusement in their small town of Pulaski, in Giles County, Tennessee, in 1866. It took root, though, in the social chaos and bitterness of the immediate postwar years in many regions in the South. Within a year, its rituals and initiation ceremonies gave way to more systematic acts of abuse against the independence of the freedpeople. In August 1866, the Giles County Freedmen's Bureau agent, Captain George E. Judd, reported a heightening hostility toward Yankees and the freedmen. "The people do all they can to degrade them [blacks]," said Judd, and keep them down to what they see fit to call their proper place." "The consequence," the agent continued, was that blacks had to fight their way against the abuse of the whites and from being cheated out of the proceeds of their labor." The fight had only begun. When a black saloonkeeper in Pulaski hung out a sign on the front of his place that read "Equal Rights," it was torn down the same day by a group of local whites. Such encounters and abuses escalated into much worse "outrages" in 1867–68, as the Klan spread to virtually every Southern state.[31]

The Klan was never a well-organized conspiracy; it tended to be largely rural and local in character. It thrived where the Democratic and Republican parties, as well as the two races, were in relative balance. The Klan's purposes were essentially political; it sought to maintain white supremacy and to restore labor discipline and economic dependency among the freedpeople. Klansmen, and their thousands of silent supporters, aimed to destroy the Republican Party, serve the resurgence of the Democratic Party, and overthrow radical Reconstruction. Although the Klan by itself did not succeed in overthrowing a Reconstruction government in any Southern state per se, it launched a pattern of counterrevolutionary violence and political intimidation that helped accomplish that end in the 1870s. By whippings, rapes, the burning of houses, schools, and churches, and hundreds of murders and lynchings, the Klan wanted to win back as much of a status quo antebellum as they could achieve. Their victims were teachers, black students, white and black politicians, and uncounted numbers of freedmen and their families who participated in Republican politics or gained some economic autonomy.[32]

Black politicians and delegates to conventions were especially vulnerable to Klan violence. At least 10 percent of the black members of constitutional conventions in the South in 1867–68 became victims, including seven who were murdered. The Klan often attacked only individuals. Sometimes, however, it launched wholesale attacks on communities or broke up Republican rallies. These attacks occasionally resulted in large casualties, such as one in October 1870 in Greene County, Alabama, where four blacks were killed and fifty-four wounded, or another in 1870 in Laurens County, South Carolina, where after Republicans won a local election, some 150 blacks were chased from their homes and thirteen murdered. In South Carolina alone, from the fall elections of 1870 to April 1871, formal testimony recorded some thirty-eight murders and hundreds of whippings. In Meridian, Mississippi, in 1871, local black orators were arrested for delivering "incendiary speeches." At a court hearing, gunfire erupted, and the white Republican judge and two defendents were killed. In a day-long riot that followed in Meridian, some thirty blacks were slaughtered by mobs.[33]

The majority of Southern counties did not experience Klan violence, but in those many that did, selective political assassinations destroyed the Republican Party and rendered independent black political and economic life untenable. As many as 150 people, mostly black, may have died in political violence in Jackson County, Florida, between 1868 and 1871. In some counties of northern Alabama (especially Madison, including the town of Huntsville), Klan beatings and hangings became weekly and even daily events during the election months from the presidential contest in the fall of 1868 to the Congressional canvass in August 1869. One scholar has estimated that approximately four hundred lynchings were committed by the Klan in the period 1868–71 alone across the South. Lynching is usually associated with the 1890s and the first decades of the twentieth century. But in Kentucky alone, one estimate suggests that in the first ten years after the war, at least three hundred people, mostly black, perished at the hands of lynch mobs, and that during the period 1867–71 in rural counties of central Kentucky, as many as twenty-five lynchings occurred per year.[34]

Fortunately, state governments and the U.S. Congress launched investigations of Klan violence during Reconstruction, leaving thousands of pages of testimony from which to imagine the fate and hear the voices of the victims as well as some of the perpetrators of this reign of terror. In widespread hearings, an initial collective memory of violence emerges from the interstices of fact, fable, denial, and grief. Some Southern states held hearings to determine the extent of Klan activity. In Tennessee, many freedmen, as well as Union army veterans and white schoolteachers, testified about beatings and murders. Several gave accounts of a particularly bad rampage by Klansmen on the Fourth of July, 1868, in Giles County. Among the victims was John Dunlap, a white principal of a black school who was dragged from his home in the dark of night by a mob of fifty. Dunlap described his ritual whipping: "They then stood me in the middle of the road, and ordered me to let down my pants; then turned my shirt up over my head, and fastened it. They then struck me each five licks." From Maury County, Tennessee, a black former Union soldier, Charles Belefont, testified for hundreds of others with similar nightmare

Thomas Nast depicts a black veteran holding a copy of the Emancipation Proclamation, unable to protect the dead woman and children below. The soldier's downcast eyes point to the monument's litany of murders and burnings by white rioters and Klansmen. (*Harper's Weekly*, October 10, 1868)

experiences: "They came to my house one Saturday night . . . and took me out . . . about one hundred yards and stripped me. There were nine in this gang: each one of them whipped me." Asked the reason for his beating, Belefont replied: "They said I was a damned nigger and had been a Yankee soldier." Many witnesses at the Tennessee commission hearings described the elaborate costumes and masks of the Klan, with red and white gowns, drapings over their horses, and special flags. Some blacks testified to resistance as well as their own humiliation. Lewis Stegall, from Marshall County, described himself laid out on a rock, blindfolded, his shirt pulled over his head, and his drawers ripped down. Just as Klansmen began to administer five lashes apiece, they were fired upon from the woods by his black rescuers; the mob dispersed but not before shooting and wounding Stegall. Stegall escaped and went to live in Nashville; his loss was immense. "I left half interest in thirty-six arces of cotton," said Stegall, "about twenty acres of corn, and one third of about twenty acres of wheat." Expressing a pattern that would recur again and again in such hearings over the next three years, Stegall declared: "I fear to return to my home, in consequence of the state of feeling against me, which is common to all colored men who voted the Radical ticket."[35]

In a series of Enforcement Acts in 1870–71, Congress moved to protect the rights of citizens against intimidation and terror in the South. The third, and most sweeping enactment, the Ku Klux Klan Act of April 1871, made private acts of violence, as well as any offenses against the political rights of individuals and their right to equal protection of the laws, punishable under federal law and enforceable by federal troops. The Klan Act even authorized the President to suspend the writ of habeas corpus and thus launched a bitter partisan struggle over the idea of jurisdiction and Constitutional authority. Democrats never accepted any of the Enforcement Acts and devoted much energy to their repeal. Republicans exhibited considerable hesitation about such an extension of federal power, but in the end, the sheer necessity of a forceful response to Klan violence compelled them to act. As part of this effort to stop the Klan, Congress decided to organize the KKK Hearings, the largest investigation of its kind ever attempted by the U.S. government.[36]

Composed of seven senators and fourteen representatives, the Joint Select Committee to Inquire into the Condition of Affairs in the Late Insurrectionary States first assembled in Washington, D.C., in March 1871. The first hearings, which began in May 1871, investigated only North Carolina. As those hearings ensued through the summer, other subcommittees, consisting of

Congressmen of both parties and utilizing detectives hired to assemble detailed evidence on Klan atrocities, opened hearings in South Carolina, Georgia, Florida, Tennessee, Alabama, and Mississippi. The hearings were often highly partisan, with Republican majority and Democratic minority representatives producing witnesses designed to contradict the other side. The hearings also faced enormous hostility from the Democratic Southern press, some of which conducted campaigns of misinformation. Many Southern newspapers and politicians labored hard in 1871 to convince voters that the Klan hearings were nothing more than an elaborate Republican effort to fabricate "outrage" stories as preparation for the 1872 presidential campaign. The notions of Yankee "despotism" and "bayonet rule," so crucial to the developing legend of Reconstruction that would eventually freeze Southern and national memory of the period, were widely aired during the nearly nine months of KKK investigations.[37]

These public hearings are a unique testament of how law and order collapsed in many areas of the South, and to the shuddering brutality of many white Southerners toward blacks and any whites judged to be complicitous with the Yankee conqueror. They are America's first public record where ordinary freedmen, public officials, poor white farmers, Klansmen, and former Confederate generals came before federal officials and described, or evaded, what the war had wrought—a revolutionary society that attempted forms of racial equality without the means or ultimate will to enforce them against a counterrevolutionary political impulse determined to destroy the new order. The hearings were designed to produce prosecution and justice. Some justice was achieved, but the reconciliation that the country ultimately reached ironically emerged through avoidance and denunciation of the mountain of ugly truths recorded in those hearings.[38]

Klan violence against blacks in the Reconstruction South succeeded especially in its uses of *fear*. For so many victims of the violence, the emotional and ideological legacies of their experiences endured as part of individual and community memories. These dangerous and painful memories undoubtedly caused conflicted emotions of guilt and rage, humiliation and vengeance, and profound distrust. If raw memories and bitter hostilities still drove the national political discourse during at least the decade of Reconstruction, how could it have been any different in the hearts and minds of black and white Southerners? Mob violence injected poisons into Civil War memory that only resistance, decades of time, and turns in history could begin to eradicate.

Torture, almost by definition, drives human beings beyond their limits of endurance and understanding. "Whoever was tortured, stays tortured," wrote Auschwitz survivor Jean Amery; "whoever has succumbed to torture can no longer feel at home in the world. Trust in the world . . . will not be regained." Klan violence was never so systematic as the Nazi Holocaust; the death of freedmen or white Republicans was never its sole aim. But in their testimonies many victims left clues to the burdens with which the survivors of Klan terror lived. Dragged from his house in the dark of the night in Rutherfordton, North Carolina, white Republican state legislator James Justice was pistol-whipped, forced to run through streets with "nothing in the world on but the loose shirt that I wear at night," and then beaten. Before telling his own gruesome tale, Justice described the results he had seen of Klan outrages on the bodies of black folk. "I have seen a great many persons in Raleigh," declared Justice, "who have come there and exhibited their persons to anyone who might wish to see them, with their backs lashed, and with wounds from gun and pistol-shots . . . I remember to have seen one colored man whose body presented quite a mangled appearance."[39]

Klan tortures knew no limits and sometimes collapsed into sadism and rape. In South Carolina, a white schoolteacher was dragged into a clearing, blindfolded, and forced to kiss the naked bodies of a group of assembled blacks. "They made me kiss the negro man's posterior, and held it open and made me kiss it," said the teacher, "and as well as I remember a negro woman's too, and also her private parts, and then told me to have sexual connection with her." He refused and was beaten. The mob leader then "asked me how I liked that for nigger equality." In his judicial district of North Carolina's central piedmont, Albion Tourgée reported twelve murders, nine rapes, fourteen arsons, and over seven hundred whippings (including one of a woman 103 years old). Asked if he knew of other rapes than the one he reported, North Carolina freedman Essic Harris replied: "Oh yes, several times. That has been very common . . . it has got to be an old saying." Harris spoke of a woman named Miss Sally who remarked that when the Yankees came (during the war) "she saw a heap of trouble; but she said the Yankees were gentlemen compared to these Ku Klux."[40]

In many sections of the South there were communities of the scarred as well as many mourners for the dead victims. Freedman James Beckwith testified in Columbus, Mississippi, in November 1871, that he had been attacked in his own house by a white-robed mob looking for money. Hanged twice from tree limbs, with his feet apparently dangling just close enough to the ground that he did not die, Beckwith nevertheless lost consciousness. "They hung me up," said Beckwith. "I never knew nothing. When I came to I was scrambling on the ground." Beckwith and his wife, who was also whipped, lived in fear from that point on. Asked how badly he was hurt, Beckwith replied: "I have been uneasy. I have worked and made a crop, and worked in uneasiness all the time . . . I was suffering for three months so that I couldn't see at all hardly, and I did no work for two or three weeks." A Mississippi freedman, Sanders Flint, testified about the murder of his two sons, Joseph and Willis. The three Flints had been jailed over a dispute about the division of a crop with a landowner. A mob of local white men, nearly every one of whom Flint could name, dragged their prey from the jail at night. The elder Flint somehow escaped from the mob but the two sons were later shot in the head; their discarded bodies were found some eight days later on a river bottom.[41] In the memorialization that swept over America in the decades after the war, no monuments ever commemorated the pitiful deaths of the Joseph and Willis Flints across the South. These stories and legacies, as much a part of the struggle over the meaning of the Civil War as Pickett's Charge or Sherman's March to the Sea, never found a place in the nation's epic.

Whole families experienced Klan terror together and lived with its legacy. Jackson and Jane Surratt testified in Spartanburg, South Carolina, in July 1871. The Surratts sharecropped a piece of land about one mile from the Cowpens Battle Ground of the Revolutionary War. The tale of anguish began as so many others: "Open the door or we will kill the last one of you," Jackson remembered the Klansmen shout. "I was scared and opened it; and they cried, 'Gentlemen blindfold him.' They started off with me, and they run in the house and cursed and tore and jerked my daughter out, and jerked my wife and my wife's son out of bed." Jane had her seven-month-old baby torn from her arms. Outside in the night, "they made us all lie down—my wife and all. They had us nearly naked." Jackson somehow seems to have gotten away into a swamp. But Jane Surratt and her children were whipped. Asked how badly "hurt" she was, Jane responded: "I couldn't hold my child on my lap to suckle it; I had to lay it on the bed and stand by it. I had no way to rest except on the flat of my belly." Jane Surratt worried especially about the effects of the beatings on her children. "They whipped my son miserably bad; they whipped my daughter very bad; she has not been able to do much since; I don't believe she will ever get over it." From so many accounts of doors knocked in; shots fired into small houses; hearths and beds invaded in the night; men, women, children, and old people of both genders trapped in a psychology of sleepless fright; and people dragged in their nightclothes into fields and ritually whipped, we can only conclude that thousands of black folk in many regions of the South, especially in the period 1868–71, reaped a long-lasting harvest of torture and fear.[42] They became witnesses of terror for their families and communities for generations to come.

Expressions of fear permeate the Klan hearings held in 1871, and this fear constitutes perhaps the deepest layer of the memories that blacks took into the future from the experience of violence. Statements such as "I have not felt safe," or "I was afraid they might come and whip me . . . again," and many other such passages ring through again and again from the tedium of the hearings. After being whipped while "stark naked" by two men he knew well and had been "raised with," Mervin Givens was asked why he did not bring suit against his tormentors. His answer spoke of common sense and the logic of terror: "For fear they would shoot me. If I was to bring them up here and could not prove the thing exactly on them, and they were to get out of it, I would not expect to live much longer." Essic Harris described his area of North Carolina as one where fear governed the daily lives of black folk. Asked if blacks were in a "worse condition now than when in slavery," Harris unreservedly declared: "Of course they must be. They must keep their doors barred up . . . Pretty much all the colored people have their doors barred; they are afraid to keep them any other way." Thousands of blacks simply took to the woods in regions of North and South Carolina, Georgia, Florida, and Alabama, afraid to stay in their homes after they or their neighbors had been attacked, and sometimes their homes burned. "I had laid out in the woods for months," reported a South Carolina freedman, "like I was a dromedary or a hog or a cow afraid to go in to the house; that was hard, I think, for poor negroes."[43] None who experienced these depredations could have remained unaffected in the long term by such cruelty. Fantasies of revenge or escape must have mixed in the psyches of many blacks with a fear-struck and anguish-laden silence.

The final, 632-page report of the Congressional subcommittees, submitted in February 1872, demonstrates not only the severe partisanship through which Americans interpreted Reconstruction violence, but also the dangerously divided memories that such terror had produced. In the majority report, Republicans may have exaggerated the extent of Klan organization and conspiracy, but they did so with little vindictiveness and a remarkable degree of understanding about the social and economic plight of the South in 1871.

The majority report also left no doubt about the horror of individual acts of atrocity. The authors reprinted the lengthy testimony of South Carolinian Elias Hill. Hill had been stricken since age seven with a disease that had rendered him crippled in both arms and legs. Unable to walk or even feed himself, Hill's freedom had been purchased by his father during slavery. He became a self-taught teacher and Baptist preacher, and after emancipation, he taught in a freedmen's school and wrote business correspondence for other blacks. For his work in a Union League and his alleged "political sermons," Klansmen carried Hill out of his cabin in May 1871, threw him into the yard, beat his deformed body with a horsewhip, and threatened to kill him if he would not send a public disavowal of the Republican Party to the local newspaper. Cringing on the ground, Hill was accused by his attackers of lying. "Upon honor," he cried in response. But "*they said I had no honor,* and hit me again" (emphasis added). From his experience of abuse, Hill lost any hope of living peaceably in America and made written application to emigrate to Liberia. In highlighting this story of cruelty to a crippled yet literate and publicly active man, the Republicans sought "to put the story of his wrongs in his own language" and demonstrate that Klan violence was an integral part of real politics.[44]

Although the Republican authors of the majority report exercised "forbearance and conciliation" while understanding that "reluctant obedience is all that is to be hoped for" from white Southerners, they were adamant about the need for federal enforcement and prosecution. The "list of men murdered and maltreated" in the nine South Carolina counties where the Klan ruled for months, the report argued, required "the strong arm of the government both to protect its citizens in the enjoyment of their rights" and to stave off an already "initiated war of races." The "experiment" of Reconstruction needed more time to succeed, declared the majority report in a combination of passive and active voices, and the freedpeople needed "protection."[45]

The Democratic authors of the minority report fashioned an elaborate version of the victimized and oppressed South, and argued vehemently that most of the alleged Klan violence simply had not occurred. A full-throated appeal to the tragic legend of Reconstruction informed the entire minority report. "History, till now," declared the Democrats, "gives no account of a conqueror so cruel as to place his vanquished foes under the dominion of their former slaves." The Reconstruction Acts, the Freedmen's Bureau, and the radical constitutions had all been "framed by venal adventurers and illiterate negroes." Offices in state governments were "filled with ignorance, vice, and unblushing corruption." And the South swarmed with carpetbaggers "seizing everything moveable." Thus the "oppressed" (a word used repeatedly) South, "gorged with plunder," endured the cruelties of an imperial conqueror and collected its grievances in the storehouse of memory.[46]

The minority report from the Klan hearings could have served as an initial script for Dixon's and Griffiths's *Birth of a Nation*. The struggle to control the memory, as well as the politics of Reconstruction, is everywhere apparent in the report. Democrats were fond of quoting Nathan Bedford Forrest, the former Confederate cavalry general and one of the founders of the Klan in Tennessee, whose evasive language in his testimony before the hearings left little doubt of the organization's purpose. "It had no political purpose," claimed Forrest. "I think it was for self-protection." Forging the Klan apologetics that would endure well into the twentieth century, the report declared that "Ku-Kluxism . . . was the legitimate offspring of misrule; it follows and disappears with its parent."[47] The vigilante war carried on by the Klan and its minions during Reconstruction left an indelible and voluminously documented legacy. North and South would yet find a way to sentimentalize and reconcile even this element of the war's aftermath. But the failure of racial reconciliation, so crucial to any ultimate working through of the meaning of the Civil War, took root in the Klan's reign of terror in 1868–71. The contested legacy of Klan violence deformed understandings of history, unsettled black memories for decades, inspired white Southerners in their struggle for self-determination and local rule, and most immediately, played a pivotal role in the electoral politics of the 1870s.

THE ELECTION OF 1872 pitted increasingly incompatible memories of war, emancipation, and Reconstruction against one another. Throughout the Ku Klux crises of 1871 and into the election year of 1872, Frederick Douglass remained a vigilant voice for the emancipationist legacy of the war. As the Republican Party prepared to renominate President Grant in June 1872 and fend off the insurgency in its own ranks known as the Liberal Republican movement, Douglass described what he saw as the gravity of the coming election. "The fruits of ten years of labor, suffering, and loss are at stake," wrote the former slave. What hung in the balance in the coming election was the "freedom, equality, and national harmony" forged by the "suppression of a gigantic slaveholding rebellion." Disgusted by what he perceived as the "deceitful cry that all the questions raised by the war . . . are now settled,"

Douglass warned that "the slave demon still rides the southern gale, and breathes out fire and wrath." Douglass had long interpreted the Klan, Democrats, and the survival of Southern rebellion as a unified political force. While black life and human rights were so insecure, Douglass could not stomach the drumbeats for reconciliation. Douglass resented what he called "this cry of peace! peace! where there is no peace."[48] To him, the election of 1872 was still a referendum on the meaning of the war and the survival of Reconstruction.

In 1872, the first Grant administration listed under the weight of corruption and cronyism. Although Grant had stood up to the Klan and used federal authority to put it out of business in the South, the Republican Party under his leadership had become a formalized organization ruled by patronage and ridden with scandal. For much of the party, the wartime idealism and the egalitarian vision of the radical Republicans survived without passion as so many slogans on old banners. By 1871, a "reform" insurgency, led by the German-born Carl Schurz, a former Union general, and by influential intellectuals and editors such as E. L. Godkin of the *Nation,* had developed within the Republican ranks (it eventually grew into a formidable coalition). At heart, these were men who had always been contemptuous of the activist state that radicals such as Thaddeus Stevens had fashioned out of the war. They were proponents of classical finanicial liberalism: laissez-faire government, free trade, and the gold standard as moral principles. They believed deeply in the ideas of tradition and progress. The reformers were middle-class and well educated, fearful of class conflict, and determined to curb what they perceived as the dangers of mass politics and universal suffrage.[49]

One of the liberal reformers' targets, therefore, was the very existence of Reconstruction in the South. These "best men," as they fashioned themselves, wanted governments, North and South, led by each region's "natural leaders." They tended to oppose federal action against the Klan on Constitutional grounds, and favored universal amnesty for ex-Confederates. Godkin led this rhetorical retreat from Reconstruction just as the new order had taken a foothold in the South. "Reconstruction and slavery we have done with," he declared in March 1872, "for administrative and revenue reform we are eager." Demonstrating the stark differences in how the legacies of the war were defined within the old Republican coalition, the *Nation'*s editor answered Douglass's condemnations of "rebels," old and new. "Reconstruction" concluded Godkin, "seems to be morally a more disastrous process than rebellion."[50]

At the national level, Liberal Republicanism emerged out of alliances of reform Democrats and Republicans in at least three upper South states: Virginia, Tennessee, and Missouri. In speeches in St. Louis in September 1870, and a year later in Nashville, Carl Schurz launched a crusade for civil service reform, tariff reduction, and various other economic measures such as land grants to railroads. But the South, Reconstruction, and a swelling chorus of reconciliation were primary themes of Schurz's speeches. "Every sensible man knows that the Civil War is over," he told the faithful in St. Louis. Any "necessity for exceptional measures for . . . the protection of loyal people" [enforcement of Reconstruction] had "ceased to exist." To Southern blacks, Schurz gave direct advice: "repel those who . . . strive to seduce and make tools of you, as your most dangerous enemies [carpetbaggers]." In Nashville, Schurz demanded that the Civil War Constitutional Amendments be upheld, but advocated amnesty for all ex-Confederates, cessation of all federal intervention, and "local self-government" in the South by leaders of "property and enterprise." His call for "fraternal feeling" between the sections and the races seemed hollow at best to blacks while Klan violence continued unabated and the Klan hearings received widespread press coverage.[51]

During the Liberal Republicans' ill-fated convention in Cincinnati, held in May 1872, this collection of strange political bedfellows (all alienated from Grant, but of very different persuasions on tariffs, corruption, black rights, and other issues) nominated the quixotic Horace Greeley. Divided and without discipline, the Liberal Republicans woke up after three days of a convention with a candidate that most of the leading lights of their movement opposed, even despised. Greeley's protectionism was at odds with one of the new party's founding principles, and the former abolitionist and advocate of black rights now sounded more like a Democrat when he addressed any Reconstruction issue. The central cause around which a reform coalition could be held together was the contest between Reconstruction and reconciliation.

Since his role in paying Jefferson Davis's bail in 1867, Greeley had been a crusader for sectional reunion. In 1871, Greeley fashioned himself an agricultural reformer and embarked on a lengthy speaking tour of Mississippi, Louisiana, and Texas, ostensibly to speak on farming improvements for the Southwest. But at nearly every stop, he addressed Southerners about the need of reconciliation for agricultural and business growth, and for the development of railroads. In his letters back to the *Tribune*, Greeley began to carve out an eventual campaign strategy. From Memphis, he observed that perhaps two-thirds of former slaveholders, complaining about labor discipline, would gladly "have their slaves back again." Greeley wrote of the planter class with genuine sympathy and declared that "years must pass before they can be reconciled" to the new regime. From Vicksburg, Mississippi, he offered many observations on the conditions of the freedmen and claimed that he had "conversed with no black who was not hopeful and confident as to the future of his race." When Greeley returned to New York, he spoke to a reception at the Lincoln Club-Rooms in Union Square. All the death and sacrifice of the war could have been avoided, Greeley now believed, if Northerners and Southerners had simply traveled and communicated more directly with one another. Half a million men had died, the old editor claimed, simply "because the North and South had failed to understand each other." While assuring the New Yorkers that the Klan was "no myth," Greely believed that if universal amnesty had been instituted right after the war, "there would have been no Ku Klux in 1871." But Greeley was ready for new issues. "Gentlemen," he proclaimed, "the past is past . . . I am weary of fighting over issues that ought to be dead."[52] Thus Greeley readied himself for a run against Grant and Reconstruction. Greeley seemed to believe that all the nation needed to attain from the travails of Reconstruction was a bad memory.

Greeley the reconciliationist was popular in the provinces. Many white Southerners and Democrats across the country signed on early to the idea of a Greeley-led third party. Although the Liberal Republican campaign failed, it is a compelling measure of the degree and character of the reconciliationist impulse in America during Reconstruction. For many, the Greeley candidacy represented a racial, class, and sectional resurgence all at once. Cassius M. Clay wrote to Greeley from Kentucky in February 1872, condemning "the continued persecution of the South by not granting amnesty and by continually decrying them as rebels." The editor of the *Weekly Caucasian* in Lexington, Missouri, calling himself an "out and out unreconstructed rebel," urged Greeley to run for President as a means of ending Grant's "reckless, corrupt, debauched . . . administration."[53] This mixture of sincerity, unholy alliance, and opportunism produced a potent force for sectional reunion that could not yet fully crystalize electorally. But in time, it provided a base for other kinds of political and cultural victories.

For many white Southerners it made good sense to suspend the function of the Democratic Party for an election, to join all the apparent anti-Grant, anti-corruption sentiment as a means of achieving their goals of local autonomy and white supremacy. An Arkansan informed Schurz that the "most extreme and prominent Rebels here consider you [Schurz] as the Redeemer of the country." H. S. Foote of Mississippi endorsed the Liberal Republicans because they promised "future fraternal relations between Northern and Southern men" and an end to the "grinding oppression of carpetbag governments." And a Kentuckian, declaring himself a "friend to the colored race," offered support to the new movement because he felt comfortable that the Liberal Republicans would restore Southerners to "equality" and return blacks to their proper place.[54] The American reunion ultimately grew in many fertile soils—pure sentiment, genuine fervor for healing, white racial solidarity, the mutuality of soldiers' valor, and business interests. But here in 1872, even Yankee moral reformers posed as redeemers of the South.

When Greeley accepted the Liberal Republican nomination in 1872, he put into play one of the longest lasting slogans in the history of the American reunion. He embraced the "New Departure from jealousies, strifes, and hates" and declared his confidence that "the masses of our countrymen, North and South, are eager to *clasp hands across the bloody chasm* which has too long divided them" (emphasis added).[55] In July, the Democratic Party endorsed, or rather accepted, Greeley as its candidate. Many Democrats found Greeley's bizarre campaign hard to champion. But in the end the combined themes of "honesty and peace," code words for many different aims, kept large numbers of Democrats under the Liberal Republican banner. Although a failure at the polls, the appeal to reconciliation drew Democrats like a beguiling siren song. Humiliated by the blunder in nominating Greeley, and eager for an alternative, Schurz may have put it best in his own admission of why he felt "no escape" from his own movement's odd creation. He would support Greeley, Schurz told Godkin, because reunion rhetoric could appeal "strongly to those who are in contact with the South and feel the full importance of . . . the pacification and regeneration of that part of the country."[56]

Hence, in one disjointed address after another, especially on a campaign tour of New Jersey, Pennsylvania, Ohio, Indiana, and Kentucky during September 17–29, when he delivered some two hundred speeches, Greeley beat the only drum he and his strange coalition possessed. In Pittsburgh, Greeley offended Union veterans who had just recently held a large convention in that city to endorse Grant. He chastized the soldiers for their continued loyalty to their former general, calling their stand "pseudo-heroic." Greeley paid dearly for that blunder at the polls. In Erie, Pennsylvania, Greeley was met by a local black delegation seeking to shake his hand; he offended them as well, appearing "as though he would gladly forgo the pleasure of the meeting." And in Jeffersonville, Indiana, in an apparent appeal to Democrats, the candidate declared that his long past as an "enemy of slavery," and his advocacy of "the rights, the dignity . . . of free labor . . . might have been a mistake." Greeley kept trying to bridge the "bloody chasm," harping on what the *New York Times* called his "old hobby of 'reconciliation.'"[57]

For their part in 1872, the Republicans responded by flogging the Liberal Republicans and their new friends, the Democrats, with the "bloody shirt." When the Greeley campaign resorted to sending former Confederate generals such as John B. Gordon (a Georgia Democrat and Klan operative) into Northern states like Indiana to preach the gospel of the white "superior race" and the "trampled, bleeding, impoverished South," Republicans responded with their own tales of oppression. Imagery of Ku Klux violence filled Republican speeches. "Go vote to burn school houses, desecrate churches and violate women," Benjamin Butler proclaimed in Massachusetts, "or vote for Horace Greeley, which means the same thing."[58] To lose this rhetorical battle about the terms of reconciliation would be tantamount to reversing the battlefield verdicts of 1865 and denouncing the relative success of the federal counterattack on the Klan.

The elitist persuasion of reform liberalism had very little appeal among blacks. Frederick Douglass stumped for Grant everywhere the Republicans would unleash him. Sickened by the "hand clasping across the bloody chasm business," Douglass pilloried the Greeley-led Democrats as the party that had "murdered half a million loyal men to destroy the government and perpetuate slavery." No Republican orator clarified the stakes in 1872 quite like Douglass. The opposition served up a "great love feast of reconciliation cooked by Mr. Greeley" where "Southern brethren are indirectly promised the first seats at the common table." Such a political meal was premature and simply could not be served to the majority in 1872.[59] The Greeley campaign stumbled early and never regained its feet. Grant, running on a platform that still pledged enforcement of the Civil War Amendments, won decisively with 55 percent of the popular vote and by carrying every Northern state. The "bloody chasm" was still both meaningful and politically useful. Within weeks of the election, exhausted and humiliated, Greeley died.

But somethng else died as well in that election. The 1872 campaign spelled the final collapse of Republican radicalism. Because he loathed Grant and wanted to find other moral paths to protect civil rights, even Charles Sumner, as faithful a champion of black equality as the U.S. Senate had ever seen, had joined the Liberal Republican movement. In July 1872, Sumner responded to a request by black citizens in Washington, D.C., for his counsel on the election. Sumner vehemently endorsed Greeley over Grant, reaching into the past to portray the editor as the "life-long abolitionist" and the President as the offender of black equality who, "except as a soldier summoned by the accident of war, never did anything against Slavery." Sumner urged blacks not to worry about the Democrats joining the Liberals; they had "changed" and had signed on to a "sacred covenant" led by an old abolitionist. Sumner wanted the "two sections and the two races . . . lifted from the ruts and grooves in which they are now fastened, and instead of *irritating antagonism* without end, there shall be *sympathetic cooperation.*" In this strange political year, Sumner suspended judgment about the price of forgetting. That such language of reconciliation was directed at black voters by one of their champions is indicative of how inexorable the process of reunion would be in America. "I am against the policy of hate," concluded Sumner. "Pile up the ashes; extinguish the flames; abolish the hate."[60] Sumner enjoyed enormous respect among blacks, but his "just say no to hate" impulse did not make sense to most blacks. The price of suspending memory was just too great to follow a reconciliationist agenda less than a decade after emancipation.

What Douglass called the "peculiar" election left much confusion about just what the Republican Party had come to represent. Under the heat of the third party challenge, Republicans in Congress cut tariffs and passed an amnesty bill, returning citizenship and the franchise to some twenty thousand ex-Confederates. Perhaps most importantly, while defeating the "clasping hands" strategy of the Greeley campaign, Republicans had themselves participated in a vast airing of the idea of reconciliation. Most Republicans were not opposed to reunion; most did not share Douglass's desire to thwart the reconciliationist legacy until the emancipationist legacy could be permanently secured. In the 1872 election, Reconstruction (meaning federal enforcement of the new regime of black civil and political liberty) had been thrown on the defensive; it was a cause served by memory more than by active commitment. In his classic Reconstruction novel *A Fool's Errand,* Albion Tourgée captured with wry insight the waning of radicalism among aging abolitionists. "I don't wonder," says the carpetbagger-hero Comfort Servosse to his oldest friend, "that men who had been in what our modern slang denominates the 'racket' of the antislavery reform should be tired. I fully realize that a lifetime of struggle takes away a man's relish for a fight. Old men never become missionaries." In the spring of 1873, after Grant's second inauguration, Douglass worried about the "fatigue" and "repose" of the Republican Party.

He summed up much recent political history and looked clear-eyed at the future. "The apparent powerlessness of the enemy," said Douglass in one of the last editorials in his failing newspaper, "makes us careless about the use of our strength."[61]

In that same spring, 1873, an economic depression hit America and ravaged the economy. The Panic of 1873 permanently shifted the relationship between labor and capital, and opened fissures of class and labor conflict in ways that Americans had never experienced. If Democrats and racial violence had not put Reconstruction into permanent retreat, economic crises surely did over the ensuing four years. The yearnings for peace and reconciliation (which were often equated with better business growth and relations) now went hand in hand with economic fear, with financial and intellectual elites entrenching themselves ideologically in order to protect private property against the challenges of workers organized in unions and western farmers gathered in Granges. Memories of the war and struggles over the unfinished business of Reconstruction now merged with daily emergencies of economic survival or ruin. These persistent economic agonies of the Gilded Age, coupled with labor violence and farmers' revolts, eventually made soldiers' reunions and monument building attractive for their essential "respectability." Old soldiers were to serve as the people's equivalent of the "best men" who ran newspapers, magazines, and companies and who increasingly denounced labor unionism and other forms of political democracy. Speaking forcefully for his class, E. L. Godkin identified the "labor question" as the "disease of which this Christian civilization of ours is to perish." Unchecked, workers' pursuit of "equality of conditions," argued Godkin, "will eventually prove fatal to art, to science, to literature, and to law."[62]

As widespread joblessness swept through America's major cities in 1874–75, giving rise to a desperate "Work or Bread" movement among the thousands of unemployed, Northerners began to celebrate Memorial Day by routinely decorating Confederate graves like those of the Union dead. This "same attention" to the Confederate dead, said the reconciliationist *New York Tribune*, now under the editorship of staunch Liberal Republican Whitelaw Reid, showed "that time is softening the asperities growing out of a long civil war."[63] The whole social fabric needed healing and rebuilding; somehow, confidence had to be secured from the past, since it did not exist in the present. Modes of military memory served as a bulwark against all manner of social disorder that might rise up from the laboring masses. The war and black freedom were slowly but surely becoming the history transferred to memory, to be invoked as occasions and political imperatives demanded. Civil War memory was the nation's sectional and racial baggage, hauled into the future; in the final years of Reconstruction, the weight of that baggage, continually laden with the debris of newer conflicts, got only heavier.

DESPITE ITS DEBACLE in 1872, the Democratic Party's role in carrying the weight of Civil War memory shifted startlingly in its electoral victories in the off-year Congressional elections of 1874. Due to the depression, and to widespread distaste for the Grant administration's scandals, the 1874 elections took on more drama than ordinary Congressional contests. Attacking the new civil rights bill pending in Congress, fanning the flames of white supremacy, and generally benefitting from Republican disaffection from Grantism, Democrats pulled off one of the biggest political upsets in American history. "The Republican Party Struck by Lightning," shouted a headline in one of that party's own papers in Buffalo; "Busted. The Radical Machine Gone to Smash," announced the gleeful *Louisville Courier-Journal.* The Democrats not only captured the House of Representatives for the first time since before the war, but they did so by turning overnight a Republican majority of 198–88 into Democratic control by 169–109. Democrats won nineteen of twenty-five governors' races, and in state after state overturned the Civil War era's political landscape. Even in Massachusetts, the governorship was lost to a Democrat for the first time since 1858. In the South, the Democratic victory meant the destruction of many state Republican parties for the rest of the century; it also restored to Democrats the statehouses and governorships of Arkansas, Alabama, and Florida, leaving only four remaining ex-Confederate states to be "redeemed" from Reconstruction.[64]

Riding economic discontent, the appeal of home rule, and in some states the continued use of terror, Southern "Redeemers" (white Democrats) carried on a counterrevolution that by 1875 eventually had returned them to power in every Southern state but three (Louisiana, South Carolina, and Florida). Mississippi joined the ranks of the "redeemed" in 1875 through the infamous "shotgun policy," an especially violent campaign of abuse and intimidation of black voters that was unstopped by federal intervention. In these years of Southern redemption and the steady Northern retreat from Reconstruction, Republicans paid dearly for their recent history of support for black liberty and equality. White fears of an imagined racial equality, coupled with economic insecurity and increasing hostility toward the activist state, drove Reconstruction into the ground. The black writer and historian William Wells Brown put it succinctly in 1874: "There is a feeling all over this country that the Negro has got about as much as he ought to have." Most Northern whites retreated to the legal doctrine of "guaranteed rights" and considered the Fourteenth and Fifteenth Amendments to be all the nation ever owed the freedpeople.[65] Millions of white Southerners, joined by large numbers of white Northerners, now targeted those very Constitutional changes for either destruction or neglect.

With dire consequences for the emancipationist legacy of the war, the Republican Party had become by 1875–76 the party of memory, and the Democrats the party of the future. Politically, a decade after Appomattox, the meaning and memory of the revolution of 1863 faltered in the face of the counterrevolution of 1874. Republican Congressman James Garfield acknowledged that his party's disaster in 1874 had resulted from "a general apathy among the people concerning the war and the negro." And in the winter of 1875, at a meeting in Faneuil Hall in Boston about federal intervention in the violent and chaotic politics of Louisiana, Wendell Phillips was shouted down when he spoke up for protection of black rights, prompting the *New York Times* to conclude that "Wendell Phillips and William Lloyd Garrison are not exactly extinct from American politics, but they represent ideas in regard to the South which the majority of the Republican party have outgrown."[66]

Indeed, many Northern papers ran increasingly derisive stories about blacks and Republican rule in the South, many of which served the creation of the tragic legend of Reconstruction. The *New York Tribune's* correspondent interviewed South Carolina black legislator Beverly Nash in May 1875. Nash is portrayed as shrewdly corrupt and enriching himself while ignorant of public policy. "Reputed to have $100,000 laid up," Nash babbles in dialect during an evasive interview. On only one issue does he seem direct and certain. Asked if he thinks Grant should run for a third term in 1876, Nash demonstrates that Republicans stand for nothing but organizational loyalty supported by ignorant freedmen in office. "It ain't no use talkin', Sah," says Nash, "ef Grant gets de nomination, we're guine for him. South Carolina'll vote for de Devil ef he runs on de Republican ticket . . . We'd go for Grant, I reckon, 'cause he's de Boss Devil!" The interview ends with Nash portrayed as a false "High Churchman" who urges people to attend services while he bilks money from the "pockets of the oppressed people of South Carolina."[67] In such widely circulated racist parodies of Southern black politicians, the myth of carpetbag rule gained long-lasting legitimacy.

As America prepared to celebrate the centennial of its independence in 1875–76, African Americans confronted a complex dilemma of allegiance, hope, and memory. Their liberty and rights were the result of the Second American Revolution, although they had always appropriated the ideology of the first. Black freedom was the child of civil war; black rights were the products of blood, destruction, and fierce political conflict. No true national consensus ever gathered around the cause of black liberty and equality except as it was necessary to restoring and reimagining the republic itself. But Americans generally had run low on imagination about racial matters by the time of the centennial. Whether the nation's "new birth" of freedom would be sustained was an unsettled question. Egalitarianism and humanitarianism were tired traditions, and black freedom itself now depended for survival on a ripening sectional reconciliation. The situation was cause for worry and celebration.

On July 5, 1875, Frederick Douglass gave an oration at Hillsdale, outside of Washington, D.C., entitled "The Color Question." Douglass reflected in racialized terms on the impending American Centennial. He fiercely claimed the historical birthright of blacks in America; they "had never forsaken the white man in any great emergency." But at this hundredth anniversary of the founding, the nation, Douglass feared, would "lift to the sky its million voices in one grand Centennial hosanna of peace and good will to all the white race." As a black citizen, he dreaded the day when "this great white race has renewed its vows of patriotism and flowed back into its accustomed channels." Douglass, worried about the hold of white supremacy on America's historical consciousness, looked back upon fifteen years of unparalleled change for his people and asked the core question in the nation's struggle over the memory of the Civil War: "If war among the whites brought peace and liberty to the blacks, what will peace among the whites bring?"[68] (emphasis added). For more than a century since Reconstruction, through cycles of great advancement and periods of cynical reaction in American race relations, Douglass's question has echoed through American political culture.

At that celebration on July 5 outside Washington, John Mercer Langston, the black former abolitionist and now Howard University law professor, also spoke. Both orators mixed their appeals to a beleaguered African American patriotism and citizenship rights with an insistence on black self-reliance. In the face of the demise of Reconstruction and the Democratic Party's counter-revolution, this dualism had special poignance. "We must not beg men to do for us what we ought to do for ourselves," challenged Douglass. With even more verve, Langston demanded that "the hour has come for us to manage our own institutions." "If we have colored banks," he announced, "we must have colored bankers; if we have colored schools, let us have our own teachers." This combination of rights language with the self-reliant impulse for institution-building marks in 1875 the pathway of most black ideological struggles well into the twentieth century. Both Douglass and Langston seemed to be readying their black audience for the long haul; they might be losing to-

During Reconstruction and its aftermath, Frederick Douglass, former slave, abolitionist writer, and renowned orator, was among the most persistent voices of an emancipationist vision of Civil War memory. (Library of Congress)

day's political battle on the ground, but perhaps they could organize, create their own conditions, and still win the war over memory. They were quite right to ask loudly, as Douglass did, "in what position will this stupendous reconciliation leave the colored people?"[69]

That very same day in Vicksburg, Mississippi, an answer to such a question rang out with terrible clarity. In conjunction with the centennial, and anticipating what a black observer called the "general feeling of amity and fraternity . . . setting in on all sides, both south and north," some two hundred to three hundred black folk from the countryside joined as many from the city for a ceremony at the Vicksburg courthouse. The event was led by white Republican circuit court judge George F. Brown, and two of the most prominent black politicians in Mississippi, superintendent of state public education T. W. Cardozo, and Secretary of State James Hill. A black minister delivered a reading of the Declaration of Independence. Judge Brown spoke with moderation about the "progress of the country." Hill gave more of a political speech, one that was "not ultra," said the correspondent of the *Christian Recorder,* but "not so guarded and discreet" either. Then a white mob entered the courthouse, ordered the meeting dispersed, and began to beat the black participants as they rushed to the doors and widows in a "panic." Within twenty minutes, some fifty white men had gathered in the courthouse yard, and after a pistol shot signal, the mob opened up with rifles on the remainder of the black crowd, killing two immediately and mortally wounding several others. "Thus ended the ninety ninth anniversary of American freedom (?)," wrote an eyewitness. The observer, identifying himself only as "Veni Vidi" ("I came, I saw"), laid the blame for this particular massacre at the feet of the "now generous and forgetful northern yankee," and on the "*New York Tribune*" for its "continually feasting these red-handed gentry." Veni Vidi saw the very meaning of national reconciliation in the Vicksburg killings at the Fourth of July celebration. "Boston . . . and Ohio," he wrote, "hold the coats of Georgia and Mississippi, while they slay the common victim of northern prejudice and southern hate." The correspondent's recourse was to appeal to future justice, and most poignantly, to the memory of the pivotal passage in Lincoln's Second Inaugural Address: "If it please God that every drop of blood drawn by the lash shall be compensated by another drawn with the sword before this war shall close . . . 'the judgments of the Lord are true and righteous altogether.'"[70] From the perspective of the emancipationist legacy, the Declaration of Independence lay shredded on the ground along with the dead victims in Vicksburg and a dozen other

Mississippi towns. By 1875, the use of Lincoln's 1865 final call to arms to crush slavery seemed only a sad remnant of a glorious past.

By 1875–76, there were no federal swords of retribution authorized for use in Mississippi or any other Southern state. The will for federal intervention to stop violence and intimidation by white "liners" against blacks and white Republicans had all but vanished. General William T. Sherman summed up and endorsed this loss of will in 1875. "Outside help sooner or later must cease," he wrote to his brother John, "for our army is ridiculously small, in case of actual collision. It is only the Memory of our War Power that operates on the Rebel Element now. They have the votes, the will, and *will* in the End prevail."[71] Sherman's summation reminds us that the complex drama of Reconstruction—the test of political wills, ideologies, and the durability of revolutions—in the end turned on which memory might prevail: the revolution named and enforced in Lincoln's Second Inaugural, or the Southern Democrats' counterrevolution of the mid-1870s? The freedman casting his ballots and serving in office, or the same freedman shot dead on the ground? The revolution of black freedom or the redemption of white supremacy?

If 1874 was a "referendum on Reconstruction," then the 1876 presidential election gave the country a referendum on reunion. The Republican and Democratic parties faced each other for the first time since before the war as relative equals, represented in both sections. Given the sordid record of scandal of the outgoing Grant administration, the Republicans needed a perceived reformer and an uncontroversial figure at the top of their ticket. They found him by going to their geographical strength in the Midwest, and nominated Rutherford B. Hayes, a Civil War veteran, conservative, and three-term governor of Ohio. Hayes was the first choice of few Republicans, but he was acceptable to all. Importantly, he was a reconciliationist: he wrote carefully in his letter of acceptance that he believed in "honest and capable local self-government" for the South.[72] In such codes, Hayes signaled a Republican abandonment of the last vestiges of Reconstruction.

The Democrats nominated one of the richest men in America, the New York corporate lawyer Samuel J. Tilden. In addition to serving as counsel to railroad kings and bankers, Tilden had helped prosecute and dislodge the Tweed Ring in New York; he therefore carried superb "reform" credentials (in the common use of the term in those years). Tilden's nomination by a party with such commitments to the South, white supremacy, and Reconstruction is yet another measure of the extent to which sectional reconciliation had come to define the Democrats. The character of the reunion they had sought in 1868, and the one they achieved in 1876, were variations on the same themes.

In the North in 1876 the Democrats ran against the depression and corruption. Thrown on the defensive, Republicans resorted to a habitual, if still useful, rhetoric of the bloody shirt. In the South, Democrats faced determined, although desperate campaigns by Republicans to survive in the three "unredeemed" states. Democrats responded with their own tried and true tactics of violence and intimidation. During 1876, a widespread reign of terror swept over South Carolina, and black voters and Republican politicians in Louisiana, Mississippi, and other states endured economic and physical pressures—and were sometimes murdered. So effective was Democratic intimidation of Republicans in Mississippi that a federal official there called the white population "one vast mob." Cowed Republicans in several states begged the Congress and Grant for protection. Several hundred deputy marshals were dispatched to precincts across the South for the November elections, but their presence turned out to be only symbolic and wholly ineffective against the abuse they encountered. In many largely Republican (meaning black) precincts, few votes were cast.[73]

The election itself ended in a celebrated, if sordid, dispute; it was so close in the electoral college that when returns in the three pivotal states of Louisiana, Florida, and South Carolina were challenged by both sides, the contest could only be settled constitutionally in the U.S. Congress. So much fraud and imtimidation took place in the disputed states that no one may ever know who really won those elections. Undoubtedly, Tilden won the popular vote, and in the weeks and months following the election great tension enveloped the country. Democrats threatened war and promised militias to a cause of "Tilden or Fight." Republicans believed with equal fervor that in a completely fair election Hayes would have won. Rumors spread that in the South, fear and confusion had set in among the freedpeople, many of whom believed that a Democratic victory would mean the reestablishment of slavery. Without the votes counted (or settled) for the three disputed states, Tilden held a margin in the electoral college of 184–166, one vote short of the necessary number for victory. The nineteen electoral votes in the three states, if penciled into Hayes's column, would give him the White House by 185–184. In the count at least, this is precisely what happened. But the disputed election of 1876 was not really settled by numbers; it ended in an elaborate process of deal making at a series of conferences between Democrats and Republicans.

During the tense winter months of 1876–77, as the House of Representatives assembled a returning board to try to "count" the ballots from the disputed states, the politics of fear and blood memory seemed to rule over newspaper rhetoric. The *Chicago Tribune* ran columns about "Confederate mobs" rising up in Southern cities. Even the reconciliationist *New York Tribune*, which held out for Hayes, tried to drive a sectional wedge between Northern and Southern Democrats. Honoring the "high courage" of white Southerners, the *Tribune* put the deaths of "half a million men" at the feet of "Northern Copperheads" (Democrats). "Memories are yet longer, when sealed with blood," proclaimed an editorial. "Perhaps the Northern Democrat fancied that the South had forgotten. But graves last longer than monuments; the South can forget everything sooner than it forgets its dead." The *Atlanta Constitution*, while advocating peace, printed rumors of semisecret militias drilling in upstate New York under names such as "Sons of Liberty" and the "Phalanx of Loyal Brotherhood." The *Constitution* also condemned Republican radicals like Oliver P. Morton of Indiana, whom it labeled a "revolutionist" eager to "precipitate a war in which" he might "officiate in bomb-proof positions."[74] But in 1877 the bloody shirt, waved in both North and South, did not prevent the two political parties from fashioning an agreement that preserved the Union, promoted economic expansion, and concluded the final chapter of Reconstruction.

The Compromise of 1877 was, indeed, about *interests,* the desires and needs of Southerners and Northerners as they bargained a divided election result into a plan for political reunion and economic development. Southerners wanted "home rule" and all federal troops removed from their states, demands that Republican managers had promised early in the crisis. Indeed, in February 1877 Congress eliminated the appropriation that would have kept soldiers stationed in the South. Many Southern politicians also wanted major subsidies for internal improvements—new levies, dredged harbors, and at least one transcontinental railroad with a Southern terminus. Manufacturing companies, railroads, and financial firms all wanted a sectional settlement and feared the rhetoric of war. A reunion and an end to agitation over black rights and Reconstruction would be good for business, and many companies flooded Congressmen with petitions urging peace and support of a bill to establish an independent commission to count the votes in the disputed states. In the end, the commission, which consisted of eight Republicans and seven Democrats, voted 8–7 for Hayes as the victor in each disputed state.[75]

Throughout most of the winter of 1877, Democrats sustained an exasperating filibuster against the possibility of Hayes taking office. But for two days in late February, four Southern Democrats and five Ohio Republicans met secretly at the Wormley Hotel in Washington and reached the final arrangements of a sectional and partisan compromise. The Democrats promised no reprisals against Southern Republicans, and agreed to end their filibuster and allow Hayes to be peacefully inaugurated as President. The Republicans pledged at least one and possibly two cabinet posts to Democrats in Hayes's administration, gave assurance of money to build the Texas-Pacific Railroad, and agreed to help Democrats take control of the governments in the remaining unredeemed states. On March 4, with much of the nation breathing a sigh of confused relief, Hayes was privately inaugurated at an indoor ceremony in the White House, thus avoiding any possible violence or disruption. At the heart of the Compromise of 1877 was the understanding that Hayes would institute a "new Southern policy," one that would leave the South alone to deal with all questions of governance and race relations. As for black voting rights, even Grant himself had told his cabinet that he had come to see the Fifteenth Amendment as a mistake, a law that "had done the Negro no good." By April, Godkin's *Nation* had rejoiced in the compromise and announced that the "negro will disappear from the field of national politics. Henceforth, the nation as a nation, will have nothing more to do with him."[76] A reconciliationist vision mixed with racism stood triumphant, ushering the emancipationist vision of the Civil War into an increasingly blurred past.

SOUTHERN CONSERVATIVE redeemers now increasingly had much in common with those Northern Republicans who sought to further the ends of commerce and thwart labor activism. These two former enemy persuasions were already becoming an odd sort of political coalition, a strange but effective memory community devoted to the ends of national reconciliation and good business. But the compromise, and the version of memory upon which it was based, had enormous stakes. In a section entitled "Memories of Reconstruction" in *An American Dilemma* (1944), Gunnar Myrdal examined the place of the tragic legend of Reconstruction in American memory. "These memories" (the story of black domination, carpetbagger corruption, and federal tyranny), wrote Myrdal, served the South as "cherished . . . symbols of regional allegiance." For Northerners and the nation as a whole, he wrote, "playing up the venality . . . of the Reconstruction governments and touching lightly the pride and prejudices of the revolting South is . . . a means of reconciling the wounds of the Civil War." Peering back through the decades, Myrdal observed a historical "popular demand of the American whites for rationalization and national comfort" in their collective memory of the Civil War and Reconstruction. Myrdal understood that all important matters of collective memory serve deep social needs. The Southerner, said Myrdal, "needs to believe that when the Negro voted, life was unbearable." Myrdal captured with remarkable insight the meaning and character of the Civil War's aftermath in American memory. "The myth of the horrors of Reconstruction," he concluded, had become with time a set of "false beliefs with a purpose."[77] That purpose was the American reunion, achievable in the end only through new regimes of racial subjugation, a fated and tragic struggle still only in its formative years. The sections needed one another, almost as polar opposites that made the center hold and kept both an industrial economy humming and a New South on the course of revival. Some of the war's greatest results, the civil and political liberties of African Americans, were slowly becoming sacrificial offerings on the altar of reunion.

FIVE

Soldiers' Memory

One man, whose leg was amputated close to his
body, uttered an inarticulate jabber of broken
screams, and rolled, or rather bounced from side to
side of a pile of loose cotton, with such violence that
two hospital attendants were fully occupied in holding him. Another, shot through the body, lay speech-
less and dying, but quivering from head to foot with
a prolonged though probably unconscious agony. He
continued to shudder thus for half an hour, when he
gave one superhuman throe, and then lay quiet for
ever.

—CAPTAIN COLBURNE, wounded and in a field hospital near Port Hudson,
Louisiana, in John W. De Forest, *Miss Ravenal's Conversion from Secession to Loyalty*
(1867)

WHEN SOLDIERS REMEMBER their war experiences, especially from
combat or from prison, it is often the ironic details and twists of fate that
prompt memory. Writing of British World War I veterans who wrote memoirs and narratives, Paul Fussell observes that "irony-assisted recall" is what
draws soldiers back to their memories, enabling them to give shape and co-
herence to their experience. Similar to Fussell's veterans of the Great War,
Civil War soldiers saw innocence collide with evil, beauty with hideous destruction, heroism with venality, absurdity with idealism, and with time they
were to write, perhaps with less modernist disillusion, about those ironies.
Countless veterans of combat and extreme physical suffering faced a psycho-

logical struggle to work through their experiences. Memories that deflected the horror often induced their recall. In an unpublished reminiscence, South Carolinian William Porcher Du Bose left this observation of his experience at the battle of Second Manassas in 1862. Wounded by a bullet that grazed his back and tore off his clothing, Du Bose wandered "through ranks of wounded and slain men" into the town of Leesburg, Virginia. "As I passed through the little town," he wrote,

> suddenly the sound of a piano came to me and I saw a little ahead of us quite an illumination. I rode up on the pavement and in the dark looked in. There were a number of officers, beautifully dressed, and a number of ladies—a scene so utterly out of keeping with all we had known this past month, that it was indelibly impressed upon my mind. By the side of the young lady at the piano and with his back to me was one officer whose appearance seemed . . . familiar. As he turned I recognized Colonel Frank Faillard, who had been through all the battles of the days before . . . He looked very fresh and gay. These little touches of home scenes, right in the midst of war, of which I have a number in my mind, are painted there for always.[1]

During the first fifteen years or so after the conflict, Civil War soldiers' memory did not lay dormant in a state of silence. In order to understand soldiers' recollection, we should first know something of what they carried in their memories. Some veterans had suffered starvation, humiliation, and disease in prisons and hospitals; their traumas and bitterness would be the most difficult to heal. Some would never heal. Many had empty sleeves and pant legs; some were addicted to morphine as a result of the primitive state of medical care and understanding of drug dosage. Thousands upon thousands had marched untold miles, agonized in the loneliness of camps and in fields, forests, and trenchworks. Many veterans had learned leadership; others saw too many politically appointed officers lead too many men to their graves. They had bonded with their closest friends, and sent many home in boxes or seen them buried in ditches all over Virginia, Tennessee, or Georgia. They had fought for their families and abandoned or caused untold suffering for the same families. They had committed acts of savagery and acts of humane courage.

Soldiers on both sides believed fiercely in their causes—Southern independence and saving the Union, black freedom and racial slavery. Almost everyone on both sides claimed that they had fought for "liberty." They had saved life and destroyed life; freed slaves, and abused civilians. Many Civil War soldiers came away from the war respecting their enemies as noble and courageous soldiers. Others had learned to hate as never before, and never fully relinquished their contempt for their enemies. On the Northern side, hundreds of thousands of veterans carried home a legacy of victory, which politically and emotionally had many uses as well as costs. Confederate survivors carried home the legacies of defeat and faced an enormous physical and spiritual challenge of renewal. Most veterans were still young, in their twenties or thirties. They had just experienced their greatest adventures and stored away some of their worst nightmares.[2]

As in other large-scale wars, most Civil War soldiers did not readily talk or write about their conflicted emotions in the immediate postwar period. But they did leave many impressions of their burdens of memory. In soldiers' responses to the end of the war and its aftermath, we can see the seeds of both the deep political and racial strife of Reconstruction and the ultimate soldiers' reconciliation that dominated American culture by the 1880s and 1890s. In April 1865, a white Union soldier, William Park, wrote from near Mobile, Alabama, of "excitement" surging through the camp since the news of Lee's surrender. But joy turned to shock at the news of Abraham Lincoln's assassination. Soldiers gathered in small groups to read newspapers and a shot was fired every half hour in tribute to the fallen President. Park struggled with his hatred of the roughly four thousand Confederate prisoners recently taken in the siege of Mobile. "Most of the boys are in for exterminating the Rebels altogether," wrote Park, "it was sad news to the Soldiers, and it has made an impression on their harts that will never be forgotten." Rather than guard any more prisoners, said Park, he would prefer to "shoot them down."[3]

Hatred and retaliation were visceral experiences and caused memories to surface for many soldiers. In April 1864, when Confederate general Nathan Bedford Forrest captured the federal outpost in western Tennessee at Fort Pillow, he either ordered or allowed his men to slaughter most of the Union soldiers. Of the 557 Union troops engaged, 262 were black, and most were massacred by Forrest's men after they had surrendered. According to Union reports, federal tents containing wounded men were set afire, some black soldiers were shot in the water of the Mississippi River as they attempted to escape, and still others were buried alive. A month later at the battle of Resaca in northern Georgia, the 105th Illinois captured a Confederate artilleryman. As the large, shirtless man emerged from under a gun carriage, he sported a tattoo that read "Fort Pillow." He was immediately bayonetted and shot by his Yankee captors. As the war became more vicious in 1864 and the armies remained in daily contact, revenge against prisoners became more common. A Massachusetts lieutenant wrote from the Virginia front in May 1864 that Confederate prisoners increasingly tried to surrender, "but our boys fire at them so they cannot. Our men are much opposed to taking prisoners since the Fort Pillow affair, that has cost the Rebels many a life that would otherwise have been spared." Indeed, Fort Pillow became a symbolic rallying cry of remembrance for many people. In January 1865, an Ohio black woman named "Lizzie" wrote to black soldiers in the *Christian Recorder,* reflecting on the nature of memory and the extraordinary transformations of the war. The year just ended was "long to be remembered by all," said Lizzie, but she especially admonished the soldiers, when discouraged on "wearisome marches . . . not to forget Fort Pillow."[4]

Many soldiers had experienced bloodlust and unbridled violence. Edward Porter Alexander, a Confederate general on Lee's staff by the end of the war, eventually wrote one of the least partisan and most highly regarded of Southern memoirs. But he left poignant evidence of his hatred of his enemies in 1864. "I always feel like kicking their prisoners all around," said Alexander.

Combat and atrocity were part of what black and white veterans had to remember, as in this artist's depiction of the Fort Pillow massacre in Tennessee in 1864. (Reprinted in *Harper's Pictorial History of the Great Rebellion,* 1868)

"It is my greatest comfort to know that I have killed some of them with my own hands, I have shot them with muskets and artillery and have seen them fall and afterwards went there and found them dead." Many soldiers saw the increasing violence of the war as a necessary means of not only killing men, but also killing the other society's morale. No one represented this kind of destructive warfare as much as William Tecumseh Sherman. In 1864–65, Sherman wrote to his wife, Ellen, describing his campaigns in Georgia and arguing that "immense slaughter is necessary to prove that our northern armies can and will fight. That once impressed will be an immense moral power." Sometimes this advocacy of violence was embedded in a steadfast devotion to cause; it served as a counterbalance to the romanticized image of Yankee-Rebel fraternization during the war.[5] These urges to "exterminate," to see one's enemies dead, to seek pleasure in killing, and to establish the "moral power" in "slaughter" were honest expessions of what many soldiers felt and carried with them into civilian life.

Some soldiers had learned to hate war itself. After more than two years of battles and campaigns, a Mississippi cavalry captain, Walter Nugent, declared war "an unmixed evil [of] . . . blood, butchery, death, desolation, robbery, rapine, selfishness, violence, wrong . . . palliated only when waged in self-defense." Only a "sense of duty," he concluded, kept him at his post. The young Oliver Wendell Holmes Jr., three times wounded and suffering dreadfully during the Wilderness-Spotsylvania campaign of May–June 1864, spoke for many soldiers undergoing battle fatigue and near psychological collapse: "I tell you many a man has gone crazy since this campaign began from the terrible pressure on mind and body." Holmes would later eloquently lead in remembering a much different war, one full of mystic glory, of rugged individualistic struggle and valor shared by all warriors on both sides. In time, few veterans were encouraged to remember, at least out loud, the terror of the Kentucky lieutenant (Union) who watched his company nearly wiped out in a battle near Atlanta in 1864. "As my men were being carried by me to the rear, groaning, and terribly mangled," wrote Henry Clay Weaver, "about a dozen of the survivors collected around me as if I were their only remaining support, I sat on a log and cried like a child."[6] Such stories appeared frequently in soldiers' wartime letters, but they only rarely became public in veterans' postwar memory rituals.

The dehumanizing aspects of war remain in old soldiers' souls as the dark underside of memory against which other recollections have to prevail. Although he might only rarely return to such a memory, no soldier could ever truly forget what he saw if he survived the charges through the cornfields at Antietam in 1862 or the Bloody Angle at Spotsylvania in 1864. Charles Brewster, an adjutant and lieutenant in the Tenth Massachusetts, left an unforgettable description of what he saw at Spotsylvania after the most savage and sustained fighting of the war:

> The most terrible sight I ever saw was the Rebel side of the breast work we fought over the other day. There was one point on a ridge where the storm of bullets never ceased for 24 hours and the dead were piled in heaps upon heaps and the wounded men were intermixed with them, held fast by their dead companions who fell upon them continually adding to the ghastly pile . . . When I looked over in the morning there was one Rebel sat up praying at the top of his voice and others were gibbering in insanity others were groaning and whining at the greatest rate . . . it is a terrible terrible business to make the best of it.

Brewster survived the war, became involved in veterans' organizations, and attended Blue-Gray reunions in the 1880s. His vision of hell faded with time into more useful and comfortable sentiments.[7]

Black veterans too had many divided emotions to work through in their memories. One black soldier wrote from Chapel Point, Maryland, in May 1865, complaining bitterly of watching a "Private Burke" of the Twenty-second U.S. Colored Troops "a little awkward in his movements" after just being released from hospital, "struck senseless and bleeding to the ground with a tremendous blow from a sword in the hands of an arrant coward and brute, his Company commander." The writer raged at the irony: "how inconsistent to laud the brave soldier as hero, and yet kick him like a dog." Other black soldiers, however, overflowed with pride at the revolution they had helped bring about in 1865. Private W. A. Freeman of the same Twenty-second U.S. Colored Troops reacted with scorn at suggestions by the American Colonization Society that blacks emigrate to Liberia. At war's end, Freeman took as his references the "blood of our comrades . . . the tears of our widows and mothers . . . the prayers of our ancestors who have died in oppression," rather than any call to missionize Africa. As a soldier patriot, he claimed ownership of the country: "with the nation we have suffered, and as a part of this great nation, we must rise with it." These triumphal sentiments, which sound almost like inscriptions on monuments, soon faced the divergent attitudes among many white Union soldiers still stationed in the South who, as volunteers, considered their duty over with the cessation of hostilities. Enforcement of emerging Reconstruction policies were not within their ken. A Maine soldier wrote home that his only duty in the confused situation of the summer of 1865 seemed to be "keeping the Niggers from killing the whites." This Mainer, Henry Gay, did not like "peacekeeping" and the knotty business of trying to help freedmen negotiate new work arrangements with former owners. "I tell you it is not much like the Soldering that we had last year, but I do not like to be a Solder in peaceable time there is not eny fun in it."[8] Little wonder that when white veterans gathered in later years, they had so little to say about the aftermath of the war in the South. Black veterans, especially those who had been targets of rioting mobs or mounted Klansmen, tended to remember the early Reconstruction years more readily.

But black veterans also had their own peculiar ironies to process in memory. Garland H. White, chaplain of the Twenty-eighth U.S. Colored Troops, was among the first black troops to enter Richmond in early April 1865. Twenty years before, White had been sold to the Georgia politician Robert Toombs while the planter was visiting Richmond. As Toombs's body servant, White had escaped in Washington, D.C., and traveled to Canada like many other fugitives in the 1850s. Among the multitude of freedpeople who gathered around the conquering black soldiers that fateful day in Richmond was a group of "broken-hearted mothers looking for their children." "I cannot express the joy I felt," wrote White, as he encountered his own mother, Nancy White, after twenty years of separation. For every such reunion among the freedpeople there were as many heartsick and permanent losses of family connections in the first years of freedom. In poignant contrast to his reunion with his mother, two weeks later White was ordered to accompany a Private Samuel Mapps of the Tenth U.S. Colored Troops, an ex-slave from Virginia, to his execution by firing squad for insubordination and attempting to kill his captain. White prayed with the young soldier and then watched him shot. "It was the saddest spectacle I ever witnessed," wrote the helpless chaplain, "and I hope never to witness another the longest day I live."[9]

Black chaplains were often the only commissioned officers of their race in African American regiments. They served important roles as advisors and leaders, but they had little control over the breakdown that occurred between white officers and black troops during the early postwar occupation of the South. Idleness, drunkenness, and sexual misbehavior plagued many units in 1865–66, and reprisals for collapsed discipline were frequent. Moreover, some white officers, concerned for their own postwar livelihoods, stole the payroll from their own troops. Worst of all, as the debate over black suffrage ensued, most white officers openly opposed giving the vote to the black soldiers they had commanded. Black troops, of course, had endured countless discriminations in pay, promotion, and medical care. It had become very difficult, wrote one soldier, H. S. Harmon, to comply with officers asking black soldiers "to forget old grudges and prejudices . . . the cruel and unjust treatment."[10] Mixed with remembrance of the heroism of Fort Wagner and numerous other battles, such mistreatment would always remain part of black Civil War memory. With time, however, even black veterans and their communities preferred a heroic and progressive memory to ugliness and betrayal.

In one of his many letters to the *Christian Recorder,* Henry McNeal Turner, chaplain of a black regiment, described a scene in May 1865, as African American troops marched with the victorious Union armies through North Carolina. Leaving Raleigh, Turner's regiment reached the town of Smithfield, where they encountered a burned bridge and no other way to cross a river than to remove their clothes and wade, "chin deep," to the other side. "I was much amused to see the secesh women," observed Turner, "watching with the utmost intensity, thousands of our soldiers, in a state of nudity. I suppose they desired to see whether these audacious Yankees were really men, made like other men, or if they were a set of varmints." As Southern women "thronged the windows, porticos and yards, in the finest attire imaginable," Turner's "brave boys would disrobe themselves, hang their garments upon their bayonets and through the water they would come, walk up the street, and seem to say to the feminine gazers, 'Yes, though naked, we are your masters.'" In this scene, charged with sexual and political symbolism, Turner captured a memory that haunted the white South for generations to come: naked black men with muskets, striding out of a river into a town's streets with an audience of white women.[11]

Even when clothed again, the black soldiers in Turner's dispatch seemed almost otherworldly. "The rebel party stops," said Turner, "and looks back at these magic lords, swaggering on in their exultant conquest, and seems to be musing as to whether they are actually in another world, or whether this one is turned upside down." So much of the Southern and national struggle with Civil War memory in the coming decades churned with tormented energy in order to invert Turner's scene. Who could safely manage by the 1880s or 1890s to tell the story of wet, naked black soldiers, muskets thrust over their heads and holding their clothes as trophies, marching through a North Carolina town, haunting the gaze of Confederate women? Even imagining

Thomas Waterman Wood's *War Episodes: The Veteran* (1866) depicts a black former soldier, maimed but proud of his sacrifice. (The Metropolitan Museum of Art, Gift of Charles Stewart Smith, 1884)

this scene in popular fiction, or as an alternative to *Birth of a Nation* in early film, is historically impossible. But such are the ways of historical memories; some survive and are refashioned into mythologies, and others are erased altogether. For Turner's part, by the 1880s and 1890s he had become a distinguished and controversial AME bishop who gave up faith in black equality in America and led a back-to-Africa emigration movement.[12]

DURING THE FIRST few years after the war, veterans joined civilians in universal mourning. Locally and nationally, veterans' organizations materialized around the ritual of Memorial Day. Some initial sparks of mutual respect between Northern and Southern soldiers were evident in the immediate aftermath of the surrender at Appomattox, as well as in many regions of the South as ragged Confederates returned to their homes under the watch of Union occupation troops. Black soldiers, it can be safely said, were never welcome as occupying forces, but white men who had experienced the agonies of war and campaigning found more than tobacco and hard tack to share with their former enemies.

Time was necessary for reminiscence to be culturally salable, or even psychologically necessary, for many veterans. None other than Robert E. Lee may have spoken for thousands of Southern veterans (and even some Northerners) in 1869 when he declined an invitation to come to Gettysburg to help that town's Battlefield Memorial Association mark and begin to erect memorials on the famous landscape. Lee claimed he "could not add anything material," but more importantly, he thought it "wiser . . . not to keep open the sores of war, but to follow the examples of those nations who endeavoured to obliterate the marks of civil strife and to commit to oblivion the feelings it engendered." As president of Washington and Lee College in Virginia, Lee urged young Southerners to pursue "peaceful industry," and he personally avoided reading books or newspapers about the war.[13] In his careful words, Lee represented one kind of soldier—those who simply wished to forget as much and as fast as possible, some for their personal peace, others because it served the political ends of reconciliation. And this need to forget war, and to reconcile the physical and psychological ravages of soldiering, arose all over America, regardless of section. Already, though, many ex-soldiers in both sections were organizing to contest which feelings and experiences should be cast into oblivion.

Thus historian Gerald Linderman's terms for and periodization of soldiers' memory—"hibernation" (1865–80) and "revival" (post-1880)—are instructive. But they may be a bit too schematic. While veterans' organizations like the Grand Army of the Republic concentrated on local fraternalism, charity to widows and orphans, achieving modest pensions, and struggling to build fledgling memberships during the 1870s, mass-marketed battle accounts and subscription histories kept the war alive in the public imagination. During the confusion and turbulence of Reconstruction, most soldiers' war memories were hibernating; the men were set apart from civilians by the experience of combat. Many veterans retreated from things martial, and a still divided nation expected such a muted remembrance from its multitudes of former soldiers.[14] But many other veterans' memories underwent a crude sorting out. Soldiers' memory may have been more in a stage of incubation than hibernation—stored and unsettled, more festering than sleeping, and growing into a cultural force.

As Americans mourned their dead and fought bitterly over Reconstruction, new mass-market magazines published war stories, some of them written by veterans. The prototypical American magazines, *Harper's Weekly* and especially the more literary *Harper's Monthly*, led the way in producing wartime fiction (more than two hundred short stories about the war by 1865). *Harper's* generally stopped publishing war fiction after Appomattox, but the *Atlantic Monthly*, *Lippincott's*, and *Galaxy* picked up the slack in the growing literary marketplace. The *Atlantic*, with a circulation that peaked at fifty thousand by 1870, covered politics extensively and published some thirty-five war stories before 1876. *Galaxy* reached 23,000 subscribers by 1871 and ran some twenty-one war-related tales, most of which were adventures, or dramas about families severed or reunited. Founded in 1868 in Philadelphia, *Lippincott's* opened its pages to Southern writers, embraced a spirit of reconciliation well before Reconstruction ended, and at least implicitly made the war a primary theme. In California, the *Overland Monthly* (1868–75), edited by Bret Harte, printed some nine war stories that were somewhat more raucous than eastern tastes allowed. And in the South, new magazines emerged to attempt to pick up where the venerable *Southern Literary Messenger*, which died with the fall of Richmond, had left off. In 1866 in Charlotte, North Carolina, former confederate general Daniel H. Hill founded *The Land We Love*, a magazine devoted not only to literature and agriculture, but also to publishing battle narratives by former Confederate soldiers. Hill's journal straddled a desire for reconciliation on one hand with embittered pieces on Northern prisons and stories of mourning on the other. Before being absorbed into the *Southern Magazine* (1868–75) in 1869, *The Land We Love* reached 12,000 subscribers, some of whom were in the North. Together, the two journals became the organ of the newly founded Southern Historical Society, and were published as *SHS Papers* (first issued in 1876).[15]

Moreover, subscription histories of the war sold widely during and immediately after the conflict. As part of a new mass-market culture, these histories provided readers with a mixture of thrilling battles, depoliticized war as popular entertainment, partisan tomes that stressed the politics of causation as well as the war's results, and works that simply allowed the reader/consumer to compile war material like Victorian collectors.[16] How much soldiers were the readership for these magazines and books is not easy to determine, although they had become avid readers of newspapers and popular fiction during the war. Certainly, many veterans suffered from battle fatigue, lingering disease, and the psychological stress of transition to civilian life. But the image of the Civil War veteran, sullen and silent during the first decade and a half after the war, needs to be measured with caution. The literary war began early as a contest over war guilt or vindication, and as a genre of romance tending toward reconciliation.

Novels on war themes were not plentiful in American culture before the 1880s, with one stunning exception. Union combat veteran John W. De Forest, who also wrote extensively for magazines, published *Miss Ravenal's Conversion from Secession to Loyalty* in 1867. The Connecticut-born De Forest lived and traveled abroad extensively in the Near East and in Europe during the 1850s. He served three years in a Connecticut unit, where he reached the rank of captain. After the war De Forest worked as an agent in the Freedmen's Bureau in South Carolina until 1868. In *Miss Ravenal's Conversion*, De Forest fashioned a story of controlled romance and conflicted North-South family relations; most importantly, he described battle and its aftermath in modern terms. His captain Colburne narrates his own as well as other soldiers' inner world of fear, while describing the most realistic battle and hospital scenes any American writer had yet produced.[17] With the exception of Ambrose Bierce, no other American writer wrote of war quite as realistically, including Stephen Crane in *Red Badge of Courage* (1895), until after World War I.

De Forest wrote with riveting clarity of men about to experience battle. His veterans were "a row of stern faces, bronzed with sunburn, sallow in many cases with malaria, grave with the serious emotions of the hour, but hardened by the habit of danger." Frail human bodies crumble, or imagine how they will crumble, under huge trees slowly felled by an enormous artillery bombardment. The "hasty stares of alarm" and the "ghastly backward glare of horror . . . eyes projecting . . . chin shaking." on the part of some of De Forest's soldiers take readers to the frightful interior of battle. Wounded badly himself and in near delirium, Colburne traverses the nightmare of field hospitals. He takes whiskey as he sickens at seeing a man's foot blown off with "shattered bones projecting clean and white from the rags of raw flesh." Through Colburne's eyes and emotions, readers saw the horror of war. A dead man "blackening in the scorching sun . . . his brains bulging from a bullet-hole in his forehead," and others in "every imaginable condition of mutilation" were scenes for which most American readers of the late 1860s were not prepared. De Forest's war realism was far ahead of his time, and the book did not sell well.[18]

Americans were deeply aware of loss in the late 1860s, but they were not ready to have war depicted in all its savagery. The critic William Dean Howells praised *Miss Ravenal's Conversion* profusely, describing the book in 1872 as "proof that we are not so much lacking in an American novelist as in a public to recognize him." Howells later urged De Forest to read Leo Tolstoy's *War and Peace* when it appeared in English in 1886. After reading it, De Forest wrote to Howells: "Let me tell you that nobody but he [Tolstoy] has written the whole truth about war and battle. *I* tried, and I told all I dared, and perhaps all I could. But there was one thing I did not dare tell . . . the extreme horror of battle, and the anguish with which the bravest soldiers struggle through it."[19] In the hands of less skilled writer-veterans, such realism as De Forest's would with time occasionally creep into soldiers' reminiscence, but only as token nods to the dark underside of war. The *daring* necessary to capture a full realism about war-making fit neither the tastes of Victorian America nor the growing imperatives of sectional reconciliation.

No wartime experience, however, caused deeper emotions, recriminations, and lasting invective than that of prisons. Civil War prisons were, by and large, hellholes of disease, misery, and death. They left bitter wounds in the psyches of individual men and their families on both sides. Prison horror, and the hatreds it fostered in both sections, infested social memories of the war during the Reconstruction years as nothing else did. Deep at the heart of bloody shirt rhetoric on both sides was a layer of real hatred rooted in the vast casualty lists of those who died wretched deaths at Andersonville in Georgia, Camp Douglas in Illinois, and dozens of other places. By one official federal count, 193,743 Northerners and 214,865 Southerners were captured and imprisoned in some way during the war. The death toll was approximately 30,000 Union and 26,000 Confederate soldiers.[20] These 56,000, approximately the same number as all American deaths in the Vietnam War, left a legacy of blame and victimization that not even the highly organized and sentimentalized reminiscence industry by the 1880s and 1990s could efface.

In the summer of 1866 Dorence Atwater, a Union veteran, and Clara Barton, the famed nurse, led an expedition to the site of Andersonville, Georgia, to record the names of all the dead buried in the cemetery at that most notorious prison. The pamphlet they published, *A List of the Union Soldiers Buried at Andersonville,* sold widely for twenty-five cents. Thousands of households across the North received verification from this document that their loved one was indeed one of the victims of Confederate neglect, or alleged terror, in the hinterland of Georgia. The numbers by state were telling markers of the local significance of such reports during the immediate postwar years. Nearly two years after the bloodletting had ended, the deaths of 2,500 New Yorkers, 1,828 Pennsylvanians, 1,051 Ohioans, 672 Michiganians, and 78 Rhode Islanders were enough to bring widespread mourning to thousands of Northern communities.[21]

In her report to the nation published with the pamphlet, Barton urged Northerners to listen to the victims: "After this, whenever any man who has lain a prisoner within the stockade of Andersonville, would tell you of his sufferings, how he fainted, scorched, drenched, sickened . . . though the tale be long and twice told, as you would have your own wrongs appreciated . . . I charge you listen and believe him." Barton said she had received three thousand letters of inquiry about the Andersonville dead, revealing a "bitter anxiety" all over Northern society. She counseled patience with prison survivors; their experiences, she claimed, were worse than the "distant gaze" of civilians could ever see. Barton shared De Forest's daring, but their differing forms of early realism about the war found only audiences of necessity in the war-sickened society.[22]

Many Northerners responded with natural forms of bereavement, and the prison legacy helped foster the popularity of Memorial Day rituals. Some veterans posts kept detailed records and files on such topics as prison "atrocities" and "barbarities." Others converted their hatred born of prison death and treatment into political reaction. A man from Buffalo, New York, whose son had survived a winter at Belle Isle, a Confederate prison in the James River at Richmond, wrote to Thaddeus Stevens in 1866 insisting on political "guarantees" of punishment against the "criminals" responsible for Southern prisons. The man, A. Noble, believed that his son had been rendered a "beast of the field frozen and starved" by Jefferson Davis, "the barbarian . . . Lee the Christian? soldier," and other "ferocious villans of Salisbury, Danville, or Andersonville."[23] These hatreds were lasting elements of Civil War memory; the prison story always remained the most vexing aspect of soldiers' narratives.

Northern soldiers' memory was rekindled as well by newspaper dispatches and books stemming from travelers' accounts of visits to old battlefields in the South. As Reconstruction politics ebbed and flowed, veterans could read about, or even visit, many of the scenes of war. By the 1870s, the South had emerged as a major tourist attraction for the growing middle class of Northerners who could afford to travel. Promoted heavily by magazines and railroads, the South—its climate, its exoticism, and even its history—became less a place of political and social problems and more the object of tourists' curiosity. Before the war, it had long been the source of a rich travel literature that helped readers explore a slave society; immediately after the war such literature was a means of understanding the conditions of a conquered land.[24]

Many travelers' accounts, meant not as promotional literature for the South, analyzed the conditions of the freedpeople and the vicissitudes of Reconstruction politics. But many travelers' guides were updated, or new ones produced, to include Civil War battlefields in tourist itineraries. One of the most remarkable series of travel accounts was the result of a three-month tour in 1869 by Russell H. Conwell, a twenty-six-year-old Union veteran writing for the Boston *Daily Evening Traveller*. Beginning his journey in Arlington Heights, Virginia, at the former residence of Robert E. Lee, which had been turned into a massive federal cemetery, Conwell dwelled on the irony that the Confederate general's estate had been converted into "one great graveyard" of the Union dead. Stunned at how "shattered and ruined" much of Virginia's countryside still appeared, he remarked that the war had "transformed the 'Garden of the South'" into the 'Graveyard of America.'" Conwell applauded the government's efforts to establish national cemeteries. "But scarcely a day passes," he wrote, "when the plough of the farmer tilling the soil, or the spade of the Negro hunting lead, does not disturb in their secret resting-places the bones of Union soldiers."[25] These dark and morbid images no doubt found deep resonance among Conwell's Northern readers. His columns included one reminder after another of Northern men buried all over the South.

Conwell gave his Northern audience a rich mixture of Southern exoticism, war ruins, poor whites and "darkeys" aplenty, as well as many vivid descriptions of well-known battle sites. His accounts were all about remembering the war, but they were transmitted through a combination of the sacred and the humorous. No one could have resisted his story of attending a wedding near Williamsburg, Virginia, of a crippled Union veteran from New Hampshire who had returned South to find the young Virginia girl who, during the Peninsula campaign of 1862, had helped him to safety after he had been badly wounded. Seven years later, the bride's father still hated Yankees with a passion. But the wedding occurred nonetheless, and an odd feast ensued for a racially mixed crowd of poor whites and blacks, with raucous dancing to the tunes of a "black fiddler placed upon a high bench in one corner." The happy couple, we are told, moved North to Madison, Wisconsin, perhaps to escape the clutches of the bride's father, who moaned that he was "ever to be cussed with a d——n Yankee son-in-law." Conwell met many friendly white Virginians who "greeted us . . . with generous smiles" and told their war stories in a circle of chairs in a barroom or on a store porch. But in Alexandria, just across the Potomac from Washington, he encountered many unreconstructed Southerners. "Their acts and words in any other land would bring hundreds of them to the gallows," wrote Conwell. "Portraits of Jeff Davis and Lee hang in all their parlors, decorated with Confederate flags. Photographs of Wilkes Booth . . . effigies of Abraham Lincoln hanging by the neck with a darkey hung at each heel, together with Confederate songs, mottoes, and keepsakes, adorn their drawing rooms."[26] In such images, Conwell recorded the origins of Confederate and Lost Cause nostalgia.

Conwell repeatedly took his readers to cemeteries and half-buried ruins and earthworks of the war. They were the "surest and saddest prompter of memory," he wrote. Around old battlefields he encountered a steady stream of lead and bone hunters who sold their scrap findings to eek out a living. At Cold Harbor battlefield, he "met several Negroes with large sacks, collecting the bones of dead horses which they sold to the bone-grinders of Richmond." In South Carolina, at the remains of Fort Wagner on Morris Island overlooking Charleston harbor, Conwell met an "old darkey soldier" whom he claimed had been part of the Fifty-fourth Massachusetts regiment and wounded in its famous charge on July 18, 1863. The black veteran and his family lived in a "bomb-proof" at nearby Battery Gregg and made a living "digging for old iron in the sand." "The products of his industry," recorded Conwell, "reminded us of the stacks in a New England hay field. He sells it by the ton and is putting his money in the bank."[27] Such a poignant image of the Reconstruction South—blacks harvesting lead and iron left by the war in the sand—might have induced some Northern readers to retreat from and others to support the recently enacted Fifteenth Amendment.

As Conwell walked on the beach near the former Fort Wagner, he reflected on how the sea had already washed in and claimed the burial trench of Colonel Robert Gould Shaw and his black troops. "Old haversacks, belts, bayonet scabbards, and shoes" were still strewn on the sand. In the surf at his feet, human skulls and bones "lay grinning upon the shore and filled us with sad sensations, which still haunt our dreams. The sad and the beautiful, how strangely combined!" As Conwell mused over this extraordinary sight, he observed skulls imbedded with seashells "in their ears, mouth, and eyes" as though "set in frames of diamonds." Conwell likened the mounds and the bones around Fort Wagner to the "inspiring sensations which the traveller feels as he treads the Plains of Marathon" in Greece. The whole scene, he believed, was a living memorial to the "cause of human freedom." Conwell concluded with a recognition that he had been carried away with his "enthusiasm," and that he had been "sent to describe and not to moralize."[28] For decades to follow, this would be the dilemma of soldiers' memory—how to describe without moralizing, especially about the subject of the black Union dead and the freedom they fought for.

Southern readers did not have to wait long after Appomattox for a thoroughly romantic conception of the war to emerge from Confederate soldiers' pens. A veteran of four years in the Army of Northern Virginia, part of it as a staff officer for J. E. B. Stuart, Virginian John Esten Cooke embarked on his "big ambition" of making himself "*the* writer of the South." Before his death in 1886, the prolific Cooke had ennobled the Southern soldier in many works and submerged the war's horrors in a flood of sentimentalism and adventure. Cooke declared that "there is nothing intellectual about fighting. There is really nothing heroic or romantic or in any way calculated to appeal to the imagination." Yet he delivered a romantic war to his readers, and he was quite successful in reaching his ambition. He lived the life of a country squire on an estate, The Briars, in the Shenandoah Valley. There, on his dining room wall, hung a portrait of the calvary commander J. E. B. Stuart signed, "Yours to count on, J. E. B. Stuart."[29]

In his earliest novel, *Surry of Eagle's Nest* (1866), Cooke announced, "Nothing delights more your old soldier returned from the wars, than to fight his battles o'er again, boast of his exploits, and tell the children . . . what wonders he has seen." Cooke's real four years at war, as his diaries indicate, had been anything but the "amusement" he now craved. But only a year after the war ended, he lured an increasingly Northern, as well as Southern, audience into a web of sentiment. "Come!" Cooke beckoned. "Perhaps as you follow me, you will live in the stormy days of a cavalier epoch: breathe its fiery atmosphere, and see its mighty forms as they defile before you, in a long and noble line." Combining literary ambition with a genteel Lost Cause outlook, Cooke demonstrated that some soldiers were ready early to refashion war memories into cultural and political dividends. Romantics like Cooke understood their audiences and the emerging material order of the Gilded Age. One of the author's admirers, the sculptor Edward V. Valentine, wrote to Cooke in 1872 praising the author's Virginia "heroes" as alternatives to the culture of "prosaic, commonplace, money-worshipping barbarism" of the time.[30] Southern soldiers' romances provided the cultural underside of Civil War memory; they resisted Reconstruction and glorified the Confederacy while at the same time slowly fueling the spirit of reunion. Cooke demonstrated how easily for some the horrible memory of combat and campaigning could be converted into purposeful nostalgia.

During the 1870s most Civil War veterans were not yet ready to embrace Cooke's romantic renderings of their experiences. Veterans' organizations languished in membership. The Grand Army of the Republic, the principle Northern veterans' organization, was founded in 1866 in Illinois by a former Union Army surgeon, Dr. Benjamin Franklin Stephenson, and two soldier-politicians, General John A. Logan and the Illinois governor Richard Oglesby. The GAR caught on around the country in local posts devoted to fraternalism, but in its early years it was also a political force—a "voting machine" for Republicans. The GAR developed elaborate rituals of rank, hierarchy, and discipline. A "grade" system, designed to attract men to military order, actually ruined the organization's cohesion in the early years. By the early 1870s, the GAR's annual encampments had dwindled in size, and the number of posts had fallen off steeply. By 1875, the GAR was all but defunct formally in nine states, and barely hanging on in some five other states. By 1876, the national GAR membership stood at 26,899, a mere 2 percent of potential participants. No doubt a general level of forgetting ensued among veterans in the 1870s; just as American politics turned decisively away from Republican-inspired Reconstruction, and as the Panic of 1873 set in, many Yankee veterans began to worry about their livelihoods more than their war memories or reputations.[31]

In the South, Confederate veterans who gathered in local reunion societies and specific unit groups, often called "survivors' associations," began to write their own versions of the war. In 1869, in New Orleans, where many ex-Confederate officers had settled, the Southern Historical Society (SHS) was founded particularly as a means of preserving a Confederate tradition and forging a Southern version of the war's history. In 1873 the SHS moved to Virginia and fell under the firm control of the Virginia generals, especially Jubal Early. In 1876, the *Southern Historical Society Papers (SHS Papers)*, under the aggressive editorship of Rev. J. William Jones, began to vindicate the Confederacy (especially its soldiers), draw nationwide sympathy to its cause, and fight the literary war with Northern magazines and books. Although a regionwide Confederate veterans' association did not emerge until 1889, when the United Confederate Veterans (UCV) was founded, among Southern ex-soldiers the 1870s were hardly a time of silence.[32]

Many Southern veterans were eager to have their stories told, and some set about the task of writing histories. Edward Porter Alexander began to collect battlefield reports and recollections immediately after the war for a history of his corps. A former comrade, Dudley McIver Du Bose, wrote to Alexander from Georgia in September 1866, encouraging his efforts. "We did as much hard fighting, marching, and suffering as any men ever did for the cause of Constitutional liberty," said the Georgian. "Future historians and future generations will acknowledge it and give us due credit, if they can only get at the true facts." Such veterans wanted their suffering and their political cause honored and defended.[33]

In September 1869, James Kemper responded to Alexander's request for muster rolls of several Confederate regiments in his former command. Kemper had been badly wounded on the third day at Gettysburg and spent two days unconscious in field hospitals. "You ask me for what I recollect of Gettysburg," he cautiously answered. "The request is hard to meet . . . it is like getting out of my existence to go back to Gettysburg." So prompted, though, Kemper proceeded to write a long recollection of the third day at Gettysburg, including ten lines of Shakespeare and a reference to "Milton's description of the war of artillery between the contending hosts of Heaven." Kemper recalled making his men "lie flat down on the ground, a precaution which poorly protected them for the enemy's hail of shot pelted them and ploughed through them, and sometimes the fragments of a dozen mangled men were thrown in and about the trench left by a single missile." As if in a trance, Kemper continued to remember seeing James Longstreet sitting tall on his horse while under incessant fire, "his bearing . . . the grandest moral spectacle of the war." Kemper's men, he maintained, had "the solemn composure, it is said, marked the Spartans at Thermopylae." Fearing for his faulty memory, Kemper signed off to get back to his legal duties, but not before declaring his reminiscence a "pleasant task."[34] Some men needed their memories prompted by the right agent; but once stimulated, the past flowed into the present.

While vacationing in Saratoga, New York, in 1873, former general and presidential candidate John C. Breckinridge wrote to Jubal Early objecting that the diehard Virginian had accused him of being too devoted to "progressive ideas to care for the preservation of our history. You will know better some day. I seek no man's society who speaks of us as 'traitors,' nor will I associate with our former adversaries upon the basis of mere sufferance." Ex-Confederates had many scores to settle among themselves, but many were not hiding from their memories within the first decade after the war. P. G. T. Beauregard lamented to Early how the war and now the Panic of 1873 had brought "sad distress" and "poverty and ruin" to "most of our best people." But Beauregard rejoiced in the chance to join with old comrades to preserve their heroic past. "I believe now, as I did when I fired the first gun in 1861 and one of the last in 1865," said Beauregard, "that the cause we upheld was a just and holy one." He looked forward to the formal organization of the Southern Historical Society: "after having taken as active part in *making* history, to see that it is correctly *written*."[35]

For many years Charles Colcock Jones of Savannah, Georgia, collected service records and battle reminiscences from many Confederate veterans all over the country for his own military history. Many veterans sent him extraordinarily detailed accounts of their unit's experiences in specific battles, and of their personal wounds, successes, and failures. Many would send both their wartime and postwar photographs. Alexander Lawton wrote to Jones in 1866 using twelve pages to describe the history of his brigade, as well as his leg wound at Antietam. But he worried because "the loss of all proper material, other than memory, prevents me from being more detailed and specific."[36] Some of these veterans spent part of the rest of their lives attempting to recall and reshape their experience with little but memory to rely upon. Others were certainly willing to send Jones or other would-be historians their service records without reflecting, at least on paper, about the nature and meaning of their war memories. Reflection had its costs for veterans; motivations to pay those costs were as varied as the thousands of men inclined to remember.

The *SHS Papers* provided many ex-Confederate writers and many more readers an outlet for their views and their memories. The pages of the papers served as a community of memory and advocacy. One of the first issues included Commodore Matthew F. Maury's "Vindication of Virginia and the South," an elaborate defense of secession, followed by a speech, "Camp Fires of the Boys in Gray," by former private Carleton McCarthy from an 1875 reunion of the Richmond Howitzers. In Maury's vision, the war came only as necessity after heroic Virginians had failed to conciliate the aggressive, abolitionist North. McCarthy's speech indicated how in the 1870s the political aims of officers' memory mixed with emotional, fraternal needs among the rank and file. "The soldier may forget the long, weary march, with its dust, heat and thirst," said McCarthy, "and he may forget the horrors and blood of the battlefield . . . but the cheerful, happy scenes of the camp fire he will never forget!"[37] Both writers, in effect, were saying "never forget" to their comrades—one in the name of political vindication and the other, on behalf of camaraderie.

In 1877, the pages of the *SHS Papers* boiled with disputes over whether General James Longstreet's allegedly slow reactions had been responsible for the Confederate failure at Gettysburg, as well as other military controversies. The papers served as the forum in which Southerners amassed documentation and opinion in order to clarify their past as they saw it. In March and April, 1876, the *SHS Papers* devoted two entire issues and over two hundred pages to a spirited defense of the South's record on prisons. The Northern "charge of cruelty," wrote the editor, stood "triumphantly refuted." In the literary war, one could simply declare victory and then prepare for the next round of dispute. Through roughly the end of the 1870s, the *SHS Papers* concentrated largely on rationalizing Confederate defeat, and on compiling documentation to buttress the argument that the South's loss was inevitable in the face of overwhelming numbers. By the 1880s, like their Northern counterparts, the directors of the *SHS Papers* had devoted themselves more to commemorative matters—to monument unveilings, battle reminiscences, and speeches and essays that deepened the hold of the Confederate tradition on Southern life.[38]

In a similar vein, Southern veterans began to write memoirs in the 1870s. Among the most successful was that of George Cary Eggleston who, like Cooke, had been a staff officer under J. E. B. Stuart. Eggleston was Indiana born, but he migrated to Virginia in 1857 and fell in love with the planter's life. In 1874, Eggleston published *A Rebel's Recollections*, provoking some

Northern scorn. He sought only "kindly feelings" and the "final burial of the animosity existing between the sections"; but his was a reconciliation on Southern ideological terms. Eggleston's narrative went through four editions with G. P. Putnam's in New York, and set a pattern for many to follow (his success indicated that a reconciliationist conception of the Lost Cause was already good business). He pleaded with Yankee readers to put themselves "in the place of the Southerners," to see through "their eyes" the issues of the war. Anticipating multitudes of other such memoirs, essays, and fiction, Eggleston insisted that all true devotion to any cause was heroic and right. He defended secession; the Confederacy was not a revolution, merely the result of self-defense in the name of honor and necessity. The image of the victimized soldier informs much of the book and may be a reason for its popularity with Northern readers. A genuine reconciliation based on mutual experience was already taking hold among soldiers. Eggleston's Confederate soldiers demonstrate essentially superhuman devotion to cause and an extraordinary fatalism during the last year of the war. "Our condition," he wrote of the 1864–65 Virginia campaign, "was not unlike that of condemned men." And finally, he ends his memoir with a full tribute to the "faithful" slaves, "diligent throughout" the war in defending their masters' families and property. Eggleston admitted that blacks wanted their freedom, but in portraying them as loyal retainers, he offered an early version of what later became a staple symbol of Confederate veterans' culture.[39]

Memoirs caught on among Northern veterans in the 1870s as well. William Tecumseh Sherman's two-volume *Memoirs,* published in 1875, is a Civil War classic, a reknowned soldier's personal story told clearly in a unique voice. The famous general, who lived in St. Louis, relished soldiers' reunions and was one of the most popular postwar lecturers. But apparently concerned that Southerners such as Early and the Virginians would dominate the country's understanding of the history of the war, and frustrated at the slow pace of the federal government's massive *Official Records of the War of the Rebellion,* the first volumes of which were not published until 1880, Sherman resolved to write his story. An avid reader of Dickens, Shakespeare, and Scott, and a devotee of the theater, Sherman wrote with passion and suspense about his life and his war. The entire second volume is the story of the Atlanta campaign from the spring of 1864 through the March to the Sea and to the end of the war a year later. Critic Edmund Wilson declared Sherman's *Memoirs* "amazing" for their honest emotions, brilliance of description, and "gift of self-expression."[40]

For Sherman's legions of readers (the *Memoirs* sold ten thousand copies in the first three weeks), including thousands of his own veterans spread all over the Midwestern states, the *Memoirs* were a way to relive some of the most dramatic events of the war. By whatever means, Sherman understood much of the art of autobiography; he drew his reader into a narrative that builds to resolutions, and he created a fascinating, if harsh, character in himself. The Sherman we meet is the ruthless warrior who wreaked an unprecedented war of physical and social destruction on Georgia. He has an enormous appetite for war, and the reader cannot help being swept up in the general's aura as conqueror, God's own Devil delivering necessary death that the republic might live. This is not a book arguing for reconciliation among warriors, but a victor's explanation of why the war was waged with calculated cruelty. But it is also a life story of a complex man with many vulnerabilities: he loved his men, and often held his enemies in contempt. His racist convictions about blacks made him a reluctant liberator and an opponent of black rights; he thrived on war and hated some of its results.

With the possible exception of Ulysses S. Grant, rarely was a man's life so thoroughly made by war as that of Sherman. He only rarely wrote of the carnage of battle and then with relative control. When Confederates placed "torpedoes" (mines) in the path of his march toward Savannah, Sherman observed a "handsome young officer" awaiting amputation after an explosion had killed his horse under him, "literally blowing off all the flesh from one of his legs." Sherman was livid: "This was not war, but murder, and it made me very angry." He also took time in the *Memoirs* to describe a lone freedman straying into the line of an artillery bombardment. "The ball (a thirty-two pound round shot) struck the ground," wrote Sherman, "and rose in its first ricochet, caught the negro under the right jaw, and literally carried away his head, scattering blood and brains about."[41] In these details, Sherman fashioned an engrossing narrative, mixing some realism with a triumphant adventure.

As though he were trying to answer the Southern vindicationists who amassed documentation to justify their versions of Confederate defeat, Sherman laced his *Memoirs* with generous amounts of his own reports and letters from his campaigns. Sherman's voice in those letters, as well as those in the frequent replies from Grant, General Henry Halleck, and some Confederates, make for some of the most revealing material in the work. His lengthy exchange of letters with General John B. Hood, Confederate commander at Atlanta, illuminates the character of just or unjust war in the summer and fall of 1864 in Georgia. Hood believed that Sherman's order to depopulate Atlanta of all civilians transcended "in studied and ingenious cruelty, all acts ever before brought to my attention in the dark history of war." Sherman replied that he had not conducted warfare in any ways that Confederates had not already practiced. "God will judge us in due time," replied Sherman to his foe, "and he will pronounce whether it will be more humane to fight with a town full of women and the families of a brave people at our back, or to remove them in time to places of safety." And to the claim that he should have given notice before shelling Atlanta, the terse Sherman declared that he "was not bound by the laws of war to give notice of the shelling of a 'fortified town, with magazines, arsenals, founderies, and public stores'; you were bound to take notice. See the books."[42] In Sherman's *Memoirs,* the nation's consumers of war memory read one of the first, and certainly one of the most probing, literary reflections ever written on the character of modern warfare.

But Sherman the memoirist was not all toughness. The book has many lyrical touches. Sherman captures the moment of departing from Atlanta on the March to the Sea: "Then we turned our horses' heads to the east; Atlanta was soon lost behind the screen of trees, and became a thing of the past. Around it clings many a thought of desperate battle, of hope and fear, that now seem like the memory of a dream; and I have never seen the place again." Veterans of Sherman's army must have been moved by that passage when they read it by their hearthstones in the North. They must have smiled in recognition as they read Sherman's descriptions of his men marching through Covington, Georgia, "color-bearers unfurling their flags, and the bands striking up patriotic airs." As the "white people" came out to "behold the sight," the "negroes were simply frantic with joy." Sherman was not religious, he disdained all apocalyptic conceptions of the war, and he was hardly an abolitionist. But he could not resist depicting the freedpeople "clustered about my horse," as they "shouted and prayed in their peculiar style, which had a natural eloquence that would have moved a stone."[43]

Any reader looking for the meanings of the war in the general's narrative did not have to look hard for them. The thoughtful nonsoldier looking to vicariously experience the war found much to appreciate as well. "To be at the head of a strong column of troops," wrote Sherman wistfully, "in the execution of some task that requires brain, is the highest pleasure of war—a grim one and terrible, but which leaves on the mind and memory the strongest mark." And for veterans who needed a realistic definition of "true courage," they found it in the final chapter, entitled "Military Lessons of the War." "All men naturally shrink from pain and danger, and only incur their risk from some higher motive, or from habit," Sherman maintained. "So . . . I would define true courage to be a perfect sensibility of the measure of danger, and a mental willingness to incur it, rather than that insensibility to danger of which I have heard far more than I have seen."[44] Given the character of so many of the battle accounts that flowed off American presses in the two decades to follow, Sherman's early effort was truly "amazing."

Early memoirists on both sides were vindicationists for their causes as well as for their personal records. They wanted to set the record straight as they saw it. But they were also aware that readers' tastes for soldiers' stories, while broad, had their limits when it came to realism. Most important, early memoirists believed that they wrote in a contest with time and with their former enemies' versions of the war. Many were ready for reconciliation, but they preferred it on the terms of their choosing, and through narratives that they themselves told.

IN MARCH 1877, the Philadelphia *Weekly Times* launched a series of articles by former Union and Confederate soldiers and some civilians, fifty-six of which were published in 1879 in an eight-hundred-page book, *Annals of the War*. The series ran until the late 1880s and eventually accumulated some 850 reminiscences, making it a good deal larger than its more famous competitor, *Century* magazine's "*Century* War Series," published between 1884 and 1887 and then issued in a lavishly illustrated and highly popular four-volume set, *Battles and Leaders of the Civil War* (1887). The *Weekly Times'* editor, Alexander K. McClure, believed that such a collection of narratives would correct "the grave errors of the hastily compiled . . . strongly partisan histories" that had appeared during and since the war. McClure's *Annals* was an initial effort at reconciliation through recollection, one boldly driven by the quest for the "truth" of history, a word used by the editor six times in a short introduction. With a sense of urgency, authors on both sides unabashedly declared their own pursuit of impartial "truth" and "facts" as a starting point in what were, by and large, passionately partisan essays. McClure courted controversial essays and solicited famous generals as well as lesser-known staff officers. He invited many Southerners to write for his paper; indeed, in the next decade, he joined with other Northerners in writing with full sympathy for the South, especially its successful economic revival.[45] Some authors sincerely embraced McClure's reconciliationist impulse; others were motivated by money or sought to puff up their reputations and settle feuds. Veteran officers in the late 1870s were anything but shy about remembering their war and trying to shape its popular memory.

While aiming to provide a forum for healing, accuracy, and multiple points of view, *Annals* accomplished a different end—it illuminated many of the bitterest memories of modern warfare. Confederate general Joseph E. Johnston, who had surrendered to Sherman in North Carolina in April 1865, attempted a point by point refutation of numerous facts about the Atlanta campaign in volume two of Sherman's *Memoirs*. Johnston, who had published his own blandly written memoir in 1874, began paragraph after paragraph with page numbers from Sherman's work, then proceeded to declare how the Union general's descriptions were "misinformed," "highly improbable," or "extremely inaccurate."[46] This kind of chapter and verse feud lent itself to a great amount of partisan heat, but little light. Johnston's essay reflected a growing trend in war reminiscence—the quest to claim moral victories about battlefield judgments, maneuvers, and even strategic outcomes through documents and disputed details. These new battles on paper not only served the ends of personal aggrandizement, but they also engaged questions of *how* the war was waged in front of a growing readership, and diverted some embittered emotions to the pursuit of facts and accuracy.

Many charged legacies resisted diversion, however. Former Confederate general John D. Imboden wrote a passionate exposé in *Annals* on the "incendiarism" of Union general David Hunter during the Shenandoah Valley campaign of 1864. As though preparing a legal brief, Imboden portrayed Hunter as a vicious war criminal for burning numerous homes, hanging a civilian, and torching the Virginia Military Institute in Lexington. Hunter emerges as a Yankee fiend unleashed by higher powers to wage uncivilized war. "The memory of General David Hunter," wrote Imboden, "will live . . . through the generations" to "illustrate how far the passions, fanaticism, and hate engendered by civil war can drag a man down from the boasted civilization of our age . . . to the barbarism . . . of . . . 'The Dark Ages.'" Imboden artfully concluded his essay with a long letter from Henrietta E. Lee, whose beautiful home the Union commander had ordered burned. The gendered message about cowardly warfare conducted by power-drunk Yankees is clear. Mrs. Lee writes to Hunter:

> Hyena-like, you have torn my heart to pieces! for all hallowed memories clustered around that homestead; and, demon-like, you

have done it without even the pretext of revenge, for I never saw or harmed you . . . Your name will stand on history's page as the Hunter of weak women and children; the Hunter to destroy defenseless villages and refined and beautiful homes . . . the Hunter of Africa's poor sons and daughters to lure them on to ruin and death of soul and body; the Hunter with the relentless heart of a wild beast, the face of a fiend, and the form of a man. Oh Earth, behold the monster!

Imboden did not invent his stories about burnings; cut off from supply lines, harassed by partisan guerrillas, and under orders to take the war to the society around them, Hunter's troops did indeed destroy civilian property.[47] But he did set up a distinct comparison between the Lost Cause as noble defense and Yankee marauders, between the victimized Southern civilian gentry and the ravages of military tyranny. Such an article revived bitter memories, but the story probably played well among many readers in the wake of Reconstruction's demise.

Imboden's essay and others like it, such as one by former Confederate general John McCausland—who in July 1864 led a raid that burned the town of Chambersburg, Pennsylvania, in retaliation for Hunter's deeds—provided a kind of memorialization by accusation and justification for the horror of modern war.[48] Indeed, partisan bitterness is so palpable in many of the essays in *Annals* that one can only conclude that the political reconciliation taking place in the late 1870s rested uneasily on a festering, unresolved popular memory by both sides of the savagery of 1864–65. That festering memory at least had to be expressed and worked through, and the emerging reminiscence industry provided one outlet.

Readers who sought romance and war adventure could find at least some in the *Annals*. John Esten Cooke weighed in with a panegyric to J. E. B. Stuart. A few pieces detail the dedication, daring, and heroism of various units, especially cavalry. The "morale" of Lee's army was fiercely defended in a classic Lost Cause article by J. William Jones, editor of the *SHS Papers*. Moreover, some articles tugged at the heartstrings of soldiers' reconciliation, such as Confederate general Richard Taylor's "The Last Confederate Surrender." Taylor surrendered his command in May 1865 in Alabama. Since he and his men were treated with honor and without retribution at that time, Taylor wondered "what years of discord, bitterness, injustice and loss would not our country have been spared had the wounds of war healed by . . . the hands that fought the battles." Taylor struck a chord many veteran writers would later echo: if soldiers had determined the terms of Reconstruction instead of "ambitious politicians," all would have been better. And for those veterans who merely needed to relive the time when they felt most alive, some *Annals* writers gave them just what they needed—like former Confederate colonel William Allan, in his piece on Stonewall Jackson's Valley campaign of 1862. Addressing his fellow veterans of the Army of Northern Virginia as if he were speaking at a post meeting, Allan hoped that his article "may, by touching the electric chord of association, transport us for a time into the presence of the majestic dead, and of the mighty drama, the acting of which was like another and higher life." Yearning for values from their youth all but lost in the Gilded Age, Allan dreamed of days of the war when "patriotism was a passion . . . when duty was felt to be the sublimest word in the language . . . [when] sacrifice outweighed selfishness."[49]

The predominant tone of the *Annals* is one of settling scores. The unsavory underside of the war surfaced in essays on the New York draft riots of 1863 and on business fraud by the Union government. Even awkward attempts at realism about combat and battle crept into two essays, one on Shiloh and the other on Fredericksburg. Descriptions of the insufficiently buried bones of the dead sticking out of the ground at Shiloh, observed four years after the battle, and of the living soldiers lying among the dead during the aftermath of the battle of Marye's Heights at Fredericksburg, were at least macabre pulses in a mass of writing that otherwise avoided the carnage. As a whole, in the *Annals* in 1877–79, a Philadelphia newspaper gave more than equal space to Southerners—accounts by Confederates seeking "truth" and a fair hearing essentially carry the day. Concerned that Confederates were dominating debates over war memory, former Union colonel William Brooke-Rawl wrote that "we begin to distrust the memory of those days, and almost to question the general belief that the battle of Gettysburg was a victory for the Union arms." Indeed the discussion had reached a point, he said, where many Union veterans wondered "whether they were even present" at Gettysburg.[50]

The essays in *Annals* offer an unwitting measure of the place of blacks in white soldiers' popular memory. In many of the stories, blacks play peripheral, sometimes supportive, roles. In Imboden's essay on Hunter's destruction of homes, a slave woman gives an axe to her white owner, who uses it to kill a Yankee vandal invading the house. A piece by Edward Spencer, "Confederate Negro Enlistments," ostensibly surveys the Confederacy's debate late in the war over whether to enlist and arm black troops, but its backdrop is a fulsome picture of faithful slaves protecting plantations and serving as body servants to Confederate soldiers. Spencer's article contributed mightily to the Lost Cause myth of black loyalty to the Old South, to the Confederacy, and even to slavery itself. Drawing upon General John B. Gordon's testimony before the Ku Klux Klan hearings in 1871 as authority, Spencer paid tribute to the "good conduct of the negroes" in the war, especially house servants, who "did not much want to be free." Using long quotations from Gordon about the "kindliest relations" of masters and slaves, Spencer assured readers that slaves "were happy because they were treated kindly and had few cares." He even claimed that some blacks served as Confederate soldiers. "A good many of these servants who followed their master afield," wrote Spencer, "albeit not fond of bullets, are known to have now and then taken 'hot shots' at the 'Yankees.'"[51] Loyal slaves also appeared in *Annals* in pieces about Confederate leaders and campaigns. But in this first major collection of war reminiscence, written largely by soldiers, black folk and their emancipation were otherwise invisible. Blacks were bystanders, beneficiaries of a foggy, unexplained freedom, bit players in a catalogue of stories about the character of both the warriors and their war-making. The use of blacks as curious props, noble victims, or devoted servants in soldiers' war stories would intensify in the 1880s.

BUT BLACK VETERAN voices were not altogether silent in the 1870s. They told stories diametrically opposed to faithful slave tales. George Washington Williams enlisted in the Union army in the summer of 1864. Barely fifteen years old at the time, he enlisted under an assumed name of either William or George Steward. Williams served in the Forty-first U.S. Colored Troops and was wounded in the assaults on Fort Harrison (near Richmond) during September 28–30, 1864. Williams returned to his unit and served out the end of the war; he was present at the fall of Petersburg in April 1865. Williams's unit was then sent with many other black troops to garrison duty on Island Brazos on the barren coast of Texas. After a sojourn fighting with republican rebels in Mexico, Williams returned to his hometown of Bedford Springs, Pennsylvania, in 1867 as a veteran with little education and few prospects for employment. He reenlisted and spent another year in the army with the Tenth Cavalry in Indian Territory on the western plains, where he sustained a gunshot wound through the lung. When Williams was discharged from the U.S. Army in 1868, he was not yet nineteen years old.[52]

Williams briefly attended the newly founded Howard University and Wayland Seminary in Washington, D.C., before enrolling at Newton Theological Seminary near Boston. With enormous dedication to his studies, Williams became the first African American graduate of Newton in 1874. Williams pastored the Twelfth Baptist Church in Boston for two years and began to pursue his passion for the study of history. Skilled as an orator and a writer, Williams served as the first editor of the *Commoner*, a journal in Washington, D.C., with pretensions of national prominence, and then moved to Union Baptist Church in Cincinnati in early 1876. In Avondale, Ohio (near Cincinnati), on July 4 of that year, Williams delivered one of his first significant public addresses. "The American Negro from 1776 to 1876" was a remarkable Fourth of July oration aimed at centennial consciousness.[53] But primarily it was a virtuoso expression of the centrality of black people in American history and of the role of black soldiers in winning the Civil War. The lengthy, sometimes florid, address was a black soldier's claim to glory in the nation's memory.

For a young man not yet twenty-seven, Williams had thought carefully about the problem of collective memory. He warned about the fleeting character of a nation's remembrance. "There is nothing immortal but truth," he declared. "The good that men do lives after them, and is not interred with their mortal bodies. The monuments we erect to the mighty dead must yield under the blighting hand of time." A decade later Williams would lead an effort to build a national monument to black Civil War soldiers, but for now he performed as their public advocate. Throughout his speech Williams portrayed American history as a dialectic between the two forces of slavery and freedom, and described African Americans as founders and preservers of the republic. "We claim a loyalty to American ideas, institutions, manners, progress, and liberty," announced Williams, "second only to Americans themselves!" He delivered a trenchant explanation of how emancipation resulted not from "an edict of humanity, but as a war measure . . . an absolute necessity . . . by the irresistible force of the logic of the nation's position."[54] Clearly, Williams saw himself as the young purveyor of a new, heroic history among his people and for the nation at large.

Flushed with a romantic sense of historical change, Williams spoke as though telling the nation's new creation story. When black soldiers arrived on the landscape of the beleaguered Union war effort in 1863, "the nation was breathless," declared the young minister-veteran. "Our army was awestruck while the whole civilized world watched with peculiar interest the move-

SIX

Soldiers' Faith

If it is our business to fight, the book of the army is a
war-song, not a hospital sketch.

—OLIVER WENDELL HOLMES JR., "The Soldier's Faith," Memorial Day address, Harvard University, May 30, 1895

WITH A WRY SENSE of insight, Confederate veteran Carleton McCarthy
observed how the Civil War possessed the American imagination by the
1880s. "A real good hearty war like that dies hard," wrote McCarthy. "No
country likes to part with a good earnest war. It likes to talk about the war,
write its history, fight its battles over and over again, and build monument after monument to commemorate its glories." If soldiers' reminiscence and
veterans' activities were not completely in "hibernation" in the 1870s, the two
ensuing decades certainly did bring an intensified "revival." Civil War reminiscence became a lucrative industry after 1880, and the place of the veteran,
both as public figure and as writer, underwent a flourishing rehabilitation.
The Grand Army of the Republic (GAR), which had lagged in membership
during the 1870s due to economic depression, the political strife over Reconstruction, and a general desire to forget the war, reemerged dramatically, late
in the decade, as part of a wave of fraternalism in the country at large. In 1880
the GAR claimed 60,000 members, and in the next five years the order's rolls
exploded to 270,000. In 1890, the GAR's numbers peaked at more than
400,000 and the organization achieved enormous influence as a lobbying
group for pensions and other policies. Thousands upon thousands of aging
soldiers participated regularly, largely out of public view, in fraternal rituals

that included delivering war narratives and memoirs, and in the fellowship of local posts at "campfire" meetings all over the United States.[1]

Very much in public view, these same veterans, South and North, attended hundreds of reunions held under state, national, and unit or army auspices. The major armies of both North and South gathered in associations at annual banquets that continued to meet into the twentieth century. By the 1880s, the veterans' reunion in an American city had become a major commercial event, with city governments, state legislatures, chambers of commerce, advertising firms, and railroad companies vying for their business. In 1880, at the eleventh annual reunion of the Society of the Army of the Potomac in Burlington, Vermont, the lakeside city "swarmed with visitors who tested it to its utmost capacity" because various railroads had granted fare reductions to veterans and their families.[2] As honored saviors of the Union, or noble embodiments of the Lost Cause, veterans in both sections were as familiar among the civilian population as the flags and music that surrounded their events. The former soldiers were the living reminders that the current society, however drab and materialistic, had evolved out of a more heroic time.

By the time Walt Whitman's now famous lines in *Specimen Days* were published (1882), they might have been read as a commentary on the burgeoning reminiscence industry emanating from veterans' culture: "the real war will never get in the books. In the mushy influences of current times, too, the fervid atmosphere and typical events of those years are in danger of being totally forgotten." Whitman lamented an absence of the authentic experience that many veterans seemed incapable of recovering in their writing. To the poet of death, "a hundred unnamed lights and shades of camp . . . will never be written—perhaps must not and should not be." Whitman's "marrow of the tragedy" remained all but lost in the hospitals and the cemeteries of the war. He ached for the unreachable stories, "the untold and unwritten history of the war—infinitely greater (like life's) than the few scraps and distortions that are ever told or written."[3] For an increasingly pliable audience, thousands of those "scraps" flooded the marketplace by the "mushy" 1880s.

Sometimes people reminisce because they truly wish to relive part of their past. Sometimes objects, or aide-mémoire, from the past induce a stream of remembrance where none may have been intended. Often reminiscence takes the form of wistfulness, a melancholy contemplation of the sheer transience of human experience. Or it is communal, stimulated by an audience of like-minded rememberers. Whatever the stimulous, we reminisce, writes the philosopher Edward S. Casey, "not only to savor, but to understand, or re-understand." And almost always, we reminisce not merely to render the past retrievable, but to serve present interests and needs. As though voicing the sentiments of the multitude of Civil War veterans who tried their hand at writing about their experiences, Casey declares: "I do the reminiscing not for the sake of the past as past but for the sake of myself."[4] At stake in reminiscence, therefore, is the dual need for personal understanding as well as personal recognition.

As veterans gathered in their posts or at annual encampments, they delivered formally written narratives, often called war "papers" or "sketches." They took the forms of battle, campaign, or prison accounts, and often merely recollected adventurous anecdotes. Here and there in the vast array of such narratives, a veteran would reflect with a sense of humor and irony on the craft of reminiscence. In 1889, choosing as his subject a tribute to "the Army Mule," Henry Castle addressed a Minnesota veterans' gathering by poking fun at his comrades' pride. "The longevity of a mule is proverbial," said Castle. "The endurance of a hallucination is, perhaps, equally great . . . the mules employed in the army are nearly all dead,—not so the hallucinations. There still survives in every town and village in the North at least one man who habitually asserts, who is willing to verify by affidavit . . . that he put down the Rebellion." By 1891 G. W. Burnell, a Wisconsin veteran, worried that the stories of all the great battles "and most of the little ones" had already been told. "The future historian will not be troubled for lack of chronicles," he wrote. "His trouble . . . will be their superabundance." And from a New York veteran, Peter Michie, came this flourish of honesty about soldiers' memory in 1893: "We know that these reminiscences cannot be strictly true . . . The greatest heroes of the war are still in the land of the living, for they are ourselves, and in telling our stories we generally so proportion the details with each repetition as to magnify more and more our personal prowess and tone down our errors until with frequent telling we end with actually believing ourselves to be the very heroes our stories make us out to be."[5] As old soldiers sought recognition for their war service, they received abundant inducement not only from their own organizations, but also from major magazines, which increasingly commissioned veterans to write narratives for series about the war.

By far the most important such series was that launched by *Century* maga-

zine. From November 1884 to November 1887, *Century* published hundreds
of articles lavishly illustrated with engravings, drawings (many made from
photographs), and maps in perhaps the most ambitious attempt ever to retell
a war by its leading participants. The series stemmed from an initial proposal
in the July 1883 issue by associate editors Clarence C. Buel and Robert
Underwood Johnson to commission eight to ten articles by officers on both
sides in key battles. As a major magazine of taste and high culture, presided
over by a poet, Editor-in-Chief Richard Watson Gilder, *Century* threw itself
into courting old soldiers to write about war. As Johnson observed, one of
the greatest obstacles the journal faced was the "literary inexperience of men
of action."[6] But Johnson and Buel surmounted that problem with a strong
editorial hand and a great deal of money to motivate their unusual authors.
Century continued to publish articles about the war well after 1887, and in
1888 it issued a four-volume set, *Battles and Leaders of the Civil War,* a model
to this day for all historical series based primarily on eyewitness accounts.

The editors' initial concern that war articles in an elite literary journal
might lose readership dissipated quickly as the series increased circulation in

Shortly after the war, Union veterans' units, such as this Grand Army of the Republic Post in
Melrose, Wisconsin, began to meet in their post halls for comradeship and regular readings of
war papers. (Wisconsin Veterans Museum, Madison)

the first six months from 127,000 to 225,000. "I should fear that a cry would be raised against us," Buel wrote to Gilder in July 1884, "that the *Century* had become a military magazine." He also wondered whether "women would take an interest in the series?" But such fears were assuaged, in Buel's words, because "the air is infectious with the whole war idea." Johnson believed that *Century* had chosen just the right "psychological moment" to pursue the series because the war had reached its twentieth anniversary, enough of the leading generals still lived, and sectional hostilities had dissipated enough to allow point-counterpoint battle narratives to unfold.[7] But the confidence to launch such a series rested in its ultimate purpose—to use war recollections as a depoliticized vehicle of sectional reconciliation.

The *Century* editors quite purposefully intended to shape a culture of reunion. They explicitly solicited articles that allowed for a "symposium . . . from a non-political point of view." They sought writing that was "accurate as well as picturesque." But most importantly, they structured the series and the subsequent *Battles and Leaders* as a means to reunion through the mutual recounting and understanding of all soldiers' valor. The *Century's* "main principle," wrote Johnson, was to "soften controversy" by the editorial "exclusion of political questions." A reader looked in vain for any discussion of the causes or consequences of the war. Even the central question of secession remained absent. This was the time to gather the old soldiers and induce them to remember the epic of the war itself before it was too late. As one writer put it, "unless such memories are recorded in a permanent form before the veterans of the war pass away, they will be lost forever." But equally, the editors considered their mission to be one of healing. The editors were proud, as Johnson said, to play referee when "the contemplation of sacrifice, resourcefulness and bravery in foes (upon which we took every occasion to lay stress) became an element of intersectional reconciliation."[8] What would be understood for all time, they hoped, was how and on what scale the war was fought—how there was glory aplenty on both sides. Why the war came and how it had transformed America were not the subjects of this prolonged soldiers' symposium; the issues of slavery and race were resoundingly silent.

For its vast readership, now growing significantly in the South, the *Century's* reconciliationist strategy worked well. The editors courted the highest-ranking living generals to write for the series. Some were utterly unwilling or wary of controversy and turned them down, as did Ulysses Grant repeatedly until his financial life collapsed and he softened to *Century's* overtures. Buel and Johnson conducted extended literary courtships of leading Southern generals such as Joseph E. Johnston and James Longstreet to induce these reluctant writers to perform for attractive sums. The leader of the Lost Cause, Jubal Early, declined to write, allegedly because he believed that "one could not write fairly for pay!" Many other ex-Confederates, such as P. G. T. Beauregard, who wrote five articles, were all too ready to accept their opportunities for literary fame. Many bitter controversies erupted during the course of producing the *Century* war series, largely over personal feuds and issues of responsibility at various battles. But most of these disputes were confined to the voluminous correspondence the editors carried on with authors so that, as Johnson put it, "the general reader never knew the violence of it."[9]

The aim of reconciliation through battle recollection was a success with many readers. C. A. Leonard wrote to Gilder in 1886, telling him that the war series "has made your magazine many warm friends in the South." Because of *Century's* "eminent fairness," Leonard offered to send the editors a special photograph of Robert E. Lee, which hung in the "sheriff's office" of his town (Richmond, Kentucky), for use as an illustration. Many ex-Yankee soldiers bought into the spirit of reunion. A Union veteran wrote from Boston wondering if *Century* had considered publishing articles by the Reverend William Jones, editor of the *Southern Historical Society Papers (SHS Papers)* because "it would afford very many of us ex soldiers an opportunity of reading the Confederate side of the question." Many former soldiers began to imagine themselves writers and promised *Century* that if allowed into its pages, they would toe the line of nonpartisanship. An ex-Confederate from Colorado wrote that his piece was written "from a Southern standpoint, and yet, I flatter myself, without partisan bias." After the series had run its course and *Battles and Leaders* rested on tables in thousands of homes, many veterans continued to offer themselves as would-be authors for *Century's* money. John O. Casler, a veteran of the Stonewall Brigade from Virginia, wrote from his new home in Oklahoma City, promising that his essay "contains nothing referring to the causes of the war or the right or wrong of it and will be interesting to all classes."[10]

Along with many other forums for reminiscence, the *Century* series prompted many an ex-soldier who would otherwise never have attempted to write anything to imagine himself a writer. Many did so because reminiscence was a way to make money. Indeed, the *Century* series fostered, perhaps more than any other source, the *commodification* of Civil War memory. As word got out that *Century* was paying good money, Johnson and Buel were flooded with letters, half-completed stories, promises for stories, and even relics that war participants (or their wives and children) wanted to bring to light in the magazine. In 1886 an Alabaman offered his eyewitness account of the Union attempt to reinforce Charleston Harbor in January 1861, provided the editors would "place a money estimate on it. I can give you references." "What will you pay for the exclusive right to use the photo and sketch?" queried a North Carolina librarian claiming to have a picture of the first Confederate soldier killed in the war. Some would-be authors wrote to the editors with remarkable audacity. "Say what you can afford to pay for it," suggested one veteran who "saw nothing more valuable . . . in my opinion than what I now send you." Cutting a hard sell, the veteran concluded: "buy it and it is yours. Reject it and it is mine." One author, W. H. Chamberlain, who actually was published, wrote at the beginning of the series wondering if the editors could "examine my article and fix a price for it in time to make your cheque available for the coming demands of Santa Claus."[11] Never had memory possessed such commercial value in America.

Many women wrote to the *Century* during the war series, offering documents as well as experiences for sale. Women from both North and South were frequently the custodians of their fathers' or brothers' wartime letters. They worked studiously to transcribe old letters and shape them into coherent form, often writing long papers of commentary to accompany such collections. Mrs. H. G. Coutler of Indiana offered one such collection to *Century* in 1885, including a thirty-page manuscript, "written in order to preserve in the family a somewhat connected record of the times." Helen O'Donnell had collected the war letters of a cousin in a Michigan regiment, and in 1890 offered to write "quite a readable paper under some such title as 'A Batch of War Letters'" based on her compilation. Frequently these reminiscences, mixed with documents, were collaborative family creations where wives, daughters, and sons fashioned a war record and a story for their veteran of choice. A New Jersey veteran, Robert McAllister, wrote with gratitude for the ten dollars *Century* had sent him for use of his letters and diary from the Spotsylvania campaign of 1864. He told the editors that his family understood the importance of the intergenerational memory that the magazine promoted. His daughter had "written on the field" and was assembling all his war papers. "We want our children and our children's children to know all about it," McAllister assured the magazine.[12]

Some women readers of the *Century* war series caught the bug to be in print. "Having seen the accounts of the late war in your magazine," wrote

Mrs. H. C. Goldsmith of Baltimore in 1889, "I feel actuated to write my experiences, which are many and varied." Mrs. C. B. Kent, a former nurse from North Dakota who had served at the Johnson's Island prison in Sandusky, Ohio, vehemently disputed ex-Confederate claims in the *Century* of inhumane treatment in Northern prisons. Southerners should not complain, she maintained, because they were allowed to make their own coffins at Johnson's Island and constructed their own "very pretty cemetery." Many women had their own unique war commodities to sell to *Century*. A Miss Rebecca Brumback wrote in 1886 offering to sell some of her deceased sister's twenty-year-old poems as long as the editors made clear "what would you be willing to pay for them."[13] Clearly, *Century* did not suffer a loss of women's readership due to the war series. But war reminiscence was a family affair across America, and many women had their own memories, their own stories and relics, to market to the New York magazine. Moreover, just like male veterans, they sought simple recognition for their experiences.

Like men, some women sought to write for *Century* because they were desperate for money. In 1891 Susie J. Bishop, a poor woman in "the mountains of Virginia" who described herself as "unmarried, delicate, penniless, and almost alone in the world," sent her "sketch" of a wartime incident to the editors. Old and caring for "some orphans," Bishop insisted on the truth of her story (which does not survive) and begged the editors to give her a hearing and to keep her letter private. She did not wish to haggle with Johnson or Buel, since she was "too poor to find stamps or time for many trials of its acceptance with editors." "My only wish for its publication," she assured them, "was the hope of remuneration."[14] There is no record that Susie Bishop ever placed her story. But when a poor woman in the Virginia mountains resorted to writing up an episode for potential pay, we can see that Civil War memory had become a creature of the mass market, and like all markets, it produced winners and losers.

Famous generals fared much better financially with *Century* than the Susie Bishops. Indeed, the purpose of the war series was to enlist the living military leaders to tell their story about the whole war in a linear, chronological manner from 1861 to 1865. The exact rates that *Century* paid to its authors are difficult to discern, but many were paid very well. The magazine itself, by Johnson's accounting, made a $1 million profit on the entire enterprise. Nearly a year after Johnson and Buel began their long and testy literary courtship of Joseph E. Johnston, the Confederate general received an offer of $500 for the two articles he had produced, which he personally considered "extravagant." Former Confederate cavalry general Stephen D. Lee, president of the Agricultural and Mechanical College of Mississippi, initially refused to write for *Century* in 1885, but by 1887 he had received fifty dollars for his article "The First Step in the War," a six-page account of the firing on Fort Sumter. At first, James Longstreet also declined to write, especially about Gettysburg. But the *Century* editors soon wore him down and, with his amanuensis Josiah Carter, city editor of the *Atlanta Constitution,* Longstreet eventually did write on Gettysburg and other battles. The various payments sent to him and to Carter demonstrate the magazine's determination to obtain writings from certain former generals who would otherwise never have produced them.[15]

Century's elitism in courting primarily high-ranking officers as authors had the unanticipated effect of prompting many of the rank and file to fashion themselves as writers. The reminiscence industry as a whole (in print media and in veterans' posts) promoted a kind of *democratization* of memory, especially among whites. Indeed, it is hard to imagine another time in American history when so many ordinary people were inspired, indeed encouraged, to tell their stories, which were then readily published. The Civil War produced a democratic, vernacular form of autobiography. Much of this flood of writing never made it into print. But the sheer volume of such material that was published, the variety of people yearning to be heard, demonstrates a vast reservoir of stories from the war era by people from across the economic and social spectrum who wanted to be counted as participants in this epic event.

Century did not welcome very many ordinary voices, but it did publish early in the series a piece by Warren Lee Goss, "Going to the Front: Recollections of a Private." Goss, a former Massachusetts soldier, had written one of the most bitter prison narratives (he survived Andersonville) in 1869. But by 1884, Goss wrote, as he put it, a story of much "lighter" fare. The essay is an engaging piece on the early enlistment and departure of raw Union troops from New England. Goss tugged at aging veterans' memories, describing mothers' tearful farewells to their sons, detailing the contents of his first knapsacks, and relating the awkwardness and naivete of some of the youthful recruits. "Drilling looks easy to a spectator, but it isn't," Goss remarked. "Old soldiers who read this will remember their green recruithood and smile assent."[16] *Century* did not commission any pieces about the horrors of combat, scenes of carnage, nor especially, at first, any stories about death and disease in prisons. But it did encourage old soldiers to remember the more savory joys and bracing hardships they had shared.

By the mid-1880s, the aim was to keep the veterans smiling. And many of them wanted the chance to write like Goss. In 1885, R. K. Beecham, a former private in a Wisconsin regiment, wrote from Nebraska claiming that he had read Goss and could offer a better first-hand account of events. Beecham was proud of surviving four years in the army, seven months of which were in prison. But he was also short on cash and resented all the attention lavished on generals. "I am aware that only men of note, Generals &c, whether on this or that side of the line matters but little—are in demand as writers or lecturers," wrote Beecham. But he was certain that he could "make such sketches interesting to the public." Beecham pleaded his poverty and got right to the point. "Of course it is not honor I am looking for now," he said, "but a chance for bread and butter, and I can do a great deal of writing for $100." His class, and perhaps even sectional, resentments rang through with remarkable honesty. "I would really like to know . . . as a matter of business," Beecham continued, "how much you paid Beauregard for his article and how much you paid the private." Beecham sent the editors a poem he had just written to give them "some idea of the genius that is running to waste in Nebraska," and then signed off: "I am willing to work cheap."[17]

Many who sent in batches of letters or diary material hoping for publication did so out of similar class interests. An Ohioan offered his brother-in-law's wartime letters in 1888 as a record of the "experiences of the lower grades and common soldiers." *Century* had opened its doors to members of the broadest memory community, but the editors had no intention of doing business with them. The lower grades had to find other paths to recognition. Some correspondents persistently pleaded their cases as potential authors. A Philadelphia veteran, Isaac W. Heysinger, determined to "correct false history," pursued Buel for the better part of a year, sending his poems, promising to write hair-raising stories about the "wonderful phantasmagoria of war," and defending his favorite general (George B. McClellan).[18] But this audacious Philadelphian never made it into print with *Century.*

Some old soldiers, infirm and living in veterans' homes, eagerly read the *Century* series. Thomas Lee wrote from the National Military Home in Dayton, Ohio, in 1888 offering to sell his elaborate handmade maps and lists, detailing in precisely printed capital letters his entire war record of "twenty-six battles and eight war hospitals." Lee said he had spent ten years preparing his record, including some "thirty-two plans showing my principle position in each battle, and my place in U.S. hospitals when I was wounded and hurt." Such a proposition from a man describing himself as "nearly totally disabled" suggests that *Century* and other publications had tapped into a vast and unchanneled source of veterans' popular memory.[19]

The image of an old man in an Ohio soldiers' home, spending his days crafting and poring over his maps and lists and then writing to editors in his own unique diction, suggests how desperate some veterans were for simple recognition of their wartime experience. Thomas Lee claimed to have more than one hundred copies of his battle plans and five hundred of his war record. Immersed in the precious details of his war experience, Lee told his story the only way he could—in the maps and tabulations that gave him an element of control over what may have been a shattered mind and body. In remembering war, writes the novelist Tim O'Brien, the veteran knows that "the thing about a story is that you dream it as you tell it, hoping that others might then dream along with you, and in this way memory and imagination and language combine to make spirits in the head." Ordinary Civil War veterans too had spirits in their heads looking to get out, but by the 1880s and 1890s, fewer and fewer Americans wanted to recollect the horror or the meaning of the war. Most were willing participants in a relentless accumulation of detail about troop movements and locations on maps. And yet in 1890, when a Georgian named Berry Benson sent *Century* a manuscript, "A Confederate Sergeant's Adventures," along with his "War Book," photographs, and some drawings by his son suggested as illustrations, he insisted on one condition: "A story of adventure like this, without comment, would seem to be an encomium on war, and I would not think it right . . . War is hateful and debasing and mankind is far enough advanced to abolish it." *Century* eventually sent Benson a check, but did not publish his piece.[20]

BEGINNING IN 1877, the principal GAR newspaper, the *National Tribune*, which was edited from Washington, D.C., by former soldier and pension agent George Lemon, welcomed the common soldier to write for its pages. The *Tribune* ran a regular feature in the 1880s and 1890s called "Fighting Them Over," which consisted largely of first-person accounts of battles and camp life. The *Confederate Veteran*, founded in 1893 by Sumner Archibald Cunningham in Nashville, Tennessee, achieved widespread popularity and a national readership. Featuring especially the common soldier's story, the western theaters of the war, and a rising tide of white supremacy, the *Confederate Veteran* reached a circulation of over twenty thousand by the end of the 1890s. Moreover, rank and file Confederate veterans founded and one edited (William N. McDonald, a former private) the *Southern Bivouac* in Louisville, Kentucky, in 1882. The *Bivouac,* which lasted until 1887 when it was purchased by *Century,* reached a circulation of fifteen thousand by 1886 and printed all manner of soldiers' reminiscence and poetry. It took a reconciliationist stand toward Yankee veterans while holding to numerous Lost Cause conventions, especially the frequent inclusion of "darky" stories about loyal slaves during and after the war.[21]

Most importantly, especially for Union veterans, the local posts of veterans' organizations, which sponsored formal papers and lectures, gave the ordinary ex-soldier an outlet for reminiscence. In monthly and annual meetings from Maine to Kansas, Union veterans gathered to read formal papers to each other. Although most of these papers never had a public audience, they were published in multi-volume sets, ten volumes covering 1878–1915 in the small state of Rhode Island alone.[22] No other historical experience in America has given rise to such a massive collection of personal narrative "literature" written by ordinary people. They published themselves, and provided each other with audiences. If any former private, captain, or brevet-general was willing to write an account, it was generally published.

In a real sense, Civil War veterans were America's first Civil War "buffs." The modern phenomenon of thousands of Americans of all walks of life time-traveling, reading, engaging in reenactments, buying popular magazines, launching newsletters, preserving battlefields, collecting weapons, and generally passing to the next generation an insatiable fascination with the Civil War and all its minute details began in the narratives, handmade maps, and remembrance of that war's veterans. Most of the general public could hardly have tolerated the steady diet of papers on "The Sinking Creek Valley Raid," "The Battle of the Boys," "The Left Attack at Gettysburg," "On the Right at Antietam," "Amusing the Enemy," or "The Last Ditch." But in fraternal communion, the old boys in Blue and Gray did sit through countless such papers. A popular, multi-edition memoir by a Southern veteran, former private Carleton McCarthy, may have caught the outcome of much soldier reminiscence in its title: *Detailed Minutiae of Soldier Life in the Army of Northern Virginia, 1861–1865* (1882).[23] Veterans burrowed into their memories and, in many ways, buried their imaginations in their war experiences. They relived and remade those experiences; they reassembled the chaos and loss inherent to war into an order they could now control. While doing so, they cleaned up the battles and campaigns of the real war, rendered it exciting and normal all at once, and made it difficult to face the extended, political meanings of the war.

Here and there in the war papers veterans did write with a certain realism about combat; most poignantly, an unforgiving bitterness survived in narratives about prison experience. After reading the *Century* for many months, a Kansas veteran detected in 1885 that the articles were written "under restraint." J. B. Mansfield understood the "sore spot that, like a soldier's wound they treat as though it had not got sufficiently healed so that it will answer to take its bandage off . . . for fear of a secondary hemorrhage." The editors did not welcome Mansfield's offer to "uncover all those sore spots if you want it done." *Century* particularly resisted publishing anything about prison experience until after its war series and *Battles and Leaders* had already run their successful course. Rhode Islander Thomas H. Mann started writing to *Century* as early as May 1884, offering a narrative on his survival of Andersonville prison. Fearing the loss of Southern circulation and aiming at reconciliation, *Century* avoided prison narratives. The magazine paid Mann one hundred dollars for his piece shortly after he submitted it, but did not publish him until 1890, when the editors had deemed it safe to take up such stories. When he made it into print, Mann assured readers that he had revised an earlier manuscript, "leaving out much of its bitterness, and nearly all the explosive adjectives and personal opinions." Warren Lee Goss, himself the author of a best-selling Andersonville narrative and a collaborator with Mann, understood *Century's* reticence about opening the prison question. "I do not wonder you 'hang fire' in taking up 'Andersonville,'" Goss wrote the editors in 1889. "The handling of the subject in your magazine at present would be apt to kill your influence South because it will certainly lead to angry recrimination on both sides."[24]

By 1890 *Century* had sent out circular letters soliciting articles on prison experience, and it received many responses. In 1888–91, *Century* published seven prison narratives, reaching for a balance of Northern and Southern reminiscence. Although the prison story was still calculated by *Century* to promote fraternalism, it proved a vexing subject for the culture of reconciliation. It was the one topic that still evoked bitterness and horror. James McCann, an Illinois veteran who had survived twenty months in eight Confederate prisons, tried his hand at a narrative in 1890. He informed *Century* how harrowing the task loomed for him. When he returned from the war a wrecked man, friends tried to convince him to enter school, "but they could not prevail on me . . . I could see no future then and felt the greater part of the time as though I had awoke out of a nightmare. And felt as though my days were numbered." *Century* wanted tales of hardship, survival, and escape, but it did not welcome veterans' nightmares. "I have tried to write the memoirs several times," wrote McCann in private, "but the effect on my brain I could not bear."[25] Realism and its accompanying pain lurked in many prison survivors as late as the 1890s, but the culture of reconciliation could only narrowly accommodate them.

Many Southerners reacted to *Century's* new interest in prison stories with hostility and their own appeals to write. In 1890, a Texas veteran accused the editors of "bad temper" after reading an Andersonville narrative. He warned *Century* that the magazine had a wide readership in the South, but if it continued to sacrifice its "spirit of fairness" to the prison issue, Southerners would "spend their money with their friends." Henry H. Price wrote from Central Plains, Virginia, demanding the chance to "act as amanuensis" for the many Confederates who had died in Northern camps. Price accused Yankees of "heartless . . . premeditated" cruelty against Confederate prisoners. "You . . . should give both sides a hearing," Price instructed the *Century* editors. "Dare you have the moral courage to publish 'the truth' from the other side, or do you still prefer to cater to a morbid . . . appetite for one-sided stories . . .? Dare you publish this!"[26]

Prison stories, and occasional reminiscences of the horror of combat, make up a significant subgenre of veterans's war papers. In 1900, a Kansas veteran opened his narrative with the acknowledgment that the "treatment of prisoners by the Rebels" was an "old story," but it merited recounting because it was "the blackest page in the book." A Rhode Islander called his prison experience "cruel as cruel could be under the nineteenth century civilization." Clay MacCauley spoke for many veterans of both sides who never reconciled their sufferings. The infamous sites of Civil War prisons, he wrote, were forever "those places of terrible memory." Although some prison narrators tried to convert their tales into feelings of mutual suffering between the Union and Confederate survivors, this story of personal agony never really belonged in the culture of reconciliation. The recollected reality of men fighting over bones like dogs, or of floors "covered with vermin," men insensible with "despair and degradation" and "doomed to suffer a living death," as the Kansas man O. R. McNary related, released the one strain of soldiers' memory that was unwelcome and unassimilable in the national reunion. Prison memory lacked heroics, personal resolutions, and the life-affirming elements of humane reconciliation, even among soldiers. Much of the horror in these memories remained out of public view during the 1880s and 1890s.[27]

So too the recollections of the worst of combat tended eventually to be buried in veterans' war papers, if openly expressed at all. In "How Does One Feel under Fire?" (1898) another Kansan, Frank Holsinger, described the extreme "mental strain" of battle. He remembered the "zip of a minie," and the "awful *thud* as some poor fellow falls by your side with that awful groan and agony of death." In battle, said Holsinger, "you are scared." In the disastrous battle of Fredericksburg, he remembered the dying and wounded all around him and his rush to "escape capture," a travail from which he ended up "deathly sick" and "vomited." He tried to describe the "terror" he felt as a wounded soldier lying helpless on a field, "alone with my thoughts," the "main artery cut" in his arm, trying desperately to improvise a tourniquet from a canteen strap. He remembers screaming "water! water!" But then he abruptly gives up on the narrative, concluding: "Who can portray the horrors coming to the wounded?"[28] Clearly some veterans needed to tell and hear these stories by the turn of the century. But such reflections had little if any public audience; rather, they were rare punctuations in the reminiscence culture of veterans' meetings.

Much of the prose in veterans' war papers, in critic Thomas Leonard's apt phrase, hovered "above the battle." Soldiers' narratives by the 1880s, writes Leonard, tend to be a "sort of petty realism—the recollection of such trivial, everyday details of life at the front that the battlefield seemed like a normal environment and suffering was lost sight of." Former soldiers wrote with what today seems a rather formal diction and pomposity. Perhaps they had, as Mark Twain once suggested, read too much Sir Walter Scott. Remembering the preparation for battle, an Ohio veteran in 1884 honored his "Confederate hosts, ready to welcome us 'with hospitable hands to bloody graves.'" He respected his enemies because "we had tried their temper on many a well-fought field." In such indirection, many old soldiers remembered and foreshadowed battle and death. "Ten thousand voices" of soldiers singing "John Brown's Body" were the "wild, weird music of the night before" the battle of the Wilderness. Many in this chorus "never sang again, unless in the angel choir of the vast unknown." Shifting between past and present tense in their attempt to describe battle, some men wrote as though they were fashioning dramatic commentary for tour guides. As though veterans needed to remember the horror of combat, but without too much realism, they sometimes submerged battle in a sea of purple prose. "The ground drank its full of blood, and grew slippery to the foot," went a description of the Wilderness. Flags often came in for especially grandiose treatment. "Torn, riddled or bloody as the old rag may be . . . to the soldier . . . it is the emblem of all he loves," wrote the Ohioan. "I have seen a shell tear off the arms of a color-bearer, and seen him clasp the bleeding stump about the flag as he fell, bathing it in his dying blood."[29]

Many veterans were quite self-conscious about the character and limitations of reminiscence and of the battle piece as autobiography. An Illinois veteran writing in 1886 admitted that "kind memory" had "thrown a mellow light over" his topic, the Shenandoah Valley campaign of 1862. Such exercises in remembrance, said John S. Cooper, "had also given a tinge of adventure and romance, to say nothing of military glory, to our campaign." Cooper acknowledged, "in the case of army life, pretty much as in our recollections of childhood and early manhood, that all the unpleasant details of daily experience drop out of memory, leaving only those pleasant recollections which we love to recall." Another Illinoisan remarked with humility that he could "not attempt a word picture to do that which no painter has ever been able to do with his brush—namely, to make a battle scene realistic."[30] But such circumspection did not stem the tide of details that poured forth in veterans' narratives and letters.

Perhaps ex-soldiers were obsessed with detail in their remembrance of the war simply because they found pleasure in the pursuit of geographical and operational facts. A revived passion for war details, for stories, and for the sheer delight of shared reminiscence became, for many veterans, an end in itself, a pastime of enduring psychological value. No doubt some veterans found in the ceaseless accumulation of campaign detail a healthy form of forgetting; in the arcane, horror and tragedy could be displaced. Veterans of all ranks also craved recognition; they wanted their sacrifice, their place in the drama, acknowledged. Once the collective culture had embraced war remembrance on a large scale, individual veterans, their egos at stake, did not want to be left out. And finally, many old soldiers were genuinely concerned to "get the story right"—or to "correct errors," as they frequently said—because they believed that accuracy about the war determined how future generations would understand what had happened and who was responsible for victory and defeat. They found refuge in the belief that near perfect accuracy was attainable, necessary, and vindicating.[31]

As ordinary ex-soldiers read the *Century* series and imagined themselves writers, they contributed, perhaps unwittingly in many cases, to the very displacement of the real war that the magazine fostered. When veterans wrote from the South promising "a stirring and well-written semi-historical military romance founded upon the incidents of the war between the states," or from the North offering a mixture of a "true strange story of the late war, my . . . experience with . . . Libby prison, and my late discovery of my rebel captor, an unpublished joke or anecdote of Prest. Lincoln," they served the ends of forgetting.[32] They offered such memories as entertainment and as the currency of soldiers' reconciliation.

Many veterans of all ranks thrived on such "work" as they aged and even in the immediate aftermath of the war. Sometimes they sent each other autographs to be collected. Those veterans writing unit histories carried on extensive correspondence with former comrades, receiving long, detailed narratives of troop movements, changes in command, and casualty counts from particular battles. Sometimes one veteran wrote to another without the slightest reflection, recording his entire service record. Other times, a veteran would detail the story of how he was wounded, his precise position while sitting on his horse, and the place where "the minnie ball passed through my right leg a few inches below the knee." After telling such a story and providing twelve pages of extraordinary detail, Confederate veteran Alexander Lawton apologized to Charles Colcock Jones: "the loss of all proper material, other than memory, prevents me from being more detailed." In some GAR posts, the accuracy of war sketches was also seen as a measure of moral rectitude. The form used to conduct interviews upon which war stories were recorded at posts in Philadelphia and Minneapolis demanded that "great care and mathematical accuracy must be observed in the matter of Names, Dates, Localities and Events."[33] The details of a man's war record were the markers in his life, symbols of some control exercised over an untidy, even a lost, past.

Perhaps no man did more to collect and record the details of a single battle than John B. Bachelder did for the battle of Gettysburg. A journalist and historian, Bachelder accompanied the Union army during the Peninsula campaign in 1862, and he began his lifelong observations at Gettysburg shortly after the July 1863 battle. Eventually serving as an unofficial "government historian," Bachelder made it his life's passion to determine the precise military topography of the three days' battle at Gettysburg. In November 1864, the state of Pennsylvania chartered the Gettysburg Battlefield Memorial Association, which became Bachelder's base of operations. By 1864, Bachelder had already spent more than eighty days walking over and sketching the twenty-five square miles of the battlefields around the Pennsylvania town. In that year, his "isometric drawing" of the battle went on sale; shortly after the war, the drawing was the basis of a collaboration with the artist James Walker, who painted a large canvas *The Repulse of Longstreet's Assault,* which depicted, in Bachelder's words, "a literal rendition of the subject." The Bachelder-Walker collaboration launched during the rest of the century a genre of such realist paintings of battles, many reaching massive, panoramic size. But most importantly, Bachelder's quest for "literal" detail encompassed thousands of interviews with surviving soldiers of both armies, some of them in hospitals. By 1873, the year when he published his own battlefield guidebook for Gettysburg, Bachelder had interviewed "the officers of every regiment and battery of the Army of the Potomac." Moreover, in the 1880s, when Congress appropriated $50,000 to research and formally mark the battlefield, Bachelder solicited detailed accounts from as many veterans as possible.[34]

During the 1860s and 1870s, Bachelder had great difficulty convincing Confederate veterans to come back to the scenes of their failure at Gettysburg. Ex-Confederates were also embroiled in a bitter interstate feud between Virginians and North Carolinians over both who was most responsible for defeat during Pickett's Charge on the third day at Gettysburg and who, indeed, had performed with the highest valor. These internecine disputes were conducted primarily in Southern newspapers and magazines, and in the *SHS Papers.* But by the 1880s, Blue-Gray reunions had become more common at Gettysburg, and hundreds of veterans on both sides wrote to Bachelder, plumbing their memories for every notion they could recall about their unit's location on three days in July twenty to twenty-five years before.[35]

Because they were aging and living amidst the unheroic culture of the Gilded Age, veterans were eager to see their names on monuments. Some offered Bachelder elaborately bound volumes of their journals and war records, which they had "put away" for their "children." Full of self-serving exaggeration, veterans, understandably, tended to place their own units at the center of the most decisive action. Many admitted the flaws in their memories; they told of heroism and sometimes of defeat and loss. Their primary subjects were their own bravery and the mathematical detail it required to record it. Many tried with numbing exertion to help Bachelder in "marking the spot" of their regiment at a given time of day during the battle. "I located the place so certainly that I can tell you just as well on paper as if I were on the spot," wrote one Pennsylvania veteran of his regiment's location on Cemetery Ridge.[36]

As with modern-day Civil War buffs, ex-soldiers who had experienced combat lived with a sense of their own mental battlefield; they came to know its detailed topography, its stone walls, its rising or declining ridges, its coppices of trees. In letters to Bachelder they explored this malleable topography of memory. Even those who complained that "the dust of twenty years is upon the map, and the forgetfulness of all these years is upon the memory of our Gettysburg fight" spent hours preparing handmade maps and sketches and did their best to help Bachelder in his colossal attempt to recover and record their past drama. Ultimately, by the 1880s, virtually all veterans wanted public recognition for their individual and collective bravery. Andrew Cowan wrote to Bachelder in 1885 complaining that, in reports as well as paintings, his New York artillery battery came "very near not being mentioned at all." He wanted his men *"mentioned,"* he admonished the historian.[37] The worst fate for old soldiers in the revival of popular fascination with the war was to go unrecognized. When that did occur, veterans had their interior battlefields to fall back into; but in a culture where memory had become such a desired and negotiable commodity, public recognition—on maps, monuments, and in books—was the more valuable possession.

Soldiers' nostalgia for the war came increasingly to be wrapped in patriotic visions of what they had accomplished for the larger society. Such visions, in time, crystalized as abiding myths.[38] Old soldiers on both sides wanted the nation to remember the general cause and outcome of the war in increasingly particular terms. For the vast majority of Yankee veterans, the idea that they were the saviors, the deliverers, of the nation—that the republic had survived and been renewed by their blood—became an article of faith. In their view, such sacrifice deserved the eternal gratitude of the republic. For their part, Confederate veterans embraced the myth that they had never fought for slavery, never really engaged in "rebellion" at all, and that their struggle for independence failed only because it was overwhelmed by numbers and resources. Increasingly, these two ennobling visions of why men had fought were so widely rehearsed that consideration of slavery, emancipation, and Reconstruction became bad taste at best, and bad politics at worst.

Despite efforts to keep sectional conflict blunted in veterans' culture by the 1880s, statements of these two mythic variations on soldiers' memory abound in narratives, letters, and reunion speeches. They carried a politics of soldierly difference that tended toward manly reconciliation. Old soldiers were splendid symbols around which to forge reunion; they had all fought heroically and deserved recognition, regardless of which side of a stone wall they had stood upon. The culture of veterans' reminiscence in the 1880s and 1890s acknowledged a distinction between the causes for which North and South had fought, but no difference in the moral righteousness and valor with which they had performed their duty.

The official oration at a Northern soldiers' reunion was never complete without the requisite tribute to the veterans as saviors of the nation. "I salute you—Veterans of the War!" proclaimed Daniel Dougherty at the 1881 reunion of the Society of the Army of the Potomac. "Soldiers who conquered rebellion! Deliverers of your Country! Preservers of the Union!" Such language became so commonplace that some orators eventually searched for ways to extend its reach. Former general and Freedmen's Bureau director Oliver Otis Howard ended a reunion speech in 1894 by dwelling on "what was gained by the war." It was "not enough that slavery was abolished," said Howard, "all our institutions . . . were then at stake." Howard named his list: "The American family! The American School! The American Churches! The American Ballot!" The great legacy of Union soldiers, claimed Howard, was that they gave their children these institutions "completed, rounded out, intact."[39] Their work, therefore, had permanently saved and transmitted a way of life.

Standard Confederate commemorative speeches abounded with the refrain that they had fought for "liberty" and "right" and that their sacrifices were all the more heroic because of the odds they faced. An argument still continued to flow between the commemorations of Confederate and Union veterans. The typical unveiling or reunion speech in the South rang with the refrain of Colonel Richard Henry Lee's oration in Virginia in 1893: "As a Confederate soldier and as a citizen of Virginia I deny the charge, and denounce it as a calumny. We were not rebels; we did not fight to perpetuate human slavery, but for our rights and privileges under a government established over us by our fathers and in defense of our homes." So deeply held were these beliefs that a postwar generation Virginian and writer for the *Washington Post*, Charles K. Moser, wrote in 1906 to the Union veteran Joshua L. Chamberlain in a sincere spirit of reunion, but with undaunted certainties about the South's cause. "Not as a Southerner, but as a lawyer," wrote Moser, "I insist that we were never 'rebels,' according to the Constitution." "I admit the error of the South in secession," Moser continued, "deplore the institution of slavery (as an economic but not as an ethical crime) and give to Northerners the same rights of moral and ethical conscience . . .

to be neither blinded by prejudice nor led astray by the injection of moral issues never involved."[40] With these ground rules, reunion among many soldiers and their descendants took a grudging but inevitable hold.

Myths are the deeply encoded stories from history that acquire with time a symbolic power in a culture. In *Mythologies* (1957), Roland Barthes suggests that myths are clusters of ideas and values that have lost "the memory that they were ever made." Indeed, Barthes might have had in mind the Civil War veterans' obsession with detail and their quest for recognition through reminiscence when he wrote that myth "organizes a world which is without contradictions because it is without depth, a world . . . wallowing in the evident . . . a blissful clarity: things appear to mean something by themselves."[41] As veterans of both sides aged, the differences in their remembrance of cause, while still evident and necessary in acts of commemoration, could not hold back their own and the culture's need to cultivate the mutual ties in soldiers' memory. The national reunion required a cessation of talk about causation and consequence, and therefore about race. The lifeblood of reunion was the

By the 1890s, Confederate veterans would gather for formal reunions, sometimes donning their old uniforms and shouldering their muskets, as in this photograph of the "Old Guard of Richmond," R. E. Lee Camp No. 1. (The Museum of the Confederacy, Richmond, Virginia)

mutuality of soldiers' sacrifice in a land where the rhetoric and reality of emancipation and racial equality occupied only the margins of history.

ON THOSE MARGINS, other kinds of memories flowed. White Union veterans' narratives were by no means devoid of discussion of the place of black soldiers in the war. Many volumes of war sketches contain at least one paper on "The Negro as Soldier," or "Reminiscences of Two Years with the Colored Troops." A mixture of romantic racialism and sincere admiration for the black men they commanded animated many of the pieces on black troops, written by white former officers. In 1890, an Indiana veteran, William H. Armstrong, paid tribute to the "stubborn bravery" of black soldiers in many battles, but occupied much of his essay with self-serving honor to the white officers who commanded their regiments. Armstrong also demonstrated a common white fascination with the racial mixture of black soldiers, maintaining that a "large percentage" of them were of "mixed blood." "While in every other creature," he said, "the product of a crossing of blood with a higher order . . . enhances its worth and elevates its character, it has in the case of this wonderful people been a deterioration and a stigma of disgrace." Armstrong relished telling of the irony of one of his black artillery gunners killing in battle his own white "half brother" in the Confederate army.[42]

The gallantry of black soldiers appeared as well in collections of sentimental war poetry by Northern women. In a book of poems dedicated to the GAR, Kate B. Sherwood offered her tribute to "The Black Regiment at Port Hudson." The special heroism of black soldiers animates Sherwood's message, even through the sentimental trappings:

> What did they wrest from the breach,
> Under the guns at Port Hudson?
> The right to be men; to stand forth
> Clean-limbed in the fierce light of freedom,
> And say, *"We are men! We are men*
> *By these scars, by these wounds!"* And what then?

It is remarkable how many white former Yankees remembered their black troops, as well as the ex-slaves they encountered in the South, through some prism of characters from Harriet Beecher Stowe's *Uncle Tom's Cabin*. A Rhode Island veteran reminisced about his leadership of black troops in the occupation of Louisiana in 1864. "Excursions into the surrounding country" afforded "conversations with the colored people whose sad memories of the old slavery days recalled so vividly the experiences of Uncle Tom and his associates in Mrs. Stowe's famous tale."[43] Mrs. Stowe's characters forever riddled the racial and historical imaginations of Americans, black and white. In their memories, Northern white soldiers, even if they had not actually seen Uncle Tom or Little Eva in Louisiana, knew they were there.

Some white officers who had commanded black troops fought vigorously, if unsuccessfully, for the equality of blacks in society as well as in veterans' organizations. Some white Yankee narrators, though, simply wrote histories of the black soldier's role in all of America's wars, paying full honor to their services and claiming that history as the black man's right to "be fully equal, in all respects," as another Rhode Islander insisted in 1905. Such histories were almost always based on George Washington Williams's work, *A History of the Negro Troops in the War of the Rebellion* (1888). Some white officers even quoted a version of Williams's epigrammatic line: "The part enacted by the Negro soldier in the war of the Rebellion is the romance of North American history." Black abolitionists and the authors of slave narratives had been quoted before by whites, but for perhaps the first time, white American writers now cited a black *historian* as their authority. As an active GAR member, Williams said he had "heard with deep interest, at camp-fires and encampments, many narratives of the heroic conduct of Negro soldiers." By the final decade of the century, however, the more normative story was that found in the war paper of a Wisconsin veteran, William Ruger, in which he waxes nostalgically about a recent Blue-Gray reunion on the battlefield at Chickamauga in Georgia. To Ruger, it seemed "like a dream . . . an experience of a lifetime." He was overwhelmed by the "messages of peace and good will," by both sides' singing "our National Anthem," and by ex-Confederates' pinning a badge on his lapel. He was so carried away with his remembrance of the reunion that he could only conclude: "I fear that I have taken more than my allotted time, and while I had intended to say something in regard to the negro and the negro problem at the South, I will close, thanking you for your kind indulgence."[44] Like many Northerners, Ruger had simply run out of time for or interest in the place of race in Civil War remembrance.

Black Union veterans, of course, had thousands of stories of their own to tell. A recent count of black soldiers and sailors who served in the Civil War gives a total of 188,571. Of that number, approximately 37,000 perished, over 90 percent of whom died of disease. This overall 20 percent death rate among black troops was 3 percent higher than that of white troops, and the disease rate was 30 percent higher than that of whites. By 1890, about half of all the white men who had joined the Union and Confederate forces in the war were still alive, but less than 30 percent of African Americans had survived. Once all Union veterans had gained access to pensions after 1887, and black veterans had achieved relative equality with their applications, one scholar has estimated that African American soldiers and their survivors received at least $273 million during the life of the system (which ended in the 1930s).[45] Blacks among the Blue were by no means absent from the cultural and political insistence on the part of Union veterans that they had saved the nation and deserved its largesse.

Many black veterans fully embraced the fraternalism (which had long been a tradition in black communities) and patriotism of Union veterans' culture. By the 1880s, virtually all GAR posts were segregated. With a few rare exceptions, black veterans resisted the discriminations of the GAR and society as a whole and formed their own posts, held their own parades, and sought opportunities to write their own war papers. In Worcester, Massachusetts, Amos Webber meticulously kept a "Thermometer Book" in which he recorded weather patterns, a host of other natural phenomena, and a wide variety of the social and political history of his town and the nation from 1870 until just before his death in 1904. Webber's "memory books" give new meaning to the veterans' preoccupation with detail. Webber was a fiercely patriotic black citizen who saw himself as one of those saviors of the republic; he worked steadily for decades as a loyal employee at a wire factory, thrived on his fraternal organizations, and almost never missed a parade, soldiers' reunion, or church convention. This proud veteran of the Fifth Massachusetts Cavalry represented every conservative value the GAR advanced, but he was also different—he demanded and celebrated the equality of his people, and he struggled with anguish to comprehend racism.[46]

Amos Webber was among the more than three hundred black veterans who gathered in their own independent reunion in Boston's Tremont Temple in August 1887. Some four thousand people in all, mostly black, attended the ceremonies from all over the Northeastern states, and some from as far as Ohio. A soloist accompanied by a choir of fifty sang stirring renditions of the national anthem, "We Are Rising as a People," and the "Battle Hymn of the Republic" as the "veterans shouted themselves hoarse." The resolutions of this black soldiers' convention demanded that the federal government safeguard "full and equal protection of the laws" and enforce the Civil War Constitutional Amendments. They explicitly called on their white comrades and the general citizenry to recognize the "patriotic Negro soldier and his kin." In closing, these black veterans registered their dissent from the increasing Blue-Gray "fraternizing" occuring among ex-soldiers across the country. "Conciliation and peace with enemies are grand," concluded the convention, and "when coupled with justice to faithful allies they are sublime." The horizon was not all dark. At the end of their ceremonies, the black veterans took a steamer down the coast to Hingham, Massachusetts, where a white GAR post welcomed them in tribute. Together the white and black veterans, in their racially distinct units but with common cause, marched to the grave of former governor John A. Andrew, who had played a pivotal role in black recruitment during the war. Amid flowers and speeches, citizen Webber and his comrades achieved genuine recognition.[47]

For other black veterans, the story was not as satisfying. Many suffered with their health, and if they were lucky enough to live in the right Northern community, found a place in a soldiers' home. Black veterans in the South fared worse because of deteriorating race relations and much less access to organizational or fraternal support. Here and there in the North, an individual or a handful of black veterans managed membership for a time in a regular GAR post. But by the 1880s and 1890s segregation was the norm. In New Bedford, Massachusetts, the all-black Robert Gould Shaw post of the GAR claimed eighteen members by the mid-1880s and a women's auxiliary of forty by the mid-1890s. These small numbers were barely enough to keep the post functioning in its rituals, and its paltry relief fund peaked at $4.50 in 1891. Occasionally a black veteran achieved high rank in the GAR, as did James H. Wolff, a Boston lawyer, when he became senior vice-commander for the Department of Massachusetts in 1905. And the New Bedford black community could claim an authentic war hero in Congressional Medal of Honor winner Sergeant William H. Carney. During the Fifty-fourth Massachusetts regiment's celebrated assault on Fort Wagner in South Carolina in July 1863, Carney carried the flag to the parapet and planted it there; when the regiment retreated, he carried off the colors under fierce fire and was seriously wounded three times. Carney served as chief marshal at the 1887 black veterans' reunion where he was "rapturously received," and as wider religious and fraternal organizations adopted him as their symbol, he became, along with Robert Smalls, the closest thing to a national black war hero from the Civil War. When he died in 1908, flags in Massachusetts flew at half-mast, making him only the second African American so honored.[48]

Some black veterans wrote autobiographies in which their war service played a prominent role. Most of these narratives were ascension stories, tales of the arc of achievement from slavery to freedom.[49] Moreover, the black soldier's story did not lack historians to tell it. In the same year (1888) that Williams published his history of black soldiers, Joseph T. Wilson, a native of New Bedford, Massachusetts, and a veteran of both the Second Regiment of the Louisiana Native Guards and the Fifty- fourth Massachusetts, brought out *The Black Phalanx,* a chronicle of the black soldier's experience from the Revolution to the Civil War. Both books served as compilations of facts and as witnesses to the heroism and honor of black veterans. Wilson's book, which was impressively illustrated, combined melodramatic prose with narrative bulk to deliver a vigorous defense of black manhood and devotion to country. Another African American veteran, George Mike Arnold, published a historical essay in 1887 paying tribute to black heroes of numerous battles and making the case for how emancipation had freed "not only . . . black people, but the whole American nation." Arnold's aim was to overcome the black soldier's invisibility in the nation's memory. Calling for a national monument to black soldiers in a moving conclusion, Arnold worried about a forgetful society's reversion to racism and violence. "Those killed in the war are accounted for," he declared. "How shall we account for those murdered by the horde that was . . . directed by the ghost of slavery, the spirit of hate and prejudice . . .?" For his part, Williams delivered sermons and campfire speeches at predominantly white GAR post meetings in several cities during the 1870s, and in 1881 he received the organization's appointment to a term as judge advocate for a year.[50] Most of all, Williams used his influence and eventually his book to push for the creation of a national monument to the black soldier.

Models for monuments to emancipation had been circulated for two decades. The controversial Freedmen's Memorial in Washington, D.C., where artist Thomas Ball's Lincoln stands with outreached arm over the kneeling slave, had been unveiled in 1876. Working through his close friend, Senator George F. Hoar of Massachusetts, Williams helped draft a bill for federal funding of a black soldier monument to be constructed near Howard University in Washington, D.C., and placed prominently in a park named for Robert Gould Shaw. In *History of the Negro Troops,* Williams laid out in detail a design for the monument, including the inscriptions to be placed on the four sides. Each respectively recorded the number of the black Union dead, the soldiers' "earned . . . right to be free" by virtue of their sacrifice in "449 engagements," the total numbers and process by which black men had been recruited, and finally a list of sixteen major battles in which blacks had served. Williams further proposed four figures by which the black warriors would be represented, one each for the artilleryman, the cavalryman, the infantryman, and the sailor. The actual size of the structure was never determined, and an estimated price of only $100,000 appeared in the proposed bill. In 1887, the monument bill was introduced in both houses of Congress, and the Senate Library Committee held hearings in which Williams himself testified. Although the bill actually passed the Senate in December 1887 by a vote of 31 to 19, with 26 voting absent, it fell into oblivion in the House of Representatives. Williams had traveled and labored extensively for the creation of the black soldiers' monument, speaking at white veterans' meetings and drumming up grassroots support. But all was for naught at this juncture in history. The black soldier would be immortalized magnificently in Augustus Saint-Gaudens's Shaw Memorial in Boston, unveiled in 1897. But the monument Williams had imagined in the nation's capital would not materialize until a very different era more than a century later.[51]

Williams intended the monument to educate both blacks and whites. Black folk memory about the heroism of the black soldier could forever be reinforced by such an edifice at the heart of the nation's capital. And white memory, he believed, could not remain ignorant of black glory; white prejudices, rooted in imagery of "the poor, patient Negro . . . his sufferings and degradation," might be altered forever. The "soldiers' faith" that inspired Williams, in spite of the failure of the monument effort, was that "the story of the civil war is forever an object lesson." He put his faith in what he considered America's epic story of human liberation and national regeneration, and as an advocate, he wrote some of his most passionate prose:

> The songs of a nation are the heartbeats of patriotism, but the surest way to teach national history is in monumental marble and brass. The deathless deeds of the white soldier's valor are not only embalmed in song and story, but are carved in marble and bronze. But nowhere in all this free land is there a monument to brave Negro soldiers, 36,847 of whom gave up their lives in the struggle for national existence . . . a republic that remembers to defend its defenders . . . can never decay.

The soldiers' faith that Williams sought to commit to stone was very different from that emerging on a thousand town squares all over the country. Virtually all monuments to the standing common soldier represented a generic white figure standing at rest.[52] Williams's emancipationist vision collided tragically with the commonplace notion of a white man's war, a war between men of equally strong character and devotion on both sides, a vision destined to reconcile the sections, celebrate a common American manhood, but largely ignore race and black freedom.

Most black Civil War veterans had their own mythic sense of cause to preserve. In season and out, wherever an audience gathered, they fought the nation's forgetfulness. By liberating slaves and themselves, black soldiers insisted that they had helped to remake America. In 1887, George Arnold declared that African American soldiers had "washed the blood scars of slavery out of the American flag, and painted freedom there; they snatched the black lies out of every false star upon its folds and set in their stead the diadem of liberty . . . They tore the Dred Scott decision from the statutes and wrote there, 'All men are equal before God.'" In 1895, at the Cotton States Exposition in Atlanta, Christian A. Fleetwood, a black Medal of Honor winner and War Department employee from Washington, D.C., delivered a speech titled "The Negro as a Soldier." Fleetwood attacked white America's ignorance of black history, especially its "absolute effacement of remembrance of the gallant deeds done for the country by its brave black defenders."[53] Black veterans no doubt had their own kind of interior battlefield where they cherished their "truth" and nurtured memories that they tried to pass on to the next generation. But they were losing the struggle over which kind of soldiers' memory would prevail in the public culture. Their loss in this contest over memory was one part of the disaster that beset African Americans in the emerging age of Jim Crow.

IN THE 1880s and 1890s, the practice of reconciliation and fraternalism emerged as dominant in veterans' culture. Unyielding partisanship still wafted from an occasional Northern or Southern reunion speech or a campfire war paper. But the prevailing theme was the equality of soldiers' sacrifice on both sides. In 1883–84, the *Southern Bivouac,* while devoted to upholding the honor of the Confederate veteran, ran articles and sentimental poetry urging soldierly reconciliation. Now and then poems that turned on Blue-Gray mutual suffering filtered into a Union veteran's war paper as well. As regimental monuments began to mark the landscape at the Gettysburg battlefield, soldiers' dedication speeches and tourist guidebooks portrayed the site as the "Mecca of American Reconciliation." At many dedications of the common soldier monuments in Northern towns, such as one in Sharon, Connecticut, in 1885, orators celebrated how after twenty years the "unutterable bitterness and destruction" could now be "obliterated . . . forgotten," how the results of the war had been rendered permanent, "the error of slavery ended; every foot of our soil free to labor."[54] Monument unveiling rhetoric tends toward hyperbole. But these sentiments of reconciliation reflected real needs for social cohesion in a nation growing into something other than what many believed the war had wrought.

Some of the earliest Union veterans' narratives, even occasionally one about prison experience, included tales of how the two sides "fraternized" with one another. A Rhode Island veteran, writing in 1876, fondly remembered his Confederate guards in "A Trip to Richmond as Prisoner of War." He recalled one Rebel saying with comaraderie, "if you and I could have the say in this war, we'd settle it soon I reckon." In a short but extraordinary paper "Mosby and His Men," delivered in 1887 by a Wisconsin veteran, J. A.

In 1889, the Duke Tobacco Company of Durham, North Carolina, published a promotional album that combined cigarette advertisements with profiles of Confederate and Union heroes. (W. Duke Papers, Perkins Library, Duke University)

Watrous, the famous Confederate guerrilla commander John Singleton Mosby was in attendance as a special guest. Watrous joked about how valuable Mosby had been to the "Union cause": the Confederate raider's tactics had been so ruthless (he hanged some Union prisoners) that straggling had ended abruptly in sections of Virginia since no Yankees wanted to fall into Mosby's hands. Mosby had long since become a Southern scalawag, a Republican Party functionary, and an advocate of reconciliation through recognition by Southerners of the failure of their cause. Still, his legendary and bloody reputation makes his presence at a Wisconsin Union veterans' meeting remarkable. According to Watrous, veterans on both sides now had a common foe at the bar of memory: "the arch-conspirators of 1860 and 1861, who precipitated the war, and were careful to avoid the battle front." The Wisconsin veteran was convinced that Father Time had done his work well. "He has plastered and splintered the bloody chasm," he wrote, and joined the veterans together, "shoulder to shoulder and heart to heart,—fairly Siamese-twinned them." In this spirit, all could have faith that "the day is coming when the gray-haired men of the war of 1861–5 will meet and fraternize as soldiers, scarcely halting to ask each other whether they wore the blue or the gray."[55]

Blue-Gray fraternalism crystallized around the values of manliness, valor, sacrifice, and a mutual sense of honor. Sectional reconciliation was, of course, good for business and investment, and some Blue-Gray fraternalism was staged in part as a means of cementing commercial ties between Northern money and Southern economic development. New South boosters like Henry W. Grady of Atlanta were adept manipulators of reconciliationist Civil War memory and master promoters of nostalgia. Grady, who had come of age after Appomattox, became a major voice of reunion through commerce and understanding. In a speech before the New England Society of New York in 1886, which no Southerner had ever addressed, he joked about his fellow speaker, General William T. Sherman, being a "careless man about fire." Then he delivered the story of a noble South that had rebuilt its society with self-respect, now knowing that in the war "her honest purpose was crossed and her brave armies beaten." In Grady's vision, an "omniscient God" had settled the war issues, including slavery, which had been "swept forever from American soil," and had delivered the nation to higher glory and growth. Preaching comity and industrial investment, Grady assured his Yankee business audience, though, that "the South has nothing for which to apologize . . . The South has nothing to take back."[56] Grady was roundly cheered by bankers and generals alike.

In the 1880s many companies in North and South appealed to customers with elaborate advertisements that used themes of Civil War reconciliation. The Duke Tobacco Company of Durham, North Carolina, used history to sell cigarettes. In 1889, they produced an elaborate multicolored souvenir album, "The Heroes of the Civil War." It consisted of twenty-nine pages juxtaposing one Confederate with one Union war hero, beginning with Lee and Grant. With fancy ads for Duke, Cameo, and Turkish Cross-Cut cigarettes adorning the page, the company announced that by issuing the commemorative album it hoped to inspire "kindly feeling" between the sections. The Civil War, said the Duke management, was "a strife so full of deeds of valor on both sides that one would fain pass by the cause of the strife and admire the individual."[57] Those famous generals, dead and alive, depicted in colorful sketches by the Duke Company and in many other places, had become commodities; their images were salable memories in the name of good will and good business. Amidst the tone and tenor of such a flood of sentiment for national reunion, the war's causes and consequences dissolved.

Among veterans on both sides, a "culture of character" emerged as a core ideology. Old soldiers tended to measure each other as preservers of an older, more wholesome society, one uncorrupted by materialism. Such a culture of individual honor set against the crassness of the materialistic Gilded Age conditioned veterans of one section to accept their former enemies as comrades. They came to see their war experience as a special, shared possession. "Those days were full of horrible sights," wrote Samuel C. Armstrong, the founder of the black college, Hampton Institute, in 1884, of his experience at Gettysburg, "yet in all these sickening scenes there was, I think, no hatred; the malice and rascality engendered by war is at the rear. There is a certain mutual respect among those who accept the wager of battle." Northerners especially offered both tacit and explicit olive branches to their former foes. As Union veteran and Andersonville survivor John McElroy put it in 1883, "wars come to husk off the invidious surroundings of place and circumstance, and show us the real grain of manhood in everyone's nature."[58] Increasingly, Northern and Southern veterans began to display their character and their condition of aging manhood at Blue-Gray reunions held all over the country.

In July 1888, George L. Kilmer of the Abraham Lincoln post of the GAR in New York published a list of twenty-four Blue-Gray reunions of one kind or another between 1881 and 1887. By May 1889, Kilmer had reported at least three more reunions brought to his attention from the earlier period of 1875–79. Kilmer believed that these gatherings demonstrated a shared "faith" among soldiers, and that increased "business relations" and intersectional migration had helped foment these events. Some meetings consisted of Southern or Northern veterans' groups touring the other section's cities and being ceremonially received by their former foes. The assassination in 1881 of President James A. Garfield, a former Union general, prompted some Blue-Gray communion, such as two meetings between the GAR post of Carlisle, Pennsylvania, and Confederate veterans of the Luray Valley in northwestern Virginia. Historical anniversaries in the South or the North also provided occasions for Blue-Gray soirees, such as the Bunker Hill centennial in Boston in 1875, where some Confederate veterans from Maryland and South Carolina marched in a parade, and the Yorktown centennial of 1881, where a Trenton, New Jersey, GAR post staged a meeting with the Association of the First Virginia Regiment. Many reunions took place at former battlefields, sometimes on anniversaries, such as in May 1884 at Fredericksburg, Chancellorsville, and the Wilderness in Virginia, and in October 1887, at Kennesaw Mountain in Georgia. Moreover, when GAR National Encampments were held in border state cities, such as in Baltimore in 1882, Confederate veterans living in the area sometimes attended with special recognition.[59]

But this soldierly kindness and healing did not always come as easily as many politicians and business leaders wished to portray it. At Gettysburg the story was mixed. A first attempt to gather the Blue and the Gray in 1874 was abandoned when it became clear that it was simply too early for soldiers to mingle at the scene of such sensitive memories. Reconstruction politics delayed such fraternalism; as long as the "bloody shirt" was so useful on both sides in the struggles over the meaning and aftermath of the war, Blue-Gray reunions were not easy to organize. Confederate veterans were also deeply divided among themselves, especially between Virginians and North Carolinians, over who was most responsible for their decisive defeat at Gettysburg. Indeed, many ex-Confederates found it extremely painful to return to Gettysburg at all, at least until the late 1880s. But in 1887, on the twenty-fourth anniversary of the battle, some five hundred members of the Philadelphia Brigade veterans' organization met at the Pennsylvania town with two hundred members of the Pickett's Divison Association from Virginia. On July 3, 1863, these units had met in some of the most celebrated combat of the war along the stone walls of Cemetery Ridge at Gettysburg, in what quickly become known in Civil War lore as Pickett's Charge. They first gathered in two lines in the town square—the Union veterans decked out in special white helmets, blue flannel shirts, and badges—and shook hands. After many speeches acknowledging each other's valor, the two groups mingled at the "High Water Mark" on the battlefield where the charge had climaxed. In the evening the members of both groups pitched tents on the very ground of their battle, shared stories, and exchanged hats and other mementos— including in one case locks of hair. A witness observed that it was "hard to tell which is the [Philadelphia] brigade and which is Pickett's division."[60] This meeting inspired poetry and praise from much of the national press.

But all was not sweetness in Blue-Gray relations in these years. An open dispute ensued in 1887 over whether the federal government, or individual Union units, should return captured battle flags to the ex-Confederates. President Grover Cleveland had suggested the return of the flags, but ran into stern official opposition from the GAR. The silver anniversary reunion staged at Gettysburg in 1888 was somewhat of a disappointment to the promoters of reconciliation, because only about three hundred Southerners attended and some Union veterans had reached at least a temporary resolve that their own heroism at the great battle risked oblivion if such affairs continued to stress mutual valor over victory and defeat. As one editor of a veterans' journal wrote in June 1888, "No God-knows-who-was-right bosh must be tolerated at Gettysburg. The men who won the victory there were eternally right, and the men who were defeated were eternally wrong."[61] With time, though, an "everyone was right" bosh did overtake the practice of Blue-Gray fraternalism, and Gettysburg would be the site of some of its most remarkable examples.

Some bitterness still fluttered in the air, but intersectional reunions continued in the 1890s, complete with elaborately staged ceremonies. On Memorial Day weekend in 1895, the city of Chicago hosted a remarkable gathering of distinguished Confederate and Union generals as well as a throng of rank-and-file veterans. The occasion was the unveiling of a large monument in Oakwood Cemetery to the 6,229 Southern soldiers who had died in the Camp Douglas prison compound in Chicago during the war. The event was the brainchild of John C. Underwood, a Kentucky Confederate veteran who had worked for many years to stage intersectional reunions in the interest of comity and better "business relations." Underwood's earlier efforts at such gatherings in Philadelphia in 1885 and Columbus, Ohio, in 1889 had been largely failures. But in 1890 he enlisted the civic resources of Chicago, abuzz with building for the Columbian Exposition of 1893, to plan his Confederate celebration in Lincoln's home state.[62]

On the night the veterans arrived in Chicago, a glamorous reception was held at the Palmer House hotel. Surviving Confederate generals in attendance included Wade Hampton, recently retired from the U.S. Senate and working as a government railroad commissioner, former governor of Virginia Fitzhugh Lee, and Mississippian Stephen D. Lee. Holding court in the middle of the lobby, ear trumpet in hand, was James Longstreet, the scalawag who was reviled by some Lost Causers but still considered a hero at these events. The "hundred" or so "beautiful" and "aristocratic" women attending the reception were decked out in combinations of U.S. and Confederate flag pins. Some veterans were on crutches and many carried "empty sleeves." This scene of gendered frivolity, and of pathos and respect, gave way to a banquet and speeches that revealed some of the underlying themes of the event. Ferdinand Peck, head of the Chicago Citizens Committee, welcomed the old Confederate soldiers in the interest of "fraternal feeling" and "closer commercial relations and business union between the citizens of our country, thus enlisting in a larger degree of investment of the capital of this section in developing the vast resources of the southern states." Responding for the United Confederate Veterans, Stephen D. Lee continued the commercial theme: "We accept your friendship . . . we invite you again to invade us, not with your bayonets this time, but with your business. We want to hear in our land the voices of your industries."[63]

The following day an enormous parade to Oakwood Cemetery involved, in Underwood's estimate, one hundred thousand people; they gathered near the large, $25,000 shaft and statue of the common Confederate soldier who had died in Northern prisons. In his dedicatory speech, Wade Hampton declared that such a ceremony on Northern soil "inaugurates a new era, a new departure." "Say if you please that they were mistaken," continued Hampton, "that they were wrong, no brave man on earth can fail to do honor to their courage." The Chicago press joined in the admiration of such a ceremony. The *Chicago Tribune* believed it "constituted an epoch in the life of the Nation and the formal close of the period of ill-will engendered by the war of the rebellion." Even the progressive *Chicago Inter-Ocean* gushed at the dedication parade as "unparalleled in history . . . yesterday it mattered not who wore the blue or wore the gray."[64]

Such spectacles of reconciliation were emotionally irresistible for most people; they carried a redemptive, uplifting appeal. They embodied patriotism, a new nationalism, and the human need for healing. But they were also the occasion for their organizers to proclaim the terms of such reconciliation. For John Underwood, the purpose of the Chicago reunion was "harmonious forgetfulness." "It is not now profitable to discuss the right or wrong of the past," declared Underwood, "neither should the question be raised as to the morals of Massachusetts selling her slaves and South Carolina holding hers, nor as to the profit of merchandising the negro on the block in New York or from the sugar cane fields of the Mississippi 'coasts' and cotton plantations in other parts of the South."[65] In this vision of the terms of Blue-Gray reunion, slavery was everyone's and no one's responsibility. America's bloody racial history was to be banished from consciousness; the only notions of equality contemplated were soldiers' heroism and the exchange of the business deal.

Later that year one of the most spectacular reunions occurred at the dedication of the Chickamauga and Chattanooga National Military Park, September 18–20, 1895. An estimated fifty thousand people attended, including Vice President of the United States Adlai E. Stevenson and numerous state governors. Several hundred tablets and more substantive monuments had already been erected by the time of the dedication, and many more were planned by the states. Virtually every surviving general of the Civil War attended the Chickamauga reunion, and most offered their portion of oratory. Ex-Union veteran Willard Warner complained that "endless discourse" about the "bloody chasm" had become a "farce." Warner declared forgetting a soldier's national duty: "Occasionally we hear a preacher, belated in being born too late for the fight, who makes war by speech or pen, or women, broomstick in hand, who show fight, but the soldiers of the two armies and the mass of our people are serenely at peace. Is it not about time we had ceased talking of the bloody chasm?" General Lew Wallace, author of *Ben Hur: A Tale of the Christ* (1880) and the former governor of New Mexico, captured the tone of the entire reunion. "Remembrance! of what?" he proclaimed. "Not the cause, but the heroism it invoked."[66]

Remarkably, in their speeches, many governors and some generals did take up the subject of the "results of the war." But they did so in arguments that neatly fit the narrative of blameless, fated reconciliation among former foes. Alabama governor W. C. Oates, a Confederate veteran, told his Southern comrades to stand "proud," for they "fought for a just cause, which though lost, was partially won." Oates addressed the centrality of slavery in the war's causation, acknowledging it as the "Pandora's box of our American politics." But he painted a picture of benevolent masters fated to their lot. "Cruelties" were practiced, he admitted, but he argued repeatedly that "the negroes simply passed through the fiery furnace of slavery to reach civilization, which was the only road by which they could have obtained it." Similarly, Union general James A. Williamson could rejoice that the destruction of slavery brought "freedom and equality before the law" to blacks, but in common with much of white America, he declared that "it may take generations to solve this problem, and so much depends upon what that class of our citizens may ultimately do for themselves."[67] In a 365-page report of the proceedings of the Chickamauga reunion, there is no evidence that a black veteran attended the festivities. By 1895, any serious discussion of racial reconciliation at Blue-Gray reunions would have been considered either arcane or inflammatory.

A major concern of some veterans, especially those among the educational and business elites, was to pass along to the next generation a set of soldiers' virtues—honor, devotion, sacrifice, love of country. This concern was vividly shown in 1890 when Henry Lee Higginson, a former soldier and wealthy businessman, donated a major piece of real estate to Harvard University as "Soldiers Field." The athletic fields of Harvard, which run for many acres on the south side of the Charles River, were dedicated by Higginson to six of his former classmates and fellow soldiers who were killed in the war: James Savage, Charles Russell Lowell, Edward Barry Dalton, Stephen George Perkins, James Jackson Lowell, and Robert Gould Shaw. All six were either Massachusetts-born Brahmins or Harvard men of longstanding New England roots. Higginson explicitly wanted the the new fields called "the Soldiers Field," and Harvard president Charles Elliot accepted them as the way "to promote manly sports . . . and to commemorate the soldier of 1861."[68]

Some four hundred people, including much of official Harvard and Boston's elite society, attended Higginson's dedication speech in Sever Hall. Higginson paid moving tributes to the lives and deaths of his six comrades. He quoted from the final letter Charles Lowell had written to him before being killed in battle. "Don't grow rich," admonished the soldier who died of wounds received at the battle of Cedar Creek in 1864, "you'll find it much more difficult to be a useful citizen." "Don't seek office," Higginson quoted the young Lowell as saying, "but don't 'disremember' that the useful citizen holds his time . . . and his life always ready at the hint of his country." Higginson made duty and service in the new age of materialism his central theme. Addressing the students, Higginson declared his "chief hope" that the new playing field "will help to make you full-grown, well-developed men, able and ready to do good work of all kinds . . . that it will remind you of the reason for living, and of your own duties as men and citizens of the Republic."[69] Higginson's auditors that day were so moved, and so desperate for a renewed sense of heroism and devotion to sacrifice, that they flooded him with letters of congratulations.

The letters to Higginson and his wife Ida provide an excellent index to class and gender anxieties twenty-five years after Appomattox. The speech must have been beautifully delivered; it clearly moved the audience emotionally with imagery of brilliant youth shattered and destroyed by war. The athletic fields were to be their monuments where new generations living in national peace could learn what it means to be a man and engage in spirited physical contests of honor. Charles Thorndike thought Higginson had demonstrated that "one could be both rich and also the most useful of citizens." Lincoln Ripley Stone saw in the address a message about service as self-denial for a culture driven only by "money, pension, rather, pension, pension!!" Many of Higginson's correspondents wrote in profoundly personal and religious terms. Mary Putnam read the speech "with a deep and sacred sense of happiness." Vincent Yardley Bowditch told Higginson that after reading the address "tears came thick and fast, a thing I don't often indulge in . . . you stirred me more than I can express." Bowditch kept his dead brother's picture on his office wall, "between Bob Shaw and Billy Putnam . . . all heroes of the noble army of martyrs."[70] Indeed, in this local memory community, as in a thousand others North and South, a cult of the fallen soldier occupied walls, town greens, cemeteries, and psyches.

Higginson's gift of the Soldiers Field, especially its vision of selfless duty, inspired many to special memories and thoughts. William James felt in the "*aftertaste*" of Higginson's speech a message of "simplicity and originality" that would "stick in those boys as long as they live." Henry Cabot Lodge asked for another copy in order to "send it to Theodore Roosevelt," and Edward William Hooper found in the oration a "moral tonic" for a "life so comfortable and pleasant." Retired president Rutherford B. Hayes wrote admiringly from Ohio: "We are drifting away from the golden days. We must not drift away from their nobleness." Many of Higginson's friends read the speech aloud with their children and reflected at length on its meaning for the next generation. "What men they were!" wrote Charles Fessenden Morse. "I have two boys coming along who I hope some day will play in the 'Soldier's Field.' They at least shall know the story of it and of the men for whom it is a memorial." Mary Louisa Cabot remarked on "how little the young people of today whom I see, *realize* the war and what it was to us older ones, and I long to bring it up now strongly to them."[71]

Moreover, some men wrote to Higginson expressing their pain at not being in the war. Silas Weir Mitchell, the psychologist who studied the effects of battle on soldiers as well as the controversial question of women's hysteria, wrote that "over it [the speech] I choked like an hysterical girl, and for a little was glad no one [came] by." "I was the elder among four brothers," Mitchell confessed, "and it was decided that I must remain at home with my mother. Three went to war. My duty was clear but I never cease to regret that I too was not in it." This confession of survivors' guilt and longing to have been a soldier no doubt speaks for many aging nonveterans of the Gilded Age who forever remained on the margins of this cult of manliness and heroism. Some among the younger generation worried that football just could not replace the glory of battlefields. Higginson's nephew George Russell Agassiz wrote to his uncle: "You make a fellow feel what a moral education was the experience of your generation in the war, and how little our play battles at football or rowing take the place of it." Many women felt instructed and transported by Higginson's speech. Elizabeth Rogers Cabot believed that she had received a message "all mothers" could read to their "sons" and "grandsons," and Lucy B. Lowell heard a warning to the young against "the danger of corruption in public men." Roxana L. Dabney felt rapture in the expression of the soldierly ideal. Since reading the speech, she "felt that this world was ever more beautiful than I have thought it."[72] Nostalgia seemed to possess these reactions to Higginson's martial idealism; the war was far in the past, but his correspondents, old and young, still needed it.

The flood of responses to Higginson's tribute to six Harvard men among the Union dead demonstrates an abiding yearning among these Brahmins for a revival of the martial spirit, for a sense of commitment to ideals, for *meaning* amid their anxieties and ambitions in the age of capital. Higginson's speech was deeply sincere in every expression of love for his brothers, of duty and devotion, but underlying these moving messages was the idea that a good man could still be both rich and heroic. Even more, he could aspire to a higher passion and help make epic history when he understood the call of duty.

BY THE 1890s, what Oliver Wendell Holmes Jr. came to call the "Soldier's Faith" had taken hold of veterans' culture and the national reunion as a whole. On Memorial Day, May 30, 1895, Holmes delivered his extraordinarily muscular and eloquent address, "The Soldier's Faith," to the graduating class at Harvard University. The speech is at once a forceful lecture to the younger generation and a paean to war as authentic, instinctive experience. Holmes offered his young auditors a secular creed that dared them to take risks, court danger, and embrace the strenuous life. Holmes stressed the value of suffering, the "divine folly of honor," the joy of "combat and pain," and the "incommunicable experience of war" as the truest inspiration for the "passion of life." Amidst the social upheavals of the 1890s, Holmes's primary target was the perceived comfort and greed of commercial culture. "War is out of fashion," he bemoaned, "and the man who commands attention is the man of wealth. Commerce is the great power." Holmes urged the young men to a higher manliness, "to pray not for comfort, but for combat; to keep the soldier's faith against the doubts of civil life." The only time Holmes referred directly to the Civil War was to identify the former foes as the Union's instructors in a soldier's values: "These things we learned from our noble enemies in Virginia or Georgia or on the Mississippi thirty years ago." In Holmes's vision, the only enemies left by 1895 were the "temptations of wallowing ease."[73]

Rooted in this ideology of manliness and an antimodern scorn for commerce and materialism, which many veterans ironically felt deeply ambivalent about, the soldiers' reunion, both metaphorically and in reality, had become by the 1890s the dominant mode of Civil War memory. If the old soldiers could find each other, bridge every bloody chasm, and celebrate their former strenuous life, then the rest of society could follow in step. That the emancipationist legacy of the Civil War was lost amidst the celebration of a soldiers' faith and that racism never emerged as an enemy of society equal to "wallowing ease" tell us much about that epoch's memory. When the Blue and the Gray gathered for reunions, and the press and photographers swarmed to record their spectacles, they were men from a simpler and more compelling time. As new generations of Americans came of age, as millions of immigrants flooded the country's shores, and as racial hatred and violence reached unprecedented levels, the old veterans provided a mother lode of nostalgia to an age that needed escape from its cities, its boardrooms, its dangerous and confusing machines, and its economic panics. These old veterans did not fight about something fundamental to national self-definition or human freedom as much as they represented a prior heroic age, a time of authentic, romantic experience.

Such was Holmes's warning to the young in 1895. "Out of heroism," he declared, "grows faith in the worth of heroism." Holmes's veterans offered an alternative, backward-glancing faith to the age in which worries about technology emerged, religion struggled with doubt, men's and women's roles were shifting irrevocably, the struggle between labor and capital threatened to overturn the social order year in and year out, and America's racial and ethnic pluralism challenged white Protestant dominance. In famous words that captured deeper sentiments than many who experienced the overwhelmingly warlike and violent twentieth century may wish to admit, Holmes described soldiers' memory as it reached a kind of glorious repose in the late Gilded Age:

> I do not know what is true. I do not know the meaning of the universe. But in the midst of doubt, in the collapse of creeds, there is one thing I do not doubt, that no man who lives in the same world with most of us can doubt, and that is that the faith is true and adorable which leads a soldier to throw away his life in obedience to a blindly accepted duty, in a cause which he little understands, in a plan of campaign of which he does not see the use.[74]

In this church of soldiers' fraternalism, the only enemies left, by and large, were in civilian society. As American society slid slowly into a racial nightmare, most veterans on both sides were having an "adorable" reunion.

SEVEN

The Literature of Reunion and Its Discontents

Thomas Nelson Page was not lying in his eulogy of
the mammy . . . Page's feeling is honest if child-like.
I am sure that he loved his mammy to death.

—STERLING A. BROWN, "The Muted South," 1945

DURING THE LATE nineteenth century, literature was a powerful medium for reuniting the interests of Americans from both North and South. In an era of tremendous social change and anxiety, a popular literature that embraced the romance of the Lost Cause, the idyll of the Old South's plantation world of orderly and happy race relations, and the mutuality of the "soldiers' faith" flowed from mass-market magazines as well as the nation's most prominent publishing houses. The age of machines, rapid urbanization, and labor unrest produced a huge audience for a literature of escape into a pre–Civil War, exotic South that, all but "lost," was now the object of enormous nostalgia. Thousands of readers took sentimental, imaginative journeys Southward and into idealized war zones, guided and narrated by faithful slaves. But the romance of the plantation as well as of the war also bred its discontents. A small but important group of dissenters, some of them veterans and some from the postwar generation, could not escape the reality of their experience and refused to allow the nation to do so.

The story of reunion was in the air, and not all the storytellers were romantics. By the summer of 1885, the nation had watched for most of a year as its greatest living Civil War hero lay dying. The drama of Ulysses S. Grant's passing was all the more poignant because of the financial disaster he and his family had experienced in 1884. After leaving office as President and taking a celebrated world tour with his wife, Julia, and after courting but not receiving a third-term nomination by the Republicans in 1880, Grant settled into a ill-fated career as a bank president and investor. With his son, Ulysses Jr., he ventured a hundred thousand dollars in a Wall Street brokerage firm, run by a young would-be titan, Ferdinand Ward. Within two years, Ward's shady dealings brought the firm, Grant & Ward, to financial ruin. In the spring of 1884 General Grant, who occupied a fancy house just off Fifth Avenue in New York City, lived in humiliation; swindled out of his savings, he was a national charity case.[1] But the general had one more campaign to fight, and one more victory to win. During his final year, the sixty-two-year-old Grant wrote his *Personal Memoirs,* a Civil War classic and one of the best-selling books of the nineteenth century.

Amid the flood of sentimental literature about the war in the 1880s, and the growing stack of self-aggrandizing soldiers' reminiscences, Grant's two-volume *Memoirs* were unique. He wrote without flair and with an almost stoic detachment. His diction is unmarred by pompous excesses; he seems immune to the pathos embedded in so many Civil War memoirs. Critic Edmund Wilson admired how the general could write with a "propriety and purity of language." Grant does have a few scores to settle, but he does so without vindictiveness; he passes judgments on other officers' abilities, but without malice. As Wilson contended, Grant understood humiliation and failure in his own life, and he "did not care to pass humiliation on."[2] Grant's *Memoirs* stand as a great personal achievement of a dying man trying to retrieve his family's well-being, a massive best-selling work that both resisted the dominant sentimentalism of its time and promoted reconciliation. Grant's book was restrained realism in the service of reunion.

The nearly 1,100 pages of the *Memoirs* consist primarily of Grant's account of his experience in the Mexican and the Civil War. Grant told an often compelling story of his rise from his father's leather store in Galena, Illinois, to his command of the largest armies in the world. Grant portrays himself as a humble and reluctant leader; he was one of so few in his region with West Point training and war experience that he quickly rose in the ranks. That initial rise was at once a good American story and an effective literary device foreshadowing this simple Midwesterner's ascent to glory. Grant simply finds himself at war out of duty, and in command out of necessity. He implies a lack of ambition, but there is no lack of confidence conveyed in his remembrance. After an anxious Galena meeting to raise volunteers in April 1861, Grant concludes with the assurance that "I never went into our leather store after that meeting, to put up a package or do other business."[3] The reader knows the path to greatness has begun.

Grant's *Memoirs* are not without political commentary. He explained secession as the result of overzealous politicians, and he had great sympathy with the nonslaveholding Southern whites, "the young men who would have the fighting to do in case of war." "They too needed emancipation," he declared of their lack of education and need of economic uplift. "I do not know that the Southern people were to blame for this condition of affairs," Grant wrote in a tone that fit the 1880s spirit of reconciliation. He was, however, convinced of slaveowners' responsibility for secession and war. Their [slaveholders'] belief that "the ownership of slaves conferred a sort of patent of nobility—a right to govern independent of the interest . . . of those who did not hold such property" drove the country into division.[4] Grant did not pronounce any further on war guilt because his primary story was his military campaigns, which he narrated with an austere clarity and a keen sense of logistical detail.

Grant's view was from headquarters; it is the unembellished story of his decisions in an ever-enlarging panorama of war. When the Confederate commander Simon Bolivar Buckner, his three-year classmate at West Point and old friend, surrenders at Fort Donelson in the general's first great triumph of the war, Grant sidesteps the romance. We are treated to the two generals' exchange of letters (in script in the original edition), and to a brief account of their "very friendly" conversation. But Grant quickly moves on to descriptions of Southern soldiers moving in and out of Union lines, some leaving because "they had had war enough." In describing this early turning point in Northern morale (March 1862), Grant simply lets his letter to Buckner speak for itself: "No terms except an unconditional surrender can be accepted. I propose to move immediately upon your works." With that, he briefly reports: "The news of the fall of Fort Donelson caused great delight all over the North. At the South, particularly in Richmond, the effect was correspondingly depressing."[5]

Grant's eye for military detail, his command of geography, and his memory of troop placements are extraordinary, as demonstrated in his writing of the April 1863 battle of Shiloh in Tennessee. He allows himself no flourishes about the spring setting around Shiloh, the macabre clash between beauty and horror that has moved poets and novelists since. Grant's terse prose and his positioning of himself above the carnage allowed him (and his readers) to overlook some of the real war. "The very objectivity of Grant's method of de-

scribing the war always works to eliminate its tragedy," concludes Edmund
Wilson. Grant almost dropped his commander's detachment while remembering his encounter with an abandoned Confederate field hospital. "I saw
an open field in our possession on the second day, over which the Confederates had made repeated charges the day before, so covered with dead that it
would have been possible to walk across the clearing, in any direction, step-
ping on dead bodies, without a foot touching the ground."[6] The tragedy almost grips the author, but only momentarily.

In his long account of the Virginia campaign of 1864–65, Grant also
brushes close to the essential tragedy of the undertaking. Preparing his reader
for the battle of the Wilderness and the sustained killing to follow, Grant al-
ludes to the horror he could not describe. "This would not be accomplished," he wrote with fitful control, "without as desperate fighting as the
world has ever witnessed; not to be consummated in a day, a week, a month,
or a single season." To Grant, the war's aim of saving the Union made it
worth the price in human suffering. With a soldier's stoicism in retrospect,
and with suspense and homespun language, Grant set up his reader for the
final push: "We had to have hard fighting to achieve this. The two armies had
been confronting each other so long without any decisive result, that they
hardly knew which could whip."[7] Without reflecting deeply on causes, Grant
conveyed how the Civil War had become a struggle over fundamentals, a
totalizing, modern war over tragically divergent visions of America's future,
fought with enormous heroism on both sides. Grant was the professional soldier who would bludgeon and surround his enemy, whatever the price, all the
while understanding that his primary duty was to sustain the effort, however
long it took.

Some of Grant's most careful and personal writing focuses on Lee's surrender at Appomattox. It is here that Grant contributed most, perhaps unwittingly, to the culture of reconciliation in 1885. If the Lost Cause was born at
Appomattox in the dignified manner of Robert E. Lee's surrender, and in his
attribution of defeat to "superior numbers and resources," surely the spirit of
reunion was, in part, born there as well. After his historic meeting at the
McClean House where terms were exchanged, Grant ordered a cessation of
the firing of any salutes, or any other celebrations among his own army. He
insisted on no "unnecessary humiliation" of the defeated Confederates. They
"were now our prisoners, and we did not want to exult over their downfall."
Grant could hardly contain his deep admiration for Lee, who seemed "too
manly" to show his "feelings." But Grant remembered his feelings in terms

that ultimately reinforced Lost Causers, reconciliationists, and war romancers of almost any persuasion. "My own feelings," wrote Grant, "which had been quite jubilant at the receipt of his [Lee's] letter, were sad and depressed. I felt like anything rather than rejoicing at the downfall of a foe who had fought so long and valiantly, and had suffered so much for a cause, though that cause was, I believe, one of the worst for which a people ever fought, and one for which there was the least excuse. I do not question, however, the sincerity of the great mass of those who were opposed to us." Here were the terms of the American reunion rendered in probably the most oft-read chapter of one of its best-selling works: shared grief at war's costs coupled with Northern respect for the *sincerity* of Southern devotion to their cause, even when that cause was judged repugnant. The war was drained of evil, and to a great extent, of cause or political meaning. A politics of forgetting attached itself readily to the Union hero's depiction of two mystic days at Appomattox where Grant and Lee, the plebeian and the aristocrat, met "cordially" in "very pleasant conversation."[8] The reunion was a consummation forged out of soldiers' dignity—the blessed peace, surpassing politics, that Grant had driven Lee to help him forge at Appomattox. As Grant prepared to die, he mirrored the culture he was about to depart.

Grant died from throat cancer on July 22, 1885, at Mount McGregor in upstate New York, the retreat to which he had retired in his last months to finish the *Memoirs*. Gilded Age Americans desperately needed a hero, and the nation had kept vigil as the general raced against death to complete his book. New York City was Grant's final resting place; he was entombed in Riverside Park, overlooking the Hudson River. The elaborate New York funeral and the more than two weeks of press commentary between Grant's death and the day of burial produced the most extraordinary outpouring of national grief and reconciliation since the war. Twenty years after Lincoln's funeral train had passed through New York on its way to Illinois, Grant's body lay in state at the City Hall in lower Manhattan for two days, as 250,000 people filed past.[9]

New York adorned itself in mourning decorations as never before. On every street and back alley, "a hundred miles of thoroughfare blackness fluttered and swayed," remarked the *New York Times*. The great metropolis stopped in its busy tracks and reflected on the meaning of the twenty years since the war. The rich on fashionable avenues festooned their homes with all manner of tasteful drapery, public buildings competed with one another over their demonstrations of civic grief, and a lone African American bootblack living at a corner on the Upper West Side nailed a sign on the front of his small shack that read: "He Helped to Set Me Free."[10]

On August 8, as the enormous funeral pageant wound its way northward through Manhattan all the way to 125th Street, there were moments when Northerners made it clear they were burying their former leader. Some Union generals had insisted that some 17,000 Yankee veterans line Fifth Avenue as the catafalque passed. In a united movement, the old soldiers removed their hats and placed them over their hearts. Persistently, though, Grant's funeral provoked a flood of reconciliationist symbolism. The press could not stop reflecting upon the theme of reunion. "This summer finds the country in perfect peace," announced *Harper's Weekly.* "The old Slave States would not restore slavery if they could. There is a better and friendlier understanding between them and the Free States than has ever been known." In this understanding, the war had become an affair of states, and not of race and ideology. In civic proclamations and church memorials all over the country, Grant's passing was invoked as a moment of national unity. Some Confederate veterans' groups in the South passed resolutions of honor and sympathy for their former foe. And most poignantly, President Grover Cleveland, the first Democrat elected chief executive since the war, appointed the twelve pallbearers for the New York funeral, among whom were two former Confederate generals, Joseph E. Johnston and Simon Bolivar Buckner, Grant's old West Point roommate who had surrendered to him at Fort Donelson. The presence of those two former Confederate leaders as pallbearers among General William T. Sherman, General Philip Sheridan, and Admiral David Porter made a lasting mark on the memory of reunion. In Norfolk, Virginia, on the day of Grant's funeral in New York, members of the Stonewall Camp of Confederate Veterans and the Farragut Post of the Grand Army of the Republic (GAR) met in a public expression of sympathy.[11] Grant would have approved.

BY THE MID-1880S and throughout the 1890s, American culture was awash in sentimental reconciliationist literature, published especially in successful magazines. *Scribner's* and *Lippincott's* were perhaps the earliest literary pilgrims at the altar of Southern romance and Negro dialect stories, but as in its war series, *Century* took the lead by the 1880s, joined by *Harper's Weekly* and *Monthly,* in forging a widely popular literature of reunion. Many other magazines competed for the vast, often largely Northern and female, audience looking for an increasingly nostalgic depiction of American slavery and the Civil War epoch. *Cosmopolitan, McClure's*—and in the nineties, even one of the most Yankee journals of all, *Atlantic Monthly*, published in Boston—courted Southern writers and stories of the Old South.[12] In these magazines, with hundreds of thousands of subscribers, and in a host of best-selling novels as well, an American genre was reborn and Civil War memory fell into a drugged state, as though sent to an idyllic foreign land from which it has never fully found the way home.

Northern novelists had plied their readers with reconciliation themes, especially stories of the universal bravery of soldiers and intersectional kindness, well before 1880. But in the 1880s, Southern writers and themes became the darlings of American fiction as never before. With a few distinct exceptions, such as Albion Tourgée's novel about Reconstruction and the Ku Klux Klan, *A Fool's Errand* (1879), the ideological character of the war, especially the reality of emancipation, had faded from American literature. Bitterness had no place in fictions where every conflict was resolved, usually in intersectional marriages, and where life itself was portrayed in naive terms. The reality of war itself, much less its causes and consequences, remained hidden away in packaged sentiment. Real hatreds and real politics fell by the way, displaced in a flood of marriage metaphors that transformed them into romance.[13]

No writer captured with more insight the meaning and significance of this Southern offensive in the literature of the 1880s than Tourgée. Tourgée was a veteran of two enlistments in the Union army, the first in a New York regiment where his back was badly injured at the first battle of Bull Run, and the second as an officer in the 105th Ohio Volunteers, where he was wounded at the battle of Perryville in Kentucky in 1862 and later captured in Tennessee in early 1863. Tourgée spent four months in Confederate prisons and later fought at the bloody battle of Chickamauga in September 1863. These experiences, his conviction that the Union forces had indeed fought for black freedom and the dawn of racial equality, and his fateful life as a carpetbagger judge in North Carolina during Reconstruction forever shaped Tourgée's literary and political consciousness. As a novelist, and especially in much of his journalism and nonfiction, Tourgée sustained a one-man counterattack on the emerging "plantation school" of Southern literature while appealing for an emancipationist vision of the war. Indeed, Tourgée's writing provides the

literary equivalent of Frederick Douglass's oratory in the development of
Civil War memory in the late nineteenth century.[14]

"The short but eventful lifetime of the Southern Confederacy," Tourgée
wrote in an influential essay in 1888, "the downfall of slavery, and the result-
ing conditions of Southern life" had furnished American novelists their "richest and most striking material." Tourgée understood that defeat is often more
interesting than victory, loss and tragedy more compelling than success by
arms or economic prowess. Tourgée chided the "realists" for missing these
truths. As the Victorian man of letters, Tourgée declared that "pathos lies at
the bottom of all enduring fiction. Agony is the key to immortality. The ills
of fate, irreparable misfortune, untoward but unavoidable destiny: these are

Among veterans who became writers, none represented the emancipationist vision more
prolifically than Albion W. Tourgée, the author of numerous satires on reconciliation.
(Chautauqua County Historical Society, Westfield, N.Y.)

the things that make for enduring fame." The sheer "woefulness and humiliation that attended its downfall," according to Tourgée, is what made the "history of the Confederacy" so attractive in America's cultural memory. He resented the facile sentimentalism of Northern acquiescence to this romantic inducement to national forgetting. But he led the way in acknowledging its sources in the human imagination.[15]

Tourgée allowed that the South's sins had given America a more intriguing, authentically tragic, history. The South and its war were the seat of "catastrophe," and the "eternal refrain of remembered agony." By the 1880s, the South had been "glorified by disaster," as though its ruins had become America's classical past, a terrible and fascinating civilization that multitudes wished to redeem and admire because it was lost. Beguiling because so gothic, the South's evil could now be addressed as something that really did not exist. The South was "a civilization full of wonderful contrasts," said Tourgée, "horrible beyond the power of imagination to conceive in its injustice, cruelty, and barbarous debasement of a subject race." Yet failed evil fascinates, and the South remained "exquisitely charming in its assumption of pastoral purity." It even "believed," claimed the Yankee writer, "that the slave loved his chains and was all the better physically and morally for wearing them."[16] In this latter assumption a literature, and a good deal of Civil War memory, found a strange home.

In 1887, Tourgée reflected on the explosion of writing on Civil War themes. American readers had come to love the war, Tourgée contended, because by the mid-1880s the political culture had practiced a perverse combination of "oblivion" and "morbid sentimentality" about the conflict. In the interest of reconciliation, questions of "right" and "wrong" in the war and its aftermath were all but banished from political discourse during and after Reconstruction. The very essence of the war's meaning and responsibilty were, in Tourgée's view, sacrificed on the altar of reunion. The "unparalleled benignity" of the American people, he wrote, "has gone so far that there was even a tendency to forget altogether the fact that a war could not be waged for the preservation of the Union unless some one was responsible for the attempt to destroy it."[17]

In a discursive book of nonfiction, *An Appeal to Caesar* (inspired by the election of 1884, in which New York governor Grover Cleveland became the first Democrat to win the presidency since the 1850s), Tourgée laid out an elaborate critique of national forgetting about the war, as well as a vigorous call for the enforcement of black civil and political rights. As Americans revived their interest in the war itself, they seemed to believe that one side fought for a "holy principle" and the other for "sacred rights"; everybody could claim the mantle of righteousness in what Tourgée termed the "wonderful conflict." Tourgée suggested that what citizens needed to "remember of the great war of yesterday is not the battles, the marches, the conflicts,—not the courage, the suffering, the blood, *but only the causes that underlay the struggle and the results that followed from it.*" As a political advocate, he made the spirited argument that "because a people battle manfully for what they believe to be right, it does not follow that when the conflict is ended the cause of difference should be forgotten." But four years later, he virtually admitted defeat: "The man who fights and wins is only common in human esteem. The downfall of empire is always the epoch of romance." Hence Tourgée's famous realization of 1888: "not only is the epoch of the war the favorite field of American fiction today, but the Confederate soldier is the popular hero. Our literature has become not only Southern in type, but distinctly Confederate in sympathy."[18] That statement has reverberated down through the career of Civil War memory.

Tourgée's insights into Civil War memory at this pivotal juncture remain to haunt us in our own time, especially his commentary on the consequences of the reconciliationist vision for African American liberty and memory. "The Negro," he wrote, "has of late developed a capacity as a stock character of fiction which no one ever dreamed that he possessed in the good old days when he was a merchantable commodity." Blacks were cast in one of two roles, Tourgée observed. Either they were the "devoted slave who serves and sacrifices for his master and mistress," or the "poor 'nigger' to whom liberty has brought only misfortune." Indeed, the faithful slave, and his or her older cousin, the unfortunate freedman, were the star characters of sentimental plantation fiction and the sine qua non of the literature of reconciliation.[19]

Tourgée was at least one white writer who resisted the charms of such twisted visions of the past and pointed to the dire consequences for blacks. "About the Negro as a man, with hopes, fears, and aspirations like other men," he said, "our literature is very nearly silent." Worse yet, such a literature full of happy darkies, steadfastly loyal uncles and aunties, only made the burden of black memory harder to bear. Whatever the reality, slavery carried with it a social burden of shame, as well as countless personal "rankling memories of wrongs." Where could African Americans look for a noble, meaningful past? Tourgée seemed to ask with piercing honesty. "To the American Negro the past is only darkness replete with unimaginable horrors," he asserted. "Ancestors he has none." Expressing an idea that lingers in modern African American cultural memory at the beginning of the twenty-first century, Tourgée named the pain in black memory. "The remembrance of this condition is not pleasant and can never become so," he contended. "It is exasperating, galling, degrading. Every freedman's life is colored by this shadow. The farther he gets away from slavery, the more bitter and terrible will be his memory of it."[20] Tourgée may not have fully understood all the ways that black communities coped with and used their American pasts in the late nineteenth century. But by expressing their plight in relation to how they were represented in popular literature, how the passage of blacks from slavery to freedom settled into the national imagination, Tourgée identified some of the most enduring dilemmas in Civil War remembrance. He dared to say, in season and out, that the war and its aftermath were all about race.

In the 1880s and 1890s, a literary calculus was at work in sentimental fiction about the South and the war. The freedpeople and their sons and daughters were the bothersome, dangerous antithesis of the noble catastrophe that the Confederacy's war increasingly became in reminiscence and fiction. Omnipresent, growing instead of vanishing, Southern blacks had to have their place in the splendid disaster of the war, emancipation, and Reconstruction. So in the works of several widely popular writers they were rendered faithful to an old regime, as chief spokesmen for it, and often confused in—or witty critics of—the new. The old-time plantation Negro became the voice through which a transforming revolution in race relations and the remaking of the republic dissolved into fantasy and took a long holiday in the popular imagination. As a companion to "local color" literature, a genre already well cultivated by John Esten Cooke immediately after the war, the plantation tradition took center stage and swept over American literary tastes in the post-Reconstruction era.[21]

Nations build memories in the same way that religions build followings. In the wake of the war and Reconstruction, the defeated South, as well as the victorious North, needed a new religion of nationhood. The crushed South was inevitably the object of this national mission work. In political and material terms, a "New South" clearly emerged by the 1880s, with a legion of boosters, investors, and business agents leading the crusade. But the movement for a New South, and inherently therefore for sectional reconciliation, needed a mythos in which to flourish; the "new" demanded an "old" counterpoise for emotional fuel and sustenance. Religion transplants and inspires the imagination, wrote George Santayana. "The vistas it opens and the mysteries it propounds are another world to live in; and another world to live in—whether we expect ever to pass wholly over into it or no—is what we mean by having a religion."[22] The hold of the plantation legend, and the image of the faithful slave, can be understood in these terms. In the Gilded Age of teeming cities, industrialization, and political skulduggery, Americans needed another world to live in; they yearned for a more pleasing past in which to find slavery, the war, and Reconstruction.

The Virginian Thomas Nelson Page, and a host of imitators, helped resurrect just such a world. Page delivered an almost retrievable world of idyllic race relations and agrarian virtue. "Our sacred past we felt to be safe in your keeping," an admirer wrote to Page in 1888.[23] The soot of factories, the fear of new machines, the unsettling dynamism of the New South could dissipate in the rarified air of gracious, orderly, old plantations; an unheroic age could now escape to an alternative universe of gallant cavaliers and their trusted servants.

Page, who grew up on a small plantation in Hanover County, Virginia, was only twelve years old when the war ended in 1865. As grand master of pathos, nostalgia, and Negro dialect stories, Page created a world of prewar and wartime Virginia inhabited by the thoroughly stock characters of Southern gentlemen ("Marse Chan"), gracious ladies ("Meh Lady" or the "Mistis"), and the stars, the numerous Negro mammies and the unwaveringly loyal bondsmen ("Sam," "Unc' Billy", "Unc' Edinburgh," or "ole Stracted"). In virtually every story, loyal slaves reminisce about the era of slavery—"befo' de war"—before freedom left them lonely, bewildered, or ruined souls in a decaying landscape. Their function in the new order is to tell stories of the old days; they are the sacred remembrancers of the grace and harmony of the Old South. "Marse Chan: A Tale of Old Virginia" is Sam's reverent remembrance of his beloved master, with whom he went to war and then carried home to his grave on the distant hill. "Ez 'tis, I remembers it jes' like 'twuz yistiddy," says Sam. "Yo' know Marse Chan an' me—we wuz boys togerr. I wuz older'n he wuz, jes' de same ez he wuz whiter'n me." As this widely popular story warms to its theme, Sam speaks his most famous lines:

> Dem wuz good ole times, marster—de bes' Sam ever see! . . .
> Niggers didn' hed nothin' 't all to do—jes' hed to ten' to de feedin'
> an' cleanin' de hosses, an' doin' what de marster tell 'em to do; an'

In Thomas Nelson Page's story "Marse Chan: A Tale of Old Virginia" (1887), the slave boy Sam is allowed to hold his newborn "master" while his owner and a dozen other faithful slaves look on in admiration. (Drawn by W. T. Smedley, from *The Works of Thomas Nelson Page*, New York: Charles Scribner's Sons, 1912, vol. 1)

when dey wuz sick, dey had things sont 'em out de house, an' de
same doctor come to see 'em whar ten' to de white folks when dey
wuz po'ly. Dyar warn' no trouble nor nothin'.[24]

In this former Eden that Sam describes, swarms of Northern readers were introduced to a world they had all but destroyed in war.

Page's fiction, told invariably by a black voice, was one tale after another of
sectional reunion, usually through love and marriage. To thousands of
Northern readers of the 1880s and 1890s, their literary reunion was served up
with the mesmerizing and reassuring music of black dialect. Much of the
emotional impact of this literature was due to the fact that black voices narrated to white audiences the stories of courtships, of Blue-Gray fraternalism,
of reconciliation itself. A civil war among whites—the torn fabric of the nation—is mended by the wit, wisdom, and sacred memories of faithful blacks.
What whites had torn asunder they might rediscover in the language of former slaves; they needed the freedmen, after all, to remind them of what *their*
war had ruined. And the sensible freedmen made no demands of their own;
they did not even have real lives of their own to be remembered. Their "freedom" in the midst of the war became only a rarely mentioned disjuncture, a
reality only as it was refused, a strange misfortune lost in the mists of reconciliation.

In another of Page's most popular stories, "Meh Lady," an old ex-slave,
Unc' Billy, narrates a story of the war on a Virginia plantation. Billy, the
headman, and his wife, Hannah, are the indispensable, loyal slaves of "mistis"
and her daughter, Meh Lady. Battles occur nearby and the war ravages the
land. Marse Phil, the family's lone son, is killed in the Confederate army, re-
trieved from the battlefield by Billy and Meh Lady, and carried home for
burial. A Yankee officer who is distant kin happens by the plantation on his
way to a cavalry battle; the spark of romance begins between this Captain
Wilton and Meh Lady. Wilton is, of course, wounded grievously in battle,
but he survives as Billy again sets out for the bloody field, fetching and carrying him home to the care of Meh Lady. Nursed back to health, and protecting the plantation from maurauding Yankees with the family sword, Wilton
falls in love. But he must return to war, and the inevitable occurs. Richmond
falls, "mistis" goes all but mad and dies, and the plantation declines into ruin
and is almost sold. With Billy lamenting the collapse of this civilization, we
encounter the war through the eyes of loyal black Confederates: "We wuz
rich den, quarters on ev'y hill, an' niggers mo' 'n you could tell dee names;

dee used to be thirty cradlers in de harves'-fiel' an' binders mo' 'n you kin count." In the end, Wilton returns to the plantation (he was after all "half Virginian") and marries Meh Lady, who collapses in torment but relents to wed this "enemy." Billy and Hannah play matchmakers, body servants, and lone witnesses to this stock North-South wedding. "Ole Billy" gives Meh Lady away, and as the newlyweds sit on their porch in the late evening, and Billy and Hannah on theirs, the world is transformed into blissful memory and the old plantation comes back to life in a vision. Billy leaves the reader sighing: "an' de moon sort o' meltin' over de yard, an' I sort o' got to studyin', an de ain' no mo' scufflin', an' de ole times done come back ag'in . . . an' I smell de wet clover-blossoms right good."[25] In Page's stories, all the "scufflin'" was gone and the blacks were happy; national reconciliation took place in marriage vows, and there had never really been any need for racial reconciliation. The Uncle Billys of the South gave the ladies away to good Yankees. How better to forget a war about slavery than to have faithful slaves play the mediators of a white folks' reunion?

Page struck it rich in this vein of American popular memory. He became a rage on the literary circuit, and he came to represent the Southern gentleman turned author, one who defended the South's honor while his tales explicitly served national reunion. He gave readings of his dialect stories all over the North as well as the South. "You have no idea how many people in this state rejoice at your success," read a typical friend's letter from Kentucky in 1886. In Henry Grady's invitation in 1888, asking Page to headline his season of lectures by Southern authors at his new Piedmont Chautauqua in Salt Spring, Georgia, Atlanta's great promoter assured the Virginian that he had "thousands of friends" and "no more devoted constituency" than in Georgia. The sensation surrounding Page's first successful stories in *Century* prompted every major magazine editor to seek his work. H. M. Alden, the editor at *Harper's*, considered "Marse Chan" "so good" that he courted Page aggressively in 1885 and 1886 for his next stories. *Lippincott's* magazine so admired the stories that *Harper's* had managed to secure that it sought "novelettes" from Page with "enough dialect." And Charles Scribner began in 1885 to help Page convert his stories into books. Bessie Paschal Wright, a reader and critic for *Harper's*, wrote that Page had "written the most perfect Negro story of the kind in the English language—life like, pathetic, beautiful, true." And Joel Chandler Harris, emerging himself as one of greatest of black dialect writers, wrote to Page in his customary self-effacing manner. "I can but feel how crude, how awkward and unfinished are my own writings in comparison

Thomas Nelson Page was a principal creator of the Plantation School of sentimental literature about the Old South, the romance of reunion, and the mythology of faithful slaves. (From the frontispiece to *The Works of Thomas Nelson Page,* New York: Charles Scribner's Sons, 1912, vol. 12)

with the picturesque and brilliant 'Marse Chan' and the historic 'Unc' Edinburgh.' I would rather have written these two sketches than everything else that has appeared since the war—or before the war, for that matter."[26] Page both invented and rode the crest of a sentimental national reunion fashioned out of literary enterprise and his own silky brand of genteel minstrelsy.

Led by Page, most plantation romancers were proponents of the New South movement. In Page's view, what "fell upon the South" in the wake of the war was "destruction under the euphemism of reconstruction. She was crucified; bound hand and foot . . . laid away in the sepulchre . . . sealed with the seal of government, and a watch was set. The South was dead and buried, and yet she rose again." He concluded therefore, especially on the question of race, that "the New South is . . . simply the Old South with its energies directed into new lines." Page was no pure apologist for the Old South; in fact, he could be quite critical of slavery and the South's lack of literary culture, and most of his white characters had opposed secession.[27] But in his vision of the South as sacrificed on a cross of slavery, and therefore as America's chosen and redemptive region, he satisfied many of the deepest needs of the Lost Cause—a reunified nation on Southern terms, white supremacy as the means of redemption.

The works of Joel Chandler Harris, the creator of the Uncle Remus tales, present a somewhat more complicated problem in Civil War memory. Harris grew up in middle Georgia with decidedly different roots than Page. Born in 1848, the illegitimate son of a seamstress and an Irish worker who abandoned his family, Harris spent his youth in a village surrounded by black folk, slave and free. Shy and insecure about his education, he nevertheless rose from writing local humor for a Savannah newspaper to the editorship of the South's most prominent paper, the *Atlanta Constitution,* at age twenty-seven. In 1877, Uncle Remus first appeared in the paper as a fictional old black man who wandered into the *Constitution's* offices with tales of the city. Quickly, though, Harris invented another venue for Remus: the old man told stories in a country setting to a small white boy about plantation life before the war. Remus was a rapid sensation. In 1879, Harris first had Remus tell stories of "Mr. Rabbit and Mr. Fox." In allegories of the triumph of agility over strength, of guile over privilege, the trickster over the whole world of power, Brer Rabbit became one of the most popular characters to emerge from nineteenth-century American literature. By 1880, Harris's collection *Uncle Remus: His Songs and Sayings* was published to national and international acclaim.[28]

In his dialect tales, as well as his short stories, Harris wrote about white yeoman farmers, free blacks, and even fugitive slaves. Harris was certainly a romancer in his depiction of plantation life, but his stories are largely not about cavaliers and moonlight swooning. He was certainly a proponent of reconciliation on mostly Southern terms, but Harris's targets were also the greed and industrialism of the New South. He seemed to favor progress of a sort, but preferred that it remain agricultural and pastoral. His heroes were more often yeomen than planters and colonels. Most important of all, he infused the literary reunion with the authority of Uncle Remus's voice. First published in 1877 as "Uncle Remus as a Rebel," but then in 1880 in *Uncle Remus: His Songs and Sayings* as "A Story of the War," Harris rendered a classic tale of reconciliation. Indeed, in this short story, published in the number one best-selling book of 1880, Harris may have set the literary tone for the reconciliationist eighties.[29]

In the original newspaper version of the story, Remus protects the plantation in Georgia as the Yankees come. Remus shoots and kills a Yankee sharpshooter, John Huntingdon, who is about to kill his master, "Mars Jeems." But in the much more widely read 1880 version, the Yankee is only wounded and loses an arm. Remus helps nurse and save Huntingdon, who then marries Miss Sally, Mars Jeems's sister. The story is being told in 1870 for Miss Theodosia Huntingdon of Burlington, Vermont, the visiting sister of the saved Yankee. In this postwar setting, Remus now lives in Atlanta, the employee of the Huntingdons. Remus's day as a "famous warrior" becomes the perfect Southern recipe for reconciliation. Remus is a thoroughly faithful slave who defends his white folks; he astonishes the Vermonter as he "spoke from the standpoint of a Southerner." Miss Theodosia further indignantly queries: "you shot the Union soldier, when you knew he was fighting for your freedom?" Remus admits that "cole chills run up my back" when he saw his predicament, but when he thought that "Mars Jeems guine home ter Ole Miss en Miss Sally, I des disremembered all 'bout freedom en lammed aloose."[30] Remus saves the Confederate family, saves the Union soldier whom he has wounded as a loyal rebel, and then gives himself and his labor to all in happy reunion. Uncle Remus, therefore, was the ultimate Civil War veteran—he fought on both sides, he saved the Union, and as the old representative of his race, he demanded nothing in return.

Perhaps most poignantly, the "little boy" to whom all the Brer Rabbit stories were told is the son of the North-South marriage that Remus had so deftly arranged. Harris's artistic achievement was to create a world where on the one hand the Civil War never really needed to have happened, but on the other, all the deception, cunning, and bare-bones competition the underdogs of life could muster was necessary for their very survival. In the Gilded Age, millions of Americans who were becoming more endeared to the South as their source of nostalgia needed to believe in both premises. They needed increasingly to believe that their terrible war had little to do with race. But at the same time, they needed melodious black voices telling them tales of a little creature's heroism against the forces of power and privilege. Uncle Remus delivered both messages.

Harris sustained the reconciliation theme in many other ways over the course of the 1880s and 1890s. Black loyalty to masters, to home places, and even to the South is a primary theme for Harris. In an 1891 story, Harris has a runaway slave named Ananias, who has fought in the Union army, return to his old plantation in Georgia because he "bin brung up right dar, suh—right 'longside er Marster en my young mistis." The fully realized independence of blacks is simply impossible in Harris's vision of the postwar South. In "An Ambuscade," a faithful slave named Plato carries his wounded master, Jack Kilpatrick, home from the battlefield to the family plantation. Kilpatrick and a Yankee sharpshooter, an Irishman named O'Halloran, had traded supplies between the lines. After the fall of Atlanta, the lines of the armies seem to be quite fluid in central Georgia. A Union surgeon, Pruden, dresses the Confederate's wounds, and the combination of loyal slave, Yankee doctor, Irish-Union soldier, and the suffering one's sister, Flora, bring the lad back to life. The doctor, believing he is caring for a wounded Union soldier, falls in love with the tender and caring Flora and they ultimately marry.[31] Love conquered war, loyalty prevailed over emancipation, and an Irish brogue provided the comic relief in a story where all kinds of reconciliations were plausible.

In "The Comedy of War," Harris places Private O'Halloran again at the center of an explicitly reconciliationist story. He and the Confederate, Kilpatrick, exchange sharpshooter's fire until they arrange a regularized rendevous for the trade of tobacco and coffee between the lines. As both armies amass for what may be a battle on the farm of Squire Fambrough, who has a son fighting in each army, Harris delivers every stock image of reconciliation. In the climactic scene, the two Fambrough brothers find each other on their own father's land, and their sister, fair Julia, finds a lover and future husband in a dashing Confederate Lieutenant named Clopton, whose loyal body servant, Tuck, is searching the countryside for his master to provide him food and clothing. The soldiers are all part of the O'Halloran-Kilpatrick scheme of Blue-Gray commerce as they encounter the incensed Squire Fambrough and his daughter. Tuck appears and discovers his long sought "Marse Dave Henry," and father, brothers, and sister all meet tearfully as O'Halloran complains that "soon the cousins will be poppin' out from under the bushes" in this "family orgie." "Me an' this Johnny will just go an' complate the transaction of swappin'," scoffs the Irish Yankee.[32]

As Tuck, the slave, joins the scene, he relishes some of the coffee beans about to be swapped. Then, just before a courier rides through announcing that "Lee has surrendered!" Harris provides the clinching reconciliation scene:

> The Irishman regarded the negro with curiosity. Then taking the dead branch of a tree he drew a line several yards in length between himself and Kilpatrick.
>
> "D 'ye see that line there?" he said to the negro.
>
> "Dat are mark? Oh, yasser, I sees de mark."
>
> "Very well. On that side of the line you are in slavery—on this side the line you are free."
>
> "Who? Me?"
>
> "Who else but you?"
>
> "I been hear talk er freedom, but I ain't seed 'er yit, an' I dunner how she feel." The negro scratched his head and grinned expectantly.
>
> "'Tis as I tell you," said the Irishman.
>
> "I b'lieve I'll step 'cross an' see how she feel." The negro stepped over the line, and walked up and down as if to test the matter physically.
>
> "'T ain't needer no hotter ner no colder on dis side dan what 't is on dat," he remarked. Then he cried out to his young master: "Look at me, Marse Dave Henry; I'm free now."

The young Confederate was reading a letter brought him by Tuck from his mother. "All right," he replies, waving his hand to the slave without taking his eyes off the letter. "He take it mos' too easy fer ter suit me," says Tuck. Then he calls out one final time to Clopton: "Oh Marse Dave Henry! Don't you tell mistiss dat I been free, kaze she'll take a bresh-broom an' run me off'n de place when I go back home." In the voices of an Irish brogue and an African American slave dialect, the reader is treated to the fullest, if fanciful, of all reconciliations: the Union restored, emancipation noted with the wave of a hand, warriors as brothers again, and the Irish and the blacks telling the stories. Harris may have meant these stories to entertain, but he surely sought to paint his own pictures of reunion as well, to provide the culture of reconciliation, as he says in one of the section headings of "The Comedy of War," with a strong dose of "commerce and sentiment."[33]

NOSTALGIA FOR slavery times and for the war epoch did not come only from the pens of Southern writers and the popular magazines that promoted the literature about Dixie. Some Northerners were attracted to yet other mythologies about the place of slavery in Civil War memory. Such was the crusade by the 1890s, led by an Ohio university professor, to collect the lore of the Underground Railroad. In reality, the alleged network of "depots" and "conductors" by which fugitive slaves excaped to freedom in the North and in Canada had never been as elaborate as legend portrayed it. Blacks themselves, in cooperation with Quakers and other white abolitionists, especially in eastern cities and out on the long border between slavery and freedom, had been the primary operatives of clandestine escape. There were many heroic whites involved in what is called Underground Railroad activity, but the self-willed heroism of black fugitives, their families, and their accomplices in "vigilance committees" has never quite broken through the mythic coating surrounding this story. Such realities have never deterred the apparently infinite need in American society to believe in an organized, secretive crusade by whites and blacks together to free slaves in the antebellum era.[34]

In 1892, Wilbur Siebert, a young history instructor at Ohio State University, began his personal quest to collect and record the story of what he called "the Road." Siebert's passion for the story of the Underground Railroad materialized in thousands of circular letters he mailed out all over the Northern states, soliciting recollections of or information about the famous clandestine traffic. In these letters, Siebert asked his correspondents for names, routes, incidents of escapes, and general reflections on the character of the system.[35] Over time he compiled some thirty-eight large scrapbooks containing the wealth of information sent to him. In 1898, he published his popular book, *The Underground Railroad*, which promoted the history and the legend of this central abolitionist story. Siebert's book, along with the collection process that produced it, reflected the sentimental retrospection of many Northerners as the century came to a close.

Siebert's work is less about the creation of reunion literature per se than about the scope and character of the audience for romantic memory of the Civil War era. He tapped into a vast reservoir of Northerners eager to claim their places, or that of their parents, in a heroic legacy, this time not so much as soldiers in the war, but as veterans of the "old liberty life guard," as one Connecticut man called his father. In his book, Siebert defended the use of reminiscence as a historical source, especially when such material was collected from abolitionists. He believed that the work of "old time abolitionists" with fugitive slaves fleeing to freedom would be too dramatic to be forgotten. "Not only did repetition serve to deepen the general recollections of the average operator, but the strange and romantic character of his unlawful business helped to fix them in his mind."[36] Relying on this dubious theory of memory, Siebert fashioned this popular American story. In one escape after another where "valuable pieces of ebony" were hidden in caves, attics, garrets, haymows, and cellars, where helpless fugitives were saved and shown the North Star at midnight by heroic station keepers, and where duped slave catchers were always sent just off course, Siebert cultivated Northerners' desires to participate in the reminiscence industry. One Iowa correspondent sent a long handwritten sketch proclaiming the Underground Railroad as the new source of romance, one sure to "furnish a rich field in which to delve for genuine material with which to adorn the historic page." The story, said the Iowan, as though writing a promotional advertisement, would "thrill the heart and quicken the pulse of the eager student of the grand progressive movement of human liberty in the past" and furnish "hairbreath escapes, perilous journies by land and water, incredible human suffering" for a wide readership.[37]

Siebert also collected existing literature from local newspapers and journals, which itself provided a trove of published reminiscence literature. He drew upon a long series of Underground Railroad recollections in 1893–94 in newspapers all over the Middle West. Local pride is always at stake in Underground Railroad lore. Is there a county from Massachusetts to Iowa that does not claim to have one or more "depots"? This all started in the 1890s as the legend took hold of the American imagination. Lucy Maynard Salmon wrote to Siebert from Vassar College, describing a visit to her uncle in Illinois when she "was shown an old attic where the negroes were concealed. He told me he could recall some thirty-seven (I think) different persons he had aided in escaping." Such was Siebert's evidence. Many respondents sent the professor hand-drawn maps of counties, regions, and townships where those coveted "routes" had carried fugitives to freedom. Town newspapers in various states ran stories about their local connections and heroes of the fugitive slave traffic.[38] An existing "literature" on the Underground Railroad, therefore, already abounded before Siebert primed the pump of reminiscence among ordinary people.

Several themes emerge in the responses Siebert prompted. Many correspondents engaged in filial piety. "My father's house was always a hiding place for the fugitive from slavery," wrote an Illinoisan in 1896. "Many were the trials and hardships these abolitionists endured and narrow escapes in carrying fugitives from one place to another." The beknighted conductors were the heroes of the narratives that filled the letters to Siebert. A Connecticut man, Erastus Blakeslee, eulogized his father: "If there was anything in his whole career of which he may have been said to be proud of in his old age, it was his connection with the antislavery movement." Blakeslee assured Siebert that his "father and mother always received" fugitives with the "greatest kindness." Siebert got what he wanted: repeated stories about the good and the true—humanity helping humanity. There is much truth embedded in these tributes. But there are also many self-serving tall tales, and a late Gilded Age yearning to bask in the moral glow of the old abolitionist generation. A seventy-three-year-old man, H. D. Platt, wrote to Siebert from Nebraska in 1896, rejoicing in the "memories of a holy life left by our godly parents." He relished the chance to declare his "fascination about the 'UGRR' biz. that fires me up."[39]

Without question, one of the true white heroes of the movement was Calvin Fairbank, an Ohioan who made numerous raids into Kentucky to lead fugitive slaves to freedom. He was captured and imprisoned more than seventeen years in Kentucky jails, where he received, reportedly, thousands of lashes. Released in 1864, Fairbank lived a long life and wrote a memoir in 1890. In 1897, the *Boston Transcript* printed excerpts of the narrative, feeling assured that "among the people, so multitudinous in these days, eager to claim antislavery descent and to aver that their parents and grandparents were assistants on the Underground Railroad, there ought to be sufficient customers for Calvin Fairbank's book to exhaust the edition in a week."[40] Indeed, Siebert's quest to record this story demonstrated for all time the need of Americans to claim literal or symbolic "descent" from the glory of the Underground Railroad. In retrospect at least, the Northern culture of reconciliation needed its antislavery past; the two impulses were complementary components of the doctrine of progress.

Many of those who answered the professor's call were seeking what we might call an alternative veteranhood. For women and civilian men, it was a way of saying that they too had served in the great cause. For some, homespun tales of helping slaves escape may have been a kind of white alternative slave narrative, a mode of participating in a literary tradition. As in soldiers' battle narratives, alleged Underground Railroad operatives recited their battles with slave catchers, and they remembered virtually no defeats. One Ohioan sent a copy of a paper he had written for a history class at Harvard in which he claimed "there were men and women there who would have burned at the stake rather than refuse aid to fugitives."[41]

Such living martyrs were everywhere in the story as Siebert collected it. These soldiers had fought with pitchforks and cleverness, and sometimes with old flintlocks. A local heroine of Adams County, Ohio, was remembered for resisting slave hunters with "a kettle of boiling water on the stove as her only means of defense." Many rescuers were themselves portrayed as victims who overcame their adversaries, and invariably, outwitted the sluggish slave catchers, who were sometimes put up for the night while their horses rest. In the morning the horses are lathered and weak because they had been used through the night to spirit fugitives northward. A story from Marysville, Ohio, of a "fearless and uncompromising abolitionist," Udney H. Hyde, confirms the symbolic link to veteranhood. Hyde's leadership of hair-raising rescues of fugitives provided "one of the causes" of the Civil War, argued an 1897 article sent to Siebert. Although Hyde "was not a soldier" in the war, his two sons "fought clear through it." The elder Hyde, concluded the article, deserved "a recompense as so many of our brave boys in blue are so deservedly receiving today."[42] Siebert struck a chord of nostalgia so deep that it is sometimes difficult to separate truly heroic abolitionism from romantic adventure stories.

What is clear is that many of Siebert's respondents used their chance to reminisce as a means of displacing conflicted racial assumptions and anxieties. Some just enjoyed telling their own versions of darky stories—tales of helpless black vagabonds, rescued in comic, keystone cops style from hapless slave hunters. Some wrote as though mimicking the routines of minstrel shows. From Illinois, George Churchill delivered a version of the typical escape story: "A slave would somehow learn that if he would cross the Mississippi on a certain night at a certain place, that he would see a white man who would immediately start to run or walk away from the black man, who followed his leader like a dog and always in a path that led safely past the wrong places and to safe stations." Then came the punch line: "If caught the white man was escaping from his black pursuer who might have been a robber." By asking for "incidents," Siebert received more than one blackface story. One reminiscer broke with form and told of a venal ancestor, a grandfather who would catch fugitive slaves and sell them back into slavery for money. "Many people knew of grandfather's capturing runaways," wrote H. C. Pemberton from Cleveland, "and one . . . conceived a scheme to get him in trouble." The noble soul blackened his face to deceive the old man, thereby turning the tables and reversing the capture scene. H. D. Platt sent his version of comic relief in a tale of a neighbor who tried to discover the "four 'big Niggers' hiding in our house." "Disguised with burnt cork as a fugitive," the neighbor tried to gain admittance, and presumably, become one of the slaves. Later the "fixed up 'nigger'" is himself revealed as he washes his hands and face.[43] Some whites enjoyed telling of their first experiences of "slumming it," and inadvertently showed what their imaginations owed to blackface minstrelsy.

Masking and role reversal stories fascinated these creators of Underground Railroad lore, and many relished telling about having "a great deal of fun" saving "the darkies." From Hillsboro, Ohio, arrived a long tale of "conductors and brakemen" who "managed to get some amusement" in the midst of their "serious business" of freeing fugitives by reversing roles; they would "play the Kentuckian" on a "new found abolitionist" in the region, accusing their new neighbor of "stealing niggers" and "abolition lies" until just the right moment to reveal the trick. Perhaps borrowing from Joel Chandler Harris's story, "Free Joe and the Rest of the World," one writer described a grandmother telling fireside stories of "Old Black Joe" to her young granddaughters. Joe had escaped to freedom in Canada earlier through the help of this very woman (now the grandmother). He returned, asking for shelter, and the woman, not knowing it is really Joe, allows him to stay with hesitation and fear about black criminals. During the night a robber dressed in a black mask invades the house. The old woman faints as Joe saves her and the homestead from the evil white robber in black mask.[44]

To his credit, Siebert did not exploit the racial elements of the stories he collected. But the raw material does reveal an interesting racial dimension in Northern Civil War memory among Siebert's correspondents. The minstrel show character "Jim Crow," ragged, grotesque, even barbaric, seems to have dominated their memories when they characterized the fugitive slaves they assisted to freedom. Rarely were the fugitives ever named; they were usually a subjective mass of dark folk, still somehow associated with a plantation world. Some respondents showed an extraordinary fascination with miscegenation, with "white" slaves and mulatto runaways. A woman in Iowa was especially content to have helped a mulatto youngster to freedom. As he rode in the wagon with her, she was "struck with . . . his great pathetic eyes so common in the mixed bloods . . ., and I was more rejoiced to be aiding him on his road to freedom than . . . had he been a coarse and stolid specimen such as we sometimes met."[45] The trope of the tragic mulatto enervated a kind of Civil War memory where solving racial questions seemed remote compared to marching in the cavalcade of national reunion.

The mimicry of slaves, especially the use of blackface, served emotional needs among whites. The audience of a minstrel show, wrote Nathan Huggins, "had ingrained in its imagination a view of the Negro that was comic and pathetic. The theatrical darky was childlike; he could be duped into the most idiotic and foolish schemes; but like a child too, innocence would protect him and turn the tables on the schemers." In the stories sent to Siebert, the schemers are vanquished by the cleverness and courage of the rescuers, combined with the natural innocence of the fugitive slaves. Alive in remembrance of Underground Railroad days was this need among white Americans to displace a whole variety of pent-up anxieties about achievement, striving, success, and responsibility, which were made only more acute by the business culture of the Gilded Age. The minstrel darkies had, by definition, violated all rules of stage decorum. They were, as Huggins wrote, "loose and undisciplined creatures of appetite." They were bizarre in movement and voice. Perhaps by the 1890s, amidst the racial tensions of the emerging Jim Crow society, this is what the fugitive slave of yore had become in some sectors of Civil War memory—a symbol of secret warfare against convention, manners, propriety, even law and order. Perhaps they offered what people want from nostalgia—what Huggins called a "pleasurable escape into naturalness."[46]

It is striking to note how many of the Siebert respondents emphasize that their efforts, and those of the Union cause in the war, *permanently* destroyed slavery and its related problems. In Underground Railroad reminiscence, it was as if the victory had long been won and the race problem banished by emancipation. After providing a tale of a black woman who had "passed in my care," who swam the Mississippi River avoiding "alligators" because "they thought she was one," and who exuded "African heathenism," Willis Boughton, a professor at Ohio University, concluded his letter: "I thank God it's all over now." After remembering for Siebert how "our hearts have ached" so many times over "the terrible revolting things connected with American slavery," Mrs. Levi Monse Gould concluded with a typical flourish: "But thank God we have lived to see the curse removed from our fair land, though it came through a *baptism of blood* . . . Thank God too for the Emancipation Proclamation of our devoted Abraham Lincoln, which struck the shackles of slavery from four million human beings, and now they no more need an Underground R. R. to liberty—*they are free*."[47]

Siebert was well warned in the letters not to believe much of what was written in county histories, nor to rely heavily on the fallible memories of old people. But he filled his scrapbooks nonetheless and wrote his history; there were so many good-hearted folk determined to claim their antislavery credentials that the professor could not resist their appeal. Even ex-President Rutherford B. Hayes responded, giving Siebert an interview in 1893. Hayes was proud of being one of the "young lawyers" who had defended fugitive slaves in Ohio. With a sense of finality and nostalgia, Hayes remembered approximately forty cases and told Siebert that "during three or four winters this thing was an important part of my life." Many respondents claimed a closeness to John Brown and his various travels through the Middle West, and even more remembered the Underground Railroad through scenes of *Uncle Tom's Cabin*, often declaring personal knowledge of incidents that Harriet Beecher Stowe made famous in the novel.[48] All of this adds up to a mythos of accomplished glory, a history of emancipation completed. For so many of his correspondents, Siebert had offered an opportunity to stroll down memory lane, to open a closed book of joyful, even amusing, experience. Only rarely did the story of the Underground Railroad emerge in his research as a struggle over race that continued in a new time. Not only had reunion trumped race, but the war itself had bludgeoned the problem of slavery out of history. In the nineties, the story of slavery and its destruction had become the subject of nostalgia, of self-congratulatory adventure tales. Masked in this comforting haze was a real history of Underground Railroad heroism, as well as the deteriorating condition of American race relations.

SENTIMENTALISM was a hard spell to break. American readers, wrote Edmund Wilson, did not want "to be shown the realities" of either the war itself or the unresolved torment of racial oppression. In Wilson's words, an understanding seemed to rule American popular fiction: "the old issues must be put to sleep with the chloroform of magazine prose." Against this thick growth of the romance of reunion, literary *realism* tried to get traction. As the arbiter of a new realism, first as editor of *Atlantic Monthly* and then of *Harper's Monthly* by the late 1880s, William Dean Howells tried to lead the public imagination away from highbrow taste and convention to allow the stories and dialects of the lowly—the "real" people—to have center place in American fiction. Howells believed that much of sentimentalism was "false" to the people it depicted. As though he had Thomas Nelson Page and his legion of admirers in mind, Howells disdained novels "that merely tickle our prejudices and lull our judgment, or that coddle our sensibilities, or pamper our gross appetites for the marvelous."[49]

From 1886 to 1892, in his "Editor's Study" section of *Harper's*, Howells kept up a remarkable critical assault on sentimentalists. "It's fun, having one's open say . . . and banging the babes of romance about," he wrote to a friend just after beginning the column. "Realism," wrote Howells in 1889, "is nothing more and nothing less than the truthful treatment of material." No subject should remain taboo to realism, according to Howells. "Nothing God has made," he said in 1886, "is unworthy of notice." The realist's "soul" should be "exalted, not by vain shows and shadows and ideals, but by realities, in which alone the truth lives." Having just read S. Weir Mitchell's *In War Time* (1885), in which the doctor who had treated so many victims of the war sympathetically created the character of a "coward," Howells wrote his friend admiringly. "The thing is done wonderfully," he told Mitchell. "I don't care for what people call 'art'; I like nearness to life, and this is life, portrayed with conscience, with knowledge . . . and with a most satisfying . . . simplicity and clearness, which is the only 'art' worth having." In his public column, which hardly fit the same imperatives driving the *Century* war series emerging at the same time, Howells gushed at how Mitchell had done "justice to the gentleness that goes with the timidity" of a "cowardly nature."[50] How the epic campaigns, or stories of leadership and valor, could fit together in the same popular remembrance with the full range of emotion and terror caused by modern war, including cowardice, has always been a paradox in Civil War memory. Our first modern war did not spawn a fully modern literary memory.

For realism to truly engage the Civil War and its aftermath required writers to grapple with an overwhelming array of what Daniel Aaron called "uncongenial truth" about the struggle. Most writers resisted this imperative. Realistic writers seemed to know that they had fought a modern war full of savagery on both sides, but that reconciliation dictated deflection of such terrors. The greater urge was to conceal or forget altogether the horror of the war and celebrate a reunified nation. The horror that remained in the imagination was that which the soldiers could own, quietly, in their hearts or at small veterans' post meetings. In the words of Englishman John Ruskin, who was appalled at the level of destruction in the Civil War, Americans came to write about their Armageddon as though they were "washing their hands in blood and whistling."[51]

Those realist writers who did struggle to portray what they had experienced in combat tried to counter the "epauletted history" written by famous generals. In his sprawling novel *Figs and Thistles* (1879), Albion Tourgée wrote from the limited angle of the common soldier. As he began his account of the experience of his character Markham Churr in the first battle of Bull Run, Tourgée acknowledged that "the soldier's story of the battle is . . . only the tale of his own day's fighting. Madame History takes no account of anything less than a Colonel, rarely coming below a General." At home in Ohio, convalescing from wounds he received at Bull Run, Markham tells his tales of battle to friends and neighbors. Markham remembers his first awareness of "real, earnest war," which emerged as he watched two fellow soldiers "whipped" for desertion. "Trembling like a leaf" while marching into battle on that July morning near Manassas, Markham speaks in romantic tones about the beauty of nature's settings, now invaded by armies and screaming shells. A stream his regiment fords "sparkled and glowed beneath the sun like molten silver." Tourgée mixed a romantic style with realist aims as he described battle. Cannon shots "whizzed by so near I could almost have reached it with my hand," Markham recalls. When a shell hits his men, he hears a "strange, dull thud, some half-uttered groans. Something warm splashed up in my face. There was a horrible sickness in my heart." Thus bloodied, Tourgée recollects through Markham the bravery and chaotic retreat of that first major battle of the war. Embedded in this autobiographical-fictional battle narrative is Tourgée's reflection on the noise and the silence of combat. As though he were trying to capture the helplessness of all soldiers in the face of modern warfare, Tourgée spoke as the writer nearly muted by horrible experience:

> The roar of battle is over and above the soldier, but with him who fights there is a sort of silence which seems all the more terrible from the fact that it seems unnatural. You hear what a comrade says when he is stricken; you answer an inquiry of one on your right . . . and of one on your left, without for a moment ceasing to

fire. The roar of battle is terrible, but its silence is still more fearful. The turmoil is above and about the soldier, but the silence with him and of him. So too, he does not see everything that is being done in the range of his vision, but the few things which his eyes note are photographed on his memory forever.[52]

Many critics have contended that in Victorian America, Civil War veterans who turned authors simply could not comprehend or describe the reality of what they had experienced in war. But there certainly was no lack of fascination with battle. The younger nonveteran Stephen Crane was obsessed with it. Crane's great work, *The Red Badge of Courage* (1895), in critic Thomas Leonard's view, epitomized the realists who were "connoisseurs of the violence endured, but not of the violence inflicted." It should not surprise us, though, that few American writers about the war penetrated outward from the shell of sentimentalism that enveloped American letters by the 1890s. The pressures of a reinvigorated manliness and a new patriotism in the industrial age, the cluster of ideas fueling the Holmesian version of soldiers' memory, and the overpowering culture of reconciliation forged around veterans made a modernist, disillusioned literature of war unlikely in the Gilded Age. Tourgée's commentary on the noise and silence induced by combat left a telling reminder of one of the war's deepest legacies: he could neither forget nor fully recapture the actual war he had helped make. Although the larger culture would stomach endless stories about manly character in the face of battle, it did not much wish to hear about the war's political meanings and legacies. The American reunion could only afford to incorporate a small allotment of blood and terror into its story of renewal and mutual glory. The Henry Flemings who ran from battle, as in Crane's *Red Badge*, had to come back to their regiments; the initiation to war was more important than its long-term ravages, more enduring than the war's consequences.[53]

Crane, who was born six years after the Civil War, had an insatiable craving to discover the connections between imagined and real war. But *Red Badge* is hardly a naturalistic depiction of war. Instead it renders the interior, psychological struggle of a young private with his own vainglorious terror of battle, with his "thousand-tongued fear." The story is far more metaphorical than realistic. The work broke with conventions of sentimentalism in a host of ways. But Crane does not describe war; instead, he fashions a series of compelling images drawn especially from nature. The vast armies are like "serpents crawling from the cavern of night," tents were "strange plants" springing from the ground, and campfires and bursting shells are war's "blossoms." When Henry Fleming seeks refuge in a "chapel"-like grove in the forest after running from battle, he pushes aside the "green doors," steps on to "pine needles . . . a gentle brown carpet," and is confronted with the grotesque corpse of a soldier. Crane mocks the sentiment and pretensions of heroism in battle while telling a tale of a young man's initiation to manhood. In *Red Badge*, as well as in a series of short stories that Crane wrote on Civil War subjects, causes and ideology are absent. But he gave to literary Civil War memory the most probing and ironic treatment of the individual's confrontation with fear—fear of physical destruction, of shame and cowardice, of those terrible "mountains" of life itself, as Crane put it, that people just cannot climb. He also injected a dose of honesty into the late-nineteenth-century's manly quest for self-justifying wounds. In a short story, "The Veteran" (1896), Crane portrays Henry Fleming as an old man, surrounded by eager and impressionable young men. They want to know what battle was like: "The veteran looked down and grinned. Observing his manner, the entire group tittered. 'Well, I guess I was . . . pretty well scared sometimes. Why in my first battle I thought the sky was falling down. I thought the world was coming to an end. You bet I was scared.'"[54]

In narratives and reminiscence—as well as in fiction—realism, and sometimes disillusionment, did burst through in the writings of some veteran-authors. "Realities of War," a piece published in 1881 in a soldiers' paper, *The Veteran*, quoted at length from an unidentified "popular writer" about the grim results of infantry charging cannon. The "roar" of a cannonade "shuts out all sound from a battle-line three miles long," declared the writer. "Shrieking" shells "hunt out, and shatter, and mangle men until their corpses cannot be recognized as human." With prurient realism, the writer described "men's legs and heads . . . torn from bodies, and bodies cut in two." After these characterizations of battle, the author abruptly declares: "For what! . . . men cannot pass from caisson to gun without climbing over rows of dead. Every gun and wheel is smeared with blood; every foot of grass has its horrible stain. Historians write of the glory of war. Burial parties saw *murder*." Moreover, in the best of soldiers' memoirs, moments of realistic description slip through the controlled style of the campaign narrative. In Edward Porter Alexander's *Military Memoirs of a Confederate* (1907), he could not resist a substantial aside on the wintertime suffering of his men during the Chickamauga campaign of December 1863. So desperate were Confederate troops for shoes for both men and horses that Alexander described men dragging dead animals out of a river and stripping the hoofs for shoes and nails. "Our men were nearly as badly off," remembered Alexander. "I have seen bloody stains left on frozen ground where our infantry had passed. In the artillery we took the shoes from the feet of the drivers to give to the cannoneers who had to march."[55]

But few Civil War novelists wrote from the perspective of burial parties or blood-stained grass and snow. One has to look hard for these kinds of battle descriptions; they emerge only infrequently from the underside of reminiscence literature and veterans' commentaries. By 1905, as though responding to Holmes's "Soldiers' Faith" or Theodore Roosevelt's cravings for war, an Illinois veteran, E. J. Harkness, delivered a decidedly antiwar sketch to his organization. "Not all the glamour and glitter with which poets, historians and orators have invested war can disguise its real character," wrote Harkness. "In its last analysis war is an appeal from reason to the brute in man, and however lofty the principles at stake, the reflex influence of actual warfare upon man is most demoralizing. War is the enemy of all social order . . . It is chiefly for its effect on human character and its disregard of human life that war is to be deplored." Such an expression was rare in soldiers' reminiscence at the turn of the century. It was all but nonexistent at veterans' reunions. It may have been tempered by the Spanish-American War and America's bloody guerrilla war in the Phillipines by the time Harkness wrote his reflections. His audience was, of course, tiny. But it demonstrates that such attitudes toward war did emerge among Civil War veterans, and some committed them to paper. Harkness fully acknowledged the "sublime heroism" of soldiers on both sides, and insisted that the Union cause was completely "justified." But with uncommon circumspection, this former union major cautioned that "all human estimate must fail" in ultimately judging the meaning and the "cost" of the Civil War.[56]

On a more popular level, readers could find ample horror and realism, if they so chose, in the prison narratives published in several waves after the war. The first wave came in the war's immediate aftermath (1865–66), when some twenty-six published accounts of prison experience appeared. Most of these were stories of Confederate atrocity against Union soldiers. Narratives continued to be published through the 1870s, although in smaller numbers. A second cluster of prison accounts appeared in the 1880s in conjunction with debates over increasing Union veterans' pensions. John Ransom's widely read narrative, based on a fabricated diary he claimed to have kept in Andersonville, appeared in 1881. Ransom had lost his teeth due to the scurvy he had contracted in prison, and he lobbied Congress to allow pensions to any veteran who could prove he had been confined as a Confederate prisoner. A third wave of narratives emanated from *Century* magazine between 1889 and 1891, as the success of the war series gave its editors the confidence to enter into such a controversial subject despite their reconciliationist stand. The several prison narratives published in *Century* proved only a mixed success, because virtually no one could write about such experiences in a nonpartisan way. The pieces tended toward adventurous escape themes rather than scenes of pestilence and death. In his 1890 account, T. H. Mann acknowledged he had revised his original version, "leaving out much of its bitterness, and nearly all the explosive adjectives."[57]

But those readers who wanted their fill of realistic prison suffering could turn to a huge collection of narratives published in 1890. In *Prisoners of War and Military Prisons,* all manner of stories emerged—escape, intrigue, theft, heroism, and venality. Many prison narratives included tales of slaves helping white soldiers escape through the Southern countryside, often taking the form of "darky" and "sambo" stories, where the blacks are alternately comical, faithful, and devious. Many Yankee soldiers likened themselves to slaves, even to the victims of the Middle Passage of the Atlantic slave trade. By seeing the underside of Southern society under great duress, many Northern prisoners came to fear that they had themselves become the "niggers."[58]

Above all, readers of the 1890 collection encountered one description after another of the war's suffering. A screaming man, "gangrened . . . his body near the wound filled with maggots" and denied amputation by a Confederate surgeon, was a typical story. The book abounds with descriptions of half-dead men released to Sanitary Commission officials. Such "awful reality" included one group thus depicted: "Some had become insane; their wild gaze and clenched teeth convinced the observer that reason had fled; others were idiotic; a few were lying in spasms . . . the hair of some was matted together, like beasts of the stall which lie down in their own filth. Vermin were over them in abundance."[59] If descriptions of blind, ulcerated, and demented men moving from life to death constitute realism, then by the 1890s such tales were certainly available to American readers. Most readers were clearly more attracted to Page's faithful slaves or stories of soldiers' heroism. But on the underside of the literary reunion festered this refuse of discontent and disillusion. In the culture of reconciliation and new nationalism, there were still too many hospital and prison sketches lying around for comfort, many of them published, and still others that lurked as spirits in the heads of veterans.

No one wrote with more disillusion about the war than Ambrose Bierce. Bierce was nineteen when he enlisted in April 1861 in the Ninth Indiana regiment, in his hometown of Elkhart. His extended family was antislavery; one of his uncles had provisioned John Brown with weapons during his Kansas exploits in 1856–57. Of all those ex-soldiers who survived to attempt serious literature, Bierce had probably experienced the most combat. From the battle of Shiloh in April 1862 through Murfreesboro, Chattanooga, Chickamauga, and Kenesaw Mountain (where he was badly wounded in the head by a sharpshooter's bullet on June 23, 1864), Bierce became a young, seasoned veteran. After a three-month convalescence, and suffering fainting spells, he returned to his regiment and took part in the bloody battle of Nashville in December 1864, where his unit again suffered severe casualties. By the time he was mustered out in January 1865, war had entered his soul forever. After the war, Bierce moved to California and became a journalist, writing primarily as a social critic and satirist for the San Francisco *Examiner*. Due to the grimness of his war stories, he was often rejected by eastern publishers and magazines. But in 1892 his book of short stories, *Tales of Soldiers and Civilians,* was published at the expense of a wealthy friend. A failed marriage, as well as the suicides of his son and two of his own literary protégés, marred Bierce's later life. He made at least two tours of the Southern battlefields of his youth while an old man, the last at the age of seventy-one in 1912, almost fifty years after the horrors he had seen at Chickamauga. He reveled in memory, in the release from the civilian existence in which he had never found happiness, as he trudged many more miles around the old battlefields in Tennessee and Georgia. Bierce relished his vain effort to recover the excitement of his war days, "when all the world was beautiful and strange." In 1913 he traveled to Mexico, likely as an observer rather than as a member of Pancho Villa's rebellion. He died mysteriously, probably in January 1914, caught somehow in the crossfire of yet another war.[60]

Rather than revealing a survivor's guilt or gratitude, Bierce seemed to have a survivor's contempt, an almost adoring hatred, for war. If, as Andrew Delbanco has argued, the Civil War "was the great divide between a culture of faith and a culture of doubt," a time when Americans watched as "death, gorging itself, mocked belief," then Bierce may have been the lyricist of this new America. His stories and personal accounts of battle are riddled with the randomness of soldiers' deaths. As critics have stressed, Bierce was "permanently warped" by his long exposure to campaigning and combat; death may have been his "only real character." But the fate of soldiers facing the hideous

In his short stories, essays, and poetry, Union veteran Ambrose Bierce provided the most vivid example of discontented realism amidst the flood of romantic reunion literature in the 1880s and 1890s. (Library of Congress)

destructiveness of modern warfare, the seductive evil at the heart of battle—that "theater of chance" where no man's will seems ultimately to control
outcomes—were Bierce's subjects.[61] Death was surely his obsession, but so
too were the sounds, smells, terror, and emotional rush of the contest of war.

Although Bierce's short stories are more surrealistic than realistic, no writer
sustained more lurid clarity about the hold of the war on his or her imagination. His military-topographical sensibility remained with him all his days.
"To this day," he remarked in 1887, "I cannot look over a landscape without
noting the advantages of a ground for attack or defense . . . I never hear a
rifle-shot without a thrill in my veins. I never catch the peculiar odor of gun-
powder without having visions of the dead and dying." He acknowledged the
"history" as "some fifty years old" during his battlefield tour in 1912, "but it is
always with me . . . making solemn eyes at me." Bierce endures in Civil War
cultural memory precisely because his work is so antiheroic, so at odds with
the modern nostalgia for Blue-Gray valor, so utterly bleak and unredemptive.
The twisted circumstances, the coincidences, the manipulative irony do become predictive in Bierce's stories.[62] But this troubled man's work nonetheless
haunts the landscape of Civil War memory.

Bierce had little formal education and was apparently quite self-conscious
of such a lacking, but he could turn a phrase. In his "What I Saw of Shiloh,"
part of his collection *Bits of Autobiography*, Bierce demonstrated that his fascination for remembering battle was not merely macabre. A battery of artillery
inspires confidence among the infantry as it "dashes up to the front, shoving
fifty or a hundred men to the side as if it said, 'Permit me!'." Then the cannon "squares its shoulders, calmly dislocates a joint in its back, sends away its
twenty-four legs and settles down with a quiet rattle which says as plainly as
possible, 'I've come to stay.' There is a superb scorn in its grimly defiant attitude, with its nose in the air; it appears not so much to threaten the enemy as
deride him." Bierce's Shiloh reminiscence contains one of the most artful and
honest characterizations in Civil War literature of the exhilaration of impending battle. A headquarters flag "hanging limp and lifeless" suddenly
"lifted its head to listen." Then came the thunder of long-range guns "in regular throbbings," and soldiers felt the "strong, full pulse of the fever of battle"
as the "flag flapped excitedly." A bugle calling the men into line "goes to the
heart as wine and stirs the blood like the kisses of a beautiful woman." "Who
that has heard it calling to him above the great guns," asked Bierce, "can forget the wild intoxication of its music?"[63]

But Bierce's account of surviving the charges and countercharges of his regiment on the second day at Shiloh is replete with horror. Marching in the dark of night, writes Bierce, "we struck our feet against the dead" of the previous day's fighting, and "more frequently against those who still had spirit enough to resent it with a moan." The futility of death on such a scale became Bierce's preoccupation. Surgeons' tents "were continually ejecting the dead, yet were never empty. It was as if the helpless had been carried in and murdered, that they might not hamper those whose business it was to fall tomorrow." The dead and living men still mired in the mud in all manner of contortions inspired Bierce's sense of the grotesque. A live victim lay face up, "taking in his breath in convulsive, rattling snorts, and blowing out in sputters of froth which crawled creamily down his cheeks, piling along side his neck and ears." From his horrifying head wound, "the brain protruded in bosses, dropping off in flakes and strings." Bierce remembers refusing the request of one of his men to bayonet the suffering man: the proposal was "cold blooded . . . unusual, and too many were looking." In his writing, Bierce needed to make his readers look at these scenes over and over, insisting on careful description of the "postures of agony" among the dead.[64]

Relentlessly, Bierce's target was Civil War sentiment and romance. He clearly admired bravery and daring, but for those still standing at the end of their day at Shiloh, he offered only the solace that "lead had scored its old-time victory over steel; the heroic had broken its great heart against the commonplace." In his short stories, Bierce's characters suffer deaths that are alternately absurd and heroic, hideous and mystical; fratricide or patricide are at the heart of many tales. Some of his best stories are dreamlike journeys away from war and execution, only to end in wrenching, utterly determined death. Bierce tried in many instances to enter the realm of death itself, as though it were a condition, a place, a state of consciousness that he could inhabit. Peytan Farquhar, the Alabama planter who escapes his own hanging in "The Occurrence at Owl Creek Bridge," plunges into the water and eventually runs deliriously through forests toward his plantation home. He begins to feel the pain in his neck near the end of his journey: "All that day he traveled . . . the forest seemed interminable; nowhere did he discover a break in it, not even a woodman's road. He had not known that he lived in so wild a region. There was something uncanny in the revelation." In sight of his beautiful wife reaching out to him from the porch of his plantation house, Farquhar is ripped out of the dream and dangles as the hanged man on the bridge. "A blinding white light blazes all about him with a sound like the shock of a cannon," writes Bierce, "then all is darkness and silence!"[65]

In "One of the Missing," a "brave scout" named Jerome Searing is ordered out to find the position of the Confederate forces who have withdrawn. He takes a position in a small abandoned house to observe the Confederates moving southward, only to be struck by an artillery shell from long range. Searing awakes, or so it seems, to discover himself buried under unmovable debris, and with his musket loaded, cocked, and pointing directly at his own head. For a moment he believes himself dead and tries to remember his burial service. Confused and terrified, unable to dislodge his limbs, and with rats running over his body, Searing finds "a great silence, a black darkness, an infinite tranquility . . . conscious of his rathood." He continues to fight to free himself, but eventually "the whole record of memory was effaced." Searing is ultimately discovered, an already long dead and almost indistinguishably yellowed and dust-covered corpse, by Union troops moving on to find the enemy.[66] Bierce hated sentiment and he never stopped recollecting the corpses.

Bierce's cynicism knew few bounds. He loathed reformers and their causes, advocated capital punishment, and by the turn of the century viewed crime as a new state of war. He lampooned romanticism, dialect stories, and nostalgia wherever he found it. In 1902, he attributed the romantic urge to "contentment . . . the dull monotony of modern life, the depressing daily contact with things we loathe . . . railways, steamships, telephones, electric street-cars." Science and invention had made the world "a spectacular extravaganza," warned Bierce. "Man has employment for all his eyes and all his ears. Yet always he throws a longing look backward to the barbarism to which eventually he will return." With Tourgée, Bierce lamented the decline of satire in the American literary imagination. "Satire cannot co-exist with so foolish sentiments," he complained, "as 'the brotherhood of man,' 'the trusteeship of wealth' . . . tolerance, Socialism, and the rest of it. Who can lash the rascals naked through the world in an age that holds crime to be a disease, and converts the prison into a sanitarium?" Bierce even held soldiers' sentimentalism in a certain contempt; he never attended reunions, even of his own regiment.[67]

But in his uniquely perverse way, Bierce's writing remains significant in Civil War memory for yet another reason. His very quest to expose pretense, to uncover the horror and ludicrousness of war from the soldiers' point of view, left open the avenue to reunion. What Bierce understood best was the nature of soldiers' sacrifices. He knew the living were luckier than the dead; he comprehended, in one macabre tale after another, that a man's will and bravery at Shiloh or Chickamauga did not save him. In his world of war, fate was the only God. Therefore, soldiers were in the end victims of a nation's folly, the wretched killers necessary to make the great machine work. Hence Bierce had no trouble reconciling with his former enemies. He may have enlisted as a youth with his family's abolitionist feelings, but in the long run, he embraced little if any ideological cause. In his poetry, Bierce the reconciliationist comes through most explicitly. In "The Confederate Flags," he took up the issue, opposed by many in the GAR in 1887, of whether battle flags should be returned to the South:

> If we were victors, then we all must live
>> With the same flag above us;
> 'Twas all in vain unless we now forgive
>> And make them love us.
>
> Let kings keep trophies to display above
>> Their doors like any savage;
> The freeman's trophy is the foeman's love,
>> Despite war's ravage. . .
>
> Give back the foolish flags whose bearers fell,
>> Too valiant to forsake them.
> Is it presumptuous, this counsel? Well,
>> I helped to take them.[68]

A foeman's love, cordoned off from all civilian manipulations, owned like an emotional investment in soldiers' hearts, may have been the only kind of sentiment this old veteran permitted himself.

In "The Hesitating Veteran," Bierce raised the issues of race and black freedom. By the 1890s, he confessed ambivalence about emancipation, the act of "that sentimental generation" in a time when "there were hate and strife to spare." But

> That all is over now—the reign
>> Of love and trade stills all dissensions,
> And the clear heavens arch again
>> Above a land of peace and pensions.
> The black chap—at the last we gave
>> Him everything that he had cried for,

Though many white chaps in the grave
   'Twould puzzle to say what they died for.

I hope he's better off—I trust
   That his society and his master's
Are worth the price we paid, and must
   Continue paying, in disasters;
But sometimes doubts press thronging round
   ('Tis mostly when my hurts are aching)
If war for Union was a sound
   And profitable undertaking. . .

No mortal man can truth restore,
   Or say where she is to be sought for.
I know what uniform I wore—
   O, that I knew which side I fought for!

Such ambivalence about the meaning of black freedom did not deter Bierce's admiration for the Confederate dead; indeed, it probably inspired it. On a visit to a national cemetery in Grafton, West Virginia, near one of his old battlefields, he visited many graves of the Confederate "unknown." In a piece called "Bivouac of the Dead," Bierce slipped into his lone sentimental pose. The "neglected and obscure" location of these graves moved the old Union veteran to a tribute. Whoever these men were, "they were honest and coura-geous foemen, having little in common with the political madmen who per-suaded them to their doom and the literary bearers of false witness in the aftertime." As though referring to all soldiers on both sides, these men, Bierce said, "did not pass . . . from the era of the sword to that of the tongue and pen. Among them is no member of the Southern Historical Society. Their valor was not the fury of the non-combatant." The Confederate dead in this lonely corner of West Virginia, where Bierce himself might have lain, were "blameless gentlemen."[69]

In these expressions, Bierce exposed his own agony in understanding the aftermath of the war, his struggle to know just what to do with all the mem-ory of the dead and dying who kept crawling back before his eyes. He held no ideological brief about the war; the dead seemed to be his companions as he satirized war itself and the sentimental society that would romanticize it. Bierce's ultimate tragedy was that in the America where he grew old, in a society tortured by racism, he found no higher meanings in Civil War cemeteries nor on his old battlefields than the precious deaths he recollected. In this he embodied in the bleakest way the character of the American reunion. His very discontent was part of what made the nature of that reunion irrepressible.

As THE SENTIMENTALISM represented by Thomas Nelson Page achieved nearly a stranglehold on the cultural memory of the war era, and as the Lost Cause developed into a full-fledged mythology across American society, the very dominance of such memory bred resistance, especially among the postwar generation. No writer offered a more artful challenge to the hegemony of Lost Cause ideology, or to the reunion wrapped in the retrospective make-believe world of faithful slaves and the mysticism of Blue-Gray fraternalism, than W. E. B. Du Bois. Du Bois was born in February 1868 in Great Barrington, a small town nestled in the Berkshire hills of southwestern Massachusetts. He grew up during Reconstruction and came of age during the era of Jim Crow. His remarkable education at Fisk University in Nashville, Tennessee (1885–88), at Harvard (1890–95), and two years studying at the University of Berlin (1892–94) made him the most educated black man in America. After writing his first two books, *The Suppression of the African Slave Trade* (1896) and *The Philadelphia Negro* (1899), Du Bois began to write the essays that would become *The Souls of Black Folk* (1903). Living in segregated Atlanta, Georgia, between 1897 and 1903, and teaching at Atlanta University, Du Bois wrote and assembled the thirteen essays and one short story that became his masterpiece.[70]

Souls is an extended meditation on racial prejudice, political leadership, the economic oppression of black laborers in the South, and the development of African American culture both before and after emancipation. Above all, it is a tragic vision of American history, a gripping revelation of the triumphs, betrayals, and legacies that, in the wake of emancipation, shaped the lives of black folk through the first years of the twentieth century. In *Souls,* Du Bois takes his readers on many journeys to sacred *places* of memory. In "Of the Black Belt," Du Bois is guide on a sojourn to the "crimson soil of Georgia." In vivid imagery he describes a "monotonous" quality of the landscape of the former Cotton Kingdom, yet he "did not nod, nor weary of the scene; for this is *historic ground.*" Du Bois combines rich descriptions of nature with the social history of the legions of sharecroppers. Here is a more believable Georgia (or South) than that presented in Harris's Uncle Remus tales or in Page's stories of faithful old retainers and magnolia-draped intersectional weddings. Here is a landscape where the grace of the Old South seems truly vanished in the wind, where only the "black tenant remains" and the "shadow-hand of the master's grand nephew or cousin or creditor stretches out of the gray distance to collect the rack-rent remorselessly." Remnants of the big houses, the "parks and palaces of the Cotton Kingdom," remain, but that "merry past" now lies in "silence . . ., ashes, and tangled weeds." Du Bois depicts this "Egypt of the Confederacy" as a society built by the blood and toil of generations of blacks, and as a "cause lost long before 1861."[71] His "Black Belt" is a tragic, forsaken landscape, the project of no New South booster, no place for exotic escapes by nervous Yankees or vacationing white Southerners.

On every level, Du Bois's journey through Georgia, a motif he repeated in other writings, was an imaginative way to dissent from the traditional image and history of slavery and the South. The "cause lost" is unmistakable. He frequently allows the voices of the freedmen themselves to tell the story. In a scene framed by the "bare ruin of some master's home," an old ex-slave says: "I've seen niggers drop dead in the furrow, but they were kicked aside, and the plow never stopped. Down in the guard house, there's where the blood ran." Du Bois combined the beauty of nature, the sweep of history in epic proportions, and the painful ruck of the freedmen's daily lives to forge an indelible memory that countered the romance of the Lost Cause and national reunion. There are no happy darkies in his Black Belt, and race relations have not been better off left to the South's own devices—despite the central argument of Page's important book, *The Negro: The Southerner's Problem* (1904), which also explicitly assumes Negro inferiority. In that genteel manifesto of white supremacy, the master of the plantation school of literature directly confronted the young African American scholar. "Some of the 'Afro-Americans,'" wrote Page, "with the veneer of a so-called education, to judge by recent works written by certain of them, presume to look down . . . and assume a fine scorn of the relation which once existed all over the South between the old-time Southerner and the old-time darky, and which still exists where the latter still survives." Page's pathos about the "cherished" memory of old darkies among white Southerners did indeed meet with Du Bois's scorn. Du Bois's vision of Black Belt Georgia concludes with a description of a prison farm, his metaphor for the whole setting and the despair of black debtors. "It is a depressing place," wrote Du Bois, "bare, unshaded, with no charm of past association, only a memory of forced toil—now, then, and before the war. They are not happy these men whom we meet throughout this region." Du Bois blurred the tenses in depicting a landscape and a people who seemed to inhabit another time, trapped in a past they cannot escape, but he avoided the cheerful nostalgia of the "old-time Negroes" so central as the talking props of the Lost Cause drama and of sentimental fiction.[72]

Souls is historical literature that breathed a heavy sigh of tragedy into America's optimistic sense of itself. In Du Bois's own time, many perceptive readers wondered about the book's somber tones. In 1906, his mentor, William James, wrote to Du Bois congratulating him on the power of *Souls,* but questioning the despair of the book. "You must not think I am personally wedded to the minor key," Du Bois answered. "On the contrary I am tuned to the most aggressive and unquenchable hopefulness. I wanted in this case simply to reveal fully the other side to the world."[73] The endless tension between pain and beauty, between the full range of suffering and the persistence of possibility in American history, between the ways Reconstruction built a new country at the same time it all but crushed its own creation, is what Du Bois sought to capture by bringing the black experience to the center of the story of the age of emancipation.

Du Bois's most direct challenge to the history of the war and Reconstruction as it stood at the turn of the century comes in the second chapter of *Souls,* "Of the Dawn of Freedom." In a combination of descriptive history and theatrical pageantry, he created a new framework in which the plight of the freedpeople might be seen. At times, Du Bois speaks in the voice of a prophet. Urging the reader to cast his or her vision to the rear of the grim parade of history, he identifies three images in the procession of Sherman's march across Georgia at the end of Civil War: "the Conqueror, the Conquered, and the Negro." As though he were trying to get Americans to alter their gaze from the soldiers' tales of battle and campaigns, he offered an alternative but equally epic vision. "Some see all significance in the grim front of the destroyer," wrote Du Bois, "and some in the bitter sufferers of the Lost Cause. But to me neither soldier nor fugitive speaks with so deep a meaning as that dark human cloud that clung like remorse on the rear of those swift columns . . . In vain were they ordered back . . . on they trudged and writhed and surged, until they rolled into Savannah, a starved and naked horde of tens of thousands."[74] Here were the nameless freedpeople, liberated and self-liberated in a terrible war, given equal billing in this memory theater with the tragic Southern planters and the awesome symbol of Yankee destruction and victory, William Tecumseh Sherman.

Then, in a stunning metaphor about passion and memory in the New South, Du Bois characterizes "two figures" that typified the postwar era and demonstrated the power of its legacy:

> the one a gray-haired gentleman, whose fathers had quit themselves like men, whose sons lay in nameless graves; who bowed to the evil of slavery because its abolition threatened untold ill to all; who stood at last, in the evening of life, a . . . ruined form, with hate in his eyes;—and the other a form hovering dark and mother-like, her awful face black with the mists of centuries, had aforetime quailed at that white master's command, had bent in love over the cradles of his sons and daughters, and closed in death the sunken eyes of his wife,—aye, too, at his behest had laid herself low to his lust, and borne a tawny man-child to the world, only to see her dark boy's limbs scattered to the winds by midnight marauders riding after "damned niggers."

Without a pause, Du Bois pressed the issue. "These were the saddest sights of that woeful day," he concluded, "and no man *clasped the hands* of these passing figures of the present-past; but hating, they went to their long home, and hating their children's children live today." Past and present met in this imagery with frightful intensity; the picture Du Bois paints is an alternative vision of the meaning of the Civil War. Here were not the customary forms of old soldiers who had met in battle and could now "clasp hands across the bloody chasm" in the time-honored slogan of many a Blue-Gray reunion.[75] Rather, Du Bois's "two figures" are *veterans* of another conflict, the primary players in the tragedy that caused the war of the Blue and the Gray. Du Bois's alternative Civil War veterans are an old male slaveholder—the broken symbol of wealth, power, and sexual domination—and an old black woman, representing "Mammy," mother, and survivor. The heritage of slavery lives on in these "passing figures of the present-past," demonstrating that racial reconciliation, unlike sectional reconciliation, demanded a confrontation with the hostility rooted in rape, lynching, and racism. Bridging this chasm remained the unfinished—and for many, all but unknowable—work of the culture of reunion.

EIGHT

The Lost Cause and Causes Not Lost

The capacity to live in the past by memory also
emancipates the individual from the tyranny of the
present. He can choose, if he wants, to reverse a present trend of history in favor of some previous trend.
He can, if he wishes, seek asylum from present tu-
mults in a past period of history, or use the memory
of a past innocency to project a future of higher
virtue.

—Reinhold Niebuhr, *Faith and History,* 1949

The relics were ready; over the doorway of elegant rooms the
names of states were emblazoned in gold. Swords, epaulets, field glasses,
Bibles, spurs, bits, saddles, blankets, uniforms, letters, even a pair of slippers
made from the original carpet were all in position. The windows were cur-
tained with Confederate flags; a platform stood in the main room beneath
portraits of Jefferson Davis, Stonewall Jackson, and Joseph E. Johnston. On
the platform stood a table draped with a tattered Confederate battle flag. On
Saturday afternoon, February 22, 1896, the Ladies Memorial Association was
ready for the formal exercises that dedicated the White House of the Confederacy in Richmond, Jefferson Davis's executive mansion in 1861–65, as the
"treasure house of Confederate history and relics." Women made up the entire committee that had managed the rehabilitation of the three-story mansion. The Reverend Moses Hoge delivered the opening prayer. Hoge declared
the mansion a place of "sacred trust," a "shrine" to "sorrow-shrouded glories

of our departed Confederacy," as well as a means of "turning from the strifes and sorrows of the past" in order to "face the future."[1]

Of the two orators of the day, Governor Charles T. O'Ferrall took the podium first. As a New South governor, O'Ferrall represented the Lost Cause as a holy heritage, the story in which white Southerners would always nourish their "fealty to traditions" and honor the matchless bravery of their soldiers. O'Ferrall recited central tenets of the Lost Cause creed, especially that of a Confederacy "whose life was crushed out of it under the Juggernaut wheels of superior numbers and merciless power." But he also urged the gathering to hold "no lingering feeling of bitterness" and proclaimed his fellow Virginians "loyal sons and daughters of the Union." Such a claim, though, rested securely on Southern terms. In their new patriotism, said O'Ferrall, Virginians had "no retractions to make, no recantations to sing." They would remain "true to ourselves, to our martyred dead . . . to our traditions and civilizations."[2]

Above all, O'Ferrall paid tribute to the Southern women who had endured the war and restored the mansion as a museum. As "Spartan wives and mothers" and "ministering angels," women had saved Southern civilization. The cause not lost and the reason for the dedication, O'Ferrall maintained, was "Southern women's love for the memories of a generation ago; Southern women's devotion to the cause." Finally, he laid the ultimate burden of the Lost Cause on the war generation's daughters. "Oh, women of the Confederacy, your fame is deathless," proclaimed O'Ferrall. "Young maidens, gather at the feet of some Confederate matron in some reminiscent hour, and listen to her story of those days . . . how God gave her courage, fortitude, and strength to bear her . . . sufferings . . . and live." Two generations of white Southern women grew up with at least some sense of this burden-inspiration; they were to be the caretakers of Lost Cause tradition.[3]

O'Ferrall then turned the lectern over to the principal speaker of the occasion, former Confederate general Bradley T. Johnson. Johnson, who had a controversial military record, was a popular Confederate memorial speaker. Along with Jubal Early, D. H. Hill, and others, he had led the effort in the 1860s and 1870s to preserve Confederate traditions in Virginia. Johnson had long been a major spokesman for an especially unreconstructed brand of Lost Cause ideology. The occasion of the opening of the White House of the Confederacy was George Washington's birthday, as well as the thirty-fifth anniversary of Jefferson Davis's inauguration as president of the Confederacy. Declaring Washington the "first rebel president," Johnson gave the Lost

Cause its longest lineage. The occasion, he said, "commemorates an epoch in the grandest struggle for liberty and right that has ever been made by man."[4] The revolution of 1861 was merely the continuation of that of 1776. By the 1890s, secession had become a sacred act, even to many who had opposed it at the moment of truth.

Johnson too honored the women, extending special thanks to Thomas Nelson Page for his stories of the sacrifices of mothers and wives. Then he served up a potent mixture of Confederate triumphalism and white supremacy. To him, there was nothing "lost" about the South's cause. "The world is surely coming to the conclusion," announced Johnson, "that the cause of the Confederacy was right." White Southerners had only "resisted invasion!" the General insisted. With a historical logic that came to dominate popular, as well as scholarly, understandings, Johnson boldly declared that the "South did not make war in defense of slavery; slavery was only the incident, the point attacked." And the attack had been that of a "free mobocracy of the North" against a "slave democracy of the South." By all manner of "deliberate intent," Northern interests had made social and political war on Southerners who were "ambitious, intellectual and brave, such as led Athens in her brightest epoch and controlled Rome in her most glorious days." Here, indeed, was the full-blown myth of the Lost Cause—a glorious, organic civilization destroyed by an avaricious "industrial society" determined to wipe out its cultural foes.[5]

Since Johnson had begun with the premise that "success is worshipped, failure is forgotten," his rhetorical sleight of hand may have been hardly detectable to his audience. Above all, Johnson delivered a racial message at this special occasion. In a classic statement of proslavery ideology, Johnson defined slavery as "the apprenticeship by which savage races had been educated and trained into civilization by their superiors." Fueled by the profits of Yankee industrialists, the North had waged a war of social destruction. "The negro . . . against his will, without his assistance," said Johnson, "has been turned loose in America to do the best he can in the contest with the strongest race that ever lived." According to the former general, the South itself had been made the "slave" to Northern banks and stockholders, and worst of all, to ballots in the hands of "these children" (blacks). Slavery had provided the "sentiments, the family of a people" that held the South together. Industrial society had no such sentiment. A corporation, like the Yankee armies, understood only "conquest"; "not a tradition hallows it, not a memory sanctifies it," lamented the old soldier. Johnson summed up the legacy of the Civil War in a declaration to which many Americans had come to at least benignly acquiesce. "The great crime of the century," he concluded, "was the emancipation of the Negroes."[6]

THE LOST CAUSE took root in a Southern culture awash in an admixture of physical destruction, the psychological trauma of defeat, a Democratic Party resisting Reconstruction, racial violence, and with time, an abiding sentimentalism. On the broadest level, it came to represent a mood, or an attitude toward the past. It took hold in specific arguments, organizations, and rituals, and for many Southerners it became a natural extension of evangelical piety, a civil religion that helped them link their sense of loss to a Christian conception of history. Like all great mythologies, the Lost Cause changed with succeeding generations and shifting political circumstances.[7]

From the late 1860s to the late 1880s, diehards, especially though not exclusively in Virginia, tended to shape the Confederate memory. They made Robert E. Lee into the God-like embodiment of a leader whose cause could be defeated only by overpowering odds. Thus ennobled in a revolution crushed by industrial might, and newly emboldened by a sense of righteousness born of successful resistance to radical Reconstruction, the Lost Cause emerged by the 1890s as that oft-told explanation of history that O'Ferrall and Johnson had represented at the dedication of the Confederate Museum. But by the 1890s, and until at least World War I, the Confederate memorial movement came under the control of new leadership and organizations, especially the United Daughters of the Confederacy (UDC) and the United Confederate Veterans (UCV). The mass of rank-and-file former Confederates (the majority of whom now lived in states west of the eastern seaboard) formed the grassroots of Lost Cause ritual activity. During this surge of Lost Cause sentiment Southerners succeeded, by and large, in helping shape a national reunion on their own terms. By the turn of the century, the Lost Cause (as cultural practice and as a set of arguments) served two aims—reconciliation and Southern partisanship. For natural reasons, some Lost Cause traditions began to wane in the wake of the Spanish-American War of 1898, and through the patriotic upheavals of World War I. But many of the assumptions of Confederate memory forged over fifty years endured to haunt America into the 1920s and beyond.[8] Especially in racial terms, the cause that was *not* lost, as Johnson had insisted in 1896, reverberated as part of the very heartbeat of the Jim Crow South.

Throughout the spread of the Lost Cause, at least three elements attained overriding significance: the movement's effort to write and control the *history* of the war and its aftermath; its use of *white supremacy* as both means and ends; and the place of *women* in its development. From the earliest days of memorial activity, the diehards were determined to collect and write a Confederate version of the history of the war. Frequently disclaiming partisanship, and eager to establish what they so frequently called the "truth of history," diehard Lost Cause advocates, many of them high-ranking officers and political leaders of the Confederacy, forged one of the most highly orchestrated grassroots partisan histories ever conceived.

From his prison release in 1867 to his death in 1889, Jefferson Davis set the tone for the diehards' historical interpretation. In private and public utterances, Davis's fierce defense of state rights doctrine and secession, his incessant pleas for "Southern honor," and his mystical conception of the Confederacy gave ideological fuel to diehards. It was forever a "misnomer to apply the term 'Rebellion'" to the Confederacy, Davis wrote in 1874. "Sovereigns cannot rebel." Diehards could look to Davis for endless expressions of solemn faith. "We may not hope to see the rebuilding of the temple as our Fathers designed it," Davis counseled a friend in 1877, "but we can live on praying for that event and die with eyes fixed on the promised land."[9]

In his two-volume, 1,279-page memoir, *The Rise and Fall of the Confederate Government,* Davis wrote what may be the longest and most self-righteous legal brief on behalf of a failed political movement ever done by an American. He placed responsibility for secession and the war entirely at the feet of the North. The South's action was merely to protect its natural rights against the "tremendous and sweeping usurpation," the "unlimited, despotic power" of the federal government. Every war measure enacted by the Lincoln administration or by Congress, from confiscation to emancipation, was a further step in the "serpent seeking its prey." In his defense of the Confederacy, Davis developed a case for what James McPherson has called the "virgin-birth theory of secession: the Confederacy was not conceived by any worldly cause, but by divine principle."[10]

In language that became almost omnipresent in Lost Cause rhetoric, Davis insisted that slavery "was in no wise the cause of the conflict, but only an incident." Moreover, he contributed a defense of slavery itself that was as direct as any written in the postwar South. "Generally," Davis claimed, African Americans' ancestors "were born the slaves of barbarian masters, untaught in all the useful arts and occupations, reared in heathen darkness, and, sold by heathen masters, they were transferred to shores enlightened by the rays of Christianity." In this benevolent environment now crushed by Yankee armies and politicians, blacks had been

> put to servitude . . . trained in the gentle arts of peace and order and civilization; they increased from a few unprofitable savages to millions of efficient Christian laborers. Their servile instincts rendered them contented with their lot, and their patient toil blessed the land of their abode with unmeasured riches. Their strong local and personal attachment secured faithful service . . . Never was there happier dependence of labor and capital on each other. The tempter came, like the serpent of Eden, and decoyed them with the magic word of "freedom" . . . He put arms in their hands, and trained their humble but emotional natures to deeds of violence and bloodshed, and sent them out to devastate their benefactors.[11]

Davis helped give the Lost Cause its lifeblood. Here again were the faithful slaves, the natural-born laborers in the idyll of the Old South performing a new service—they were the broken symbols of lost glory and Yankee idiocy. It is telling to observe that virtually all major spokespersons for the Lost Cause could not develop their story of a heroic, victimized South without the images of faithful slaves and benevolent masters—the "sovereigns" of a state had to be protecting something besides principles on parchment. And so, in such reasoning, was the Civil War about and not about slavery.

Davis had many predecessors upon whose work he built his mystical defense of the Confederacy. The diehard era (1860–late 1880s) of the Lost Cause emerged in several polemical books in the immediate postwar years, and especially in new magazines founded as the vehicles of Southern vindication. In his book *The Lost Cause* (1866), Edward Pollard warned that what the South had lost on battlefields it would carry on in a "war of ideas." Only two years later, with his militancy under more control and no longer urging Southerners to still take up arms, Pollard wrote a campaign tract, *The Lost Cause Regained* (1868), in which he counseled reconciliation with conservative Northerners on Southern terms. Those terms coalesced in a central idea. "To the extent of securing the supremacy of the white man," wrote Pollard, "and the traditional liberties of the country . . . she [the South] really triumphs in the true cause of the war." Alfred Taylor Bledsoe, a former professor of mathematics at the University of Virginia and undersecretary of war in the Confederacy, led the diehards in the defense of secession. His *Is Davis a Traitor, or Was Secession a Constitutional Right before 1861?* (1866) and *A Constitutional View of the Late War between the States* (1868–70) laid out a vehement justification of state rights doctrine. Most importantly, Bledsoe created a polemical magazine, the *Southern Review,* in Baltimore in 1867. Along with D. H. Hill's *The Land We Love,* founded in 1866 in Charlotte, North Carolina, the *Southern Review* kept up an intensive defense of the Confederate legacy until the end of Reconstruction. Indeed, the political and racial struggles over Reconstruction policy itself became central themes of these magazines, most of which faded away with the steady growth of political reconciliation in the late 1870s.[12] In organizations, however, the Lost Cause found new and more permanent footing.

The earliest Confederate veterans' groups formed around two aims: charity to members and families, and as the Charleston, South Carolina, Survivors' Association put it, to create "a Southern history." In these first years after the war, Confederate veteran activists devoted themselves to the most basic duty of memorialization, tabulating elaborate rolls of honor of both the living and the dead. But with meager resources at the local levels, they sought to carry on the battle for historical memory as well. In 1869, the leader of the New Orleans Survivors' Association invited his counterpart in Charleston to share in this historical enterprise. "We wish to collect," wrote Reverend B. M. Palmer to Edward McGrady, "everything that can illustrate the history of our Southern country . . . to publish volumes of transactions, spreading before our people and before the world the very documents from which all true history is to be drawn." Within the South Carolina association, a Rock Hill veteran wrote to the leadership, endorsing as its central objective "the necessity of transmitting the *truth* to posterity."[13] In its earliest manifestations, therefore, the Lost Cause was born out of grief, but just as importantly, it formed in the desire to contend for control of the nation's memory. Whatever the extent of Union victory on the battlefield, the verdicts to be rendered in history and memory were not settled for good at Appomattox.

From its beginnings in New Orleans in 1869, in its original circular letter, the Southern Historical Society (SHS) declared its object to be the "collection, classification, preservation, and final publication" of the Confederate story. The founders of the SHS announced that their society would not represent "purely sectional" interests, "nor that its labors shall be of a partisan character." But in all its work the organization sought to "vindicate the truth of history."[14] Many ex-Confederates put enormous faith in history as their source of justification. While the history they had lived ruined them, the history they would help write might redeem them.

The editor of the *SHS Papers,* J. William Jones, and the society's members who wrote so vigorously, labored as though they were under a literary siege. Like all polemicists, in the sheer repetition of the word "truth" they claimed credibility and sought justification. The SHS's fifth annual report acknowledged contributors of "material for a true history of the war," offered its aid to writers "elucidating the truth of Confederate history," and praised supporters for choosing the "cause of truth" over money with their donations of personal collections. For all to see, the official seal of the SHS, blazoned on the cover of every volume, contained the slogan: "Truth Is the Proper Antagonist of Error." The SHS worked from the assumption that the war's victors would never do them justice in the history books or in the emerging memoir literature. Based on the collection they had assembled in the offices reserved for them in the Virginia state capitol, the SHS leadership put their faith in the power of documentation.[15] These ex-soldiers demanded respect and would try to argue their way to righteousness before the bar of History.

In the early years of forging Lost Cause ideology, diehards fashioned a historical creed, demanded discipleship, and worked with urgency to counter Northern histories. "Our adversaries leave no stone unturned to defeat us through the South," wrote former general John B. Gordon in 1872 as vice president of a publishing firm. "Their offensive books" demanded answers, Gordon maintained. "We must meet their attacks when it seems wise to do so." To the charge from Jubal Early that he had become too infected with "progressive ideas to care for the preservation of history," the former presidential candidate and Confederate general John C. Breckinridge assured Early that he "would know better some day. I seek no man's society who speaks of us as 'traitors,' nor will I associate with our former adversaries upon the basis of mere sufferance." Early told a fellow diehard in 1871 that he kept very active fighting Northerners' false history. "Every now and then," he wrote to D. H. Hill, "I manage to land a bomb against the enemy, in the way of exploding some of their lies, and that affords me some consolation." In his windy way, P. G. T. Beauregard rejoiced over the creation of the SHS. "After having taken an active part in *making* history," he wrote to Early, the job of the generals was to "see that it is correctly *written.*" Robert S. Dabney, a chaplain and chief of staff for Stonewall Jackson during the early part of the war and one of the most unreconcilable of the diehards, saw the Lost Cause as a sacred trust that required theological devotion and a strong sense of denial. In his *A Defense of Virginia and through Her of the South* (1867), Dabney was obsessed with historical judgments about the war and Southern slaveholding. He believed the South had "been condemned unheard," and that the "pens" of its "statesmen" had been too silent. In the tradition of the older proslavery writers, Dabney praised the South as an "organic" society, the bulwark against all the disorder now championed by radical Republicanism. In one of the most desperate expressions of the diehard spirit, Dabney called on Southerners to wield the pen and count on God. Yankees would ultimately meet their just fate, Dabney believed, "in the day of their calamity, in the pages of impartial history, and in the Day of Judgment."[16]

Until his death in 1894, Dabney was never at home in the world the war had made. Almost as much as he hated Yankee rule, he eventually condemned the New South movement for its materialism and anti-agrarianism. Dabney believed Southerners needed major literary works that would do for them what John Fox's *Book of Martyrs* had done for seventeenth-century English Protestants. "The South needs a book of 'Acts and Monuments of Confederate Martyrs,'" he told D. H. Hill in 1873. Dabney argued that Southern writers should model the pathos of *Uncle Tom's Cabin,* but in reverse. "Paint the picture skillfully," he urged, "of Southern martyrdom under ruthless abolition outrages." He called for "helpless sufferings of *weakness* under the brute hand of merciless *power.*"[17] This was not quite the kind of Lost Cause that Thomas Nelson Page would give the nation, but it did eventually find its author in Thomas Dixon's *The Clansman* (1905) and its immortal place in motion pictures in D. W. Griffith's *Birth of a Nation* (1915).

As in most lost causes, ex-Confederates had scores to settle with each other as well as with their former enemies. In their canonization of Lee, Virginians in particular sought to make James Longstreet the scapegoat for the Southern loss at Gettysburg. In a speech at the dedication of the Lee Chapel in Lexington, Virginia, in January 1873, William Nelson Pendleton, Lee's chief of artillery, attacked Longstreet. Longstreet was a Georgian and scorned by the diehards for renouncing Lost Cause sentiments and urging his fellow Southerners to get on with rebuilding their economy as early as 1867. He was especially vilified for being "so slow" in his attacks on the second and third days of the battle of Gettysburg. A bitter controversy raged until the end of the century over these charges against Longstreet and lasted even longer in the enduring Lee legend. In spite of ample evidence to demonstrate that Lee himself had deeply respected Longstreet, this dispute had a long life in the pages of the *SHS Papers* and elsewhere because essential tenets of the Lost Cause were at stake—the military and moral infallibility of Lee, and the myth of Confederate invincibility.[18]

By the late 1870s, diehards were no longer merely explaining defeats; they had a victory to bequeath to history as well. From the beginning, Lost Cause diehards attacked Reconstruction policy nearly as much as they appealed for history true to the Confederate cause. After acknowledging Ulysses Grant's appeal for "peace," Jubal Early ended an article on federal numerical superiority during the war with a diatribe against the current situation in the South in 1870. The elections of 1870, claimed Early, were "superintended by armed agents of the United States Government . . . for the purpose of perpetuating the power of the ruling faction, through the instrumentality of the ballot in the hands of an inferior race." When John T. Morgan addressed the 1877 annual meeting of the SHS, he portrayed the period 1868–77 as the "nine years war of Reconstruction" and the era of "dishonorable oppression for an unworthy cause." Reconstruction, Morgan maintained, had been the "second war." "If we have now met in peace and reconciliation upon the broad concessions, mutually accepted, that the war was not a crime," he said, "we need not inquire who was right or who was wrong." In such language, Lost Cause advocates found a victory narrative. They had won the second war over Reconstruction; they had thrown off "Negro rule" and redeemed their states. In a speech to a group of veterans of the Army of the Tennessee in July 1878, Jefferson Davis made the victory over Reconstruction an explicit element of Lost Cause ideology. The normally morose Davis described a cause reflowering in a new season. "Well may we rejoice in the regained possession of local self-government," Davis said, "in the power of people to . . . legislate uncontrolled by bayonets. This is the great victory . . . a total non-interference by the Federal Government with the domestic affairs of the States."[19] By regaining home rule, defeating black equality, and throwing off all vestiges of Reconstruction, the South had found a new cause: a story of redemption and victory that could serve the ends of both diehards and reconciliationists.

ALTHOUGH SOME diehards remained thoroughly unreconstructed for the rest of their lives, what made possible the reconciliationist phase of the Lost Cause (1880s and beyond) is that Southerners found they could transform loss on the battlefield into a reunion on terms largely of their own choosing. New South promoters and Lost Cause diehards may have differed somewhat over how slavery should be remembered, but most shared a refurbished commitment to white supremacy and a desire for renewed economic growth. Reconciliationist spokesmen of the Lost Cause could announce acceptance of the Thirteenth, Fourteenth, and Fifteenth Amendments, as John Goode did at a monument unveiling in Culpeper, Virginia, in 1881, but equally claim that "all powers of the earth could not compel us to write the word 'traitor' with our own hands upon the graves of our heroic and martyred dead." At the same unveiling ceremony, Virginia's ex-governor James Kemper and future governor Fitzhugh Lee (both former generals) declared that they had "never done any treason" in a cause more "free of crime" than any in history.[20] Keeping diehards like Early in check, Kemper and Lee were conservatives who helped usher their state into the era of reunion with a proud and respected sense of their Lost Cause.

As Southerners began to unveil their local soldiers' monuments, and as their victory over Reconstruction became part of their narrative of Confederate heritage, Lost Cause orators moved from mournful to more triumphant tones. At the October 1878 unveiling of the Confederate monument in the town square of Augusta, Georgia, one of that state's most popular Lost Cause voices, Charles Colcock Jones Jr., argued that the South had fought for "liberty" and "freedom" and had lost only because it had been "overborne by superior numbers and weightier munitions." Then he quickly shifted to a victory narrative. The ultimate verdict of the war awaited the history of their own time. "Nothing has been absolutely determined except the question of comparative strength," said Jones. "The issue furnished only a physical solution of the moral, social, and political propositions." To Jones, the South could still win the war politically. The "political privileges" and "vested rights" of Southerners, he declared, "are, in a moral point of view, unaffected by the result of the contest."[21]

Thus was the Lost Cause transformed into national reunion on Southern terms. A Memorial Day speaker in Baltimore in 1879 invested such sentiments even deeper in local pride and vindication. At bottom, argued A. M. Keiley, it was "love of state and love of home" for which Southerners fought the war. In a speech that was otherwise not very reconciliationist, Keiley announced that he found "reconciliation easy with him who says, 'I answered the summons of Massachusetts or Ohio,' for I answered the summons of Virginia, and hers alone." Keiley predicted that each year "this platform of reconciliation will more and more assert itself" and the nation would revive from its roots in state sovereignty and local rule.[22] Keiley may have been only partly right with this prediction; a new nationalism fueled the reunion, as did fear of radical populism. But retreats to this sense of "home," and all the vestiges of control over social institutions and race relations that it implied, were at the heart of the American reunion. For Lost Cause advocates, a narrative of loss had become a narrative of order, revival, and triumph.

The Lost Cause became an integral part of national reconciliation by dint of sheer sentimentalism, by political argument, and by recurrent celebrations and rituals. For most white Southerners, the Lost Cause evolved into a language of vindication and renewal, as well as an array of practices and public monuments through which they could solidify both their Southern pride and their Americanness. In the 1890s, Confederate memories no longer dwelled as much on mourning or explaining defeat; they offered a set of conservative traditions by which the entire country could gird itself against racial, political, and industrial disorder. And by the sheer virtue of losing heroically, the Confederate soldier provided a model of masculine devotion and courage in an age of gender anxieties and ruthless material striving. For those who needed it, the Lost Cause became a tonic against fear of social change, a preventative ideological medicine for the sick souls of the Gilded Age. It also armed those determined to control, if not destroy, the rise of black people in the social order.[23]

In the 1880s Americans digested the soldiers' literature of reunion in magazines and memoirs along with the evolving Lost Cause mythology. Two signal events at decade's end marked the change in both the leadership and the character of Confederate public memory. In December 1889, Jefferson Davis died during a visit to New Orleans. Cities and towns held memorial services as the entire South seemed to go into mourning. Davis had made a celebrated public tour of the South in 1886 accompanied by his daughter, Winnie (the "daughter" of the Confederacy, since she had been born during the war), during which he was cheered by huge crowds. Indeed, Winnie Davis, who appeared in white dresses and became the object of veterans' adoration, was forced to play the symbolic model of purity and perfect young womanhood at many public gatherings. She became a gendered icon of the social order—the cause and the future—for which Southern white men had fought. Often aloof or rash in his defense of Confederate memory, Davis himself emerged before death as a hero, a symbol of the South's "suffering" both during the war and through Reconstruction. A floral inscription, "He Was Manacled for US," adorned the front of his train during the triumphal 1886 tour. White Southerners used these occasions to proclaim the glory of their failed revolution and to refurbish their self-respect. "There never has been anything at the South equal to the ovation which Mr. Davis has received," wrote D. H. Hill in 1886. "You know that I have no reason to like Mr. Davis, but he has suffered for us and is our representative man. We ought to honor him in order to honor ourselves."[24] However harshly Davis himself rejected reconciliation, the Lost Cause now served as a regenerative force in the New South's reunion with the North.

In the spring after Davis's death, on May 29, 1890, Richmond unveiled the giant equestrian statue of Robert E. Lee in a suburb on what would become Monument Avenue. Led by Jubal Early and other former officers of Virginia, a Lee cult evolved immediately after the general's death in 1870. This Virginia coalition of mystic diehards sought through the SHS and the Association of the Army of Northern Virginia to create a memorial to Lee that would actively revive Confederate history and memory. Their canonization of Lee as a blameless Christian soldier, a paragon of manly virtue and duty who soared above politics, was not really challenged by their competitors. It was the politics of the design as well as the national meanings of the Lee monument that motivated the two competing groups. A Richmond "ladies committee" composed of upper-class matrons, entered the Lee monument movement in the 1870s, especially as fund-raisers and as critics of artistic designs. And under two Virginia governors, Kemper in the 1870s and Fitzhugh Lee in the late 1880s, the Lee Memorial Association took over official control of the campaign. Intense controversy marred both the fund-raising and the artistic competitions. But in 1886, Governor Lee managed to solidify all the factions under one committee, which pushed the project to completion and gave the commission to the French artist Antonin Mercie. The diehards had opposed several previous designs as simply not true likenesses of "Marse Robert," and Early even objected to the use of Maine marble for the base of the statue (he was overruled by the governor, who acknowledged that Richmond marble companies had colluded to keep their prices high). In the end, the women's committee, led by Sarah N. Randolph, won control over the design, the governor chose the site (in a new suburb, symbolic of future progress), and Early was left with the consolation of being master of ceremonies at the unveiling.[25]

Attended by a crowd estimated between 100,000 and 150,000 people, the unveiling of the giant Lee equestrian was an extraordinary event held on the weekend of the national Memorial Day. The parade of some twenty thousand participants to the outskirts of the city was festive in every way. Bands played "Dixie" and other Southern airs, and countless Confederate flags

The unveiling of the Robert E. Lee monument in Richmond on Memorial Day, 1890, marked the entry of the Lost Cause into the national mainstream. (The Museum of the Confederacy, Richmond, Virginia)

mixed with U.S. flags along the march. The orator, Archer Anderson, treasurer of the Tredegar Iron Works, set the tone for the Lee remembered, the man of "moral strength and moral beauty." The monument, said Anderson, stood not for "a record of civil strife, but as a perpetual protest against whatever is low and sordid in our public and private objects." As General Joseph E. Johnston pulled the cord to unveil the statue, deafening cheers ensued in the huge throng.[26] Sectional hostility was not an overt theme of this public ritual. But clearly, Southern pride rose restored on that odd landscape on the outskirts of a new, but as yet undeveloped, Richmond. Twenty-five years after a massive civil war, the military leader and the heroic symbol of the side that lost now sat high astride his horse, looking northward on a nation soon to incorporate him into its own pantheon. Reconciliation now appeared to be dependent upon the dead leader of the cause that lost. More than ghosts emerged from the Richmond unveiling of 1890; a new, more dynamic Lost Cause was thrown into bold relief as well. Early and his Virginia diehards had lost influence, but the Lee legend was now something the whole country had to interpret.

Some Northern newspapers openly objected to the aggressive display of Confederate flags in Richmond. The Republican *New York Press* reported that it received more letters "denouncing the liberal display of rebel flags" than it could print. The *Chicago Inter-Ocean* declared in "sorrow, not in anger" its regret at the "unfurling and waving of the flag of the so-called Confederate States" at the unveiling. The *Minneapolis Tribune* lamented that the "Lee cult is much in vogue, even at the North, in these days." The Minnesota editors disclaimed the "fashion" of surrounding Lee with "a sort of halo of moral grandeur, military genius, and knightly grace, as a man of finer and better mold than his famous antagonists." The *Salt Lake Tribune* (Utah), also Republican, was willing to condone such an "ostentatious display of affection for their dead" on the part of ex-Confederates, as long as they continued to confess that their defeat was "mercy in disguise." All was understandable, claimed the Utah paper, because "human affections have their way; and as the mother loves best her crippled child, so it is natural for a people who have been defeated in a cherished project . . . to return . . . and to bewail it with all their hearts."[27] In the far-off West, the unveiling of the Lee monument in Richmond apparently seemed a benign exercise.

But the Lost Cause on display in Richmond in 1890 was less an act of mourning and more of a celebration. Southern newspapers rejoiced over the Lee monument and its surrounding events declaring, as the *New Orleans Pic-*

ayune did, that on this Memorial Day the South had demonstrated that its hero was among the "truest of Americans," and that Lee belonged in the nation's "common heritage." The *New York Times* echoed this sentiment, placing Lee at the heart of reconciliation. Lee's "memory," announced the *Times,* was "a possession of the American people, and the monument . . . a National possession."[28] This mixture of reactions indicates that a debate still ensued in the land about just how much the Lost Cause ought to be incorporated into national culture. But that incorporation was well under way and critics could hardly have stopped it.

African Americans reacted to the Lee cult generally, and the Richmond monument specifically, with a combination of silence and defiance. As early as 1871, when the Lee cult took root, Frederick Douglass denounced its potential as a source of Southern political revival. Douglass feared a "devoutly cherished sentiment, inseparately identified with the 'lost cause.'" He denounced the "bombastic laudation of the rebel chief" and lamented that he could "scarcely take up a newspaper . . . that is not filled with *nauseating* flatteries of the late Robert E. Lee." "It would seem," he wrote as though trying to answer Early and the diehards, "that the soldier who kills the most men in battle, even in a bad cause, is the greatest Christian, and entitled to the highest place in heaven." By 1890, Lee certainly had his high place above the landscape of Richmond, as well as in national Civil War memory. But the three blacks who survived politically on the Richmond city council voted against the city's appropriation for the monument. Those who wore the "clinking chains of slavery," wrote John Mitchell, editor of the *Richmond Planet,* had a perfect right to "keep silent" about the monument. The black editor denounced the Lee monument, its fund-raising committees, and the spectacle of its unveiling. In this era of labor unrest, Mitchell chose to remind white Virginians that blacks also participated in Memorial Days, North and South. "He [the Negro] put up the Lee Monument," warned Mitchell, "and should the time come, will be there to take it down. He's black and sometimes greasy, but who could do without the Negro?"[29]

Silence or rhetorical condemnation were about the only options open to blacks in 1890. Their place in the Confederate commemoration, as well as in the Lost Cause, had become carefully prescribed. Mitchell reported hearing an "old colored man" who "after seeing the mammoth parade of the ex-Confederates on May 29th and gazing at the rebel flags, exclaimed, 'The Southern white folks is on top—the Southern white folks is on top!'" Who can really know what an elderly black man in Richmond must have felt looking up at the giant Lee statue: Fear? Outrage? A sense of irony and inevitability? Perhaps he might even have laughed at the extraordinary extent that white folks would go to forget while remembering. According to Mitchell, the old man took heart. "A smile lit up his countenance as he chuckled with evident satisfaction, 'But we've got the government! We've got the government!'"[30] The Republican Benjamin Harrison had defeated Grover Cleveland in the 1888 presidential election. But the old black man's hope notwithstanding, Republican commitments to black rights had steadily eroded since Reconstruction. The Lee monument now represented a South seeking reunion and respect, a society poised to forge a new racial system that would reinvigorate the cause Lee had fought for, even though the legend makers, along with thousands of sincere believers, would endlessly claim that he and his men never made war for slavery. The Lost Cause thus transformed into a new cause.

The old man in Mitchell's article had reasons to mix his smile with dread. Blacks remained quite active in Virginia politics during the 1880s in a fledging Republican Party as well as a variety of "readjuster" tickets. Yet even Virginia, which was not nearly as notorious as its neighbors to the South in its record of racial violence, had averaged two lynchings per year in the 1880s, while its governors, including Fitzhugh Lee, had remained silent. As the celebration of the Lee monument was taking place in Richmond, the U.S. Congress was about to debate Henry Cabot Lodge's "Force Bill," a law that would have reinforced an 1870 enactment enabling the federal government to supervise all phases of registration and voting in national elections. Born of the Republican Party's desire to end the Democratic Party's widespread practices of fraud and intimidation in some Southern state elections, the Lodge bill passed the House of Representatives but failed narrowly in the Senate. That defeat was a harbinger of the great upheaval to come in the 1890s in American society and politics. Indeed, the bitter Congressional debates over the Lodge force bill were a public symposium on the memory of emancipation and Reconstruction. The unveiling of the Lee monument came just before the final substantive national debate the country would have in the nineteenth century over the black man's right to vote and the responsibilities of the government to protect that right. Moreover, between August and October 1890 the state of Mississippi convened a constitutional convention and passed the first explicit disfranchisement law aimed at blacks. Through a variety of contrivances—property qualifications, literacy tests, and a poll tax, all of which were replicated over the next two decades in each former Confederate state—blacks were effectively eliminated from Southern political life.[31]

As the Lost Cause found its new, forward-looking voice of reconciliation, the Southern terms on which it flourished included the demeaning of black people as helpless, sentimental children and the crushing of their adult rights to political and civil liberty under the Fourteenth and Fifteenth Amendments. In the next two decades Jim Crow danced his steps at hundreds of Confederate monument unveilings and veterans' parades. High atop his monument in Richmond, Lee represented many of the inspirations Southerners now took from their heritage: a sense of pride and soldierly honor, an end to defeatism, and a new sense of racial mastery.

DURING THE 1890s, three entities took control of the Lost Cause: the United Confederate Veterans (UCV), founded in 1889; a new magazine, the *Confederate Veteran,* founded in 1893 and edited in Nashville by Sumner A. Cunningham; and the United Daughters of the Confederacy (UDC), founded in 1894. Both the UCV and the UDC grew rapidly as organizations that complemented one another. The UCV was born in New Orleans in June 1889, out of a growing impulse among local veteran organizations to amalgamate into larger groups. Survivors' associations and associations of particular armies had long engaged in fraternal support and local remembrance. But as the national reunion took hold, so too did ex-Confederates seek more national forms of expression. The UCV's first commander-in-chief was former U.S. Senator and then governor of Georgia, John B. Gordon. Gordon was a New South politician with heroic credentials, and he provided an eloquent voice for both Confederate memory and reconciliation on Southern economic and political terms. By 1896, the UCV had 850 local camps, and by 1904, they had 1,565. The geographical distribution of UCV camps included at least one in 75 percent of the counties of the eleven former Confederate states. The best estimate of membership in the UCV seems to be 80,000 to 85,000 in 1903, a peak year.[32] Appealing to the interests of the ordinary veteran, especially against the fears and trials of 1890s economic collapse and political turmoil, the UVC became a safe haven of comradeship and celebration for the full range of Lost Cause attitudes and rituals.

For its part, the UDC spread across the South and also established some chapters in the North. By 1900, the UDC boasted 412 chapters and 17,000 members in twenty states and territories. By World War I it may have had as many as 100,000 members engaged in a wide variety of memorial activities. The generally well-heeled UDC women were strikingly successful at raising money to build Confederate monuments, lobbying legislatures and Congress for the reburial of Confederate dead, and working to shape the content of history textbooks. They distributed tens of thousands of dollars in college scholarhsips to granddaughters and grandsons of Confederate veterans. The UDC ran essay contests to raise historical consciousness among white Southern youth, and by the turn of the century they had launched an ongoing campaign to designate "War between the States" as the official name for the conflict. In all their efforts, the UDC planted a white supremacist vision of the Lost Cause deeper into the nation's historical imagination than perhaps any other association. Working largely from women's sphere as guardians of piety, education, and culture, many UDC members nonetheless led public-activist lives; although most opposed women's suffrage, many of their leaders were intensely political people. Behind, and often at the center of, every Confederate reunion (their pictures adorning the pages of nearly every issue of the *Confederate Veteran*) were UDC women, old and young, the "auxiliaries," "sponsors," and "maids of honor" without which the Lost Cause could not have dominated Southern public culture as it did.[33]

The UDC served its patrician class interest, but its activists both eroded and hardened the bonds of Southern womanhood. UDC women included advocates of women's suffrage as well as those who opposed it. Women such as Lila Meade Valentine of Richmond might grow up ensconced in the planter class and weighted down with the full burden of the Lost Cause as well as the expectations of a Southern "Lady." But some, as in Valentine's case, became gradualist, progressive reformers and persistent crusaders for women's rights. Valentine embraced most tenets of the Lost Cause, but also became president of the Equal Suffrage League in Virginia. Within women's sphere, and while preserving a genteel white supremacy, women like Valentine believed the "New South Lady" could be the agent by which the whole South could transcend the legacies of defeat and Reconstruction.[34]

At a proliferating array of veterans' reunions that Southern cities competed to host, and in oratory and writings, Confederate memory transformed into a set of arguments for a cause not lost. Ex-Confederates still had much to mourn, but the Lost Cause now appeared more as chapters in a victory narrative. This new ideology still nurtured dogmatism and mysticism, but it took hold in five potent arguments. First, veterans and the Daughters continued to glorify the valor of Southern soldiers and to defend their honor as defensive warriors who were never truly beaten in battle. Second, Lost Cause advocates of the 1890s especially promoted the Confederate past as a bulwark against all the social and political disorder of that tumultuous decade. Third, the UCV and the UDC established history committees that guarded the Confederate past against all its real and imagined enemies. Fourth, contrary to the norm in Blue-Gray fraternalism, many Lost Cause writers and activists during the reconciliationist era were not at all shy of arguing about the *causes* of the war. Fifth, and most strikingly, a nostalgic Lost Cause reinvigorated white supremacy by borrowing heavily from the plantation school of literature in promoting reminiscences of the *faithful slave* as a central figure in the Confederate war. Together, these arguments reinforced Southern pride, nationalized the Lost Cause, and racialized Civil War memory for the postwar generations.

Sentimental journeys into Civil War memory had become a national pastime. In *The Mind of the South,* Wilbur Cash observed that "the growth of the Southern legend was even more sentimental than it was grandiloquent." It was both. Under the influence of Thomas Nelson Page and others, the Lost Cause spread by pathos and pompousness. In his fictional stories, Page touched every chord of Lost Cause emotion. "The Gray Jacket of 'No. 4'" (1892) ends with a Confederate veterans' parade where, in a crowd rising as a "tempest" at the sight of the old soldiers,

> Men wept; children shrilled; women sobbed aloud. What was it! Only a thousand or two of old or aging men riding or tramping along through the dust of the street, under some old flags, dirty and ragged and stained. But they represented the spirit of the South; they represented the spirit which when honor was in question never counted the cost; the spirit that had stood up . . . against overwhelming odds . . .; the spirit that is the strongest guaranty to us today what the Union is and is to be; the spirit . . . glorious in victory . . . yet greater in defeat.

And in his nonfiction such as *The Old South* (1892), Page gave Lost Cause ideology full voice. The heroism of the South almost surpassed understanding, according to Page. The North had arrayed the "world against her . . . its force was as the gravitation of the earth—imperceptible, yet irresistible."[35] The South had lost, but only by gloriously resisting the engines of nature itself.

Here was the South as America's fallen man, the source of sacrificial blood for the remission of national sins—"greater in defeat." Hence the reunion was dependent upon a New South still draped in images of the Old. As with soldiers' reminiscence, such sentimentalism met with a warm welcome among powerful Northern publishers. In 1890, Richard Watson Gilder imperiously rejoiced at "how much more national" Northern periodicals had become because of the presence of Southern writers. "It is well for the North, it is well for the nation," said Gilder, "to hear in poem and story all that the South burns to tell of her romance, her heroes, her landscapes; yes, of her lost cause."[36] Thus did Gilder and other Northern editors nurture the rise of the Confederate Lost Cause as a national heritage.

In 1896 a Southerner, Albert Morton, attended a UCV reunion in Richmond and a GAR reunion in Saint Paul, Minnesota. He found a "marked contrast" between the two events. Both involved enormous crowds and festooned streets. In Richmond, Morton found "tumultuous" enthusiasm, the singing of Confederate songs by "thousands of throats," and tears everywhere as women kissed old flags and people cheered wildly for the marching veterans. In the more staid Saint Paul, Morton was disappointed at a parade where "the heart was lacking." He found himself "astounded at the apathy, the woodenness of the onlookers." Hardly anyone cheered the Union veterans as they marched by; Morton saw even a "cripple who hobbled along on his crutches amidst profound silence." Judging by the character of these reunions, Morton concluded: "I felt, as I watched the blue coated veterans pass, that I would rather have been a soldier under the Southern cross."[37] When it came to commemorating the war, Southerners seemed to have more passion and more fun.

Moreover, in 1894, the *Confederate Veteran* reported a story of a Southern mother and her son attending a production in Brooklyn, New York, of the play *Held by the Enemy*. The boy asks his mother, "What did the Yankees fight for?" As the orchestra strikes up "Marching through Georgia," the woman answers: "For the Union, darling." "Painful memories" bring sadness to the mother's face as she hears the Yankee victory song. Then, earnestly, the boy asks, "What did the Confederates fight for, mother?" Before the mother can answer, the music changes to "Home Sweet Home," which fills the theater with "its depth of untold melody and pathos." The mother whispers her answer: "Do you hear what they are playing? *That* is what the *Confederates* fought for, darling." "Did they fight for their *homes?*" the boy counters. With the parent's assurance, the boy burst into tears, and with the "intuition of right," hugs his mother and announces: "Oh mother, I will be a Confederate!"[38] Apocryphal or not, this tale represents a place that the Confederate veterans and their cause had reached in American popular culture. They had lost the war in 1865, but were winning the hearts of millions and providing a healing balm for the worried and disruptive society of the 1890s. Their conservative rebellion now seemed an antidote to the new ethnic invasion of America's shores, and especially to farmers' and workers' revolts. In the bewildering technological and industrial society, and amidst resurgent racism, a white boy growing up in America in the 1890s might find safe havens in the past and present by just *being a Confederate.*

Many Confederate Memorial Day speakers embraced memories of the Old South as a way of denouncing the New. At an 1895 gathering in Savannah, Georgia, the orator, Pope Barrow, rejected all "prating of a 'N——— South.'" He set the Lost Cause off as the protector of the real America now under threat. "The Southern people are the Americans of Americans," proclaimed Barrow, "and ex-Confederates of today are representatives of an American army—not an army made up largely of foreigners and blacks fighting for pay . . . I believe in the Old South." These code phrases for racial supremacy and nativism often spilled into more explicit expressions. At Memorial Day ceremonies in Nashville in 1894, a U.S. district judge, G. R. Sage, embraced reconciliation by warning of impending threats to the American political order. "How soon the crisis may be upon us . . . we do not know," offered Sage. But he called on North and South to "stand shoulder to shoulder and present a united . . . front against the vicious and revolutionary and communistic elements which threaten the public safety." At a reunion in Waco, Texas, another judge, George Clark, told assembled veterans that their cause was "not lost" and "could not be lost" in the nation's new hour of peril. Pointing to a Confederate flag, Clark declared that it stood for "the right of the enjoyment of our liberty and that equal dignity of right to enjoy the fruits of our labor." Clark made the new enemy clear. He called on his comrades to join ranks "against the aggressions of government, against the aggressions of anarchy, against the aggressions of communism in every shape."[39] In the 1890s the Lost Cause emerged as a useful weapon against radicalism and a bulwark against social diversity and disorder. Indeed, many of our controversies at the turn of the twenty-first century over the continuing presence of Confederate symbols, especially the battle flag, can be traced to this era when the Lost Cause changed its skin and became both a force of reunion and reaction.

During this second era of Lost Cause discourse, its advocates accelerated the fight to control historical interpretation of the Civil War. UCV and UDC history committees, in conjunction with a proliferation of state history associations, engaged in what one historian has called "a grand crusade to secure in the hearts and minds of the region's young" what it had lost on battlefields, and to "immunize southern children against democratic reforms then threatening the South's ruling class." "Thought is power," declared Mary Singleton Slack at a Louisville, Kentucky, meeting in 1904. She called on the Daughters to build the "greatest of all monuments, a thought monument" for the "pulsing hearts and active brains" of Southern youth.[40] Slack captured much of what was at stake in the struggle to control Civil War memory in turn-of-the-century America.

Since the 1860s every organ of Lost Cause thought had declared itself a bulwark against prejudiced Yankee history. In 1893, as S. A. Cunningham launched his *Confederate Veteran,* he announced a "fraternal" mission of peace. "Bitterness," he said, would not be his stock in trade. Above all else, though, Cunningham declared that his magazine would "vindicate the truth of history at all hazards." The *Confederate Veteran* became the voice of the UCV, the clearinghouse for Lost Cause thought, and the vehicle by which ex-Confederates built a powerful memory community that lasted into the 1930s. Many veterans wrote to Cunningham expressing their love for the journal, which with "every succeeding year," wrote a Tennesseean, "adds luster to the Lost Cause." Similar to the role that *Century* played with its war series in the 1880s, the *Confederate Veteran* attracted hundreds of poems, copies of war records, and reminiscences from old soldiers and their wives and families. New South reconciliationists, as well as the most unreconstructed rebels, seemed to find their interests met in Cunningham's popular repository of Confederate heritage.[41]

Cunningham himself was no towering intellect, but he was a dogged defender of the South and a tireless organizer of veterans' activities. He was often at odds with the UCV leaders, who practiced too much Blue-Gray fraternalism for his taste. Cunningham made white supremacy central to the magazine's vision, welcoming to its pages frequent tributes to "faithful slaves" and denouncing the racial equality attempted during Reconstruction. Eventually, Cunningham all but banished the terms "Lost Cause" and "New South" from the journal because they did not sufficiently vindicate the Confederacy's wartime goals. His brand of reconciliation folded easily into the South's new victory narrative. "No! No! Our cause was not lost because it was wrong," he announced in 1909. "No! No! Our cause was not lost for the reason that it was not wrong." Cunningham reprinted or endorsed hundreds of speeches from reunions and dedications, none more forcefully than Bradley T. Johnson's tribute to Confederate triumphalism and white supremacy at the opening of the Confederate Museum (quoted near the beginning of this chapter), which he contended "should become a part of the education of every child in the South."[42] In endless refrains about true history and nonpartisanship, the preservers of the Confederate tradition built one of the most enduring and partisan mythologies in American experience.

As early as 1899, UDC chapters endorsed a pro-Southern textbook and began their decades-long crusade to fight what many perceived as a Yankee conspiracy to miseducate Southerners.[43] When UDC women took up the cause of history they did so as cultural guardians of their tribe, defenders of a sacred past against Yankee-imposed ignorance and the forces of modernism. They built moats around their white tribe's castles to save the children from false history and impure knowledge. But they did so by manning the parapets and by constant incursions into enemy territory. Many UDC leaders were anything but pious, quietistic women adorning irrelevant parlors with approved books. They were activists eager to fight to control America's memory of slavery, the Civil War, and Reconstruction. They delivered public speeches, wrote in the popular press, and lobbied Congressmen. On a popular level, they may have accomplished more than professional historians in laying down for decades (within families and schools) a conception of a victimized South, fighting nobly for high Constitutional principles, and defending a civilization of benevolent white masters and contented African slaves. If the Lost Cause now marched to a victory song, the UDC provided much of its spirit and its righteous indignation.

Many UDC activists harbored abiding memories of wartime loss and suffering. Janet Weaver Randolph, the founder and spirit of the Richmond UDC chapter, was seventeen when the war ended in 1865. She spent the entire war on her family's 179-acre farm near Warrenton, in northern Virginia. Her thirty-eight-year-old father had died of typhoid as a Confederate private, and her mother had been captured and detained as an alleged Confederate spy while trying to reach relatives in Philadelphia for financial help. The Weavers boarded and cared for wounded men on both sides, and young Janet's memorial work began even before the war ended with Sunday rituals of placing flowers at gravesites of dead soldiers. In 1880, Janet Weaver married Norman V. Randolph, a Confederate veteran active in the Lee Camp in

Richmond. She was a founding member of the women's group that converted the White House of the Confederacy into a museum, and with time she became the UDC's most effective lobbyist with politicians. Her long efforts to get the Congress, War Department, and two Presidents to reinter the Confederate dead from Northern cemeteries to their various Southern homes, as well as to erect monuments to the prison dead at Northern sites, resulted in an extensive reburial of Southern soldiers in Arlington National Cemetery in 1903. Fiercely loyal to the Lost Cause, Janet Randolph nevertheless used her memorial work to struggle against some of the barriers encircling women's sphere. In an interview in 1916, she called herself an "uneducated woman" who had grown up with the hardships of the war. "The women who spend their all to get the advantage of even a few months at the University," she complained, "are not accorded the degrees that will rank them with the men. Do you call this chivalry to women? Is it placing them on that lofty pedestal our opponents so delight to talk of?" Randolph reflected on the obstacles in her own life and seemed to recognize that she lived on the cusp of a new age. "I am not a suffragist," she said, "but it is just such injustice that will cause the women of Virginia to become suffragists."[44]

The UDC woman who may have had the greatest influence on Southern historical consciousness was Mildred Lewis Rutherford of Athens, Georgia. Serving as historian general of the UDC from 1911 to 1916, Rutherford gave new meaning to the term "diehard." A prolific lecturer, writer, and organizer, Rutherford was the most conspicuous woman among many who prompted local chapters to conduct essay contests and to solicit reminiscences—the collection of which, along with similar efforts by the *Confederate Veteran* and some libraries, produced an extensive oral history of the Lost Cause. From the late 1890s onward, Rutherford was active in historical work, and for twenty-seven years she was principal of the Lucy Cobb Institute, a school for girls in Athens. She considered the Confederacy "acquitted as blameless" at the bar of history, and sought its vindication with a political fervor that would rival the ministry of propaganda in any twentieth-century dictatorship. She assembled dozens of scrapbooks, documenting every conceivable aspect of the Lost Cause and white supremacy. Rutherford traveled the country in period gowns with hoop skirts and delivered speeches entitled "Wrongs of History Righted" or "Historical Sins of Omission and Commission." Her conception of Southern history included large doses of romantic plantation imagery. "How restful the old life was!" went a typical expression. "What a picture of contentment, peace and happiness it presented! It was something

Mildred Lewis Rutherford of Athens, Georgia, historian general of the United Daughters of the Confederacy from 1911 to 1916, traveled the country lecturing and organizing in support of the Lost Cause and white supremacy. (The Museum of the Confederacy, Richmond, Virginia)

like our grandmother's garden." She seemed to borrow directly from Page's stories. "The Negroes under the institution of slavery were well-fed, well-clothed, and well-housed," she claimed. "How hard it was for us to make the North understand this!" Rutherford's absolutism flowed in endless recitals of the "horrors" of Reconstruction. She peddled the theory of black racial decline since emancipation. Had blacks "benefitted by freedom"? she asked in speeches. "As a race," she answered, "unhesitatingly no!" Slave health had been exemplary, she claimed. "I never saw a case of consumption . . . and now negroes are dying by the hundreds yearly. I never heard of but one crazy negro before the war. Now asylums cannot be built fast enough to contain those who lose their minds."[45]

For all who would listen, Rutherford fashioned Confederate memory into a revival crusade and the Old South into a lost racial utopia. In an era when patriotism and history instruction were thoroughly conflated in the public schools, Rutherford insisted that the Confederacy be ranked in glory with the American Revolution. She lectured teachers to display and teach about the Confederate battle flag, and urged that pictures of Confederate heroes be hung in every school. She provided to instructors lists of Civil War causes (five primary and ten "aggravating"), all of which placed responsibility at the feet of abolitionists. And Rutherford spoke with utter certainty that the American reunion was a victory for Southern righteousness. "While we are trying to right the wrongs of history and literature," she declared in 1915, "let us be very careful to do it in the spirit of truth and peace. Surely the South can best stand gracefully for peace, for she has the most to forgive."[46]

The UCV entered this history crusade earlier than the UDC, and the fervor of its efforts no doubt inspired the women. Under the leadership of former general Stephen D. Lee, the UCV Historical Committee issued a remarkable report at its 1895 reunion in Houston, Texas. The committee portrayed itself as a political force engaged in a moral struggle for the soul of the South. They urged a social and educational awakening that would demand "vindication of the Southern people, and a refutation of the slanders, the misrepresentations, and the imputations which they have so long and patiently borne." The committee defended the right of secession and rejected slavery as the cause of the war. "Slavery," said the UCV committee, "was the South's misfortune, the whole country's fault." "The true cause of the war between the states," it further argued, "was the dignified withdrawal of the Southern states from the Union . . . and not the high moral purpose of the North to destroy slavery, which followed incidentally as a war measure." The target of the report was "New England historians" who had foisted upon the country histories full of "prejudice" and "passion." In the need to organize themselves into an "influential agency" of a proper historical memory, the UCV committee demonstrated above all else its embrace of a particular conception of history.[47] The implicit assumption at work in its report was that history, especially for those who judge themselves aggrieved, is at heart a form of political advocacy. Historical memory, therefore, was a weapon with which to engage in the struggle over political policy and a means to sustain the social and racial order.

The UCV's attempt to produce a "deeper, surer . . . permanent mode of vindicating the South" was nothing less than a political movement, a quest for thought control aimed at shaping regional and national memory of the war. The Historical Committee ranked school histories of the United States in three categories: first, Northern books that were "pronouncedly unfair to the South"; second, Northern-authored works that were "apparently fair" but still judged "objectionable"; and third, "Southern histories," those that passed all of some nine tests, including whether a book had properly represented the "unparalleled patriotism manifested by the Southern people in accepting" the war's "results." Eight books, all written by Southerners, made the recommended list. Mildred Rutherford and the UDC produced similar approved lists and condemnations of Northern histories. "We are absolutely powerless if we permit ourselves to be dominated by the book trust," she charged, "and allow Northern publishing houses to place books unfair to us in our schools." Everywhere she went, Rutherford urged that "no library should be without" approved Southern histories and "all of Thomas Nelson Page's books."[48] In such constant appeals for "truthful history," Lost Cause ideology, especially the notions that slavery really did not cause the war and that Reconstruction was the vicious oppression of an innocent South and the exploitation of ignorant blacks, sunk deeper with each passing year into the South's and the nation's memory.

No argument in the Lost Cause formula became more an article of faith than the disclaimer against slavery as the cause of the war. In reunion speeches, committee reports, and memoirs, it is remarkable to note the energy Southerners spent denying slavery's centrality to the war. Some, like John B. Gordon in his *Reminiscences* (1903), allowed that slavery was the "immediate fomenting cause" of conflict, "the tallest pine in the political forest around whose top the fiercest lightnings were to blaze." But "responsibility" for slavery, he contended, could not be "laid at her [the South's] door." So familiar and ubiquitous were these arguments that they flowed effortlessly from Southern pens. "It was not the desire to hold others in bondage," contended a Richmond Memorial Day orator in 1894, "but the desire to maintain their own rights that actuated the Southern people throughout the conflict." At a Franklin, Tennessee, Memorial Day in 1901, an orator carried the argument about responsibility to its utopian conclusion. "In 1861," declared Judge H. H. Cook, "the southern people were the best informed, most energetic, the most religious, and the most democratic people on earth." They had "no classes" and "perfect equality" among whites. As for the slaves, who had been imposed on them by Northern traders, they had nobly "civilized and Christianized 4,000,000 of this unfortunate race."[49] The Lost Cause imagined millions of willing and contented slaves in its nostalgic remembrance, with slaveholders in the role of providers and mentors for African bondsmen.

So eager were ex-Confederates to deny responsibility for slavery's existence, as well as their role in causing it, that it would have been impossible to grow up in the South from 1890 to World War I and not have heard or read such arguments many times over as the common sense of white Southern self-understanding. Many Confederate veterans wrote of their refusal to "be handed down to the coming generation as a race of slave-drivers and traitors." The stock Confederate Memorial Day speech contained four obligatory tributes: to soldiers' valor, women's bravery, slave fidelity, and Southern innocence regarding slavery. Robert E. Lee, grandson of the famous general, hit all of these chords at an Atlanta gathering of five thousand people in April 1911, but with an assertion of Southern innocence he twisted history inside out. "If the South had been heeded," said Colonel Lee, "slavery would have been eliminated years before it was. It was the votes of the southern states which finally freed the slaves."[50] In such strange logic, the Lost Cause not only absolved Southerners of responsiblity for slavery, but made them the truest abolitionists. Protected by such mists of sentiment, the past could be anything people wished.

With time, women's organizations and state departments of education took over much of the responsibility for historical work, publishing elaborate guides containing defenses of secession and condemnations of the antislavery movement.[51] From this combination of Lost Cause voices a reunited America arose pure, guiltless, and assured that the deep conflicts in its past had been imposed upon it by otherworldly forces. The side that lost was especially assured that its cause was true and good. One of the ideas the reconciliationist

Lost Cause instilled deeply into the national culture is that even when Americans lose, they win. Such was the message, the indomitable spirit, that Margaret Mitchell infused into her character Scarlett O'Hara in *Gone with the Wind* (1936), and such, perhaps, is the basis of the enduring legend of Robert E. Lee—through noble *character,* he won by losing.

IF LOST CAUSE ideology gained long-term strength from its success in controlling history books, and by banishing slavery from the war's causation, it drew its staying power from the image of the faithful slave and the overall ideology of white supremacy. An outpouring of loyal slave narratives in the *Confederate Veteran,* in reminiscences collected by the UDC, and in popular musical entertainments produced the vernacular equivalent of Page's fiction. The image of the loyal slave may be one of the most hackneyed clichés in American history, but no understanding of the place of race in Civil War memory is possible without confronting its ubiquitous uses in turn-of-the-century culture. From its beginning, admiring readers of the *Confederate Veteran* urged its editor to reach out to the younger generation and counter the "tons of literature giving the dark side of slavery." "Let each issue of your paper contain something telling the bright side," wrote Manly B. Curry, son of a Tennessee veteran, "of the corn shuckings, the quiltings, the barbecues, the big meetings, the weddings." Show that "the slaves enjoyed life," Curry urged Cunningham, "and were not eternally skulking in dark corners dodging the whip." Cunningham needed little prodding; he saw contemporary race relations as the best reason to promote stories of faithful slaves of yore. In a 1905 issue of the magazine devoted largely to material about "old-time darkies," Cunningham offered a "lesson" for "young negroes": "Their aspirations for social equality will ever be their calamity. If they will observe the situation as it really exists, they will see that not an old-time negro lives in the South to-day faithful to white people who has not among them sustaining friends." In such devotion, Cunningham believed, young blacks should find their models for life. "The only solution of this matter is for negroes to accept the situation," the editor concluded; "treat the whites with deference, and they will soon realize the best they need ever hope to exist between the races."[52] In its racial fervor, the Lost Cause seemed to find new energy from the growth of national reconciliation and a segregated society.

Some Confederate reunions and United Daughters of the Confederacy events honored elderly blacks-deemed "loyal slaves" or "faithful Confederates"-for their service to their former owners and to the Lost Cause. (From *Confederate Veteran,* July 1910)

These young men, representing the third generation of emancipated blacks in 1913, offer a powerful response to the "faithful slave" ideology as they pose with dignity and confidence. (From *Crisis,* February 1913)

From the mid-1890s to as late as 1930, the *Confederate Veteran* published hundreds of tributes to faithful slaves, often written by former masters. Stories of "Negro devotion," of faithful servants saving their masters from wartime battlefields, of old blacks paying tribute to their old "marster" or "mistiss," and photographs of old slaveowners with their surviving ex-slaves became regular features in the magazine as well as in newspapers. The zeal with which white Southerners marshaled the faithful slave idea to support the Lost Cause tells us more about tensions in the Jim Crow South than it does about antebellum history. "It is my fixed opinion," declared B. G. Humphreys, a Mississippi politician, in 1903, "judging the negro who grew to manhood in slavery and the negro who has grown to manhood in freedom, that as a race he reached his zenith in all those qualities which make for civilization . . . under the old regime." As though he might have heard some early blues or work songs that he found repulsive, Humphreys longed for "the songs that have come down to us from the old plantation" because they were "not the songs of the caged bird; there is no wailing of the soul crying out to its God for deliverance."[53] This Mississippian left a telling statement of how much some white Southerners were affected by black music, but in the long run how little they comprehended it.

In dialect poems written in the voices of loyal slaves, in "darky" minstrel performances, and in unpublished family reminiscences, white Southerners strove to convince themselves that emancipation had ruined an ideal in race relations. Festivals under such titles as "Old Plantation Days," at which ex-slaves would swap staged stories with Confederate veterans, became common in Southern public culture. Such an event in Grant Park in Atlanta in 1913, sponsored by the Country Collective Society, featured black storytellers and hominy tastings by "uncles" and "captains." UDC chapters nationwide made "Stories of Faithful Slaves" one of their primary subjects of essay contests. In an essay denying any role for Lincoln's Emancipation Proclamation in freeing the slaves, Fanny Selph, historian of the Nashville UDC, reassured her readers that the "tie between master and servant was not only beautiful, but it was strong." She invoked "tender memories" of all "black mammies" and honored the loyalty of black laborers since the war in protecting the South from "the low class of foreigners." This fidelity had enabled the South to "preserve in its purity our Anglo-Saxon population," contended Selph. "We have been spared the great troubles that come from anarchy, strikes, and labor agitations which have disturbed the North and East." Loyal slaves, who never really wanted their freedom, were far more prominent in the Southern imagination in 1915 than they had ever been in 1865. In a reminiscence dictated to her daughter, North Carolinian Bertha Lucas Smith recited how the slaves at the family plantation, Meadow Hill in New Hanover County, had been a "happy and contented lot." "Life held all happiness," it seems, until the war came, when in its final year, "every male slave except old Uncle Jim left my Father to join the yankee forces." The runaways further demonstrated their "loyalty" by stealing their master's box of special papers, thinking it contained money. Smith's nostalgic remembrance includes a tribute to the "true heroism" of white Southern women, but her main message remained one of incredulity at how such a "happy past" could have vanished.[54]

Such nostalgia was rooted in an assumption that the slaves had protected their masters during the crisis of their own freedom. Or, as an Alabaman put it in 1914 in advocating a monument to faithful slaves, "exceptions to the affectionate loyalty of the negroes were practically unknown." In this flood of testimony about faithful blacks at the heart of Civil War memory, history gives way completely to mythology. The thousands of slaves who escaped to contraband camps, joined the Union army and navy, or fled when opportunities came while working in Confederate hospitals or on railroads and fortifications—as well as the daily revolution that occurred in the master-slave relationship during the war—had been steadfastly repressed in Southern memory. The "faithful slave" was of course not a complete fiction. The complex, ambivalent, fearful reaction of many slaves to the prospect of freedom and their often heroic protection of their owners' property from Union forces all gave some basis to the claim of fidelity. But ignored were the myriad ways that blacks joined the revolution for their own freedom. Lost to near oblivion in white memory by the early twentieth century were the countless wartime testimonies of planters about the "defections" and "betrayals" of their most trusted slaves. The stories of the Louisiana planter who saw a "perfect stampede of the negroes" in his parish and observed one of his plantations "cleaned out" in an apparent work stoppage had no place in Lost Cause memory. The South Carolina planter's admission in 1865 that "we were all laboring under a delusion" that slaves were "content, happy, and attached to their masters" fell into a record that the UDC did not care to collect by 1900. All those planters "betrayed by *pet* servants," in the words of another Louisianan during the war, fell silent in the new paradigm of Lost Cause memory, only to be rediscovered more than a half-century later by scholars working with new questions and assumptions.[55]

The compulsion to remember faithful slaves led many Southerners to advocate formal monuments in their honor. At least one such monument was erected before World War I, as part of a remarkable ensemble of memorials in Fort Mill, South Carolina. The brainchild of Samuel E. White, a Confederate veteran and local cotton mill owner (the richest man in the area), the Fort Mill faithful slave monument was dedicated in May 1896. Beginning in 1891, White brought about four monuments on the village green: a standard soldier monument, a monument to Confederate women, a monument to the local Catawba Indians who had supported the Confederacy, and a marble obelisk to loyal slaves. This unique paean to slavery included two panels, one depicting a mammy sitting on the porch of a columned mansion, holding a child in her arms, and the other a male laborer sitting on a log holding a sickle, his hat lying restfully on the ground. In such repose, with images of dedicated labor and loving care, the faithful slave received a permanent place in the Lost Cause landscape. White's inscription summed up a well-rehearsed story: "Dedicated to the Faithful Slaves who, loyal to a sacred trust, Toiled for the support of the Army with matchless Devotion, and with sterling fidelity guarded our defenseless homes, women, and children during the struggle for the principles of our 'Confederate States of America.'" At the unveiling, White found some local blacks to pull the cords (probably mill employees) and to provide part of the huge audience.[56]

The idea of faithful slave and mammy monuments had only begun its career of inspiration in Lost Cause circles. Indeed, beginning at least as early as 1905, the UDC carried on a campaign for nearly two decades to erect mammy memorials in every state, and lobbied Congress for a national mammy memorial in Washington, D.C. Support for mammy monuments was widespread within the UDC; many elite white women believed that they "must remember the best friend of their childhood," as Mrs. B. Bryan wrote to Janet Randolph in Richmond in 1910. Randolph, however, was not so sure; she frequently favored relief efforts for poor black children. "While remembering these poor little creatures," Randolph wrote in a public letter, "remember the old negro. No monument to them, if you please, until we have attended to their earthly wants." Such a progressive impulse found less enthusiasm within the UDC, however, than building monuments that advanced the organization's social agenda. The national effort for a mammy memorial ebbed and flowed during the World War I era, culminating in the passage in 1923 of a $200,000 appropriation in the Senate to build such a monument on Massachusetts Avenue near Sheridan Circle. The monument design, by the Hungarian-born George Julian Zolnay (a popular sculptor of

Confederate memorials), provided for a large fountain and a majestic mammy sitting as if on an altar, surrounded by three children. The bill failed, however, in the House of Representatives. The nation was only narrowly spared the ironic spectacle of unveiling a major memorial to faithful slaves on a prominent avenue in Washington only one year after the dedication of the temple of freedom and union the country has known ever since as the Lincoln Memorial.[57]

Short of building stone memorials, many Southerners went to great lengths to acknowledge former loyal servants as actual Confederate veterans. Ex-slaves participated at some Confederate reunions in various capacities, primarily as laborers and cooks. In 1900 in Brazos County, Texas, a black farmer, Henson Williams, and his son were murdered by whites while plowing in a field. Because he had "fought through the civil war as a Confederate soldier," the local UCV camp buried him with honors and threatened to lynch his assailants. At an occasional UCV parade or ceremony, an old black man or two would appear in uniform and march as a "veteran." In Memphis, Tennessee, in 1904, Preston Roberts, called "Uncle Pres" by the Confederate veterans, was given a "cross of honor" by the local UDC. Roberts had been a cook for Nathan Bedford Forrest's cavalry during the war. The *New York Sun* wrote admiringly of Roberts as a "typical antebellum darky" and so loyal a "negro rebel" that during the war he would relieve weary soldiers on picket duty, shoulder the musket himself, and sleeplessly defend the men "whose chattel he was." Similarly, the *Atlanta Journal* marveled in 1900 at "Uncle" Amos Rucker, "the only colored United Confederate Veteran member" who had marched with a Georgia camp. Rucker, who had also been a camp cook in the war, marched in a suit of gray with Confederate buttons and badges, and he seemed to fulfill white expectations for Negro authenticity. Although the Atlanta reporter acknowledged that his type was hardly seen anymore "outside of the novel," Rucker "never wanted to be free," and his hair was "like Uncle Ned's of song fame." Blacks who participated in Confederate memorial events, and who even courted the designation of "veteran," no doubt had complex motives. Old black servants who could secure white witnesses to vouch for them actually received modest pensions in some Southern states.[58]

In her capacity as historian general of the UDC, Mildred Rutherford assembled a massive collection of the racist underworld of the Lost Cause. Essay contests on the glories of the Ku Klux Klan and personal tributes to faithful slaves fill several of her scrapbooks. A Louisiana chapter claimed to have received more than three thousand essays on Confederate generals in one year. Northern chapters in such cities as Chicago, Dayton (Ohio), and New York all gave annual essay prizes. In 1915 in Seattle, Washington, a young girl received the annual "loving cup" for her prize piece honoring the men of the Klan. Rutherford was inundated with hundreds of reminiscences of every kind, many of which focused on the lives of white women and their relationships with faithful blacks. Demonstrating that the racial dimension of women's Lost Cause activism was not confined to the deep South, the Los Angeles chapter of the UDC sent Rutherford an especially large batch of faithful slave essays in 1915. Many women wrote about battles and wartime policies, some choosing condemnation of emancipation as their theme; others wrote of the oppression of Reconstruction. Rutherford did not confine her collecting duties to written texts; included in her scrapbooks are scores of photographs and postcards of Klansmen, lynchings, and especially "loyal" ex-slaves.[59] All UDC members and leaders were not as virulently racist as Rutherford, but all, in the name of a reconciled nation, participated in an enterprise that deeply influenced the white supremacist vision of Civil War memory.

Mrs. A. B. Lindsey, a member of the Lancaster, Virginia, chapter of the UDC in 1913, paid effusive honor to the "fidelity" of her former slaves. "Uncle Nelson," admired as a "life-long Democrat," was always in the "foremost ranks of every Red Shirt parade." If Nelson "lacked courage, it was a weakness of nature." And "Aunt Nancy," the laundress, was remembered lovingly because "she literally dropped from the ironing table, for she worked much harder after freedom than before." Lindsey spiced her narrative with her own poem, "What Mammy Thinks of Freedom," which concluded with the lines: "Ef dis is freedom—God forbid! / I calls it simply knabery. / An' w'en I gits ter hebben, Lord, / I hope I'll find it's slabery." Lindsey ended with a warm sense of assurance about the travail she saw in the New South. "In God's providence slavery came and went," she concluded, "and while the race question of today is a vexing problem, we can always feel sure that white supremacy is God-given and will last." In such explicit terms, the UDC collected the past and imagined the present.[60]

The men of the UCV embraced no less explicit forms of white supremacy in their imaginings. At a reunion in Augusta, Georgia, in 1903, the popular orator J. C. C. Black held the veterans spellbound. With cheering men standing on chairs and tables, waving hats and canes, Black proclaimed: "We did not fight to perpetuate African slavery, but we fought to preserve and perpet-

uate for our posterity the God-given right of the freedom of the white man."
For the "supremacy of the white man," Black continued, the veterans must
carry on a new "war of moral suasion" in the new age. The only struggle over
"bondage" in the Civil War epoch had been that inflicted on Southern whites
by their postwar Northern oppressors. And the only liberation to be commemorated, he maintained, was that of "Anglo-Saxon emancipation."[61] In
such language, the Lost Cause emerged in the early twentieth century as a
Southern narrative of racial victory, a major force in the collective memory in
which the American reunion flourished.

BY THE TURN of the twentieth century the reunion was all but a fully
completed political fact, and the short adventure of the Spanish-American
War helped solidify it. But the Southern terms from which the reunion drew
its life had to be defended at all costs. White supremacy, a hardening of traditional gender roles, a military tradition and patriotic recognition of Confederate valor, and a South innocent of responsibility for slavery were values in
search of a history; they were the weapons arming the fortress against the
threats of populist politics, racial equality, and industrialization. For UDC
and UCV leadership, those values were a social elite's last, best protection
against the progressive and democratic society they most feared. Among
some in the new generation of Southern intellectuals, defending the Lost
Cause became a positive, mystical vocation. Just after 1900, Douglass
Southall Freeman, who grew up in Lynchburg, Virginia, surrounded by Confederate veterans whom he all but worshipped, launched his successful career
as Robert E. Lee's prolific and loyal biographer and one of the South's most
partisan historians. For Freeman, the Lost Cause was Virginia's civil religion.
His deepest appeals were to the mysticism of Confederate heroism amidst the
battlefields around Richmond where, as he proclaimed in a 1918 speech,
"wind and water, and sky and ground alike, are vocal with the chords of our
dead fathers. Oh! did a people ever live in the midst of such great traditions
as ours? To count ourselves Virginians, men, is to count ours the greatest heritage ever given to a people."[62] In real-life policies as well as in mysticism, the
Lost Cause had a hold on the American imagination.

Just as reminiscence reflects essentially the need to tell our own stories, so
too crusades to control history demonstrate the desire to transmit to the next
generation a protective and revitalizing story. An almost desperate need for
sectional and racial justification compelled Lost Cause history crusaders to

equate virtually any form of Southern defense with "truth." Hence one of the conclusions in the UCV Historical Committee's 1897 report: "Works in vindication of the course of the South before and during the civil war will be invaluable . . . but controversial literature is not history, and is out of place in political instruction." The need to convert Southern defeat into a victory narrative was never so explicit as in that same committee's 1900 report. In the postwar South, the UCV maintained, the Confederate veteran had won several "victories of peace." "First, came the political victory, from which he rescued his State from the carpetbagger and adventurer," argued the report; "second, came the social victory, by which he restored the time-honored institutions and redeemed the social fabric; third, came the industrial victory, by which he readjusted the labor system and created the industrial progress of the South; fourth, came the financial victory, by which he recuperated his own wasted fortune." This story, and these terms, had so firm a hold on the popular Southern historical imagination that the UCV committee could conclude without the slightest irony: "This association has ever been the promoter of patriotism and reconciliation between the several sections of our common country, and the advocate of nonpartisan history."[63]

In 1900, William Faulkner was a three-year-old boy growing up in New Albany, Mississippi. He would eventually drink in Southern Civil War memory and then reimagine it as few others in American letters. Given the character of the "history" demanded by the Lost Cause, it is little wonder that a new generation of Southern writers had by the 1920s rebelled against its strictures and insisted in a variety of ways on forging a literary "renascence." Robert Penn Warren may have retrospectively captured this need to break out of an inheritance of doctrinaire tradition in his tribute to Faulkner's work in 1946. Warren pondered the condition of Southern memory and the treatment of blacks laced throughout Faulkner's writing:

> If respect for the human is the central fact of Faulkner's work, what makes that fact significant is that he realizes and dramatizes the difficulty of respecting the human. Everything is against it, the savage egotism, the blank appetite, stupidity and arrogance, even virtues sometimes, the misreading of our history and tradition, our education, our twisted loyalties. That is the great drama, however, the constant story.[64]

The Lost Cause left just such a legacy; it was not essentially inhuman in character, but its very existence depended upon dehumanizing a group of people.

And as a reactionary revitalization movement, it constricted creative impulses and stultified historical understanding. The Lost Cause made itself a ready target; it forced a confrontation with the past that bred a Faulkner, a Warren, a Flannery O'Connor, and many others in white Southern letters. Piety rarely lasts forever as a substitute for knowledge among those determined to probe the depths of human drama, and twisted loyalties can produce good literature.

But the Lost Cause had always bred dissenters. The scalawags, ex-Confederates who joined the Republican Party during Reconstruction, were the first dissenters from Lost Cause ideology. The much maligned James Longstreet of Georgia, former colonel and legendary partisan cavalry leader in Virginia John S. Mosby, political leaders such as James W. Hunnicut in Virginia, James Lusk Alcorn of Mississippi, Amos T. Ackerman of Georgia, and Thomas Settle Jr. of North Carolina, and many others embraced new economic development and acted with a spirit of unionism to resist Lost Cause mythology. Moreover, in the wake of Reconstruction the "Readjuster" movement in Southern politics brought another form of rejection to the Lost Cause. Successful expecially in Virginia, the Readjusters took their name from a growing, class-based resistance to the insistence of conservative Democrats (the Bourbons) on paying off all public debts from the war era in order to preserve state "honor." The Readjusters demanded repudiation of those debts, and instead favored public investment, the expansion of schooling, and economic development that served ordinary people, black and white.[65]

Led in Virginia by the former Confederate general, railroad entrepreneur, and brilliant political organizer William Mahone, the biracial Readjuster insurgency swept to power in that state in 1879–83, taking control of the governor's office, the legislature, and six of ten seats in Congress, and sending Mahone to the U.S. Senate. Mahone's amazing success, especially his sincere willingness to build a biracial coalition, demonstrated the possibilities for an economically and racially just New South. Mahone's New South vision, contrary to Grady's or Page's, had no place for Lost Cause doctrine. "I have thought it wise to live for the future," Mahone wrote to a fellow former Confederate in 1882, "and not the dead past . . . while cherishing honorable memories of its glories." The Readjuster phenomenon caught on to a lesser degree in several other Southern states, but by the mid-1880s the Democrats' rabid appeals to white supremacy had swept Mahone and others out of office almost as quickly as they had appeared.[66]

The great hopes represented by the Readjusters—that the color line might be broken and that education might be truly modernized and democratized—resurfaced in the 1890s with the even larger Populist movement. With its roots in the resistance of farmers' alliances to the power of banks, railroads, and grain elevators in the 1880s, Populism took its urgency from economic depression in the 1890s. At the heart of Populism was a rebellion against oligarchy and privilege, and therefore, by its very character, it was hostile to Lost Cause tradition. For a while during the upheaval of the nineties, the Populist revolt forced a viable two-party system into Southern politics, and most importantly, it brought blacks into political life more vigorously than at any time since radical Reconstruction. The Populists, whether their leaders fully intended it or not, threatened to overthrow the political, if not the social, color line.

But for most white Southerners in the 1890s, the growing rage to separate the races, to crush black liberty, and to kill alleged black criminals in hideous public rituals festered in raw memories of Reconstruction. The "fusion" tickets, forged in some states between Populists and Republicans, threatened conservative white Southerners as nothing had since 1868–70. When Thomas L. Nugent, the Populist candidate for governor in Texas in 1894, condemned his former party, the Democrats, for abandoning their principle of "equal rights to all, special privileges to none," or when the Georgia Populist Tom Watson appealed to class as a means for blacks and whites to "daily meet in harmony . . . and wipe out the color line," the leaders of the Lost Cause—the UCV or Democrats in state houses—mobilized their crusade to control the nation's history and the South's social order.[67] It is no coincidence that the UCV, UDC, and *Confederate Veteran* all emerged in force in the very years that Populism peaked in power.

The model dissenter in Southern literature was George Washington Cable, who after 1885 lived the remainder of his life as an expatriate of a sort in Northampton, Massachusetts. Cable's dissent from the sentimental literature of reunion contained a political challenge that only grew in significance with time. In his extraordinary essay "The Silent South," first published in the *Century* in September 1885, Cable reasserted his "faithful sonship" to the South. He wrote with near mystical admiration for the Robert E. Lee monument in New Orleans, Cable's hometown. Lee's image might yet be the source of a more humane, progressive Southern spirit. The marble Lee "symbolizes our whole South's better self," he wrote, "that finer part that the world not always sees; unaggressive, but brave, calm, thoughtful, broad-minded . . . and, in the din of boisterous error round about it, all too mute." With more subtlety and intelligence than perhaps any other nineteenth-century white Southern thinker, Cable challenged "traditionists" to alter their habits of "evasion," to "move on" and cease their fears of miscegenation and "social equality" with blacks. Demanding that the future must offer civil and political equality to blacks, Cable taught his own history lessons. He took his critics back to the dreaded era of "Reconstruction agony" and asked them to remember their own deepest impulses. They were governed, he charged, by "our invincible determination—seemingly to us the fundamental condition of our self-respect—never to yield our ancient prerogative of holding under our discretion the colored man's status, not as a Freedman, not as a voter, but in his daily walk as a civilian." Reaching out for reason and comity with his critics, Cable only demonstrated how irreconcilable his views were with the racial vision of Lost Cause tradition. "This attitude in us," he claimed, "with our persistent mistaking his [freedman's] civil rights for social claims, this was the taproot of the problem."[68] Cable and Lost Cause "traditionists" might agree about the "taproot" of Southern racial woes, but not on their own mistakes. That "daily walk" of black civilians haunted debate over whether memory or the future should reign in the South.

With the professionalization of history in the 1890s, the training of scholars in "scientific" seminars under Herbert Baxter Adams at Johns Hopkins University or William A. Dunning at Columbia, new forms of Lost Cause dissent came on the scene. Some young historians, such as William E. Dodd, John Spencer Bassett, William P. Trent, and eventually Ulrich B. Phillips countered the control that veterans and the Daughters exercised over historical memory. In 1902, Dodd complained in the *Nation* about how the UCV had forced history teachers to "subscribe unreservedly to trite oaths" about Southern righteousness on secession and a war that had nothing to do with slavery. Most Southern professional historians did participate in Confederate Memorial Days and other celebrations, and many of their works were either cautiously or openly supportive of Lost Cause arguments. Many who did criticize orthodoxy in Southern memory or society, however, paid a price.[69]

In 1901, Bassett, a product of Johns Hopkins and a professor at Trinity College (later Duke University) in Durham, North Carolina, founded the *South Atlantic Quarterly* to "counteract the reactionary feeling in the Southern press in matters on which tradition had developed ideas provincial and intolerant." In 1903, Bassett created a storm of protest with an article "Stirring Up the Fires of Race Antipathy," in which he attacked racial demagoguery among politicians, condemned lynching, and suggested that blacks might one day rise and demand their equality. Almost incidentally, Bassett remarked that Booker T. Washington was the "greatest man, save General Lee, born in the South in a hundred years." These opinions drove some members of the Trinity board of trustees and much of the white North Carolina press to seek Bassett's ouster. His case became a cause célèbre of free expression in higher education. By a vote of 18 to 7, Bassett retained his job, although many faculty distanced themselves from his views. Bassett believed in black inferiority and segregation. But he was one of the first Southern historians to study African American history. He wrote two books on slavery and black religion in North Carolina, and more than any other professional white Southern historian of his time, he engaged the black experience seriously as a scholar, essayist, and reviewer. The staunchly conservative historian Walter Lynwood Fleming interpreted Bassett's provocative 1903 essay as a "martyrological, superior, new Southern, jackassical attitude . . . toward all things of the Old South." Bassett was purposefully provocative. But he also simply sought the freedom to write history as he found it. In 1906, he left his native North Carolina and took a teaching position at Smith College, where he became Cable's permanent neighbor in Northampton, Massachusetts.[70]

Other such cases of historical orthodoxy and academic freedom rocked Southern universities. In 1911, native Southerner Enoch M. Banks, a professor of history and economics at the University of Florida, wrote a fiftieth-anniversary piece on secession in the New York–based *Independent*. In the spirit of "a free estimate of our past," he said, "and a frank realization and acknowledgement of its errors, where errors are found," Banks offered his assessment of the birth of the Confederacy. He declared that the "fundamental cause of secession and the Civil War, acting as it did through a long series of years, was the institution of slavery." Banks believed that "calm history" would demonstrate that those who work for the "best interests of advancing civilization are in the right in the highest and best sense of the term right." He concluded, therefore, in assessing responsibility for the war, that "the North was relatively right, while the South was relatively wrong." A whirlwind of protest and defense ensued. The UDC called for Banks's resignation, he was condemned in the Florida press for his "false and dangerous" views, and rumors circulated that the state would cut off funds to the university. Although he was defended by some Southern newspapers, including the *Atlanta Constitution*, Banks resigned his teaching position, ruined by the irony that his effort at "calm history" could so easily be blown away by sudden storms of Lost Cause dogmatism.[71]

Perhaps the most intriguing, if mercurial, dissenter to the Lost Cause was the "Gray Ghost," John Mosby. Mosby's exploits during the war—he was the guerrilla cavalry leader who raided Union forces and supply trains, captured a Union general out of his own headquarters, and even hanged prisoners—made him one of the conflict's most romantic figures. Educated at the University of Virginia before enlisting as a private in 1861, Mosby remained fiercely proud of his military service throughout his long life (he died in 1916). But in 1872, he became a scalawag and worked for Grant's reelection in Virginia, beginning a long relationship with the Republican Party that would land him appointments in the foreign service as well as the Justice Department. As a dissenter from Lost Cause mythology, Mosby set a standard for candor. He loathed Confederate reunions and refused to participate in large veterans' organizations, although he did relish the small meetings with comrades in his former command, the mysterious Forty-third Battalion Virginia Cavalry.[72]

Mosby's political stand during Reconstruction made him one of Virginia's most prominent political exiles; after 1877, he lived most of the rest of his life in San Francisco, Washington, D.C., or abroad, and for one sixteen-year period, he never set foot back in Virginia. The Virginia diehards never forgave Mosby's apostasy from the Lost Cause. They slandered him as a turncoat, as "the most serviceable partisan Grant has in Virginia." During the election campaign of 1872, Mosby lamented his loss of place in the South. "It is but seldom now that I receive a word of cheer from a Southern source," he wrote to Alexander H. Stephens, "and the last few months have been to me like a passage through 'the Valley of the Shadow of Death' so great has become the intolerance of our poor infatuated people." Mosby's political realism led him to support the Republican Rutherford B. Hayes in 1876. In a public letter to a former Confederate comrade that year, he warned that the Lost Cause was a dead end. "You speak of the bitter hostility of the North toward the South," he said. "Well, four years of hard fighting is not calculated to make men love each other; neither is an everlasting rehearsal of the wrongs which each side imagines it has suffered going to bring us any nearer to a better understanding. Peace can only come with oblivion of the past." Mosby was dead as a Virginian. "I did change my politics because politics changed," he reminisced in 1897. "I did not, according to the cant of the day, 'go with my people.'"[73]

Mosby had firm ideas about how the meaning of the war ought to be remembered and how Confederate soldiers ought to seek public respect. "I have never apologized for anything I did during or since the war," he wrote in

1895. "How little we know about the future," he wrote of the spring of 1861, when he followed the "tocsin of war." "It was our country and we fought for it and we did not care whether it was right or wrong." In 1910, breaking completely with normative Lost Cause arguments, Mosby declared that "I committed treason and am proud of it." He participated in numerous literary feuds and disputes, and frequently complained about the orthodoxy of the Lee cult. Mosby was hardly reluctant to "take sides with truth," he said in 1910, but "the whole trouble I have is butting up against the popular belief in the infallibility of Gen. Lee."[74]

Most importantly, Mosby contributed some of the most candid expressions by any ex-Confederate about the place of slavery in the South's cause. He remained hostile or ambiguous on racial equality. But while a former slaveowner himself, he viewed slavery apologetics by the 1890s as the most debilitating element of the Lost Cause. "I don't go to reunions," he told an old comrade, "because I can't stand the speaking." He despised the "oratorical nonsense" of so many speakers who recycled the ideas that the South neither fought for nor was responsible for slavery. Referring to one such speech, Mosby reacted: "Why not talk about witchcraft if as he said, slavery was not the cause of the war. I always understood that we went to war on account of the thing we quarrelled with the North about. I never heard of any other cause of quarrel than slavery." Mosby spurned virtually all Lost Cause arguments about slavery. "I can't see how setting the negroes free could have saved the Union," he remarked in 1894, "unless slavery was the cause of the breach." And in 1902, he left a telling guide to all lost causes in a letter to a member of his battalion. "Men fight from sentiment," wrote Mosby. "After the fight is over they invent some fanciful theory on which they imagine that they fought."[75]

In 1907, Mosby also reacted to an especially righteous report of the UCV Historical Committee written by George Christian, in which slavery was depicted as as a system of "patriarchal" happiness. Mosby wrote to a friend in "disgust." "According to Christian the Virginia people were the abolitionists and the Northern people were *pro-slavery,*" complained Mosby. "He says slavery was 'a patriarchal' institution. So were polygamy and circumcision." Mosby denounced the idea that "Old Virginians" (founding fathers) were antislavery. Then he delivered a dagger at the heart of Lost Cause mythology:

> Now while I think as badly of slavery as Horace Greeley did I am
> not ashamed that my family were slaveholders. It was our inheri-

tance. Neither am I ashamed that my ancestors were pirates and cattle thieves. People must be judged by the standard of their *own* age. If it was right to own slaves as property, it was right to fight for it. The South went to war on account of Slavery . . . I am not as honored for having fought on the side of slavery—a soldier fights for his country—right or wrong—he is not responsible for the political merits of the course he fights in. The South was my country.[76]

If such honesty and spirit of debate had prevailed in Southern confrontations over the Lost Cause, the career of Civil War memory in America might have been different. That it did not and could not tells us much about the tragic interdependence of race and reunion. That the Mildred Rutherfords prevailed in Southern memory over the John Mosbys demonstrates how and why the Lost Cause left such an enduring burden in national memory.

NINE

Black Memory and Progress of the Race

> We do not forget that even in the North much
> greater consideration is shown the white man who
> attempted the dissolution of this government than to
> the black man who served it. The poetry of the
> "Blue and the Gray" is much more acceptable than
> the song of the black and the white.
>
> —CHRISTIAN RECORDER, July 13, 1890

IN THE THREE DECADES following the twentieth anniversary of emancipation, several strains of black Civil War memory—what we might call *attitudes toward the past*—emerged in American culture: the slave past as a dark void, a lost epoch, even as paralytic burden; a celebratory-accommodationist mode of memory, rooted in Booker T. Washington's philosophy of industrial education and the "progress of the race" rhetoric that set in all over a culture obsessed with the "race problem"; a view of black destiny that combined Pan-Africanism, millennialism, and Ethiopianism—the tradition (more a theory of history than a political movement) that anticipated the creation of an exemplary civilization, perhaps in Africa or in the New World, and which saw American emancipation as one part of a long continuum of Christian development; an African American patriotic memory, characterized by the insistence that the black soldier, the Civil War Constitutional Amendments, and the story of emancipation ought to be at the center of the nation's remembrance; and a tragic vision of the war as the nation's fated but unfinished passage through a catastrophic transformation from an old order to a new one. These strains of memory are not definitive; all could overlap and flow into one another. Together they form the conflicted determination of a people to forge new and free identities in a society committed to sectional reconciliation, even at the cost of forgetting the legacy and claims of its African American citizens.

ON NEW YEAR'S DAY, January 1, 1883, in Washington, D.C., an American flag hung at the end of a banquet room on Ninth Street, and a sumptuous feast for more than fifty men filled the table bedecked with flowers and candles. At half past seven in the evening, the twentieth anniversary to the day of the signing of the Emancipation Proclamation, former U.S. senator from Mississippi Blanche K. Bruce called the distinguished gathering of African American leaders to the table in honor of Frederick Douglass. The *Washington Bee* remarked that "never before in the history of the American negro has there ever been such an assemblage of leading colored men." The elaborate dinner honored the sixty-four-year-old Douglass, the famed abolitionist, autobiographer, and now elder statesman of the Republican Party establishment. On this occasion, Douglass served as black America's principal symbol of a people's journey from slavery to freedom.[1]

The guests represented a who's who of two generations of black politicians, civil servants, journalists, writers, professors, ministers, and soldiers. Prominent among them were Bruce as chair, the pan-Africanist scholar Edward Blyden, the former emigrationist, soldier, and politician Martin Delany, and the heroic wartime boat pilot and later Congressman from South Carolina Robert Smalls. Professors Richard T. Greener and James M. Gregory of Howard University were but two among a group of academics. The young historian George Washington Williams led the contingent of writers. The Reverend Benjamin T. Tanner, editor of the *Christian Recorder*, and T. Thomas Fortune, the bold, young editor of the *New York Globe*, headlined the ranks of newspapermen. The War Department clerk and Congressional Medal of Honor winner Christian A. Fleetwood appeared and was addressed as "Captain." Douglass's two sons, Charles and Lewis, veterans of the Fifty-fourth Massachusetts regiment, attended the tribute to their father. Among the gathering were Congressmen and members of legislatures from South and North, men who owned their own businesses and ministers of prominent churches. Some among them had disagreed fiercely with one another about issues and strategies for best advancing the race—and many had argued with Douglass himself, a fact the guest of honor freely acknowledged.[2]

Rivalries were left at the door. Perhaps most important of all, the generational divide was put aside for at least one evening of celebration. This was a night to contemplate the meaning of emancipation and to celebrate what the men present believed to be the new founding for their country and their people.

As the gentlemen settled in for a long evening (they did not adjourn until 3 A.M.), some forty-one toasts were offered to virtually every aspect of black life and aspiration, as well as to heroes of the antislavery cause. It was a men-only banquet (no women writers or leaders were invited), and one toast was offered to "the ladies." When introduced, Douglass delivered a speech in which he reached for the lodestar of recent American history. To hear Douglass on these occasions must have been to feel one's inheritance, to almost see history flowing as a procession in time. Who were black people in America at this moment of remembrance in 1883? According to Douglass, they were a people reborn with emancipation, and a new nation had been born as well. "This high festival of ours is coupled with a day which we do well to hold in sacred and everlasting honor," Douglass declared, "a day memorable alike in the history of the nation, and in the life of an emancipated people." Reflection on this day, continued the aging orator, opened "a vast wilderness of thought and feeling . . . it is one of those days which may well count for a thousand years."[3]

Fortune later recollected the evening as a transcendent experience. Normally, said the New York editor, he found Washington, D.C. "depressing" and "nauseating" in its political cynicism. "But the Douglass banquet, a spontaneous tribute of love, respect, honor, and veneration," he declared, "bridged over many a sigh . . . Indeed, the Douglass banquet was an event in the history of the race." Fortune forgot for the moment his own harsh criticism of Douglass's symbolic role and acknowledged the event as one for the transmission of memory, where "tender youth" were instructed by "mature age." Douglass, in Fortune's words, "bent low his majestic head of snowy whiteness and received with pleasurable emotions the homage of a host of men of his race, the majority of whom were unborn or in their infancy when he was thundering against the iniquity of the slave power." What unified the disparate gathering, Fortune believed, was the "cause of the race" and "gratitude and love" for Douglass.[4] With a combination of that love and differing agendas, the young men present that night went forth to do battle for America's memory of their freedom.

Douglass, no doubt, made their hearts pound and their throats choak. He filled the room with Civil War memory and gave to the occasion an incantatory refrain that he used some fifteen times in a breathless expression of the nation's rebirth. "Until this day," he said,

> Slavery, the sum of all villainies, like a vulture, was gnawing at the heart of the Republic; until this day there stretched away behind us an awful chasm of darkness and despair of more than two centuries; until this day the American slave, bound in chains, tossed his fettered arms on high and groaned for freedom's gift in vain; until this day the colored people of the United States lived in the shadow of death . . . and had no visible future . . . until this day it was doubtful whether liberty and union would triumph, or slavery and barbarism. Until this day victory had largely followed the arms of the Confederate army. Until this day the mighty conflict between the North and the South appeared to the eye of the civilized world as destitute of moral qualities. Until this day . . .

From the hour of emancipation, Douglass argued, the American republic had risen from its historic "spell of inconsistency and weakness," and black folk had seen the "first gray streak of morning after a long and troubled night." In these visions, Douglass lent more than sermonic flourish to the narrative of black Civil War memory. He took the central idea in Lincoln's Gettysburg Address—national rebirth and redefinition—and rendered it palpable as "felt history."[5] Here was the emancipationist vision of Civil War memory given the mythic power it would need to survive in the national imagination and in black communities. Against those heralding reconciliation and those carrying the banner of the Lost Cause, Douglass urged vigilance at the flame of black freedom and justice.

ALL ACROSS the land in that anniversary year of 1883, as well as for decades to follow, blacks continued to commemorate emancipation and Union victory. Their world had undergone a seismic change in 1861–65, and they did their best to forge a memory community that could keep their story at the center of national attention. Commemorating black freedom and the preservation of the Union came easy on days of celebration, but not in daily life or in the nation's treacherous politics of memory. While Southern Lost Cause advocates struggled to win a long-term victory out of what they came to see as the short-term defeat of the Confederacy, blacks and their white allies sustained a determined, if divided, struggle to themselves avoid the wasteland of lost causes. Remembering the thrill of emancipation, experiencing the pride of citizenship, witnessing the growth of black education and intellectual achievement, and building new black institutions all afforded the emancipationist vision fertile ground in which to take root.[6]

The story of the centrality of slavery and emancipation to Civil War history and memory made sense to most blacks. But the comfort for African Americans in looking back was not easily achieved. The clanging of the medals on a black veteran's jacket at a parade, the freedom anthems sung at commemorations, or the swarming crowds at black exhibitions about racial "progress" sometimes rang hollow against the screeching realities of lynchings, the degradation of blackface minstrelsy, the bleakness of poverty, and the insults of segregation. African Americans could not afford the despair born of short-term defeats, however; their sense of history had to embrace a long view, a faith that at least since 1863 time, God, and the weight of history might be on their side. As Ralph Ellison aptly put it, "Negro American consciousness is not a product (as so often seems true of so many American groups) of a will to historical forgetfulness. It is a product of our memory, sustained and constantly reinforced by events, by our watchful waiting, and by our hopeful suspension of final judgment as to the meaning of our grievances."[7]

With confidence and watchful waiting, black communities remembered their war and emancipation on all anniversary occasions. During 1883, black GAR posts held marches and public meetings from Massachusetts to Ohio, sometimes joining with white veterans in integrated gatherings. In Ohio, black GAR posts, which mobilized veterans of three regiments and booked special excursion trains, planned the largest gathering ever of their members for August in the town of Chillicothe. In New York, the Thaddeus Stevens post met in lower Manhattan in January 1883 for speeches and glee club entertainment. The following month, the William Lloyd Garrison post welcomed several other black posts from as far away as Hartford, Connecticut, and mixed with white veterans at the Bridge Street AME Church in Brooklyn for a full dress march and a choir performance. The Shaw Guards (named for Colonel Robert Gould Shaw) in Boston held frequent meetings, bringing together the surviving black rank and file with white officers of the Fifty-fourth and Fifty-fifth Massachusetts regiments. On Memorial Day,

1883, at Rainsford Island, Massachusetts, Julius C. Chappelle, the lone black member of that state's legislature, addressed a public ceremony conducted by black veterans. Chappelle predicted that the day was at hand when all civil rights will "be accorded us in South Carolina as well as we now enjoy in Massachusetts, in Texas as well as in Maine." For at least one stunning moment in Richmond, Virginia, on that same Decoration Day, 1883, a newly organized black GAR post in the former Confederate capital joined with a post from Worcester, Massachusetts (and probably at least one other Northern black post) in a parade to a cemetery. Most remarkably, some members of the R. E. Lee post of Confederate veterans participated as well, formally present-

Emancipation Day (January 1) became a major celebration in African American communities, North and South, as seen in this storefront in Richmond, Virginia, in 1888, which is decorated with flags, bunting, and a banner displaying Abraham Lincoln's image. (Cook Collection, Valentine Museum, Richmond, Virginia)

ing floral arrangements to the black veterans and to a black women's memorial association. The circumstances of this interracial cooperation on Decoration Day can only be surmised. But surely William Mahone's Readjuster movement (with its interracial political appeal) influenced the occasion. The Readjusters had just peaked in their control of the Virginia government, although they were soon to be overthrown in that year's fall elections.[8] Such possibilities for racial reconciliation amidst the culture of national reunion and white supremacy in the South were doomed to a sporadic and short life.

But confident memory prevailed at many black commemorations in that special year. On February 14, 1883, a Lincoln Day gathering of blacks from several towns met despite snowstorms in Meriden, Connecticut. Positioned around the hall were shields bearing the names of at least two dozen black and white abolitionist heroes, including Harriet Beecher Stowe, Lucretia Mott, James McCune Smith, Frederick Douglass, William Lloyd Garrison, Wendell Phillips, Robert Purvis, William Wilberforce, and others. On the walls were hung pictures of Lincoln, John Brown, Charles Sumner, James Garfield, U. S. Grant, and the late Republican governor of Connecticut Marshall Jewell, who had just died. Several white politicians addressed the gathering. Local black leaders, such as Walter H. Burr of Norwich, also spoke, delivering reminiscences of the antislavery movement, calls to action for "wiping out the color line," and tributes to black veterans. The racially integrated celebration ended with the singing of "John Brown's Body" and "America."[9] Such scenes large and small, some integrated and many not, would be repeated at countless emancipation celebrations for the next three decades, with similar symbols adorning halls or the altars of churches.

One of the most extraordinary celebrations during 1883 occurred in Washington, D.C., in April, on the twenty-first anniversary of the abolition of slavery in the District of Columbia. Washington blacks differed over whether to conduct such a celebration at a time when the condition of their people was anything but secure. But the April 16 parade was one of the most elaborate that blacks had ever staged in an American city. The line of march was a mile and a half long, with several bands and some 150 "chariots" and carriages. The procession was led by Colonel P. H. Carson, who in his uniform and feathered hat reminded watchers of Toussaint L'Overture; he was followed by eighteen mounted black policemen. Then followed a dozen military companies, groups of veterans, and drill teams. Behind the military contingents marched representatives of more than twenty-five civic organizations and social clubs, including the Ethiopian Minstrels, the Sons and Daughters of Liberty, the West Washington Union Labor Association, various district queens in their decorated chariots, the Brick Machine Union, the Cosmetic Social Club, the Knights of Labor with four horses and the Goddess of Liberty on a throne, the Paper Hangers Union, and the Rick's Park chariot carrying two beer kegs. Following this demonstration of black Washington's social life and labor activism came the proud representatives of some ten fraternal orders.[10]

Later that evening at the First Congregational Church, Frederick Douglass spoke to a racially mixed audience and called them to vigilance in the cause of black liberty and citizenship. "As the war for the Union recedes into the past," admonished Douglass, "and the negro is no longer needed to assault forts and stop rebel bullets, he is in some sense of less importance. Peace with the old master class has been war for the negro. As the one has risen the other has fallen." The implications of the cultural turn toward reconciliation for blacks could hardly have been more starkly expressed. Douglass left the celebratory audience that night with a cautionary tale of how and why "the negro" was America's "inexhaustible topic of conversation." What loomed as the greatest legacy of the war, he asked? "Americans can consider almost any other question more calmly and fairly than this one," he declared. "I know of nothing outside of religion, which kindles more wrath, causes wider differences, or gives force . . . to . . . more irreconcilable antagonisms." In the face of rising fears about the betrayal of their rights and new forms of violence, Douglass asked his listeners for clear-eyed forbearance. "There is no modern Joshua who can command this orb of popular discussion to stand still," he said. "As in the past, so in the future, it [the race question] will go on."[11] However resplendently they celebrated, the struggle of the race against the swell of the reunion, Douglass insisted, would never really end.

Throughout the spring and summer of 1883, a debate ensued among black leaders over whether to convene a national convention to bring their grievances to the attention of the nation. State conventions of black civic and religious leaders were still common occurrences in these years, with some advocating independence from the Republican Party. But other black spokesmen believed that the day for separate black conventions had passed with the war and the Constitutional victories of Reconstruction. Still others, like Fortune, resisted a convention initially planned for Washington, preferring a Southern city where "the problem for solution is to be found." Eventually a national assembly of more than one hundred black leaders from virtually every state met in Louisville, Kentucky, in late September. After intense debate, the assembly officially refused to endorse President Chester Arthur and the Republican Party. The convention's resolutions included an appeal to memory. The delegates announced their gratitude for "the miraculous emancipation" and adopted the language of national rebirth. But the bulk of their eleven resolutions were demands for the enforcement of civil and political rights, protests against prevailing economic conditions, and an insistence on equal education for black youth. The convention pronounced the provisions of the Fourteenth Amendment and the civil rights legislation of Reconstruction "nothing more than dead letters."[12] Twenty years after emancipation, it threw a bleak picture of African American conditions at the feet of the nation.

Douglass delivered the keynote address at Louisville, striking the year's mixed chords of proud remembrance and embittered betrayal. His widely reprinted speech challenged the nation to acknowledge the birthrights of African Americans. "Born on American soil in common with yourselves," he said to whites (the nation), "we, like yourselves, hold ourselves to be in every sense Americans," and having "watered your soil with our tears, enriched it with our blood . . . we deem it no arrogance . . . to manifest now a common concern with you for its welfare." Douglass then provided the Civil War generation's precursor of Du Bois's famous statement that "the problem of the twentieth century is the problem of the color line." The "feeling of color madness" and the "atmosphere of color hate," he declared, pervaded churches, courts, and schools, and worse, the deepest "sentiment" of ordinary people. So conditioned were whites to see blacks as inferior, said Douglass, that "in his [the Negro's] downward course he meets with no resistance, but his course upward is resented at every step of his progress." In Douglass's metaphors, the color line stalked like a wild animal and infected human organisms like a dreaded disease. "In all relations of life and death," he told the American people, "we are met by the color line. It hunts us at midnight . . . denies us accommodation . . . excludes our children from schools . . . compels us to pursue only such labor as will bring us the least reward."[13]

But Douglass asserted that where the "laws were righteous" the right could yet prevail. Black freedom, he reminded those who would listen, had not come from the "sober dictates of wisdom, or from any normal condition of things." Emancipation and the nation's new founding, he cautioned, "came across fields of smoke and fire strewn with . . . bleeding and dying men. Not from the Heaven of Peace amid the morning stars, but from the hell of war." The long legacy of that central fact, Douglass believed, guaranteed an enduring passion of "deadly hate and a spirit of revenge" at the heart of all attempts to work through the memory of the war.[14] That the revolution of 1863 came from the "hell of war," and that forces were now arrayed to permanently reverse that revolution, remained the tortured challenge before African Americans and the nation as a whole.

The delegates from the Louisville convention had hardly returned home when the U.S. Supreme Court landed a bombshell in the lap of black America. A group of civil rights cases had been pending before the Supreme Court throughout the year, including one in Kansas and another in Missouri of blacks denied accommodations at inns, a case from California of rejection from a theater, and a variety of instances of exclusion from first-class railway cars. The ruling in *United States v. Stanley* (also known as the civil rights cases) held that the equal protection clause of the Fourteenth Amendment applied only to states; a person wronged by racial discrimination, therefore, could look for redress only from state laws and courts. In effect, the decision meant that the discriminatory acts of private persons were beyond the safeguards of the Fourteenth Amendment and federal jurisdiction. In relegating enforcement of civil rights laws only to state authority, the court struck down the Civil Rights Act of 1875, rendering the entire meaning and intent of the Civil War Constitutional Amendments "sacrificed," as the lone dissenter, John Marshall Harlan, put it. The door was now open for the eventual passage of Jim Crow laws across the South.[15]

In the variety of African American responses to the 1883 Supreme Court decision, we can discern differing modes of black Civil War memory. At a mass meeting in Washington, D.C., Douglass tried to capture the pain and fear most blacks felt. "We have been . . . grievously wounded . . . in the house of our friends," he proclaimed. The Chief Justice in these years, Morrison R. Waite, was an Ohio Republican, and there were only two Southerners, both Republicans, and one Democrat from California on the high court. Douglass described a "national deterioration" of moral and political commitment to black rights with the "increasing distance from the time of the war." Justice for blacks, he contended, had lost ground from "the hour that the loyal North . . . began to shake hands over the bloody chasm." According to Douglass, the country was undergoing a failure of morality and national memory. The *Christian Recorder* counseled defiance, calling the decision "humiliating" and "maddening" and urging blacks to structure their lives within a segregated society. "Husband your resources," the AME organ told its readers, "know once and for all that you must depend upon yourself." The commemorative spirit of an anniversary year now gave way to a deepening sense of betrayal. The *New York Globe* said the decision had made blacks feel "as if they had been baptized in ice water." The *Boston Hub* thought the ruling "worthy of the Republic fifty years ago," and the *Detroit Plaindealer* said the decision came "like an avalanche, carrying our fondest hopes down the hill of despair."[16]

Black clergy reacted to the civil rights decision with heightened appeals for racial self-reliance and uplift. Convinced that white prejudices could never be conquered, the Reverend I. F. Aldridge advised blacks "to get property, land, money, education, religion . . ., and we will get our rights and justice before the Supreme Court of heaven." Aldridge spoke for conservative black ministers who counseled against agitation for civil and political liberty and instead urged the race to "come together as one man, and build churches, hotels, railroads, and everything else to our interests." The reverend represented an old and persistent strain of black social thought, a variation of which Booker T. Washington would fashion into a national movement within a decade. As the weeks after the decision passed, Benjamin Tanner, editor of the *Christian Recorder*, took a somewhat more moderate position, cautioning readers to keep the peace and to put faith in the Constitutional separation of powers to right the recent judicial wrong.[17]

But as blacks debated the meaning of the Supreme Court's ruling, perhaps the harshest reaction came from AME bishop Henry McNeal Turner. Already a staunch proponent of black emigration to Africa before 1883, Turner, never one to mince words, stepped up his calls to leave the country. He demanded a more intense race pride among blacks, and he gave up on American political institutions. "Those who suppose . . . that the remedy for our ills is to be found in national legislation or supreme court decisions," he wrote in June 1883, "are greatly mistaken." In an interview with a Saint Louis paper in November 1883, Turner charged that the Supreme Court decision absolved "the Negro's allegiance to the general government, makes the America flag to him a rag of contempt . . . reduces the majesty of the nation to an aggregation of ruffianism, opens all the issues of the late war." Turner's position was uncompromising: "As long as that decision is the law of the land I am a rebel to this nation."[18]

Howard University professor B. K. Sampson, claiming the court action was "not a finality," probably spoke for a large segment of educated blacks in resisting Turner. Sampson despised the decision, but he invoked African American sacrifice in a litany of Civil War battles and counseled confidence that "the public mind is softening as it ripens." Blacks could "afford to be loyal still," Sampson believed, because "Christianity and civilization" were on their side. As Turner spent the next twenty years trying to civilize and redeem Africa, other African Americans, with divergent views of the past and competing strategies of uplift, would struggle with how best to live with the realities that the civil rights decision had put in motion. With the color line sharpening, the black community faced decisions over just how to compete for its place in America's collective memory. Should blacks embrace or reject the nation they had helped to preserve and reinvent? Should they celebrate their own past, or lament its agonies? Should they fight the Lost Cause and segregation, or retreat into group self-development? Should they, in season and out, remind the country of their former enslavement, or simply not look back? Most African Americans heeded some version of the warning of Joseph C. Price, the young black educator and founder of Livingstone College in Salisbury, North Carolina. "The South was more conquered than convinced," said Price in 1890; "it was overpowered rather than fully persuaded. The Confederacy surrendered its sword at Appomattox, but did not there surrender its convictions."[19]

LATE-NINETEENTH-CENTURY blacks commonly referred to the era of slavery as a kind of historical void, a long dark night of denial and futility. For many this attitude flew in the face of experience and memory. Freedpeople knew that they had lived useful, creative lives; they could see what they had built and remember what they had imagined. For many, their faith reminded them that they were forever part of a purposeful history. Many others had to face a past they could never come to terms with, a formative experience that may have impoverished their minds and ravaged their bodies. Remembering slavery was, thus, a paradoxical memory: it was a world of real experience, one complicated by relationships with whites that were both horrible and endearing and enriched or traumatized by their own family and community relations. Slavery was also a collective racial experience in which it was difficult to take pride when the larger society looked on with so much amusement and contempt. Indeed, any perusal of the heart-rending advertisements in black newspapers by the 1880s for loved ones separated from families during slavery or the war demonstrates both the vitality and the destruction of family life. Looking back was not easy, but it was also unavoidable.

The emotional legacy in the personal advertisements was one of loss. The search for kin in newspapers began even before the war ended. In the summer of 1865, the national black paper, the *Christian Recorder*, ran numerous appeals demonstrating that slavery and emancipation had caused a new diaspora. Writing from Crawsfordsville, Indiana, Elizabeth Ann Jackson sought the whereabouts of two sisters and two brothers last seen in Virginia. Sold away from Virginia to New Orleans ten years before, Hannah Cole hoped to find her son, John, "the only child I have and I desire to find him much."[20] Sale and separation dominated the memories of many ex-slaves seeking their lost families.

By the 1880s, many freedpeople still desperately searched and waited. Thomas Cooper wrote from New Jersey, hoping for news of his mother, father, two brothers, two sisters, and his only daughter. In the chaos of the war, he had last seen his daughter in Kentucky and recollected that the rest of his family had been "sold in Virginia by William Goult." Many who submitted these notices could remember precise details of masters, traders, buyers, and locations in the South. They remembered many facts, but had no control over fate. Celia Poole of Iowa could name her owners and buyers through more than twenty years of haze, but she was left only to write: "When quite young, I was sold with my mother and brother Aaron to traders. My mother was sold again soon after leaving home. Since then I have never heard of her." Searching for her mother in 1880, another woman's plea reflected her namesake: separated from her mother in 1852, she "was sold to a speculator by the name of Alex Hopkin and was brought to Georgia [from North Carolina] . . . my name is Patience."[21]

In 1881, Albert Butts of Brooklyn, New York, still advertised for his brother, William. "We parted at the battle of Antietam," wrote Albert, in a war memory oddly out of place amidst the soldiers' reminiscences of the 1880s. Thousands of black women spent their aging lives trying to reassemble lost families dislocated by emancipation's diaspora. The Butts brothers, probably camp hands or gravediggers for the Union forces, no doubt had many war stories to tell. But no major magazine solicited the tales of many freedpeople and black war veterans. If they had, the culture of reconciliation taking hold in the 1880s might have included the epic of emancipation. That epic would be uncovered nearly a century later in scholarship and by the re-discovery of slave narratives.[22] But as Blue-Gray fraternalism grew in popularity, no such understanding of the effects of slavery and emancipation on African Americans penetrated the historical consciousness of most Americans.

The names, places, and unrequited hopes expressed in freedmen's advertisements provide a glimpse of how ordinary black individuals and families privately, as well as publicly, rejected the plantation legend. As Thomas Nelson Page's and Joel Chandler Harris's endearing uncles narrated story after story of slave loyalty and nostalgia for the Old South, black survivors of slavery named the names of "speculators" who had sold them and their kin into a deeper South. It was America's national tragedy that the memories of slavery that were popularized and sold in the last decades of the nineteenth century were the romantic fantasies of dialect writers, not the actual remembrance of ex-slaves themselves. Unfortunately, stories of slave sales, of displaced black migrants seeking new lives in new places, of the deprivation and humiliation of slavery, did not sell in a culture eager to purchase tales of reunion and soldiers' glory. How could a nation reunify itself by telling its epic through the experience of slavery and its consequences? Far better to root the new national narrative in a heritage of mutual heroism and in yearning for a lost civilization crushed by industrialization and an unavoidable war. To this day, at the beginning of the twenty-first century, much of Civil War nostalgia is still rooted in the fateful memory choices made in the latter two decades of the nineteenth century. As the *Christian Recorder* put it in 1890, "the poetry of the 'Blue and the Gray' is much more acceptable than the song of the black and the white."[23]

By the 1880s and 1890s, North or South, in a city or in a sharecropper's shack, where did most African Americans look for a safe haven in the past? Where could they find themselves a part of some uplifting history in the age of Progress? In what narrative did they root their fragile citizenship? What American story could they own? For many, looking back into the past forced an encounter with the shame of slavery. In an age that exalted self-made business titans, when Christianity stressed personal responsibility, and in a culture riven by theories of inherent racial characteristics, blacks carried the stigma of bondage. When Tourgée wrote in 1888 of blacks facing a slave past of "only darkness replete with unimaginable horrors," he only echoed a discourse well under way among blacks themselves. Bondage had left the collective "injury of slavery," said *Christian Recorder* editor Benjamin Tanner in

1878. "The very remembrance of our experience is hideous." In 1887, Tanner's paper ran a poem, "Keep Out of the Past," by Emma Wheeler Wilcox, which had an unmistakable meaning for blacks:

> Keep out of the past! for its highways
>   Are damp with malarial gloom.
> Its gardens are sere, and its forests are drear,
>   And everywhere moulders a tomb . . .
>
> Keep out of the past! It is haunted.
>   He who in its avenues gropes
> Shall find there the ghost of a joy prized the most,
>   And a skeleton throng of dead hopes. . .
>
> Keep out of the past! It is lonely
>   And barren and bleak to the view,
> Its fires have grown cold and its stories are old,
>   Turn, turn to the present, the new!

Hence, in a thousand settings, from magazine articles to sermons, from emancipation exhibitions to anniversaries, and in private communication, many blacks tended to consider slavery as an American prehistory that was painful to revisit. As the black sociologist Kelly Miller put it, "in order to measure . . . progress, we need a knowledge of the starting-point as well as a fixed standard of calculation. We may say that the Negro began at the zero point, with nothing to his credit but the crude physical discipline of slavery."[24] With this notion of emancipation as the *zero point* of group development, blacks risked reflection on their past and measured their progress.

Among the remarkable range of memories expressed in interviews with ex-slaves conducted in the twentieth century are many expressions of the sheer agony of remembering slavery at all. Delia Garlic, who had been sold several times and enslaved in three states, told of the sale of her "babies" to "speculators." "I could tell you 'bout it all day, but even den you couldn't guess de awfulness of it." Some former slaves may have exorcised their anger in the act of reconstructing their memories. "I's hear tell of dem good slave days," said a Texan, Jenny Proctor, "but I ain't nev'r seen no good times den." Her story was one of separation from kin and "cotton patch" labor. Born around 1858, Sarah Wooden Johnson of Petersburg, Virginia, wondered why her interviewer, Susie Byrd (also black), wanted to know so much of her past.

"Now don't ax me no mo' 'bout dat," Sarah admonished Susie. "What in de world is you gwine do wid all dis here longy, longy go stuff . . .? Ha, ha, ha. Say you is writin' hist'ry? A slave ain't had no say so of his own 'til de 'render [surrender] come and he was sot free. Glory, glory gal! . . . Dat's back stuff honey. Dis here is new time. Let dat be." Angry or painful memories are not the same thing as shame. Indeed, it is difficult to know when ex-slaves felt shame or when they merely exhibited a stoical disposition to not look backward. In ex-slave memory, one finds expressions of shame sometimes mixed with conservative nostalgia and intraracial contempt. Former North Carolina house servant Sarah Debro looked back at age ninety and declared: "My folks don't want me to talk about slavery, they's shame niggers ever was slaves. But, while for most colored folks freedom is the best, they's still some niggers that ought to be slaves now." Debro seems never to have abandoned her sense of class distinction as handmaid to her mistress. "I look back and thinks," she said. "I ain't never forgot them slavery days, and I ain't never forgot Miss Polly and my white starched aprons."[25]

At the end of the 1930s, when most of the slave narratives were recorded as part of the federal WPA project, the novelist Richard Wright, in his lyrical history of African Americans, *Twelve Million Black Voices* (1941), left a pained expression about the endurance of slavery's shadow. "When we compare our hopelessness with the vast vistas of progress around us," wrote Wright, "when we feel self-disgust at our bare lot, when we contemplate our lack of courage in the face of daily force, we are seized with a desire to escape our shameful identification."[26] A profound sense of grievance over the ravages and legacies of slavery and sharecropping, about the numbing persistence of poverty, animate Wright's work. That desire among blacks to escape the past was many decades old by the time Wright penned his proletarian manifesto of black history.

Black intellectuals of the late nineteenth century differed, often fiercely, over just how historically minded their people ought to be. At Storer College in Harpers Ferry, West Virginia, on Memorial Day, May 30, 1885, Alexander Crummell, one of the most distinguished black intellectuals, gave a commencement address, "The Need of New Ideas and New Aims for a New Era," to the graduates of the institution founded for freedmen at the end of the war. Crummell, an Episcopal priest educated at the abolitionist Oneida Institute in upstate New York and at Cambridge University in England in the 1840s, had spent nearly twenty years as a missionary and an advocate of African nationalism in Liberia (1853–71). Although Crummell could not resist acknowledging Harpers Ferry's associations with John Brown as a setting "full of the most thrilling memories in the history of our race," he hoped to turn the new generation of blacks, most of whom were born just before or during the war, away from dwelling "morbidly and absorbingly upon the servile past"; instead, they should embrace the urgent "needs of the present." As a minister and theologian, and as a social conservative, Crummell was concerned not only with racial uplift—his ultimate themes were family, labor, industrial education, and especially moral improvement—but also with the unburdening of young blacks from what be perceived as the "painful memory of servitude."[27]

Blacks, Crummell believed, were becoming a people paralyzed by "fanatical anxieties upon the subject of slavery." Black leaders seemed to "settle down in the dismal swamps of dark and distressful memory," and ordinary black folk fashioned life "too much after the conduct of the children of Israel." In his stern rebuke, Crummell made a distinction between memory and recollection. Memory, he contended, was a passive, unavoidable part of group consciousness; recollection, on the other hand, was active, a matter of choice, and dangerous in excess. "What I would fain have you guard against," he told the Storer graduates, "is not the memory of slavery, but the constant recollection of it." Such recollection, Crummell maintained, would only degrade racial progress; for him, unmistakably, "duty lies in the future."[28]

Prominent in the audience that day at Harpers Ferry was Frederick Douglass. According to Crummell's own account, his call to reorient African American consciousness away from the past met with Douglass's "emphatic and most earnest protest." No verbatim account of what Douglass said at Harpers Ferry that day survives, but his many anniversary and Memorial Day speeches during the 1880s offer a clear picture of what he may have said. A healthy level of forgetting, said Douglass in 1884, was "Nature's plan of relief." But in season and out, Douglass insisted that whatever the psychological need of avoiding the woeful legacy of slavery, that legacy would resist all human effort at suppression. The history of African Americans, he remarked many times in the 1880s, could "be traced like that of a wounded man through a crowd by the blood."[29] Better to confront such a past, he believed, than to wait for its resurgence.

In his many postwar speeches about memory, Douglass would often admit that his own personal memory of slavery was best kept sleeping like a "half-forgotten dream." But he despised the politics of forgetting that the culture of reconciliation demanded. "We are not here to visit upon the children the sins of the fathers," Douglass told a Memorial Day audience in Rochester in 1883, "but we are here to remember the causes, the incidents, and the results of the late rebellion." Most of all, Douglass objected to the historical construction that portrayed emancipation as a great national "failure." The growing argument (made by some blacks as well as whites) that slavery had protected and civilized blacks, while freedom had gradually sent them "falling into a state of barbarism," forced Douglass to argue for aggressive vigilance about memory. The problem was "not confined to the South," Douglass declared in 1888. "It [the theory of black degeneration coupled with historical misrepresentations of emancipation and Reconstruction] has gone forth to the North. It has crossed the ocean. It has gone to Europe, and it has gone as far as the wings of the press, and the power of speech can carry it."[30]

Crummell and Douglass had great respect for each other, but they had very different personal histories and different agendas. Crummell had never been a slave; he achieved a classical education, was a missionary of evangelical Christianity and a thinker of conservative instincts, and had spent almost the entire Civil War era in West Africa. He returned to the United States twice during the war to recruit blacks to emigrate to Liberia, while Douglass worked aggressively as an advocate of emancipation and recruited approximately one hundred members of the Fifty-fourth Massachusetts regiment. Crummell represented a brand of black nationalism that combined Western Christian civilizationalism and race pride. He contended that the principal problems faced by American blacks were moral weakness, self-hatred, and industrial primitiveness. Douglass, the former slave, had established his fame by writing and speaking about the meaning of slavery; his life's work and his very identity were inextricably linked to the transformations of the Civil War. The past made and inspired Douglass, and he had risen from slavery's prison; there was no meaning for him without memory, whatever the consequences of "recollection." The past also had made Crummell, but his connections to many of the benchmarks of African American social memory were tenuous and informed by African nationalism and Christian mission. For Douglass, emancipation and the Civil War were *felt* history, a moral and legal foundation upon which to demand citizenship and equality. For Crummell, they were potentially paralyzing memories—not the epic to be retold, but merely the source of future needs.[31]

Remembering slavery and emancipation thus became a forked road. Douglass's and Crummell's differing dispositions toward the past represent two directions that black thought could go in the 1880s. Both sought racial uplift, but one would take the risk of sustaining a sense of historic grievance against America as the means of making the nation fulfill its promises; the other would look back only with caution and focus on group moral and economic regeneration. Crummell sought to redeem Africa, and to inspire moral values in the freedpeople by the example of an elite black leadership. Douglass embraced the same values but sought to redeem the civil and political rights established by the verdicts of Fort Wagner and Appomattox. Crummell had tried to be a founding father of Liberia; Douglass dearly wished to see himself as a founding father of a reinvented American republic. With differing aims, Crummell and Douglass both sought to teach a new generation of African Americans how to understand and use the legacy of slavery and the Civil War era, how to preserve and destroy the past.

That past lingered in the writings of many blacks who joined the chorus of racial uplift ideology in the late nineteenth century. In one of her moralistic poems, Frances Ellen Watkins Harper, a novelist and lecturer, wrote of the "Dying Bondman" (1884) who had once been a chieftain in Africa. On his deathbed he pleads with his kind master for his freedom:

> "Master," said the dying chieftain,
>   "Home and friends I soon shall see;
> But before I reach my country,
>   Master, write that I am free;"
>
> "For the spirits of my fathers
>   Would shrink back from me in pride,
> If I told them at our greeting
>   I a slave had lived and died . . ."

"Precious token" in hand, the old man dies "free" of the burden of telling his kinsmen in heaven that his life was forever stained with slavery. The idea of slavery as the burdensome past informed much black religious writing, whether or not, as was often the case, the authors converted that burden into evidence of racial progress. Slavery had "blasted" the "higher powers" of "the Negro," wrote one AME minister, and had forced him to drag its legacies around like "a relic of the infirmity of those years he carries in his heart and brain." Uplift advocates were acutely aware of the servile past. The novelist Pauline Hopkins wrote in the preface of her romantic novel about Reconstruction, *Contending Forces* (1900), of her sincere desire "to do all that I can to raise the stigma of degradation from my race." Such a quest was particularly poignant for black women, who carried a special burden in seeking bourgeois respectability in a society that had for so long defined them only in maternal or sexual terms.[32]

The future beckoned, but the past remained a heavy weight to carry. Forgetting might seem wise, but also perilous. To face the past was to court the agony of one's potential limitations, to wonder if the rabbits really could outwit the foxes or whether some creatures in the forest just did have history and breeding on their side. "As slavery was a degrading thing," Crummell had said in his Storer address, "the constant recalling of it to the mind serves, by the law of association, to degradation." Long before Du Bois wrote of a struggle with the "double consciousness" of being American and black, African American freedmen had to decide how to look backward and forward. Many may have been like the characters Toni Morrison created in *Beloved* (1987)—haunted by slavery's physical and psychic tortures, but desperate to live in peace and normalcy. When Paul D says to Sethe, "me and you, we got more yesterday than anybody, we need some kind of tomorrow," Morrison imagined herself into the heart of late-nineteenth-century black memory. Memory is sometimes that human burden we can live comfortably neither with nor without. Douglass believed that black memory was a weapon and that its abandonment was dangerous to his people's survival. Crummell argued that a people can "get inspiration and instruction in the *yesterdays* of existence, but we cannot healthily live in them."[33] The story of black Civil War memory demonstrates that both were right.

W ITH EMANCIPATION widely viewed as a new creation, as the zero point of black racial development, a vast "progress of the race" rhetoric took hold in African American life and letters by the end of the nineteenth century. Part of this discourse was driven by the imperatives of uplift ideology: for the race to rise, build its own institutions, and defend itself against racist attacks and assumptions about group degeneration, the race's spokesmen had to demonstrate black advancement. Slavery might not always be mentioned in claims of racial progress, but it was the obvious presence behind most such expressions. The "progress of the race" and its implicit acknowledgment of slavery's legacy was, therefore, an inherent part of Booker T. Washington's accommodationist social philosophy and uplift strategy.

From the earliest stage of his public career to its end in 1915 during the fiftieth anniversary of the Civil War, Washington gave countless addresses in which he portrayed emancipation as the time when "the Negro began life" anew. Such an assumption owed much to the then common view of black folk's African background as a cultural, linguistic, and moral void. "When the Negro went into slavery," Washington said in 1903, "he was without anything which might properly be called a language; when he came out of slavery he was able to speak the English tongue . . . when he entered slavery he had little working knowledge of agriculture, mechanics, or household duties; when he emerged . . . he was almost the entire dependence in a large section of our country for agricultural, mechanical and domestic labor." Moreover, in terms of religion, Washington contended in 1905, Africa equipped blacks only with "barbarous . . . fetishism . . . a childish way of looking at and explaining the world." Out of bondage, they emerged Christians. Hence, Washington summed up the historic situation of blacks in America: "Slavery presented a problem of destruction; freedom presents a problem of construction. The latter requires patience, time, courage and toil, but in the end we shall reach our goal."[34] Booker Washington was a goal-driven man; he forged a compelling attitude toward the past and carried much of his people with him for nearly two decades.

Black ministers and editors frequently stressed how blacks faced a multiple need for "healing" from their African legacies of "ignorance," "poverty," and "immorality," as Benjamin Tanner put it. The greatest "wound" left by slavery and the African heritage, said Tanner in 1880, was the "curse of self-disrespect." With these notions of African deficits, and the call for blacks to have "faith in one another," Tanner and others embraced the uplift ideology for which Washington became famous. For many black leaders, especially those inclined to a millennial view of history, slavery had been part of God's design, an anguished but perhaps necessary passage to a new age for the black race. In his autobiography, *Up from Slavery* (1901), Washington made his own contribution to the image of the loyal slave. The "kindly and generous nature" of most slaves, and their refusal to harbor any "feelings of bitterness against the whites" during and after the war, led Washington to conclude that black folk had undergone a beneficent "school of slavery." He condemned slavery as an institution, but in such a way as to portray it as a necessary stage in a people's development. The slave experience showed "how Providence so often uses men and institutions to accomplish a purpose." Hence Washington's famous assertion that "notwithsanding the cruel wrongs . . . the black man got nearly as much out of slavery as the white man did."[35]

The doctrine of divine Providence was very old in American religious thought, and black clerics, as well as secular leaders, employed it to varying ends. Bishop Henry McNeal Turner was a profound believer in Providential design. Turner believed that "slavery was a providential institution, not a divine institution." "There is a God that runs this universe," he said in 1888, and during slavery, he "was not asleep or oblivious to passing events." His faith in such a doctrine fueled Turner's optimism and energy for emigration to Africa, but it also led him to some odd assumptions about just how emancipation emerged out of the very war he had known so intimately. Turner attended Jefferson Davis's funeral in 1889, and at the impromptu call of white mourners, delivered a speech in which he praised Davis's steadfastness in the Confederate cause because it eventually led to black freedom. Such were the designs of Providence, Turner believed. *Christian Recorder* editor Benjamin Lee objected to Turner's logic about emancipation, as well as to the circumstances in which he delivered it. If a "mantle" was to be placed on Davis as "some merit due" for instigating emancipation by leading the Confederate revolution, said Lee, "as well throw the mantle over Satan . . . or Judas." Lee argued that Davis and "all his class" ought to be remembered by blacks only for their "characteristic deadness."[36] Measures of progress started with many different yardsticks, and emerged from a spirited debate over both the character of black history and the relative balance between God's sovereignty and human agency.

Turner's devotion to the doctrine of God's reign over history sustained him through decades of embitterment at America's betrayal of black rights. Although his emigrationism followed directly from his sense of Christian mission to the African "heathen," he did not share a belief in the African cultural void. Soon after arriving in Sierra Leone on his first of three visits to West Africa, Turner wrote back to America of the astonishing richness of African cultural and material life. "What fools we are," he wrote in November 1891, "to suppose these Africans are fools!"[37] Indeed, in this identification with a glorious African past, the religious-historical tradition of Ethiopianism took root among nineteenth-century African Americans.

Ethiopianism drew its inspiration from the most quoted verse in black religious thought: Psalms 68:31, "princes shall come out of Egypt and Ethiopia shall soon stretch forth her hands unto God." As a religious world view, it became a vision of black destiny, an explanation for slavery and emancipation, and a framework for collective memory. In Pan-African thought by the late nineteenth century, the terms Egypt and Ethiopian had become synonymous with Africa and Africans, as well as a source of devotion to a theory of human development and the redemption of African peoples and cultures.[38] For Turner and many other black religious thinkers, Ethiopianism provided a way to explain a long historical continuum in which the agonies of slavery, the transformations of the Civil War, and the evils of racism and lynching in the 1890s fell into their appointed places in God's historical logic.

Black millennialism combined romanticism about African culture with a Christian, and in some ways distinctively black, view of history itself as a sacred drama. It combined apocalyptic tragedy with the optimism and determinism of the Second Coming of Christ. From sermons, and from the "race histories" and theological works written by blacks by the turn of century, a spiritually reassuring form of memory emerged that helped many people cope with despair in the age of Jim Crow. Many blacks found not only a link to a glorious, if unrealizable, African background, but also a historical theodicy that provided them the spirit to redeem Africa, even if only symbolically. Such a theodicy also bred an especially useful critique of America, of its racism and its, as yet, unredeemed history. Perhaps African peoples were scattered into the Americas for a divine purpose; perhaps the Civil War's apparent inevitability was all God's plan. Out of suffering, even degradation and near destruction, would come the glory and prophecy of the lowly race rising to improve and rule the world in its final stage of development.[39]

So went the arguments of many black theologians and historians, including George Washington Williams, whose histories of African Americans are stories about the fulfillment of an ultimate and sacred American progress. In the work of Peter Thomas Stanford, we find a thoroughgoing religious history. Born a slave in Hampton, Virginia, Stanford escaped to New York when he was twelve, where he was eventually converted to Christianity and educated through the support of Harriet Beecher Stowe and Henry Highland Garnet. In *The Tragedy of the Negro in America* (1898), Stanford told the story of slavery and emancipation as simply "God's record," in which all human history was a working out of divine justice, and black experience in America was a journey toward freedom. Slavery thus became the necessary travail of a race destined to rise from its suffering to redeem Africa and much of the rest of the world as well.[40]

A sense of chosenness informs virtually all black millennial thought. As the Pan-Africanist Edward Blyden put it, God had ordained slavery, black Christian conversion, even American racism itself as a motivator, and he held the interior peoples of Africa in readiness "until the time arrived for the emancipation of her children in the Western world."[41] In this vision, black Civil War memory in America was not so much the beginning of a new history at year "zero" as it was one crucial turning point in the long chronicle of international race development and the coming of God's rule over history itself. Millennial expectation could take all shame out of the heritage of slavery; past suffering could be a badge of honor on the march to the new day coming. While during the Gilded Age many white Americans ached nostalgically for another world to live in—one of Southern gentility and military valor —black millennialists converted their pasts into a new future in which to live. With God as the only monitor of memory, and not publishers, presidents, or business elites, black millennialists plotted the historical reversals inherent in what Turner had called the "grand sequel" to slavery and the war.

Some black theologians, namely J. Max Barber, Theophilus Gould Steward, and James T. Holly, took black millennial history to its ultimate extent. They aimed to provide not only a usable past, but a sense of ultimate "racial triumph" for black folk in America. Writing just after the turn of the century, Barber interpreted emancipation as a millennial age in which black people would reverse the racial hierarchy and replace the "degenerating, morally putrid . . . avaricious white man" with the "virile, puissant races in whose hearts there is mercy and justice." Worldwide, blacks were about to "have their turn at the wheel." In such interpretations, old collective memories could be discarded and new ones imagined. Steward, an AME minister writing in 1888, saw the end times at hand. The Saxon race had "accomplished its mission," he contended, and would end in self-ruination from its bloody reign of "conquest." White corruption of Christianity had given birth, though, to a truer Christianity that the darker races would carry forward into the millennial age. Hence the great events of the nineteenth century in America were merely the ordinary historical markers of God's design and the emancipated slaves were his victorious agents.[42]

Holly, the Protestant Episcopal bishop of Haiti, also writing in the 1880s, saw the millennium unfolding in three historic ages, or "dispensations." The first phase of history, which had belonged to the Semitic race, was when the Holy Scriptures were written and preserved. The second phase, the evangelical age of Christianity, belonged to the Europeans, who spread the gospels across the globe. And the third phase, which was to belong to the Hamitic race, would be ushered in by apocalyptic warfare, after which the thousand-year reign of the millennium would begin. During the latter stage of history, black peoples, the "elect among nations," would assume the "crowning work of the will of God . . . when Ethiopia shall stretch out her hands directly unto God."[43] Black millennialists fashioned a racial memory that made a potentially shameful past both purposeful and ultimately a long prelude to moral and historical triumph. As an attitude toward the past, toward Africa, and toward America, Ethiopianism would remain enormously useful, though never dominant, in black thought, as late as the semicentennial of emancipation.

Although millennial thought was common among religious blacks, many leaders did not share Washington's notion of slavery as a "school," nor Turner's as a "providential institution." Crummell, for one, declared himself in "amazement that men of sense and reason can thus travesty plain, common English, and talk such senseless stuff" as slavery the "schoolmaster!" Himself a missionary, Crummell maintained that blacks "would have been more blessed and far superior, as pagans, in Africa than slaves on the plantations of the South." In the context of fierce disagreements over emigration among blacks in the 1880s, T. Thomas Fortune declared the notion of Africans being brought to America to "prepare themselves to evangelize Africa" as "so much religious nonsense boiled down to a sycophantic platitude." Moreover, the Reverend A. L. Ridgel, a staunch advocate of emigration, had no patience with the idea of slavery as providential. "I don't believe that Providence had anything to do with the establishment and perpetuation of an institution so vile and degrading," wrote Ridgel in 1896. Precisely because slavery's "imprint" was so "deep and lasting" on blacks, Ridgel urged them to emigrate to Africa where, he believed, they could build a confident future not possible in America.[44]

SUCH STERN disagreements notwithstanding, Booker T. Washington's deep investment in "progress" rhetoric, in patriotism, and in an accommodationist approach to race relations informed a great deal of African American commemorative activity. Indeed, in many ways, Washington became America's ultimate proponent of reconciliationist Civil War memory. In his most celebrated oration, delivered at the Cotton States Exposition in Atlanta on September 18, 1895, Washington had virtually the entire nation as his stage. Remarkably, on the very same day that a black Southerner would leap into fame with a speech to white people in Atlanta, the massive Blue-Gray reunion was under way some 150 miles north at the Chickamauga battlefield (see Chapter 6).[45] An elixir of reunion and race filled the commemorative and festive air along the axis from Chattanooga to Atlanta that September.

In this era of massive expositions and world's fairs, it was Atlanta's turn to represent the South and to try to match the Chicago Columbian Exposition of 1893 in grandeur. The president of Tuskegee Institute stole the show, and his fame rang from front pages of newspapers across the country. Invited as the representative black orator among a series of speakers in a packed auditorium, Washington delivered one of the most important addresses in the long history of national reunion. Indeed, Washington's "Atlanta Compromise" speech is most often remembered as the signature statement in the Wizard of Tuskegee's accommodationist social philosophy—by his critics as a racial surrender to white supremacy and inequality, and by his defenders as a necessary strategy of educational and economic uplift in the segregated South.[46] But the speech was also part of Washington's long effort to merge sectional and racial peace into a single cause of black progress. Thirty years after Appomattox, he took the stage on a sweltering evening in Atlanta, looked out upon a huge racially mixed audience of former slaves, Confederate veterans, and their descendants, and gave all those who wished it a license to forget the war, to agree on the mistakes of Reconstruction, and to put the South's vexing race problem on a course of permanent settlement. Washington had a prescription for nearly everyone's still ailing memory of the Civil War.

A black man addressing whites in such a setting was a rare event in the South. Washington rode in a three-hour parade of carriages, which included companies of white and black militia troops. Blacks were relegated largely to the rear of the procession, and in the great hall where the opening ceremonies took place, they were cordoned off in a Negro section. Just as it became Washington's time to speak, a band played the "Star Spangled Banner" and the "audience cheered"; then the band played "Dixie," and the throng "roared with shrill hi-yi's." Washington broke the tension by celebrating the Exposition as the means to "do more to cement the friendship of the two races than any occurrence since the dawn of our freedom." Washington spoke as a native and proud Southerner dropping his ideological tithe into the well of resentment over Reconstruction. "Ignorant and inexperienced,"

Booker T. Washington was a major spokesman for a reconciliationist vision of Civil War memory, which he hoped would enable black Southerners to achieve racial peace and economic progress. (Tuskegee University Archives, Tuskegee, Alabama)

the freedmen had started wrongly at the "top instead of at the bottom" of life. They had foolishly pursued political office and voting rights rather than "real estate or industrial skill." Then the skilled orator offered the promise of black labor to the South's future, and gave the speech its famous refrain. "Cast down your bucket where you are," Washington proclaimed to blacks many times over, weaving it through a metaphor of a lost ship at sea encountering a friendly vessel. Washington delivered a set of promises and bargains; blacks would forget their "grievances" and embrace their "opportunities." They would "live by the productions of our hands" and prosper by the maxim that "there is as much dignity in tilling a field as in writing a poem."[47]

Washington then drew whites intimately into the metaphor, asking them to fulfill the bargain of racial peace by casting down their buckets as well among the very work force that had cleared the South's forests and built its cities, the "patient . . . unresentful people" who did not, like foreign workers, engage in "strikes and labor wars." Thrusting his hand in the air, Washington offered another soon-to-be-famous deal: "In all things that are purely social we can be as separate as the fingers, yet one as the hand in all things essential to mutual progress." White and black Southerners would march to economic growth and out of depression together. Washington asked whites to "remember the path" blacks had traversed since starting out in 1865 with only "a few quilts and pumpkins and chickens (gathered from miscellaneous sources)." He maintained that both races were bending over the same "altar" of remembrance, "both starting practically empty-handed three decades ago." In millennial tones, Washington ended with an appeal for the "blotting out of sectional differences and racial animosities," and for faith that "our beloved South" would soon know a "new heaven and a new earth."[48] White women threw flowers and blacks wept in the aisles as the white dignitaries on the stage swarmed gleefully about the orator. The reconciliationist vision of Civil War memory had a new voice and a new bargain, rooted in the strange but beguiling dream that economic progress would render remembering unneccessary. As the late day sun flashed horizontally through the auditorium windows, the crowd cheered in delirium and the Civil War and Reconstruction seemed truly over.

Viewed overnight as spokesman of his race, Washington was now heralded by whites, and some blacks, as the "Moses" of his people. As hats were thrown in the air and "the fairest women of Georgia stood up and cheered" the black man, wrote the *New York World*'s correspondent, James Creelman, "it was as if the orator had bewitched them." Perhaps he had. The opening ceremonies had been the "most hopeful day in the history of the negro race," said Washington the next day in self-congratulation, "the day for which Garrison and Douglass and Grady [Henry] worked and prayed." Folding the two great abolitionists into the same breath with the New South's famous promoter, announcing that the "year of jubilee of the negro" had arrived in the place where "Sherman and Hood fought," Washington demonstrated his keen determination to serve as the South's and the nation's reconciler.[49] The elements of the deal made a much weaker combination than Washington would ever admit; his dreamy coalition of Northern financiers, white Southern conservative segregationists, and masses of Southern blacks had no chance of wresting from American society a new racial and economic utopia.

Yet for many months and from diverse quarters, Washington's prescriptions seemed to embody sweet reason and excited many supporters. Indeed, many black admirers responded to the possibilities in the speech, not to its dangers; they were inspired by the message of *success* implied by Washington's performance before a white audience. The Reverend Frances J. Grimké wrote of the "great satisfaction" the race felt that Washington held center stage at "so important an occasion." The free-lance journalist and self-styled black nationalist John Edward Bruce admired Washington's ability to "strike the happy mean" at Atlanta. "You hold the key to the solution of the problem of the century," Bruce assured Washington. "The Negro" must make "himself intellectually, morally, and industrially the equal of the white man." And from New York, one of Washington's protégés, T. Thomas Fortune, informed his leader: "It looks as if you are our Douglass and I am glad of it." Since Douglass had died earlier the same year, these responses may reflect a yearning for national leadership among black Americans. But it also implied that the deeper meanings of Washington's prescriptions had not yet become the primary subject of debate; fame, and the possibilities of a new day in race relations, seemed to drive the hopes of many blacks. Indeed, William Casler, a black teacher from Knoxville, Tennessee, was so inspired that he suggested to Washington that his expression, "separate as the fingers, yet one as the hand in all things essential to human progress," be inscribed on a lapel button, "as worn by Grand Army men" and "sold on Exposition grounds at the Negro exhibit."[50] In such genuine enthusiasm, the marketing of memory and hope knew no bounds.

Many Atlanta blacks boycotted the Exposition because of the segregation practiced in the city. To the wider public, however, the Negro building was the great curiosity of the fair. An impressive structure, 276 feet long and 112 feet wide, it had been built largely by black workmen. Over the main entrance decorated relief work represented past and present in the black experience. On one side a slave mammy appeared with a log cabin, rake, and basket in 1865; on the other side Frederick Douglass's face joined representations of a substantial house, a well-fed mule and plow, a stone church, and symbols of racial progress in science, art, and literature. After passing under this contrast of "old" and "new negro" symbolism, visitors could observe numerous exhibits of wares produced in the various black colleges and secondary schools, as well as many works of art, including three paintings by Henry Ossawa Tanner and Edmonia Lewis's bust of Charles Sumner.[51] The Tuskegee and Hampton institutes assembled the largest displays of the "industrial work."

Perhaps the most unusual exhibit in the Negro building was one assembled by Henry McNeal Turner, who had recently returned from a trip to West Africa. Labeled "Uncivilized Africa," Turner's collection of swords, knives, and spears, oils, cloth, and bird specimens were meant to depict the undeveloped life of the "heathen," as the press and even Turner himself referred to West Africans. On a stroll with a newspaper reporter, Turner objected to all the talk about the exhibits representing the "new Negro." "There is nothing new in all this fine work," insisted the bishop. "The negroes always did the finest kind of work in the South." Always available for a good quote, Turner next turned his contrarianism on the "Dahomey Village," located on the midway of the exposition. Insulted by the white huckster outside the show urging visitors to see the "wild cannibals" of Africa, Turner confronted the man. With a crowd nearby cheering him on, Turner dressed down the carnival employee with a speech about white ignorance of Africa, ending with the exhortation for all to hear: "Stop your lying about the negro!"[52]

It takes nothing away from Booker Washington's leadership skills to note that his fame in the aftermath of Atlanta in 1895 was very much the creation of whites. He had been chosen to speak largely by the whites who organized the exposition because they judged him "safe." Racial tensions in the South of the mid-1890s, after several years of lynching, turmoil over Populist politics, and a deepening economic panic, were as potentially explosive as they had ever been. One white Northerner attending the Atlanta speech observed that as the platform guests arrived an hour late in the hot auditorium, many whites angrily shouted, "what's that nigger doing on the stage?"[53] Professor

Washington won over a hostile white audience, but one that, by and large, wanted to believe in racial peace, as long as it blossomed in a firmly segregated society, with blacks knowing their place as efficient but politically inactive laborers. Washington delivered the tonic that seemed to awaken hope on many fronts, North and South, among whites and many blacks. Atlanta dearly wanted Yankee investments; the spokesman of the black race who had built the tradition of industrial schools performed as broker of the deal, pacifier of the past and prophet of the new day.

What Page's loyal slave narrators had not yet accomplished for the Northern mind, Washington helped to complete. John Cochrane, a Union veteran and lawyer practicing in New York, wrote to Washington of his complete wish fulfillment after reading the Atlanta speech. "Bless God, the 'day of Jubilee' am come. As a white man and old time abolitionist and ex Union Veteran I bless God . . . for the great speech which He told you to make." Cochran seemed to see now the true end of the war. "The old gulf is bridged—the ax is buried forever," he said, "not to be unburied on Election Day!" The *Chicago Inter-Ocean* heralded Washington's performance at Atlanta as the advent of the "new negro." But most important was the "amazement" with which the white audience responded; the real story, said the Chicago reporter, was the "awakening of the white race . . . to the possibilities of the colored people."[54] Everyone saw what they most wanted to see. But all was not hopeful among Washington's own race in the aftermath of his famous speech.

While some black newspapers fell in line behind the strategy of economic racial advancement and Bookerite reconciliation, many protested. In his *Voice of Missions,* Henry McNeal Turner complained that Washington "will have to live a long time to undo the harm he has done our race." Another writer in the same paper, George N. Smith, thought the labeling of Washington as the next Douglass "as unseemly as comparing a pigmy to a giant—a mountain brook leaping over a boulder, to a great, only Niagara." And the *Atlanta Advocate* lampooned Washington as "Prof. B. T. or Bad Taste Wash," who was "so representative of the Negro that his hat flies off, the moment a red headed white newsboy is introduced to him." In Washington, D.C., the Bethel Literary and Historical Association, an organization of intellectuals and artists that met frequently to deliver formal papers, held its October 1895 meeting as a discussion of the Atlanta address. Some at the meeting spoke in defense of Washington's accommodationism, but many others who vehemently opposed it dominated the debate. Francis Grimké reported carefully to Washington that "there were a few who thought you were playing into the hands of the Southern Whites." As the turn of the century approached, and as the Lost Cause gained considerable sway over the American historical imagination, blacks and whites alike had to position themselves in relation to Booker Washington's brand of reconciliation on Southern terms. It combined a black Southerner's appeal for national reunion, a faith in markets, a doctrine of patience and self-reliance, an acquiescence in Jim Crow social legislation, and the Wizard's persistent belief that "progress is a law of God and progress is going to be the negro's eternal guiding star in this fair land."[55]

Bookerite reconciliation was a complex mixture of purposeful forgetting, a theory of "race-development" (blacks were only in an early stage), devotion to industrial education, and sincere appeals for interracial cooperation. Washington tailored his appeals to memory to particular audiences. At the annual conference of the AME Church in May 1900, he portrayed the past as "broken-hearted," a "storm" out of which the nation would "reap the whirlwind." But quickly, Washington stressed that "our [blacks'] duty is to face the present and not to wail over the past" in "useless debate" over who was "responsible . . . for slavery." No one could fully disagree with the famous orator when he offered such direct prescriptions as "Our knowledge must be harnessed to the things of real life."[56] With such inspirations and bromides, Washington served up a hopeful vision of sectional and racial reunion.

At the Birmingham, Alabama, Lyceum in March 1899, Washington, as expected, stressed the "bond of sympathy" across the South between ex-slaves and former masters. Then, with a combination of dialect stories and a recital of the accomplishments of Tuskegee Institute in industrial education, he won over the audience of 250 potentially hostile whites. Moreover, that same month in Boston, he recited his version of the history of emancipation. "Faithful slaves" who had been the "bulwark" of plantations awaited the defeated white Southerner when he returned from the war. And with time white Southerners had come to realize how dependent they were on black labor and skill. "Debts" (between whites and blacks) had accumulated "in every direction" since Reconstruction. Slavery had been "almost as much permanent injury" to whites as to blacks, Washington contended. "The wrong to the Negro is but temporary, but upon those committing the crimes the results are eternal." The Negro "can afford to be wronged," he assured the New Englanders, but whites "cannot afford to wrong him" without their "proudest and bluest blood . . . being degraded."[57] In these expressions before white audiences, Washington did not talk of "debts" incurred by two generations of sharecroppers or about what the nation might owe the victims of waves of lynchings (at least not yet). His was a moral reconciliation that he hoped to convert into material change. But at the center of America's dilemma with the memory of the war and its aftermath was the tragic fact that racial reconciliation could never be based solely on the powerless morality that Washington preached in his call for a reunion of ex-slaves and ex-masters around mutual economic need.

Washington carried such a message through to his last days: material progress by blacks would foment white admiration and, therefore, lead to the truest form of national and racial reconciliation. In a tribute to Harriet Tubman in Auburn, New York, in June 1914, where the former liberator of fugitive slaves had recently died, Washington linked past and present in his peculiar way. Tubman was best remembered, he declared, as a symbol of the "law-abiding Negro," a leader who "brought the two races nearer together and made it possible for the white race to know the black race." By reciting the acreage of land ownership and the numbers of houses, grocery stores, dry goods stores, shoe stores, drug stores, and banks owned by blacks fifty years after freedom, Washington found the best evidence that "the work of Harriet Tubman was not in vain." Tubman had long been a malleable icon of America's antislavery past. But Washington's appropriation of this revolutionary activist who broke many laws to liberate slaves, in order to create a narrative of "racial friendship," showed less the measure of "progress" than the bankruptcy of Bookerite reconciliation.[58]

Measuring racial progress, however, became a major preoccupation in black America around the turn of the century. Numerous thick books appeared that included the statistical advancement by blacks in literacy, property ownership, and many other categories; biographical sketches of scores of prominent men and women; the successful growth of schools, colleges, churches, and businesses; and short histories of black participation in wars and other national affairs. These compilations were often informed by a Bookerite agenda of uplift and accommodationism, as well as by a general desire for pride and respectability. Laced with photographs of professors, ministers, journalists, orators, and writers, including women who led the club movement and created institutions of social uplift, such books as H. F. Kletzing and W. H. Crogman, *Progress of a Race; or, The Remarkable Advancement of the Afro-American* (1897), G. F. Richings, *Evidences of Progress among Colored People* (1900), and J. L. Nichols and W. H. Crogman, *Progress of a Race* (1920) were inspired by an unflappable faith that demonstrating blacks' improved condition in the industrial age would conquer white racism, unify blacks, and provide the only sure path to reconciliation. "Race prejudice is bound to give way before the potent influences of character, education, and wealth," Kletzing and Crogman confidently assumed. According to Richings, black artists and educational leaders of all sorts were representing "the race in educating the white people up to a better knowledge of what the race can do."[59]

The purpose of these works seemed to be to cheer the race on to higher aspirations, to emotionally empower the young; they were encyclopedic pep talks within the black community of memory. To read these volumes is to enter huge storehouses of uplift ideology, as though encountering thousands of anecdotes from Booker T. Washington speeches without a narrative line. In schools, in families, and among black youth, these books provided much needed reminders of black success, repositories of seemingly self-made achievement. By an almost endless array of measures, each book attempted to show how far black folk had come since, and in spite of, slavery. Some were even forthright in addressing the history and agony of slavery; they included pictures and stories of ex-slaves against which progress could be judged. In the age of Jim Crow, all these measures of group capacity were of no small importance to a people for whom it was never fully safe to remember or forget.

Although Washington controlled some of these publications on racial advancement, "progress of the race" rhetoric had been a main theme in African American newspapers and schools for decades. An inherent part of the education at a college like Hampton Institute was the persistent effort to measure black progress. By the 1890s it was a custom to gather the year's graduates for a day-long symposium during commencement week to "discuss . . . the position of the Negro in the South today, to note improvement . . . as well as any retrogression." All manner of material, social, and occupational measures were considered at each year's assessment, and always in the background was remembrance of slavery as the starting line. To become a young educated black man or woman in the late nineteenth century was to enter a society where your own intellectual capacities were always under suspicious measurement in the white world and under a nearly constant self-scrutiny and tabulation in the segregated black world. At the heart of uplift ideology was a drumbeat about moral improvement as equal to, if not greater than, intellectual endeavor. It may be fine, argued Frances E. W. Harper, to train young blacks to "be brilliant and witty; eager, keen, and alert for the main chance," but the most important "factor in human progress" was to educate the young as "moral athlete[s]." Harper counseled the "spirit of self-surrender" as the guiding principle of black education and progress.[60]

African American newspapers became repositories for both celebrations of black progress and intense debate about the obstacles of Jim Crow and violence. For every naysayer among blacks who decried the lack of economic and social progress, there were more eager to defend the race. When the lawyer T. McCants Stewart criticized blacks for their lack of independent achievement in 1897, a Bryn Mawr, Pennsylvania, minister, H. C. C. Astwood, answered that "race men" had succeeded in every profession outside of politics. "The progress made by the American Negro since reconstruction," said Astwood, "is the most remarkable and marvelous shown by any race in history." Many blacks made it their passion to collect the "facts and figures" of black achievement and publish such numbers well before "progress of the race" books were published. In 1889–90, John G. Jones of Philadelphia worked for eighteen months tabulating the wealth in real and personal property holdings by blacks in every state and territory, concluding with a total of $263,000,000. Jones intended his findings as an answer to all those who suggested that blacks were dying out, or that they would be better off emigrating to Africa. He converted his progressive statistics into a declaration of belonging: "We are American citizens by birth, and here is where we propose to live and die." Moreover, many black ministers asserted the race's achievements, but did so as part of an embittered response to the heightened racism and obsessive talk of the "Negro question." "The progress of the Negro is creating such an excitement," wrote N. H. Jefferson in 1887, "that obstructions and hindrances are thrust across his pathway by his brother in white to impede him." And in 1889 the Reverend L. J. Coppin declared it "almost miraculous how well they [blacks] have done in so short a time," but in his travels in the South he found "an iron-handed opposition to the negro's elevation . . . the lines between the races never so closely drawn."[61]

ON THE UNDERSIDE of "progress of the race" rhetoric festered anger and great disappointment at the declining state of race relations in America as the nation reconciled. In 1888 a black New Jersey minister, William Yeocum, lamented that whites just did not comprehend how steadfastly blacks had earned their "citizenship." No Americans had greater reverence for public schools, said Yeocum, and if whites would open their minds to black progress, they would see that African Americans did not engage in such acts as the "Haymarket massacre in Chicago" and that "the colored American citizen does not go on the strike" or "carry his point with deadly dynamite." "Although sometimes shot down and hanged without judge or jury," concluded Yeocum, "there are no Anarchists and Communists found among the colored people." These appeals did not fall completely on deaf ears in the New South era, as some urban white business and civic elites began to organize to control or improve race relations within the segregation regime. As one historian of lynching has said, the "tensions between progress and tradition" were especially acute in the South's struggle to modernize, eventually forcing many respectable whites to try to "strip away much of the legitimacy of lynching." But increasingly, deep frustration mixed with progress rhetoric among black spokesmen. The AME minister and future bishop Reverdy Ransom stressed that blacks were "loyal to the American flag and . . . imbued with the spirit of American institutions," but were, nevertheless, "practically shut out from many trades and useful callings . . . entirely upon color." Too much progress rhetoric rang hollow to Ransom. "Although we have had emancipation proclamations, constitutional amendments, civil rights bills, and that hot-bed of oppression now popularly called the 'new South,' the colored race in America has never yet been accorded a full and equal chance in the race of life."[62]

As lynching and lawlessness against blacks increased in the 1890s, discussions of progress had to share space with outrage over violence. In 1893, a black Georgian, J. M. Lee, complained that news of a lynching had become virtually a weekly occurrence in his state. In response to preachers' appeals to scripture and the law as a means of dealing with mob terror, Lee said "the Negro . . . must fight for his rights. Nothing shorter than a Winchester or a gatling gun will stop this lynching." Ida B. Wells, a journalist and crusader against lynching, drew her extraordinary passion from personal experience and a sense of unbounded grievance. The aim in much of her anti-lynching writing was not only exposure, but also to deliver a compelling critique of America's self-definition as a land of liberty and progress. In *A Red Record* (1895), a catalogue of lynching horrors and appeals for activism, Wells urged the "Negro . . . to speak for himself" about lynching. And in so doing, Americans would have to swallow hard their sense of innocence. "With regret," charged Wells, blacks

> must disclose to the world that degree of dehumanizing brutality which fixes upon America the blot of a national crime. Whatever

faults and failings other nations may have in their dealings with their own subjects or with other people, no other civilized nation stands condemned before the world with a series of crimes so peculiarly national. It becomes a painful duty of the Negro to reproduce a record which shows that a large portion of the American people avow anarchy, condone murder and defy the contempt of civilization.[63]

With every exposure of a fabricated rape charge as the basis for a lynching, Wells exploded the doctrine of progress and tried to disturb the calm in the culture of national reconciliation.

In *The Reason Why the Colored American Is Not in the World's Columbian Exposition* (1893), a widely distributed pamphlet, Wells compiled a stinging and ironic treatise on both black achievement and outrage. Among chapters by Frederick Douglass on the legacies of slavery, her own discussion of gruesome lynching details, and a concluding piece by her future husband, Ferdinand L. Barnett, documenting the many attempts black women had made to gain access to planning the exposition, Wells placed an essay on race progress by I. Garland Penn, soon to be the chief black organizer at the Atlanta Cotton States Exposition. Penn recorded the wealth held by blacks, state by state, the numbers of schools and churches, blacks in the various professions, and some seventy-five patents for inventions issued to African Americans. Juxtaposing measured black achievement with extremely graphic accounts of lynchings, Wells demonstrated the unsettled and anguished place of "progress of the race" discourse in African American life by the turn of the century. Wells insisted that the quantifiable material and professional success of blacks coexist in the same story with images of black men's bodies hanging from lampposts, riddled with bullets, burned on woodpiles, or dragged through city streets chased by fiendish relic hunters.[64] American memory, she hoped, could be forced to digest both sets of images. One of the burdens of black memory was that progress and horror had to occupy the same narrative.

On Emancipation Day, January 1, 1909, in Augusta, Georgia, a black Baptist minister, Silas X. Floyd, delivered the speech "Abraham Lincoln: Sent of God" at a large celebration sponsored by churches, fraternal orders, and the local Lincoln League. Floyd was young, charismatic, and a prolific writer of, among other works, a black history for children. He admonished those blacks who wished to forget that "our race was once enslaved in this country." "Did you ever see . . . a Confederate veteran who desired to forget that he once wore the gray," asked Floyd, "or who was unwilling to teach his children that he once proudly marched in battle behind Lee and Gordon, Jackson and Johnston? Did you ever see a Union soldier who was ashamed of the part which he took in the Great War, or who felt humiliated to tell his children about it?" Floyd reminded his people that they too had a great story to tell and preserve:

> And don't you remember that, when the children of Israel under the leadership of Moses were on the march from Egypt . . . to Canaan . . . don't you remember that, after they had safely crossed the Red Sea, the Lord commanded them to set up memorial stones by which the event should be remembered? And yet some old Negroes wish to forget all about slavery—all about the past—and stoutly maintain that we have no right to be celebrating this day that brought freedom to our race . . . may God forget my people when they forget this day.

Floyd's speech reflects many dilemmas that Southern blacks faced. The youthful minister represented the postfreedom generation challenging the slavery generation. Just who should determine how and if the narrative of remembrance is written in any culture is always a generational conflict. Floyd raised some of the central questions confronting blacks as they contemplated their past in America: the meaning of more than two centuries of slavery, and the meaning of emancipation in the Civil War. How to look back, and then forward, with pride and confidence? How to tell the tale that they too had marched with Grant, stormed Fort Wagner, and lurched toward freedom through fear and hardship? Indeed, how to understand and declare their history in the Jim Crow South? When the children of Israel assembled their memorial stones, they too were obedient and reluctant in the face of God's commands, inspired and frightened by their faith, their heroism, and their history.[65]

TEN

Fifty Years of Freedom and Reunion

The bitterness of civil war is not so insurmountable
as that of one involving a question of race dominance.

—CHARLES FRANCIS ADAMS II, "Lee at Appomattox," 1901

IN BOSTON on Memorial Day, May 31, 1897, a slow drizzle fell in the
morning as an immense crowd gathered to witness a parade and the unveiling of a unique Civil War monument. Nearly 3,500 cadets, seamen, militia,
and mounted police marched to the corner of Boston Common in front of
the golden-domed State House. Among their ranks were some 140 survivors
of the black Massachusetts Fifty-fourth and Fifty-fifth infantry and the Fifth
cavalry. They gathered to welcome Augustus Saint-Gaudens's masterpiece,
the Robert Gould Shaw Memorial, to the landscape of Civil War memory.
The stunning bronze relief depicts Colonel Shaw, commander of the
Fifty-fourth, astride his horse, sword drawn, with stiff back and determined
visage, marching southward down Beacon Street. Behind, and as though surrounding Shaw, march his black volunteers, ladened with knapsacks and can-
teens. With muskets darting upward at angles, their bodies arched forward,
the soldiers flow inexorably toward their fate. The faces of the troops
(twenty-three in all on the relief) capture their individuality, their shaven
youth and bearded middle age, their dignity and resolve. Shaw, born a
Boston Brahmin, selected at twenty-six to command this experimental black
regiment in the spring of 1863, almost floats on his horse, even on the shoulders and courage of his men. As the monument sweeps the eye forward, it
foreshadows a tale of how commander and men will die together. On the

beach below Battery Wagner, on Morris Island guarding Charleston harbor, July 18, 1863, 40 percent of the Fifty-fourth's 630 men fell dead or wounded in a futile military charge. At Fort Wagner, blacks demonstrated their valor as men. Shaw was killed with his men, while leading them up to the parapet, and the next morning the Confederates buried the officer and his troops, white and black together, in a trench in the sand.[1] The emancipationist vision of Civil War memory has no greater symbol than the Shaw Memorial.

By the 1890s, on battlefields, in cemeteries, and in city squares, the American landscape contained thousands of Civil War monuments, many of them designed to fit artistic formulas. The Shaw Memorial was (and still is) different. Like the Jackson or Lee monuments in Richmond, the Shaw Memorial moved people emotionally. The events it commemorated compelled viewers to acknowledge that wars have meanings that go beyond manly valor. Saint-Gaudens's relief forced the thoughtful citizen to ask how a struggle in the 1860s between white Northerners and Southerners over conflicting conceptions of the future became a struggle for blacks over whether they had any future in America at all. The monument also asserts with majestic anguish that in the nation founded by the Declaration of Independence, black men had to die by the thousands in battle or of disease in order to be recognized as men, much less as citizens. The Shaw Memorial reveals a narrative of authentic tragedy at the heart of the Civil War. In 1935, W. E. B. Du Bois may have captured best the tragic sense one can encounter in gazing at the Shaw Memorial: "How extraordinary, and what a tribute to ignorance and religious hypocrisy, is the fact that in the minds of most people . . . only murder makes men. The slave pleaded; he was humble; he protected the women of the South, and the world ignored him. The slave killed white men; and behold, he was a man!"[2]

The men of the Fifty-fourth regiment carried the highest aims of the Union cause, and inevitably became the perfect target for what the Confederacy preserved. Their heroism represented not merely physical courage in battle; it stood for their audacious faith as black men to join up, salute, train, suffer, and give their lives for the chance to belong in their own land. The men of the Fifty-fourth, and by extension all black soldiers, marked the boundary between the promises of equality that soldiering might provide and betrayals of that equality in political life. As they move forward with one will on Saint-Gaudens's relief, with no hesitation in their step toward death, they breathe a new narrative into American history—a story of movement toward racial equality. It is a narrative of tragedy, one that cannot be served up with pure moral clarity and tidy reconciliation. It is a story that invokes thoughtfulness of cause, consideration of ideological memory—not mere wistfulness. The Shaw Memorial forced viewers to confront a critical issue in Civil War remembrance: did they remember the meanings of the war, or merely the drama of the fight? Had they chosen by the 1890s to feel and see only the spectacle of battle, the equality of white heroism on both sides, or the unending challenge of the war's political consequences? Were they ennobled by Saint-Gaudens's monument, or deflected by it? Did they recognize the degree to which the black civic future had been sacrificed to national reconciliation? How could they have reunion and still deal with race?[3] Such a separation in popular thought haunted Civil War memory in the 1890s and formed one of the most tangled legacies of the conflict.

Saint-Gaudens's flying angel above the marching soldiers has always lent itself to ambiguity, but the meaning of his relief has never represented a generic heroism. The monument has always had deep local meanings—the Brahmin class celebrating itself in a memorial to one of its own. But from the day of its unveiling, the Shaw Memorial invoked special reactions, as though something deep in the war's meaning had been forever realized in bronze.

At the unveiling of Augustus Saint-Gaudens's Shaw Memorial in May 1897, many black survivors and white officers of the Massachusetts Fifty-fourth regiment marched together. (Massachusetts Historical Society)

On the day after the unveiling ceremonies, the *Boston Transcript* editorialized with "special gratification" that the Shaw monument brought new artistic fervor to Civil War memorialization. From this sculpture, the paper continued, "there comes at last a genuine exhalation of the magnificent, colossal tragedy, the mingled splendor and horror, the pageantry and squalor, the thrilling romance and the unspeakable brutality of the War of the Rebellion." And over the century since its appearance, perhaps no Civil War monument has inspired as much poetry as the Shaw Memorial, the most famous of which is Robert Lowell's "For the Union Dead" (1961), which stands as the best modernist work in a long tradition of Shaw poems by James Russell Lowell, Ralph Waldo Emerson, William Vaughn Moody, John Berryman, Paul Lawrence Dunbar, and many others. In the familiar published version of "For the Union Dead," Lowell muses magically and sardonically about the specialness of Saint-Gaudens's work by contrasting it with the dulling effects of time and forgetting represented in the endless "stone statues of the abstract Union soldier" adorning New England town greens, where "they doze over their muskets and muse through their sideburns." But in his many drafts and revisions of this poem, Lowell left a line not ultimately published, though it signals the meaning he pursued. The monument, he wrote, was "our most felt authentic memorial."[4] Lowell's "our" is a New England, Yankee voice; but it also speaks for national meanings under duress in the 1890s, and under revival and torment in the 1960s and beyond.

After the monument unveiling in 1897, much of the crowd filled the Boston Music Hall for speeches. The hall was packed, with hundreds standing in aisles and corners. Along with other dignitaries, Saint-Gaudens himself sat on the stage in a back row, and numerous survivors of the Fifty-fourth regiment occupied chairs to the speaker's right. William James, the philosopher from Harvard University, delivered the official oration. James's brother, Garth Wilkinson ("Wilky") James, one of the officers in the Fifty-fourth regiment, had been seriously wounded in the assault on Fort Wagner and never fully recovered. In a special finale, Booker T. Washington, representing blacks, gave a short but memorable tribute to the soldiers and to the occasion.[5]

James's speech included an earnest demand for civic virtue while hitting several meaningful chords of Civil War memory. He worried that the "abstract soldier's monument . . . reared on every village green" might in time lull Americans into forgetting the "profounder meaning of the Union cause" represented in the black regiment that fought for freedom. As sectional reconciliation swept over American culture, James used this occasion of profound remembrance to observe the force of collective forgetting: "Only when some yellow-bleached photograph of a soldier of the 'sixties comes into our hands, with that odd and vivid look of individuality . . . do we realize the concreteness of that by-gone history, and feel how interminable to the actors . . . were those leaden-footed hours and years. The photographs themselves erelong will fade utterly, and books of history and monuments like this alone will tell the tale." James answered his own challenge; he declared his listeners bound by their humanity to distinguish between the meaning and the fight. Nations should build monuments to "civic courage" and not merely to "battle instinct," James insisted. Such monuments would distinguish the "moral service of them [the soldiers] from the fortitude which they display." James's erudite address, likely not what much of the audience most wanted that day, was nevertheless a determined expression of the emancipationist meanings within the valorous fight.[6]

After James concluded, the assembled sang the "Battle Hymn of the Republic" and then Booker Washington took the podium. The audience, said a reporter, "quivered with an excitement that was not suppressed." "Tears glistened in the eyes of the soldiers and civilians on the platform" as Washington cast Shaw in a Christlike image and invoked the names of former governor John Andrew and abolitionist George L. Stearns, who had together led the recruitment of black troops. Washington then addressed the veterans on stage: "To you . . . the scarred and scattered remnant of the 54th regiment, who with empty sleeve and wanting leg, have honored this occasion with your presence, to you your commander is not dead." As he did this, Sergeant William Carney, the first black to win the Congressional Medal of Honor, rose from his chair with the regiment's old battle flag in his hand. Carney had been wounded three times at Fort Wagner while carrying the colors, which "never touched the ground." According to Washington, the "dramatic effect" of this moment was like nothing else he ever experienced at any oratorical occasion. As Carney rose, "for a number of minutes the audience seemed to entirely lose control of itself."[7]

Washington, a master of the short oration, surged on. He spoke of slavery as the system that had "bound master and slave, yea, North and South, to a body of death." Full atonement could not be attained even by "shot and sword, nor by blood and tears." He offered his customary gesture of quoting a Southern ex-slaveholder, whose "quivering lips" had informed a black audience that God had set whites free as well by ending slavery. And in a remarkable passage, Washington addressed racial reconciliation. "The black man," he said, "who cannot let love and sympathy out to the white man, is but half free. The white man, who would close the shop or factory against the black man seeking an opportunity to earn an honest living, is but half free." Only on a path of complete forgiveness, Washington believed, could the country find "the full measure of the fruit of Fort Wagner." Washington ended with his favorite themes of sectional reconciliation and black economic self-reliance. He extended his heart to "those who wore the gray as well as those clothed in blue," and took a few swipes at the mistakes of Reconstruction (especially premature black suffrage). The emotional power of Washington's speech was unmistakable. As the conservative Populist, he guided his audience from the valor and sacrifice of Shaw and his men in 1863 to the glorious new challenges on the "field of peace, in the battle of industry, in the struggle for good government, in the lifting up of the lowest to the fullest opportunities." When he finished, Governor Roger Wolcott immediately shouted, "Three cheers for Booker Washington!"[8]

Although the Shaw Memorial was planted permanently on the Boston landscape, its artistic power could never alone render its meanings stable. As a monument to black freedom, it stood virtually alone in the national landscape of Civil War memory. By 1897, the sectional reunion was all but complete politically and culturally, and a racial apartheid was steadily becoming the law of the land. Most Southern governors, and many Congressmen and Senators, were Confederate veterans. Here and there in the South, a lone black politician was still elected to office, one even to the U.S. Congress in 1896. But the slow wave of disfranchisement and segregation laws had begun to roll over Southern political life. By 1897, the farmers' revolt and the Populist movement, which had threatened to realign American politics on class and racial lines, had run its course as the country faced yet another cycle of economic depression. The Republican candidate and Union veteran William McKinley, who in 1896 defeated the prairie-Populist-turned-Democrat William Jennings Bryan, had been inaugurated President just two months before the unveiling of the Shaw Memorial. And the *Plessy v. Ferguson* Supreme Court decision, which enshrined the "separate but equal" doctrine (announced to virtually no press coverage or public outcry), was but a year old when Boston turned out to honor the survivors of the Fifty-fourth.

By the late 1890s, it was the rare Memorial Day speech that did not pay equal honor to Confederate and Union veterans. Indeed, on the night before the unveiling in Boston, Henry Lee Higginson, veteran, entrepeneur, and friend of Shaw, delivered the official oration in Sanders Theater in Cambridge. He paid a moving tribute to Shaw and the black soldiers who had "atoned," he said, "for the sin of slavery." Higginson could only lay such a burden of atonement on black soldiers because he earlier had absolved white Southerners of any specific responsibility. Higginson intended nothing "harsh toward our brothers of the South." In his view, "the sin of slavery was national, and caused the sin of disunion."[9] This notion of slavery as the national original sin shared by all had helped pave the way to reunion; it implicated and absolved everybody all at once. No one had been truly wrong; heroism and devotion alone had rendered everyone right. In a popular culture infused with white supremacy and sectional comity, and in a legal system increasingly governed by racial separation, Saint-Gaudens's masterpiece took its place as an inspiring exception.

As the Shaw Memorial appeared, monuments to faithful slaves began to dot the Southern landscape, and their depiction at the center of so much plantation literature reached a peak of popularity. The UDC and the UCV were launching their organizational crusades to preserve Lost Cause ideology and foster reunion on Southern terms. Indeed, at the seventh annual UCV reunion in Nashville, held only three weeks after the unveiling of the Shaw Memorial and attended by some fifteen thousand veterans, the keynote address provided a measure of the distances between some Southern and Northern, and especially black and white, memories. John H. Reagan of Texas, a former member of the Confederate cabinet, delivered a long survey of how slavery was the "cause" of the war, but only as an "inheritance" entailed on the South by Europe. The "ex-Confederates," Reagan confidently asserted, "were not responsible for the existence of African slavery . . . and were not responsible for the existence of the great war which resulted from the agitation."[10] Neither William James nor Booker Washington addressed the question of the war's responsiblity. White Southerners claimed that high ground of argument as their own.

Moreover, the most vital context in which to measure the distances between emancipationist and white supremacist or reconciliationist memories is the explosion of racial violence in the 1890s. Between 1897 and 1906, whites lynched at least 884 blacks in America. At the end of the decade, the black novelist Charles Chesnutt, in *The Marrow of Tradition* (his novel based on the Wilmington, North Carolina, massacre against that city's black community in 1898), offered a trenchant summation of America's twisted racial condition. The "weed" of slavery had been cut down, Chesnutt wrote, but "its roots remained, deeply imbedded in the soil, to spring up and trouble a new generation." As lynchings increased at a frightening rate, those "roots" seemed to sprout all over the American landscape, and not only in the South. Only three days after the unveiling of the Shaw Memorial in Boston, a large mob in Urbana, Ohio, a town forty miles from Columbus, broke into a jail housing a black man named Charles Mitchell who had been accused of assaulting a white woman, and convicted of the crime in a trial of a "few minutes." Although two in the mob were killed, a detachment of Ohio National Guard could not stop the fury. Mitchell was hanged from a tree in the town square on June 3, 1897, in front of spectators that included "hundreds of women." It is difficult to account for the distance between the honor paid to Sergeant Carney and his comrades in Boston and the inhumanity and death delivered to Charles Mitchell in Ohio. And yet they are parts of the same narrative of triumph, betrayal, and tortured memory. When Paul Lawrence Dunbar, the most prominent of black poets, wrote his "Robert Gould Shaw" in 1900, he could breathe little hope from the monument or the story:

> Why was it that the thunder voice of Fate
>> Should call thee, studious, from the classic groves . . .,
> Far better the slow blaze of Learning's light,
>> The cool and quiet of her dearer fane,
> Than this hot terror of a hopeless fight,
>> This cold endurance of the final pain,—
> Since thou and those who with thee died for right
>> Have died, the Present teaches, but in vain![11]

By 1900 the flame of emancipationist memory still burned, but it lit isolated enclaves in a darkening age of racial antagonism. The noble pose of Saint Gaudens's black soldiers, striding forward, seemed to strain under too much ugly irony in Dunbar's "present."

WILLIAM MCKINLEY was the last Civil War soldier to serve as President of the United States. In an age ruled by spoilsmen and robber barons, and in a culture increasingly devoted to a revival of violent games and war itself as the tests of manhood, McKinley believed in Christian virtue, conciliation, and unity. In the 1896 campaign, the Republicans appealed forcefully for the

Union veteran vote as they had ever since the war. But this time, they did not wave the "bloody shirt"; instead, they wrapped McKinley in a conservative class appeal against William Jennings Bryan's Populist insurgency from within the Democratic Party. In 1894, a businessman from Massillon, Ohio, Jacob S. Coxey, had led a march of unemployed workers and their families from his hometown to Washington, D.C., to demand federal aid to create jobs and issue paper currency. His march caught on around the country, but when Coxey's peaceful charges reached the Capitol grounds they were clubbed and arrested by police. Populism in its various forms had a potent class appeal. With such social unrest, the Pullman strike, the lingering economic depression, and "Coxey's army" as backdrop, Republicans mobilized the aging Billy Yanks to march against the new and dangerous "disunionists" (Bryan's appeals to the "struggling masses"). The Republican press likened the Democrats (called "Popocrats") of 1896 to the secessionists of 1861. White Southerners were portrayed as victims once again of radicals in their midst. The Republican rallying cry in 1896 was the memory of sectionalism from the war and the place of Yankee soldiers in thwarting it. Numerous surviving Union generals barnstormed the Midwest on a whistle-stop campaign tour, urging crowds of thousands to uphold the social order as they had in 1861. By this economic and emotional appeal for reconciliation as protection against the "mob," McKinley carried key Midwestern states and won the White House against Bryan's revivalist-Populist campaign.[12]

Along with high tariffs, personal character seemed to be McKinley's only political platform. He had experienced war and never wanted to see it again. Yet McKinley's faith in progress and the harmony of interests, his devotion to the principle that a President should never lead public opinion but follow it, that real power in the federal system rested in Congress and not the executive, were all thrown into disarray when the battleship *Maine* exploded in Havana harbor on February 15, 1898, killing 260 Americans. Shortly afterward, McKinley wrote to a friend: "I have been through one war; I have seen the dead piled up, and I do not want to see another."[13]

By the mid-1890s, however, American investments in Cuba had reached $50 million and annual trade totaled $100 million. In search of naval bases, markets, and spheres of influence (notably the Caribbean), the United States had discreetly extended its power around the globe for two decades, and many responded positively to the bellicose rhetoric of empire. With the British as their model, and Rudyard Kipling's poetry providing their cadence, Americans were well conditioned by their own history to

Take up the White Man's burden—
  Send forth the best ye breed—
Go bind your sons to exile
  To serve your captives' need;
To wait, on heavy harness,
  On fluttered folk and wild—
Your new-caught sullen people,
  Half devil and half child.[14]

Infused with imperial language, nationalism, and racial supremacy, the Spanish-American War provided Americans, North and South, with new ways to cement their reunion. At the same time, it exposed the racial paradoxes of that American reunion.

Despite McKinley's sincere personal agony, he acquiesced in a Congressional declaration of war on Spain in April 1898. For four months of a "splendid little war," the United States fought the Spanish colonial forces over the official cause of Cuban freedom and independence. With a resurgence of the martial ideal, the jingoistic press exploited popular racism to fan hostility to the Spanish and their dark-skinned subjects in the Philippines. Americans mobilized on land and sea. For some, like Assistant Secretary of the Navy Theodore Roosevelt, the war with Spain offered the desired experience of combat that many in the post–Civil War generation had missed. The sons of the Blue and the Gray now had their war. Roosevelt resigned his civilian appointment, recruited his own cavalry unit, and sought his manly destiny in the charge up San Juan Hill in Cuba. In all, 460 Americans died in battle in the Spanish-American War, though due to terrible medical hygene and poor camp organization, another 5,200 died of disease.[15] The glorious foreign adventure made America a world power, but it had many unanticipated domestic consequences as well. Its reverberations were a full national debate over imperialism, a complex black response of patriotism mixed with fierce resistance, a new urgency to control the darker races of the world, and new drumbeats for sectional reunion.

From the Spanish-American War and the ensuing Philippine colonial war that lasted until 1903, African Americans learned once more that their own lives were the measuring stick of their country's contradictions. Blacks both embraced and rejected the new Manifest Destiny; like white men, black men were eager to prove their manhood and patriotism, to uphold traditions they too had built. But virtually all African Americans, whether conservative nationalists or militant war resisters, responded to America's foreign expansion from their own precarious position in the nation's deteriorating race relations. How could they help Cubans or Filipinos achieve freedom from Spain when they had not yet managed their own liberation? Some, like the commencement speaker at Hampton Institute in 1898, argued that blacks could not "afford to be blinded by resentment." Their bravery would "win . . . due recognition," said T. E. Rose, from the American people, and make white and black men who "fight side by side . . . friends in peace."[16] Most blacks, though, came to believe that charity began at home, and the dangers they faced in their own communities demanded their vigilance more than those three thousand or more miles away.

Approximately ten thousand blacks enlisted and served in the American forces in the Spanish-American War. Indeed, Booker Washington promised to recruit that many himself if by their service blacks could better secure their rights. As war seemed imminent, Washington told Secretary of the Navy John D. Long that blacks were eager to enlist, if necessary, to demonstrate "gratitude" for past "lives laid down" for their "freedom and rights." Initially, many blacks saw in the war, as in other national crises, a potential "blessing in disguise," as a Californian put it—an opportunity to exhibit loyalty, which would in turn erode white prejudice and lead to greater black liberty. Others feared that unwillingness to serve would imperil them among war-feverish whites. "It is highly probable that out of the nation's necessity will spring the race's opportunity and from between the dragon teeth of cruel war may be wrung concessions that years of sulking could never bring about," declared the *Wisconsin Weekly Advocate*. Black patriotism and expansionist fervor were genuine. Some believed that increased contact with "colored" foreigners could only serve the interests of African Americans. Others just argued for national devotion and birthright. "Our forefathers labored . . . fought . . . and died to perpetuate this country and leave a heritage to us," insisted the *Iowa State Bystander*. "Let us be men and show loyalty and we shall be rewarded."[17]

But in the intensive debate that ensued in the black press over whether African Americans should support the war, those in resistance seemed to prevail. The war threw black security and rights into bold relief. John Mitchell Jr., editor of the *Richmond Planet,* urged support for the war once it had been declared, but only if black men could serve under black officers above the rank of lieutenant. In May 1898, Mitchell launched a propaganda campaign under the slogan: "No Officers, No Fight!" The idea caught on widely in the black press. At its root, Mitchell's slogan carried the insistence on real political gains at home before any blacks should die abroad. Writing from the city where the huge Lee monument stood high above the emerging Monument Avenue of Confederate heroes, Mitchell offered the black side of a bargain. "We are not rushing forward now to die," he announced. "We have done our part of that kind of serious business, for sixty thousand victims of the Ku Klux Klan, the white-caps, the lynchers, the miscellaneous hordes of red-handed murderers are sleeping beneath the sod, and souls . . . go marching on."[18] In this variation on the legacy of "John Brown's Body," Mitchell demonstrated that the subtext of virtually all black response to the Spanish-American and Philippine wars was violence toward blacks at home.

Many blacks felt irreparably betrayed when, only a week after the destruction of the *Maine* in February, Frazier B. Baker, a black postmaster in Lake City, South Carolina, was murdered by a white mob. The lynchers set fire to the post office and Baker's adjoining house, killing Baker and his infant son. Some blacks hoped that because Baker was a federal official the government would now have to act against such violence. Representing black Chicagoans, Ida B. Wells-Barnett went to Washington to lobby for federal action by the attorney general. But the government's attention was solely focused on the impending war abroad, and no action was ever taken against Baker's murderers.[19]

Black editors voiced their communities' outrage. One declared that if "Remember the *Maine*" was "the white man's watch-word," then "remember the murder of postmaster Baker . . . should be the Negro's." The antiwar *Kansas City American Citizen* sought retribution and called the South a land of "anarchy" ruled by the mob, to whose "sulphurious dictum, all law and reason bend the quivering knee." Other papers urged Southern blacks to enlist, but only to fight the war at home, "to kill off some of their drunken, cut-throat neighbors who make a pastime of hanging, shooting, and burning men, women, and children" or to "avenge the wrongs of their brothers in the past thirty years." So much had lynching become the hideous underside of black life in America that most blacks could only view the nation's excursion into imperialism through this violent prism. Frederick Douglass's son-in-law, Nathan Sprague, resigned from the Republican state committee in Maryland in 1899 in protest against McKinley's imposition upon Filipinos of "a warped civilization" that permitted its own colored citizens to be "lynched and burned at the stake." And Douglass's son, Lewis H. Douglass, veteran of the Fifty-fourth Massachusetts, feared that because Filipinos were so readily dubbed "niggers" American imperialism only meant "the extension of race hate and cruelty, barbarous lynchings and gross injustice" around the globe among peoples of color.[20]

By 1899, when black anti-imperialist sentiment had reached full flower, domestic violence included images of the Wilmington, North Carolina, and Phoenix, South Carolina, "riots," each a series of lynchings and wholesale massacres of black folk surrounding the elections of November 1898. The savage lynching of Sam Hose in Atlanta in April 1899 also provoked public protest. Hose, a tenant farmer who killed his landowner in self-defense and fled in fear, was pursued for a week by a posse of white men. Falsely accused of raping the landowner's wife and other crimes, Hose was hanged and burned by a large crowd that had assembled from several counties. Against the background of expansion abroad, increasing disfranchisement, segregation, and mob violence at home, a gathering of black leaders in Massachusetts wrote a remarkable open letter to President McKinley. On October 3, 1899, in a mass meeting of the Colored National League at the Charles Street Church in Boston, the letter was read aloud by its principal author, the former slave and prominent lawyer Archibald H. Grimké. The tone and purpose of the letter was in stark contrast to Booker Washington's approach to dealing with Presidents and other white officials. Grimké directly addressed McKinley on the "oppressions" suffered by black folk, and "your [the President's] incomprehensible silence on the subject of our wrongs in your annual and other messages to Congress." The letter was an open challenge to McKinley's moral leadership by formerly loyal black Republicans (some now seeking political independence), and it was written in the form of a "demand." Grimké appealed to memory as a way of conveying the depths of black outrage. "Are you silent," he queried McKinley, "because without any fault of our own we were enslaved and held for two centuries in cruel bondage by your forefathers? Is it because we bear the marks of those sad generations of Anglo-Saxon brutality and wickedness, that you do not speak?" Although it addresses McKinley as representative of Americans generally, the letter nevertheless was a personal appeal: "Is there no help in the federal arm for us, or even one word of audible pity, protest and remonstrance in your own breast, Mr. President . . .?"[21]

After an extended history lesson about the "social degradation" practiced against blacks from 1619 to 1863, Grimké reached his main theme—present-day violence. "The terror wrought at the South," he said, "is so complete, so ever-present, so awful, that no negro's life or property is safe for a day who ventures to raise his voice to heaven in indignant protest." After a recital of the riots and lynchings to which McKinley never responded (Wilmington, Phoenix, and Sam Hose among them), Grimké's letter condemned the President's failure to react with anything except his infamous claim that the Southern outrages had "no federal aspect." Southern lynchers had "out barbarized barbarism," claimed the Boston petitioners, and with these sentiments they condemned American imperialism, asking in the end: "Do the colored people of the United States deserve equal consideration with the Cuban people?"[22]

McKinley was an inveterate conciliator, especially toward the South. Indeed, the furthering of sectional reconciliation was one of the President's explicit war aims. The bitter appeal to McKinley by Massachusetts blacks vividly illustrates how even though the Spanish-American War served the ends of reunion by uniting North and South against a common external foe, it also exacerbated racial antagonism. In the wake of the war, McKinley toured the South to urge support for the peace treaty and America's new territorial acquisitions in the Caribbean and the Pacific. At Atlanta's celebration of the peace, McKinley touted the war's "magic healing, which has closed ancient

As the United States went to war with Spain in 1898, this cartoon celebrated the reconciliation of the Confederate and Union veteran, both draped in the national flag as they gaze out on a burning Cuba. (From *Chicago Inter-Ocean*, May 30, 1898, in *Cartoons of the War of 1898 with Spain*, Chicago: Belford, Middlebrook & Co., 1898)

wounds and effaced their scars." The President viewed parades of Confederate veterans and stood proudly for the playing of "Dixie." "Sectional feeling no longer holds back the love we bear each other," he told the Georgia legislature. And as chief federal spokesman, he announced that the time had arrived when "in the spirit of fraternity we should share with you in the care of the graves of the Confederate soldiers." All the dead from the Civil War, said McKinley, simply embodied "American valor." Two decades of soldiers' reconciliation had inevitably prepared the ground for these statements, but without the war with Spain, and the South's embrace of the cause, such reconciliation would not have matured so readily. By 1900, some 128 Confederate dead buried around Washington, D.C., were reinterred in Arlington National Cemetery. In 1903 the first Confederate Memorial Day service was held there, and slowly, with UCV endorsements, the Congress passed, and President Theodore Roosevelt signed in 1906, a bill requiring federal care of Confederate graves in Northern cemeteries.[23]

Blacks knew that white Southern support for the war and its consequences did not bode well for them. The *Norfolk Recorder* advised blacks in 1898 that "the closer the North and South get together by this war," the harder they would "have to fight to maintain a footing." And the Massachusetts public letter to McKinley chastized him a year later for his effusive appeals for reconciliation: "When you made your Southern tour . . . we saw how cunningly you catered to Southern race prejudice and proscription." But Southern support for the war and expansion became an overwhelming force by which reunion trumped appeals for racial justice, no matter how eloquently made. This deepening racialization of American patriotism, the growing alliance between white supremacy and imperialism, had profound consequences for race relations and for the nation's historical memory.[24] National unity in foreign policy, especially a war against a darker race, gave the promoters of Jim Crow in the South a freer hand than ever in fashioning a segregated social system. White Southerners saw in the war with Spain a way to demonstrate their new loyalty and to gain from Northerners a robust recognition of their honor. Both aims were achieved many times over.

After news of the first death in the war, a sailor from North Carolina named Worth Bagley, Northern and Southern papers gushed with reconciliationist sentiment. Since the South had furnished the "first sacrifice of this war," commented the *New York Tribune*, "there is no north and no south . . . we are all Worth Bagley's countrymen." The *Atlanta Constitution* agreed, declaring Bagley's blood "the covenant of brotherhood between north and south," and a culmination of the "reconciliation that commenced at Appomattox." Some Americans proposed folding the Union and Confederate Decoration Days into one, and apparently with all seriousness S. A. Cunningham, editor of the *Confederate Veteran,* advocated brown, rather than blue or gray, as the color of soldiers' uniforms for the campaign in Cuba.[25]

Symbols of reunion abounded everywhere. Confederate veterans Hannis Taylor and Fitzhugh Lee were ambassador to Spain and consul to Havana respectively, and both were staunch interventionists. Moreover, Lee and another former Confederate general, Joseph Wheeler, were reappointed major generals for the war with Spain. Some ex-Confederates were so proud of Wheeler's role in the new war that they claimed a kind of vindication for themselves. Edward Porter Alexander told Wheeler that by his service in the U.S. Army, "you honor again the Old Cause" and "captured that prize for the memory of the Confederate Army." At the 1898 UCV reunion, Commander John B. Gordon gave a full endorsement to the war, urged Southern boys to be "wrapped in the folds of the American flag," and predicted that the conflict would bring the "permanent obliteration of all sectional distrusts." The heartthrobbings of reconciliation were so intense that a Detroit paper concluded that after the war with Spain, "nothing short of an archaeological society will be able to locate Mason and Dixon's line." Some songsters redrafted the "Battle Hymn of the Republic" and "Dixie," exchanging lyrics and tunes. And in Congressional debates over appropriations for the war, some members fell all over themselves trying to outdistance one another in reconciliationist patriotism. A Kentuckian responded to a Massachusetts Congressman's appeal for unity: "we who were defeated in the late unpleasantness will be glad as the citizens of a common country to touch elbows with the men of Massachusetts and see who can go farthest for the honor of our country."[26]

Southerners had their own serious debates over imperialism, especially during the protracted Philippine occupation. Some invoked memories of Reconstruction more readily than they sought recognition of Southern valor and opposed the establishment of "carpetbag rule" in Pacific islands. Most Southerners missed no opportunity to remind Northerners to do their part in preventing anything like Reconstruction from ever happening again in America. More than anything else, white Southern politicians feared the millions of colored people who might now become American dependents, and might even flood the borders. South Carolina Congressman, "Pitchfork" Ben

Tillman, one of the most virulent of racial demogogues, served up his anticolonialism as pure white supremacy. Tillman lumped African Americans, Polynesians, and Malays into one nonwhite group that "God Almighty made . . . inferior and lacking in moral fiber." He resisted "injection into the body politic of the United States . . . ten millions of the colored race, one half or more of whom are barbarians of the lowest types."[27] Racism could serve the ends of both imperialism and anti-imperialism. Whatever their attitudes toward American expansion abroad, as the twentieth century took hold, surviving ex-Confederates and their children could comfortably embrace the domestic reunion at home on terms of their own making.

IN THE FIRST decade of the twentieth century, American society reeled under the transformative pressures of urbanization, immigration, and industrialization. In 1860 the urban population of the United States was approximately 20 percent, but by 1900 it had reached 40 percent. New York and Brooklyn consolidated in 1898 and two years later reached a population of 3 million. Similarly Chicago, which had a population of only 30,000 in 1850, reached 1.7 million in 1900, while in the same period Philadelphia grew from a city of 560,000 to 1.3 million. The war, emancipation, and Reconstruction wrought an emerging urban order in the South as well. New Orleans more than doubled in size from the war until 1910, rising from 169,000 to 339,000. But whole new cities grew out of the war's aftermath, such as Atlanta, which increased in population by over 300 percent by 1910 to a figure of 155,000. Richmond and Nashville expanded by 100 and 155 percent respectively to become cities of well over 100,000 inhabitants. And cities like Birmingham, Alabama, or Dallas and Fort Worth, Texas, which had hardly existed in 1860, were now emerging industrial centers. To add to this domestic urban growth, almost 14 million immigrants came to America between 1860 and 1900. Another 14.5 million arrived in the period 1900–15, mostly from eastern and southern Europe.[28] In this new, pluralistic society, which teemed with racial, religious, and ethnic turmoil, the reunion of North and South reached its culmination.

In the decade leading to the fiftieth anniversaries of the war and emancipation, varieties of reconciliationist and white supremacist memory fused into a potent force, while emancipationist memories were thrown on the defensive. For the South, the spread of urbanization and the challenge of ethnic infusion were always corollaries to the "race problem," a new kind of disorder against which white supremacists reacted with fervor. Thomas Nelson Page spoke for multitudes of white Southerners in 1904 when he wrote of the "question which ever confronts the South . . . which . . . still keeps the South 'one section' and the rest of the nation the other. This is the ever-present, ever-menacing, ever-growing Negro Question." And the previous year, W. E. B. Du Bois opened *The Souls of Black Folk* with the telling line: "Between me and the other world there is ever an unasked question . . . How does it feel to be a problem?" While he admitted that "being a problem is a strange experience," he concluded: "Merely a concrete test of the underlying principles of the great republic is the Negro Problem." Somehow, in the chasm of ignorance and embittered memory that lay between these two perceptions of the Negro Problem, the one as menace and the other the measure of democracy, Americans, black and white, had to decide just what reunion and race meant in a modern society. While trapped in the same tragic fate, the sections reconciled as the races divided.[29]

As the nation lurched toward the Civil War semicentennial, an ever-expanding sectional reconciliation served as a counterweight to economic and social change. The reunion had always been good for commerce. Southerners continued to welcome Yankee investment dollars, while the growing concentration of the races in cities prompted their legislatures to draft increasingly rigid Jim Crow laws. Symbols and rituals of reconciliation appeared everywhere. Veterans' reunions and monument unveilings (by the semicentennial in virtually every hamlet, town, and city) served as public gestures of social cohesion in the distended industrial age. Nostalgia for the heroic and romantic pasts of the battlefield and the plantation found robust markets. Commercial flag producers began to include the Confederate battle flag, along with the stars and stripes, in their advertisements. Indeed, one ex-Confederate living in Colorado tried to find support for having the stars and bars incorporated into a corner of the United States flag. The Blue and the Gray clasping hands became a popular symbol of social peace in a time when the disorder of race riots, labor strife, class antagonism, and bewildering immigrant diversity dominated social consciousness. Handclasping and intersectional marriages appeared everywhere in popular culture. "The Wedding of the Blue and the Gray" was a sprightly number in George M. Cohan's 1906 musical comedy, *George Washington, Jr.,* a show better known for having introduced "You're a Grand Old Flag." In the story, a Northern youth's father has arranged for him to marry the daughter of a European nobleman, but the boy wants to marry a Southern girl named Dolly. When the father disowns his son, the son disowns his father and proclaims himself "George Washington, Jr." The plot is resolved as the couple sings the duet: "Our Grand Daddies of the North and South, Shook hands one fine day . . . So we'll drink to peace and our Grand Daddies, at the wedding of the Blue and Gray."[30]

As veterans aged and began to die off precipitously after the turn of the century, Blue-Gray reunions occurred in many places and proportions. Sometimes two regiments gathered to commemorate an anniversary of a wartime encounter or arranged exchange trips—as veterans from Springfield, Massachusetts, and Petersburg, Virginia, did in 1910. Elsewhere annual reunions of either the UCV or the Grand Army of the Republic, or anniversaries of specific battles, included large-scale Blue-Gray fraternalism, such as those conducted at Memphis and Manassas in 1911. The return of captured battle flags, long a hotly contested matter between veterans' organizations in both sections, had remained in dispute even in the aftermath of the Spanish-American War. In spite of intensified nationalist feelings, some Union veterans refused to budge on releasing the flags to the Southern states. But by 1905, while deliberating on the bill to require federal care for Confederate graves, Congress, without protest, authorized the return of all battle flags in government possession. The "captured banners" were shipped to Richmond and other points South. Although ex-Confederates had never been shy of waving their battle flag to convey its many regional and racial messages, the U.S. government had now relinquished these last tangible "trophies" of the war.[31] In the name of reconciliation, Grant's lenient terms at Appomattox had transfigured in forty years into a slow surrender of a different kind. The age of Jim Crow was not only the creation of aggressive Southern legislatures, but the result of the North's long retreat from the racial legacies of the war.

During these years American Presidents, in retirement, in office, or as aspirants, thumped the drums of reunion. In 1900, the eager candidate and self-styled hero of San Juan Hill, Theodore Roosevelt, saw among the many "good features" of the Spanish-American War "the unity it brought about between the sons of the men who wore the blue and of those who wore the gray." And in 1910, "Colonel Roosevelt," as he was so widely called even after his presidency, assured Southerners that intersectional commercial congresses would foster the "complete disappearance" of any remaining "misunderstanding" between those who "wore the blue or the gray." Invoking images of the Blue and Gray provided a kind of mantra for anyone who needed to serve the political or business interests of sectional comity and social cohesion.

President William H. Taft crafted reconciliationist speeches to fit his audiences. At a gathering of Confederate veterans in New Orleans in 1909, Taft assured the old men that "we've got beyond the time . . . when we discuss the war . . . all who were in the bloody four years contest are proud of the courage and fortitude shown by both sides." With the language of forgetfulness and fraternalism, Taft readied the nation for the Civil War's fiftieth anniversary season. "What any Americans did then," he declared, "we all cherish as a common heritage." In presidential rhetoric, the Civil War had become necessary and good for the country. As Taft told another Blue-Gray meeting in Virginia, the sections united with a "confession that all that was done was well done, that the battle had to be fought."[32] These official expressions left little room for national debate on just what meanings and consequences Americans should ponder apart from battlefield valor. Such attitudes were not new; they were only rendered more conclusive by rhetoric from high places.

In formal history, especially in the seven-volume work of James Ford Rhodes, *History of the United States from the Compromise of 1850* (1893–1906), Americans had a popular nationalist-reconciliationist interpretation of the war to savor. Born in 1848, Rhodes grew up in a Democratic Party family in Cleveland, Ohio, where his father, a successful businessman in coal mining, taught him to oppose the Emancipation Proclamation and most other Republican Party influences during and after the war. Rhodes's own success in the coal and iron industry, which strengthened economic ties between North and South, may have, in part, predisposed him to a reconciliationist vision of the Civil War and Reconstruction. Although an amateur, Rhodes represented the new generation of American historians who came of age after the Civil War, began writing in the 1890s, and were no longer invested in questions of war guilt.[33]

Rhodes argued that slavery was the essential, "sole cause" of the war, but in such a way as to absolve white Southerners of specific responsibility. He portrayed slavery as more a curse imposed from without than a crime committed by the South and the nation. Rhodes removed blame from the ledger of accounts in Civil War memory. As a natural, economic juggernaut, cotton fueled the growth of slavery, and due to forces largely out of human control, the nation tumbled like gravity into the "irrepressible conflict." Rhodes left no doubt of his belief that slavery was an inhumane institution and that it formed the "unrighteous cause" for which Southerners fought. But he opened the door of national imagination wide to the admiration of beleaguered Southern leaders, especially Robert E. Lee. He reinforced the idea that exemplary men can choose the wrong, or doomed, side in a great war, a notion that Lost Cause promoters had tried to teach Americans. Similarly, Rhodes gave strong endorsement to the cultural revival of the martial ideal and the worship of soldiers' valor. His widely read narratives of battles and campaigns were the experiences of glorious warriors on both sides, and prisons and plunder, the harsh underside of the war, were portrayed as the outcomes of war itself rather than the acts of military leaders.[34] By the turn of the century, Americans had an epic history of the Civil War to match the expectations of its emerging collective memory. Rhodes's *History* contained honor and sympathy in full supply for both sections.

But perhaps most importantly, Rhodes held that Reconstruction had been a colossal mistake, and that the South had been victimized by misguided or viscious radicalism. When Rhodes reached the postwar "race question," his sympathies rested firmly with the South. "No large policy in our country," he wrote, "has ever been so conspicuous a failure as that of forcing universal negro suffrage upon the South." Rhodes believed that the radical Reconstruction policies constituted nothing short of the "oppression of the South by the North," and chastized the radicals for their misunderstanding of "the great fact of race."[35] With his stellar reputation for fairness well established, by the time his Reconstruction volumes appeared in 1905–1906, Rhodes had set the stage for William A. Dunning and his many students who, as professional historians, were to plant so deep the tragic legend of Reconstruction that it simply became an article of faith in American historical understanding. The reconciliation not only reunited North and South, but it also welcomed a victimized South back to full honor. The victors of Southern redemption over Yankee carpetbaggery and treachery held as high a place in national memory as the victors at Gettysburg or Appomattox. And beneath all, the "race question" festered like a national illness on which memory fed. In the national memory, the alleged wrongs of Reconstruction tarnished, if not overwhelmed, the values of the revolution of 1863.

In reviews and in voluminous correspondence with historians and readers, Rhodes received many accolades on his "conspicuous impartiality and justice," as Lord Acton put it from England in 1898. In 1895, the *Critic* honored Rhodes for his "studied fairness." And A. V. Dicey wrote from England: "As I read your book I see more clearly that the conflict was so inevitable that one can perhaps hardly blame greatly the men engaged in it on either side." At least in Rhodes's class, Americans seemed desperate for a historian's "fairness in dealing with a period when passion raged fiercely." It was as though the intent of the editors of *Century* a decade earlier had finally found full fruition. Tom L. Johnson, a Southerner engaged in the steel business in Cleveland, praised Rhodes's work for its "perfect fairness to the southern people." And the son of a radical Republican, Charles S. Ashley of Ohio, complimented Rhodes for holding "the scales remarkably even in discussing . . . public sentiment in both North and South."[36]

Alhough Rhodes's nationalist interpretation would come under severe criticism from progressive historians such as Charles Beard, over time many distinguished historians passed lasting judgments on the great amateur. In the turn-of-the-century context, wrote Frederick Jackson Turner in 1928, Rhodes's "*History* marked an important turning point in the relations between North and South. He carried his calm judgment and fairness into a field that up to that time had still been largely a battlefield among historians." In the years of Rhodes's influence, the UDC still struggled mightily to control school textbooks in the South.[37] But for the broadest American audience, Rhodes had made a *civil* war comfortable to remember. Healing of the sections advanced to nearly full completion as justice between the races sunk deeper into a void.

Another Northerner, Charles Francis Adams II, took a step further than Rhodes and fused reconciliationist and white supremacist memory. The son of Charles Francis Adams I, the American minister to Great Britain during the Civil War and a Union cavalry veteran, Adams had amassed a fortune in mining, railroad, and real estate by the end of the 1880s. By the turn of the century Adams had become a soul mate of Rhodes, joined the ranks of gentlemen scholars, and fashioned his own peculiar defense of secession, the Confederacy, and Robert E. Lee. Most interestingly, he parlayed his deep Yankee lineage (grandson and great-grandson of two Adams Presidents) into a conspicuous condemnation of Reconstruction and support for white supremacy. In long letters, Adams prodded Rhodes to stress cotton even more as a cause of the war, to downplay slavery, and to condemn Reconstruction.[38]

Southern audiences were eager to hear Adams's lectures on their own turf and to bask in the Bostonian's respect for their history. In 1902 he delivered a vigorous defense of secession in Charleston, South Carolina, in which he exhibited his racial obsessions and his sympathies with the South. "The Southern people have the dead-weight of Africanism tied to them," he declared in the speech's afterword. "The races are segregating," he wrote approvingly. "In all these respects an increasing separation of the two species, living perforce not side by side but together, is bad for both." The South deserved the North's aid and comfort in managing its "handicap . . . the presence in its civilization of a vast, imperfectly assimilated mass of barbarism veneered."[39]

The glorification of Lee as a tragic hero became one of Adams's favorite topics. In "Lee at Appomattox," delivered in Worcester, Massachusetts, in 1901, Adams praised Lee for his magnanimity at the war's end, arguing that the Confederate general singlehandedly saved the country from guerrilla war. But even in this romantic recreation of Lee's last days of command at Appomattox, Adams invoked the evils of Reconstruction and racial equality as a central theme. The deepest legacies of the war era, Adams made clear, were racial. He gave the "Lee's Centennial" address at Washington and Lee University, in Lexington, Virginia, in 1907. Standing on the altar in the college chapel, in front of Lee's recumbent tomb where the general's calm, knightly head in marble looked toward the sky, Adams spent many pages glorifying Lee's "character," his national image as a "great man,—great in defeat . . . well-nigh the highest type of human development." Here, in one of the most sacred sites of the Lost Cause, where Lee had served as college president for four years until his death in 1870, Adams brought his message of solidarity with the South. Never, he maintained, had "a people prostrate after civil strife . . . received severer measure than was inflicted on the so-called reconstructed Confederate States." Two days later when Adams departed, all the students from Washington and Lee gathered at the train station to send him off with a rousing ovation.[40] How complete the reunion on Southern terms must have seemed to those young white Virginians.

A year later in Richmond, Adams reminded his large Southern audience of the "hateful memory of what is known as the Reconstruction Period" and acknowledged that out of those memories "the portentous Race Question looms up!" "The African," he claimed, as though imitating Southern racial demogogues, was a "distinct alien" who had caused the American ideal of assimilation to break down. Appealing to all manner of racist assumptions, short of outright endorsement of lynching, Adams showed his personal hand: "I stand abashed and silent in the awe-inspiring presence of this awful and mysterious Afro-American Sphinx." He reinforced the story of Yankee oppression and Southern victimhood during Reconstruction. "The reconstruction policy of 1866," he said, "was worse than a crime . . . as ungenerous as it was gross." The only conclusion to be drawn was to leave the race question alone, to "be worked out in the South."[41]

Hence there is little wonder that at a Confederate Memorial Day ceremony in Norfolk, Virginia, the following spring (1909), Hilary A. Herbert, ex-secretary of the U.S. Navy, pronounced Southerners "reconciled" to the defeat of their "battle for . . . independence." But then he rejoiced that the South had "triumphed . . . over carpetbag and negro rule." Yankee money or power "did not awe us," declared Herbert, "and *we won*" (emphasis added). Herbert concluded with a message that struck the central theme of the reunion:

> I am glad to say that we are making in all our State Legislatures a noble use of our victory. There is no law among our statutes that does the negro injustice. New constitutions have been devised for the benefit of both races, and I honestly believe that now we have reached the solution . . . of the negro problem which has been the curse of America.[42]

The Southern victory over Reconstruction replaced Union victory in the war and Jim Crow laws replaced the Fourteenth Amendment in their places of honor in national memory. As the fiftieth anniversary of the conflict arrived, just what had been won or lost in the Civil War epoch reached this shaky consensus.

A SEGREGATED society demanded a segregated historical memory. The many myths and legends fashioned out of the reconciliationist vision provided the superstructure of Civil War memory, but its base was white supremacy in both its moderate and virulent forms. Emancipationist visions had long been on the defensive in the national marketplace, but they were by no means absent. Booker Washington, under increasingly severe attack from black activist leaders of the Niagara movement, founded in 1905, and the National Association for the Advancement of Colored People (NAACP), founded in 1910, could still command center stage.

Washington's reconciliationist gestures at times seemed to have no limits. In November 1902, he invited General John B. Gordon, the commander of the UCV and former governor of Georgia, to speak at Tuskegee. Some 1,800 students, teachers, and citizens of the town filled the college auditorium and "jumped to their feet . . . with salvos of welcome" as the old Confederate soldier took the podium. To this black audience, Gordon delivered the lecture

"The Last Days of the Confederacy." After describing the pathetic demise of the Army of Northern Virginia at Appomattox, Gordon paid tribute to "the Negro race who with so much faithfulness befriended and cared for the wives and sisters of the Confederate soldiers who went to the front of a war having for its issue the continuation of slavery." On this day at Tuskegee, everyone was a loyal Southerner. "I declare to you that the Southern white man is the best friend the Negro in the South has," the old general assured the black youth. Before closing, Gordon also "paid a beautiful tribute to the old plantation songs sung with so much power" by the students.[43] Here was a kind of racial reconciliation unique to the South; wrapped in ceremonial paternalism, promoted officially by Tuskegee, the old and new met on scripted Southern terms of forgetting.

Gordon was widely known, both in politics and in memorial activities, as a conciliator of the sections. As UCV spokesman, he went out of his way to foment good relations with Union veterans, and in the case of his appearance at Tuskegee, with some blacks. A year later, Gordon published a romantic autobiographical article in *Scribner's* about his first command during the war. Embedded in it is his well-honed argument, one perfectly resonant with reconciliationist thinking in these years, that "the Negro" and "slavery" had caused the war—but that the South had never been responsible for the origins of the problem. Not all Southern blacks responded with kindness to Gordon's brand of reconciliation. When the UCV commander died in January 1904, H. A. Rucker, the black collector of customs for the port of Atlanta, refused to lower the flag to half-mast on the federal building as ordered, much to the chagrin of local Confederate veterans.[44]

Many black leaders in the early years of the century took increasingly critical stands on the costs of sectional reunion and tried to shape a historical memory devoted to racial justice. Every group in American society sought a usable past, and blacks needed it desperately. But for blacks who followed Du Bois's efforts to counter Washington's accommodationism with protest, the need was not merely for a positive history with which to build self-respect, but also for one that could counter the increasingly racist social memory they faced in American life. Du Bois was by no means ungenerous in sympathy toward the white South in the first decade of the century; he sought understanding with its "best elements" across the color line. But among his many concerns about Washington was the Wizard of Tuskegee's leadership, as Du Bois put it, "not of one race but of two,—a compromiser between the South, the North, and the Negro." "The growing spirit of kindliness and reconciliation between the North and South," wrote Du Bois, "ought to be a source of deep congratulation to all, and especially to those whose mistreatment caused the war." But he worried: "If that reconciliation is to be marked by the industrial slavery and civic death of those same black men, with permanent legislation into a position of inferiority," then blacks were "called upon by every consideration of patriotism . . . to oppose such a

Northern born and Harvard educated, W. E. B. Du Bois became a fierce critic of national reconciliation and an eloquent voice of the emancipationist vision of Civil War memory. (Special Collections and Archives, W. E. B. Du Bois Library, University of Massachusetts, Amherst)

course by all civilized means."[45] The Du Bois–Washington conflict over social and political strategy should be seen not only as a division over philosophy and leadership methods, but also as a dispute over how and if blacks should embrace the American reunion to which their rights were increasingly sacrificed.

In the ubiquitous discussion of the "Negro Problem," emancipationist memory of the Civil War era seemed forever under duress. When Americans spoke of the "Negro Problem" or "Race Problem," many referred to blacks as the obstacle to national progress, as a people to be reformed or eliminated, as a social crisis demanding solutions. Or they might mean segregation and disfranchisement and how to combat or cope with these challenges. Many blacks preferred to banish endless debate over the Negro Problem in favor of going after its root causes—racial prejudice, legal discrimination, and lynching. But American society dragged it into every consideration of black life, and inherently forced virtually every black commentator to confront it as a struggle over remembering and forgetting. Some fought with historical and statistical analyses of black progress and demonstrations of patriotism. Many said that it was a white problem. "I say there is no negro problem," wrote the lawyer D. Augustus Straker, "but a race prejudice [among whites] . . . seemingly ineradicable." S. C. Cross named the irony more specifically. If one is referring to "trampling innocent, helpless men, women, and children in the dust," he said, "smothering their aspirations . . . submerging them beneath the tides of tyranny and treachery . . . even roasting them alive at stakes in chains . . . then there is a Negro Problem." And most poignantly, in a 1905 address memorializing William Lloyd Garrison in Faneuil Hall in Boston, AME bishop Reverdy C. Ransom probed the meaning of the intersection between the race problem and reunion. "We would see the wounds left by the War of the Rebellion healed," declared Ransom,

> but we would have them healed so effectually that they could not be trodded upon and made to bleed afresh by inhuman barbarities and unjust legislation; we would have the wounds of this nation bound up by the hands of those who are friendly to the patient, so that they might not remain a political running sore. We would have the bitter memories of the war effaced, but they cannot fade while the spirit of slavery walks before the nation in a new guise. We too, would have a reunited country; but we would have the re-

union to include not only white men North and South, but a union so endearing, because so just, as to embrace all of our fellow-countrymen, regardless of section or of race.[46]

In this appeal for healing with justice, Ransom defined the tragedy, as well as the course not taken, in Civil War memory.

The interdependence of reunion and the "Race Problem" in Civil War memory is stunningly exhibited in a scene from James Weldon Johnson's novel, *The Autobiography of an Ex-Colored Man,* published anonymously in 1912. The protagonist is riding the train southward to Macon, Georgia. Because he is passing for white, he rides the Pullman car. A robust conversation ensues between four characters: a Northern, "Jewish-looking man," who is a cigar manufacturer experimenting in Havana tobacco in Florida; a "slender bespectacled young man" from Ohio, who teaches at a state college in Alabama; a "white-moustached, well-dressed" man, an old Union soldier who "fought through the Civil War" and has numerous investments to attend to in the South; and a loud, "tall, raw-boned, red-faced man" who is a Texas cotton planter. The discussion moves from mundane matters—the weather, crops, and business—to politics, and then quickly to the "Negro question." The Jew is portrayed as the diplomat, taking all sides at once, opposing no one. The young Northern professor had believed in black rights and opportunity, but a year in the deep South had given him compassion fatigue; he now confessed that he thought the race question should be left to white Southerners.[47]

A contentious debate ensues, however, between the old soldier and the Texas planter. The debate is one between generations and between conflicting conceptions of the meaning of the Civil War. The young Texan reflects Southern collective memory well and argues that the "Civil War was a criminal mistake on the part of the North and that the humiliation which the South had suffered during Reconstruction could never be forgiven." The old Union soldier retorts that the "South was responsible for the war and that the spirit of unforgetfulness on its part was the greatest cause of present friction." At issue was the meaning of black freedom. The Texan assures the audience of listeners that the Anglo-Saxon race will always rule the world, while the Northerner gives a neo-abolitionist commentary on the "moral responsibility" to help uplift blacks socially and guarantee their "essential rights of men." The Union veteran bests the New South planter in education and eloquence. After a long exchange about the meaning of what a "race" actually is and a requisite query from the Texan to the Old Yankee of whether he would allow his daughter to "marry a nigger," this discussion among white men ends in laughter, with almost everyone taking a drink from the Texan's flask of whiskey. Reconciliation conquers antagonism. The race question is debated, but in the end, dissolves in newfound relationships among white men of means. Johnson's protagonist watches with a "chill . . . sick at heart" over what he heard from the planter, but admits to an odd sense of admiration for the steadfastness with which Southerners "defend everything belonging to them."[48]

Johnson captured many elements of Civil War memory in this single scene: worn-out Yankee liberalism, noble neo-abolitionism on the part of an old soldier, white ethnic indifference to Southern and racial issues, and white Southern hostility to any variety of the emancipationist legacy of the era. All of them are busy making money, except the gaunt Ohio professor; he also does not drink from the flask. That Johnson's passing protagonist, black but not black, observes this conversation is a fitting metaphor for one of the ways many African Americans would have to watch the semicentennial of *their* Civil War—as deeply interested and implicated observers, the underlying subject of many articles and symposia but segregated and, to most whites, invisible.

SEGREGATION AND racism had not stopped African Americans from commemorating emancipation as the benchmark of their history. In 1901, Archibald Grimké demonstrated that whites had no monopoly on the pathos and patriotism of Memorial Day rhetoric. His address to black veterans in Boston included a recital of Civil War causation. "The wrong done the negro by this country [slavery]," said Grimké, "soon overflowed upon the country itself." Emancipation had not come by any sudden moral transformation of the nation; it had been "wrenched from the hands of an unwilling country." But in this regeneration of blacks and the nation, Grimké discovered a patriotic narrative. "Need I repeat to you, veterans," he proclaimed, "how in numbers nearly two hundred thousand strong, our colored boys in blue left their blood and their bones in every Southern state . . .?" Grimké paid tribute to radical Reconstruction as the "best and wisest" policy and described the current state of race relations as the same "battle of ideas" over which the "great war" was fought. Before ending with a moving description of the Shaw Memorial, Grimké argued that the "unification of the sections" could only be achieved if blacks received their full liberty as citizens.[49] In these arguments and tones, black patriotic memory found its voice.

Black newspapers and magazines had long run retrospectives on black leaders and heroes, especially Civil War soldiers, and these features increased as the semicentennial approached. In speeches, poetry, and magazine essays, Frances Harper and Pauline Hopkins worked to forge a positive view of black history. Persistently, Harper, as one of the characters in her novel *Iola Leroy; or, Shadows Uplifted* (1892) says, wanted to prevent her people from "forgetting the past," and instead would "have them hold in everlasting remembrance our great deliverance." Likewise, Hopkins used the past for models of uplift, by writing long biographical sketches in the *Colored American* magazine on Washington, Douglass, Blanche Bruce, and others, many of them in romantic prose designed to inspire the younger generation to self-improvement.[50]

Some black editors also tried to raise historical awareness. In 1909, T. Thomas Fortune's *New York Age* called for a usable history for black youth. "The Negro . . . will get more of race pride and self-confidence out of his own history," he said. "Let Negro students study Negro history. Let Negro schools teach Negro history." A kind of antiquarian commemorative spirit took hold as well in black communities. In the 1880s and 1890s, the *New York Age* offered for sale a wall chart containing several black heroes, and by 1911 it advertised twenty-by-twenty-four-inch photogravures of several black historical figures for three dollars each. Other papers ran full-page pictorials of "The Ten Greatest Negroes," and the AME Church in 1899 produced a "Souvenir Historical Chart" featuring Bishop Richard Allen and several events in the history of the denomination. Inevitably, elements of black historical consciousness were put toward commercial ends. By the semicentennial the Frederick Douglass Shoe Company of Lynn, Massachusetts, was selling by mail order a Fred Douglass brand for men and a Phillis Wheatley brand for women. And the National Afro-Art Company provided eleven-inch busts of Allen, Douglass, Washington, and other "eminent leaders" for only $1.25 each.[51] Such collecting, as well as the consumer appeal now attached to black history, fit the new era of mass-market culture. But it may also have represented for many black families a form of empowerment or social aspiration, a way of displaying a heroic past and deflecting the shame of slavery. These icons were objects through which the "double consciousness" of being black and American could be joined and played out publicly in a segregated society.

Exhibitions were colossal civic and financial enterprises in America by the turn of the century, and blacks eagerly embraced the era of the fair. Indeed, the patriotic-progressive mode of black Civil War memory had no greater forum than these emancipation exhibitions, which though they emerged in full flower decades earlier, became especially significant as the fiftieth anniversary of freedom arrived. The celebration of Emancipation Day (January 1)—or Freedom Day, as it was sometimes called—began even before the Civil War ended. From hamlets to cities, blacks celebrated the anniversary of their liberation in a wide variety of ways. Its commemoration may have fallen off somewhat as the Jim Crow period took hold in the South, as well as because of reluctance to reflect on slave origins, but it never ceased. Moreover, "Juneteenth," the commemoration of June 19, 1865, when slaves received word of their emancipation in Texas during the war, survived in some Southern black communities, both as an actual celebration and as a cultural concept. In 1878, the *Christian Recorder* complained that blacks celebrated emancipation on "such days as suits them" with "no fixedness." The *Recorder* urged general agreement on one day and the lobbying of Congress for a "national holiday, to be observed by the colored race and their friends everywhere."[52]

Such a national day never materialized around emancipation, but by the mid-1880s, blacks had begun planning their own large exhibitions in major cities and were engaged in a degree of "monument fever" as well. In tune with the industrial expositions of the Gilded Age, these fairs collected and displayed black material and educational progress. One such festival of "all branches of industry, agricultural, mechanical and inventive" occurred in New Orleans in 1885. According to a newspaper account, it touted twenty years of "prodigious progress" and covered 34,220 square feet with "16,000 distinct exhibits." Setting a pattern that would be followed later, every state except Maine and Oregon was represented by a black delegation, which brought together the work of photographers and artists of all kinds; inventions, including a new "quartz mill" from Utah; and the wares of carriage makers from Georgia. These exhibitions served many ends in local black communities; their "progress of the race" themes advanced reconciliationist Civil War memory by demonstrating black success in the industrial economy and by buttressing the needs of race pride and national patriotism.[53]

Around the centennial of Abraham Lincoln's birth in 1909 and the semicentennial of the war in 1910–11, black commemorative activity emerged everywhere. Lincoln had always been a central part of African American emancipation celebrations; in the desperate circumstances of the age of Jim Crow, he became even more important symbolically to black citizens. The idea that "Lincoln freed the slaves" has been treated more recently with considerable scholarly and public skepticism. But at many black gatherings commemorating freedom, Lincoln's image was still front and center. Lincoln as icon had come to represent much more than a personal or presidential act of emancipation. The "Proclamation" itself, almost always read at these occasions, had come to represent to blacks their own kind of national treasure, their own founding document. It was "the issuance of their Magna Carta" that they should celebrate on January 1 every year, declared the National Afro-American Council in 1906, an organization created by Fortune.[54] Whether blacks saw the Emancipation Proclamation as the foundation of their citizenship, or whether they viewed Lincoln as their liberator, most had generally adopted their own civic logic: in segregated America, where their rights were temporarily crushed, if Lincoln had not freed the slaves, then the nation had not; and if the nation had not freed them, then they had no future as citizens. For many blacks, Lincoln's place in emancipation stood as a symbol of necessary and humane statecraft, an official declaration of their belonging in the land of their birth, secured by blood in war and sanctioned by the highest authority of the nation. Lincoln's portrait at the front of a black church at an emancipation celebration was a collective statement of citizenship and identity. Blacks, of course, also recollected how as refugees, soldiers, and camp hands they had freed themselves. But theories of self-emancipation had little historical grounding in the early twentieth century, and were of marginal value in wresting the right to vote back from white supremacists and Jim Crow "reformers." Strategically, and with genuine sentiment, therefore, blacks honored Lincoln in season and out, but especially on the days when they remembered their freedom as a national matter.

Behind public anniversary celebrations, a kind of commemorative spirit can be discerned among ordinary black folk. In 1910 Mary White Ovington, a white social worker and one of the founders of the NAACP, recorded the recollections of several ex-slaves in Southern Alabama. Ovington found an interesting range of old folks who told of personal pain, hardship, family breakups, labor conditions, progress toward property ownership, and insights as well as tall tales about the war and emancipation. A woman identified only as "Granny" recited the most compelling story. Very old, with African features, Granny told of being sold away from her four children in North Carolina, sent in the slave trade westward to Alabama, and forced to give birth to a fifth child fathered by her new, cruel master. She remembered crying when the master's son died in the Confederate army, because he was a "kind chile." She related tales of being whipped, of her desperate fears of running away, and of how she survived only on her faith in "Master Jesus."[55]

As Ovington was about to leave, she asked Granny about the photograph of Lincoln on the mantle in her cabin. "I love dat face, Miss," Granny answered. "I love it so dat der lady down here, she done gib me der picture. Dose eyes, dey follow me, dey's so kind. I don' know how ter tell you how much I lub dat man dat made us free—an' all der oders, too, dat helped." Granny and Ovington are both reminded of a lyric from a plantation song as they "looked out on the fields where men guided the mules in the plowing," and the ex-slave concludes: "I's see a heap o' sorrow an' trouble, but it's ober for me. I t'ank de Lord dat I's free; dat us all, chillen, an' women, an' men, is free."[56] This interview is likely a collaborative work of nostalgia, a dose of neo-abolitionist pathos, and a genuine window into freedpeople's memory all at once. The old woman's retrospective mixture of sorrow and celebration provided a kind of literary keynote for the public events that followed during the semicentennial season of emancipation.

The states of Georgia, New York, Pennsylvania, Illinois, and New Jersey gave appropriations of varying amounts for emancipation expositions. Cities as large as Washington, D.C., Chicago, Philadelphia, Atlantic City, New Orleans, Atlanta, Richmond, and Los Angeles and as small as Savin Rock, Connecticut; Zanesville, Ohio; Corpus Christi, Texas; Keokuk, Iowa; and Quincy, Illinois, had their own celebrations. Black associations of all kinds, such as the National Baptist Convention, Freedmen's Relief Committee of Philadelphia, and National Association of Colored Nurses, held anniversary events. Celebrations were nearly as common in the South as the North. Under the leadership of journalist and politician Charles N. Hunter, Raleigh, North Carolina, had conducted Emancipation Day events for many years. In that city in October 1913, the Negro State Fair and the Ex-Slaves Association of North Carolina hosted a reunion of former bondsmen. Crowds of two thousand to three thousand people were not uncommon at some of the smaller occasions, which often took on festive airs; speeches were often relegated to a minor role in favor of barbecues and baseball games. In 1914 in

Quincy, Illinois, the orators were rejected by the crowd, which went to the ball game where the Quincy Wonders defeated a team from Paris, Missouri, 7 to 6 in "an interesting fray." Similarly, in August of the same year (celebrations were moved to summer for outdoor pleasure), black folk from all over western Illinois were much more interested in the all-women brass band and in the game between the Galesburg and Rock Island baseball teams than in emancipation rhetoric. In some communities, designated emancipation days became an alternative Fourth of July, occasions for amusement in a culture where working people more and more chose their own leisurely pursuits over formal political or civic events.[57]

But large-scale expositions were very much the project of black leadership of all persuasions. As early as 1908, Booker Washington, along with President Taft, advocated that blacks plan for emancipation celebrations of the semicentennial. And in late 1911, Washington's National Negro Business League put out a formal call for local celebrations of black "progress" on every scale. Major R. R. Wright of Georgia, a veteran of the Spanish-American War, led a campaign to obtain a $250,000 appropriation from Congress for a national emancipation exhibition, which he hoped to host in Savannah, Georgia. Wright was president of Georgia State Industrial College and had for some years through his Georgia Fair Association conducted successful, small-scale expositions of industrial progress in his state. In February 1912, Wright, his son, R. R. Wright Jr., editor of the *Christian Recorder,* I. N. Ross, a minister in Washington, D.C., and W. E. B. Du Bois, editor of the NAACP's *Crisis,* testified before the U.S. Senate Committee on Industrial Expositions. The elder Wright laid out the case that since 1876, the federal government had spent $25 million on expositions, and that blacks deserved 1 percent of that for their celebration of emancipation. Wright's son delivered a litany of statistical measures of black progress since freedom, especially in "material development." Then Du Bois addressed the senators, suggesting that they be "a little chary of expositions" because they were so numerous and expensive. But he promised in detail an exposition that would be "distinctly educational" in a host of sociological, historical, and artistic forms. He envisioned a unique "African exhibit" culled from the world's museums, and he signaled the "historical pageant" on which he was already at work. Reverend Ross concluded from the "moral side of this question," urging the senators to extend this gift to blacks as a vision of hope to the "discouraged and despondent." After some testy debate in which one Southern senator, announcing himself a "radical on the race question," rejected the idea that "two races . . .

can live on the same soil without one being subservient to the other," the appropriation easily passed. Unfortunately, later that summer the bill languished in the House of Representatives and died.[58] A federally funded national exhibition, such as Wright had envisioned, never materialized. But despite Congress's rebuke, the enthusiasm within black communities for an exhibition continued to grow.

In 1914, after the actual fiftieth anniversary had passed, a black group in Richmond, Virginia, led by a lawyer, Giles B. Jackson, requested $55,000 from Congress for an exposition in the former Confederate capital. This time, for peculiarly Southern, reconciliationist reasons, Congress approved the measure. In debate, Senator Thomas Martin of Virginia represented a "liberal" racial outlook of a sort, declaring himself a close observer of blacks and arguing that they had made "astounding" progress considering their obstacles. Martin was all for a celebration of "fifty years of their freedom." Senator James Vardaman of Mississippi held firm to the "radical" racist banner. Whites had "assisted" blacks in every way, said Vardaman, but making "citizens and voters of them" ought "never be done"—hence he opposed any appropriation to celebrate emancipation. A third Southern senator, Frank White of Alabama, held up a version of the "conservative" racial tradition, reaching deep into Lost Cause mythology. White supported the bill as a way of honoring the "loyalty" of former slaves during the war—"more," he said, "for what they did for us during the struggle in which their freedom was the issue than for what they did for us in other times." White said blacks deserved white gratitude because they "camped with us . . . marched with us . . . supplied our every want . . . guarded our homes and protected our women and children," and "carried their dead masters back to their wives."[59] In this romantic imagery, Thomas Nelson Page's fictions arrived triumphantly as a force on the floor of the U.S. Senate. Transformed once again into *Confederate veterans* and loyal slaves, blacks were allowed their celebration as payment for wartime service. An emancipation commemoration on these terms would not in the least transgress the Jim Crow social and political structure that these very politicians had helped to construct.

The Richmond "National Negro Exposition" ran for three weeks in July 1915. The fair received endorsements from President Woodrow Wilson and from Virginia governor Henry C. Stuart. In his official proclamation, Stuart encouraged "the negro in his efforts to solve his industrial problem," and in a careful use of Lost Cause tradition, he identified "the fidelity displayed by slaves during four years of war" as the "chain which links in enduring bond of friendship the best elements of both races." The exposition garnered widespread press coverage, especially of its midway and entertainments, and of the forthright manner in which it promoted the conservative-accommodationist aims of the "gospel of Booker T. Washington," as a Northern paper wrote with condescending admiration.[60]

The Richmond midway featured numerous vaudeville acts, including a Wild West show, high-wire and ladder acts, acrobats, minstrel singers, a roller skate act, a contortionist lady, and "all sorts of wonderful and alarming freaks." With two acts per day, a special attraction was the white diving girls—a group of "shapely aquarian artists . . . somewhat scantily attired" who passed the judgments of a "self-appointed committee of censors." The third day of the fair, in an interesting expression of segregated life in Richmond, was designated "White Folks Day," when the mayor and other white citizens visited the exhibition in large numbers, especially to observe demonstrations of the handiwork of black schools. During the second week of the show, Giles Jackson's committee of organizers staged a pantomimic pageant, *The Answer to the "Birth of a Nation,"* involving three hundred black schoolchildren performing such scenes as "a skiff landing the first slaves" in Jamestown, "a cotton plantation . . . with appropriate songs," and "closing with the negro entering the door of opportunity." This attempt to respond to D. W. Griffith's *Birth of a Nation* (which had just opened in American theaters in February) within the context of such an accomodationist-reconciliationist spectacle indicates how many competing elements of black memory could coexist in a single memorial event. But irony was the lifeblood of the semicentennial season; in preparing for anticipated crowds of blacks visiting Richmond for the exposition, a city in which there was only one black hotel, Jackson negotiated to borrow the housing facilities of Camp Stuart, a recent site of a Confederate veterans' reunion.[61]

Many other exhibitions of various sizes occurred in 1913–15. The clearest theme linking them all was the celebration of black progress and achievement in the professions, business, education, inventions, women's status, and the arts. In New Jersey an organizing committee worked for more than a year, dividing themselves into some thirty-seven "leagues," each devoted to sending out questionnaires and gathering facts and statistics on everything from needlework and dressmaking to real estate and music. Some even conducted "house-to-house canvasses" to gather such data. One of the more striking features of the Atlantic City event was an assembly on the boardwalk of black Civil War veterans in their uniforms mingling with two companies of black

Boy Scouts. In Chicago, some 135,000 people attended an exposition that combined the memory of Lincoln with modern black material progress, especially in technology and inventions. An editor of a black newspaper in Topeka, Kansas, rejoiced over all the commemoration of freedom, especially what he called "these cheering statistics."[62]

The accumulation of social scientific data about black achievement spread even more widely as new "progress of the race" books appeared, such as the *Negro Year Book* (1913), which was produced for many successive years by Monroe N. Work, the superintendent of records and research at Tuskegee Institute. Work's book became a kind of statistical bible by which newspapers far and wide reported the myriad measures of black advancement since slavery. Moreover, many major magazines and journals put out special issues commemorating emancipation and black progress for the semicentennial. In September 1913 the *Annals of the American Academy of Political and Social Science* published an issue devoted to "The Negro's Progress in Fifty Years." Some twenty-four essays, by eleven blacks and six Northern and seven Southern whites, covered subjects such as business and labor conditions, population growth, sharecropping, public health, criminality and debt, urban migration, and the growth of literacy. The collection ended with a piece by Washington on "Industrial Education and the Public Schools" and one by Du Bois on "The Negro in Literature and Art." However cast in data, these essays were markers of the relationship of past and present; some are social science in the service of an optimistic, interracial memory of emancipation, and others justify the segregated society forged by the national reunion. Du Bois was clearly not comfortable appearing in this volume; his own piece was a token nod to the arts and not his best work. He admired essays by Kelly Miller, R. R. Wright, Monroe Work, and other black contributors, as well as articles by some of the whites, such as that written by J. P. Lichtenberger, the journal's editor, which cast the growth of black literacy as a "phenomenal race achievement." But a segregationist, white-supremacist purpose motivated several pieces in the volume, such as Howard Odum's on the need for separate black schools, Ray Stannard Baker's on confidence in the white South when it came to black voting rights, and Thomas Edwards's idyllic picture of tenant farming.[63] In the myriad explorations of "Negro Progress" during the fiftieth anniversary season, the "Negro Problem" mixed in knotty contradiction with visions of optimism and measures of advancement.

By far the most elaborate commemoration was organized in New York City by Du Bois and other artists and civic leaders. This "National Emanci-

Staged at New York City's Twelfth Regiment Armory in October 1913, the National Emancipation Exhibition was one of the largest among hundreds of such celebrations. The appeal to African and Egyptian cultural roots is evident in the wall paintings and obelisks on the Temple of Beauty in the Great Hall of Freedom. (From *Crisis*, December 1913)

The *Star of Ethiopia* pageant was the central attraction of the 1913 emancipation exhibition in New York. The photo shows a portion of the 350-member cast. (From *Crisis*, December 1913)

pation Exposition" was staged at the Twelfth Regiment Armory, on Sixty-second Street near Broadway, October 22–31, 1913. The state of New York appropriated $25,000, and nine blacks served on the Emancipation Proclamation Commission appointed by the governor. Du Bois embraced the exposition fever as much as anyone; his social scientific and Victorian earnestness were in full form for the New York event. "With detailed charts, models, moving pictures, maps and a few typical exhibits," he said, "a complete picture of the present conditions will be presented, while a magnificent pageant . . . with music and costume, will give the historic setting." He promised "no endless repetition and country-fair effect," only "one fine and dignified presentation of great facts in simple form, with a frame of beauty and music."[64]

In this era of pageantry, Du Bois synthesized progressive and celebratory black remembrance, making grand appeals to public memory as social reform. The New York exposition had some fifteen divisions of Negro life and labor—all represented by booths, photographs, and other displays—and an extraordinary Temple of Beauty in the Great Court of Freedom, complete with Egyptian wall paintings and obelisks. Among the many art works was an eight-foot-high grouping of sculptures, *Humanity Freeing the Slave,* by Meta Warrick Fuller. Some three thousand people attended the opening ceremonies, half of them white.[65]

But it was *The Star of Ethiopia* pageant, written by Du Bois, with dramatic direction by Charles Burroughs and music by J. Rosamond Johnson, that provided the most remarkable element of the exposition. With a cast of 350 people, the pageant depicted five epochs in six eipsodes (or "gifts," as Du Bois put it) of African and African American history. The "gift of iron" from prehistoric African societies gave way to the "gift of the Nile" from ancient Egyptian civilization, to the "gift" of the "faith of Mohammed," to America where blacks experience slavery and the "gift of humiliation" (complete with the singing of spirituals and a "Dance of Death and Pain"), to the age of the "gift of Struggle toward Freedom" led by "brave maroons and valiant Haytians" Crispus Attucks and Nat Turner. The final episode brings the age of emancipation and its aftermath, the "gift of Freedom," with William Lloyd Garrison, John Brown, Abraham Lincoln, David Walker, Frederick Douglass, and Sojourner Truth all playing roles amidst marching black Union soldiers and a chorus of "O Freedom!" The music consisted of several marches, including the famous theme from Verdi's *Aïda* and Coleridge Taylor's "Bamboula," numerous spirituals and black folk songs, and considerable use of "Tom Toms." The key symbolic figure in the performance was Ethiopia herself, played by a tall black woman, who provides the "Star" at pivotal moments of deliverance. From the numerous drafts that Du Bois and Burroughs wrote, it is clear that they intended a story of tragedy, transcendence, and redemption, of romantic African origins and American transformation. As a theatrical representation of African American historical memory, there had never been anything quite like it. The pageant was performed four times during the celebration, playing to 14,000 spectators; some thirty thousand (mostly black) in all attended the Exhibition.[66]

Du Bois staged *The Star of Ethiopia* two more times, in 1915 in Washington, D.C.'s American League ballpark, and in Philadelphia in 1916 to commemorate the Fourteenth Amendment. The pageant represented almost all modes of black memory—particularly the progressive, patriotic, and Ethiopian—and it exposed the problem of just how much black people generally wanted to reflect on slavery or Africa. Given its epic level of pomp and romanticization, as well as its cost, all of which caused considerable jealousy and sniping, the pageant came under criticism in the black community. "What a task that was!" Du Bois declared in 1915. "I have been through a good many laborious jobs and had to bear on many occasions accusations difficult to rest under, but without doubt the New York Emancipation Exposition was the worst of all my experiences. Such an avalanche of altogether unmerited and absurd attacks it had never been my fortune to experience." Some people saw pageantry as a vulgar art form, and some blacks also saw an uncomfortable backward glance on slavery as a hundred bondsmen danced their mournful steps on stage. In a variation on the Washington–Du Bois split, some simply complained that the exhibition should have emphasized "industrial" rather than "intellectual" achievement. Those critics wanted an exposition about "work and progress," not one about "African curios." Du Bois defended himself and the pageant. "This was the one new thing in the dead level of uninteresting exhibitions," he wrote. "We had our ups and downs . . . it was difficult to get hold of the people . . . more difficult to keep them." As though defining the universal burden of historians engaged in public memory disputes, he concluded: "This is what the people want . . . this is the gown and paraphenalia in which the message of education and reasonable race pride can deck itself."[67]

But Du Bois wrote in many voices during the semicentennial season. Sometimes with angry editorials, and other times with satire, parable, or poetry, he forged the tragic vision of black memory as forthrightly as anyone. In these years, Du Bois's poetry and short fiction were replete with images of death and rebirth, of Christ figures and resurrections. In April 1913, he published a poem in the *Crisis* called "Easter-Emancipation, 1863–1913." The "I" pronoun of this long, enigmatic poem is the slave woman as Christ figure, who is repeatedly crucified and enveloped in the "folding and unfolding of Almighty wings." Through her many agonies and deaths come life and freedom. These apocalyptic visions were somber medicine for the fiftieth anniversary of emancipation. They were warnings about evil and sorrow in the past and the persistent betrayals of the present.[68]

In his January 1913 editorial "Emancipation," Du Bois reminded his readers that the American people had not freed the slaves "deliberately and with a lofty purpose," but in a war to "destroy the power of the South." Facing the challenge of black equality, Du Bois said, "the nation faltered, quibbled and finally is trying an actual *volte-face* [about-face]." Turning away from historical responsibility, Americans had built "barriers to decent human intercourse . . . between the races that today few white men dare call a Negro friend." Far too many, North and South, Du Bois despaired, "would greet the death of every black man in the world with a sigh of relief." On the cover of that special emancipation issue of the *Crisis* (the most popular black magazine) was an extraordinary drawing by Laura Wheeler of an elderly black man with eyes and head slightly bowed in sad dignity.[69]

A year earlier Du Bois had written his most striking fiftieth anniversary piece. Modeled on Jonathan Swift's story "A Modest Proposal," Du Bois called his satire "A Mild Suggestion." Similar to Johnson's parable on the Pullman car, Du Bois placed five characters on the deck of a ship: a Little Old Lady, a Westerner, a Southerner, a New Yorker, and a Colored Man. They are discussing the "Negro Problem" within hearing of the Colored Man, and suggest the usual solutions of education, work, and emigration. Finally they ask the black man his opinion. He sits down and lays out his "perfect solution." He urges rejection of education because it will only lead to "ambition, dissatisfaction and revolt," scorns work because it can only foment job competition and the disruption of social circles, and refuses emigration because it is impractical. Instead, he proposes that on January 1, 1913, "for historical reasons," each white American who has a black friend invite him to dinner. This, he thought, would encompass "black mammies and faithful old servants of the South." Those blacks without such an invitation would be urged to come to white churches and YM and YWCAs. There they would be seated in a fully integrated manner at dinner. All remaining blacks in the country should be "induced to assemble among themselves at their own churches or at little parties and house warmings." Stragglers and vagrants should be rounded up and watched. Then, he suggested, at the ringing of a bell, or "singing of the national hymn," blacks at the dinners were to be given cyanide of potassium pills, those at the large meetings were to be dispatched with stilettos, and all others shot with Winchester rifles. With the Southerner staring and forgetting "to pose," the Westerner gazing in "admiration," the New Yorker "smiling," and the Little Old Lady in "tears," the Colored Man concludes: "The next morning there would be ten million funerals, and therefore no Negro problem."[70]

No celebratory voice here, no cant about progress, and no nostalgia. Only a prophetic call to a national conscience, the bitterest of protests against everything from lynching (the NAACP counted more than seventy in 1913) to the meaning of segregation. Du Bois would not let his black or white readers think about Emancipation Day, past or present, without a stinging reminder from his Colored Man who, while admitting that his solution "may seem a little cruel," asks: is it "more cruel than present conditions?" Satire has always worked best in worlds of absurdity; so much of segregated America and the semicentennial of emancipation and the Civil War formed just such a world. Swift himself said in 1728 that satire is motivated not merely by ridicule, but by "a public spirit, prompting men of genius and virtue to mend the world so far as they are able."[71] In the culture of reunion, Du Bois planted this stark reminder that another kind of mending had eluded America.

Most readers of Du Bois's unforgettable short story would have been black. But black Civil War memory in its many forms did reach white America as well. On January 1, 1913, on page one, the *New York Times* published James Weldon Johnson's poem "Fifty Years." Reprinted in black newspapers and delivered as a reading at numerous commemorations to follow, Johnson's poem is a striking statement of African American birthright. As though banishing the shame of slavery from memorial consciousness and transcending progress rhetoric to a higher plane of tragic but true patriotism, Johnson insisted on an honored place for blacks at the Civil War's semicentennial. Seven verses into the poem, he struck his central theme:

> Then let us here erect a stone,
> To mark the place, to mark the time;
> A witness to God's mercies shown,
> A pledge to hold this day sublime.

And let that stone an altar be,
    Whereon thanksgivings we may lay,
Where we in deep humility,
    For faith and strength renewed may pray . . .

For never let the thought arise
    That we are here on sufferance bare;
Outcasts, asylumed 'neath these skies,
    And aliens without part or share.

This land is ours by right of birth,
    This land is ours by right of toil;
We helped to turn its virgin earth,
    Our sweat is in its fruitful soil.

Johnson claims the center of America's historical memory by right of birth and by right of labor. In the poem's middle he claims it by right of soldiering, of "blood" and devotion to the "flag": "We've bought a rightful sonship here, / And we have more than paid the price." As the poem reaches its hopeful ending, Johnson celebrates the abolitionist tradition as America's national destiny and rejects any shame for blacks in the legacies of slavery.[72] Like the freedpeople in Charleston who marched around the planters' Race Course and created Memorial Day in 1865, demonstrating their freedom as the true meaning of the Civil War, at the fiftieth anniversary of emancipation Johnson converted that same meaning into the war's core memory. The assertion and coexistence of this emancipationist memory with all the forces arrayed against it in 1913 demonstrate just how vital it remained. And yet it also testified to how divided Civil War memory had become in fifty years and the extent to which blacks had become alienated from the national community's remembrance of its most defining event.

Epilogue

Only fools forget the causes of war.

—ALBION W. TOURGÉE, *An Appeal to Caesar*, 1884

THE SEMICENTENNIAL of the Civil War stimulated a flood of memories and commemorative activities. In the years that brought Americans to the eve of World War I, the press was full of retrospective consciousness about the Civil War; newspapers and magazines ran special features and series about leaders and battles, and avidly reported reunions and exhibitions. In the spring of 1911, the *New York Times* urged its readers to "avoid needless celebration" of Civil War anniversaries. "All the battles of the civil war were won by American soldiers," declared the *Times*. "All the heroes of that war were Americans." These sentiments did not stop the paper, however, from running many lengthy commemorative sections on one fifty-year anniversary after another, from Fort Sumter in 1911 through to Appomattox and Lincoln's assassination in 1915.[1]

Understandably, the dominant mode of memory was reconciliation. In admiring the "love feast" between soldiers of both sections about to occur at Manassas in 1911 on the fiftieth anniversary of the first battle of Bull Run, the *Nation* acknowledged that the "Civil War day by day" features of many newspapers might annoy the South. But its editor felt confident that when remembrance emphasized "reconciliation rather than conflict," Americans on all sides would embrace their Civil War as a "triumph of brotherhood." Still, the occasional white writer in a Northern journal urged caution in probing issues such as race and slavery in relation to the war. In a 1912 essay in the *Atlantic Monthly*, "The Slave Plantation in Retrospect," Winthrop Daniels warned that "despite the lapse of almost half a century, the embers of the great conflict in which slavery perished are still hot, if one but deeply stir the ashes." From pulpits on Lincoln's birthday, Sunday, February 12, 1911, some rabbis and ministers in New York called their congregations to vigilance about the legacy of emancipation. Joseph Silverman reminded an interracial audience at Temple Emanu-El that "though the war is ended and the slaves are freed . . ., there are many white Americans carrying on a war as bitter and unjust as that carried on against the Negroes fifty years ago." And the Free Synagogue invited Reverdy Ransom, pastor of the Bethel AME Church, to address its congregation. Ransom celebrated black progress since emancipation, and then called on Jews and blacks to join as "co-partners" against the "veritable inferno" of racial prejudice that both groups faced in forgetful America.[2] The reunion at the semicentennial emerged triumphant, in great part because American culture had succeeded in keeping considerable distance between those who stirred and those who doused the embers of conflict.

In January 1913, Dudley Miles, a French literature professor at Columbia University, published "The Civil War as Unifier," an essay that fashioned a master narrative of reunion. The Civil War's "true significance," wrote Miles, was the rapidity of sectional reconciliation afterward. Contrary to the aftermath of so many other civil wars and revolutions, the American conflict "deepened and spread the sense of nationality" across the land. Miles pointed to several "episodes" of public reconciliation during the fifty years since the war, from Mississippian L. Q. C. Lamar's eulogy of Massachusetts senator Charles Sumner in 1874 to Southern poet Sidney Lanier's nationalistic verses at the Philadelphia centennial celebration in 1876, from Grant's death and funeral in 1885 to Henry Grady's "New South" speech to the New England Society of New York in 1886. He stressed the new "scientific history" that had come of age by the 1890s and served the ends of reunion, and in Southern historical fiction, especially the North's embrace of it, he found the most influential bond of "love" between the former foes. The Spanish-American War of 1898, mutual grief over President McKinley's assassination in 1901, and the return of Confederate battle flags in 1905 all gave Miles confidence that "what makes our Civil War unique is this remarkable sequel . . . an unexampled obliteration of sectional animosities."[3]

In a Southern journal, Miles seemed to speak for the country itself as he declared a "very easy explanation" for such an outcome to fratricidal war. "Electricity . . ., industry . . ., and commerce" had knit the nation back together. The "torrent" of a "swifter age" had "swept away the bitter memories" in favor of trade and economic growth. Miles also stressed a special "restraint" and "political temper" in the American people that helped them forget the past and cement a new nation. In this vision, the Civil War was the good war, a necessary sacrifice, a noble mutual experience that in the long run solidified the nation. In a piece published on the fiftieth anniversary of black emancipation, Miles steadfastly avoided even mentioning slavery, except to acknowledge that the triumph of reunion had been made possible, in part, by the North's recognition of the South's need to overcome the "burden of a crushing social problem" in its own ways. These code words had become so common in American writing that in national memory, the Civil War was now the glorious fated event in which slavery and racial division were "removed," banished from the national story.[4] In this collective victory narrative, the Civil War, followed by an interlude of bitterness and wrongheaded policy during Reconstruction, became the heroic crisis survived, a source of pride that Americans solve their problems and redeem themselves in unity. Much of the emancipationist vision of Civil War memory was so ill-fitted to this reunion narrative that during the semicentennial it simply had to coexist in isolation from national remembrance of an epic fight and an intersectional inheritance of reunion.

At Gettysburg, July 1–4, 1913, an extraordinary festival of reconciliation provided the exclamation mark of the American reunion at its fiftieth anniversary. Behind the enormous tent city, President Wilson's flying appearance, and all the scenes of Blue-Gray fraternalism was a tremendous organizational effort. Public money paid for the transportation and care of the more than fifty thousand veterans who came to the Pennsylvania town as honored guests from every corner of the country. Some one hundred veterans arrived from California, ten of them Confederates. Vermont sent 669 men, four of them listed as Confederates. Nevada and Wyoming were the only states not accounted for at the reunion. The whole event was a logistical and financial triumph. Not only did a small army of souvenir salesmen flood the streets of the town of Gettysburg, but no fewer than forty-seven railroad companies operating in and through Pennsylvania alone were paid a total of $142,282 for the transportation of veterans. One hundred and fifty-five reporters from the national and international press covered the event, which was headlined (along with stunning photographs) during the week of the reunion.[5]

Where Wilson came to declare the "quarrel forgotten," the nation also witnessed a marvel of efficiency. The Great Camp, covering 280 acres and serving 688,000 meals prepared by 2,170 cooks, laborers, and bakers using 130,048 pounds of flour, warmed the hearts of even the most compulsive advocates of Taylorism, the popular theory of industrial and management efficiency. Frederick W. Taylor's popular *Principles of Scientific Management* had just been published in 1911, and the Taylor Society had been founded in the same year as the Civil War centennial began. The forty-seven miles of "avenues" completed on the battlefield, lighted by five hundred electric arc lights, provided a perfect model of military mobilization and mass production. Some thirty-two automatic "bubbling ice water fountains" throughout the veterans' quarters offered a delightful example of American technical prowess. Efficiency advocates warmly approved the extraordinary "preparedness" of the Red Cross and the army medical corps in their efforts to provide first-class hospital care for the veterans during the encampment. The average age of veterans at the event was seventy-four, and the Pennsylvania Commission's report celebrated the fact that only nine of the old fellows died during the reunion, a statistic many times lower than the national average for a

Reconciliation was the theme of the day at the 1913 Gettysburg reunion of Union and Confederate veterans, as represented by this group of "Old Soldier Fiddlers" clasping hands on stage in preparation for a concert.

group of that age and number. Efficiency enthusiasts could marvel at the ninety modern latrines (men's and women's) constructed all over the encampment. The press was full of celebration of such efficiency. The *Philadelphia Inquirer* marveled at the "more painstaking care, more scientific preparation and a better discipline than has ever before been known on such an occasion . . . there never was anything better done in our history."[6] To many, the reunion seemed as much rooted in technological progress, the unity implied in electrification and mass organization, as in the Blue and Gray clasping hands.

The theme of the reunion from its earliest conception in 1909 was national harmony and patriotism—a "Peace Jubilee" as the planning commission announced. Fifty years after Pickett's Charge (and the Emancipation Proclamation, which was utterly ignored during the week's ceremonies), Frederick Douglass's haunting question from 1875—"what will peace among the whites bring?"—received a full-throated answer. Only obscure references exist of the attendance of any black veterans at the 1913 reunion. In a travel memoir, New Jersey veteran Walter H. Blake compiled a reminiscence of his journey to Gettysburg for the event. Blake claimed that "there were colored men on both sides of the lines." The Pennsylvania Commission "had made arrangements only for negroes from the Union side," lamented the New Jersey veteran, "forgetful of the fact that there were many faithful slaves who fought against their own interests in their intense loyalty to their Southern masters."[7] The idea of the faithful slave had penetrated deep into the Northern imagination; Thomas Nelson Page still hovered above even Yankee remembrance.

Numerous black men worked as camp laborers, building the tent city and distributing mess kits and blankets. But nowhere in its published report does the Pennsylvania Commission indicate how many black veterans, if any, attended the reunion. By the commission's rules, black GAR members with documented honorable discharges were eligible to participate. But research has turned up no evidence that any did attend. It may have been especially difficult for black veterans to respond to the reunion's tone and purpose. One of Walter Blake's anecdotes is what he calls a "very pretty little incident" in which "a giant of an old negro, Samuel Thompson," was resting under a shade tree. Some Confederate veterans came up to shake hands with "the old darky" and exchange greetings. It is not made clear whether Thompson was a veteran or not. Blake declares this incident another triumph for kindness and concludes without the slightest sense of irony: "no color line here."[8]

The ceremonies at Gettysburg in 1913 represented a public avowal of the deeply laid mythology of the Civil War that had captured the popular imagination by the early twentieth century. The war was remembered primarily as a tragedy that forged greater unity, as a soldier's call to sacrifice in order to save a troubled, but essentially good, Union, not as the crisis of a nation in 1913 still deeply divided over slavery, race, competing definitions of labor, liberty, political economy, and the future of the West. Holmes's idea of the "soldiers' faith" prevailed at the Gettysburg reunion, as it had for more than two decades of Blue-Gray fraternalism. Devotion itself was the theme of the day, and among old soldiers, understandably so. They had come to see and feel the impulses of their youth. For most of the veterans, whether in their private tents, listening to brass bands or lone fiddles, or standing erect in front of news photographers, the four anniversary days were a transcendent experience.

The veterans, as well as the gazing crowds, had come to commemorate a glorious fight; and in the end, everyone was right, no one was wrong, and something so transforming as the Civil War had been rendered a mutual victory of the Blue and the Gray by what Virginia governor Mann called the "splendid movement of reconciliation."[9] Behind the podiums and bunting,

The 1913 Gettysburg reunion, attended by some 53,000 white veterans, was a segregated affair where the issues of slavery, emancipation, and racial equality were absent and the only role for blacks was as laborers distributing blankets. (Record Group 25, Pennsylvania State Archives)

out beyond the throngs of beautiful, if old and frail, men, beyond the spectacle of the tent city and smells of campfires, was a society riven with racial strife. It was a white man's experience and a white nation that the veterans and the spectators came to celebrate in July 1913. Any discussion of the war's extended meanings in America's omnipresent "race problem" was simply out of place. Wilson's "righteous peace" was far more the theme than Lincoln's "rebirth of freedom." At this remarkable moment when Americans looked backward with deepening nostalgia and ahead with modern excitement and fear, Jim Crow, only half-hidden, stalked the dirt paths of the veterans' tent city at Gettysburg. He delivered supplies, cleaned the latrines, and may even have played the tunes at the nation's feast of national memory. Jim Crow stalked the streets and backroads of the larger nation as well, and he had recently arrived with a new mandate in the bureaucracies of the federal government. The Civil War had become the nation's inheritance of glory, Reconstruction the legacy of folly, and the race problem a matter of efficient schemes of segregation.

Reconciliation is, of course, a noble and essential human impulse. But it must be understood within historical time, and as similar to any other political process that results from contests of human wills. Press reports and editorials about the Gettysburg reunion indicate just how much a combination of white supremacist and reconciliationist memories had conquered all others by 1913. The issues of slavery and secession, rejoiced the *Washington Post,* were "no longer discussed argumentatively. They are scarcely mentioned at all, except in connection with the great war to which they led, and by which they were *disposed of for all time.*" To the extent that slavery involved a "moral principle," argued the *Post,* "no particular part of the people was responsible unless, indeed, the burden of responsibility should be shouldered *by the North for its introduction*" (emphasis added). The *New York Times* hired Helen D. Longstreet (widow of Confederate general James Longstreet) to write daily columns about the Gettysburg reunion. She entertained *Times* readers with her dialogues with Southern veterans about the value of Confederate defeat and the beauty of "Old Glory." She also challenged readers to remember the sufferings of women during the Civil War and to consider an intersectional tribute to them as the theme of the next Blue-Gray reunion. The nation's historical memory, concluded the *Times,* had become so "balanced" that it could never again be "disturbed."[10]

The editors of the liberal magazine *Outlook* were overwhelmed by the spirit of nationalism at the Gettysburg reunion and declared it a reconciliation of "two conceptions of human right and human freedom." The war, said the *Outlook,* had been fought over differing notions of "idealism": "sovereignty of the state" versus "sovereignty of the nation." Demonstrating the degree to which slavery had vanished from understandings of Civil War causation in serious intellectual circles, the *Outlook* announced that "it was slavery that raised the question of State sovereignty; but it was not on behalf of slavery, but on behalf of State sovereignty and all that it implied, that these men fought." So normative was this viewpoint that the *Outlook*'s special correspondent at the reunion, Herbert Francis Sherwood, could conclude that the veterans' "fraternity . . . showed that no longer need men preach a reunited land, for there were no separated people." Such was the state of historical consciousness in Jim Crow America. Slavery (and the whole black experience) had no place in the formulas by which most Americans found meanings in the Civil War. The *Outlook* was both accurate and oblivious in its interpretation of the reunion; thus it could conclude without blinking that "both sides" had fought for "the same ideal—the ideal of civil liberty."[11] This is, of course, the equality of motive in Civil War memory for which Southern advocates had pleaded for decades. In both romance and reality, the Lost Cause had become the desideratum of national reunion.

Reporters from every section of the country registered their sense of awe at the symbolism of the Gettysburg celebration. The *San Francisco Examiner* declared the "jubilee" to be the "supreme justification of war and battle." Now "we know that the great war had to be fought, that it is well that it was fought," announced the *Examiner:* "a necessary, useful, splendid sacrifice whereby the whole race of men has been unified." Such martial spirit and claims of ritual purging were answered (albeit by a minority voice) in the *Charleston News and Courier.* The newspaper in the city where secession began urged readers not to glorify the "battle itself," for it was a "frightful and abominable thing." If war "thrills us," declared the *News and Courier,* "we lose a vitally important part of the lesson." But the *Brooklyn Daily Eagle* kept the discussion on a higher plane, allowing simultaneously for a recognition of Northern victory, Southern respect, and faith in American providential destiny:

> Two civilizations met at Gettysburg and fought out the issue between them under the broad blue sky, in noble, honorable battle . . . In one . . . the family was the social unit—the family in the old Roman sense, possibly inclusive of hundreds of slaves. In the other,

the individual was the only social unit. Within half a century those two civilizations have become one. Individualism has triumphed. Yet . . . with a fuller recognition than ever before the war, of the charm and dignity and cultivation of what has yielded to the hand of Fate . . . The ways of Providence are inscrutable.[12]

This neatly packaged nostalgia from a Northern paper offered mystic honor to the Lost Cause of patriarchal "family" structure, combined with an uneasy celebration of the victory of individualism in the age of industrialization, all justified by God's design. In this reconciliationist vision, a homegrown beneficent Fate governed American memory. Such a depoliticized memory, cleansed of any lessons about the war's unresolved legacy of racial strife, had indeed fostered reconciliation among soldiers, politicians, businessmen, and scholars. But sectional peace had its costs.

Homilies about reunion, though altogether well meaning, masked as much as they revealed. Naturally, monuments and reunions had always combined remembrance with healing and, therefore, with forgetting. But racial justice took a different fork on the road to reunion. Not out of overt conspir-

At the culmination of a reenactment of Pickett's Charge on July 3, 1913, members of the Philadelphia Brigade Association and the Pickett's Division Association clasped hands across the stone wall they had fought over fifty years earlier. (Record Group 25, Pennsylvania State Archives)

acy, not by subterfuge alone, did white supremacist memory combine with reconciliation to dominate how most Americans viewed the war. This result emerged from the process of history itself, from all the ways that public and private memories evolve. Thus the Gettysburg reunion took place as a national ritual in which the ghost of slavery, the very questions of cause and consequence, might be exorcised once and for all—and an epic conflict among whites elevated into national mythology. That mythology was the product of fifty years of cultural evolution, of the growth and erosion of memories in response to events and social tensions. But it also grew in carefully cultivated soil, the harvest of human choices made by powerful leaders and ordinary folk. Collective memories are the source of group self-definition, but they are never solely the result of unthinking decisions.

Black newspapers of the era were wary, even resentful, of the celebration at Gettysburg in 1913. As segregation deepened and lynching persisted, many black opinion leaders observed history and memory wielded in such a way as to write blacks out of the story. "We are wondering," declared the *Baltimore Afro-American Ledger*, "whether Mr. Lincoln had the slightest idea in his mind that the time would ever come when the people of this country would come to the conclusion that by the 'People' he meant only white people." The *Afro-American* identified the stakes of this contest for America's national memory: "Today the South is in the saddle, and with the single exception of slavery, everything it fought for during the days of the Civil War, it has gained by repression of the Negro within its borders. And the North has quietly allowed it to have its own way." The *Afro-American* asserted the historic loyalty of blacks to the nation and pointed to President Wilson's recent forced segregation of federal workers. The "blood" of black soldiers and lynched citizens," it argued, was "crying from the ground" in the South, unheard and strangely unknown at the Blue-Gray reunion.[13]

These reactions in the black press are especially telling given the Wilson administration's increasingly aggressive program of racial segregation in federal agencies, enacted that summer of 1913. Federal departments in Washington were large employers of African Americans. On the day after Decoration Day, the official segregation of black clerks in the Post Office began. And on July 12, only a week after Wilson spoke at Gettysburg, orders were issued to create separate lavatories for blacks and whites working in the Treasury Department. These and other segregation policies, stemming in part from the many white Southerners who had come to Washington with the Wilson adminstration, caused deep resentment and protest among blacks, led largely by the National Association for the Advancement of Colored People (NAACP). Such policies, and the sense of betrayal they caused among blacks, prompted Booker T. Washington, no friend of the NAACP, to declare that he had "never seen the colored people so discouraged and bitter" as they were in the summer of 1913. That summer, the NAACP launched a campaign against segregation practices in the federal government.[14]

By 1913 racism in America had become a cultural industry, and twisted history a commodity. A segregated society required a segregated historical memory and a national mythology that could blunt or contain the conflict at the root of that segregation. Most Americans embraced an unblinking celebration of reunion and accepted segregation as a natural condition of the races. Just such a celebration is what one finds in the *Atlanta Constitution's* coverage of the Gettysburg reunion. The *Constitution* declared that "as never before in its history the nation is united in demanding that justice and equal rights be given all of its citizens." No doubt these sentiments reflected genuinely held beliefs among white Southerners that Jim Crow meant "progress" and "reform." The *Constitution* gushed about the "drama" and "scale" of the symbolism at the Gettysburg reunion, even its "poetry and its fragrance." But most important was "the thing for which it stands—the world's mightiest republic purged of hate and unworthiness, seared clean of dross by the most fiery ordeal in any nation's history."[15] Such were the fruits of America's segregated historical consciousness after fifty years. Racial legacies, conflict itself, the bitter consequences of Reconstruction's failure to make good on the promises of emancipation, and the war as America's second revolution in the meaning of liberty and equality had been *seared clean* from the nation's master narrative. But that clean narrative of a Civil War between two foes struggling nobly for equally honorable notions of liberty, of a sentimentalized plantation South to which Americans of the hectic industrial age could escape, of soldiers' devotion in epic proportions to causes that mattered not, could not rest uncontested forever across American culture.

THE CIVIL WAR'S fiftieth anniversary season left countless examples of Americans looking backward and forward. A young George S. Patton, a captain in the U.S. Army and the grandson of a Confederate officer in Lee's army, was part of the detachment of troops sent to Gettysburg to help "police" the 1913 reunion. The brash Patton loved to visit Gettysburg and confessed to a "strange fascination" for the place, as well as a desire to "have been there" in 1863. But in 1913, with his duty confined to distributing blankets to veterans, Patton expressed only contempt for the old Civil War soldiers: "They are a disgusting bunch dirty and old and of the people who 'God loves.'" The nation may have seemed at peace, but the generations were not. Patton was eager for his own war.[16]

Contrasts of new and old, modernity and tradition, were everywhere in American culture. For one month in February and March 1913 in New York City, the celebrated and controversial *Armory Show* of modern art caused an enormous stir. Its 1,600 works of art, often treated with irreverence in the press, attracted one hundred thousand viewers and enduring attention. "To be afraid of what is different or unfamiliar, is to be afraid of life," read a typical line in one of the *Armory Show's* catalogs.[17] But this casting off of tradition and innocence was a far stretch from the deeply conservative aims of the United Daughters of the Confederacy, who had reached the peak of their influence in 1913—through their funding of monuments, efforts to control Southern textbooks, lobbying of Congressmen, and their ubiquitous essay contests whereby Southern youth could exhibit the "truth" of the Lost Cause. As guardians of culture and memory, the UDC led those who saw modernity itself as their principal enemy.

In the fall of 1913, a seventy-one-year-old Ambrose Bierce made a last tour of his old battlefields in Tennessee; he lumbered fifteen miles around the Chickamauga and Chattanooga landscapes and at Shiloh found the graves of some former comrades in his Indiana regiment. He wrote his last letter in December 1913, en route to Mexico, where he vanished in a mysterious death. In 1913, the eighteen-volume Plantation edition of Thomas Nelson Page's collected works had just been published, and President Wilson appointed the writer the U.S. ambassador to Italy. Page's universe of sentimental and racist abstractions were now available in one well-marketed set. Oliver Wendell Holmes Jr., who kept his Civil War uniform hanging in his closet, sat prominently on the Supreme Court, and was not yet halfway through his thirty-year presence there in 1913. Holmes had converted his unsentimental view of life as governed by conflict and fate into a judicial philosophy that understood law as the product of "experience" and the "felt necessities of the time." Holmes's "soldiers' faith" had directed him forever away from root causes and premises about law, life, or history. AME bishop Henry McNeal Turner and the ever-powerful Booker T. Washington, his influence now openly defied by other blacks but not yet eclipsed, were both still active in their paradoxical ways in 1913. Both men, one born free and a veteran of the war who eventually denounced America, and the other born a slave who rose to be the most prominent voice of reconciliation, would die in 1915, celebrated as visionaries of how to remember and forget. In 1913, a thirteen-year-old girl named Margaret Mitchell was growing up in Atlanta, Georgia, surrounded by an abiding Lost Cause tradition she would eventually represent more popularly than any writer ever. And in Oxford, Mississippi, a sixteen-year-old boy named William Faulkner was about to drop out of high school as he drank in an environment and a burden of memory he would later represent more probingly than any American writer.[18] Their time would come two decades later, during the Great Depression, when an astonishing American appetite reemerged for the nostalgia and the Lost Cause of the Old South. Millions would flock to buy the story of Scarlett O'Hara's struggle in *Gone with the Wind* (1935) to cope with the crushed but ennobled South in the aftermath of the war; not nearly as many would embrace so eagerly Thomas Sutpen's fierce ambitions and the legacies his family coped with on the real and psychological landscapes of Mississippi in *Absalom! Absalom!* (1935).

In 1913, Harriet Tubman, the grand old half-forgotten warrior of the Underground Railroad, herself a veteran of service with Union troops in the war, died at ninety-three in Auburn, New York, where local Civil War veterans led her funeral march. In 1890, after many years of rejected requests, she had received a federal pension, but only as a widow after her husband, Nelson Davis, a Civil War soldier, had died. Also in 1913, in early summer, amidst all the attention to Blue-Gray fraternalism and the planning of emancipation exhibitions, W. E. B. Du Bois, a New England child of the Reconstruction years, took a seven-thousand-mile journey all over the western United States as spokesman of the NAACP. He delivered twenty public lectures to an estimated 18,000 people in eighteen cities from Fort Worth, Texas, to Kansas City, Missouri, to Seattle, Washington. He spoke in huge auditoriums and at small dinners in his honor. Everywhere, Du Bois saw and admired the forward-looking, hopeful attitudes of black communities in the American West. Among the 500,000 blacks in those eighteen cities, he found "energy and alertness . . . new ambition and determinedness . . . to fight segregation." He felt the "tragedy" that overlay Fort Worth and Atlanta, cities that had recently experienced race riots or lynchings. But in Los Angeles he observed a "gospel of fight and self-assertion," and in Tacoma he was greeted officially by the mayor and spoke to a large interracial audience. Contrasts of old and new met Du Bois at every turn: here a Jim Crow railcar, there a group of young black professionals brimming with confidence.[19] Perhaps it was this trip that gave Du Bois the ultimate confidence to lead and mount the extraordinary emancipation exhibition and the *Star of Ethiopia* pageant later that fall in New York.

That spirit of confidence would be crucial to blacks because also in 1913, D. W. Griffith and Thomas Dixon began their collaboration to bring to the motion picture screen *The Clansman,* Dixon's fiercely racist epic about the victimized South and the heroism of the Ku Klux Klan. The alienation of the emancipationist vision, and of the basic substance of black memory, from mainstream popular remembrance of the Civil War era received no greater long-term stimulus than when *Birth of a Nation* premiered across the country in the spring of 1915. Dixon, the North Carolina–born author of the extraordinarily successful white supremacist novels *Leopard Spots* (1903) and *The Clansman* (1905), which was adapted to the stage with sensational success in 1906, possessed a boundless desire to "teach the north," he said, "the young north, what it has never known—the awful suffering of the white man during the dreadful reconstruction period. I believe that God . . . anointed the white men of the south . . . to demonstrate to the world that the white man must and shall be supreme." Griffith, who grew up in Louisville, Kentucky, came of age in the heyday of the Lost Cause. A lover of the Southern martial tradition and Victorian melodramas, and eager to portray a lost rural innocence in the new urban age, he was in New York by 1908, acting and making short films. As the fiftieth anniversary of the war approached in 1909–11, Griffith made several Civil War melodramas. In these films, stock scenes and characters abound: rebel soldiers going off to war with black fieldhands cheering, genteel but sturdy Southern white women, Confederate and Union soldiers (sometimes brothers) shaking hands while wrapped in the folds of their flags, and ubiquitously, loyal slaves saving or dying for their masters.[20]

When Dixon and Griffith connected in New York, the filmmaker was leading a group of pioneers making scores of short movies that fed the growing American appetite for the visual image. During the semicentennial, American theaters were saturated with Civil War films lasting fifteen to twenty-five minutes, with some 98 produced in 1913 alone. These films virtually all followed ritual plots full of nostalgia, reconciliation, brave if defeated Confederates surrounded by their virtuous women, and countless uncles and mammies protecting plantations and arranging marriages of the Blue and Gray. The films' subtitles repeatedly portrayed the slaves as "happy, contented, and well cared for . . . joyous as a bunch of school children," as though the obsequious characters on screen did not adequately convey the message. Black characters in these films themselves carry the historical lesson that slavery was not the cause of the war, and its destruction was the lingering misfortune of the nation and the black race. Not only do black mammies and butlers die saving their white folks from marauding Yankees, but in some films, whole families and slave quarters defend plantations, and thereby the South, from its destruction. In one film, *The Old Oak's Secret*, Old Mose even hides his master's will in a tree because he cannot face its manumission clause.[21] With these characters, Griffith and others established a stereotype for blacks that would stand for decades as essentially the only image allowed in the movies.

In *Birth of a Nation*, Griffith and Dixon gave their well-plied audiences the message not only that blacks did not want their freedom, but also that emancipation had been America's greatest and most dangerous disaster. With its stunning battle scenes and suspenseful chases, *Birth of a Nation* made cinematic history. But it was the racial dramas that Griffith foisted on to the semicentennial that left the deepest imprint. The lasting significance of this epic film is that by using powerful imagery, buttressed by enormous advertising and political endorsement, it etched a story of Reconstruction that has lasted long in America's historical consciousness. The war was noble on both sides, the film says, but Reconstruction in the South was directed by deranged radicals and sex-crazed blacks, especially those mulattos given unwarranted political power. The very lifeblood of civilization, of familial survival, was at stake for the exploited South; hence, white Southern men had to take law and history into their own hands. The South not only wins in the end in *Birth of a Nation;* it also transforms emancipation, the potential second founding of the American nation, into a reign of racial terror and the necessity of a third creation by the heroic, hooded riders of the Ku Klux Klan. When Gus, a renegade black soldier who has symbolically raped and murdered a white girl, is thrown upon the ground by Klansmen who have castrated and murdered him, the "nation" achieves a rebirth quite unlike the one Lincoln and Douglass had in mind in 1863.[22]

The NAACP and other black organizations, as well as some white dissenters (Southern and Northern) protested and condemned *Birth of a Nation* in 1915. It opened first in Los Angeles with the title, *Clansman,* but after Dixon himself saw the final cut in New York, he urged the new title on Griffith. Dixon and Griffith were both master promoters, and they managed screenings at the White House and in Congress. In many cities, NAACP chapters, often armed with thousands of pamphlets and enacting their first direct-action protests, sought to get the film banned or at least portions of its content censored. Furor and anger from black communities stalked the movie in city after city, but it did not stop Dixon, Griffith, and their company from staging *Birth of a Nation* in New York with hooded white cavalry outside the theater as a promotion. In Boston, black protesters led by William Monroe Trotter, the militant editor of the *Guardian* and fierce critic of Booker Washington, achieved some success in getting the most offensive scenes banned by censorship boards. After violence and brawls at theaters, Massachusetts governor David Ignatious Walsh banned the film in Boston for reasons of public safety. Through his network of loyalists, Booker Washington supported Griffith's right to show the film. Among blacks generally, the issue of censor-

Few events carry more poignancy for the emancipationist vision of the Civil War than the March on Washington in August 1963, the 100th anniversary year of black freedom. At the final crescendo of his "I Have a Dream" speech, Martin Luther King Jr. imagines a day when his people are "free at last" in a land of true racial reconciliation, but only after an unforgetta-ble reminder that a century after the Civil War, black people are still "not free." (Photograph by Bob Adelman, Magnum Photos, New York)

ship became a knotty one; some were never comfortable with banning art, and others launched efforts to make their own counter films. But protest over *Birth of a Nation* reinvigorated direct-action resistance and inaugurated a new era of dissent in the realm of popular culture. At one point in the Boston protests, Trotter led a group of blacks who had been thrown out of the state capitol to the front steps of the golden-domed building. As he spoke in condemnation of Griffith's vision of the Civil War, the Shaw Memorial, with its proud black soldiers marching to freedom, stood immediately beneath them on Boston Common.[23] In the end, no amount of partial bannings could stop millions from seeing *Birth of a Nation*. It would always be out there as a set of images that emancipationist memory of the Civil War would have to counter.

And so it was that in 1913–15 Civil War memory was both settled and unsettled; it rested in a core master narrative that led inexorably to reunion of the sections while whites and blacks divided and struggled mightily even to know one another across separate societies and an anguished history. Reconciliation joined arms with white supremacy in Civil War memory at the semicentennial in an unsteady triumph. Just how enduring that triumph would be was a matter of degree, time, and place. Beleaguered but hardly invisible, emancipationist memory lived on to fight another day. The "peace among the whites" that Douglass had so feared in 1875 had left the country with a kind of Southern victory in the long struggle over Civil War memory. But because of the enduring significance of race in American society, and because it would take another political revolution and the largest mass movement for human rights in our history to crush the nation's racial apartheid system that had been forged out of the reunion, the first fifty years of remembering the Civil War was but a prelude to future reckonings. All memory is prelude.

Notes

Prologue

1. Robert Penn Warren, *The Legacy of the Civil War* (1961; rpr. Cambridge: Harvard University Press, 1983), 4, 7, 60; William Dean Howells, quoted in Allan

Gurganus, *Oldest Living Confederate Widow Tells All* (New York: Ivy Books, 1984), epigraph.

2. Paul H. Buck, *The Road to Reunion, 1865–1900* (New York: Knopf, 1937). Buck's book won the Pulitzer Prize for history in 1938. It was a pioneering achievement in the use of innovative sources to write cultural history. Buck also essentially ignored racial questions, or considered them historically insoluble—an outlook that garnered considerable popularity in the 1930s.

3. Reinhold Niebuhr, *Faith and History: A Comparison of Christian and Modern Views of History* (New York: Scribner's, 1949), 129.

4. Mary Johnston, *Cease Firing* (1912; rpr. Baltimore: Johns Hopkins University Press, 1996), 457; W. E. B. Du Bois, editorial in *Crisis* (April 1912). *Cease Firing* followed *The Long Roll* as Johnston's two-volume epic fiction of the Southern armies in the whole of the Civil War. She was one of the best writers in her time of combat scenes, as well as of the epic romance of the Confederate cause.

5 W. E. B. Du Bois, *The Souls of Black Folk* (1903; rpr. Boston: Bedford Books, 1997), 45.

1. The Dead and the Living

1. For the various drafts of the Gettysburg Address, see Roy P. Basler, ed., *The Collected Works of Abraham Lincoln,* vol. 7 (New Brunswick: Rutgers University Press, 1953), 17–23.

2. "Wilson a Stranger in Old Yorktown," *New York Times,* July 4, 1913. On Virginia's suffrage restriction, see J. Morgan Kousser, *The Shaping of Southern Politics: Suffrage Restriction and the Establishment of the One-Party South, 1880–1910* (New Haven: Yale University Press, 1974), 178–181. For use of the term "disrecognized," used in the memoir of an ex-sharecropper, see Theodore Rosengarten, *All God's Danger: The Life of Nate Shaw* (New York: Knopf, 1974), 116.

3. Telegram, Woodrow Wilson to Ellen Axson Wilson, Washington, D.C., June 28, 1913; and letters, Wilson to Ellen Axson Wilson, June 29, 1913, Wilson to Mary Allen Hulbert, June 29, 1913, in Arthur S. Link, ed., *The Papers of Woodrow Wilson,* vol. 28 (Princeton: Princeton University Press, 1978), 11–13. Wilson, of course, has the date wrong for Lincoln's address at Gettysburg (November 19, 1863, not July 4).

4. *Fiftieth Anniversary of the Battle of Gettysburg: Report of the Pennsylvania Commission, December 31, 1913* (Harrisburg, Pa.: n.p., 1915), 39–41, 36–37. One hundred fifty-five reporters from the national and international press covered the event, which was headlined (along with stunning photographs) in most newspapers during the week of the reunion. On commemorations at Gettysburg, see Edward Tabor Linenthal, *Sacred Ground: Americans and Their Battlefields* (Ur-

bana: University of Illinois Press, 1991), 89–126; and John S. Patterson, "A Patriotic Landscape: Gettysburg, 1863–1913," *Prospects* 7 (1982), 315–333.

5. On the suffragettes and the Boy Scouts at the Gettysburg reunion, see *Washington Post,* June 28, 30, July 2, 6, 1913; *Columbus, Ohio Citizen,* July 1, 1913; *National Tribune,* July 10, 1913; *CV* (August 1913); *London Times,* July 4, 1913; *Louisville Courier-Journal,* July 4, 1913.

6. Mann speech reprinted in *Fiftieth Anniversary of the Battle of Gettysburg,* 144, 174–176.

7. *Washington Bee,* June 7, 1913.

8. "Address at the Gettysburg Battlefield," July 4, 1913, in Link, ed., *Papers of Woodrow Wilson,* vol. 28, 23–25.

9. Ibid.

10. *Fiftieth Anniversary of the Battle of Gettysburg,* 176–178.

11. Edward Everett's speech is reprinted in Garry Wills, *Lincoln at Gettysburg: The Words That Remade America* (New York: Simon & Schuster, 1992), 233–240, 241–245.

12. "Gettysburg Address," in Basler, ed., *Collected Works,* vol. 7, 23.

13. Wills, *Lincoln at Gettysburg,* 38, 40. On the 1912 election and Wilson's Progressivism in relation to race, see Nell Irvin Painter, *Standing at Armageddon: The United States, 1877–1919* (New York: Norton, 1987), 268–272.

14. *NY,* July 5, 1913.

15. Wills, *Lincoln at Gettysburg,* 38, 147. On Douglass, see David W. Blight, *Frederick Douglass' Civil War: Keeping Faith in Jubilee* (Baton Rouge: Louisiana State University Press, 1989), 59–121.

16. "Our Work Is Not Done," speech delivered at the Annual Meeting of the American Antislavery Society, Philadelphia, December 3–4, 1863, in Philip S. Foner, ed., *Life and Writings of Frederick Douglass,* vol. 3 (New York: International Publishers, 1952), 379, 385.

17. Ibid., 383–385.

18. Ibid., 385.

19. Ibid.

20. Abraham Lincoln, "Annual Message to Congress," Dec. 8, 1863, in Basler, ed., *Collected Works,* vol. 7, 36, 49–51, 53.

21. "The Mission of the War," delivered many times across the North during late 1863 and throughout 1864, in Foner, ed., *Life and Writings,* vol. 3, 388, 390, 396–397. During 1864 and the early months of 1865, the themes Douglass stressed in this speech were echoed in many such speeches by other black orators and intellectuals. Novelist and orator Frances Ellen Watkins Harper traveled the circuit with a speech by the same title, "The Mission of the War." See announcement and extract of speech, *CR,* December 31, 1864, January 7, 1865. In a speech

on November 15, 1864, just after Maryland had declared itself a free state, Harper proclaimed: "Oh! how grand the words! How inspiring the theme! Breathing to worn and weary hearts the music of redemption and freedom . . . The Union of the past, thank God, is gone. Darkened by the shadow of a million crimes, it has sunk beneath the weight of it guilt, and now we stand upon the threshold of a new era." On the idea of regeneration and the religious tradition of apocalypticism during the Civil War era, see James H. Moorhead, *American Apocalypse: Yankee Protestants and the Civil War, 1860–1869* (New Haven: Yale University Press, 1978); James H. Moorhead, "Between Progress and Apocalypse: A Reassessment of Millennialism in American Religious Thought, 1800–1880," *Journal of American History* 71 (December 1984), 524–542; and Drew Gilpin Faust, *The Creation of Confederate Nationalism: Ideology and Identity in the Civil War South* (Baton Rouge: Louisiana State University Press, 1988).

22. Douglass, "Mission of the War," 401.

23. "The Million Dead, Too, Summed Up," *Specimen Days* (1882), in Walt Whitman, *Complete Prose Works* (New York: Appleton, 1910), 73. See also Ralph Waldo Emerson, *Journals* (1862), and Emerson to Thomas Carlyle, Concord, December 8, 1862, in Louis P. Masur, ed., *"The Real War Will Never Get in the Books:" Selections from Writers during the Civil War* (New York: Oxford University Press, 1993), 126, 137.

24. "The Real War Will Never Get in the Books," *Specimen Days* (1882), in *Complete Prose Works*, 74.

25. Horace Traubel, *With Walt Whitman in Camden* (1905; rpr. New York: Rowan & Littlefield, 1961), 6, 194–195. On Whitman's work in the hospitals, see David S. Reynolds, *Walt Whitman's America: A Cultural Biography* (New York: Knopf, 1995), 421–432. On death and its meanings in nineteenth-century America, see James J. Ferrill, *Inventing the American Way of Death, 1830–1920* (Philadelphia: University of Pennsylvania Press, 1980); Lewis Saum, "Death in the Popular Mind of Pre–Civil War America," *American Quarterly* 26 (December 1974); and Drew Gilpin Faust, 'A Riddle of Death': Mortality and Meaning in the American Civil War," the Fortenbaugh Memorial Lecture, Gettysburg College (Gettysburg, 1995). Another poet, Emily Dickinson, observed the war and came to see death from a very different perspective than that of Whitman. See Shira Wolosky, *Emily Dicksinson: A Voice of War* (New Haven: Yale University Press, 1984), 5–6, 40–45, 51, 116–117, 163–164.

26. Walter Lowenfels, ed. and comp., *Walt Whitman's Civil War* (New York: Knopf, 1960), 15–16.

27. Sculley Bradley and John A. Stevenson, eds., *Walt Whitman's Backward Glances* (Philadelphia: University of Pennsylvania Press, 1947), 44–45. "A Backward Glance o'er Travelled Roads" was first published in "My Book and I,"

Lippincott's Monthly Magazine (January 1887). See also "Convulsiveness," *Specimen Days* (1882), in *Complete Prose Works*, 71.

28. Whitman to Louisa Van Velsor Whitman, Washington, D.C., March 22, 1864, June 7, 1864, in Lowenfels, ed., *Walt Whitman's Civil War*, 152, 163. "A Glimpse of War's Hell-Scenes," *Specimen Days*, in *Complete Prose Works*, 49–50.

29. On Whitman's mystical unionism, see Daniel Aaron, *The Unwritten War: American Writers and the Civil War* (New York: Knopf, 1973), 56–59; and Reynolds, *Walt Whitman's America*, 414–421.

30. On Whitman's work in the Johnson administration, see Reynolds, *Walt Whitman's America*, 467–470.

31. Edwin Haviland Miller, ed., *Walt Whitman: The Correspondence* (New York: New York University Press, 1964), vol. 2, 15; Floyd Stovall, ed., *Whitman: Prose Works* (New York: New York University Press, 1963), vol. 1, 326. On Whitman's racial views, see Aaron, *Unwritten War*, 59–62; Reynolds, *Walt Whitman's America*, 464–474; and Geofrey Sill, "Whitman on 'the Black Question': A New Manuscript," *Walt Whitman Quarterly Review* 8 (Fall 1990), 69–75.

32. "O Magnet-South" (1866), in Walt Whitman, *Leaves of Grass*, Emory Holloway, ed. (1897; rpr. Garden City, N.J.: Doubleday, 1926), 394; from a conversation with Horace Traubel, in Lowenfels, ed., *Walt Whitman's Civil War*, 235. On the cult of the fallen soldier, see George L. Mosse, *Fallen Soldiers: Reshaping the Memory of the World Wars* (New York: Oxford University Press, 1990), 4–11, 70–106.

33. Clara Barrus, *Whitman and Burroughs, Comrades* (Boston: Houghton Mifflin, 1931), 339; "Reconciliation" (1865–66), in *Leaves of Grass*, 269.

34. Thomas B. Wester to Editor, December 1864, and Henry C. Hoyle to Editor, January 15, 1865, *CR*, January 7, 28, 1865. Both Wester and Hoyle were members of the Forty-third regiment, U.S. Colored Troops. On the freedpeople in the aftermath of emancipation, see Leon F. Litwack, *Been in the Storm So Long: The Aftermath of Slavery* (New York: Knopf, 1979).

35. E. D. Townsend, Assistant Adjutant General, "Minutes of an Interview between the Colored Ministers and Church Officers at Savannah with the Secretary of War and Maj. Gen. Sherman," in Ira Berlin et al., eds., *Freedom: A Documentary History of Emancipation, 1861–1867* (New York: Cambridge University Press, 1990), ser. 1, vol. 3, 337. The full text is 331–337. The text was also reprinted in *NYTr*, February 13, 1865; and *CR*, February 18, 1865. The text for this colloquy, therefore, had a relatively large potential readership among people (black and white) closely following the course of the war during its final months. Also see Eric Foner, *Reconstruction: America's Unfinished Revolution, 1863–1877* (New York: Harper & Row, 1988), 70.

36. Berlin et al., eds., *Freedom*, ser. 1, vol. 3, 333–337.

37. Ibid., 337.

38. James Lynch to Editor, *CR*, February 4, 1865; J. McKaye, "Report of a Commission of the American Freedmen's Inquiry Commission," New York? April? 1864, in Berlin et al., eds., *Freedom*, ser. 1, vol. 3, 529–530.

39. On military labor and contraband camps, see Berlin et al., eds., *Freedom*, ser. 1, vol. 3, 19–24, 30–33, 61–64.

40. Emily Waters to my dear husband, Roseland Plantation, La., July 16, 1865; Hugh P. Beach to Thomas W. Conway, August 1, 1865; Catherine Massey to Edwin M. Stanton, July 10, 1865, in Berlin et al., eds., *Freedom: A Documentary History of Emancipation, 1861–1867*, ser. 2 (New York: Cambridge University Press, 1982), 698–700, 667. Ezra Adams, in George P. Rawick, ed., *The American Slave: A Composite Autobiography* (19 vols.; Westport, Conn.: Greenwood Press, 1972), vol. 2: South Carolina Narratives, part 1, 5.

41. "A Grand," *Christian Recorder*, January 14, 1865. On the uses and rewritings of the Declaration of Independence by various groups in American history, see Philip S. Foner, ed., *We the Other People: Alternative Declarations of Independence by Labor Groups, Farmers, Women's Rights Advocates, Socialists, and Blacks, 1829–1975* (Urbana: University of Illinois Press, 1976).

42. J. M. Wilkerson, "Celebration of the Emancipation Proclamation, Chester, Illinois," *CR*, January 28, 1865.

43. Walt Whitman, "When Lilacs Last in the Dooryard Bloomed," *Leaves of Grass*, 275–281.

44. "O Captain, My Captain," *Leaves of Grass*, 282–283.

45. "Chicago Correspondence," *CR*, May 20, 1865; Corporal William Gibson, Co. C, Twenty-eighth USCT, to editor, *CR*, May 27, 1865; "When Lilacs Last in the Dooryard Bloomed," 282.

2. Regeneration and Reconstruction

1. W. E. B. Du Bois, *Black Reconstruction in America* (New York: Atheneum, 1935), 713, 725.

2. Germaine Necker de Staël (1807), quoted in David Lowenthal, *The Past Is a Foreign Country* (Cambridge: Cambridge University Press, 1985), 114.

3. Myrta Locket Avary, ed., *Recollections of Alexander H. Stephens: His Diary Kept When a Prisoner at Fort Warren, Boston Harbor, 1865* (New York: Doubleday, 1910), 537, 539; Abram J. Ryan, "The South," a lecture in Nashville, 1878, quoted in Charles Reagan Wilson, *Baptized in Blood: The Religion of the Lost Cause, 1865–1920* (Athens: University of Georgia Press, 1980), 59. On Father Ryan, see Charles C. Boldrick, "Father Abram J. Ryan: The Poet-Priest of the Confederacy," *Filson Club History Quarterly* 46 (July 1972), 201–217. Also see Nina Silber,

The Romance of Reunion: Northerners and the South, 1865–1900 (Chapel Hill: University of North Carolina Press, 1993), 39–65.

4. John T. Trowbridge, *The South: A Tour of Its Battlefields and Ruined Cities* (1866; rpr. New York: Arno Press, 1969), 16.

5. Ibid., 18–20, 23.

6. Ibid., 34, 38–39.

7. Ibid., 143–144, 147, 150–151.

8. John Richard Dennett, *The South as It Is, 1865–1866,* ed. Henry M. Christman (1866; rpr. Baton Rouge: Louisiana State University Press, 1965), 13–19.

9. Ibid., 26–27, 29–33.

10. *Richmond Dispatch,* December 9, 1865. The opening sentence of Robert E. Lee's "Farewell Address" to his troops was: "After four years of arduous service, marked by unsurpassed courage and fortitude, the Army of Northern Virginia has been compelled to yield to overwhelming numbers and resources." The address, General Orders No. 9, was actually written by Charles Mitchell, a member of Lee's staff. See Emory M. Thomas, *Robert E. Lee* (New York: Norton, 1995), 367.

11. Joel Porte, ed., *Emerson in His Journals* (Cambridge: Harvard University Press, 1982), 528, 530; *Nation,* July 6, 1865. Also see George M. Fredrickson, *The Inner Civil War: Northern Intellectuals and the Crisis of the Union* (New York: Harper and Row, 1965), 183–198.

12. Harriet Beecher Stowe, "The Chimney Corner I," *AM* 15 (January 1865), 115. On Stowe's interpretation of the war, see Patricia R. Hill, "Writing Out the War: Harriet Beecher Stowe's Averted Gaze," in Catherine Clinton and Nina Silber, eds., *Divided Houses: Gender and the Civil War* (New York: Oxford University Press, 1992), 260–278.

13. Colonel Wheelock G. Veazey, "Oration before the Reunion Society of Vermont Officers," in Representatives' Hall, Montpelier, Vt., October 25, 1866 (Rutland: Tuttle, Gay, & Co., 1866), 5, 24, 26, pamphlet in American Antiquarian Society, Worcester, Mass.

14. John Q. Anderson, ed., *Brokenburn: The Journal of Kate Stone, 1861–1868* (Baton Rouge: Louisiana State University Press, 1972), 333–334, 339–341, 346, 355.

15. Ibid., 368–369, xxxviii–xl.

16. Mrs. Mary Jones, in her journal, March 1865, in Robert Manson Myers, ed., *The Children of Pride: A True Story of Georgia in the Civil War* (New Haven: Yale University Press, 1984), 657–658. On the struggles of Southern women to cope with the dislocations of the war, see Drew Gilpin Faust, *Mothers of Invention: Women of the Slaveholding South in the American Civil War* (Chapel Hill: University of North Carolina Press, 1996).

17. Caroline S. Jones to Mary Jones, Augusta, Ga., April 30, 1865; Eva B. Jones to

Mary Jones, Augusta, Ga., June 13, 1865, in Myers, ed., *Children of Pride,* 547, 549–550.

18. Mary Jones to Mary S. Mallard, Montevideo, Ga., November 17, 1865; Mary Jones to Mary S. Mallard, November 7, 1865; Charles C. Jones Jr., to Mary Jones, Augusta, Ga., July 28, 1865; Charles C. Jones Jr., to Mary Jones, November 30, 1865, in Myers, ed., *Children of Pride,* 556, 565, 570–572.

19. Ibid., 663–664. See *The Siege of Savannah in December 1864* (New York: Appleton, 1874); *The History of Georgia* (Boston: Houghton Mifflin, 1883); and *Negro Myths from the Georgia Coast* (Boston: Houghton Mifflin, 1888).

20. Gaines Foster, *Ghosts of the Confederacy: Defeat, the Lost Cause, and the Emergence of the New South* (New York: Oxford University Press, 1987), 74, 82. Charles C. Jones Jr. to Eva Jones, January 5, 1870, January 2, 1882, in Myers, ed., *Children of Pride,* 664–665.

21. Private R. D. Hicks to "editor," Edgefield, S.C., August 10, 1865, in MOLLUS collection, HLH, box 1; John T. Harper to Thaddeus Stevens, Philadelphia, Pa., February 16, 1866, Thaddeus Stevens Papers, LC, reel 4.

22. Frederick Douglass, "Reconstruction," *AM,* December 1866, in Philip S. Foner, ed., *Life and Writings of Frederick Douglass,* vol. 4 (New York: International Publishers, 1955), 198–199, 201.

23. Ernest Renan, "What Is a Nation?" in *Nation and Narration,* trans. Martin Thom, ed. Homi K. Bhabha (London: Routledge, 1990), 11, 19.

24. *Chicago Tribune,* April 26, 1865.

25. Whitelaw Reid, *After the War: A Tour of the Southern States, 1865–1866* (1866; rpr. New York: Harper Torchbooks, 1965), 18, 154–155; Trowbridge, *The South,* 584; Dennett, *The South as It Is,* 360 *NYTr,* May 2, 1865; and David Eckstein to Thaddeus Stevens, Stevens Papers, reel 4. See Michael Perman, *Reunion without Compromise: The South and Reconstruction, 1865–1868* (Cambridge, Eng.: Cambridge University Press, 1973), 13–25.

26. On Johnson's plan of Reconstruction, see Eric Foner, *Reconstruction: America's Unfinished Revolution, 1863–1877* (New York: Harper & Row, 1988), 176–200. On Johnson's view toward blacks, especially questions of suffrage and civil rights, see Eric L. McKitrick, *Andrew Johnson and Reconstruction* (Chicago: University of Chicago Press, 1960), 55–61, 313–315; and LaWanda Cox and John H. Cox, "Johnson and the Negro," in Kenneth M. Stampp and Leon F. Litwack, ed., *Reconstruction: An Anthology of Revisionist Writings* (Baton Rouge: Louisiana State University Press, 1969), 59–82.

27. See Foner, *Reconstruction,* 198–203; and Theodore B. Wilson, *The Black Codes of the South* (University: University of Alabama Press, 1965).

28. Marvin, quoted in Foner, *Reconstruction,* 189.

29. James S. Brisbin to Stevens, Helena, Ark., December 29, 1865, Stevens Papers, reel 4.

30. *Nation*, July 20, August 17, 1865; Charles Sumner to Francis Lieber, Boston, October 8, 1865, and Washington, D.C., May 7, 1865, Charles Sumner Papers, HU, reel 64; Stevens to Sumner, Caledonia Iron Works, Pa., Stevens Papers, reel 4. Sumner would have preferred "the exile of a considerable number of the leading rebels, say 100, or better 500." "Let them all go with their lives," he wrote, " and learn abroad how to appreciate the crime they have committed." See Sumner to Francis Lieber, August 2, 1865, Sumner Papers, reel 64. On the idea of "tragic legend" of Reconstruction, see Kenneth M. Stampp, *The Era of Reconstruction, 1865–1877* (New York: Random House, 1965), 3–23.

31. Stevens to Andrew Johnson, Caledonia Iron Works, Pa., May 16, 1865, Stevens Papers, reel 4.

32. Sumner to Francis Lieber, September 18, 1865, Sumner Papers, reel 64; Foner, *Reconstruction*, 228–239.

33. *Raleigh Tri-Weekly Standard*, April 3, 1867. On Settle, see Jeffrey J. Crow, "Thomas Settle, Jr., Reconstruction, and the Memory of the Civil War," *Journal of Southern History* 62 (November 1996), 689–726, Settle quoted 701–703.

34. Thomson Powell to Stevens, Halifax Court House, Va., February 22, 1866; A. Conroe to Stevens, December 19, 1865, Stevens Papers, reel 4.

35. Simon Corley to Stevens, Lexington, S.C., February 6, 1866; Charles J. Smith to Stevens, Rochelle, Va., January 8, 1866; A. J. Evans to Stevens, Waco, Tex., July 8, 1866; Marion Roberts to Stevens, Asheville, N.C., May 15, 1866, Stevens Papers, reels 4–5.

36. *Raleigh Standard*, May 21, 25, 1867. Over 600 black men served in state legislatures, and 16 served in Congress during Reconstruction. Twenty-two served in Congress between 1869 and 1901.

37. John Wolcott Phelps to Stevens, Brattleboro, Vt., February 13, 1866; Samuel Holmes to Stevens, St. Louis, Mo., February 24, 1866, Stevens Papers, reel 4. Phillips speech delivered at annual meeting of the American Antislavery Society, New York, May 2, 1867, reprinted in *NYTr*, May 3, 1867.

38. *Buffalo Express,* in *NYTr*, May 11, 1867.

39. Henry Wilson, speech in New Bern, N.C., April 29, 1867, in *NYTr*, May 10, 1867; Edward A. Pollard, *The Lost Cause: A New Southern History of the War of the Confederates* (1867; rpr. New York: E. B. Treat & Co., n.d.), 750–752.

40. *CG*, 39th Cong., 1st sess., May 8, 10, 1866, 2460, 2544.

41. Benjamin M. Boyer (Democrat, Pa.), ibid., May 8, 1866, 2466; Phelps and Ingersoll, ibid., May 5, 1866, 2394, 2399.

42. Ibid., May 8, 1866, 2461–2462, 2464.

43. Ibid., May 8, 1866, 2462, 2467; Stampp, *Era of Reconstruction*, 3–4.

44. *CG*, May 9, 1866, 2507.

45. *Nation*, July 6, 1865; *CG*, May 10, 1866, 2530.

46. *CG*, May 10, 1866, May 9, 1866, 2531, 2495.

47. Ibid., May 10, 1866, 2537–2539; Douglass, "Reconstruction," *AM*, December 1866, in Foner, ed., *Life and Writings*, 4, 204.

48. *CG*, May 24, 1866, 2799.

49. *CG*, May 8, 1866, 2459; 39th Cong., 2d sess., February 8, 1867, 1104.

50. *Raleigh Standard*, May 14, 1867; *NYTr*, May 4, 11–15, 1867; William C. Davis, *Jefferson Davis: The Man and His Hour* (New York: Harper Collins, 1991), 650–655. A popular book that sensationalized Davis's prison experience was published in 1866. See Charles G. Halpine, *Prison Life of Jefferson Davis*. On Halpine's book and its impact, see William Hanchett, "Reconstruction and the Rehabilitation of Jefferson Davis: Charles G. Halpine's *Prison Life*," *Journal of American History* 56 (September 1969), 271–292.

51. *Raleigh Standard*, May 14, 18, 1867.

52. Ibid., May 18, 1867.

53. Gerrit Smith to Andrew Johnson, Peterboro, N.Y., August 24, 1866, reprinted in *NYTr*, May 11, 1867; Smith to William Lloyd Garrison, Peterboro, N.Y., March 20, 1867, a published letter with subtitle, "Let Us Deal Impartially with the Sinning South and the Sinning North," copy in Francis Porteus Corbin Papers, Duke University Library; Smith quoted in Robert Penn Warren, *Jefferson Davis Gets His Citizenship Back* (Lexington: University of Kentucky Press, 1980), 84.

54. Varina Davis to Horace Greeley, Fortress Monroe, Va., October 16, 1866, November 21, 1866, Horace Greeley Papers, NYPL, reel 3.

55. Greeley to James Lawrence of Beloit, Wis., December 16, 1866; Greeley to H. Sedley, January 5, 1867, Greeley Papers, reel 2. Greeley was a master of political slogans. He helped to popularize "clasping hands across the bloody chasm" as a clarion call of reunion.

56. *Raleigh Standard*, May 18, 1867; *Richmond Whig*, May 14, 1867, quoted in James Parton, *The Life of Horace Greeley* (Boston: James R. Osgood, 1872), 498.

57. Greeley speech at Richmond AME Church, quoted in Parton, *Life of Horace Greeley*, 499, 502–505.

58. Ibid., 509–510.

59. John Jay to Greeley, Union League Club, May 16, 1967, Greeley Papers, reel 3; *New York Herald*, May 20, 1867; *Nation*, May 25, 1867; "Nasby Papers," from *Toledo Blade*, reprinted in *Raleigh Standard*, May 30, 1867; GAR meeting, in *Raleigh Standard*, May 25, 1867; *CR*, May 18, 1867.

60. B. F. White to Greeley, Zurich, Switz., June 24, 1867; Richard G. Parsons to Greeley, Washington, D.C., May 18, 1867.

61. J. E. Snodgrass to Greeley, New York, May 17, 1867, Greeley Papers, reel 3.
62. Toledo Blade, in *NYTr*, May 3, 1867.

3. Decoration Days

1. Maris A. Vinovskis, "Have Social Historians Lost the Civil War? Some Preliminary Demographic Speculations," *Journal of American History* 76 (June 1989), 35–39; Drew Gilpin Faust, *"A Riddle of Death": Mortality and Meaning in the American Civil War* (pamphlet), 34th Fortenbaugh Memorial Lecture, Gettysburg College (Gettysburg, 1995), 7–8; and Thomas L. Livermore, *Numbers and Losses in the Civil War in America, 1861–65* (Bloomington: Indiana University Press, 1957).

2. Robert N. Rosen, *Confederate Charleston: An Illustrated History of the City and the People during the Civil War* (Columbia: University of South Carolina Press, 1994), 98–147; Ravenal from St. Julien Ravenal, *Charleston: The Place and the People* (New York: Macmillan, 1906), quoted in Rosen, *Confederate Charleston,* 121.

3. Rosen, *Confederate.Charleston,* 150, 152–153.

4. Raphael Samuel, *Theaters of Memory: Past and Present in Contemporary Culture,* vol. 1 (London: Verso, 1994), esp. 3–39. On the significance of ritual for collective memory, also see Paul Connerton, *How Societies Remember* (Cambridge, Eng.: Cambridge University Press, 1989), 6–71.

5. Justus Clement French, *The Trip of the Steamer Oceanus to Fort Sumter and Charleston, S.C., Comprising the Incidents of the Excursion, the Appearance, at That Time, of the City, and the Entire Programme of the Exercises of Re-Raising the Flag over the Ruins of Fort Sumter* (Brooklyn, N.Y., 1865), 119, 65–69; Willie Lee Rose, *Rehearsal for Reconstruction: The Port Royal Experiment* (New York: Oxford, 1964), 341–345; Rosen, *Confederate Charleston,* 150–153. Also see the commemorative book Frank Moore, ed., *Fort Sumter Memorial: The Fall of Fort Sumter, A Contemporary Sketch from Heroes and Martyrs,* including "Replacing the Flag upon Sumter," from the narrative of an eyewitness, William A. Spicer, adapted by F. Milton Willis (New York: Edwin C. Hill, 1915), 29–46.

6. "Our Martyr and His Mourners," *NYTr,* May 13, 1865. On the federal reinterment program and the problem of death at the end of the Civil War, see Faust, "A Riddle of Death," 10–18. On grief from psychological and symbolic perspectives, see Maurice Bloch and Jonathan Parry, eds., *Death and the Regeneration of Life* (Cambridge, Eng.: Cambridge University Press, 1982); and Paul C. Rosenblatt, R. Patricia Walsh, and Douglas A. Jackson, *Grief and Mourning in Cross-Cultural Perspective* (New Haven, Conn.: HRAF Press, 1976). On the development of funereal practices in America, see David E. Stannard, ed., *Death in America* (Philadelphia: University of Pennsylvania Press, 1975); and James J.

Farrell, *Inventing the American Way of Death, 1830–1920* (Philadelphia: Temple University Press, 1980). Some recent social historians have paid greater attention to the scale of death in the conflict. See especially Vinovskis, "Have Social Historians Lost the Civil War?" 36–39.

7. *NYTr*, April 8, May 13, 1865.

8. Ibid.; *Charleston Daily Courier*, May 2, 1865. I first encountered evidence of this first Memorial Day observance in a document, "First Decoration Day," MOLLUS collection, HLH, boxes unnumbered. This handwritten description of the parades around the Race Course is undoubtedly based on the article by the *Tribune* correspondent named Berwick, whose name is mentioned in the description. The MOLLUS author, however, misdates the *Tribune* articles. Other mentions of the May 1, 1865 event at the Charleston Race Course include Paul H. Buck, *The Road to Reunion, 1865–1900* (New York: Knopf, 1937), 120–121. Buck misdates the event as May 30, 1865, does not mention the Race Course, gives James Redpath full credit for creating the event, and relegates the ex-slaves' role to "black hands [strewing flowers] which knew only that the dead they were honoring had raised them from a condition of servitude." In his account of his travels through the conquered South, Whitelaw Reid visited the cemetery in Charleston founded on that first Decoration Day, making special mention of the archway and its words: "Sympathizing hands have cleared away the weeds, and placed over the entrance an inscription that must bring shame to the cheek of every Southern man who passes: 'The Martyrs of the Race Course.'" See Whitelaw Reid, *After the War: A Tour of the Southern States, 1865–1866* (1866; rpr. New York: Harper & Row, 1965), 69. James Redpath claimed much of the credit for the founding of Memorial Day because of his role in the creation of the Race Course cemetery. Redpath did lead a group of ministers and missionaries who first visited the grounds and resolved to repair the site. See Charles F. Horner, *The Life of James Redpath and the Development of the Modern Lyceum* (New York: Barse & Hopkins, 1926), 111–118. At least two artists' depictions of the first Decoration Day at the Race Course exist, one by L. D. McMorris, in Horner, *Life of Redpath*, 115; and the other an illustration in *Harper's Weekly* May 18, 1867, reprinted in Rosen, *Confederate Charleston*, 155.

9. Leviticus 25:12–13, King James Version. For a case that Petersburg, Virginia, founded Decoration Day on May 9, 1866, see Mrs. Roger A. Pryor, "The Genesis of Decoration Day," *NYTr*, May 29, 1898.

10. *Charleston Daily Courier*, May 2, 1865; *NYTr*, May 13, 1865. The *Daily Courier* named five black clergy who spoke at the ceremonies, most without first names: Dickerson, Vanderhorst, Duncan, Miller, and Magrath.

11. Earl Marble, "Origin of Memorial Day," *New England Magazine* 32 (June 1905), 467–470; "Report of the President of the Ladies Memorial Association, Charles-

ton, S.C., June 5, 1916," 3, Ladies Memorial Association Papers, South Carolina Historical Society, Charleston, SCHS.

12. *The National Memorial Day: A Record of Ceremonies over the Graves of the Union Soldiers, May 29–30, 1869,* E. F. M. Faehtz, comp. (Washington, D.C: Headquarters, Grand Army of the Republic, 1870), 5–8; Buck, *Road to Reunion,* 120–121. On the disputed origins of Memorial Day, also see Michael Kammen, *Mystic Chords of Memory: The Transformation of Tradition in American Culture* (New York: Knopf, 1991), 102–103; Cecelia O'Leary, *To Die For: The Paradox of American Patriotism* (Princeton: Princeton University Press, 1999), 3, 100–107; and Lloyd Lewis, *Myths after Lincoln* (New York: The Press of the Readers Club, 1929), 304–319. Various towns claimed to have originated Memorial Day; Kammen makes special mention of Waterloo, N.Y. See "The History and Origin of Memorial Day in Waterloo, New York," pamphlet, Waterloo Memorial Day Centennial Committee. The date claimed by Waterloo is May 5, 1866. Columbus, Mississippi, also makes a claim to the first Memorial Day. See Kenton Kilmer, "The Origin of Memorial Day," History and Government Division, Library of Congress, May 21, 1958. O'Leary writes that "the exact origins of the day may never be known" (103), but the Charleston event of May 1, 1865 deserves pride of place. On the symbolic meanings and uses of Memorial Day, see W. Lloyd Warner, *The Living and the Dead: A Study of the Symbolic Life of Americans* (New Haven: Yale University Press, 1959), 248–279.

13. On Women's Relief Corps, see O'Leary, *To Die For,* 89–106.

14. "Ceremonies at Cincinnati," *National Memorial Day,* 789–790. Lee's speech confirms the thesis of Andrew Delbanco, in *The Death of Satan: How Americans Have Lost the Sense of Evil* (New York: Farrar, Straus, and Giroux, 1995), 125–153. Delbanco sees the Civil War as the hinge of his argument that Americans steadily lost a sense of evil, of divine purpose in history, because of and in the wake of the bloodletting of 1861–1865. The culture began to go spiritually flat, to embrace a doctrine of luck and chance, as it had to assess the meaning in who lived and who died as a result of such all-out war.

15. *National Memorial Day,* 249, 202, 21.

16. Ibid., 46, 112.

17. Sermon by Rev. Michael Creedon in ibid., 701–702. With what must have been at times awkward bluster, some orators found virtually no other theme than blood sacrifice. The Rev. N. Mighill, in Brattleboro, Vt., rejoiced in how it is "sweet to die for one's native land . . . they died, tens and hundreds of thousands, for dear fatherland" (710).

18. *National Memorial Day,* 97–101.

19. Speeches by Rev. L. L. Wood and Rev. William McKinley, in ibid., 710, 493.

20. *Oration by Gen. I. F. Shepard,* adjutant-general of Missouri, Memorial Day, May

30, 1870, Jefferson Barracks, St. Louis (St. Louis: Missouri Democrat and Job Printing House, 1870), 7–12, pamphlet in HU.

21. *Oration of Hon. O. P. Morton* (Gettysburg, 1870), 4–5, 13–14, 18–20, pamphlet in HU.

22. See Foster, *Ghosts of the Confederacy,* 38–45. "Reports of Memorial Day Exercises" at Magnolia Cemetery, compiled from the *Charleston Daily Courier,* 1866–1882, Ladies Memorial Association Papers, CSHS. On the ritual process, see Clifford Geertz, *The Interpretation of Cultures* (New York: Basic Books, 1973), 87–169; Victor W. Turner, *The Ritual Process: Structure and Anti-Structure* (Chicago: Aldine, 1969); and Paul Connerton, *How Societies Remember* (Cambridge, Eng.: Cambridge University Press, 1989), 41–71.

23. Rutherford reminiscence, and the varied dates of Confederate Memorial Day, in Foster, *Ghosts of the Confederacy,* 42; and Charles Reagan Wilson, *Baptized in Blood: The Religion of the Lost Cause, 1865–1920* (Athens: University of Georgia Press, 1980), 28. Rutherford's novel was Baroness Tautphoeus's *The Initials.* On Rutherford, also see "Origin of Memorial Day: Miss Lizzie Rutherford's Idea, But Mrs. Williams' Achievement," in Lucian L. Knight, *Georgia's Bi-Centennial Memoirs and Memories* (Atlanta: by author, 1933), 274–277. See also Rev. William McKinley, "Ceremonies at Winona," *National Memorial Day,* 491. On the origins of Memorial Day, see Martha E. Kinney, "'If Vanquished I Am Still Victorious': Religious and Cultural Symbolism in Virginia's Confederate Memorial Day Celebrations, 1866–1930," *Virginia Magazine of History and Biography* 106 (Summer 1998), 237–266; and Margaret Inman Meaders, "Postscript to Appomattox: My Grandpa and Decoration Day," *Georgia Review* 24 (Fall 1970), 297–304.

24. Capers, quoted in Foster, *Ghosts of the Confederacy,* 42.

25. See Foster, *Ghosts of the Confederacy,* 49–62, 55. Drawing on the work of anthropologist Anthony F. C. Wallace, Foster persuasively contends that this early memorialization by ex-Confederates can best be understood as a "revitalization movement" (56). See Anthony F. C. Wallace, "Revitalization Movements," *American Anthropologist* 58 (1956), 264–281. On the founding and character of the Southern Historical Society, also see Richard D. Starnes, "Forever Faithful: The Southern Historical Society and Confederate Historical Memory," *Southern Cultures* 2 (Winter 1996), 177–194.

26. On the unionist-emancipationist narrative, see Daniel Aaron, *The Unwritten War: American Writers and the Civil War* (New York: Knopf, 1973), xiii–xiv. Aaron calls this conception of the war the "federal epic."

27. *Proceedings of the Southern Historical Convention, Which Assembled at the Montgomery White Sulphur Springs, Va. on the 14th of August, 1873 and of the Southern Historical Society, as Reorganized, with the Address by Gen. Jubal A. Early, De-*

livered before the Convention on the First Day of Its Session (Baltimore: Turnbull Brothers, n.d.), 27–28. On Early's role at the White Sulphur Springs meeting, see Charles C. Osborne, *Jubal: The Life and Times of General Jubal A. Early, CSA, Defender of the Lost Cause* (Baton Rouge: Louisiana State University Press, 1992), 434–436.

28. Rev. J. William Jones wrote a reminiscence of Jackson, and assembled a mass of documents—including speeches and press coverage of the monument unveiling in Richmond in 1875—as an appendix in John Esten Cooke, *Stonewall Jackson: A Military Biography* (New York: Appleton, 1876). See *Richmond Daily Dispatch,* October 26–27, 1875, in Cooke, *Jackson,* 514–529, 537–545; and Wilson, *Baptized in Blood,* 18–24.

29. D. H. Hill, from *Southern Home,* in Cooke, *Jackson,* 574–576; Robert Penn Warren, *The Legacy of the Civil War* (1961; rpr. Cambridge: Harvard University Press, 1983), 15.

30. *Richmond Daily Dispatch,* October 27, 1875, in Cooke, *Jackson,* 570–572.

31. Kemper to Mrs. D. Brown, October 7, 1875, Governor's Letterbook, James L. Kemper; Jubal Early to Kemper, Executive Papers, Gov. James L. Kemper, box 4, both in Virginia State Library, Richmond; Kemper to Early, October 11, 1875, and October 23, 1875, Jubal Early Papers, LC, vol. 7.

32. Kemper to Early, October 22, 23, 1875, Early Papers, LC, vol. 7; and Jack P. Maddex Jr., *The Virginia Conservatives, 1867–1879: A Study in Reconstruction Politics* (Chapel Hill: University of North Carolina Press, 1970), 192–193. Kemper and Early mended their fences some. They were still working together to pay off bills from the Jackson statue unveiling in November 1875. See Kemper to Early, November 15, 24, 1875, Early Papers, LC, vol. 7.

33. Kemper speech, in Cooke, *Jackson,* 545–547.

34 Hoge oration in ibid., 548–549, 561, 564–565. On Hoge, also see Wilson, *Baptized in Blood,* 21–23.

35. See Buck, *Road to Reunion,* 122–126; Frances Miles Finch, "The Blue and the Gray," *AM* (September 1867), vol. 20, 369–370.

36. John A. Gilmer, "Memorial Address," Guilford, N.C., May 10, 1873, in unidentified newspaper clipping, Albion Tourgée Papers, reel 18, microfilm copy, Harvard University Library.

37. Albion Tourgée, "Memorial Address," Wilmington, N.C., May 30, 1874, in two unidentified newspaper clippings, Tourgée Papers, reel 18.

38. O. Hunter, "Reconciliation with Vengeance," in *Elevator,* n.d. (a black Raleigh newspaper), clipping in Tourgée Papers, reel 18. Hunter's letter includes an excerpt from a Memorial Day address by Tourgée, delivered in Raleigh in 1876. A gathering of blacks did occur at an unidentified location. Osborne Hunter is the brother of Charles N. Hunter, a Raleigh editor and schoolmaster.

39. C. A. Bartol, "The Soldier's Motive," May 30, 1874, in *Memorial Day Exercises of Charles Russell Lowell Encampment, Post 7, G.A.R.* (Boston: J. A. Cummings, 1874), 7, 10–12, 14, pamphlet in AAS. On veterans and the postwar revival of soldiers' ideals, especially as a mode of reconciliation, see Gerald F. Linderman, *Embattled Courage: The Experience of Combat in the American Civil War* (New York: Free Press, 1987), 266–297; Stuart McConnell, *Glorious Contentment: The Grand Army of the Republic, 1865–1900* (Chapel Hill: University of North Carolina Press, 1992), esp. 166–205; and Larry M. Logue, *To Appomattox and Beyond: The Civil War Soldier in War and Peace* (Chicago: Ivan R. Dee, 1996), 82–142.

40. *NYH*, May 29, 1877. The *NYTr*, May 31, 1877, opened its coverage of Decoration Day activities with the statement that across the country, North and South, "the spirit of reconciliation and peace seemed universal."

41. *NYTr*, May 29–30, 1877.

42. Ibid., May 31, 1877.

43. Ibid. On the political functions of parades and other public rituals, see Susan G. Davis, *Parades and Power: Street Theatre in Nineteenth-Century Philadelphia* (Philadelphia: Temple University Press, 1986); and Bodnar, *Remaking America.*

44. *NYTr*, May 31, 1877; *NYH*, May 31, 1877. On Greenwood and the rural cemetery movement, see David Charles Sloane, *The Last Great Necessity: Cemeteries in American History* (Baltimore: Johns Hopkins University Press, 1991), 44–127; and Stanley French, "The Cemetery as Cultural Institution: The Establishment of Mount Auburn and the Rural Cemetery Movement," in Stannard, ed., *Death in America*, 69–91.

45. *NYH*, May 31, 1877.

46. *The Proceedings of the Evening of Decoration Day, May 30, 1877 at the Academy of Music, City of Brooklyn, New York* (Brooklyn: Eagle Job and Book Printing Department, New York Bar Association, 1877), 4–5, copy in AAS.

47. On Pryor, see Daniel E. Sutherland, *The Confederate Carpetbaggers* (Baton Rouge: Louisiana State University Press, 1988), 102–105; Sarah Rice Pryor, *My Day: Reminiscences of a Long Life* (New York: Macmillan 1909), 280–282; Robert S. Holzman, *Adapt or Perish: The Life of General Roger A. Pryor, C.S.A* (Hamden, Conn.: 1976), 90–92; Mark Mayo Boatner, *The Civil War Dictionary* (New York: McKay Company, 1959), 674.

48. *Proceedings of the Evening of Decoration Day*, 8–9, 11. On the needless war school of interpretation, see Thomas J. Pressley, *Americans Interpret Their Civil War* (New York: Free Press, 1962), 289–328.

49. *Proceedings of the Evening of Decoration Day*, 14, 15–16.

50. Ibid., 24–25; *NYTr*, May 31, 1877.

51. *Proceedings of the Evening of Decoration Day*, 27–28.

52. Ibid., 29, 33.

53. Frederick Douglass, "Speech in Madison Square in Honor of Decoration Day," May 30, 1878, Douglass Papers, LC, reels 15, 5, 8. Also see *NYT,* May 31, 1878; and *NYTr,* May 31, 1878. Presiding over the ceremony at the Lincoln monument was Gen. Schuyler Hamilton who, according to the *Tribune,* urged the crowd to "keep alive the memory of their dead . . . by burying past antagonisms." He therefore advocated the decoration of Confederate and Union graves with equal compassion. Douglass's speech, although from a prepared text, may have been directed in part against Hamilton's tone of reconciliation. On Douglass, Memorial Day speeches, and the memory of the war, see David W. Blight, "For Something beyond the Battlefield: Frederick Douglass and the Struggle for the Memory of the Civil War," *Journal of American History* 75 (March 1989), 1156–1178.

54. Douglass, "Speech in Madison Square in Honor of Decoration Day," 9–10.

55. Grant interview in *NYTr,* May 28, 1878.

56. Sherman speech in ibid., May 31, 1878.

57. *NYTr,* May 30, 1878, May 30, 1880.

58. John D. Washburn, *Memorial Address at Lancaster,* May 29, 1880 (Worcester, Mass.: Press of Charles Hamilton, 1880), 4, pamphlet in HU.

59. *Memorial Address of Col. Thomas F. Barr, Judge Advocate, USA,* Stillwater, Minn., May 30, 1879, 4–5, pamphlet in AAS.

60. Holmes's speech was delivered to the John Sedgewick Post, no. 4, GAR. It has been published with two titles. See Oliver Wendell Holmes Jr., *Dead Yet Living, an Address Delivered at Keene, N.H., May 30, 1884* (Boston: Ginn, Heath, & Co., 1884), 4, 11–12, pamphlet in U.S. Army Military History Institute, Carlyle Barracks, Pa.; and "Memorial Day," in *Speeches by Oliver Wendell Holmes* (Boston: Little, Brown, 1934), 1–12. Excellent discussions of Holmes are found in George M. Fredrickson, *The Inner Civil War: Northern Intellectuals and the Crisis of the Union* (New York: Harper & Row, 1965), 218–221; Cruce Stark, "Brothers at/in War: One Phase of Post–Civil War Reconciliation," *Canadian Review of American Studies* 6 (Fall 1975), 174–181; and Aaron, *Unwritten War,* 161–162.

61. Albion Tourgée, "'Memorial' Day," *Chicago Inter-Ocean,* May 30, 1885, in Albion Tourgée, *The Veteran and His Pipe* (Chicago: Homewood Publishing, 1902), 70–71, 77.

62. Geertz, *Interpretation of Cultures,* 112.

4. Reconstruction and Reconciliation

1. Joel H. Silbey, *A Respectable Minority: The Democratic Party in the Civil War Era, 1860–1868* (New York: Norton, 1977), chs. 8–10, esp. 236–241.

2. William S. McFeely, *Grant: A Biography* (New York: Norton, 1981), 274–277; *NYH,* May 19, 1868; *NYT,* May 19, 1868. On the ambiguity of the slogan "Let us

have peace," see Brooks D. Simpson, *Let Us Have Peace: Ulysses S. Grant and the Politics of War and Reconstruction, 1861–1868* (Chapel Hill: University of North Carolina Press, 1991), 246–247. Simpson points out how the slogan could capture several sentiments at once: an end to bitter conflict; sectional reconciliation and the restoration of the states; and economic prosperity and renewed investment in the South.

3. On the Republican platform and its conservative directions, see Foner, *Reconstruction*, 337–338.

4. Silbey, *A Respectable Minority*, 199–210, 228–231; Foner, *Reconstruction*, 339–341.

5. *Nation*, June 28, 1868; Benjamin Tanner to Thomas O. Summers, editor of *Christian Advocate* (Nashville, Tenn.), September 24, 1868, in *CR*, October 3, 1868. In a public letter of July 30, 1868, Blair offered a manifesto of Democratic opposition: "There is but one way to restore the Government and the Constitution; and that is for the president-elect to declare these acts [Reconstruction Acts] null and void, compel the army to undo its usurpation of the South, disperse the carpet-bag State Governments, allow the White people to reorganize their own governments, and elect Senators and Representatives." See *NYTr*, September 2, 1868.

6. *NYH*, August 17, 25, 1868; *Federal Union* (Milledgeville, Ga.), June 23, 1868. Also see *New York World*, July 14, 1868; and Charles H. Coleman, *The Election of 1868: The Democratic Effort to Regain Control* (New York: Columbia University Press, 1933), 286–290.

7. *NYTr*, September 19, 1868; *Cincinnati Commercial*, September 1, 1868.

8. Blair, quoted in Foner, *Reconstruction*, 340; *Louisville Daily Courier*, October 8, 20, September 29, 1868.

9. "The Great Speech of Hon. B. H. Hill," Atlanta, Ga., July 23, 1868, recorded in *Augusta Daily Chronicle and Sentinel*, copy in the Mildred Rutherford Scrapbooks 25, Eleanor S. Brockenbrough Library, MOC. See also Gaines M. Foster, *Ghosts of the Confederacy: Defeat, the Lost Cause, and the Emergence of the New South* (New York: Oxford University Press, 1987), 95–96.

10. *Southern Watchman* (Athens, Ga.), February 19, April 22, April 15, 1868; *Daily News and Herald* (Savannah, Ga.), July 19, 1868. White attitudes toward blacks, Reconstruction issues, and the election were often expressed in racist jokes and parodies, crafted as though they were meant for the minstrel stage. See a dialect story about a white judge communicating with the foreman of a "darky jury," *Southern Watchman*, February 19, 1868. The black jury cannot reach a verdict because, though "we searched every nook, corner, crebice, and everywhere dar was in dat room," they just could not find any verdicts. See also a story alleged to have been written by a Northern journalist during the war, "A Sable Philosopher," by Gray Jackets, *Southern Watchman*, February 12, 1868. It is an interview

with a black soldier incapable of courage. Asked about standing his ground in battle, the black soldier says "No, sa, I runs . . . dat isn't my line, sa—cookin's my profeshan . . . self preserbashum am the first law wid me!" A typical joke that went around among whites during the election is in the *Louisville Daily Courier,* October 4–5, 1868: "At a late dinner party in North Carolina there sat down to table three ex-Governors, an ex-Justice of the Supreme Court, two ex-members of Congress, and some other men of honorable distinction in their State, and the only person in the room who could vote, or hold office, was the negro who waited on the table."

11. George William Curtis, letter to the Grant and Colfax Clubroom of Factoryville, Staton Island, July 28, 1868, in *NYTr,* September 1, 1868; Wendell Phillips, speech in Boston, October 27, 1868, in *NYTr,* October 28, 1868; "Empty Sleeves," *NYTr,* September 2, 1868.

12. *CR,* October 17, 1868. The reference to Wagner is the charge of Robert Gould Shaw and the Fifty-fourth Massachusetts infantry at Fort Wagner, on Charleston harbor, S.C., July 27, 1863.

13. The Rosecrans and Lee letters are both dated August 26, 1868, and are reprinted in *NYTr,* September 5, 1868. On the White Sulphur Springs meeting, see Emory M. Thomas, *Robert E. Lee: A Biography* (New York: Norton, 1995), 390–391. By 1868 Lee was president of Washington and Lee College in Lexington, Virginia. He was still under at least the threat of indictment for treason until a general amnesty was issued by President Andrew Johnson on Christmas Day, 1868, and a formal abandonment of any treason proceedings was announced on February 15, 1869. Lee died in Lexington on October 12, 1870. See Thomas, *Robert E. Lee,* 390, 416–417.

14. Rosecrans and Lee letters, *NYTr,* September 5, 1868. On the first stages of the apotheosis of Lee as as mythic hero, see Thomas L. Connelly, *The Marble Man: Robert E. Lee and His Image in American Society* (Baton Rouge: Louisiana State University Press, 1977), chs. 1–3.

15. *Columbus Sun* (Georgia), reprinted in *NYTr,* September 17, 1868; *NYTr,* September 6, 8, 1868; *Cincinnati Commercial,* September 7, 1868.

16. Henry Adams, "The Session," *North American Review,* 108 (April 1869), 613; "What Have We Won," *NYTr,* November 5, 1868; "Victory," *CR,* November 7, 1868. On the Republicans' idea of "guaranteed rights," see W. R. Brock, "The Waning of Radicalism," in Kenneth M. Stampp and Leon F. Litwack, eds., *Reconstruction: An Anthology of Revisionist Writings* (Baton Rouge: Louisiana State University Press, 1969), 496–515.

17. Wendell Phillips, "We Ask of Congress," speech delivered in Boston, December 4, 1969, in Harold M. Hyman, ed., *The Radical Republicans and Reconstruction* (New York: Bobbs-Merrill, 1967), 483–484.

18. *New National Era*, November 24, 1870; Douglass, "Address at the Grave of the Unknown Dead," Arlington, Va., May 30, 1871, Frederick Douglass Papers, LC, reel 14.

19. *Louisville Courier-Journal*, "A Decade of History," January 4, 1870, "A Radical Exclamation Point," March 12, 1870. The *Cleveland Herald* responses are reprinted in these articles.

20. Phillips, "The Fulfillment of Our Pledge," speech in Boston, April 9, 1870, in Hyman, ed., *The Radical Republicans and Reconstruction*, 498–499.

21. *CR*, February 13, 1869, December 5, 1868. On the overall notion of black destiny in America, see Leonard I. Sweet, *Black Images of America, 1784–1870* (New York: Norton, 1976), esp. ch. 5. On white attitudes toward black destiny, see George M. Fredrickson, *The Black Image in the White Mind: The Debate on Afro-American Character and Destiny, 1817–1914* (New York: Harper & Row, 1971), esp. ch. 6.

22. George P. Rawick, ed., *The American Slave: A Composite Autobiography* (19 vols; Westport, Conn.: 1972), vol. 16, Kansas, Kentucky, Maryland, Ohio narratives, part 4; vol. 2, South Carolina narratives, part 1, 17, 44.

23. Trudier Harris, *Exorcising Blackness: Historical and Literary Lynching and Burning Rituals* (Bloomington: Indiana University Press, 1984), 70, 69–94. By "racial memory," Harris does not mean the term in a biological sense, rather as a folk or community memory passed from one generation to the next. Also see Gladys-Marie Fry, *Night Riders in Black Folk History* (Athens: University of Georgia Press, 1991), esp. 110–169. Charles Chesnutt, *The Marrow of Tradition* (1901; rpr. Ann Arbor: University of Michigan Press, 1970); Pauline Hopkins, *Contending Forces: A Romance Illustrative of Negro Life North and South* (1900; rpr. New York: Oxford University Press, 1988); Walter White, *The Fire in the Flint* (New York: Knopf, 1924). The tradition of writing about violence and lynching is also represented widely in black short stories. See especially Paul Laurence Dunbar, "The Lynching of Jube Benson," in Jay Martin and Gossie H. Hudson, eds., *The Paul Laurence Dunbar Reader* (New York: Dodd, Mead, 1975), 232–239; W. E. B. Du Bois, "Of the Coming of John," in *The Souls of Black Folk* (1903; rpr. Boston: Bedford Books, 1997), 172–184; Langston Hughes, "Home," in *The Ways of White Folks* (1933; rpr. New York: Vintage, 1962), 32–48; and James Baldwin, *Going to Meet the Man* (New York: Dell, 1965), 198–218.

24. James Weldon Johnson, *The Autobiography of an Ex-Colored Man* (1912; rpr. New York: Hill and Wang, 1960), 186–187. On the scene in Johnson see Harris, *Exorcising Blackness*, 72–73.

25. George C. Rable, *But There Was No Peace: The Role of Violence in the Politics of Reconstruction* (Athens: University of Georgia Press, 1984), 15.

26. Wilbur J. Cash, *The Mind of the South* (New York: Doubleday, 1941), 56, 123,

127; Sheldon Hackney, "Southern Violence," in Hugh Davis Graham and Ted Robert Gurr, eds., *Violence in America: Historical and Comparative Perspectives* (Beverly Hills, Calif.: Sage Publications, 1979), 407. Also see C. Vann Woodward, "The Search for Southern Identity," in Woodward, *The Burden of Southern History* (1960; rpr. New York: New America Library, 1968), 17–31. Woodward stresses poverty, guilt, and defeat as central themes in the development of a distinctive Southern identity.

27. Primo Levi, "The Memory of Offense," in Geoffrey H. Hartman, ed., *Bitburg in Moral and Political Perspective* (Bloomington: Indiana University Press, 1986), 134–135.

28. On Dixon see Joel Williamson, *Crucible of Race: Black-White Relations in the South since Emancipation* (New York: Oxford University Press, 1984), 140–158.

29. Myrta Lockett Avary, *Dixie after the War: An Exposition of Social Conditions Existing in the South, during the Twelve Years Succeeding the Fall of Richmond* (1906; rpr. New York: Negro Universities Press, 1970), 203–204, 206, 384. It was reviewed widely and divergently. A measure of popular imagination about Reconstruction to which the publisher appealed is in the promotional announcement, which shouts: "No book hitherto published so fully and graphically portrays Southern life after the war, or so vividly presents race problems. The grotesque absurdities, the corruption, the tragedy, the pathos, and the humor of military dictatorship and reconstruction are intimately pictured." At the turn of the century Avary's book could be interpreted many ways (and it had negative reviews), but not least it was seen by many as a literary gesture of reconciliation. In the *Atlanta Constitution,* a Southerner, William Riley Boyd, defended Avary against a critical review by "Yankee." "Yankee" lacked appreciation for Avary's "spirit of friendliness," claimed Boyd, and he saw in the book a means of reuniting white Northerners and Southerners: "for after all we are both human if not always humane, but we are all of one blood, and it is well to learn the great lesson of how to forgive and to forget." These documents are in Myrta Lockett Avary Papers, Atlanta Historical Society, Atlanta, Ga., box 1, folder 10.

30. Avary, *Dixie after the War,* 380–381, 384, 373–378. Popular and apologetic literature on the Klan had appeared before and after Dixon and Avary in various forms. See James Melville Beard, *K.K.K. Sketches: Humorous and Didactic* (Philadelphia: Claxton, Remsen and Haffelfinger, 1877); Eyre Damer, *When the Ku Klux Rode* (New York: Neale, 1912); and William Thomas Richardson, *Historic Pulaski: Birthplace of the Ku Klux Klan, Scene of Execution of Sam Davis* (1913), no publication information, copy in Widener Library, Harvard University.

31. Allen W. Trelease, *White Terror: The Ku Klux Klan Conspiracy and Southern Reconstruction* (New York: Harper and Row, 1971), 3–10.

32. Foner, *Reconstruction,* 425–431; Trelease, *White Terror,* 49–64.

33. Foner, *Reconstruction,* 427–428; Lou Falkner Williams, *The Great South Carolina Ku Klux Klan Trials, 1871–1872* (Athens: University of Georgia Press, 1996), 19–39. One of the earliest attempts to investigate the violence occurred when the U.S. Army sent Major Lewis Merrill to York County, South Carolina. Merrill's report documented eleven murders and six hundred whippings in that county alone. See Report of Major Merrill, *Testimony Taken by the Joint Select Committee to Inquire into the Condition of Affairs in the Late Insurrectionary States,* 13 vols. (Washington, D.C., 1872), South Carolina, 1599–1606 (hereafter *KKK Hearings).* Also see Williams, *South Carolina Ku Klux Klan Trials,* 38–39. On the Meridian, Miss., events see *KKK Hearings,* Mississippi, 7–204.

34. Trelease, *White Terror,* 261–273, esp. 262–263; Rable, *But There Was No Peace,* 96; Richard Maxwell Brown, *Strain of Violence: Historical Studies of American Violence and Vigilantism* (New York: Oxford University Press, 1975), 214; George C. Wright, *Racial Violence in Kentucky, 1865–1940: Lynchings, Mob Rule, and "Legal Lynchings"* (Baton Rouge: Louisiana State University Press, 1990), 39–43.

35. *Report of Evidence Taken before the Military Committee in Relation to Outrages Committed by the Ku Klux Klan in Middle and West Tennessee,* extra session, Thirty-fifth General Assembly of the State of Tennessee (Nashville, 1868), 7–9, 13, 18–20, 23–26, 28–29. The July 4, 1868, rampage was reported to involve four hundred to five hundred Klansmen.

36. Foner, *Reconstruction,* 454–56; Trelease, *White Terror,* 383–389; Williams, *South Carolina Ku Klux Klan Trials,* 42–43.

37. Trelease, *White Terror,* 389–395. Democrats did all they could to discredit the hearings and pointed especially to the provision that witnesses were paid two dollars per diem and a mileage allowance for coming to towns to testify. Scores of black witnesses were repeatedly accused of testifying merely for money. Witnesses were also offered immunity from prosecution for anything they said in the hearings, which protected many a white Southerner who lied or shaded the truth. Some blacks were attacked as a result of their testimony, whereas no white Southerner was prosecuted solely based on his testimony.

38. See Trelease, *White Terror,* 389–410.

39. Jean Amery, *At the Mind's Limits: Contemplations by a Survivor on Auschwitz and Its Realities,* trans. Sidney Rosenfeld and Stella P. Rosenfeld (Bloomington: University of Indiana Press, 1980), 35; *KKK Hearings,* North Carolina, 103, 115–117.

40. *KKK Hearings,* South Carolina, 366; Tourgée, in *New York Tribune,* August 3, 1870, and in Foner, *Reconstruction,* 430–431; *KKK Hearings,* North Carolina, 100, 148. On rape by Klansmen in South Carolina, and on the issue of a gendered "code of honor" generally in the South, see Williams, *South Carolina Ku Klux Klan Trials,* 31–37; Harris, *Exorcising Blackness,* ix–xiii, 1–23; and

Bertram Wyatt-Brown, *Southern Honor: Ethics and Behavior in the Old South* (New York: Oxford University Press, 1983), 292–300.

41. *KKK Hearings,* Mississippi, 888–891, 803–805.

42. *KKK Hearings,* South Carolina, 520–526. On sleeplessness and fear, see Jane Surratt's testimony, *KKK Hearings,* 525. On families being whipped together, see testimony of Caleb Jenkins, *KKK Hearings,* South Carolina, 697–698.

43. *KKK Hearings,* South Carolina, 613–617, 698–700, 598; North Carolina, 99; Alabama, 720. Also see Fry, *Night Riders,* 166–169.

44. *Reports of the Committees of the Senate of the United States, 1871–72* (Washington, D.C., 1872), 44–46 (hereafter *KKK Hearings, Reports*). See Trelease, *White Terror,* 395–398.

45. Ibid., 98–99. For one of those lists of victims for a single county, Spartanburgh, see *KKK Hearings,* South Carolina, 919–922. The list contains the names of 227 people murdered, beaten, or who had their homes burned.

46. *KKK Hearings, Reports,* 439, 442, 296, 377.

47. Ibid., 448–449. For Forrest's testimony before the Congressional committee, see *KKK Hearings,* Miscellaneous Testimony, 3–24. Also see Trelease, *White Terror,* 19–20, 49–50. Forrest never openly admitted that he was the first Grand Wizard of the Ku Klux Klan, but he was widely believed to be one of its primary founders. He admitted in his testimony that during the Klan's rapid spread across the South in 1867–68, he received fifty to one hundred letters per day regarding resistance to the Reconstruction regimes, and that he employed a personal secretary to keep up with the correspondence. Forrest also gave newspaper interviews in which he discussed the Klan's character, purpose, and size. To a *Cincinnati Commercial* reporter he verified that "there is such an organization, not only in Tennessee, but all over the South, and its numbers have not been exaggerated." Forrest put the number at 40,000 in Tennessee and 550,000 across the South. Such figures can never be verified and are probably exaggerated, as are the Klan's claims to rigid organization. But Forrest's interviews were widely reprinted. See *Cincinnati Commercial,* September 1, 7, 1868; *NYTr,* September 4, 1868.

48. *New National Era,* May 30, 23, 1872, November 2, 1871. Douglass maintained a steady coverage of the Ku Klux Klan outrages in the South and of the Klan hearings throughout 1871 in his newspaper. See *New National Era,* January 26, February 2, March 2, 9, 16, 23, 30, April 6, 1871.

49. See Foner, *Reconstruction,* 488–499; John G. Sproat, *"The Best Men": Liberal Reformers in the Gilded Age* (Chicago: University of Chicago Press, 1968), 4–69; and William Gillette, *Retreat from Reconstruction, 1869–1879* (Baton Rouge: Louisiana State University Press, 1979), 56–62.

50. *Nation,* March 21, 1872, July 6, 1871.

51. Frederic Bancroft, ed., *Speeches, Correspondence, and Political Papers of Carl*

Schurz (New York: G. P. Putnam's Sons, 1913), vol. 1, 511, 517–518; vol. 2, 258–285; Foner, *Reconstruction*, 499–500.

52. *Mr. Greeley's Letters from Texas and the Lower Mississippi: To Which Are Added His Address to the Farmers of Texas, and His Speech on his Return to New York, June 12, 1871* (New York: Tribune Office, 1871), microfilm from originals in Beinecke Library, Yale University, 35–40, 44, 46, 48, 50, 55–56.

53. Cassius M. Clay to Greeley, White Hall, Ky., February 10, 1872; R. Donan to Greeley, Lexington, Mo., October 14, 1871, Horace Greeley Papers, NYPL, reel 4.

54. Ernest Wiedemann to Schurz, Hempstead, Ark., May 24, 1872; H. S. Foote Jr. to Schurz, Canton, Miss., May 22, 1872; and James (illegible) to Schurz, Lexington, Ky., July 24, 1872, Carl Schurz Papers, LC, reel 8.

55. Greeley to Carl Schurz et al., New York, May 20, 1872, Schurz Papers, reel 8.

56. Gillette, *Retreat from Reconstruction*, 64–67; R. Jones Monaghan to Schurz, West Chester, Pa., August 7, 1872, Schurz Papers, reel 8; Schurz to E. L. Godkin, June 23, 1872, Edward L Godkin Papers, HLH.

57. *NYT*, September 26, 17–25, 1872. On Democrats' support of Greeley also see Paul A. Neil to Schurz, West Bend, Wis., May 23, 1872, a petition of citizens in Chattanooga, Tenn., to Schurz, May 27, 1872, and (illegible) Chapman to Schurz, Detroit, Mich., May 22, 1872, Schurz Papers, reel 8.

58. *AC*, September 17, 21, 1872; Butler, quoted in Foner, *Reconstruction*, 509. Liberal Republicans complained repeatedly about the effectiveness of the "bloody shirt." John P. Hopkins wrote to Schurz, accusing Republicans of playing only on "the mad excitement of the past . . . dead heroes and Ku Klux horrors until the people's hair stood on end." Hopkins to Schurz, September 16, 1872, Schurz Papers, reel 8.

59. *New National Era*, August 1, 15, September 26, 1872; Gillette, *Retreat from Reconstruction*, 69–71.

60. Sumner's letter, July 29, 1872, to blacks about the 1872 election, in *The Works of Charles Sumner* (Boston: Lee and Shepard, 1870–83), vol. 15, 177–181, 184–185, 189, 192–194. The letter to Sumner, July 11, 1872, was signed by twenty-four black citizens, including physician A. T. Augusta, hotel owner William Wormley, and distinguished veteran and Medal of Honor winner Christian Fleetwood.

61. Speech by Douglass at Republican rally at Cooper Institute, New York, in *NYT*, September 26, 1872; Gillette, *Retreat from Reconstruction*, 71–72; Albion W. Tourgée, *A Fool's Errand* (1879; rpr. New York: Harper & Row, 1961), 380; *New National Era*, March 27, 1873. On amnesty, also see Foner, *Reconstruction*, 504.

62. Foner, *Reconstruction*, 512–524; *Nation*, September 5, 1872. On economic issues

and the "eclipse of radicalism," see David Montgomery, *Beyond Equality: Labor and the Radical Republicans, 1862–1872* (New York: Knopf, 1967), 335–386.

63. *NYTr,* May 30–June 1, 1874, May 31, 1875.

64. *Buffalo Commercial Advertiser,* November 4, 1874, *Louisville Courier-Journal,* November 4–5, 1874, quoted in Gillette, *Retreat from Reconstruction,* 246, 248, and on the impact of the election generally, see 236–251. On Southern redemption, see Michael Perman, *The Road to Redemption: Southern Politics, 1869–1879* (Chapel Hill: University of North Carolina Press, 1984), esp. 149–178.

65. On Mississippi, see Rable, *But There Was No Peace,* 144–162; Vernon L. Wharton, *The Negro in Mississippi, 1865–1890* (New York: Harper & Row, 1947); Brown is quoted in *Springfield Republican,* September 4, 1874. On the decline of Republican radicalism and the limits of American thought about equality, see W. R. Brock, "The Waning of Radicalism," in Kenneth Stampp and Leon F. Litwack, eds., *Reconstruction: An Anthology of Revisionist Writings* (Baton Rouge: Louisiana State University Press, 1969), 496–515. On Charles Sumner's civil rights bill and its impact on the 1874 election, see Gillette, *Retreat from Reconstruction,* 256–258; Foner, *Reconstruction,* 532–534, 553–556.

66. Theodore C. Smith, ed., *The Life and Letters of James A. Garfield,* 2 vols. (New Haven: Yale University Press, 1925) vol. 1, 521; *New York Times,* quoted in Foner, *Reconstruction,* 554. Also see James B. Stewart, *Wendell Phillips: Liberty's Hero* (Baton Rouge: Louisiana State University Press, 1986), 308–310.

67. *NYTr,* May 28, 1875. Nash was actually William B. Nash (1822–88). Born a slave in Virginia, he was brought to South Carolina as a youth and worked as a servant in a Columbia hotel. Nash held many offices in Reconstruction South Carolina and served as state senator, 1868–77. He was a distinguished and influential member of the senate, as well as a brick manufacturer and a coal-yard operator. He admitted to accepting one bribe from a railroad company in exchange for his vote. When he resigned from the senate in 1877, Nash made restitution to the state for funds he had illegally procured. See *Freedom's Lawmakers: A Directory of Black Officeholders during Reconstruction,* rev. ed. (Baton Rouge: Louisiana State University Press, 1996), 159.

68. Frederick Douglass, "The Color Question," speech delivered July 5, 1875, in Hillsdale, near Washington, D.C., Frederick Douglass Papers, LC, reel 15.

69. Langston quoted in *CR,* August 5, 1875; Douglass, "Color Question."

70. "Another Chapter of Blood at Vicksburg," *CR,* July 22, 1875; Rable, *But There Was No Peace,* 152; Wharton, *Negro in Mississippi,* 190.

71. William T. Sherman to John Sherman, February 3, 1875, William T. Sherman Papers, LC, quoted in Gillette, *Retreat from Reconstruction,* 172.

72. Gillette, *Retreat from Reconstruction,* 236–258; Foner, *Reconstruction,* 566–567.

73. Foner, *Reconstruction,* 568–569. Federal marshal J. H. Pearce, quoted in Rable,

But There Was No Peace, 182, and on the election of 1876 and the role of violence and intimidation generally, see 163–185.

74. *Chicago Tribune,* November 11, 1876; *NYT,* February 22, 1877; *AC,* November 8, 1876, January 5, 25, 1877.

75. C. Vann Woodward, *Reunion and Reaction: The Compromise of 1877 and the End of Reconstruction* (1951; rpr. New York: Anchor, 1956).

76. Ibid., 201–234; Foner, *Reconstruction,* 578–582; Gillette, *Retreat from Reconstruction,* 332–333; *Nation,* April 5, 1877.

77. See Woodward, *Reunion and Reaction,* 233. Gunnar Myrdal, *An American Dilemma: The Negro Problem and Modern Democracy* (1944; rpr. New York: Harper & Row, 1962, 20th anniversary ed.), 446–448.

5. Soldiers' Memory

1. Paul Fussell, *The Great War in Modern Memory* (New York: Oxford University Press, 1975), 29–35; William Porcher Du Bose, "Reminiscences," n.d., SHC, UNC.

2. On Civil War veterans generally see Mary R. Dearing, *Veterans in Politics: The Story of the GAR* (Baton Rouge: Louisiana State University Press, 1952); Stuart McConnell, *Glorious Contentment: The Grand Army of the Republic, 1865–1900* (Chapel Hill: University of North Carolina Press, 1992); Gerald F. Linderman, *Embattled Courage: The Experience of Combat in the American Civil War* (New York: Free Press, 1987), 266–297; Gaines M. Foster, *Ghosts of the Confederacy: Defeat, the Lost Cause, and the Emergence of the New South* (New York: Oxford University Press, 1987), 104–126; Larry M. Logue, *To Appomattox and Beyond: The Civil War Soldier in War and Peace* (Chicago: Ivan Dee, 1996), 82–148; and Thomas C. Leonard, *Above the Battle: War-Making in America from Appomattox to Versailles* (New York: Oxford University Press, 1978), 1–39. On veterans' psychological disorders, see Eric T. Dean, *Shook over Hell: Post-Traumatic Stress, Vietnam, and the Civil War* (Cambridge: Harvard University Press, 1998), 91–179.

3. William E. Park to Dear Cousin, April 21, 1865, Spanish Fort, Alabama, GLC, ML. On the reactions of black soldiers to Lincoln's assassination, see Joseph T. Glatthaar, *Forged in Battle: The Civil War Alliance of Black Soldiers and White Officers* (New York: Free Press, 1991), 208–209.

4. Albert Castel, "The Fort Pillow Massacre: A Fresh Examination of the Evidence," *Civil War History* 4 (March 1958), 38–71; Ashley Halsey, ed., *A Yankee Private's Civil War by Robert Hale Strong* (Chicago, 1961), 15–16, in Reid Mitchell, *Civil War Soldiers: Their Expectations and Their Experiences* (New York: Viking, 1988), 193; Charles Harvey Brewster to mother, May 24, 1864, in David W.

Blight, ed., *When This Cruel War Is Over: The Civil War Letters of Charles Harvey Brewster* (Amherst: University of Massachusetts Press), 304; Lizzie, "Letter from Morrowtown" (Ohio), *CR*, January 7, 1865.

5. Wiliam McWillie Notebooks, Mississippi Department of Archives and History, Jackson, Miss., in Gary W. Gallagher, *The Confederate War: How Popular Will, Nationalism, and Military Strategy Could Not Stave off Defeat* (Cambridge: Harvard University Press, 1997), 105, and see 63–111; William T. Sherman to Ellen Sherman, May 23, 1865, May 20, 1864, Sherman Papers, Notre Dame University, in Charles Royster, *The Destructive War: William Tecumseh Sherman, Stonewall Jackson, and the Americans* (New York: Knopf, 1991), 339–340.

6. Walter L. Nugent to Eleanor Nugent, November 22, 1863, in William M. Cash and Lucy Somerville Howarth, eds., *My Dear Nellie: The Civil War Letters of William L. Nugent* (Jackson: University of Mississippi Press, 1977), 148, and Henry Clay Weaver to Cornelia Wiley, August 14, 1864, in James M. Merrill and James F. Marshall, "Georgia through Kentucky Eyes: Letters Written on Sherman's March to Atlanta," *Filson Club Historical Quarterly* 30 (1956), 332, both in James M. McPherson, *For Cause and Comrades: Why Men Fought in the Civil War* (New York: Oxford University Press, 1997), 167, 169; Oliver Wendell Holmes Jr. to parents, June 24, 1864, in Mark DeWolfe Howe, ed., *Touched with Fire: Civil War Letters and Diary of Oliver Wendell Holmes, Jr., 1861–1864* (Cambridge: Harvard University Press, 1946), 149–150. Also see Linderman, *Embattled Courage,* 7–110.

7. Brewster to mother, May 15, 1864, in Blight, ed., *When This Cruel War Is Over,* 298–299, 23.

8. "Soldier's Letter," Camp, Twenty-second U.S. Colored Troops Infantry, Chapel Point, Md., May 13, 1865, signed only as "Observer," and "Letter from a Soldier," by W. A. Freeman, Private, Twenty-second U.S. Colored Troops Infantry, in *CR*, May 27, 1865; Henry W. Gay to father and mother, August 11, 1865, Civil War miscellany, U.S. Army Military History Institute, in Mitchell, *Civil War Soldiers,* 203.

9. Garland H. White, "Letter from Richmond," April 12, 1865, and "The Execution of a Soldier," *CR*, April 22, May 6, 1865. On White, also see Edwin S. Redkey, ed., *A Grand Army of Black Men: Letters from African American Soldiers in the Union Army, 1861–1865* (New York: Cambridge University Press, 1992), 133–136.

10. H. S. Harmon to editor, *CR*, October 21, 1865. On the postwar breakdown between black troops and white officers, see Glatthaar, *Forged in Battle,* 209–230.

11. Turner, "Army Correspondence," May 15, 1865, Goldsboro, N.C., *CR*, May 27, 1865. On Turner, see John Dittmer, "The Education of Henry McNeal Turner," in Leon Litwack and August Meier, eds., *Black Leaders of the Nineteenth Century*

(Urbana: University of Illinois Press, 1988), 253–272; and Stephen W. Angell, *Bishop Henry McNeal Turner and African American Religion in the South* (Knoxville: University of Tennessee Press, 1992).

12. *CR,* May 27, 1865.

13. Robert E. Lee to D. W. McConaughy, Lexington, Va., August 5, 1869, David McConaughy Collection, Gettysburg College Archives, Gettysburg, Penn. See also Marshall W. Fishwick, *Lee after the War* (New York: Dodd, Mead, 1963); Emory Thomas, *Robert E. Lee: A Biography* (New York: Norton, 1995); Linderman, *Embattled Courage,* 269.

14. Linderman, *Embattled Courage,* 266–275; McConnell, *Glorious Contentment,* 167–205.

15. On Civil War stories in popular magazines, see Kathleen Diffley, *Where My Heart Is Turning Ever: Civil War Stories and Constitutional Reform, 1861–76* (Athens: University of Georgia Press, 1992), xi–xlvii, 1–12; and Alice Fahs, "The Feminized Civil War: Gender, Northern Popular Literature, and the Memory of the War, 1861–1900," *Journal of American History* 85 (March 1999), 1461–1494. Fahs shows how a "distinctively woman's war" appeared repeatedly in wartime stories, but how it vanished in popular magazines in the postwar era, especially by the 1880s and 1890s. This redefinition of the experience as a "man's war" fits the pattern of how soldiers' memory came to dominate the national culture.

16. Alice Fahs, "The Marketplace of Memory: Popular War Histories and the Northern Literary Marketplace," manuscript, copy courtesy of the author. John S. C. Abbott's two-volume *The History of the Civil War in America* drew heavily upon wartime newspapers and demonstrated that the war could be made into a popular entertainment, especially if slavery and other ideological differences were muted. But even books that were partisan enjoyed good subscription success. Horace Greeley's massive *The American Conflict* (1867), which sold 125,000 copies in 1867, did engage the politics of the war and its causation. With *The Lost Cause* (1867), Richmond's E. A. Pollard produced nearly a Confederate equivalent of Greeley's work. G. P. Putnam's *Rebellion Record* was also a success by merely compiling the story of the war without regard to partisanship or narrative line. Like Victorian collectors, Putnam's *collected* the war for popular consumption.

17. John W. De Forest, "The First Time under Fire," *Harper's,* September 1864, 83–90. On De Forest, see Daniel Aaron, *The Unwritten War: American Writers and the Civil War* (New York: Knopf, 1973), 164–180; Edmund Wilson, *Patriotic Gore: Studies in the Literature of the American Civil War* (1962; rpr. Boston: Northeastern University Press, 1984), 669–742; Nina Silber, *Romance of Reunion: Northerners and the South, 1865–1900* (Chapel Hill: University of North Carolina Press, 1993), 107, 110–112.

18. John W. De Forest, *Miss Ravenal's Conversion from Secession to Loyalty* (1867; rpr. New York: Harper & Brothers, 1939), 244–249, 255, 257.

19. William Dean Howells, *AM* 29 (March 1872), 365; De Forest to Howells, quoted in Wilson, *Patriotic Gore*, 684. On De Forest's realism, see Leonard, *Above the Battle*, 20–23, 26.

20. William B. Hesseltine, ed., *Civil War Prisons* (Kent, Ohio: Kent State University Press, 1972), 6, based on a special issue of *Civil War History* 8 (1962). On prisons generally, see William B. Hesseltine, *Civil War Prisons: A Study in War Psychology* (Columbus: Ohio State University Press, 1930).

21. Dorence Atwater, *A List of the Union Soldiers Buried at Andersonville, Copied from the Official Record in the Surgeon's Office at Andersonville* (New York: Tribune Association, 1866), vii.

22. Ibid., viii.

23. A. Noble to Thaddeus Stevens, Buffalo, N.Y., February 2, 1866, Stevens Papers, reel 4; MOLLUS collection, HLH, box 2.

24. Silber, *The Romance of Reunion*, 66–92.

25. De Forest's articles, originally published in *Harper's*, *Atlantic Monthly*, and *Putnam's*, were eventually collected in James H. Croushore and David Morris Patter, eds., *A Union Officer in the Reconstruction* (New Haven: Yale University Press, 1948). As an example of tourist guides that incorporated battlefields into new printings, see Edward H. Hall, ed., *Appleton's Handbook of American Travel: The Southern Tour* (New York: Appleton, 1866), the ninth yearly issue of this travel guide. On traveler's accounts about the South, see Thomas E. Clark, ed., *Travels in the New South: A Bibliography, the Post-War South, 1865–1900*, vol. 1 (Norman: University of Oklahoma Press, 1962). Conwell's letters are published in Joseph C. Carter, ed., *Magnolia Journey: A Union Veteran Revisits the Former Confederate States* (University: University of Alabama Press, 1974), 3, 7.

26. Carter, ed., *Magnolia Journey*, 48–53, 12.

27. Ibid., 59–60, 22–23, 76.

28. Ibid., 77–78.

29. "Literary Record," March 1867 (a literary diary), 2, John Esten Cooke Papers, PL, DU, box 1. On the unromantic character of war, see Cooke quoted in John Esten Cooke, *Wearing of the Gray: Being Personal Portraits, Scenes, and Adventures of the War*, Philip Van Doren Stern, ed. (1867; rpr. Bloomington: Indiana University Press, 1959), xvi. The Stuart portrait is described in George Cary Eggleston, *A Rebel's Recollections* (1874; rpr. 3d ed. New York: G. P. Putnam's, 1889), 109. On Cooke's work see Thomas L. Connelly and Barbara L. Bellows, *God and General Longstreet: The Lost Cause and the Southern Mind* (Baton Rouge: Louisiana State University Press, 1982), 52–63; Wilson, *Patriotic Gore*, 192–196.

30. John Esten Cooke, *Surry of Eagle's-Nest; or, The Memoirs of a Staff-Officer Serving in Virginia* (1866; rpr. Ridgewood, N.J.: Greg Press, 1968), 9–10. *Surry of Eagle's Nest,* manuscript, Cooke Papers, box 2. Cooke, Diary, 3 vols., Cooke Papers, box 1. The diaries are quite self-consciously literary, but they also contain a good deal of commentary on Cooke's sickness and depression during his four years at the front. Edward V. Valentine to Cooke, Richmond, September 7, 1872, Cooke Papers, box 1.

31. McConnell, *Glorious Contentment,* 18–38; Dearing, *Veterans in Politics,* 80–112, 148–184.

32. Foster, *Ghosts of the Confederacy,* 49–62, 104–105; Richard D. Starnes, "Forever Faithful: The Southern Historical Society and Confederate Historical Memory," *Southern Cultures* 2 (Winter 1996), 177–194.

33. Dudley McIver Du Bose to Porter Alexander, September 5, 1866, Washington, Ga., Frederick M. Dearborn Collection of Military and Political Americana, HLH.

34. James Kemper to Edward Porter Alexander, September 20, 1869, Madison Court House, Va., Dearborn Collection, HLH.

35. John C. Breckinridge to Jubal Early, August 10, 1873, Saratoga, N.Y., and P. G. T. Bearuregard to Jubal Early, July 17, 1873, New Orleans, in Jubal Early Papers, LC, vol. 7.

36. Richard Lucian Page to Charles Colcock Jones, June 25, 1871, Norfolk, Va.; Alexander Robert Lawton to Jones, August 10, 1866, Savannah, Ga.; Daniel Harris Reynolds to Jones, March 4, 1872, Lake Village, Ark.; Edward Aylesworth Perry to Jones, April 16, 1872, Pensacola, Fla.; and William Porcher Miles to Jones, November 9, 1875, Yazoo City, Miss.; all in Dearborn Collection, HLH.

37. *SHS Papers* 1 (February 1876), 59–61, 76.

38. Ibid. (March–April 1876), 113–327, esp. 116; Starnes, "Forever Faithful," 189.

39. Eggleston, *A Rebel's Recollections,* v–vi, 3–4, 17–18, 108–37, 224–225, 243, 255–257.

40. Wilson, *Patriotic Gore,* 175. On Sherman's *Memoirs,* see John Marszalek, *Sherman: A Soldier's Passion for Order* (New York: Free Press, 1993), 460–467; Stanley Hirshson, *The White Tecumseh: A Biography of William T. Sherman* (New York: John Wiley, 1997), 355–358. On the publication of the *Memoirs* and Appleton's quest to be the publisher, see John Tebbel, *A History of Book Publishing in the United States: The Expansion of an Industry, 1865–1919,* vol. 2 (New York: R. R. Bowker, 1975), 205. On Sherman's many postwar feuds, see Michael Fellman, *Citizen Sherman: A Life of William Tecumseh Sherman* (Lawrence: University of Kansas Press, 1995), 316–340.

41. *Memoirs of General William Tecumseh Sherman, Written by Himself* (New York: Appleton, 1875), vol. 2, 194–195; Wilson, *Patriotic Gore,* 181–182.

42. Sherman, *Memoirs*, vol. 2, 119–121, 127–128.

43. Ibid., 179–180.

44. Ibid., 407, 395–396.

45. *Annals of the War* (1879; rpr. Dayton, Ohio: Blue & Gray Press, 1996), i–iv; Buck, *Road to Reunion*, 197–198. On *Annals*, see Gary Gallagher, "Introduction," *Annals of the War* (New York: Da Capo Press, 1994), v–xiv. McClure's work on the South is in Alexander K. McClure, *The South: Its Industrial, Financial, and Political Condition* (Philadelphia: J. B. Lippincott, 1886).

46. General Joseph E. Johnston, "The Dalton-Atlanta Operations," *Annals of the War*, 331–341. See Joseph E. Johnston, *Narrative of Military Operations* (1874; rpr. Bloomington: Indiana University Press, 1959). On Johnston's memoir, see Craig L. Symonds, *Joseph E. Johnston: A Civil War Biography* (New York: Norton, 1992), 361–367. Johnston's memoir sold poorly and was largely a political brief against Davis.

47. John D. Imboden, "Fire, Sword, and Halter," *Annals of the War*, 169–83. On Hunter's raids in the Shenandoah Valley, see James M. McPherson, *Battle Cry of Freedom: The Civil War Era* (New York: Oxford University Press, 1988), 737–739.

48. John McCausland, "The Burning of Chambersburg," *Annals of the War*, 770–774.

49. John Esten Cooke, "General Stuart in Camp and Field"; Richard Taylor, "The Last Confederate Surrender"; William Allan, "Stonewall Jackson's Valley Campaign," all in *Annals of the War*, 665–676, 205–219, 60–66, 693–704, 71, 749.

50. T. P. McElrath, "The Draft Riots in New York"; Henry S. Olcott, "The War's Carnival of Fraud"; Wills De Hass, "The Battle of Shiloh"; D. Watson Howe, "On the Field of Fredericksburg"; William Brooke-Rawle, "The Right Flank at Gettysburg," all in *Annals of the War*, 305–318, 619–633, 286–304, 705–723, 690, 257–266, 467.

51. Imboden, "Fire, Sword, and Halter," and Edward Spencer, "Confederate Negro Enlistments," both in *Annals of the War*, 176–177, 536–553. The public history debate in the 1990s over "black Confederates"—the alleged participation of blacks in the Confederate war effort even as soldiers—finds its roots in such articles as Spencer's. His story line of 1879 revived in the 1990s in the never-ending quest among some to establish legitimacy for the Confederacy in American memory. On "black Confederates" see Charles Kelly Brown, J. H. Segars, and R. B. Rosenberg, eds., "Forgotten Confederates: An Anthology about Black Southerners," *Journal of Confederate History Series* 14 (n.d.); Richard Rollins, ed., "Black Southerners in Gray: Essays on Afro-Americans in Confederate Armies," *Journal of Confederate History Series* 11 (n.d.); and Ervin L. Jordan Jr., *Black Con-*

federates and Afro-Yankees in Civil War Virginia (Charlottesville: University Press of Virginia, 1995).

52. John Hope Franklin, *George Washington Williams: A Biography* (Chicago: University of Chicago Press, 1985), 1–8.

53. Ibid., 8–39; George Washington Williams, "The American Negro, from 1776 to 1876," oration delivered July 4, 1876, Avondale, Ohio (Cincinnati: Robert Clarke & Co., 1876), pamphlet in HLH. In the 1880s Williams wrote two major works of history, the first serious efforts of their kind. See *History of the Negro Race in America from 1619 to 1880: Negroes as Slaves, as Soldiers, and as Citizens*, 2 vols. (New York: G. Putnam's, 1882, 1883); and *A History of the Negro Troops in the War of the Rebellion, 1861–1865* (New York: Harper & Brothers, 1888).

54. Williams, "The American Negro," 6, 9, 15, 18–21.

55. Ibid., 21–22, 24–25.

6. Soldiers' Faith

1. Carleton McCarthy, quoted in B. A. Botkin, ed., *A Civil War Treasury of Tales, Legends, and Folklore* (New York: Random House, 1960), 567; McConnell, *Glorious Contentment*, 84–93, 110; Logue, *To Appomattox and Beyond*, 94–102.

2. *The Society of the Army of the Potomac, Eleventh Annual Reunion, Report of Proceedings*, Burlington, Vt., June 16, 1880 (New York: Pease and Stuyvesant, 1870), 5. This veterans' group held its first annual meeting in 1869, with Joshua Lawrence Chamberlain of Maine as its orator. The society still held reunions at least as late as 1907. See *Society of the Army of the Potomac, First Annual Reunion, Report of Proceedings*, New York, July 5–6, 1869, 8–16. Typical of so many reunions and veterans' organizations, the Society of the Army of the Potomac published these roughly 100-page reports each year. On the financial and political attraction of veterans' reunions for cities, see McConnell, *Glorious Contentment*, 114–115.

3. Whitman, *Specimen Days* (1882), in *Complete Prose Works*, 73–75. Most of *Specimen Days* was written long before 1882, but it is virtually impossible to determine exactly the date.

4. Edward S. Casey, *Remembering: A Phenomenological Study* (Bloomington: Indiana University Press, 1987), 104–121. "When we reminisce," writes Casey, "we are not going back into the past to reconstitute it as an object of historiological inquiry. We return, rather, as persons whose present interests and needs are most fully met by reminiscing . . . Or, more precisely, the revivifying of the past that occurs so prominently in reminiscing is at the same time a revitalizing of the present in which the reminiscing is taking place" (110). By the 1880s and 1890s veterans sought a revivifying of their present—of their aging minds and bodies in a modernizing and increasingly commercial culture.

5. Captain Henry A. Castle, "The Army Mule," April 3, 1889, in Chaplain Edward E. Neill, ed., *Glimpses of the Nation's Struggle, a Series of Papers Read before the Minnesota Commandery of MOLLUS, 1887–1889* (St. Paul: St. Paul Book and Stationery Co., 1889), 338; Captain G. W. Burnell, "The Development of Our Armies, 1861–65," December 2, 1891, in *War Papers, Read before the Commandery of the State of Wisconsin MOLLUS*, vol. 2 (Milwaukee: Burdick, Armitage & Allen, 1896), 70; Brevet Brigadier General Peter Michie, "Reminiscences of Cadet and Army Service," October 4, 1893, in A. Noel Blakeman, ed., *Personal Recollections of the War of the Rebellion, Addresses Delivered before the Commandery of the State of New York MOLLUS*, 2d ser. (New York: G. P. Putnam's, 1897), 183.

6. *Century* 29 (July 1883), 27–34. In this same issue *Century* ran two articles from differing viewpionts on John Brown's raid. Robert Underwood Johnson, *Remembered Yesterdays* (Boston: Little, Brown, 1923), 189–190, 193; Robert Underwood Johnson and Clarence Clough Buel, eds., *Battles and Leaders of the Civil War*, vol. 1 (New York: Century Co., 1888), ix–x.

7. Johnson, *Remembered Yesterdays*, 189–190, 200; C. C. Buel to Gilder, July 11, 1884, Richard Watson Gilder Papers, NYPL, box 2.

8. Johnson, *Remembered Yesterdays*, 190, 192, 194; R. E. Coleton to Buel, Washington, D.C., September 5, 1887 CC, NYPL, box 118. The idea for conceiving of the series as a "symposium" may have come from one of Johnson's trusted correspondents about the project. See Francis Vinton Greene to Johnson, Washington, D.C., December 22, 1883, CC, NYPL, box 121. Vinton writes: "How would it do for the victorious general to write his account, the opposing general to reply and the victor to rejoin, a sort of limited symposium?"

9. Johnson, *Remembered Yesterdays*, 193–204, 209–210.

10. C. A. Leonard to R. W. Gilder, Richmond, Ky., July 26, 1886, M. H. Gavin to editor, Boston, n.d., Howard D. Corbyn to editor, Walserburg, Colo., April 10, 1886, CC, NYPL, boxes 118, 121, 126. John O. Casler to *Century*, Oklahoma City, December 17, 1891, CC, NYPL, box 119. The hardcover four-volume set of *Battles and leaders*, expanded and even more illustrated by such artists as Walton Taber, Winslow Homer, and Theodore Davis, sold over 75,000 copies when published in 1888. See Stephen W. Sears, ed., *Century Collection of Civil War Art*, (New York: American Heritage, 1974), 12.

11. John L. Branch to *Century*, Griffin, Ga., March 13, 1886, J. C. Birdsong to *Century* Pub. Co., North Carolina Library department, Raleigh, N.C., July 19, 1890, E. J. Harvie to *Century*, February 15, 1892, W. H. Chamberlain to Buel, November 21, 1884, CC, NYPL, boxes 117, 118, 121. Many correspondents wrote to the editors offering old family papers, wartime posters, letters with authentic signatures of famous people, and other objects and ephemera from the war. Georgian Berry Benson wrote to Buel offering photos and other memorabilia that he had

carried home from the surrender at Appomattox, including "a small cloth bag or pocket" that had been used by a prisoner to "carry earth out from the tunnel dug at Elmira" (a Northern prison). Berry Benson to Buel, Augusta, Ga., July 30, 1890, CC, NYPL, box 117.

12. Mrs. H. G. Coutler to editors, Madison, Ind., August 13, 1885, Helen O'Donnell to editor, Utica, N.Y., October 9, 1890, Robert McAllister to *Century*, Belvedere, N.J., October 9, 1888, CC, NYPL, boxes 119, 121.

13. Mrs. H. C. Goldsmith to *Century*, September 17, 1889, Mrs. C. B. Kent to editors, West Superior, Wis., September 22, 1891, Miss Rebecca Brumback to *Century*, Jacksontown (no state), April 22, 1886, CC, NYPL, boxes 117, 127, 129.

14. Susie J. Bishop to editor, "in the mountains of Va," March 26, 1891, CC, NYPL, box 117.

15. My impression is that *Century* paid generally by the word, as well as on an ad hoc basis: the more famous and hard to get, the more an author was paid. See Joseph E. Johnston to Johnson, Washington, D.C., February 25, 1884, January 20, 1885, Stephen D. Lee to editor, November 4, 1885, March 19, 1887, CC, NYPL, boxes 124, 126; Stephen D. Lee, "The First Step in the War," *Battles and Leaders* vol. 1, 74–81; James Longstreet to Johnson, Atlanta, June 10, 1884, July 31, 1884, Gainsville, Ga., November 2, 1885, James Longstreet to *Century*, September 24, 1885, January 24, 1886, *Century* Collection, NYPL, box 126. In this latter letter Longstreet informs the editors that $500 "will not meet the Gettysburg account. It has taken double the labor of others and I believe more than double the words upon which the agreement was based." Josiah Carter to Johnson, Atlanta, February 27, 1885, September 30, 1885, August 27, 1888, Josiah Carter to Buel, July 3, 1886, CC, NYPL, box 118. In the CC, NYPL, box 126, among the Longstreet letters, is a document on *Century* stationery labeled "Longstreet and Carter." It indicates payment for four battles or campaigns: Fredericksburg, Frayser's Farm, Bull Run and Md. Campaign, and Gettysburg. The totals are $2,200 for Longstreet and $515 for Carter. These are probably not the full amounts paid to the two men.

16. Warren Lee Goss, "Going to the Front: Recollections of a Private," *Battles and Leaders*, vol. 1, 149–159. See Warren Lee Goss, *The Soldier's Story of His Captivity at Andersonville, Belle Isle, and Other Rebel Prisons* (Boston: Lee and Shepard, 1869); Hesseltine, ed., *Civil War Prisons*, 252.

17. R. K. Beecham to *Century*, Neligh, Nebr., February 11, 1885, CC, NYPL, box 117. On Beecham, see Michael Stevens, ed., *"As if It Were Glory": Robert Beecham's Civil War from the Iron Brigade to the Black Regiments* (Madison, Wis.: Madison House, 1998).

18. A. W. Gilbert to Editor, Ross, Ohio, February 15, 1888, Isaac W. Heysinger to

Buel, Philadelphia, March 27, 1892, April 11, 1892, April 18, 1892, December 8, 1892, CC, NYPL, box 121.

19. Thomas Lee to editor, National Military Home, Dayton, Ohio, February 3, 1888, CC, NYPL, boxes 121, 126. On the Dayton soldiers' home, and such homes generally, see Patrick J. Kelly, *Creating a National Home: Building the Veterans' Welfare State, 1860–1900* (Cambridge: Harvard University Press, 1997), 110–112.

20. Thomas Lee to editor, February 3, 1888, Berry Benson to Buel, Augusta, Ga., October 1, 1890, CC, NYPL, boxes 117, 126; Tim O'Brien, "The Lives of the Dead," in *The Things They Carried* (New York: Penguin, 1990), 259–260.

21. McConnell, *Glorious Contentment*, 74; Foster, *Ghosts of the Confederacy*, 106–108; John A. Simpson, *S. A. Cunningham and the Confederate Heritage* (Athens: University of Georgia Press, 1994), 90–100. On the *Southern Bivouac*, see Gary Gallagher, "Introduction," *The Southern Bivouac*, 6 vols. (1882–87; rpr. Wilmington, N.C.: Broadfoot Publishing, 1992), i–xii. For two examples of the "darky" stories, see "The Last Ration" and "Humor and Pathos of the Old Regime Negro," *Southern Bivouac*, vol. 1, 217–218, vol. 2, 371–373.

22. *Personal Narratives of the Battles of the Rebellion, Being Papers Read before the Rhode Island Soldiers and Sailors Historical Society*, 10 vols. (Providence: Sidney S. Rider, 1878–1915). In the Rhode Island collection 99 narratives appear, written by 67 different men, with 51 pieces written by repeat authors. As a comparison to a larger state, see W. H. Chamberlain, ed., *Sketches of War History, 1861–1865: Papers Prepared for the Ohio Commandery, MOLLUS*, 6 vols. (Cincinnati: Robert Clarke Co., 1888–1908). Among the Ohio veterans' group, spanning 23 years of performing such papers, 110 men delivered some 132 narratives, with 36 as repeat authors. Such a pattern exists across the Northern states. The number may run into several thousands of Yankee veterans who attempted at least once, and many multiple times, to write formally about their war experience. Normally, each volume of published papers contained 20–25 pieces, and each paper ranged in length from 10 to 30 pages.

23. Brevet Major-General W. H. Powell, "The Sinking Creek Valley Raid," *War Papers and Personal Reminiscences, 1861–1865, Read before the Commandery of the State of Missouri, MOLLUS*, vol. 1 (St. Louis: Becktold & Co., 1892), 191–203; Brevet Major-General A. C. Voris, "The Battle of the Boys," in Chamberlain, ed., *Sketches of War History* [Ohio], vol. 4, 87–100; Brevet Captain Edward N. Whittier, "The Left Attack at Gettysburg" and Lieutenant Colonel Francis S. Hesseltine, "Amusing the Enemy," in *Civil War Papers Read before the Commandery of the State of Massachusetts, MOLLUS*, vol. 1 (Boston: F. H. Gilson), 75–108; Brevet Brigadier-General Rufus R. Dawes, "On the Right at Antietam" and Brevet Major Lewis M. Hosea, "The Last Ditch," in Robert

Hunter, ed., *Sketches of War History, 1861–1865: Papers Prepared for the Ohio Commandery, MOLLUS,* 1888–1890, vol. 3 (Cincinnati: Robert Clarke & Co., 1890), 252–263, 293–300; Carlton McCarthy, *Detailed Minutiae of Soldier Life in the Army of Northern Virginia, 1861–1865* (Richmond: J. W. Randolph & English, 1882).

24. J. B. Mansfield to *Century,* Effingham, Kans., August 9, 1885; Thomas H. Mann to editors, Woonsocket, R.I., May 14, May 29, June 14, July 14, December 12, 1884, February 16, 1888, April 22, August 14, August 26, 1890; Warren Lee Goss to Buel, May 14, 1889, CC, NYPL, boxes 121, 127; T. H. Mann, "A Yankee in Andersonville," *Century* 40 (July 1890), 447–461; 40 (August 1890), 606–622.

25. Frank E. Moran, "Colonel Rose's Tunnel at Libby Prison," *Century* 34 (March 1888), 770–790; W. H. Shelton, "A Hard Road to Travel out of Dixie," *Century* 40 (October 1890), 921–949; J. T. King, "On the Andersonville Cicuit," *Century* 41 (November 1890), 100–105; Horace Carpenter, "Plain Living at Johnson's Island," *Century* 41 (March 1891), 705–78l; John A. Wyeth, "Cold Cheer at Camp Morton," *Century* 41 (April 1891), 844–852; W. R. Holloway, "Treatment of Prisoners at Camp Morton: A Reply to 'Cold Cheer at Camp Morton,'" *Century* 42 (September 1891), 757–770. Also see Ann Fabian, *The Unvarnished Truth: Personal Narratives in Nineteenth-Century America* (Berkeley: University of California Press, 2000). I am indebted to Fabian for bringing many of these narratives to my attention. James McCann to editor, Champaign, Ill., August 29, September 6, September 16, 1890, April 7, 1891, CC, NYPL, box 127.

26. James Stepto Johnston to editor, San Antonio, Tex., November 6, 1890; Henry M. Price to *Century,* Central Plains, Va., August 11, 1890, CC, NYPL, boxes 124, 131.

27. O. R. McNary, "What I Saw and Did inside and outside of Rebel Prisons," December 3, 1900, *War Talks in Kansas: Series of Papers Read before the Kansas Commandery, MOLLUS* (Kansas City, Mo.: Franklin Hudson, 1906), 25, 28, 31, 36, 41; Clay MacCauley, "Through Chancellorsville, into and out of Libby Prison," *Personal Narratives . . . Rhode Island Soldiers and Sailors Society* 7 (Providence, 1904), 36, 39–40.

28. Frank Holsinger, "How Does One Feel under Fire?" May 5, 1898, in *War Talks in Kansas,* 291–304.

29. Leonard, *Above the Battle,* 208, n. 9; Robert Stoddart Robertson, "From the Wilderness to Spotsylvania," *Sketches of War History,* vol. 1, [Ohio], 258, 264–265, 284, 291.

30. John S. Cooper, "The Shenandoah Valley in Eighteen Hundred and Sixty-Two," December 9, 1886, and Captain George Hunt, "The Fort Donelson Campaign," January 25, 1899, in *Military Essays and Recollections: Papers Read be-*

fore the Commandery of the State of Illinois, MOLLUS, vol. 4 (Chicago: Cozzens & Beaton, 1907), 36–37, 61.

31. For the pleasure of detail, see A. H. Markland to editor, Washington, D.C., December 22, 31, 1884; Joseph E. Johnston to Buel, Washington D.C., January 25, 1886, May 14, 30, June 11, 17, July 1, 2, 4, August 11, September 12, December 8, 14, 15, 17, 1885, CC, NYPL, box 124.

32. Franklin Parks to *Century,* Atlanta, April 14, 1888; A. H. McKelvy to *Century,* Warren, Pa., June 28, 1890, CC, NYPL, boxes 127, 129. Letters to the *Century* disputing facts in articles are voluminous. A typical one, which complains of "manifold errors" in an article by former Confederate general John Imboden in the May 1885 *Century* about Stonewall Jackson's Valley Campaign, is Joseph Packard Jr. to editor, Baltimore, June 17, 1885, CC, NYPL, box 129. On the meaning of the human urge for detail, see Sigmund Freud, *Beyond the Pleasure Principle,* James Strachey, trans. (New York: Norton, 1961).

33. Alexander Robert Lawton to Charles Colcock Jones, Savannah, Ga., August 10, 1866, Dearborn Collection, HLH; McConnell, *Glorious Contentment,* 172.

34. John B. Bachelder, *What to See and How to See It* (Boston: John B. Bachelder, 1873), 20; Carol Reardon, *Pickett's Charge in History and Memory* (Chapel Hill: University of North Carolina Press, 1997), 69–72; David L. Ladd and Audrey J. Ladd, eds., *The Bachelder Papers: Gettysburg in Their Own Words,* 2 vols. (Dayton, Ohio: Morningside House, 1994), vol. 2, 735–737.

35. Reardon, *Pickett's Charge,* 84–182. The first attempt at a Blue-Gray gathering was in 1874, and it was a decided failure. In 1887 a much larger and more successful intersectional reunion occurred at Gettysburg.

36. Samuel Pennypacker to Bachelder, Philadelphia, August 26, 1881, John C. Kensill to H. Bassler, Ft. Wayne, Ind., February 14, 1882, *Bachelder Papers,* vol. 2, 758, 832–834.

37. William R. Ramsey to Bachelder, Philadelphia, September 30, 1883, George G. Briggs to Bachelder, Grand Rapids, Mich., March 26, 1888, Andrew Cowan to Bachelder, Louisville, Ky., November 24, 1885, *Bachelder Papers,* vol. 2, 970–971, 1255–1258, 1145–1148.

38. There are many working definitions of myth. A useful one is Richard Slotkin's conception of myth as sacred ideas ritualized in memory, or "usable values from history . . . beyond the reach of critical demystification." See Slotkin, *The Fatal Environment: The Myth of the Frontier in the Age of Industrialization, 1800–1890* (New York: Atheneum, 1985), 19. Also valuable is Roland Barthes, *Mythologies* (London: Jonathan Cape, 1957), esp. 109–159. Barthes's notion of myth as "depoliticized speech" applies well to much of the myth-making and employment of myth in Civil War memory. "Myth does not deny things," writes Barthes, "on the contrary, its function is to talk about them; simply, it purifies

them, it makes them innocent, it gives them a natural and eternal justification, it gives them a clarity which is not that of an explanation but that of a statement of fact" (143). On the nature of myth also see Kammen, *Mystic Chords of Memory*, 24–38; and Geertz, *Interpretation of Cultures*, 28–30, 33–141, 213–220.

39. Daniel Dougherty, "Oration," *Society of the Army of the Potomac, Twelfth Annual Reunion, Report of Proceedings*, Hartford, Conn., June 8, 1881 (New York: MacGowan & Slipper, 1881), 15; Oliver O. Howard, speech on Governor's Island, N.Y., September 28, 1894, Oliver Otis Howard Papers, Bowdoin College Library, New Brunswick, Maine.

40. Address by Colonel Richard Henry Lee, at dedication of a Confederate monument at Old Chapel, Clarke County, Va. (n.d.), reprinted in *CV* I (July 1893); Charles K. Moser to Joshua L. Chamberlain, Washington, D.C., February 10, 1908, Joshua Lawrence Chamberlain Papers, Bowdoin College Library.

41. Barthes, *Mythologies*, 143.

42. William H. Armstrong, "The Negro as a Soldier," *War Papers Read before the Indiana Commandery, MOLLUS* (Indianapolis: The Commandery, 1898), 316–317, 330.

43. *Kate Brownlee Sherwood, Camp-Fire, Memorial Day, and Other Poems* (Chicago: Jansen, McClurg, 1885), 116–123; J. M. Addeman, "Reminiscences of Two Years with the Colored Troops," *Personal Narratives, Rhode Island Soldiers and Sailors Historical Society* 2, no. 7 (Providence, 1880), 10–11. For a discussion of the impact of the black soldier on Northern white attitudes during and immediately after the war, see George M. Fredrickson, *The Black Image in the White Mind: The Debate on Afro-American Character and Destiny, 1817–1914* (New York: Harper & Row, 1971), 167–171.

44. George R. Sherman, "The Negro as a Soldier," *Personal Narratives . . . Rhode Island Soldiers and Sailors Historical Society* 8 (Providence, 1906), 18; Williams, *History of the Negro Troops*, xiii, x; William Ruger, "Our Soldiers as Citizens," delivered October 2, 1895, *War Papers, Wisconsin, MOLLUS*, vol. 2, 442–443. Armstrong, "The Negro as Soldier," cited Williams in a footnote (333). Other war papers would occasionally adopt his language, as in a Massachusetts essay in the late 1890s, which claimed that "the part taken by the colored soldier in the war . . . will in the hands of some future historian form a romantic chapter in the history of the progress of the Republic." See also Solon A. Carter, "Fourteen Months' Service with Colored Troops," *Civil War Papers Read before the Commandery of the State of Massachusetts, MOLLUS*, vol. 1 (Boston: The Commandery, 1900), 179. On reminiscences about the black soldier, the support of white officer-veterans, and the struggle for recognition for and by black veterans, also see Glatthaar, *Forged in Battle*, 256–264.

45. Donald R. Shaffer, "An Ambiguous Victory: Black Civil War Veterans from a

National Perspective," paper delivered at the American Historical Association annual meeting, New York, January 4, 1997 (courtesy of the author), 6–9. Also see Donald R. Shaffer, "Marching On: African-American Civil War Veterans in Postbellum America, 1865–1951" (Ph.D. diss., University of Maryland, College Park, 1996). Shaffer based his "conservative estimate" of $273 million in pension payments on a sample of 1,044 black veterans randomly selected from throughout the alphabet. Of these, 38.5 percent had a pension file at the National Archives with at least one successful application. The amount was computed by multiplying the estimated number of black pension files with a least one successful application (72,000) by the average amount paid per file ($3,759).

46. Nick Salvatore, *We All Got History: The Memory Books of Amos Webber* (New York: Times Books, 1996), 236–316, 320. On segregation in the GAR, see McConnell, *Glorious Contentment,* 213–218; and Wallace E. Davies, "The Problem of Race Segregation in the Grand Army of the Republic," *Journal of Southern History* 13 (August 1947), 354–372.

47. *Boston Globe,* August 1–3, 1887; *Boston Herald,* August 2, 1887; Salvatore, *We All Got History,* 290–291; Glatthaar, *Forged in Battle,* 262; Earl F. Mulderink, "Black Veterans and *Their* Civil War: African-American Veterans in Postbellum New Bedford, Massachusetts," paper delivered at the American Historical Association annual meeting, New York, January 4, 1997 (courtesy of author), 9, 18.

48. *Journal of the Thirty-Ninth Annual Encampment, Department of Massachusetts, Grand Army of the Republic,* meeting at Faneuil Hall, Boston, February 14–15, 1905 (Boston: Griggith-Stillings Press, 1905), 52; Mulderink, "Black Veterans and *Their* Civil War," 5–10. Carney did not actually receive his Congressional Medal of Honor until nearly forty years after Fort Wagner. Publicity posters for the 1887 Boston reunion featured Carney prominently, both with quotes and with his picture (Mulderink, "Black Veterans and *Their* Civil War," 18, n. 35). On discriminations and hardships experienced by black veterans generally, see Glatthaar, *Forged in Battle,* 252–257.

49. The autobiographies include Elijah Preston Marrs, *Life and History of Rev. Elijah P. Marrs* (Louisville: Bradley and Gilbert, 1885); Allen Parker, *Recollections of Slavery Times* (Worcester, Mass.: Charles A. Burbank, 1895); Rev. Samuel Harrison, *Samuel Harrison: His Life Story Told by Himself* (Pittsfield, Mass.: Press of the Eagle Publishing Co., 1899); Alexander Herritage Newton, *Out of the Briars: An Autobiography and Sketch of the Twenty-ninth Regiment Connecticut Volunteers* (Philadelphia: A.M.E. Book Concern, 1910); William Henry Singleton, *Recollections of My Slavery Days* (Peekskill, N.Y.: Highland Democrat Co., 1922); Peter Bruner, *A Slave's Adventures toward Freedom: Not Fiction, But the True Story of a Struggle* (Oxford, Ohio: by author, 1925); Robert Anderson, *From Slavery to Affluence: Memoirs of Robert Anderson, Ex-Slave* (Hemingford, Nebr.:

Hemingford Ledger, 1927). Many of these are available at the Schomburg Center, NYPL. One of the strangest of this genre is William H. Robinson, *From Log Cabin to the Pulpit; or, Fifteen Years in Slavery* (rpr. 1903; Eau Claire, Wis.: James H. Tifft, printer, 1913), copy in AAS. Robinson was a former slave, born in Wilmington, N.C. His tale is one of a catalogue of horrors, blood, brutality, and family breakup during slavery, as well as his service, first as a servant to his Confederate master who is killed in the war, and then as a Union soldier. Hamilton seems to be everywhere in the world and the nation, however, at crucial times in history. The narrative includes numerous apocryphal stories about hearing the guns firing at Fort Sumter as far away as North Carolina, meeting General Grant, and seeing Frederick Douglass waving while riding in Queen Victoria's carriage in London. Hamilton's varied career includes work as a singer and a banjo player for a group called the "Tennessee Singers" (not the famous Fisk Jubilee Singers), a stint as a Pullman porter, and eventually a tenure as a preacher about which he writes an extensive description of his conversion experience. It is hard to assess Hamilton's autobiography as literature; it might best be characterized as fictional history combined with a personal narrative. What is striking is that Hamilton uses Civil War imagery and place names all over the book. The book opens with numerous references to a dozen or more Civil War battles and a full-page picture of an American flag that had allegedly passed through the war "which freed the colored race from slavery and saved the Union from disruption. The old flag was fought under by the colored as well as the white boys." Some of these books served several aims: racial uplift, a particularly African American vision of their progress since slavery, and a statement of the meaning of the war and emancipation.

50. Joseph T. Wilson, *The Black Phalanx: A History of the Negro Soldiers in the United States in the Wars of 1775–1812, 1861–1865* (Hartford, Conn.: American Publishing Co., 1890); George Mike Arnold, "Colored Soldiers in the Union Army," *African Methodist Episcopal Church Review* 3 (January 1887), 257–266; Franklin, *George Washington Williams*, 169–170.

51. Kirk Savage, *Standing Soldiers, Kneeling Slaves: Race, War and Monument in Nineteenth Century America* (Princeton: Princeton University Press, 1997), 89–128; Franklin, *George Washington Williams*, 171–174; Williams, *History of the Negro Troops*, 328–330.

52. Savage, *Standing Soldiers, Kneeling Slaves*, 162–186, 189–190; Williams, *History of the Negro Troops*, 328, 331–332.

53. *New York Freeman*, August 20, 1887, in Shaffer, "An Ambiguous Victory," 16; Christian A. Fleetwood, *The Negro as a Soldier*, address delivered for the Negro Congress at the Cotton States and International Exposition, Atlanta, Ga., November 11–23, 1895 (Washington, D.C: Howard University Print, 1895), 18, copy

at Schomburg Center, NYPL. I am grateful to Donald Shaffer for bringing both of these speeches to my attention. On black veterans, also see John David Smith, *Black Judas: A Biography of William Hannibal Thomas* (Athens: University of Georgia Press, 1999).

54. See poems "Home, Sweet Home," "Bury the Hatchet," and "The Night of Battle," and the article Paul Hamilton Hayne, "The Defense of Fort Wagner," *Southern Bivouac* 1 (March, May–June 1883, April 1886, March 1886), 292–293, 354–355, 653, 602–608. The Hayne article makes a strong defense of the heroism of Confederates in defending Fort Wagner at Charleston Harbor, but not without also honoring Robert Gould Shaw and other Union officers who died there. See Isham, "Through the Wilderness to Richmond," *Sketches of War History* 1, Ohio, MOLLUS; Luther W. Minnigh, *Gettysburg: What They Did Here* (1892; rpr. Mt. Holly Springs, Penn.: Mt. Holly Printing Co., 1920), 13th edition, 134, copy in AAS; Sergeant H. Nachtigal, oration, dedication of monument to 75th regiment, Pennsylvania Infantry, October 8, 1888, in *Pennsylvania at Gettysburg: Ceremonies at the Dedication of the Monuments Erected by the Commonwealth of Pennsylvania to Mark the Positions of the Pennsylvania Commands Engaged in the Battle,* 2 vols. (Harrisburg: State of Pennsylvania, 1893) vol. 1, 406, AAS; Colonel A. N. Fenn, "Dedicatory Address," in *History of the Dedication of the Soldier's Monument, Sharon, Litchfield County, Connecticut,* dedicated August 6, 1885 (Amenia, N.Y.: Charles Walsh, 1885), 11, AAS.

55. Edward P. Tobie, "A Trip to Richmond as Prisoner of War," read November 15, 1876, in *Personal Narratives . . . Rhode Island Soldiers and Sailors Historical Society* 1, 18–19, 26–27; Captain J. A. Watrous, "Mosby and His Men," read February 2, 1887, *War Papers* 2, Wisconsin, MOLLUS, 305–307.

56. Henry W. Grady, *The New South: Writings and Speeches of Henry Grady* (Savannah, Ga.: Beehive Press, 1971), 11–12. On Grady and the ideology of New South boosterism, see Paul M. Gaston, *The New South Creed: A Study in Southern Mythmaking* (New York: Knopf, 1970). On Grady's speech in New York, and on the growth of a nationalized commerce through mass-market advertising and mail order catalogues, all of which served the ends of reconciliation, see Edward L. Ayers, *The Promise of the New South: Life after Reconstruction* (New York: Oxford University Press, 1992), 21, 81–103. Industrial growth and development were a major preoccupation of the South's business and political leaders. They produced magazines and other publications to induce Northern investment in the South as gestures both of good business and sectional reconciliation. See *The New South,* Birmingham, Ala., August 1886, copy in PL, DU.

57. *The Heroes of the Civil War,* March 1889, produced by W. Duke, Sons & Co., PL, DU. These albums were mass-produced and distributed as commemorative collectors' volumes.

58. See McConnell, *Glorious Contentment,* 103–110; Warren I. Susman, "'Personality' and the Making of Twentieth-Century Culture," in John Higham and Paul Conkin, eds., *New Directions in American Intellectual History* (Baltimore: Johns Hopkins University Press, 1979), 212–226; Samuel C. Armstrong to Bachelder, Hampton, Va., February 6, 1884, *Bachelder Papers* 2, 1002–1003; *National Tribune,* December 27, 1883, in McConnell, *Glorious Contentment,* 106. Also see William T. Sherman, "Camp-Fires of the Grand Army of the Republic," *North American Review* 47 (November 1888), 502.

59. *Century* 35 (December 1887), 330; George L. Kilmer, "A Note of Peace: Reunions of 'the Blue and the Gray,'" *Century* 36 (July 1888), 440–442; Kilmer, "Fraternization—The Blue and the Gray," *Century* 38 (May 1889), 157; Salvatore, *We All Got History,* 222–223; *The Veteran* (Worcester, Mass.) vol. 1, June 1882, 279–283, copy in Newberry Library, Chicago. Confederate veterans also participated at a Bunker Hill anniversary event in Boston in 1887. *Century* editors took pride in the reunion that they believed their war series had helped to stimulate. See "Soldiers' Memorial Services," *Century* 38 (May 1889), 156–157. On Blue-Gray reunions, also see Buck, *Road to Reunion,* 266–272.

60. Reardon, *Pickett's Charge in History and Memory,* 84–107, quote, 101.

61. On the battle flags dispute, see *NYT,* June 16–17, 1888; Reardon, *Pickett's Charge in History and Memory,* 96–97; Silber, *Romance of Reunion,* 97–98; Buck, *Road to Reunion,* 284–286; Wallace E. Davies, *Patriotism on Parade: The Story of Veterans and Hereditary Organizations in America, 1783–1900* (Cambridge: Harvard University Press, 1955), 250–260. Quote about "bosh" in *National Tribune,* June 14, 1888, in Reardon, *Pickett's Charge in History and Memory,* 110.

62. John C. Underwood, *Report of Proceedings Incidental to the Erection and Dedication of the Confederate Monument; Reception and Entertainment of Renowned Southern Generals and Other Distinguished Personages, at Chicago, Illinois; Luncheon and Banquet Given Them at Cincinnati, Ohio, and Their Military Greeting at Fort Thomas, Kentucky, May 29–June 1, 1895,* souvenir edition (Chicago: William Johnston Printing, 1896), 4–6, copy in Newberry Library, Chicago.

63. Ibid., 7–8, 23–28, 35.

64. Ibid., 35, 37, 118; *Chicago Tribune,* May 31, 1895; *Chicago Inter-Ocean,* May 31, 1895.

65. Underwood, *Report of Proceedings,* 118.

66. H. V. Boynton, comp., *Dedication of the Chickamauga and Chattanooga National Military Park, September 18–20, 1895* (Washington, D.C.: Government Printing Office, 1896), 12, 14, 140–141, 179–181.

67. Ibid., 187, 191, 275.

68. Henry L. Higginson to Charles Elliot, and Elliot's response, June 5, 1890, vol. 3 of "The Soldiers Book," two large scrapbooks prepared by Henry Lee Higginson

and Ida A. Higginson and dedicated to their son Alexander Henry Higginson, Christmas, 1894, HLH. On manliness and sports at Harvard and in colleges generally, and on Higginson's contribution of Soldiers Field, see Kim Townsend, *Manhood at Harvard: William James and Others* (New York: Norton, 1996), 80–158, 103, 106, 277. On the revival of the martial ideal in American culture broadly, see Jackson Lears, *No Place of Grace: Antimodernism and the Transformation of American Culture* (New York: Pantheon, 1981), 97–140.

69. Higginson, "The Soldiers Field," speech delivered in Sever Hall, Harvard University, June 10, 1890, in "Soldiers Book," vol. 2. Also see *Four Addresses by Henry Lee Higginson* (Boston: D. B. Updike, 1902), 3–25.

70. Charles Thorndike to Higginson, June 11, 1890; Lincoln Ripley Stone to Higginson, June 11, 1890; Mary Putnam (Lowell) to Higginson, July 9, 1890; Vincent Yardley Bowditch to Higginson, June 11, 1890, all in "Soldiers Book," vol. 1.

71. William James to Higginson, June 20, 1890; Henry Cabot Lodge to Charles Stebbens, July 27, 1890; Edward William Hooper to Higginson, June 24, 1890; Rutherford B. Hayes to Arnold A. Rand, December 24, 1890; Charles Fessenden Morse to Higginson, June 17, 1890; Mary Louisa Cabot to Higginson, June 11, 1890, in ibid., vol. 1.

72. Silas Weir Mitchell to Higginson, October 16, 1890; George Russell Agassiz to Higginson, n.d. (nephew of Higginson); Elizabeth Rogers Cabot to Higginson, June 19, 1890; Lucy B. Powell to Higginson, June 16, 1890; and Roxana L. Dabney to Higginson, n.d., 1890, in ibid., vol. 1.

73. Oliver Wendell Holmes Jr., "The Soldier's Faith," address delivered on Memorial Day, May 30, 1895, at a meeting called by the graduating class of Harvard University, in *Speeches by Oliver Wendell Holmes* (Boston: Little, Brown, 1934), 56, 58–59, 64. On Holmes, see Aaron, *Unwritten War,* 160–162; and Wilson, *Patriotic Gore,* 743–796. On similar attitudes among Southern veterans, see Ayers, *Promise of the New South,* 336–338.

74. Ibid., 59, 63–64. On martial heroism and antimodernism, see T. J. Jackson Lears, *No Place of Grace: Antimodernism and the Transformation of American Culture, 1880–1920,* New York: Pantheon, 1981), esp. 98–124, and on Holmes, 123–124.

7. *The Literature of Reunion and Its Discontents*

1. William S. McFeely, *Grant: A Biography* (New York: Norton, 1981), 478–493.

2. Ibid., 514; Wilson, *Patriotic Gore,* 142, 152. On Grant, historical memory, and the "memoir battles" he saw himself engaged in with other generals, especially Southerners, see William A. Blair, "Grant's Second Civil War: The Battle for Historical Memory," in Gary W. Gallagher, ed., *The Spotsylvania Campaign:*

Military Campaigns of the Civil War (Chapel Hill: University of North Carolina Press, 1998), 223–254. On Grant in American memory, see the forthcoming book by Joan Waugh.

3. *Personal Memoirs of U. S. Grant,* 2 vols. (New York: Charles L. Webster & Co., 1885–86), vol. 1, 230–231.

4. Ibid., vol. 1, 224–226.

5. Ibid., vol. 1, 312–314, 316.

6. Wilson, *Patriotic Gore,* 152; *Personal Memoirs,* vol. 1, 330–357, quote on 355–356.

7. *Personal Memoirs,* vol. 2, 177–178.

8. Ibid., vol. 2, 489–490, 492, 495–496. There are many celebrated responses to Grant's *Memoirs* in the literary world. One of the most poignant was the exchange, of a sort, between the English literary aristocrat Matthew Arnold and Mark Twain. Arnold wrote an essay on the *Memoirs* that was reprinted in the United States. Arnold's smug assessment included a dismissal of Grant's use of grammar: "I found a language all astray in its use of *will* and *shall, should* and *would* . . . an English without charm and high breeding." But Arnold also admired Grant's sense of himself as "humane, simple, modest" and some of the language as "straightforward, nervous, firm, possessing in general the high merit of saying clearly in the fewest possible words what had to be said." In his "Rejoinder" at a speech at the Annual Reunion of the Army and Navy Club of Connecticut, April 27, 1887, Twain declared that "Grant's grammar is as good as anybody's." "Great books," said Twain to enormous applause from the veterans, "are weighed and measured by their style and matter, not by the trimmings and shadings of their grammar. There is that about the sun which makes us forget his spots: and when we think of General Grant our pulses quicken and his grammar vanishes: we only remember that this is the simple soldier who, all untaught of the silken phrasemakers, linked words together with an art surpassing the art of the schools, and put into them a something which will still bring to American ears . . . the roll of his vanished drums and the tread of his marching hosts." See John Y. Simon, ed., *General Grant by Matthew Arnold with a Rejoinder by Mark Twain* (Carbondale: Southern Illinois University Press, 1966), 13, 56–57.

9. Thomas M. Pitkin, *The Captain Departs: Ulysses S. Grant's Last Campaign* (Carbondale: Southern Illinois University Press, 1973), 46–129; *NYT,* July 25, 1885.

10. *NYT,* July 25, August 5, 8, 1885; *Harper's Weekly,* August 8, 1885.

11. *Harper's Weekly,* August 1, 1885; *NYT,* July 25, 31, August 5, 8, 1885.

12. On magazines and the sentimentalism of reconciliation, see Silber, *Romance of Reunion,* 93–158, esp. 113–120; Buck, *Road to Reunion,* 228–241; Diffley, *Where My Heart Is Turning Ever,* xi–xlvii; and John Tebbel and Mary Ellen Zuckerman, *The Magazine in America, 1741–1990* (New York: Oxford University Press, 1991),

57–72. From 1865 to World War I is the "Golden Age" of American magazines. Tebbell and Zuckerman report 700 magazines in 1865 in the United States, 1,200 by 1870, 3,300 by 1885. *Youth's Companion* reached a subscription rate of 385,000 by 1885, and the literary journals *Scribner's* and *Harper's* (weekly and monthly) surpassed 100,000. Due to its Civil War series, *Century* exceeded 200,000 by 1885 (57–60).

13. Joyce Appleby, "Reconciliation and the Northern Novelist, 1865–1800," *Civil War History* 10 (June 1964), 117–129; Silber, *Romance of Reunion,* 115–116. With insight, Silber shows how "writers relied on a gendered metaphor to make a political statement about the power relations between the sections in the postwar period. Also see Elizabeth Young, *Disarming the Nation: Women's Writing and the American Civil War* (Chicago: University of Chicago Press, 1999).

14. Otto H. Olsen, *Carpetbagger's Crusade: The Life of Albion Winegar Tourgée* (Baltimore: Johns Hopkins University Press, 1965), 12–25. See also David W. Blight, "For Something beyond the Battlefield: Frederick Douglass and the Struggle for the Memory of the Civil War," *Journal of American History* 75 (Spring 1989), 1156–1178; and Leonard, *Above the Battle,* 26, 28–29. Tourgée's first novel was *Toinette: A Tale of the South* (New York: J. B. Ford, 1874). Between 1879 and 1883, he laid out his vision of Reconstruction and the nation's responsibility to the freedmen in several works of fiction. See *A Fool's Errand: A Novel of the South during Reconstruction* (New York: Ford, Howard & Hulbert, 1879); *Bricks without Straw: A Novel* (New York: Ford, Howard & Hulbert, 1880); *A Royal Gentleman* (New York: Ford, Howard & Hulbert, 1881), a revision of *Toinette; John Eax and Mamelon; or, The South without the Shadow* (New York: Ford, Howard & Hulbert, 1882); and *Hot Plowshares: A Novel* (New York: Ford, Howard & Hulbert, 1883).

15. Albion W. Tourgée, "The South as a Field for Fiction," *Forum* 6 (December 1888), 404. On Tourgée's critique of Southern fiction and the development of Southern myths, see Paul M. Gaston, *The New South Creed: A Study in Southern Mythmaking* (New York: Knopf, 1970), 171, 182–184.

16. Tourgée, "The South as a Field for Fiction," 411–413. See also C. Vann Woodward, *The Burden of Southern History* (1960; rpr. New York: New American Library, 1968, rev. ed.), 32–39, 134–149.

17. Albion W. Tourgée, "The Renaissance of Nationalism," *North American Review* 144 (January 1887), 2–3, 5–6.

18. Albion W. Tourgée, *An Appeal to Caesar* (New York: Fords, Howard, & Hulbert, 1884), 37, 43–45; Tourgée, "The South as a Field for Fiction," 412, 405. Robert Lively took issue with Tourgée's claim that the South won the literary war. He studied some 512 novels over a broad expanse of time and claimed that "if the northern mind were ever so completely captured, it was not held for very long."

See Robert A. Lively, *Fiction Fights the Civil War: An Unfinished Chapter in the Literary History of the American People* (Chapel Hill: University of North Carolina Press, 1957), 42–43. On the ways that sympathy for the Confederacy still has a deep hold on American popular attitudes toward the war, see Tony Horwitz, *Confederates in the Attic: Dispatches from the Unfinished Civil War* (New York: Pantheon, 1998).

19. Tourgée, "The South as a Field for Fiction," 409–410. Also see Buck, *Road to Reunion,* 242–243. Tourgée, according to Buck, "was a legion in himself," but one that could only harp on "the old issues of moral reform and justice to the Negro." Inevitability may be the ultimate explanation of some historical phenomena, but the rub comes in the assumptions we employ to make such arguments. On the faithful slave in Southern fiction about the war, see Lively, *Fiction Fights the Civil War,* 47–54.

20. Tourgée, "The South as a Field for Fiction," 409–410.

21. The term "local color" implied marginality and exoticism, but it may always have been inadequate for the complexity of this genre. Historians have suggested that it "trivialized" the writing and "condescendingly" portrayed the myriad of authors who practiced it. See Ayers, *Promise of the New South,* 340; and David Herbert Donald, *Liberty and Union* (Lexington, Mass.: D. C. Heath, 1978), 267. The genre included rich regional literatures, including what Bret Harte created for the California gold fields and mining towns; Mark Twain for the Mississippi River region; George Washington Cable for the Creoles of Louisiana; Constance Fenimore Woolson, Edward Eggleston, and James Whitcomb Riley for the Middle West, the Great Lakes, and Hossier "plain folks"; Thomas Nelson Page and many others for the "ole Virginia" planters; and perhaps most famous of all, Joel Chandler Harris for middle Georgia blacks and whites. On Cooke and local color, see Thomas L. Connelly and Barbara L. Bellows, *God and General Longstreet: The Lost Cause and the Southern Mind* (Baton Rouge: Louisiana State University Press, 1982), 52–63. On race and the genre, see Louis D. Rubin Jr., "Southern Local Color and the Black Man," *Southern Review* 6 (October, 1970), 1011–1030.

22. See Benedict Anderson, *Imagined Communities: Reflections on the Origin and Spread of Nationalism* (London: Verso, 1983), esp. 1–7, 187–206; George Santayana, from *Reason and Religion,* quoted in Geertz, *The Interpretation of Cultures,* 87.

23. Mrs. Paul Hamilton Hayne to Thomas Nelson Page, May 10, 1888, quoted in Fred Hobson, *Tell about the South: The Southern Rage to Explain* (Baton Rouge: Louisiana State University Press, 1983), 129.

24. Thomas Nelson Page, "Marse Chan," in *In Ole Virginia, or Marse Chan and Other Stories* (1887; rpr. New York: Scribner's, 1920), 4, 10. "Marse Chan" first

appeared in *Century* 27 (April 1884), 932–942, just as the editors were planning to launch their Civil War series. Indeed, such stories by Page, Joel Chandler Harris, and others often ran in the same issues as the *Battles and Leaders* articles. For a serious if rosy reading of Page, see Buck, *Road to Reunion*, 220–224. For less favorable but important readings of Page, see Wilson, *Patriotic Gore*, 604–616; Hobson, *Tell about the South*, 132–144; and Aaron, *Unwritten War*, 285–288. On the plantation legends, see Gaston, *The New South Creed*, 167–185; Catherine Clinton, *Tara Revisited: Women, War, and the Plantation Legend* (New York: Abbeville Press, 1995), 191–198, 206–213; and Francis Pendleton Gaines, *The Southern Plantation: A Study in the Development and the Accuracy of a Tradition* (1924; rpr. Gloucester, Mass.: Peter Smith, 1962), 1–142. On Page's work and its relationship to the New South Movement, see Wayne Mixon, *Southern Writers and the New South Movement, 1865–1913* (Chapel Hill: University of North Carolina Press, 1980), 32–41.

25. Page, "Meh Lady," in *In Ole Virginia*, 80, 84–85, 138. On Page's creation of this "mythos" of the faithful slaves, see Rubin, "Southern Local Color and the Black Man," 1015–1016.

26. John R. Proctor to Page, June 4, 1886, Frankfort, Ky.; Henry W. Grady to Page, April 25, 1888, Atlanta, Ga.; C. C. Buel, *Century*, to Page, September 9, 1885; H. M. Alden, *Harper's*, to Page, April 10, 1885, July 23, 1886; J. M. Stoddart, *Lippincott's*, November 23, 1886; Charles Scribner, Scribner's Sons, to Page, October 19, 22, 1885; Bessie Paschal Wright to Page, 1885, New York; Joel Chandler Harris to Page, December 31, 1885, Atlanta, Thomas Nelson Page Papers, PL, DU, boxes 1–2.

27. Thomas Nelson Page, *The Old South: Essays Social and Political* (New York: Scribner's, 1892), 4–5. See also Hobson, *Tell about the South*, 136–146. Hobson makes the telling point that in Page's work slavery is often portrayed as a curse, but all the suffering was experienced by whites.

28. On Harris, see Paul M. Cousins, *Joel Chandler Harris: A Biography* (Baton Rouge: Louisiana State University Press, 1968); R. Bruce Bickley Jr., *Joel Chandler Harris* (Boston: Twayne, 1978); Ayers, *Promise of the New South*, 340–342; Wayne Mixon, "Joel Chandler Harris, the Yeoman Tradition, and the New South Movement," *Georgia Historical Quarterly* 61, no. 4 (1977), 308–317.

29. See Rubin, "Southern Local Color and the Black Man," 1016–1022; Mixon, "Joel Chandler Harris," 309–315; Herbert F. Smith, "Joel Chandler Harris's Contributions to *Scribner's Monthly* and *Century*, 1880–1887," *Georgia Historical Quarterly* 47 (June 1963), 169–179; Michael Flusche, "Joel Chandler Harris and the Folklore of Slavery," *Journal of American Studies* 9 (1975), 347–363; Frank Luther Mott, *Golden Multitudes: The Story of Bestsellers in the United States* (New York: Macmillan, 1947), 310.

30. Joel Chandler Harris, "A Story of the War," in *Uncle Remus: His Songs and His Sayings*, illus. A. B. Frost (1880; rpr. New York: Appleton, 1926), 201–212. On the change in the two versions of the stories and the reconciliationist character of the second, see Eric J. Sundquist, *To Wake the Nations: Race in the Making of American Literature* (Cambridge: Harvard University Press, 1993), 325–327; and William L. Van Deburg, *Slavery and Race in American Popular Culture* (Madison: University of Wisconsin Press, 1984), 96–98.

31. For the Ananias story, see Joel Chandler Harris, *Balaam and His Master and Other Sketches and Stories* (Boston: Houghton Mifflin, 1891), 113–148; "An Ambuscade" is in Joel Chandler Harris, *Tales of the Home Folks in Peace and War* (Boston: Houghton Mifflin, 1898), 184–214, 293–344.

32. "The Comedy of War," in Harris, *Tales of the Home Folks in Peace and War*, 148–183.

33. Ibid.

34. See Larry Gara, *The Liberty Line: The Legend of the Underground Railroad* (Lexington: University of Kentucky Press).

35. Wilbur H. Siebert, *The Underground Railroad from Slavery to Freedom*, intro. Albert Bushnell Hart (New York: Macmillan, 1898), 1–2. For a copy of the circular letter, see Wilbur Siebert Papers, HLH, scrapbook vol. 1. The circular letters asked seven questions: about routes, period of activity, method of operation, memorable incidents, the correspondent's personal connections, names and addresses of witnesses, and a biographical sketch. See Oliver Mills to Siebert, October 18, 1894, Lewis, Iowa, Siebert Papers, Iowa, vol. 1.

36. Rev. Erastus Blakeslee to Siebert, August 28, 1896, Siebert Papers, Conn., vol. 4; Siebert, *Underground Railroad*, 11–12. On the problem of histories written from recollections and on the use as well as mistrust of oral history in the late nineteenth century, see Kammen, *Mystic Chords of Memory*, 96.

37. James Baynes to Siebert, March 14, 1896, Hodge, Iowa, H. D. Platt to Siebert, March 20, 1896, Franklin, Nebr., Siebert Papers, Ill., vol. 5; "Its Tracks Were Clouded . . .," *Felicity Times*, Felicity, Ohio, July 6, 1893, Siebert Papers, Ohio, vol. 6; no author, 4-page sketch, "Underground Railroad," from Clinton County, Iowa, Siebert Papers, Iowa, vol. 1.

38. "Reminiscences of the Underground Railroad," *Republican Leader* (Salem, Ind.) November 17, 1893–April 27, 1894, Siebert Papers, Ind., vol. 1; "Sojourner Truth," *Chicago Inter Ocean*, September 24, 1893, Lucy Maynard Salmon to Siebert, April 7, 1896, Vassar College, Poughkeepsie, N.Y., Siebert Papers, Ill., vols. 1, 5. For Siebert's local lore collecting, see series, "Local History: The Underground Railroad of Forty Years Ago," *The Spirit of the Times*, Batavia, N.Y., February 8, 15, 1896, Siebert Papers, N.Y., vol. 1; *Chicago Tribune*, January 29, 1893, in Siebert Papers, Ohio, vol. 6. Articles from *Johnson's Lakeshore Home*

Magazine are strewn throughout the 38 volumes of scrapbooks. He also collected many examples, some in transcriptions done by correspondents, of testimonials and tributes to old abolitionists taken from county histories. See, for example, Harriet K. Keeler, "Betsy Mix Cowles and the Antislavery Cause of Austinburgh, Ashtabula County, Ohio," *The History of Ashtabula County, Ohio,* 100–101, Siebert Papers, Ohio, vol. 1.

39. H. B. Leeper to Siebert, n.d., but likely 1896, Princeton, Ill.; Rev. Erastus Blakeslee to Siebert, August 28, 1896; H. D. Platt to Siebert, March 20, 1896, Franklin, Nebr.; *Boston Transcript,* September 9, 1897, in Siebert Papers, Ill., vol. 5, Conn., vol. 4, Ohio, vol. 7.

40. See *Rev. Calvin Fairbank during Slavery Times* (Chicago: Patriotic Publishing Co., 1890). On the survival of an abolitionist tradition and its transference to the next generations, see James M. McPherson, *The Abolitionist Legacy: From Reconstruction to the NAACP* (Princeton: Princeton University Press, 1975), 3–10, 299–393.

41. C. D. Booth, "Ashtabula as a Station on the UGRR," report for U.S. History 13, A. B. Hart, Harvard University, in Siebert Papers, Ohio, vol. 2.

42. "Some Stirring Events That Occurred before the War, Revived by the Death of Mrs. Martha McIntire," "Helping Runaway Slaves to Canada and Freedom, and the Timely Assistance Rendered by Adams County Abolitionists," n.d., newspaper clippings provided by O. B. Kirkpatrick, Cherry Fork, Ohio; "True Story of the Underground Railway," *Tribune* (Marysville, Ohio), September 29, 1897, Siebert Papers, Ohio, vol. 1.

43. George Churchill to Siebert, January 29, 1896; H. C. Pemberton to Siebert, January 21, 1932, Cleveland, Ohio; H. D. Platt to Siebert, March 20, 1896, Franklin, Nebr., Siebert Papers, Ill., vol. 5, Ohio, vol. 1.

44. W. E. Corner to Siebert, n.d., probably 1896; Henry M. Huggins to Siebert, October 30, 1895, Hillsboro, Ohio; "Black Joe," in *Johnson's Lake Shore Home Magazine,* September 1887, Siebert Papers, Iowa, vol. 1, Ohio, vols. 1–2, Ill., vol. 5. See Joel Chandler Harris, "Free Joe and the Rest of the World," in Harris, *Free Joe and Other Georgian Sketches* (New York: Scribner's, 1887), 1–20. "Free Joe" is a free black in slavery times in Geogia; he is a lost soul between two worlds. As Harris describes his condition, Joe "was a black atom, drifting hither and thither without an owner, blown about by all the winds of circumstance, and given over to shiftlessness" (1).

45. Mrs. E. G. Platt to Siebert, n.d., Civil Bend, Iowa, Siebert Papers, Iowa, vol. 10.

46. Nathan Irvin Huggins, *Harlem Renaissance* (New York: Oxford University Press, 1971), 248–249, 251–253, 255–256. On minstrelsy in the postwar period, see Robert C. Toll, *Blacking Up: The Minstrel Show in Nineteenth-Century America* (New York: Oxford University Press, 1974), 134–274. See especially 201–216 for

the ways that whites in blackface as well as black performers themselves portrayed, or were compelled to portray, grotesque images of the old plantation life of slavery times. Indeed, as in so much sentimental fiction, the plantation was the setting of minstrel shows. For a class analysis of minstrelsy, see Eric Lott, *Love and Theft: Blackface Minstrelsy and the American Working Class* (New York: Oxford University Press, 1993).

47. Willis Boughton to Siebert, January 5, 1894, Athens, Ohio; Mrs. Levi P. Monse Gould to Siebert, March 7, 1896, Siebert Papers, vol. 10.

48. Benjamin Blackstone to Siebert, March 9, 1896, Martinsville, Ind.; P. H. White to Siebert, September 11, 1894, Salesville, Ohio, Siebert Papers, Ohio, vols. 1, 7, Ill., vol. 7. Blackstone warns Siebert to "pay no attention to county histories as they abound in mistakes and perversions . . . county histories are written in job lots by one or more interviewers who publish biographies and likeness. My father would never be interviewed by them." After providing considerable detail about routes, White admits to Siebert: "There are many incidents connected with this work but my memory is so bad that I cannot undertake it." Interview with Rutherford B. Hayes, Spring 1893, Siebert Papers, Ohio, vol. 6. For references to John Brown, see for example, Daniel H. Wheeler to Siebert, May 29, 1900, Omaha, Nebr.; S. H. Adams to Siebert, n.d., Tabor, Iowa, Siebert Papers, Iowa, vol. 10. There are numerous references to *Uncle Tom's Cabin* in Siebert's collection. See L. M. Jewett to Siebert, March 23, 1892, Athens, Ohio; Mary C. Thorne to Siebert, March 3, 1892, Selma, Ohio; Henry Howe, "Eliza Harris's Escape," Historical Collections of Ohio, Siebert Papers, Ohio, vols. 1, 3.

49. Wilson, *Patriotic Gore*, 613; Howells, quoted in Alan Trachtenberg, *The Incorporation of America: Culture and Society in the Gilded Age* (New York: Hill and Wang, 1982), 185 (also see 182–201). On the Civil War's impact on the development of realism, see David W. Shi, *Facing Facts: Realism in American Thought and Culture, 1850–1920* (New York: Oxford University Press, 1995), 45–65.

50. Howells to Edmund W. Gosse, January 24, 1886, Auburndale, Mass., and Howells to S. Weir Mitchell, October 20, 1885, Boston, in Robert C. Leitz III, ed., *William Dean Howells, Selected Letters*, vol. 3: 1882–1891 (Boston: Twayne, 1980), 134, 152; *Harper's Monthly*, November 1889, May 1886, January 1886, in James W. Simpson, ed., *Editor's Study by Wiliam Dean Howells* (Troy, N.Y.: Whitson Publishing Co., 1983), 3, 22, 225.

51. Ruskin to Charles Eliot Norton, in Aaron, *Unwritten War*, 337.

52. Leonard, *Above the Battle*, 20; Albion Tourgée, *Figs and Thistles: A Romance on the Western Reserve* (New York: Fords, Howard, & Hulbert, 1879), 259–261, 264–277, 271–272.

53. Leonard, *Above the Battle*, 23. In a fascinating analysis, Leonard contends that the "most important legacy" of the war among writers was "silence." He demon-

strates a kind of "moral" and "political" silence in works as different as Theodore Roosevelt's *Rough Riders* (1899) and William Faulkner's *Sartoris* (1929). He also points to lesser-known writers such as Harold Frederic and Francis Grierson, neither of whom were old enough to have fought in the war, but who fashioned a local literature about the war's aftermath in their counties (Frederic—Oneida, N.Y., and Grierson—Sangamon, Ill.). See Thomas F. O'Connell, ed., *Harold Frederic's Stories of York State* (Syracuse, N.Y.: Syracuse University Press, 1966); and Francis Grierson, *The Valley of the Shadows* (Boston: Houghton Mifflin, 1909). Their stories tended to be about the farmers back home during the war, for whom the conflict remains largely a mystery. In one of Frederic's stories, a veteran returns home "shot through the tongue . . . Whenever he attempted conversation, people moved away, or began boisterous dialogues with one another to drown him out." The case for silence can be overstated. It depends on how broadly one wishes to define literature, whether to include soldiers' reminiscences as a whole. Moreover, Leonard largely ignores Ambrose Bierce. On the incapacity or refusal of novelists to confront the realism of the war, also see Aaron, *Unwritten War,* xiii–xix, 327–340. On Crane, see Christopher Benfrey, *The Double Life of Stephen Crane* (New York: Knopf, 1992), esp. 102–122, 201–219.

54. Crane, *The Red Badge of Courage: An Episode of the American Civil War,* ed. Henry Binder (1895; rpr. New York: Avon Books, 1987), 14, 17, 41. See also Benfrey, *The Double Life of Stephen Crane,* 102–122; and "The Veteran," in *The Little Regiment and Other Episodes of the American Civil War* (New York: Appleton, 1896), 186. Hamlin Garland is another writer who wrote in an antiromantic vein about Civil War experience and its aftermath. See especially his "The Return of a Private" (1891), reprinted in Eric Solomon, ed., *The Faded Banners: A Treasure of Nineteenth-Century Civil War Fiction* (New York: Promontory Press, 1992), 310–321.

55. "Realities of War," *The Veteran* (August 1881), 8–9; Edward Porter Alexander, *Military Memoirs of a Confederate: A Critical Narrative* (1907; rpr. New York: Da Capo Press, 1993), 491.

56. Major E. J. Harkness, "Reflections Concerning the War," delivered February 2, 1905, *Military Essays and Recollections, Illinois, MOLLUS,* vol. 4, 523–524, 539, 542–543.

57. On the stages and character of prison narratives, see Fabian, *Unvarnished Truth.* See also John Ransom, *Andersonville Diary: Escape and List of the Dead, with Name, Co., Regiment, Date of Death and No. of Grave in Cemetery* (Auburn, N.Y.: John Ransom, 1881). On Ransom's fabricated diary, also see William Marvel, "Johnny Ransom's Imagination," *Civil War History* 41 (September 1995), 181–189; and T. H. Mann, "A Yankee in Andersonville," *Century* 40 (July 1890),

447–461; (August 1890), 606–622. *Century* sought balance by publishing pieces on Northern prisons. See Horace Carpenter, "Plain Living at Johnson's Island," *Century* 41 (March 1891), 705–718; John A. Wyeth, "Cold Cheer at Camp Morton," *Century* 41 (April 1891), 844–852; and W. R. Holloway, "Treatment of Prisoners at Camp Morton, a Reply to 'Cold Cheer at Camp Morton,'" *Century* 42 (September 1891), 757–770.

58. Asa B. Isham, Henry M. Davidson, and Henry B. Furness, *Prisoners of War and Military Prisons: Personal Narratives of Experience in the Prisons at Richmond, Danville, Macon, Andersonville, Savannah, Millen, Charleston, and Columbia* (Cincinnati: Lyman & Cushing, 1890), 159, 266–267. On the images of blacks and uses of racial assumptions in Northern prison narratives, see Fabian, "Transient and Somewhat Fugitive Histories," 6–14.

59. Isham, Davidson, and Furness, *Prisoners of War and Military Prisons,* 388–390, 474–475.

60. Carey McWilliams, *Ambrose Bierce* (New York: Albert and Charles Boni, 1929), 28–140, 326–335; Paul Fatout, *Ambrose Bierce: The Devil's Lexicographer* (Norman: University of Oklahoma Press, 1951), 36–58, 310–318; Wilson, *Patriotic Gore,* 617–621; Aaron, *Unwritten War,* 181–183, 191–192; William McCann, ed., *Ambrose Bierce's Civil War* (1956; rpr. Washington, D.C.: Regnery Gateway, 1988), iii–xi.

61. Delbanco, *The Death of Satan,* 138, 145; Aaron, *Unwritten War,* 190; Wilson, *Patriotic Gore,* 622.

62. *San Francisco Examiner,* June 12, 1887, quoted in Fatout, *Ambrose Bierce,* 159; Bierce, quoted in McWilliams, *Ambrose Bierce,* 311; Wilson, *Patriotic Gore,* 622. Also see Aaron, *Unwritten War,* 183.

63. "What I Saw of Shiloh," in *The Collected Works of Ambrose Bierce,* 10 vols. (New York: Neale Publishing Company, 1909–11), vol. 1, 234–269.

64. Ibid., 234–269.

65. Ibid., 265; "Occurrence at Owl Creek Bridge" in McCann, ed., *Ambrose Bierce's Civil War,* 96–98.

66. "One of the Missing," in ibid., 122–123, 129.

67. "The Age Romantic" and "The Passing of Satire," in *Collected Works of Ambrose Bierce,* vol. 9, 313, 316, vol. 10, 281–284. Although Bierce did not attend veterans' reunions, as if he did not want to ruin his own memories, he did write long letters to old comrades in the Ninth Indiana on the occasion of some of their meetings. In those letters he would often describe his travels back to old battlefields and regions of campaigns. In one such letter in 1904, Bierce described the Cheat River country, where he had just "passed a few of the most interesting weeks of my life following the track of the Ninth," as if in a "kind of dreamland." See Fatout, *Ambrose Bierce,* 261–262. For Bierce's reactionary views on the

death penalty, see "The War Everlasting," *Collected Works of Ambrose Bierce*, vol. 9, 317–326.

68. "The Confederate Flags," in *Collected Works of Ambrose Bierce*, vol. 4, 336–337.

69. "The Hesitating Veteran," in ibid., vol. 4, 116–118; "The Bivouac of the Dead," in McCann, ed., *Ambrose Bierce's Civil War*, 72–73. Also see Aaron, *Unwritten War*, 189–191.

70. David Levering Lewis, *W. E. B. Du Bois: Biography of a Race, 1868–1919* (New York: Henry Holt, 1993), 1–210; David W. Blight and Robert Gooding Williams, eds., The Strange Meaning of Being Black: Du Bois's American Tragedy," introduction to Du Bois, *The Souls of Black Folk* (1903; rpr. Boston: Bedford Books, 1997), 3–8.

71. Du Bois, *Souls*, 103–104, 107, 109, 111. Chapters seven and eight of *Souls*, "Of the Black Belt" and "Of the Quest of the Golden Fleece," respectively, were revisions of an original piece, "The Negro as He Really Is," *World's Work* (June 1901), 848–866.

72. Du Bois, *Souls*, 111. See also Thomas Nelson Page, *The Negro: The Southerner's Problem* (New York: Scribner's, 1904), 163–165. In "The Old-Time Negro," Page laments at length the "passing away" of what he perceived as the once ubiquitous plantation darky, who "once . . . was as well known as the cotton-plant and the oak tree." "Their memory is still cherished in the hearts of those to whom they stood in a relation which cannot be explained to and cannot be understood by those who did not know it as a vital part of their home life," Page insisted (165).

73. Du Bois to William James, June 12, 1906, W. E. B. Du Bois Papers, University of Massachusetts, Amherst Library, reel 2.

74. Du Bois, *Souls*, 48.

75. Ibid., 54–55.

8. The Lost Cause and Causes Not Lost

1. *In Memoriam Sempiternam*, commemorative book produced by the Confederate Memorial Literary Society (Richmond: Confederate Museum, 1896), copy in MOC, 37–38, 54–56; John M. Coski and Amy R. Feely, "A Monument to Southern Womanhood: The Founding Generation of the Confederate Museum," in Edward D. C. Campbell Jr., and Kym S. Rice, *A Woman's War: Southern Women, Civil War, and the Confederate Legacy* (Charlottesville: University of Virginia Press, 1996), 131–133.

2. *In Memoriam Sempiternam*, 39–42.

3. Ibid., 40. On women and the Lost Cause, see Anastasia Sims, *The Power of Femininity in the New South: Women's Organizations and Politics in North Carolina, 1880–1930* (Columbia: University of South Carolina Press, 1997), 128–154;

W. Fitzhugh Brundage, "White Women and the Politics of Historical Memory in the New South, 1880–1920," paper, 1998, courtesy of the author; Karen Lynne Cox, "Women, the Lost Cause, and the New South: The United Daughters of the Confederacy and the Transmission of Confederate Culture, 1894–1919" (Ph.D. diss., University of Southern Mississippi); Jacquelyn Dowd Hall, "'You Must Remember This': Autobiography as Social Critique," *Journal of American History* 85 (September 1998), 444–453; and Vanessa Harris, "Three Southern Women and the Weight of the Past: Race, Gender, and Memory, 1890–1920s" (senior thesis, Amherst College, 1999).

4. *In Memoriam Sempiternam,* 43. Before the war Johnson was a lawyer from Maryland, educated at Princeton University. By 1864 he had reached the rank of brigadier general and was the officer who executed Jubal Early's orders to burn Chambersburg, Pennsylvania. See Foster, *Ghosts of the Confederacy,* 52–53, 55–56, 64–65.

5. *In Memoriam Sempiternam,* 44–46.

6. Ibid., 43, 50–52. On proslavery ideology and its survival into the New South era, as well as in the Lost Cause, see John David Smith, *Old Creed for a New South: Proslavery Ideology and Historiography, 1865–1918* (1983; rpr. Athens: University of Georgia Press, 1991), 41–68, 239–294. On the Lost Cause as a culture of "whiteness," see Grace Elizabeth Hale, *Making Whiteness: The Culture of Segregation in the South, 1890–1930* (New York: Pantheon, 1998), 43–84.

7. Definitions of the Lost Cause abound. Some scholars have employed the term "myth" to describe the character and meaning of the Lost Cause. See especially Rollin G. Osterweis, *The Myth of the Lost Cause, 1865–1900* (Hamden, Conn.: Archon Books, 1973), esp. 3–15; and Gaston, *The New South Creed,* 1–42, 215–246. Gaston's own definition of myth is useful: "Myths . . . are not polite euphemisms for falsehoods, but are combinations of images and symbols that reflect a people's way of perceiving truth. Organically related to a fundamental reality of life, they fuse the real and the imaginary into a blend that becomes a reality itself, a force in history" (9). Charles Reagan Wilson has written a treatment of the Lost Cause as a fundamentally religious movement. See Wilson, *Baptized in Blood,* 1–57. Wilson considers the Lost Cause essentially a "civil religion"—"the story of the use of the past as the basis for a Southern religious-moral identity, an identity as a chosen people" (1). Wilson contends that "the religion of the Lost Cause . . . contained ritualistic, mythological, theological, institutional, educational, and intellectual elements that were simply not present in the other aspects of the civil religion. Without the Lost Cause, no civil religion would have existed. The two were virtually the same" (13). In the most recent and thorough study of the Lost Cause, Gaines Foster eschews the terms myth and civil religion in favor of "tradition." Claiming that

the previous two terms lack precision, Foster is content to define tradition simply as "a cultural belief held over time." See Foster, *Ghosts of the Confederacy*, 7–8. Thomas L. Connelly and Barbara L. Bellows are less concerned with terminology and more with content, periodization, and the enduring elements of the Lost Cause. See Connelly and Bellows, *God and General Longstreet*, 1–5, 107–148. Also see William C. Davis, *The Cause Lost: Myths and Realities of the Confederacy* (Lawrence: University of Kansas Press, 1996), 3–14, 161–206. Davis points out that "out of any conflict, the losers create more myths than the winners . . . winners have little to explain to themselves" (175). I have no quarrel with the term "myth" and employ it here frequently. It can at times be used interchangeably with "tradition" without misleading readers (see Chapter 6). Whatever terms we employ, the Lost Cause, as Michael Kammen points out, is a classic example of "how a sense of tradition can have ideological consequences and help to define a culture or a subculture." See Kammen, *Mystic Chords of Memory*, 11.

8. See Chapter 3. On periodization of the Lost Cause, see especially Foster, *Ghosts of the Confederacy*. Foster argues that the Lost Cause traditions declined significantly as cultural practice after 1900 (163–179). See also Connelly and Bellows, *God and General Longstreet*, 107–148. On the literary dimensions of the Lost Cause and its changes over time, see Hobson, *Tell about the South*, 85–128; and Osterweis, *Myth of the Lost Cause*, 42–91.

9. Jefferson Davis to Frank Heath Alfriend, August 17, 1867, Montreal, Canada; Davis to unknown, July 6, 1874, Memphis; Davis to General C. J. Wright, December 8, 1877, GLC, ML.

10. Jefferson Davis, *The Rise and Fall of the Confederate Government*, 2 vols. (1881; rpr. New York: Da Capo Press, 1990), vol. 2, foreword by James M. McPherson, iii–iv.

11. Ibid., vol. 2, iv, 161–162.

12. Pollard, *Lost Cause*, 750; Edward Pollard, *The Lost Cause Regained* (New York: G. W. Carleton, 1868), 14. On Pollard, Bledsoe, Hill, and the magazines, see Hobson, *Tell about the South*, 88–92; Foster, *Ghosts of the Confederacy*, 49–50; and Wilson, *Baptized in Blood*, 84.

13. Edward McGrady to Rev. B. M. Palmer, May 20, 1869, Palmer to McGrady, July 7, 1869, Iredell Jones to McGrady, December 19, 1869, Papers of the Survivors' Association of Charleston, South Carolina, SCHS.

14. Copy of "Official Circular," 1869, Papers of the Survivors' Association of Charleston, SCHS; reprinted in *SHS Papers* 1 (January 1876), 39–43.

15. *SHS Papers* 5 (January–February 1877), 1, 34. At annual meetings, the SHS often passed resolutions reconfirming its pursuit of "truth" in the history of the war. See *SHS Papers* 7 (January–December 1879), 589.

16. John B. Gordon to P. G. T. Beauregard, May 10, 1872, New York, John B. Gordon Papers, Duke University Library. Gordon's publishing firm, which specialized in schoolbooks, was University Publishing Co. of New York and Baltimore. John C. Breckinridge to Early, August 10, 1873, P. G. T. Beauregard to Early, July 17, 1873, Jubal Early Papers, LC; Jubal Early to D. H. Hill, February 27, 1871, D. H. Hill Papers, SHC, UNC; Dabney, quoted in Hobson, *Tell about the South,* 97–99.

17. Robert S. Dabney to D. H. Hill, Dec. 1, 1873, Hill Papers, SHC, UNC.

18. Published in *Southern Magazine* 15 (December 1874). Pendleton delivered his Lexington speech about Longstreet many times elsewhere in the South. Early, Fitzhugh Lee, Richard Taylor, and others also wrote similar anti-Longstreet articles and speeches. See *SHS Papers* 5 (January–February 1877), 138–139, 162–194. On the Longstreet controversy, see William Garret Piston, *Lee's Tarnished Lieutenant: James Longstreet and His Place in Southern History* (Athens: University of Georgia Press, 1987); Gary Gallagher, "Scapegoat in Victory: James Longstreet and the Battle of Second Manassas," in Gallagher, *Lee and His Generals in War and Memory* (Baton Rouge: Louisiana State University Press, 1998), 140–142; and Connelly and Bellows, *God and General Longstreet,* 30–38. The first six volmes of the *SHS Papers* are replete with articles about Gettysburg; volumes 4–6 are especially devoted to the creation of the image of Lee as invincible. For an example of Early's quest to demonstrate the North's "superior numbers," see letter, November 19, 1870, in "The Relative Strength of the Armies of Generals Lee and Grant," *SHS Papers* 2 (July–December 1876), 6–21.

19. Early, in *SHS Papers,* vol. 2, 21; Morgan, in *SHS Papers,* vol. 5, 10–11, 21–22; Davis, address to Louisiana Division of the Association of the Army of the Tennessee, a ceremony in Mississippi City, Mississippi, where the veterans presented Davis with a badge and certificate of membership, in *SHS Papers* 6 (January–February 1878), 169.

20. The Goode, Kemper, and Lee speeches are quoted in "The Culpeper Confederate Monument," *Baltimore Sun,* July 21, 1881, clipping in scrapbook, Anne Bruin Papers, SHC, UNC.

21. Oration at unveiling of Confederate monument, Augusta, Ga., October 31, 1878, Charles Colcock Jones Jr. Papers PL, DU.

22. "Our Fallen Heroes," address by A. M. Keiley, of Richmond, Va., at Loudon Park, near Baltimore, Md., June 5, 1879, in *SHS Papers,* vol. 7, 375–382.

23. On the Lost Cause as a response to social tensions, see Foster, *Ghosts of the Confederacy,* 88–103, 113–126.

24. On Davis's tour, death, and funeral, see ibid., 95–98, 121–122, D. H. Hill quoted, 96. On Winnie Davis, see Coski and Feely, "A Monument to Southern Womanhood," 38; and Cita Cook, "The Creation of the Daughter of the Con-

federacy," paper delivered at the Southern Historical Association annual meeting, Birmingham, Ala., November 12, 1998, courtesy of author.

25. Savage, *Standing Soldiers, Kneeling Slaves*, 130–150; Foster, *Ghosts of the Confederacy*, 98–103. On the creation of the Lee image and the members of the Lee cult, see Thomas L. Connelly, *The Marble Man: Robert E. Lee and His Image in American Society* (Baton Rouge: Louisiana State University Press, 1977), 27–61.

26. Anderson, quoted in Foster, *Ghosts of the Confederacy*, 101; Savage, *Standing Soldiers, Kneeling Slaves*, 151.

27. *New York Press*, June 3, 1890, *Chicago Inter-Ocean*, May 30, 1890, *Minneapolis Tribune*, May 30, 1890, *Salt Lake Tribune*, May 30, 1890, in *Public Opinion* 9 (June 7, 1890), 189–192.

28. *New Orleans Picayune*, May 30, 1890, *NYT*, May 30, 1890, in *Public Opinion* 9 (June 7, 1890), 191.

29. Douglass, "Wasted Magnanimity," "Bombast," *New National Era*, August 10, November 10, 1871. See also Blight, *Frederick Douglass' Civil War*, 229; *Richmond Planet*, May 10, 24, 1890; and Savage, *Standing Soldiers, Kneeling Slaves*, 151–153.

30. *Richmond Planet*, June 7, 1890.

31. W. Fitzhugh Brundage, *Lynching in the New South* (Urbana: University of Illinois Press, 1993), 103–190. Later Virginia governors of the 1890s did work to stop lynching in the Old Dominion, as it grew steadily in other states. On the Lodge bill and Mississippi disfranchisement, see J. Morgan Kousser, *The Shaping of Southern Politics: Suffrage Restriction and the Establishment of the One-Party South, 1880–1910* (New Haven: Yale University Press, 1974), 20–30, 139–145; Rayford W. Logan, *The Betrayal of the Negro from Rutherford B. Hayes to Woodrow Wilson* (1954; rpr. New York: Collier Books, 1965), 70–82; and C. Vann Woodward, *The Strange Career of Jim Crow* (1955; rpr. New York: Oxford University Press, 1966), 82–85.

32. Herman Hattaway, "The United Confederate Veterans in Louisiana," *Louisiana History* 16 (Winter 1975), 5–37; Foster, *Ghosts of the Confederacy*, 106–107.

33. Mrs. Roy Weeks McKinney, "Origins," in Mary B. Poppenheim, et al., eds., *The History of the United Daughters of the Confederacy* (Raleigh, N.C.: Edwards & Broughton, 1956), vol. 1, 2–10; Coski and Feely, "A Monument to Southern Womanhood," 137–138; Cox, "Women, the Lost Cause, and the New South," 1–76.

34. Harris, "Three Southern Women and the Weight of the Past," chs. 1–2; Marjorie Spruill Wheeler, *New Women of the New South—The Leaders of the Women's Suffrage Movement in the Southern States* (New York: Oxford University Press, 1993), 39.

35. Cash, *Mind of the South*, 136; Thomas Nelson Page, "Gray Jacket of 'No. 4,'" in Page, *The Burial of the Guns: The Novels, Stories, Sketches and Poems of Thomas*

Nelson Page (1892; rpr. New York: Scribners, 1912), 235–236; Page, *The Old South*, 50.

36. Richard Watson Gilder, "The Nationalizing of Southern Literature: Part II—After the War," *The Christian Advocate* 10 (July 1890), 442. Also see Michael Kreyling, "Nationalizing the Southern Hero: Adams and James," *Mississippi Quarterly* 34 (Fall 1981), 383–385.

37. "Two Great Reunions," and "Why He Would Be a Confederate," *CV* 4 (October 1896), 333–335. The two reunions attended by Morton were in Richmond, July 2, and St. Paul, September 2, 1896.

38. *CV* 2 (June 1894), 182.

39. *CV* 2 (April, June, 1894), 122–123, 166; and *CV* 3 (May 1895), 130–131. S. A. Cunningham, editor of the Confederate, also adopted the occasional use of "N—— South" as a derogatory term.

40. Fred Arthur Bailey, "Free Speech and the Lost Cause in the Old Dominion," *Virginia Magazine of History* 103 (April 1995), 237; *CV* 1 (April 1893), 112; Mrs. Mary Singleton Slack, "Causes That Led to the War between the States in 1860," paper read before the Albert Sidney Johnston chapter, UDC, Louisville, Ky., March 16, 1904, Historical Records of the United Daughters of the Confederacy, comp. Mildred Lewis Rutherford, Athens, Ga., MOC.

41. J. H. Brunner to Cunningham, October 13, 1899, Hiawassee College, Tenn., S. A. Cunningham Papers, SHC, UNC. Many of the "sketches" sent to Cunningham rival anything done in Union veterans' war papers for their obsession with detail. Among the hundreds of poems sent to the magazine, most never published, are a variety of Blue-Gray reconciliation poems written especially during the 1910–15 period. Some poems, often by women, were variations on "Dixie." See the 141-page "Sketch," by Tyree Bell, Dyer County, Tenn., and numerous others, in Confederate Veteran Papers, PL, DU. The *Confederate Veteran* reached a circulation of 20,000 by 1900 in 41 states, two territories, the District of Columbia, and a few foreign countries. See Foster, *Ghosts of the Confederacy*, 106; and *CV* 8 (March 1900), 126–127.

42. *CV* 17 (July 1909), 313; *CV* 6 (August 1898), 357. See also Simpson, *S. A. Cunningham*, 90–116.

43. *Minutes of the Sixth Annual Meeting of the United Daughters of the Confederacy, 1899* (Nashville, Tenn., 1900), 72–74, MOC; Coski and Feely, "A Monument to Southern Womanhood," 138.

44. Coski and Feely, "A Monument to Southern Womanhood," 142–143; interview with the *Fauquier Democrat* (Warrenton, Va.), April 8, 1916, Mrs. Norman V. Randolph Papers, MOC. For Janet Randolph's lobbying, see Randolph to Sen. J. B. Foraker, April 15, 1903; Randolph to President William McKinley, July 24, August 8, 1900; Franklin H. Mackey to Randolph, February 16, 1898; Randolph

to "Honorable Sec. of War," early Fall 1900; W. T. Patten, Quartermaster of U.S., to Randolph, October 10, 1900; Congressman J. Wheeler to Randolph, March 2, 1899; Congressman John Lamb to Randolph, February 28, 1899, December 11, 24, 1900; and Senator Thomas Martin to Randolph, October 18, 1900, Randolph Papers, MOC, box 8A. On the reinterment in Arlington Cemetery, see Foster, *Ghosts of the Confederacy,* 153–154. See chapter on Lila Valentine, leader of the Women's Suffrage League in Virginia, in Harris, "Three Southern Women and the Weight of the Past," ch. 2.

45. An example of Rutherford's appearances in costume and her speeches is reported in a newspaper clipping from Portland, Oreg., October 1916. She wore a dress made in Paris in 1850 covered with a 113-year-old silk overdress made of Spanish lace. See clippings, Mildred Rutherford Scrapbooks 6, 60, MOC. Also see "Wrongs of History Righted" and "Historical Sins of Omission and Commision," 7, 35, in UDC Addresses, MOC; Coski and Feely, "A Monument to Southern Womanhood," 188; and Cox, "Women, the Lost Cause, and the New South," 143.

46. "Word to School Teachers," Rutherford Scrapbooks 9, MOC; "Address," June 1, 1915, and "Causes That Led to the War between the States," Historical Records of the UDC 6, 60, MOC; "Historian General's Page," *CV* 23 (October 1915), 443–445. Rutherford's list of "the five causes" were (1) the Missouri Compromise, (2) the unjust tariff acts, (3) the unjust distribution of money in the treasury, (4) the "personal liberty-bills" in violation of the Fugitive Slave Law, and (5) the election of Abraham Lincoln by a sectional party on a sectional platform. The "other aggravating causes" included: "Dred Scott case; John Brown's raid; Beecher's Bibles; Wilmot Proviso; Kansas and Nebraska bill; Uncle Tom's Cabin; vituperations from the press; falsehoods from the pulpits; the slave trade in violation of the Constitution [which she blamed on the North!]; and the Underground Railroad."

47. "Report of the Historical Committee," *CV* 3 (June 1895), 163–167. On the establishment, membership, and work of the UCV Historical Committee, see Herman Hattaway, "Clio's Southern Soldiers: The United Confederate Veterans and History," *Louisiana History* 12 (Summer 1871), 217–242.

48. *CV* 3 (June 1895), 167–170; Rutherford, "Address," delivered to group of Sons of Confederate Veterans, Richmond, June 1, 1915, Historical Records of the UDC 6, MOC. The irony in the political character of this movement to control history textbooks stems from the UCV's origins and principles. In an 1894 statement, UCV commander General John B. Gordon declared that "neither discussion of political or religious subjects, nor any political action, will be permitted in the organization." Gordon ended, however, with a seemingly contradictory reminder to the membership: "But you realize that a people without the memo-

ries of heroic suffering or sacrifice are a people without a history." See *CV* 2 (April 1894), cover page. On the issue of school and state histories in the 1890s, also see "In the Interest of School Histories," *CV* 3 (October 1895), 316; "Southern Social Relations," *CV* 4 (December 1896), 442–443; "Telling the Truth to Children" and "Correct History of Missouri," *CV* 6 (January 1898), 29. For an account of the Southern crusade to control history, especially through state histories, see Fred Arthur Bailey, "The Textbooks of the 'Lost Cause': Censorship and the Creation of Southern State Histories," *Georgia Historical Quarterly* 75 (Fall 1991), 507–533. A comparative account of textbooks is Daniel E. Boxer, "Dueling Memories: The Retelling of the Civil War in Textbooks of Boston and Richmond," (senior thesis, Amherst College, 2000).

49. John B. Gordon, *Reminiscences of the Civil War* (1903 rpr. Baton Rouge: Louisiana State University Press, 1993), 18–19; oration by Rev. R. C. Cave, Richmond, May 30, 1894, *CV* 2 (June 1894), 162; "Judge Cook's Tribute to Confederate Dead," *Nashville Banner,* May 27, 1901, HCF, fiche 271.

50. "The Causes of the War," address by Richard Henry Lee, Old Chapel, Va., at dedication of Confederate monument, *CV* 1 (July 1893), 201; Arthur Marshall, Springfield, Mo., letter to editor, *CV* 1 (November 1893), 323; "Gray Warriors Extolled by Grandson of Leader," *AC,* April 27, 1911.

51. *Memorial Day Annual, 1912: The Causes and Outbreak of the War between the States, 1861–1865* (Richmond: Department of Public Instruction and Confederate Memorial Literary Society, 1912), in Rutherford Scrapbooks 60, MOC.

52. *CV* 1 (May 1893), 136; "White People and Negroes," *CV* 13 (September 1905), 421. On the importance of mammies in white Southern lore, see Hale, *Making Whiteness,* 85–104. On the faithful slave stereotype and white tributes to former slaves, see Leon F. Litwack, *Trouble in Mind: Black Southerners in the Age of Jim Crow* (New York: Knopf, 1998), 184–197.

53. "Relations of Southern Masters to Slaves," *CV* 5 (January 1897), 21–22; "Master and His Faithful Slave," "Gratitude of a Faithful Slave," "Honor for the Old-Time Negro," *CV* 20 (September 1912), 228–230. For representative examples of photographs, see *CV* 8 (September 1900), 399–400; *CV* 11 (October 1903), 172, 407, 470; *CV* 12 (May 1904), 122–123, 125; and *CV* 19 (November 1911), 522–523. "Faithful Old Slaves; Degenerate Progeny," address by B. G. Humphrey, Port Gibson, Mississippi, *CV* 11 (September 1903), 407.

54. For examples of poetry, see "Old Mose at Gettysburg," *CV* 11 (September 1903), 407; "Long Ago—Faithful Slaves," *CV* 14 (March 1906), 117; "The Old Boatman," *CV* 23 (December 1915), 545. Women performers of dialect stories and "darky" songs were especially conspicuous in the advertisements that appeared in the *Confederate Veteran.* See Sally B. Hammer, "Mammy Susan's Story," *CV* 1 (September 1893), 270; "Negro Dialect and Slave Songs," a notice for perfor-

mances by Jeannette Robinson Murphy, *CV* 6 (July 1898), 344; and "Preserving the Amiability of Black Mammy," notice for performance of Louise A. Williams, *CV* 17 (August 1909), 427. "Ex-Slaves Tell Stories of Plantation Days at First Gathering of Old Country Society," *Atlanta Constitution,* July 3, 1913. A typical UDC chapter report of activities would include "Stories of Faithful Slaves" as one among several themes of collected reminiscence. See *CV* 24 (June 1916), 279; Fanny E. Selph, "The Emancipation Proclamation: Was It the Instrument by Which the Slaves Were Emancipated?" *CV* 23 (December 1915), 547; Bertha Simpson Lucas, "An Interesting Reminiscence of a Girl of the Sixties," recorded in 1929, Confederate Sketches, SHC, UNC. Another remarkable unpublished narrative about faithful slaves is J. Willcox Brown, "Reminiscence," 1904, typescript prepared when Brown was 71 years old and living in Afton, Va., Virginia State Library, Richmond.

55. Hugh G. Barclay, "A Monument to Uncle Ben and Aunt Maltilda," *CV* 22 (October 1914), 474; Franklin Pugh and Julia Le Grand, quoted in James L. Roark, *Masters without Slaves: Southern Planters in the Civil War and Reconstruction* (New York: Norton, 1977), 113; and Litwack, *Been in the Storm So Long,* 137, 158, 163. On the power of the idea of "faithful slaves" in the South, and on the reality of slaves who remained supportive of their masters and their home places, see Litwack, *Been in the Storm So Long,* 3–63, 149–166; and Clinton, *Tara Revisited,* 118–119, 174–177, 200–203.

56. Savage, *Standing Soldiers, Kneeling Slaves,* 155–161; "Monuments at Fort Mill," *CV* 7 (May 1899), 209–211.

57. See paper delivered by Mary M. Solari, J. Harvey Mathews chapter, UDC, Memphis, Tenn., in *CV* 13 (March 1905), 123–124. Solari demonstrates that UDC women saw multiple purposes in honoring mammies: "Erecting this monument would influence for good the present and coming generations, and prove that the people of the South who owned slaves valued and respected their good qualities as no one else ever did or will do. It would bespeak the real conception of the affection of the owner toward the slave and refute the slanders and falsehoods published in 'Uncle Tom's Cabin.'" Mrs. B. Bryan to Janet Randolph, August 13, 1910, Randolph Papers, MOC; Mrs. Norman V. Randolph, "Our Colored People's Christmas," *Richmond Times-Dispatch,* December 17, 1913, Confederate Museum Literary Society Scrapbook, 1912–15, 126, MOC. On the proposed mammy monument, see *Amsterdam News* (New York), August 22, 1923; *Goldsboro Argus* (N.C.), July 8, 1923; *Southwestern Christian Advocate* (New Orleans), October 4, 1923, in Tuskegee Clipping File. Blacks widely condemned the idea of the mammy monument, although some support existed in the South. The Baptist journal *Southwestern Christian Advocate,* as well as Eli-

jah Jones, the bishop of New Orleans, supported the movement. On Zolnay, see *CV* 5 (April 1897), 181–182.

58. *New York Sun,* April 12, 1903, January 4, 1904; *Times Democrat* (Tex., town unknown), June 15, 1900; *Atlanta Journal,* November 20, 1900; *New York Age,* March 26, 1902, in HCF, fiche 271.

59. Rutherford Scrapbooks, MOC, especially vols. 46 and 47. This massive collection includes hundreds of faithful slave narratives, many of them typescripts, and some published clippings. For the Los Angeles chapter material, and the postcards and photographs, see vol. 46. For reports from various UDC chapters, see Margaret Reintzel to Rutherford, Philadelphia, September 18, 1912; Mary Louise Johnson to Rutherford, n.d., Maryland Division; Mrs. T. T. Loy to Rutherford, Los Angeles, April 11, 1916; Mrs. J. T. Sifford to Rutherford, Camden, Ark., n.d; Mrs. J. S. Alison to Rutherford, La Vier, La., n.d; Mrs. M. D. Slaven to Rutherford, Lewisburg, W.Va., September 23, 1914; Clara Miner Lynn to Rutherford, Warren, Ariz., September 10, n.y.; Julia Bottomley to Rutherford, Chicago, October 14, 1914; Annie Jopling Lester, Dayton, Ohio, June 11, 1914; Mrs. Elliot Spaulding to Rutherford, St. Joseph, Mo., October 8, 1914; Carry A. Leazar to Rutherford, Morrisville, N.C., October 3, 1913; Mrs. W. C. Chidester to Rutherford, Seattle, Wash., September 6, 1915; file "Mississippi Mss."; file "Virginia Mss."; and over 100 reminiscences, all in Mildred Lewis Rutherford Papers, MOC, box 2.

60. Paper read by Mrs. A. B. Lindsey, "The Faithful Slave of the Older South," clipping, *Richmond Times-Dispatch,* November 23, 1913, Confederate Museum Literary Society Scrapbook, 1912–15, MOC.

61. "The White Man's Freedom," *Atlanta News,* November 13, 1903, HCF, fiche 271.

62. Address in Richmond, March 25, 1918, Douglass Southall Freeman Papers, LC, container 126.

63. "Patriotic School Histories," report of the UCV Historical Committee, *CV* 5 (September 1897), 45; "New South: Historical Committee Makes Its Report," *Louisville Courier-Journal,* June 1, 1900, 16–21, Hampton clipping file, fiche 271.

64. Joel Williamson, *William Faulkner and Southern History* (New York: Oxford University Press, 1993), 141–146; Robert Penn Warren, "William Faulkner," *New Republic,* August 12, 26, 1946, in *A Robert Penn Warren Reader* (New York: Random House, 1983), 222. On the sources of rebellion and the deep sense of history among 1920s Southern writers, see Woodward, "The Historical Dimension," in *Burden of Southern History,* 32–39; William C. Havard, "The Search for Identity," in Louis D. Rubin Jr., ed., *The History of Southern Literature* (Baton Rouge: Louisiana State University Press, 1985), 415–428.

65. Carl N. Degler, *The Other South: Southern Dissenters in the Nineteenth Century* (New York: Harper & Row, 1972), 191–229, 269–315; and Maddex, *The Virginia*

Conservatives, 233–238, 252–265. On Readjusters, see Jane Dailey, *Before Jim Crow: The Politics of Race in Post-Emancipation Virginia,* forthcoming.

66. For the Mahone quotation, and on Mahone and the spread to the Readjuster movement to other states, see Degler, *The Other South,* 275, 271–285, 288–291.

67. Thomas L. Nugent and Tom Watson, quoted in ibid., 321, 341.

68. George Washington Cable, "The Silent South," in Cable, *The Negro Question: A Selection of Writings on Civil Rights in the South,* Arlin Turner, ed. (1889; rpr. New York: Norton, 1958), 77–90, 116–118. On Cable in Northampton, see Philip Butcher, *George W. Cable: The Northampton Years* (New York: Columbia University Press, 1959).

69. William Dodd, "The Status of History in Southern Education," *Nation* 75 (August 1902), 109–111. On the professional historians and the Lost Cause, see Foster, *Ghosts of the Confederacy,* 180–191.

70. Narrative of the "affair at Trinity," and Bassett to Charles Francis Adams, November 3, 1911, Northampton, Mass., John Spencer Bassett Papers, Massachusetts Historical Society, Boston; John Spencer Bassett, "Stirring Up the Fires of Race Antipathy," *South Atlantic Quarterly* 2 (October 1903), 297–305; Fleming quoted in Smith, *Old Creed for the New South,* 145. On the entire Bassett affair, see Williamson, *Crucible of Race,* 261–271. Bassett wrote one of the most insightful reviews, certainly by a white Southerner, of W. E. B. Du Bois's *The Souls of Black Folk.* See Bassett, "Two Negro Leaders," *South Atlantic Quarterly* 2 (July 1903), 267–272.

71. Enoch Marvin Banks, "A Semi-Centennial View of Secession," *Independent* 70 (February 9, 1911), 299–303; "Free Speech Suprest," *Independent* 70 (April 20, 1911), 807–808; James W. Garner, "The Dismissal of Professor Banks," *Independent* 70 (April 27, 1911); "A Bold Defense," *Independent* 70 (May 4, 1911), 974–975; Andrew Sledd, "The Dismissal of Professor Banks," *Independent* 70 (May 25, 1911), 1113–1114; *Jacksonville Times-Union,* quoted in *AC,* April 24, 1911. Also see Foster, *Ghosts of the Confederacy,* 188.

72. Christopher L. Jones, "Traitor and Patriot: Myth, Honor, and the Lost Cause in the Life of John Singleton Mosby" (senior thesis, Amherst College, 1999); Kevin H. Siepel, *Rebel: The Life and Times of John Singleton Mosby* (New York: Da Capo, 1983). For Mosby's participation in various reunions of his former unit, usually in Alexandria, Va., see numerous clippings in John Singelton Mosby Scrapbooks 1, University of Virginia Library, Charlottesville.

73. Unnamed newspaper clipping, n.d., in William H. Payne Papers, Library of Virginia, Richmond; Mosby to Stephens, Alexander H. Stephens Papers, LC; Mosby to former Confederate comrade, *NYH,* August 12, 1876; Mosby to S. M. Yost, April 10, 1897, reprinted in clipping, unnamed newspaper, Mosby Scrapbooks 1, University of Virginia Library.

74. Mosby to Dr. A. Monteiro, February 19, 1895, San Francisco, Mosby to Judge Rueben Page, June 11, 1902, Akron, Colo., John C. Ropes to Mosby, February 16, 1896, Boston, Mosby to Lunsford L. Lomax, February 19, 1896, San Francisco, Mosby to Marcus J. Wright, February 22, 1896, San Francisco, Mosby to John C. Ropes, December 13, 1897, Warrenton, Va., in Adele H. Mitchell, ed., *The Letters of John S. Mosby* (Charlottesville: Stuart-Mosby Historical Society, 1986), 75, 83–90, 111–113; Mosby to Sam Chapman, January 21, February 15, 1910, GLC, ML; Mosby to Bradley T. Johnson, December 20, 1897, Bradley T. Johnson Papers, PL, DU.

75. Mosby to Dr. A. Monteiro, June 9, 1894, San Francisco, Mosby to Judge Rueben Page, June 11, 1902, in Mitchell, ed., *Letters of John S. Mosby,* 69, 97; Mosby to (illegible), June 22, 1894, Mosby Scrapbooks 1, University of Virginia Library; George L. Christian, "Report of the UCV History Committee," 1907, MOC.

76. Mosby to Sam Chapman, June 4, 1907, February 15, 1910, Washington, D.C., GLC, ML.

9. Black Memory and Progress of the Race

1. *Washington Bee,* January 6, 1883; Blight, *Frederick Douglass' Civil War,* 219–221.

2. *People's Advocate* (Washington, D.C.), January 6, 1883, clipping in Leon Gardiner Collection, Pennsylvania Historical Society, Philadelphia; *Washington Bee,* January 6, 1883; Abraham Lincoln, "First Inaugural Address," March 4, 1861, in Basler, ed., *Collected Works,* vol. 4, 271.

3. *Washington Bee,* January 6, 1883.

4. *New York Globe,* January 6, 1883.

5. *Washington Bee,* January 6, 1883. I draw the term "felt history" from Robert Penn Warren, *The Legacy of the Civil War* (1961; rpr. Cambridge: Harvard University Press, 1983), 4. Warren writes: "The Civil War is our only felt history—history lived in the national imagination."

6. On just what blacks faced in preserving their own sense of historical memory against the Lost Cause tradition, see Litwack, *Trouble in Mind,* chs. 1–2.

7. Ralph Ellison, "The World and the Jug," 1963, in Ellison, *Shadow and Act* (New York: Random House, 1964), 124.

8. *CR,* July 26, 1883; *New York Globe,* January 20, February 3, 24, June 9, 1883; *Washington Bee,* June 10, 1883; Degler, *The Other South,* 276–300.

9. *New York Globe,* February 24, 1883.

10. *Washington Bee,* April 21, 1883. The drill team averaged some 40 men per team. On cities, democratic civic culture, and parades, see Mary P. Ryan, *Civic Wars: Democracy and Public Life in the American City during the Nineteenth Century* (Berkeley: University of California Press, 1997).

11. *Washington Bee,* April 21, 1883.

12. *CR,* October 4, 1883. On the variety of state conventions, and especially the growing sentiment for political indepencence, see August Meier, *Negro Thought in America, 1880–1915* (Ann Arbor: University of Michigan Press, 1963), 26–41, 69–71. Richard T. Greener opposed the national convention, declaring in May: "Conventions!—there never was one that did not disgrace the race by wranglings. We need some common sense, not conventions." See *New York Globe,* May 12, 1883.

13. Douglass, "Address to the People of the United States," Louisville, Ky., September 24, 1883, in Foner, ed., *Life and Writings,* vol. 4, 373–374, 377–380.

14. Ibid., 384.

15. See speech by J. M. Gregory at the Douglass banquet, *Washington Bee,* January 13, 1883; "Civil Rights Laws," *New York Globe,* February 3, 1883. On the cases and Harlan's dissent, see Rayford W. Logan, *The Betrayal of the Negro: From Rutherford B. Hayes to Woodrow Wilson* (New York: Collier, 1954), 114–118.

16. Douglass, "Speech at the Civil Rights Mass Meeting," Lincoln Hall, Washington, D.C., October 22, 1883, in Foner, ed., *Life and Writings,* vol. 4, 393, 402; other papers quoted in *CR,* October 25, 1883. Also see Blight, *Frederick Douglass' Civil War,* 221–222.

17. *CR,* November 15, 1883.

18. Ibid., June 21, November 8, December 13, 1883.

19. Ibid., December 27, 1883; Joseph C. Price, "The Race Problem Stated," in Carter G. Woodson, ed., *Negro Orators and Their Orations,* (1925; rpr. New York: Russell and Russell, 1969), 490. On Turner, see Stephen Ward Angell, *Bishop Henry McNeal Turner and African American Religion in the South* (Knoxville: University of Tennessee Press, 1992).

20. *CR,* March 18, June 3, 24, 1865.

21. Ibid., January 1, 1880, June 14, 1883.

22. Ibid., March 17, 29, 1881. See also Ira Berlin, et al., eds., *Freedom: A Documentary History of Emancipation, 1861–1867,* 4 vols. (New York: Cambridge University Press, 1982–94). But especially see the supplementary volume, Ira Berlin and Leslie S. Rowland, eds., *Families and Freedom: A Documentary History of African American Kinship in the Civil War Era* (New York: New Press, 1997).

23. *CR,* July 13, 1890. On the often highly publicized reunions of former slaves with white families, see Litwack, *Trouble in Mind,* 189–190. On the planning of these events as "Ex-Slave Reunion Days," such as one in Tyler, Tex., in 1893, organized by blacks, see *CR,* August 4, 1893.

24. Tourgée, "South as a Field for Fiction," 409–410; *CR,* April 25, 1878, September 29, 1887; Kelly Miller, "The Negro's Part in the Negro Problem," in *Race Adjustment: Essays on the Negro in America* (1908; rpr. New York: Arno Press, 1968), 99.

25. Delia Garlic, interviewed in Montgomery, Ala., n.d., in Rawick, ed., *American Slave*, ser. 1, vol. 6 (Ala.), 129–132, and Jenny Proctor, interviewed in Tex., n.d., Rawick, ed., *American Slave*, ser. 1, vol. 5 (Tex.), 208–217, both in Ira Berlin, Marc Favreau, and Steven F. Miller, eds., *Remembering Slavery: African Americans Talk about Their Personal Experiences of Slavery and Emancipation* (New York: New Press, 1998), 8–11, 30–31; Sarah Wooden Johnson, interviewed in Petersburg, Va., n.d., in Charles L. Perdue Jr., Thomas E. Barden, and Robert K. Phillips, eds., *Weevils in the Wheat: Interviews with Virginia Ex-Slaves* (Bloomington: Indiana University Press, 1980), 163; Sarah Debro, interviewed in Durham, N.C., July 24, 1937, in Belinda Hurmence, ed., *My Folks Don't Want Me to Talk about Slavery* (Winston-Salem, N.C.: John F. Blair, 1984), 61.

26. Richard Wright, *Twelve Million Black Voices: A Folk History of the Negro in the United States* (New York: Viking Press, 1941), 46–47.

27. "The Need of New Ideas and New Aims for a New Era," address to the graduating class of Storer College, Harpers Ferry, W.Va., May 30, 1885, in Alexander Crummell, *Africa and America: Addresses an Discourses* (1891; rpr. New York: Atheneum, 1969), iii, 13–15. The speech was originally published in the *AME Review* 2 (October 1885), 115–127. On Crummell see Wilson J. Moses, *Alexander Crummell: A Study of Civilization and Its Discontent* (New York: Oxford University Press, 1990); and Alfred A. Moss, *The American Negro Academy: Voice of the Talented Tenth* (Baton Rouge: Louisiana State University Press, 1981), 19–34, 53–62. Crummell was the founder of the American Negro Academy, a group of black intellectuals that met occasionally in the 1890s and during the first decade of the new century to deliver formal papers. On the Crummell-Douglass encounter at Harpers Ferry, see Blight, "Quarrel Forgotten or a Revolution Remembered?" in Blight and Simpson, eds., *Union and Emancipation: Essays on Politics and Race in the Civil War Era,* (Kent, Ohio: Kent State University Press, 1997), 160–166.

28. Crummell, "The Need of New Ideas and New Aims," 18.

29. Frederick Douglass, "Speech at the Thirty-Third Anniversary of the Jerry Rescue," 1884, Douglass Papers, LC, reel 16.

30. Frederick Douglass, "Thoughts and Recollections of the Antislavery Conflict," speech undated, but it is at least as late as the early 1880s; "Decoration Day," speech at Mt. Hope Cemetery, Rochester, N.Y., May 1883; and "Address Delivered on the 26th Anniversary of Abolition in the District of Columbia," April 16, 1888, Washington, D.C., all in Douglass Papers, LC, reel 15. On the role of white supremacy in the development of theories of black "degeneration," see Smith, *Old Creed for a New South*, 103–196, 239–277, and on the permanence with which these ideas were held, Fredrickson, *Black Image in the White Mind*, 320–322.

31. See Moses, *Alexander Crummell*, 226–228; William S. McFeely, *Frederick Douglass*, (New York: Norton, 1991), 238–304; and Blight, *Frederick Douglass' Civil War*, 189–245.

32. Frances Ellen Watkins Harper, "The Dying Bondman," *AME Review* 1 (July 1884), 45; Rev. James M. Henderson, "The Negro in America," *AME Review* 4 (April 1888), 384; Pauline E. Hopkins, *Contending Forces: A Romance Illustrative of Negro Life North and South* (1900; rpr. New York: Oxford University Press, 1988), 13. On black women and the question of respectability, see Evelyn Brooks Higginbotham, *Righteous Discontent: The Women's Movement in the Black Baptist Church, 1880–1920* (Cambridge: Harvard University Press, 1993); and Cynthia Neverdon-Morton, *Afro-American Women of the South and the Advancement of the Race, 1895–1925* (Knoxville: University of Tennessee Press, 1989).

33. Crummell, "The Need of New Ideas and New Aims," 19, 13; Du Bois, *Souls*, 38; Toni Morrison, *Beloved* (New York: New American Library, 1987), 273.

34. "Address to the Negro Society of Virginia," November 12, 1914, in Louis R. Harlan and Raymond W. Smock, eds., *The Booker T. Washington Papers* (hereafter *BTW Papers*), 13 vols. (Urbana: University of Illinois Press, 1972–1980), 13, 170; "Address before Brooklyn Institute of Science," February 2, 1903, *BTW Papers*, vol. 7, 88–89; "Religious Life of the Negro," *North American Review*, July 1905, and *Boston Globe*, October 4, 1904, *BTW Papers*, vol. 8, 333, 84.

35. *CR*, April 22, 1880; Booker T. Washington, *Up from Slavery* (1901; rpr. New York: Oxford University Press, 1995), 8–10.

36. Henry McNeal Turner, *The Negro in All Ages: A Lecture Delivered in the Second Baptist Church of Savannah, Georgia, April 8, 1873* (Savannah, 1873), 29; *Nashville Christian Advocate*, October 8, 1888, in Edwin S. Redkey, ed., *Respect Black: The Writings and Speeches of Henry McNeal Turner* (New York: Arno Press, 1971), 74–75. On Turner's attachment to the doctrine of Providence, his speech at Davis's funeral, and Lee's response, see *CR*, January 2, 9, 1890, and Stephen Ward Angell, *Bishop Henry McNeal Turner and African American Religion in the South* (Nashville: University of Tennessee Press, 1992), 263–266. Discussion of slavery and the Confederacy as paradoxical or even as divine agents of black liberation was nothing new. Even William Still, in his massive history of the Underground Railroad in 1872, announced in his preface that "the slave auction block indirectly proved to be in some respects a very active agent in promoting travel on the UGRR, just as Jeff. Davis was an agent in helping to bring about the downfall of Slavery." See William Still, *Underground Railroad* (1872; rpr. New York: Arno Press, 1968), 2.

37. Turner, letter from Freetown, Sierra Leone, November 16, 1891, in Redkey, ed., *Respect Black*, 111.

38. See Albert J. Raboteau, "'Ethiopia Shall Soon Stretch Forth Her Hands': Black Destiny in Nineteenth Century America," in Raboteau, *A Fire in the Bones: Reflections on African American Religious History* (Boston: Beacon Press, 1995), 42. On Ethiopianism, see Wilson J. Moses, "Assimilationist Black Nationalism, 1890–1925," in Moses, *The Wings of Ethiopia: Studies in African-American Life and Letters* (Ames: Iowa State University Press, 1990), 95–105, esp. 102–103; Wilson J. Moses, *The Golden Age of Black Nationalism, 1850–1925* (Hamden, Conn.: Archon Books, 1978), 23–24, 156–157; and J. Mutero Chirenje, *Ethiopianism and Afro-Americans in Southern Africa, 1883–1916* (Baton Rouge: Louisiana State University Press, 1987), 1–3, 50–83. Raboteau considers Ethiopianism a deep tradition in black religious history and stresses the "obscure" character of the passage in Psalms 68:31 (and hence the multiple interpretations and uses it can inspire). Moses considers the tradition of Ethiopianism to be more political and religious than literary, and to have been influenced by the American tradition of Manifest Destiny. Through this outlook, he writes, blacks were given a sense of "destiny . . . to create an exemplary civilization, usually in Africa, but not only there" (102).

39. On black millennialism see Timothy E. Fulop, "'The Future Golden Day of the Race': Millennialism and Black Americans in the Nadir, 1877–1901," in Timothy E. Fulop and Albert J. Raboteau, eds., *African-American Religion: Interpretive Essays in History and Culture* (New York: Routledge, 1997), 227–253; and St. Claire Drake, *The Redemption of Africa and Black Religion* (Chicago: Third World Press, 1970). For the varieties of black millennial outlooks and for the term "race histories," see Laurie F. Maffly-Kipp, "Redeeming Southern Memory: The Negro Race History, 1874–1915," in Fitzhugh Brundage, ed., *No Deed But Memory: Essays on History and Memory in the American South* (Chapel Hill: University of North Carolina Press, forthcoming, 2000), 227–258. See Rayford W. Logan, *The Betrayal of the Negro: From Rutherford B. Hayes to Woodrow Wilson* (1954; rpr. New York: Collier, 1965). In both his prefaces (to the first and second editions), Logan reflects on just what to call this period of the late nineteenth and early twentieth centuries in American race relations. He coined the term "nadir," which has had considerable staying power. He said he was tempted to call it the "Dark Ages in Recent American History." He also quotes Henry Arthur Callis's phrase "a low, rugged plateau" and John Hope Franklin's suggestion of "the Long Dark Night" (9, 11). These terms suggest some of the reasons why millennial thought took hold among blacks at the end of the nineteenth century.

40. Peter Thomas Stanford, *The Tragedy of the Negro in America* (Boston: by the author, 1898), iii, 9. On Williams and the writing and reception of his *History of the Negro Race in America* (1882), see Franklin, *George Washington Williams*, 100–133. On the ways in which Williams infused his history with "moral mean-

ing" and millennial expectation, and on Stanford and Blyden, see Maffly-Kipp, "Redeeming Southern Memory," 227–228, 233–234, 237–240; and Raboteau, "Ethiopia Shall Soon Stretch Forth Her Hands," 45–46, 49.

41. Edward W. Blyden, "The African Problem and the Method of Its Solution," *AME Review* 7 (October 1890), 213.

42. Maffly-Kipp, "Redeeming Southern Memory," 229, 242–243; J. Max Barber, *The Negro of the Earlier World: An Excursion into Ancient Negro History* (Philadelphia: The AME Book Concern, n.d.), 28; T. G. Steward, *The End of the World; or, Clearing the Way for the Fullness of the Gentiles* (Philadelphia: AME Church Book Rooms, 1888), 71; T. G. Steward, *The Colored Regulars in the United States Army* (1904; rpr. New York: Arno Press, 1969), 12. Steward served as chaplain in a U.S. Army regiment during the Spanish-American War. In its aftermath he wrote a history of black participation in that war. On Steward, also see Litwack, *Trouble in Mind,* 468–469, 474.

43. James Theodore Holly, "The Divine Plan of Human Redemption, in Its Ethnological Development," *AME Review* 1 (October 1884), 79–85. On Steward and Holly, see Raboteau, "Ethiopia Shall Soon Stretch Forth Her Hands," 53–56; and Fulop, "The Future Golden Day of the Race," 239–242.

44. Alexander Crummell, "A Defense of the Negro Race in America from the Assaults and Charges," delivered at the Episcopal Church Congress, Richmond, Va., October 1882, in Crummell, *Africa and America,* 92; T. Thomas Fortune, *Black and White: Land, Labor, and Politics in the South* (1884; rpr. Chicago: Johnson Publishing Co., 1970), 86; *Voice of Missions,* March 1896.

45. See *Dedication of the Chickamauga and Chattanooga National Military Park, September 18–20, 1895.* In its long story on the Atlanta speech and ceremonies, the *New York World,* September 19, 1895, commented on the juxtaposition of the Blue-Gray reunion with the Exposition. The "hosts of soldiers . . . celebrating the struggle the fruits of which were exposed to the world in Atlanta . . . would have been astonished by the spectacle when Prof. Booker stepped to the front of the platform." See *BTW Papers* vol. 4, 3–4.

46. On the background for Washington's selection as orator, and the origins of the Exposition, see Louis R. Harlan, *Booker T. Washington: The Making of a Black Leader, 1856–1901* (New York: Oxford University Press, 1972), 204–211; and Ayers, *Promise of the New South,* 322–323.

47. Harlan, *Booker T. Washington,* 214–217; *New York World,* September 19, 1895, in *BTW Papers,* vol. 4, 3–8; "Atlanta Exposition Address," *BTW Papers,* vol. 3, 583–584.

48. "Atlanta Exposition Address," 585–587.

49. *New York World,* September 19, 20, 1895, in *BTW Papers,* vol. 4, 4, 9, 15–17. See also Harlan, *Booker T. Washington,* 229–236; Harlan has aptly called Washing-

ton's prescription for reconciliation a "Faustian bargain." See John Hope Franklin and August Meier, eds., *Black Leaders of the Twentieth Century* (Urbana: University of Illinois Press, 1982), 89.

50. Frances J. Grimké to Washington, September 24, 1895, Ben Bell Sr. to Washington, October 1, 1895, John Edward Bruce to Washington, October 14, 1895, William J. Casler to Washington, September 26, 1895, Timothy Thomas Fortune to Washington, September 26, 1895, all in *BTW Papers* vol. 4, 18–19, 24–26, 30–31, 46–47, 55–56.

51. *Chicago Inter-Ocean,* October 2, 1895, in ibid., 37–42; *Voice of Missions,* November 1895.

52. *Chicago Inter-Ocean,* October 2, 1895, in *BTW Papers,* vol. 4, 41–42.

53. W. J. McGee, in Harlan, *Booker T. Washington,* 216.

54. John Webster Cochran to Washington, September 21, 1895, and *Chicago Inter-Ocean,* October 2, 1895, *BTW Papers,* vol. 4, 20, 34.

55. *Voice of Missions,* October, December 1895; *Washington Bee,* November 2, 1895; *Atlanta Advocate,* in *Cleveland Gazette,* November 2, 1895, quoted in Harlan, *Booker T. Washington,* 226; Minute Book, Bethel Literary and Historical Association, October 22, 1895, Moorland-Springarn Collection, Howard University; Frances Grimké to Washington, November 7, 1895, *BTW Papers,* vol. 4, 74–75. The discussion at the October 22 meeting of the Bethel Association was led by L. M. Hershaw, a professor at Howard University. Other participants included Kelly Miller, Ida Gibbs, J. W. Cromwell, L. W. Pulies, Jesse Lawson, Frances Grimké, "and others." A stunning illustration of the difficulty Washington's approach faced came in the Montgomery, Ala., Race Conference in 1900. Washington attended this gathering controlled by white supremacists, but was not allowed to speak. Several speakers at the conference were radical racists, arguing that emancipation had been a mistake and favoring repeal of the Fifteenth Amendment. George A. Mebane, a black man and former Congressman from North Carolina, considered the Montgomery Conference an assembly of "the unreconciled, to revise and resuscitate the 'lost cause.'" See John David Smith, "No Negro Is upon the Program': Blacks and the Montgomery Race Conference of 1900," in Smith and Thomas H. Appleton Jr., eds., *A Mythic Land Apart: Reassessing Southerners and Their History* (Westport, Conn.: Greenwood Press, 1997), 125–150.

56. Booker T. Washington, "The Storm before the Calm," speech delivered before AME Conference, May 23, 1900, in *The Colored American Magazine* 1 (September 1900), 200–204. This speech to the AME annual meeting is especially interesting because Washington, while still advocating that political agitation is unwise, delivered a forthright defense of the Fifteenth Amendment, which at that time was under consideration for repeal by some Southern state legislatures.

57. "Extracts from an Address before the Birmingham Lyceum," Birmingham, Ala., March 30, 1899, and "Extracts from an Address at the Hollis Street Theater," Boston, March 21, 1899, *BTW Papers,* vol. 5, 54–57, 62.

58. "Extracts from an Address at the Unveiling of the Harriet Tubman Memorial," Auburn, N.Y., June 12, 1914, *BTW Papers,* vol. 13, 58–61.

59. H. F. Kletzing and W. H. Crogman, *Progress of a Race; or, The Remarkable Advancement of the Afro-American* (1897; rpr. New York: Negro Universities Press, 1969), 616; G. F. Richings, *Evidences of Progress among Colored People* (1900; rpr. Chicago: Afro-Am Press, 1969), 422. The first 200 pages of J. L. Nichols and William H. Crogman, *Progress of a Race* (1920; rpr. New York: Arno Press, 1969) is devoted to a history of African Americans from the slave trade to the women's club movement of the first two decades of the twentieth century.

60. *Southern Workman,* September 1895; *AME Review* 2 (July 1885).

61. *Voice of Missions,* October 1897; the Stewart piece appeared in the *New York Sun,* August 13, 1897. See also *CR,* July 10, 1890, August 18, 1887, September 22, 1887, January 3, 1889.

62. *CR,* August 9, June 28, 1888; Brundage, *Lynching in the New South,* 210–211.

63. *CR,* May 25, 1893; *A Red Record: Tabulated Statistics and Alleged Causes of Lynchings in the United States, 1892–1893–1894* (1895), in Trudier Harris, comp., *Selected Works of Ida B. Wells-Barnett* (New York: Oxford University Press, 1991), 138, 149.

64. *The Reason Why the Colored American Is Not in the World's Columbian Exposition,* in *Selected Works of Ida B. Wells-Barnett,* 46–137. Wells had 20,000 copies of this pamphlet printed and distributed. She married Barnett, a Chicago lawyer, in 1895.

65. *AC,* January 2, 1909.

10. Fifty Years of Freedom and Reunion

1. *Boston Evening Transcript,* June 1, 1897. On the formation of the Fifty-fourth and the battle of Fort Wagner, see Luis F. Emilio, *A Brave Black Regiment: History of the Fifty-Fourth Regiment of Massachusetts Volunteer Infantry* (Boston: Boston Book Company, 1894), 68–85; Peter Burchard, *One Gallant Rush: Robert Gould Shaw and His Brave Black Regiment* (New York: St. Martin's, 1965); and Glatthaar, *Forged in Battle,* 136–142. On the development of the monument, see Stephen J. Whitfield, "'Sacred in History and in Art': The *Shaw Memorial,*" *New England Quarterly* 60 (March 1987), 3–27; Sidney Kaplan, "The Sculptural World of Augustus Saint-Gaudens," *Massachusetts Review* 30 (Spring 1989), 17–36; Lois Goldreich Marcus, "The Shaw Memorial by Augustus Saint-Gaudens: A History Painting in Bronze," *Winterthur Portfolio: A Journal of*

American Material Culture 14 (Spring 1979), 1–23; and Savage, *Standing Soldiers, Kneeling Slaves,* 196–208.

2. See Savage, *Standing Soldiers, Kneeling Slaves,* 162–208; W. E. B. Du Bois, *Black Reconstruction in America, 1860–1880* (New York: Atheneum, 1935), 110.

3. See David W. Blight, "The Meaning or the Fight: Frederick Douglass and the Memory of the Fifty-Fourth Massachusetts," *Massachusetts Review* 36 (Spring 1995), 141–153; and David W. Blight, "The Shaw Memorial in the Landscape of Civil War Memory," in Thomas Brown, Martin Blatt, and Donald Yacovone, eds., *Hope and Glory: Essays on the Shaw Memorial and the Massachusetts Fifty-Fourth* (Amherst: University of Massachusetts Press, forthcoming 2000). Whitfield uses the unveiling of the Shaw Memorial as a way of showing how reunion was achieved at the cost of racial equality. He writes: "The full reunification of the United States required the suppression of the dream of racial equality that radical abolitionism had once envisioned." See Whitfield, "Sacred in History and in Art," 12.

4. *Boston Transcript,* June 1, 1897; Robert Lowell, "For the Union Dead," in *Norton Anthology of American Literature,* vol. 1 (New York: Norton, 1980), 842; fragments and revisions of "Colonel Shaw and His Negro Regiment," Robert Lowell Papers, HLH, folders 2300, 2571. In a personal note Lowell writes: "My poem, The Union Dead, is about childhood memories, evisceration of modern cities, civil rights, nuclear warfare and more particularly Colonel Robert Shaw and his negro regiment, the Massachusetts 54th. I brought in early personal memories because I wanted to avoid the fixed, brazen tone of the set-piece and official ode." On the Shaw traditon of poetry, see Steven Axelrod, "Colonel Shaw in American Poetry: 'For the Union Dead' and Its Precursors," *American Quarterly* 24 (October 1972), 523–537; and Whitfield, "Sacred in History and in Art," 21–27. On the significance of Shaw to New England intellectuals, see Fredrickson, *Inner Civil War,* 151–165.

5. *Boston Transcript,* June 1, 1897.

6. William James, "Robert Gould Shaw," in *Memories and Studies* (New York: Longman's, Green, 1911), 13, 42–43, 55–57. James searched here for what social memory theorist Frederic Bartlett called "effort after meaning" in the formation of collective memory. See Frederick C. Bartlett, *Remembering: A Study in Experiential and Social Psychology* (1932; rpr. Cambridge, Eng.: Cambridge University Press, 1961), 266–267.

7. *Boston Transcript,* June 1, 1897; Booker T. Washington, "Speech at the Unveiling of the Robert Gould Shaw Memorial," in Harlan, ed., *BTW Papers,* vol. 4, 285–286; Washington, *Up from Slavery,* 148–149.

8. Washington, "Speech at the Unveiling of the Robert Gould Shaw Memorial," 287–288; *Boston Transcript,* June 1, 1897.

9. Henry Lee Higginson, "Robert Gould Shaw," an address delivered in Sanders Theater, May 30, 1897, in *Four Addresses by Henry Lee Higginson* (Boston: Merrymount Press, 1902), 102, 72–73.

10. *CV,* June–July, 1897. The Confederate reunion was a huge celebration and part of Nashville's Tennessee Centennial Exposition. See Ayers, *Promise of the New South,* 336–337.

11. Monroe K. Work, *Negro Year Book: An Annual Encyclopedia of the Negro, 1925–1926* (Tuskegee, Ala.: Tuskegee Institute, 1925), 369; Charles Chesnutt, *The Marrow of Tradition* (1999; rpr. Ann Arbor: University of Michigan Press, 1969), 269–270; *Boston Transcript,* June 4, 1897; Paul Lawrence Dunbar, "Robert Gould Shaw," in Jay Martin and Gossie H. Hudson, eds., *The Paul Lawrence Dunbar Reader* (New York: Dodd, Mead, & Co., 1975), 320.

12. Patrick Kelly, "Taking Care of Billy Yank: The Politics of Veterans' Care in the Gilded Age and the Election of 1896," paper delivered at the conference "Memory of the Civil War in American Culture," Huntington Library, San Marino, Calif., November 6, 1999, courtesy of the author.

13. McKinley to Leonard Wood, quoted in Gerald F. Linderman, *The Mirror of War: American Society and the Spanish-American War* (Ann Arbor: University of Michigan Press, 1974), 29; on McKinley's character see 9–24.

14. Nell Irvin Painter, *Standing at Armageddon: The United States, 1877–1919* (New York: Norton, 1987), 141–155, Kipling verse, 153; Litwack, *Trouble in Mind,* 463–470. Kipling's "The White Man's Burden" first appeared in print in the United States in *McClure's Magazine,* February 1899.

15. Painter, *Standing at Armageddon,* 157. The term "splendid little war" was coined in part by John Hay, American ambassador to Great Britain. On McKinley's personal indecision regarding the war, see Linderman, *Mirror of War,* 27–36. On gender and the revival of the martial ideal, see Kristin L. Hoganson, *Fighting for American Manhood: How Gender Politics Provoked the Spanish-American and Philippine Wars* (New Haven: Yale University Press, 1998), esp. 107–132.

16. T. E. Rose, "What Should Be Our Relation to the Federal Government?" speech delivered at commencement, Hampton Institute, *Southern Workman,* July 1898.

17. Washington to John Davis Long, March 15, 1898, *BTW Papers,* vol. 4, 389; "Los Angeles Letter," *Indianapolis Freeman,* quoted in Willard B. Gatewood Jr., *Black Americans and the White Man's Burden, 1898–1903* (Urbana: University of Illinois Press, 1975), 24–25; *Wisconsin Weekly Advocate,* July 9, 1898, *Iowa State Bystander,* May 20, 1898, in George P. Marks III, ed., *The Black Press Views American Imperialism, 1898–1900* (New York: Arno Press, 1971), 70–71.

18. *Richmond Planet,* May 21, 1898, in Marks, ed., *Black Press Views American Imperialism,* 36, and on the "No Officers, No Fight!" press response generally, see

33–50. On Mitchell and resistance to the war, see Gatewood, *Black Americans and the White Man's Burden*, 30–37, 82–85; and Litwack, *Trouble in Mind*, 464.

19. Gatewood, *Black Americans and the White Man's Burden*, 31–33.

20. *Lexington Standard* (Ky.), quoted in *Cleveland Gazette*, August 17, 1898, and Sprague and Douglass, in ibid., 32, 212; *Kansas City American Citizen*, February 24, 1898, *Omaha Afro-American Sentinel*, April 2, 1898, and *Iowa State Bystander*, July 1, 1898, in Marks, ed., *Black Press Views American Imperialism*, 11, 22, 69.

21. "Not as Suppliants Do We Present Our Claims, But as American Citizens. Open Letter to President McKinley, by Colored People of Massachusetts," October 3, 1899, in Marks, ed., *Black Press Views American Imperialism*, 201–202. On the lynching of Sam Hose, see Brundage, *Lynching in the New South*, 82–84.

22. "Open Letter to President McKinley," 203–206. On Grimké's challenges to Booker Washington, see Dickson J. Bruce, *Archibald Grimké: Portrait of a Black Independent* (Baton Rouge: Louisiana State University Press, 1993), 90–91.

23. *Speeches and Addresses of William McKinley, from March 1, 1897, to May 30, 1900* (New York: Doubleday and McLure, 1900), 90, 158–159; Linderman, *Mirror of War*, 35; Foster, *Ghosts of the Confederacy*, 153–154; *CV* 11 (January 1903), 6. On the Spanish-American War and reconciliation, see Buck, *Road to Reunion*, 318–319. On McKinley's reconciliationist tours and speeches, also see his dedication of a monument at Antietam, *Baltimore American*, May 27, 1900, HCF, fische 271. The Baltimore paper gushed: "Nothing has more excited the world's surprise or forced its admiration than this healing of a breach which for a time threatened the destruction of the republic."

24. *Norfolk Recorder*, quoted in *Cleveland Gazette*, August 13, 1898, in Willard B. Gatewood Jr., "Black Americans and the Quest for Empire, 1898–1903," *Journal of Southern History* 38 (November 1972), 556; "Open Letter to President McKinley," 204. See Ayers, *Promise of the New South*, 328–329, 332–333; and O'Leary, *To Die For*, 137–149. Ayers contends that "the major effect of the war seems to have been to enlist the North as an even more active partner in the subjugation of black Americans" (333). The phrase "racialization of patriotism" is O'Leary's, and she shows how "the Spanish-American War provided a structural basis for the ideological alliance of white supremacists in the South and advocates of imperialism in the North" (142).

25. *NYT, AC*, quoted in Richard E. Wood, "The South and Reunion, 1898," *Historian* 31 (1969), 420–421, 427.

26. On Taylor and Lee, and for Alexander and Gordon quotes, see Foster, *Ghosts of the Confederacy*, 146, 148; *Detroit News Tribune*, in ibid., 427. On Bagley, also see Ayers, *Promise of the New South*, 332.

27. Ayers, *Promise of the New South*, 333; Foster, *Ghosts of the Confederacy*, 150; Tillman, in *Congressional Record*, 55th Cong., 1899, 2d sess., 6532, 3d sess., 837.

28. Vincent P. De Santis, *The Shaping of Modern America: 1877–1916* (Boston: Allyn and Bacon, 1973), 94–98; Don H. Doyle, *New Men, New Cities, New South: Atlanta, Nashville, Charleston, Mobile, 1860–1910* (Chapel Hill: University of North Carolina Press, 1990), 1–21, 261–266.

29. Page, *The Negro*, 208; Du Bois, *Souls*, 37, 43–44.

30. Foster, *Ghosts of the Confederacy*, 128–131, 158–159; O'Leary, *To Die For*, 148; A. J. Emerson, "Fraternity in National Flags," *CV* 21 (December 1913), 603; George M. Cohan, "The Wedding of the Blue and the Gray," sung by Ethel Levy and Cohan, sheet music, courtesy of Scott Sandage.

31. *NYT*, July 3, 1910; *CV* 18 (September 1910), 433; *CV* 19 (March 1911), 108; *CV* 19 (September 1911), 413, 456. On the return of flags, see *Congressional Record*, 58th Cong., 3d sess., 1905, pp. 3007, 3131; Foster, *Ghosts of the Confederacy*, 154; and O'Leary, *To Die For*, 135–137.

32. Theodore Roosevelt, "Fellow-Feeling as a Political Factor" (1900), in Herman Hagedorn, ed., *American Ideals, the Strenuous Life, Realizable Ideals: The Works of Theodore Roosevelt* (New York: Charles Scribner's Sons, 1926), 356; *Confederate Veteran* 18 (September 1910), 405; *NYT*, February 14, May 20, 1909. Also see Hoganson, *Fighting for American Manhood*, 124–125.

33. Thomas J. Pressly, *Americans Interpret Their Civil War* (New York: Free Press, 1962), 166–171.

34. James Ford Rhodes, *History of the United States from the Compromise of 1850*, 8 vols. (New York: Macmillan, 1892–1919), vol. 5, 485, vol. 1, 52–53; Pressly, *Americans Interpret Their Civil War*, 172–175.

35. Rhodes, *History of the United States*, vol. 1, 383, vol. 6, 39, vol. 7, 168, 290.

36. Lord Acton to Rhodes, Trinity College, Cambridge, Eng., June 15, 1898, *Critic* (August 10, 1895), A. V. Dicey to Rhodes, Oxford, Eng., December 3, 1894, Charles C. Smith to Rhodes, Boston, November 2, 1894, Tom L. Johnson to Rhodes, Cleveland, October 14, 1895, Charles S. Ashley to Rhodes, Toledo, Ohio, August 6, 1897, all in James Ford Rhodes Papers, MHS, boxes 1, 5.

37. Frederick Jackson Turner to Mark De Wolfe Howe, San Gabriel, Calif., January 9, 1928, Rhodes Papers, MHS box 11. Howe wrote a biography of Rhodes in 1928, and some of his correspondence from that project is in the Rhodes Papers. On the UDC's campaign about textbooks, see for example, "Review of Histories Used in Southern Schools and Southern Homes," address of Miss Anna Caroline Benning, chairman of textbook committee, delivered at eighth annual convention of Georgia division, UDC, La Grange, Ga., October 28, 1902, *CV* 10 (December 1902), 550–552.

38. Charles Francis Adams to Rhodes, December 5, 1899, April 18, 1907, Rhodes Pa-

pers, MHS box 1. On Adams's business career, see Edward Chase Kirkland, *Charles Francis Adams, Jr., 1835–1915: The Patrician at Bay* (Cambridge: Harvard University Press, 1965), 65–129.

39. "The Ethics of Secession," address delivered in Charleston, S.C., December 24, 1902, at annual celebration of the New England Society of Charleston, in Charles Francis Adams, *Studies Military and Diplomatic, 1775–1865* (New York: Macmillan, 1911), 203–231, quote, 230–231.

40. "Lee at Appomattox," paper read before the American Antiquarian Society, Worcester, Mass., October 30, 1901, in *Charles Francis Adams, Lee at Appomattox and Other Papers* (Boston: Houghton Mifflin, 1902), 1–30, quote, 16; "Lee's Centennial," address delivered at Washington and Lee University, January 19, 1907, on the centennial of Lee's birth, Lexington, Va., in Adams, *Studies Military and Diplomatic*, 291–343, quotes, 335, 338. On Adams's visit to Lexington and his memories of the speech, see *Charles Francis Adams, 1835–1915: An Autobiography* (Boston: Houghton Mifflin, 1916), 207–208; and Kirkland, *Charles Francis Adams, Jr.*, 207. Ex-Confederates cherished opportunities to publicize Adams's strong pro-Confederate views. See the coverage of Adams's speech on secession in Charleston and another to the thirteenth annual banquet of the Confederate veterans' camp of New York, *CV* 11 (January, February, 1903), 12–13, 100–101.

41. *"The 'Solid South' and the Afro-American Race Problem," speech of Charles Francis Adams, at the Academy of Music, Richmond, Virginia, Saturday, October 24, 1908* (Boston), pamphlet in HU. On Southern reactions to such speeches by Northerners, see Foster, *Ghosts of the Confederacy,* 165. "Southerners gloried in northern homage to their conquered banner and in all other signs of northern respect," writes Foster.

42. "Negro Problem Solved," *NYT,* May 15, 1909. For interesting reflections on how racism played in the development of dominant and mythic visions of Civil War memory, see Alan T. Nolan, *Lee Considered: General Robert E. Lee and Civil War History* (Chapel Hill: University of North Carolina Press, 1991), 163–171.

43. "A Press Release by Emmett Jay Scott," Tuskegee, Ala., November 29, 1902, *BTW Papers,* vol. 6, 598–599.

44. John B. Gordon, "My First Command and the Outbreak of the War," *Scribner's* 33 (May 1903), 525; "Negro Incenses Ex-Confederates," *NYTr,* January 18, 1904. For an example of Gordon's conciliation toward Union veterans, especially those not easy to accommodate (such as General Daniel Sickles), see *AC,* April 17, 1900. Sickles had sent a message of good will to the annual UCV reunion in Louisville, which some Confederate veterans had resented. Gordon responded officially: "the time will never come, while I stand on Southern ground, or among the chivalrous men of the South, when I will refuse to send a kindly mes-

sage to an enemy." On Gordon's conciliatory manner of writing, see Gary W. Gallagher, ed., *Fighting for the Confederacy: The Personal Recollection of General Edward Porter Alexander* (Chapel Hill: University of North Carolina Press, 1989), xvii, 555.

45. Du Bois, *Souls*, 67, 70, 137. For Du Bois's reflections on the possibilities for white-black relations in the South, see 133–147.

46. D. Augustus Straker, "No Negro Problem," and S. C. Cross, "The Negro and the Sunny South," in *Colored American Magazine* 5 (May–June, 1903), 414 (July 1902), 193; Reverdy C. Ransom, "William Lloyd Garrison: A Centennial Oration," in Woodson, ed., *Negro Orators and Their Orations*, 535–536.

47. James Weldon Johnson, *The Autobiography of an Ex-Colored Man* (1912; rpr. New York: Hill and Wang, 1960), 156–159.

48. Ibid., 159–166.

49. "Memorial Day and the Negro," speech delivered in Boston, 1901, n.d., Grimké Papers, Moorland-Spingarn Collection, Howard University.

50. Frances Ellen Watkins Harper, *Iola Leroy; or, Shadows Uplifted* (1892; rpr. New York, 1990), 435. For examples of Hopkins's biographical panegyrics, see Pauline E. Hopkins, "Hon. Frederick Douglass," "Famous Men of the Negro Race: Booker T. Washington," and "Famous Men of the Negro Race: Senator Blanche K. Bruce," *Colored American Magazine* 2 (December 1900), 121–132, 3 (August, October 1901), 257–261, 436–441. On Harper and the enterprise of blacks forging a popular history of their own, see Mitchell A. Kachun, "The Faith That the Dark Past Has Taught Us: African-American Commemoration in the North and West and the Construction of a Usable Past, 1808–1915" (Ph.D. diss., Cornell University, 1997), 142–171, esp. 163–164.

51. *New York Age*, December 23, 1909, clipping in Charles N. Hunter Papers, PL, DU; *New York Globe*, September 27, 1884; *New York Age*, October 5, 1911; *Indianapolis Freeman*, September 20, 1890; AME souvenir chart in Kachun, "The Faith That the Dark Past Has Taught Us," 161; *Crisis* 10 (May 1915), 47.

52. *CR*, April 25, 1878. See also William Wiggins, *O Freedom! Afro-American Emancipation Celebrations* (Nashville: University of Tennessee Press, 1987), 1–7, 35; and Kachun, "The Faith That the Dark Past Has Taught Us," 241–248. On early emancipation celebrations, also see Kathleen Clark, "Celebrating Freedom: African American Emancipation Day Celebrations and African American Memory in the Reconstruction South," forthcoming in Brundage, ed., *No Deed But Memory.*

53. *CR*, March 12, 1885. On black monument planning and "fever," see Kachun, "The Faith That the Dark Past Has Taught Us," 153–159. The black exhibitions were small compared to the world's fairs that were the rave of the 1890s. One report claimed that the Columbian Exposition in Chicago in 1893 increased the

population of the city by one-half million and added $200 million to permanent property values. See *Boston Evening-Transcript*, May 4, 1897.

54. *New York Age*, December 27, 1906, HCF, fiche 272.

55. Mary White Ovington, "Slaves' Reminiscences of Slavery," *Independent* 68 (May 26, 1910), 1131–1134.

56. Ibid., 1135–1136.

57. *Crisis* 10 (May 1915), 31–32. As editor of the *Crisis,* the NAACP's magazine, W. E. B. Du Bois monitored these commemorations, big and small. See especially *Crisis,* February–November, 1913. For Raleigh events, see *Negro Fair Bulletin,* September 16, 1913, *Raleigh Times,* August 19, September 22, 1913, *Raleigh News and Observer,* January 2, 1908, *Our Advance,* May 18, 1910, *The Baptist Sentinel,* January 9, 1908, clippings in Hunter Papers, PL, DU, box 14, *Peoria Transcript,* September 2, 1914, *Galesburg Evening Mail,* August 6, 1914, *Quincy Journal,* August 5, 1914 (Ill.), in HCF, fiche 273. In 1918 in Corpus Christi, Texas, the local paper reported that the World War had cut off the anticipated picnic. "Elaborate demonstrations have always accompanied this date in the history of the Negro, but this year about the only thing left for the Negro is the ball game." See *Corpus Christi Caller,* June 21, 1918, HCF, fiche 272. On workers and leisure, see Roy Rosenzweig, *Eight Hours for What We Will: Workers and Leisure in an Industrial City, 1870–1920* (Cambridge: Harvard University Press, 1983). On black exhibitions, amusement, and community reactions, see Kachun, "The Faith That the Dark Past Has Taught Us," chap. 8.

58. *New York Age,* January 25, 1912; Senate Report no. 311, "Hearing before the Senate Committee on Industrial Expositions," *Congressional Record,* 62d Cong., 2d sess., February 2, 1912, pp. 1–7; *CR,* February 8, April 11, 1912, *NYT,* August 5, 15, 1912, *Brooklyn Eagle,* August 4, 1912, and "$250,000 Given for Negro Show," April 26, 1912 unidentified newspaper clipping, HCF, fiches 272 and 273.

59. *Congressional Record,* 63d Cong., 2d sess., July 8, 1914, pp. 11797–11798. I am drawing on Joel Williamson's use of the terms "liberal," "conservative," and "radical" to explain white Southern mentalities on race relations. Southern liberals, according to Williamson, were the smallest group by the turn of the century, but they carried over from the experience of Reconstruction a conspicuous, articulate faith in black capacities and the progress of race relations. "Conservatives," the core of the Southern white mind, never relinquished the cardinal belief in Negro inferiority and sought in myriad ways to fix the subordinate place (Jim Crow) of black folk in American life. And the "radicals" advanced a racial vision of America where blacks had no place in society—where they would vanish, or be forced to vanish. All three of these mentalities, says Williamson, "evoked the past to meet the present." See Williamson,

The Crucible of Race: Black-White Relations in the American South since Emancipation (New York: Oxford University Press, 1984), 4–7, 36–39.

60. *Charlotte News* (N.C.), June 27, 1915, *Worcester Evening Post* (Mass.), July 8, 1915, HCF, fiche 274.

61. *Richmond Leader,* June 10, July 8, 10, 13, 15, 1915, *Richmond Dispatch,* July 7, 1915, in HCF, fiche 274. In the wake of the Richmond exhibition, Giles Jackson was accused of fraud, although from what can be determined, he was never indicted or convicted.

62. *Hackensack Record* (N.J.), September 24, 1913, *Atlantic City Press,* October 10, 1913, *Chicago Defender,* September 18, 1915, *Rockford Republic* (Ill.), August 30, 1915, *Louisville News,* August 28, 1915, HCF, fiche 272–274; *Crisis* 6 (October 1913), 297. Du Bois described the New Jersey exposition in Atlantic City as one with "many disappointments" in its scope and execution. *Topeka Capital* (Kans.), August 7, 1910, HCF, fiche 272.

63. For one of many uses of Work's book in the press, see *Chicago Inter-Ocean,* August 5, 1913, HCF, fiche 272. See also "The Negro's Progress in Fifty Years," *Annals of the American Academy of Political and Social Science* 49 (September 1913), 1–237; and *Crisis* 7 (February 1914), 202.

64. *New York Press,* July 9, 1913, *Brooklyn Standard Union,* July 19, 1913, *Brooklyn Eagle,* September 4, 1913, *New York Globe,* July 25, 1913, HCF, fiche 272; *Crisis* 6 (August 1913), 183.

65. *Brooklyn Eagle,* October 23, 1913, *NYT,* October 23, 1913, HCF, fiche 272. For photographs of the exhibits as well as the pageant, and for the fifteen divisions, see *Crisis* 7 (December 1913), centerfold; *Crisis* 11 (December 1915), 89–93; *Crisis* 6 (October 1913), 297. On pageantry, see David Glassberg, *American Historical Pageantry: The Uses of Tradition in the Early Twentieth Century* (Chapel Hill: University of North Carolina Press, 1990), 131–134; and Glassberg, "History and the Public: Legacies of the Progressive Era," *Journal of American History* 73 (March 1987), 957–980.

66. For various versions of the script for the pageant, as well as programs, and for Burroughs's draft of the dramatic "continuity," see W. E. B. Du Bois Papers, Du Bois Library, University of Massachusetts, Amherst, reel 87. One script for the "Star of Ethiopia" is reprinted in *Crisis* 7 (November 1913), 339–341. Attendance figures are in *Crisis* 7 (December 1913), 84. Also see *New York Press,* October 29, 1913, HCF, fiche 273.

67. *Crisis* 11 (December 1915), 89; Du Bois's report to Board of Directors of the NAACP, "The Pageant," 1915, and Du Bois to Joel Spingarn, November 3, 1915, Du Bois Papers, reel 5; *Brooklyn Standard Union,* July 19, 1913, *New York Evening Mail,* August 9, 11, 1913, *New York Press,* August 10, 1913, HCF, fiche 273.

68. *Crisis* 5 (April 1913), 180.

69. *Crisis* 5 (January 1913), 128–129.

70. "A Mild Suggestion," *Crisis* 3 (January 1912), 115–116.

71. Ibid., 116. Shaw and Swift quoted in Jonathan Swift, *A Modest Proposal and Other Stories*, intro. by George R. Levine (Amherst, N.Y.: Prometheus Books, 1955), 14.

72. James Weldon Johnson, "Fifty Years," in *"Fifty Years" and Other Poems* (Boston: Cornhill Co., 1917), 1–5; *NYT*, January 1, 1913.

Epilogue

1. *NYT*, March 26, April 9, 26, 1911, April 4, 11, 1915. On April 4, 1915, the *Times* ran a massive commemorative feature, "The Blue and the Gray: The Golden Anniversary of Peace within This Union," with many articles on wartime heroes and battles, all presented in a mode of national unity. The entire 24-page section, featuring a good deal of poetry, was written and compiled by Charles Willis Thompson.

2. *Nation* 92 (May 25, 1911), 518; Winthrop More Daniels, "The Slave Plantation in Retrospect," *AM* 107 (March 11, 1911), 362–369; Silverman and Ransom quoted in *NYT*, February 13, 1911.

3. Dudley Miles, "The Civil War as a Unifier," *The Sewanee Review* 21 (January 1913), 188–195.

4. Ibid., 196–197.

5. *Fiftieth Anniversary of the Battle of Gettysburg*, 31, 36–37. This report contained many photographs, with one compelling scene after another of the spirit of reconciliation as well as the generational transmission of memory. In a few of these pictures one sees black laborers and camp workers constructing the tents, serving as bakers, or passing out blankets or mess kits. Nowhere is there a photograph of a black veteran in uniform.

6. Ibid., 6, 39–41, 49–51, 53, 57–58; *Philadelphia Inquirer*, July 6, 1913.

7. *Fiftieth Anniversary of the Battle of Gettysburg*, 6; William H. Blake, *Hand Grips: The Story of the Great Gettysburg Reunion of 1913* (Vineland, N.J.: n.p., 1913), 66–67.

8. *Fiftieth Anniversary of the Battle of Gettysburg*, 25; Blake, *Hand Grips*, 66–67.

9. *Fiftieth Anniversary of the Battle of Gettysburg*, 176.

10. *Washington Post*, June 30, 1913; *NYT*, July 1–5, 1913.

11. *Outlook* 104 (July 12, 1913), 541, 554–555, 610–612.

12. *San Francisco Examiner*, July 4, 1913; *Charleston News and Courier*, July 1, 1913; *Brooklyn Daily Eagle*, July 2, 1913.

13. *Baltimore Afro-American Ledger*, July 5, 1913.

14. See Williamson, *Crucible of Race*, 364–395; Booker T. Washington, *NYT*, August 18, 1913. An especially interesting counterattack on the Wilson administration's

segregation policies in 1913 was Oswald Garrison Villard's "Segregation in Baltimore and Washington," an address delivered to the Baltimore branch of the NAACP, October 20, 1913, copy in HU. The central figure in the NAACP's often successful resistance to Wilson administration segregation schemes was Archibald Grimké, the branch director for Washington, D.C. See Bruce, *Archibald Grimké*, 184–200.

15. *AC*, July 2, 1913.
16. George S. Patton Jr., to Beatrice, May 11, 1909 and July 1, 1913, in Martin Blumenson, ed., *The Patton Papers, 1885–1940* (Boston: Houghton Mifflin, 1972), 173, 255.
17. *The Armory Show International Exhibition of Modern Art, 1913*, vol. 1: Catalogues (1913; rpr. New York: Arno Press, 1972), preface.
18. McCann, ed., *Ambrose Bierce's Civil War*, x–xi; Hobson, *Tell about the South*, 155–156; Williamson, *William Faulkner and Southern History*, 167–174.
19. *Crisis* (July 1913), 130–132.
20. See Raymond A. Cook, *Thomas Dixon* (New York: Twayne, 1974); Thomas Cripps, *Slow Fade to Black: The Negro in American Film, 1900–1942* (New York: Oxford University Press, 1977), 26–28, Dixon quote, 44.
21. Cripps, *Slow Fade to Black*, 28–32.
22. See ibid., 46–52; Michael Rogin, "'The Sword Became a Flashing Vision': D. W. Griffith's *The Birth of a Nation*," *Representations* 9 (Winter 1985), 150–194; John Hope Franklin, "*Birth of a Nation*—Propaganda as History," *Massachusetts Review* 20 (Autumn 1979), 417–434; Fred Silva, ed., *Focus on "The Birth of a Nation"* (Englewood Cliffs, N.J.: Prentice-Hall, 1971).
23. Charles Flint Kellogg, *A History of the National Association for the Advancement of Colored People* (Baltimore: Johns Hopkins University Press, 1967), 142; *Crisis* (May 1915), 40–42, (June 1915), 87; Thomas R. Cripps, "The Negro Reaction to the Motion Picture *Birth of a Nation*," *Historian* (May 1963), 244–262; Cripps, *Slow Fade to Black*, 53–65; and Nickieann Fleener-Marzec, "D. W. Griffith's *The Birth of a Nation*: Controversy, Suppression, and the First Amendment as It Applies to Filmic Expression, 1915–1973" (Ph.D. dissertation, University of Wisconsin–Madison, 1977).

Acknowledgments

DURING TEN YEARS of researching and writing this book, I have amassed countless debts that I now gratefully acknowledge. My interest in historical memory generally, and in the memory of the Civil War in particular, began in the late 1980s as I completed an intellectual biography of Frederick Douglass. Innocently and almost blindly, I ventured into this field of memory studies in the final chapter of that book, unaware that in the next decade such studies would become a subfield of American history. Other disciplines, especially anthropology, and other national historians, especially the French, were already probing the depths of collective memory. I benefited greatly from participating in 1988–90 in a working group on history and memory in Afro-American culture, organized at the W. E. B. Du Bois Institute, Harvard University, by Genevieve Fabre and Melvin Dixon. The many scholars in that group helped me to understand memory as a social and cultural force. Robert O'Meally, Nellie McKay, and Lawrence Levine became confidants on these matters, and I will be forever grateful to the late Nathan Huggins for, among other generosities, inviting a neophyte like me into such a thoughtful and supportive circle of intellectuals. Among them, this book was born, and Nathan's memory lingers in its pages. In those years and ever since, I have gained immeasurably as a scholar of African American history from the advice and counsel of Randall Burkett, the best bibliographer I know. Randall's research tips inform nearly every chapter of this book.

More institutions and individuals have helped me in this work than I can mention here. But I have received the generous aid of many research librarians all over the United States whom I thank with pleasure, especially Nancy Burkett, Joanne Chaison, and John Hench at the American Antiquarian Society; Bill Irwin and Linda McCurry at the Perkins Library, Duke University Archives; Paul Romaine and Sandra Trenholm at the Gilder Lehrman Collection, New York; the late David Thackery at the Newberry Library in Chicago; and John and Ruth Ann Coski at the Museum of the Confederacy in Richmond. John and Ruth Ann have been special friends and research partners in my effort to understand the Lost Cause and Southern memory. Librarians too numerous to mention also assisted me at the Army War College library, Carlysle Barracks, Pennsylvania; the Library of Congress manuscripts division; the National Archives; the various Harvard libraries, especially the Houghton Library and the microform reading room of the Lamont Library; the New York Public Library manuscripts reading room and the Schomburg Collection; the Massachusetts Historical Society (especially Donald Yacovone); the Moorland-Springarn Collection, Howard University; the Pennsylvania State Archives; the Southern Historical Collection, University of North Carolina, Chapel Hill; the South Carolina Historical Society in Charleston; and the Virginia State Library and the Virginia Historical Society in Richmond. Reference and research librarians at Amherst College, especially Michael Kasper, Daria D'Arienzo, and John Lancaster, and at the University of Massachusetts, Amherst, especially Linda Seidman, have answered countless calls for information and interlibrary loans.

I wish to thank the many universities, colleges, libraries, and museums that have invited me to lecture and supported my research over some eight years. They cannot all be listed individually, but special thanks go to three in particular: Loretta Mannucci and the Milan Group, which meets every other year at the University of Milan, Italy, and where I first delivered a paper on memory in 1992; the Amerika Institute, University of Munich, where I was Fulbright Professor in 1992–93 and hosted by Berndt Ostendorf, who helped me understand German and American memory; and the Du Bois Institute, Cambridge, Massachusetts, where Henry Louis Gates Jr. has extended me visiting scholar privileges for several years. I warmly thank Skip for his generosity. I am also grateful to the National Park Service for its several invitations to speak at conferences and historic sites, especially in Boston at the centennial of the Shaw Memorial in 1997, and at Ford's Theater in Washington, D.C. in 2000.

I have received a lucky man's share of grant and fellowship support to complete this project. First, two deans at Amherst College, Ronald Rosbottom and Lisa Raskin, have helped provide grants on at least four occasions to fund research assistants and all manner of expenses. To Ron I am especially grateful for his courage in letting me see his childhood Civil War scrapbooks. And to Lisa, I owe much for her extraordinary efforts to uphold my and others' scholarly aspirations at one of the best liberal arts colleges in America. I thank former president of Amherst College Peter Pouncey for many conversations about memory and for helping me find that Thucydides passage. It has been my good fortune to receive grants of varying kinds from the Whiting Foundation, the Warren Center for the Study of American History at Harvard, the Fulbright Commission, and the Gilder Lehrman Institute for American History. Bill Gienapp and Ernest May were kind and supportive hosts at the Warren Center during my year there, 1996–97. And I owe very special gratitude to Lesley Herrmann and the Gilder Lehrman Institute for a timely grant in the fall of 1998 that made possible some unencumbered time in which to complete the first draft of this book.

From my earliest forays into this topic student research assistants have aided my work immensely. They include Kevin Burke, Alec Dun, Andrew Erickson, Rachman Gill, Vanessa Harris, Christopher Jones, Shayne Klein, Dan Levinson-Wilk, Daniel Miller, Michael Sachse, Layn St. Louis, Joshua Shapiro, Chip Turner, Alena Weiserbs, and Elizabeth Wolf. Alec, Andrew, Chip, Chris, Kevin, and Vanessa especially know how much they became part of this project, and how much I am grateful for their endless searches and hours on photocopy machines.

Many friends and colleagues have talked with me, redirected my thinking, sent me research materials, and read drafts of this work. I can never thank Jim and Lois Horton enough for several years of support, confidence, and ideas. Lois read every chapter of this book in manuscript and her comments were uncommonly keen and insightful. A historian and teacher could have no better friend and colleague than Jim, with whom I co-teach summer institutes, give joint lectures, and have shared more ideas about memory than perhaps anyone. Michael Kammen has been a faithful friend and critic, as valuable a fellow traveler on the memory beat as anyone could ever want. His reading of my entire first draft was helpful in more ways than I can express; his ideas about history, culture, and potential illustrations are without end, and I am grateful for all of Michael's time and energy. Fitzhugh Brundage also read with expert care and keen intelligence my entire first draft. Fitz has perhaps more insight into what we historians are doing with memory than any other scholar I know. I am privileged to share historical and research passions with Scott Sandage, although I can never keep up with his extraordinary finds. Scott has provided me many special tips, documents, photographs, and just plain good ideas. As a reader, a historiographer, a researcher, and a historian of good sense, John David Smith has generously given his energy and insights to many chapters in manuscript, for which I am deeply grateful. Catherine Clinton has prodded me in friendly ways to think about this topic in broad terms for many years; I have used her work repeatedly and am grateful for her suggestions. As friend and scholar, Nina Silber has taught me much in recent years about the Civil War era and about ways to think about the culture of reunion. Bill McFeely has allowed me to pepper him with questions, ideas, and language over time; reading Bill's prose is always an inspiration to write. For a long time, I have learned how to be a historian from Dick Sewell, my mentor in graduate school and ever since. Dick has faithfully fed me ideas and read drafts with his keen eye for interpretation and for my howlers, several of which he caught again. I have valued the help of Edward Linenthal and Tony Horwitz, sympathetic readers and fellow preachers on the memory circuit. Ed's books are models of how to think clearly about historical memory. And at Amherst College, Martha Sandweiss, Kim Townsend, and Jeffrey Ferguson have seen me through to an end product. Marni's readings and knowledge of visual images and sources are invaluable, and have made this historian at least think about how I will do it next time. Kim's careful readings have improved Chapters 6 and 7, and his conversations about literature and history have kept me on course. With Jeff I share the "Hugginoid" legacy and an unexplainable sympatico; I owe him deeply for all the thoughts, questions, ideas, and especially for saving me from technological meltdowns.

Many other scholars, artists, and friends have given me their time and ideas, and the following is a partial list: John Adler, Peter Almond, Orlando Bagwell, Thomas Bender, Ira Berlin, Richard Blackett, Bill Blair, Steve Brier, Thomas Brown, Edward Casey, Christopher Clark, Frank Couvares, Kathleen Dalton, David Brion Davis, Maria Deidrich, David Herbert Donald, Clark Dougan, Ann Fabian, Alice Fahs, David Glassberg, Joseph Glatthaar, Robert Gooding-Williams, James Goodman, Michael Harper, Hugh Hawkins, Pembroke Herbert, Kristin Hogenson, Mitchell Kachun, Hartmut Keil, Jill Lepore, Leon Litwack, Alessandra Lorini, Waldo Martin, Louis Masur, Stuart McConnell, William McFeely, Michael McManus, Dick Newman, Greg Nobles, David Nord, Cecelia O'Leary, Alessandro Portelli, Richard Rabinowitz, Sean Redding, Bill Riches, Jon Rosenberg, Fath Ruffins, John Servos, Brooks Simpson, Werner Sollors, Marita Sturken, Kevin Sweeney, Dave Thelen, Clarence Walker, Frank Ward, Joan Waugh, and David Wills.

To my editor at Harvard University Press, Joyce Seltzer, I owe a deep debt for her professionalism and her consummate skill in seeing the whole from the parts. Julie Carlson was a marvelous copyeditor. Joyce and Julie, as well as several people named earlier, have saved me from mistakes and improved this book in countless ways. I take full responsibility, of course, for all remaining errors and imperfections.

Three final people made this book possible. Jim Blight and Janet Lang continue to inspire me with their collaborative spirit and the best model I could ever have asked for. And Karin Beckett has lived with this book as no one else. To her courage and patience, and to our shared memories, I dedicate this book.